UNITED STATES

Los Angeles

30°N

MEXICO

Oahu

Hawaii

H A W A I I

15°N

Mexico City

North Pacific Ocean

Clipperton

Kiritimati

Line Islands

0°

C O O K   I S L A N D S

Galapagos
Islands

CAN
MOA

Marquesas
Islands

F R E N C H   P O L Y N E S I A

Tuamotu Archipelago

Tahiti

Society Islands

15°S

Rarotonga

Austral Islands

Gambier Islands

Pitcairn
Islands

h Pacific Ocean

30°S

Easter

THE PACIFIC ISLANDS

Prepared for the Center for Pacific Islands Studies
University of Hawaii at Manoa
by Manoa Mapworks, 1988.

W — E

155°W

140°W

125°W

110°W

95°W

Missionary Lives

Pacific Islands Monograph Series, No. 6

Missionary Lives
Papua, 1874–1914

DIANE LANGMORE

Center for Pacific Islands Studies
School of Hawaiian, Asian, and Pacific Studies
University of Hawaii
UNIVERSITY OF HAWAII PRESS • Honolulu

Library of Congress Cataloging-in-Publication Data

Langmore, Diane.
  Missionary lives.

  (Pacific islands monograph series ; no. 6)
  Bibliography: p.
  Includes index.
  1. Missionaries—Papua New Guinea—Biography.
  2. Missions—Papua New Guinea—History. 3. Papua
New Guinea—Biography. I. Title. II. Series.
  BV3680.N5L35   1989   266'.023'40953   88-26131
  ISBN 0-8248-1163-1

∞ *The paper used in this publication meets the minimum requirements of American National Standard for Information Sciences—Permanence of Paper for Printed Library Materials*

ANSI Z39.48–1984

Cartography by
Manoa Mapworks
Honolulu, Hawaii

Figure 18 is reproduced with the permission of the Mitchell Library, State Library of New South Wales, Sydney, Australia, and may not be further reproduced without the consent of the Library Council of New South Wales.

Figures 20, 21, and 25 are from the records of the Methodist Overseas Mission held on loan in the Mitchell Library from the Uniting Church in Australia, and are reproduced with permission.

Figures 7, 8, 9, 11, 12, 13, 14, 15, 16, 17, and 19 are reproduced with the permission of the Council for World Mission.

Editor's Note

This work by Diane Langmore is the sixth volume in the Pacific Islands Monograph Series and has an important feature in common with volume 4. In *Nan'yō: The Rise and Fall of the Japanese in Micronesia, 1885–1945*, Mark R. Peattie wrote not about Pacific Islanders but about the Japanese and their activities in the islands. Despite his focus on the Japanese, Peattie helped to provide an understanding of much of Micronesia's history and why things are the way they are today.

In a similar vein, Langmore has not written about the indigenous peoples of Papua. Rather, her focus is on the more than three hundred European missionaries who served in the southeastern quarter of the island of New Guinea before World War I. Langmore presents us with a group biography of the diverse aggregation of individuals who came from several nations and four separate mission movements. She examines and dispels stereotypes about missionaries and, equally important, gives new insights about the roles of the European women involved in the mission efforts.

The impact of Christianity on Papua is well documented, and Langmore informs us about the first individuals who introduced the new faith to the area. Langmore's scholarship is impeccable, and the people she writes about were remarkable.

ROBERT C. KISTE

Contents

Figures

Tables

Preface

BETWEEN 1874 AND 1914, 327 European missionaries lived and worked in Papua. They belonged to four missions: the London Missionary Society (LMS), the Sacred Heart Mission (SHM), the Australasian Wesleyan Methodist Missionary Society (AWMMS), and the Anglican Mission. For the first decade of that period the LMS, first into the field, worked in a land free of control by any foreign government. During that time they were the main agents of European culture, as well as Christianity, in the country. After Britain declared a protectorate in 1884, the missionaries shared the former role, and to some extent the latter, with a small force of government officers. But throughout the period to the First World War, the number of European missionaries in the colony was comparable to that of government officers.[1] In 1889 the head of the Sacred Heart Mission boasted that at the headquarters of his mission alone—Yule Island—there were more Europeans than at the administrative center of Port Moresby.[2]

Moreover, by their pattern of settlement—at mission stations scattered along the coast, among the islands, and to a lesser extent inland, rather than at centralized district stations—and by the priority they gave to learning the languages of the people among whom they settled, the missionaries were generally in a stronger position to exert sustained influence on the Papuans than were the government officers.[3] Conflict between the two groups sprang frequently from the jealousy of the officials at the missionaries' influence.

The only other Europeans to have much influence on Papuan life and culture during this period were the few traders and miners who had chosen to live with Papuan women. But their influence, though undoubtedly more intimate, was also more circumscribed and less disruptive, since, unlike the missionaries, miners and traders did not come with the avowed intent of changing the lives of the Papuans.

David Knowles has observed that history, when it touches men, "touches them at a moment of significance, whether they are great in themselves, or . . . stand in great places, or like the men of 1914 are matched with great issues."[4] Whether or not the men and women who came to Papua as missionaries were great in themselves, it is clear that history touched them at a moment of significance, when traditional Papuan societies were experiencing for the first time, a sustained and powerful onslaught from an alien culture and an alien religion. Because of their central role in this process, if for no other reason, the missionaries must be seen as crucial actors in the colonial history of Papua.

What sort of influence the missionaries exerted in Papua, as elsewhere, depended on what kinds of people they were. As well as bringing a new religion, they brought a vast amount of cultural and intellectual baggage that was determined by their backgrounds, both secular and religious, their personalities, and the era in which they came.

In the modern historiography of the Pacific, missionaries have been accorded a prominent place, as a sampling of recent publications shows. Even general histories have recognized their significance as one of the earliest and most influential agents of change throughout the Pacific. Douglas Oliver's classic general study[5] charted the arrival of the pioneer missionaries and their dispersal through the Pacific and briefly contrasted some aspects of their style of work and their reception. A more recent general history by K. R. Howe[6] extended Oliver's work. Benefiting from his own insights and those of his colleagues who, over the last three decades, have rejected the imperial view of Pacific history in favor of an island-based interpretation, Howe gave greater play to the active role of the Islanders in responding to the missionaries and their message. He presented a persuasive comparative analysis of the relative success of missionaries in different parts of the Pacific, demonstrating the significance of local factors such as the presence or absence of an indigenous elite, chiefly patronage, institutionalized religion, a centralized society, and a general openness to strangers in explaining the influence of the missionaries in Hawaii, Tahiti, Fiji, Tonga, and the Loyalty Islands, as compared with Vanuatu, the Solomon Islands, or even Samoa, where Christianity was readily accepted but rapidly assimilated into traditional forms.

Recent regional studies have also scrutinized the part played by missionaries in the postcontact history of particular islands or archipelagoes. Hezel's study of the Caroline and Marshall islands[7] traced missionary activity in that area from the first ill-fated attempts of the Jesuits to reach Palau at the beginning of the eighteenth century through the settlement of workers of the American Board of Commissioners for Foreign Missions (ABCFM) on Pohnpei and Kosrae and their eventual expansion, by 1880, through eastern Micronesia. He documented their struggles against "heathen customs" such as kava drinking, hostile chiefs, established religion, and rival European interests. Macdonald, in his study of Kiribati and Tuvalu, traced "the impact of foreigners and foreign influences,"[8] including Protestant and Catholic missionaries, and explored the reasons for the failure of the ABCFM workers in the northern Gilberts in contrast to the rapid success of the LMS, and later of the Sacred Heart missionaries, in the southern Gilberts and the Ellice Islands.

Dening described the advance and retreat of the envoys of various mission societies, both Protestant and Catholic, who made their way onto the islands and beaches of the Marquesas.[9] He analyzed the difficulty they faced in transferring a religion without a sustaining cultural system and showed the confrontation of ideas as the intruders crossed the cultural boundary of the beach into the new island world. Gilson, in his study of the Cook Islands,[10] considered the factors making for the remarkably early success of the LMS missionaries in the southern islands compared with other parts of the Pacific.

The most thorough scholarly appraisals of mission activity in the Pacific are probably to be found in recent studies of particular missions. Unlike the early triumphalist accounts of missionary successes written by apologists to encourage supporters, these, in varying degrees, are sympathetic but dispassionate accounts of the foundations of various missions, their growth and development, and, generally, indigenous responses to them. Gunson provided a definitive study of the evangelical missionaries, the "messengers of grace" who arrived in the South Seas between 1797 and 1860.[11] He placed them firmly in their socioeconomic and religious context, assessed their motivations, analyzed their preconceptions and assumptions, and then followed them into the field, observing their reactions to the peoples among whom they labored as well as their perceptions of their successes and failures. A more comprehensive but less analytical study of missionary activity in Oceania is that of John Garrett.[12] In a lucid chronological narrative he traced the courses of the various bodies, Protestant and Catholic, now represented by the Pacific Conference of Churches, from their origins to their emergence as a series of distinct churches.

Latukefu[13] provided a case study of a theme that recurs in the works of Gunson and Garrett and other studies of missionary interaction with chiefly societies—the role of missionaries in local political activity. He traced and critically evaluated the part played by the Wesleyan missionaries in the development and adoption of the constitutional monarchy in Tonga.

Wiltgen's study of the founding of the Roman Catholic church in

Oceania[14] is a detailed scholarly narrative that identified the main actors in the drama of missionary expansion as it unfolded in the Pacific. His presentation of the metropolitan church that sent the missionaries is solid and sure, but his evocation of the island world that received them is more shadowy. Laracy, in his study of one particular group of Roman Catholic missionaries, the Marists in Melanesia, focused on "the relationship between forces of indigenous and exotic origin."[15] While Wiltgen's study presented this interaction mostly from an exotic viewpoint, Laracy described the encounter more from the side of the missionized Solomon Islanders, with a thorough analysis of precontact society and an assessment of the impact of the intruders on the Melanesians and their culture.

Two recent studies have described the endeavors of the Anglicans in Melanesia: Hilliard[16] presented the gentlemen of the New Zealand-based Melanesian Mission, at work in northern Vanuatu, the Santa Cruz group, and the Solomon Islands; Wetherell[17] looked at Australian-based missionaries, generally of humbler rank, in Papua New Guinea. Both followed the course of these Anglican missions from their precarious foundations to their metamorphoses by the 1940s into indigenous churches, albeit still largely controlled by expatriates. Each paid some attention to the personnel of their respective missions, their social origins, their religious formation, and their responses to the cultures that confronted them.

All these studies, and numerous other books and articles, have contributed richly to our understanding of mission activity in the Pacific. But most of them chose not to make the missionaries, either as individuals or as a social group, the primary focus of their analyses. The general histories have been concerned mainly with the shifting patterns in interactions in the Pacific, with charting the intrusion of various foreigners, and with the adaptations made by both sides after the impact of contact. Painting on such a broad canvas they could not delineate in any detail the protagonists of the contact situation. Regional studies too, generally committed to a decolonized view of Pacific history, have tended to focus on indigenous responses, active as well as passive, to the intrusion of missionaries and other foreigners. Modern studies of missionary organizations in the Pacific have, in varying degrees, examined the personnel of the mission or missions under consideration, but their interest has generally been subordinate to their dominant theme—the establishment and growth of these institutions. The missionaries themselves—their objectives and aspirations, their ideals, convictions, and opinions, their actions and responses—are rarely the central concern of such studies.

Other types of historical work can also shed light on the missionaries.

Biographers, or the best of them (for example, Gavan Daws[18]), can offer profound under standing of particular individuals, but is beyond their scope to suggest the extent to which the individual is representative of the group. Standard histories of missionary societies, such as Lovett,[19] Goodall,[20] or Findlay and Holdsworth,[21] are helpful in explaining the context within which the missionaries worked, but their sweep is too broad and their aims too diverse for them to be able to give more than a passing glance at them as individuals or as a group.

Anthropologists studying culture contact have lamented this neglect. Kenelm Burridge wrote of Australian history: "We know quite a lot about aborigines in the contact situation, but we know very little about the missionaries and others involved in the same situation."[22] T. O. Beidelman, having surveyed the literature of missionary activity in Africa, concluded:

> Unfortunately none of these works conveys much about the ordinary activities and organizations of these missionaries at the grass roots, still less about their social backgrounds, beliefs and day to day problems, economic attitudes or patriotism. . . . Nowhere do we gain any idea of how any particular station was run or what a day at a mission station was like. There is no description of the career of any rank and file missionary. In general the historical studies of missionaries represent a rather dull form of scissors and paste history.[23]

Sharing Beidelman's conviction as to the necessity of knowing who the missionaries were in order to understand their role in colonial history, I have attemped to write a group biography of the 327 missionaries who came to Papua before 1914. I have investigated their ethnic origins, their socioeconomic background, and their intellectual and religious experience in the belief that these inevitably influenced their behavior and their responses to the environment in which they found themselves. I have then looked at the missionaries in the field, exploring their way of life, their style of work, their interaction with their contemporaries, both Papuan and European, and their personal responses to the mission situation. My concern is not so much with their achievements as with their objectives and aspirations, their perceptions of the situation, and their reactions to it.

Popular stereotypes of the nineteenth-century missionary flourish. The Australian poet, James McAuley, analyzed some of the images of the missionary entrenched in common folklore.[24] The first is of the missionary who, at great personal cost, rescues heathens from the darkness of superstition, converts them, cures them, teaches them, and trains them to "wash and dress with propriety." This is the image that has been represented by missionary society propaganda and promulgated by the sermons and Sunday schools that are a half-remembered part of many childhoods. The second stereotype, that of the missionary as champion of indigenous rights against those who threaten them, is derived largely from the writings of the missionaries themselves and reinforced by other mission literature. The third and perhaps most prevalent image of the nineteenth-century missionary is that of a "narrow-minded killjoy" who introduced a sense of sin into South Sea Island paradises, destroying native dances, festivals, and arts, and who was more intent on imposing lower-middle-class Victorian prudery than promoting the more generous virtues. This image, inspired by the eighteenth-century romantic ideal of the "noble savage," draws on modern popular literature to portray the ignoble invader of paradise. Louis Becke, James Michener, and Somerset Maugham are among the writers who have perpetuated this image. Maugham's caustic portrait of the haunted, repressed Mr. Davidson in "Rain" is a fine example. "You see," Maugham had Davidson explain to a fellow passenger in the Pacific,

> they were so naturally depraved that they couldn't be brought to see their wickedness. We had to make sins out of what they thought were natural actions. We had to make it a sin, not only to commit adultery and to lie and to thieve, but to expose their bodies, and to dance and not come to Church. I made it a sin for a girl to show her bosom and for a man not to wear trousers.[25]

Music hall parodies, cartoons, and review skits seized joyfully on this stereotype, of which Noel Coward's irreverent portrait of "Uncle Harry" presented a mirror-image. This portrayal of the missionary has also become popular with writers of new nationalist histories, in reaction against the Eurocentric interpretations of colonial history with their narratives of great men and noble exploits.

The fourth image identified by McAuley, that of the missionary as one of the "sinister trio of capitalist imperialism" in league with the trader and the official, is one that has long been popular with political radicals. It found pungent expression in the *Bulletin*, which was, in the late nineteenth-century, of the "firm opinion that missionaries in the Pacific were merely one aspect of European exploitation."[26] "The Pious Pirate Hoists his Flag" (Figure 1) is regarded as a "typical May cartoon" by Margaret Mahood, who described it as showing "a black-clad missionary hoisting his skull-and-crossbones flag amid a group of cringing natives and rejoicing missioners in front of the New Hebrides Mission which is hung with posters advertising Coconut Oil and Religion and Greed and Gospel."[27] Later *Bulletin* cartoons elaborated the same theme.

The fifth and sixth stereotypes described by McAuley—the mission-

Figure 1. "The pious pirate hoists his flag." (*Bulletin*, 17 April 1886, 5)

ary as bigot and fanatic who will not let people worship God in their own way, and the missionary as underminer of traditional society—are closely related to the fourth stereotype and share the same roots in romantic literature. They have also been perpetuated, unwittingly or intentionally, by some anthropologists, especially the exponents of structural-functionalism, who have seen no further than the disruptive effects of the missionary on traditional religion and culture.[28]

Popular stereotypes presuppose that there was one identifiable creature—the nineteenth-century missionary. In this book I have attempted to measure these stereotypes against reality as it existed in Papua between 1874 and 1914, and to bring to life the missionaries as they existed in that time and place. But because differences in background, personality, and experience produced a great diversity of ideas and attitudes, and hence of behavior, it was also necessary to investigate the differences between the missionaries as well as the characteristics they shared. In Kitson Clark's useful phrase, I seek to present the men and women who were "the units covered by . . . large generalizations."[29]

The limits of this study must be stressed. The most apparent is that it is a study of culture contact that focuses solely on the missionaries and not on the host peoples. In restricting myself thus, I am not trying to perpetuate the ethnocentric heresy that Europeans were the actors in the contact situation and Papuans merely the passive reactors. For the story to be complete the other, and arguably the more important, side must be told. Papuan scholars are already recording and analyzing the wide range of their people's responses to the intrusion of the missionaries and other foreigners.[30] I hope that my work will complement theirs. H. A. C. Cairns defended studies of culture contact from a single perspective: "British attitudes and responses had a logic of their own. They were derived from a fairly consistent climate of opinion which conditioned and moulded their perceptions and reactions."[31] It is possible to identify, though more tentatively, common European attitudes and responses. To describe and interpret them, as they were manifested in the missionaries, is a limited but justifiable aim.

This study is not a mission history. All of the missions in Papua have their own official or informal histories.[32] Information about the growth and development of the missions has been given only when it casts light on the missionaries, who are the subject of this work. Moreover, the hundreds of Polynesians and Melanesians who gave heroic service in the mission fields of Papua are not treated here. Both their premissionary experience and their roles in Papua were so different from those of the European missionaries that theirs too is a separate story.

My study is limited in time and place. I did not look at the missionaries of German New Guinea, which was, for the period under consideration, a totally separate and different colony. Nor did I make more than passing reference to missionaries in other parts of the world. It is a case-study of missionaries in one particular area. Within Papua, I looked only at the missionaries who arrived in the period before 1914, described by one writer as the "golden age of missions."[33] The First

World War was no watershed in Papuan history as was the Second World War, but as far as the missions were concerned it cut off or curtailed recruitment for several years. Those who came to the mission field after the Great War were men and women who came from a different world.

A group biography, besides sharing the problems common to a single biography, has problems peculiar to itself. The first is to define the group to be studied. Writers of large-scale prosopographical studies limit the scope of their research by selecting a random sample of the category to be investigated. In a study of a small group, as in this work, it is possible to include all the individuals who make up the group. But where records are incomplete, as in this case, it is necessary to proceed in the fashion of the first prosopographers, the classical historians, by noting down a name whenever it occurred in the sources and gradually building up a file about the individual, in order even to identify the complete group.

Writers of small-scale collective biographies have generally studied groups that have been elites in their own societies: politicians, scientists, intellectuals, or high-status socioeconomic groups. For such people, biographical data and often extensive personal records are generally available. Such was not the case with the missionaries who worked in Papua, most of whom were not, in the eyes of the world, eminent people. For some, the only known noteworthy action they took in their lives was to leave their homes to work in the mission field for a few years, or perhaps only a few months. Such people left little mark on their own societies, and when mission records themselves are incomplete, it is difficult to uncover even such basic information as will allow the retrieval of the birth, death, and marriage certificates that are an essential part of the skeleton of a group biography.

But if there are few surviving records for many of the missionaries, for some there is an overwhelming amount. For instance, there are twenty-eight large boxes of the papers of the LMS missionary Ben Butcher in the National Library of Australia. Such unevenness of evidence presents obvious problems of generalization. It is tempting to rely heavily on the statement of those whose lives are well documented. But in the absence of comparative material, it is impossible to tell whether they form a genuinely random sample. Indeed, the fact that such a wealth of material about them exists suggests that they were an articulate and atypical minority.

This is a crucial but not insurmountable problem of group biography. Lacking the sociologist's option of questionnaire and interview, the group biographer must, and can, use the sources that are available, uneven as they are. Although the material that survives cannot be assumed to be representative, and is often clearly not, accidents of history do lead to the preservation of the papers of carpenters, missionary sisters, and others low in the mission hierarchy, as well as of the elite. Furthermore, if the elite are overrepresented in the sources, they were generally the opinion makers and the most influential actors in the field, and for that reason it is useful to understand their thoughts and actions as fully as possible. These can be presented without making false generalizations about the thoughts and actions of the missionaries as a group. More generally, much reading of the sources fosters an intuitive feeling for what are typical or atypical responses. This can be a dangerous exercise and one must embark on it mindful of Kitson Clark's advice: "Do not guess, try to count," but at the same time consoled by his approval of "guesses informed by much general reading and . . . shaped by much brooding on the matter in hand," provided they are presented as such.[34]

The apparently homogeneous group is in fact composed of a series of discrete or sometimes overlapping subgroups. The group cannot be characterized until the subgroups are identified and analyzed. In this study, Catholics, Protestants, liberals, Evangelicals, lay, ordained, men, women, professionals, artisans, missionaries of the seventies, the nineties, and 1914 all have to be differentiated. Final definition of the group must take accout of, and yet transcend, the variables produced by the diversity of subgroups.

The central issue in the methodology of collective biography is not, however, that of group and subgroup, but rather of group and individual. Striking a balance between the individuals and the group is an integral problem of prosopography, and one that is solved variously by different practitioners. At one extreme, for prosopographers of the "mass" school with large computerized samples, the individual is essentially a statistical unit, and the end product more a Weberian ideal type than a group composed of actual people. At the other extreme, among practitioners of the "elitist" school studying smaller and more socially eminent groups, the emphasis is on the individuals who make up the group and the end product a group portrait pieced together from individual case studies. Such studies generally have less statistical underpinning, but the individuals emerge from them with distinctive and recognizable features. The present study, from inclination as well as necessity, approximates more closely to the second type. I have tried, however, to bridge the gap by using what modest statistics are available and by presenting ideal types as well as individual portraits.

Concentrating on the individuals who make up the group introduces further difficulties into a collective biography. The group biographer, like the biographer of the individual, recognizes the importance of "peeling the skins of the onion" in an effort to understand the subjects at their innermost levels of being.[35] Issues such as parent-child relationships, childhood experiences, the processes of socialization or, in Erikson's words, the "framework of social influences and traditional institutions,"[36] which mold perceptions and develop the beliefs and attitudes that define the adult, are as important in understanding the individuals who constitute a group as in understanding the individual per se. Yet peeling 327 onions is a task of a different order from peeling 1. It is inevitable that one's knowledge and understanding will remain more superficial, especially when the evidence is not easily accessible. Moreover, it is necessary at times to resist being drawn too far down some of the tantalizing byways of individual personality which, while rich material for the individual biographer, shed little light on the group. Study of the group requires detailed charting of its exernal contours, its institutional framework, and its relation to the larger society. This, because of limitations of time and space, must be achieved, to some extent, at the expense of exploration of the inner workings of the individuals.

To focus on the individuals in a group biography raises also the problem that much of what makes up a person cannot be quantified. While it is possible to tabulate and draw statistical conclusions from such data as ethnicity, occupational and marital status, morality, and even, with caution, class origin, it is not so easy to do so for ideas, prejudices, passions, beliefs, ideologies, ideals, and principles. Even when evidence of such a nature is available, it must not only be tested, as in all biography, for irony, flippancy, insincerity, special pleading, or other such motivations, but it must also be placed in the context of the characteristic mode of speech—especially the rhetoric—of the subgroup to which the individual belongs. Distinguishing the various "tones of voice" of a number of subjects is a difficult task and, despite rigorous testing through content analysis, what can be derived is only a subjective interpretation of the attitudes behind the words.

While recent critiques of prosopography[37] have been helpful in providing a conceptual framework for this work, it is not presented as a prosopographical study. My main concern was not to identify and correlate a few significant variables among the background characteristics of the group. The model on which this work is based is, rather, the biography. It is a loosely chronological study from birth to death of 327 men and women who constituted an identifiable group. Although I have tried to identify the sociopsychological ties that bound the group, I have also tried to present them as individuals in all their diversity. The result is a group portrait.

Acknowledgments

THIS BOOK owes much to the generous assistance of descendants of missionaries who supplied personal papers or information not available from public records. I wish to express particular gratitude to those who provided not only material but also hospitality to a stranger: Bishop and Mrs. Oliver Tomkins, Mrs. Betty Beattie, Dr. and Mrs. Charles Lawes, and Mrs. Marjorie Butcher. I am also very grateful to other missionary descendants who responded to my pleas and offered information either by letter or interview: Mr. Cecil Abel, Miss Gwen Avery, Dr. Robert Ballantyne, Mr. Howard Bardsley, Mr. James Beharell, Mrs. Mary Bull, Dr. Hal Colebatch, Dr. T. O. Enticott, Mr. Richard Garran, the Reverend W. R. Francis, Ms. Margaret Saville, and Dr. L. A. Scrivin.

Missionaries, former missionaries, and officials of the four organizations gave me much help. I am especially grateful to Sister Mary Venard, FDNSC, for her patience with endless queries; to Mother Margaret Mary, Sisters Martha and Paule-Marie, FDNSC, Canon Bodger, and Sister "Paul" Fairhall for their lively recollection of former colleagues; to Fathers McMahon, Bertolini, and Black, MSC, for generously providing material from the MSC archives and to the Reverend George Carter for papers relating to the New Zealand Methodist missionaries. To the Daughters of Our Lady of the Sacred Heart at Issoudun, Rome, Sydney, and Yule Island, and to the Anglican Mission at Dogura, I owe thanks for the hospitality that made field work so enjoyable.

Numerous libraries and archives provided a wealth of source material: in Canberra—the National Library of Australia, the Commonwealth Archives Office, the Menzies and Chifley libraries, ANU, and St. Mark's Library; in Melbourne—the LaTrobe Library and the Australian Board of Missions; in Sydney—the Mitchell Library, the Uniting Church Records, and the Australian Board of Missions; in Papua New

Guinea—the New Guinea Collection, University of Papua New Guinea; in London—the libraries of the School of Oriental and African Studies, the London School of Economics, Lambeth Palace, the Church Missionary Society, and the Society for the Propagation of the Gospel. I thank the trustees of these libraries, and their staffs, especially Ms. Nancy Lutton (UPNG), Mrs. Eileen Duncan (NLA), Ms. Hazel Roberts (SOAS), and the Reverend E. G. Clancy (UCR).

Many scholars and friends have supplied particular pieces of information or made useful suggestions about sources or methodology. I thank Judy Bennett, Kenneth Cable, Geoff Cummins, Gavan Daws, Lyndsay Farrall, Stewart Firth, Bill Gammage, Jim Gibbney, James and Helga Griffin, Niel Gunson, Alan Haig, David Hilliard, Renata Howe, Ken Inglis, Hugh Jackson, Rod Lacey, John Langmore, Hugh Laracy, Martha Macintyre, Ross Mackay, Patricia Mercer, Hank Nelson, Nigel Oram, Andrew Pike, Robin and Anthony Radford, Ian Stuart, and Andrew Thornley. I am indebted to the staff of the *Australian Dictionary of Biography*, especially Chris Cunneen, for generous assistance with the collection of biographical data. To Niel Gunson, Hank Nelson, Gavan Daws, Ken Inglis, and John Langmore who read the manuscript, as a whole or in part, I owe a particular debt of gratitude for their encouragement and help.

I wish to thank the Australian National University for the scholarship that enabled me to write the thesis on which this book is based, and the Department of Pacific and South-East Asian History for providing both a congenial home and the opportunity to leave it for field work in Sydney, Papua New Guinea, and Europe. Finally, I thank most sincerely my husband John and my three daughters, Sarah, Naomi, and Kate, for allowing 327 missionaries to become part of our family life for several years.

Missionary Lives

Prologue

CHRISTIAN MISSIONARY activity in New Guinea in the late nineteenth and early twentieth centuries was largely the product of earlier religious revivals that had revitalized both British Protestantism and French Catholicism. Protestant missions were the outcome of that "great movement of the spirit" of the previous century, the Evangelical Revival.[1] Both the London Missionary Society (LMS)[2] and the Wesleyan Methodist Missionary Society—parent of the Australasian Wesleyan Methodist Missionary Society (AWMMS)—were born of the enthusiasm and earnest commitment generated by the Revival, the impact of which was also felt in the Church of England.[3] But Anglican missionary activity in New Guinea also drew its inspiration from another source—the Anglo-Catholic conviction that evangelization was the responsibility of the church, and not of a misson society.[4]

In nineteenth-century France, the fashionable skepticism of the Enlightenment and the radicalism of the Revolution gave way to an ardent and romantic Catholicism, partly inspired by Chateaubriand's *Génie du Christianisme*, published at the beginning of the century.[5] Popular piety increased and, despite periodic anticlericalism, religious congregations burgeoned. More new orders appeared in the years from 1815 to 1915 than in any previous century.[6] Many had a professed missionary intent. By 1830, a new Catholic missionary movement, largely of French origin, was under way. In 1900, about 70 percent of Roman Catholic missionaries were French.[7]

Each of these great missionary movements was felt on the mainland of New Guinea (Figure 2).[8] First was the arrival of the pioneer LMS missionaries, for whom New Guinea was the last shore of that "great tidal wave of missionary endeavour that rolled across the South Seas from East to West."[9] In 1871 Samuel McFarlane began work in the Torres Strait, and three years later, William Lawes, with his wife,

1

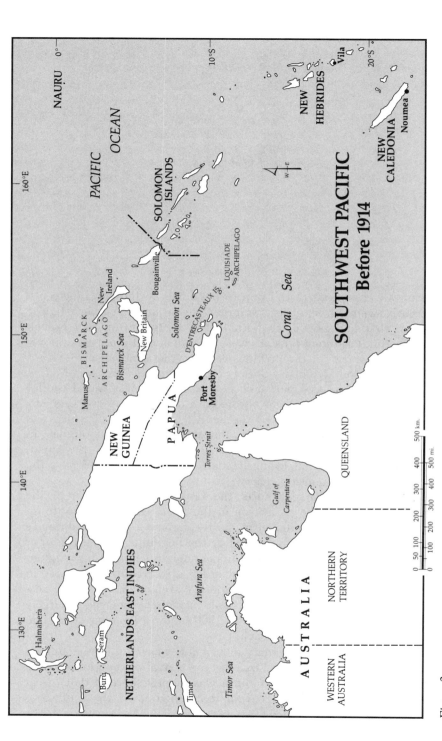

Figure 2.

Fanny, settled in a small weatherboard cottage on a hill overlooking the newly charted harbor of Port Moresby, the first missionary, and indeed the first European, to establish himself in southeastern New Guinea. Thirty-one other LMS missionaries followed McFarlane and Lawes to New Guinea (Papua)[10] in the period up to 1914. All were male and all were ordained. They settled at stations scattered sparsely along the southeastern coast, each one the center of a surrounding district, staffed by Polynesian, and later Papuan, pastors (Figure 3).[11]

The Missionaires du Sacré-Coeur (Missionaries of the Sacred Heart, MSC), a congregation founded at Issoudun, France, in 1854, came to New Guinea at the request of Pope Leo XIII. Debarred from entry by the Queensland Government, an ardent young priest, Father Henri Verjus, with two coadjutor brothers, made an illicit pioneer voyage from their *pied-à-terre*, Thursday Island, on the lugger of a sympathetic trader known as Yankee Ned. Arriving at Yule Island in August 1885, they bought land and erected primitive buildings on a site which they named Port Leo, and which was to remain the headquarters of their mission in Papua, known popularly as the Sacred Heart Mission (SHM). There, after a precarious beginning, the pioneers were joined by other members of their own congregation, and by sisters of the associated congregation, the Filles de Nôtre-Dame du Sacré-Coeur (Daughters of Our Lady of the Sacred Heart, FDNSC). Confined by the operation of a "spheres of influence" policy, they evangelized a narrow corridor through Roro and Mekeo, and expanded into the unevangelized, and largely uncontacted, mountainous interior (Figures 2, 4). By 1914, 60 priests, 65 sisters and 47 brothers had lived (and, in many cases, died) in Papua.

New Guinea was chosen as a special field of missionary endeavor by the AWMMS, to commemorate the centenary of the death of John Wesley. In 1891, William Bromilow led the pioneer party of Wesleyan missionaries to Dobu Island in the D'Entrecasteaux group, headquarters of the field determined for them by the gentleman's agreement of 1890, which had initiated the spheres of influence policy. In their energetic evangelization of the islands at the southeast tip of New Guinea, the AWMMS employed ordained Methodist ministers, missionary sisters, male lay missionaries, and South Sea Islanders, all organized, according to the dictates of Methodist polity, into districts, circuits, and stations (Figure 5). Between 1891 and 1914, forty-eight European[12] missionaries (18 ministers, 23 missionary sisters, and 7 laymen) served in the Methodist mission field in Papua.

The Anglican missionaries, whose arrival in 1891 was the eventual outcome of the intermittent concern of the colonial bishops for the Aborigines and other "heathen" of the islands near Australia,[13] also had

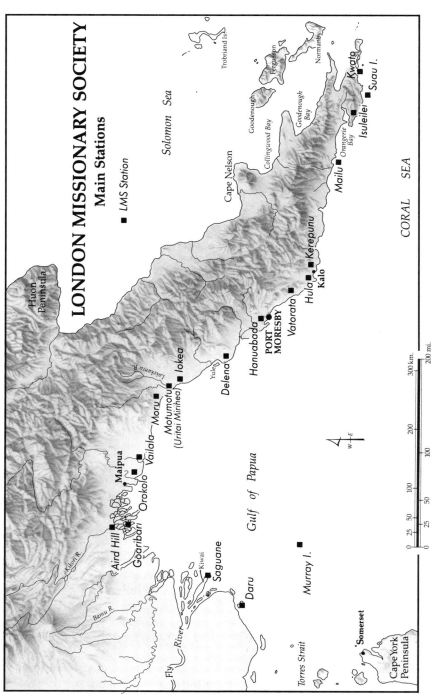

LONDON MISSIONARY SOCIETY
Main Stations

■ LMS Station

Huon
Peninsula

Solomon   Sea

Trobriand Is.

Ferguson

Goodenough

Goodenough
Bay

Collingwood Bay

■ Kwato
Isuleilei ■ ■ Suau I.

Cape Nelson

Orangerie
Bay

Mailu ■

CORAL   SEA

Kerepunu
■ Kalo

Vatorata ■
Hula ■

PORT
MORESBY ●
Hanuabada ■

Lakekamu R.

Iokea ■

Motumotu
(Uritai Mirihea) ■

Moru ■
Vailala ■

Delena ■

Yule I.

Maipua ■
Orokolo ●

Aird Hill ■ ■
Goaribari

Kikori R.

Bamu R.

Fly River

Kiwai
Saguane ■

Daru

Murray I. ■

Torres Strait

Somerset ●

Cape York
Peninsula

Gulf of Papua

W ─ E

| 0 | 25 | 50 | 100 | | 200 | | 300 km. |
| 0 | 25 | 50 | 100 | | 200 mi. | | |

Figure 3.

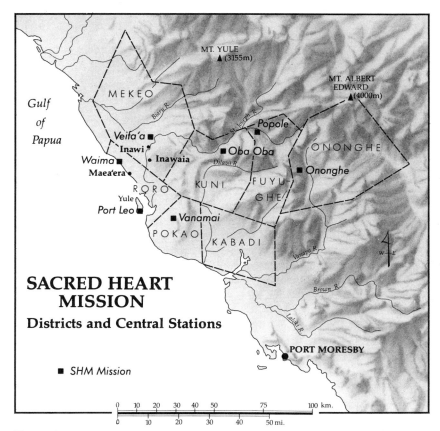

Figure 4.

their sphere determined by the agreement of 1890. They were to be responsible for the whole north coast of British New Guinea, except for a small strip at the south end that was handed over to the Methodists. In August 1891, a priest, Albert Maclaren, with three lay colleagues, bought land on the grassy plateau of Dogura at Bartle Bay and, with considerable effort, erected the large prefabricated house, shipped from Victoria, which was to be the heart of the Anglican community. Between 1891 and 1914, seventy-four Anglicans (18 priests, 28 women, and 28 laymen) served at Dogura and the other Anglican stations, which stretched from the Mamba River, near the German border, to Taupota, in the east (Figure 6).

After the First World War, other missions entered the Territory of Papua, beginning a new era that had been heralded by the arrival of a

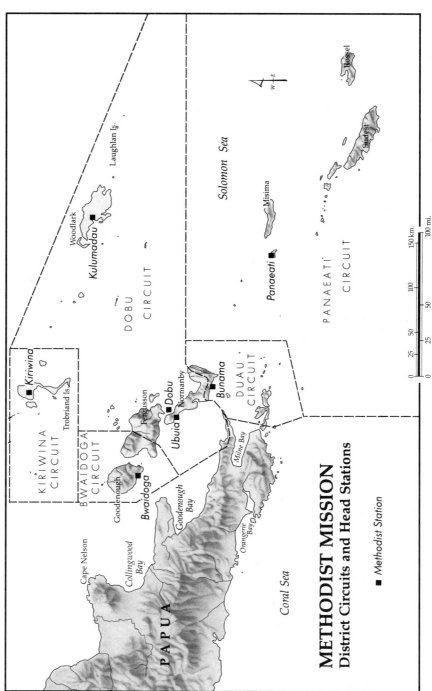

METHODIST MISSION
District Circuits and Head Stations

■ *Methodist Station*

Figure 5.

Figure 6.

Seventh Day Adventist pastor before the war. After the interruption of the war, new recruits continued to come to the four original missions as well. But the men and women recruited after the Great War were different people from those who came before, and they served in a different world. The golden age of mission was over.

CHAPTER 1

"Few Are Powerful
or Highly Born"

Origins

THE 327 EUROPEAN missionaries who worked in Papua before the First
World War came from a wide diversity of national, ethnic, and class
backgrounds, of which any simple stereotype of "the missionary" fails
to take account. The mores, values, assumptions, and aims they
brought with them to the mission field were inevitably molded by their
cultural and subcultural backgrounds, as much as by their religious formation.

In what became first a British and then an Australian colony, neither
the British nor the Australian presence was heavily preponderant in the
mission field. Of all missionaries, 45 percent came from continental
Europe, the French alone accounting for 25 percent. However, the largest single national group came from Australia, which contributed 30
percent of all missionaries, while Great Britain contributed 19 percent
(Table 1).[1]

The nationality of the missionaries was, predictably, closely correl-
ated with the mission in which they served. All of the continental European missionaries belonged to the Sacred Heart Mission, two-thirds of
them coming from France, homeland of the congregations of the Missionaries of the Sacred Heart and the Daughters of Our Lady of the
Sacred Heart. By contrast, the LMS was overwhelmingly British.
Throughout the period, it continued to draw most of its recruits for
Papua—as for its other fields—from England and Scotland. The Anglican Mission was more colonial in origin. Sixty-five percent of its missionaries were Australian born, and of the twenty-one born in Britain
seventeen were British migrants to Australia, recruited there. Most
colonial of all was the Methodist Mission. More than 75 percent of its
missionaries were born in Australia or New Zealand, and of the ten

Table 1. Country of origin of missionaries, by denomination

COUNTRY	LMS	SHM	METHODIST	ANGLICAN	TOTAL
Great Britain	30	1	10	21	62
Ireland		4			4
Australia	3	19	30	46	98
New Zealand		1	8	1	10
Canada		1			1
United States				1	1
France		83			83
Holland		22			22
Belgium		15			15
Germany		12			12
Italy		8			8
Switzerland		4			4
Austria		1			1
Spain		1			1
Unknown				5	5
Total	33	172	48	74	327

British-born, six were recruited in Australia and five in New Zealand, most of them having migrated as children with their parents and grown up in the colonies.

Within the Sacred Heart Mission, the national composition of the priesthood was notably different from that of the lay brothers. Thirty-seven of the sixty-one priests were French, and the second largest national group were the six German priests, all of whom were born after the Franco-Prussian War on the newly German soil of Alsace, but of loyal Catholic families who commonly retained an emotional and cultural allegiance to France. Of the forty-six brothers, only seven were French. Holland contributed twenty, almost half of the total, Belgium six, Italy five, Germany four, Switzerland two, and Austria, Australia, and Canada one each. The Daughters of our Lady of the Sacred Heart were, like the priests, predominantly French (thirty-nine of the sixty-five).

The French missionaries came almost entirely from those regions of France identified by Gabriel Le Bras in 1880 as containing "real" rather than "statistical" Catholics and being generally resistant to the pressures of anticlericalism to remain the "Christian regions" of France up to the mid-twentieth century.[2] Most outstanding was the strong Breton presence in the mission. With a respected clergy, an aristocracy that preserved the faith, and a distinctive syncretic religion in which Catholicism coexisted with pre-Christian ritual and beliefs, nineteenth-century Brittany was described by one historian as "the most steadfastly religious province in France."[3] Thirty-two of the eighty-three French missionaries came from Brittany, nineteen of them from one diocese, Nantes, noted for its piety.

Alsace, another region of "real" Catholics, contributed eight French missionaries to Papua, in addition to the six of German nationality. Neighboring Lorraine provided a further three. Other notably religious areas from which the French missionaries came were Savoy (4), the Pyrenees (4), the Auvergne (4), the Calvados department of Normandy (3), the Vendée (3), and the Lozère and Franche-Comté one each. A further seven missionaries came from the Loire Valley which, though more mixed in the strength of its religious adherence, was the cradle of the two congregations.

The distinction between real and statistical Catholics did not reflect a simple dichotomy between rural and urban areas. Although Paris was regarded as a city where the hold of religion was weak, Marseilles was commonly believed to be more Christian than the rural environs of Provence. Paris provided only one missionary for Papua before the First World War, Marseilles two.

Had the French orders not been subject to the anticlerical policies of the Third Republic, the congregations of the MSC and the FDNSC probably would have remained more homogeneously French. But the prohibition of teaching orders under the Ferry Decrees of 1879–1880 and the renewed and more intensified attack in 1901 under the Law of Associations, dispersed the congregations into other European countries. After a temporary exile in Barcelona, apostolic schools and novitiates were established in 1880 in Holland, first in the diocese of Bois-le-Duc and then in 1882 in the neighboring industrial town of Tilburg, and soon after in Belgium, at Borgerhout near Antwerp. These areas supplied the SHM with a number of missionaries, especially lay brothers. Seven came from the villages or small towns of Bois-le-Duc, two from the environs of Tilburg, and four from nearby Breda. Of the six Belgian brothers, all were from the neighborhood of Antwerp or the nearby towns of Mechelen and Melsele.

Despite the differences in national composition within the SHM, priests, sisters, and brothers all had predominantly rural backgrounds. The majority of priests and sisters came from the smaller towns and villages of the French provinces; the brothers came from the villages and regional towns of Holland and Belgium and, to a lesser extent, of France, Italy, Germany, and Switzerland.

The missionaries of the LMS were mostly of urban origin. Many were born and bred in towns or cities and of those born elsewhere, most had established themselves in a town, often in employment, before applying to the LMS. Two were Londoners and two others were living in London when recruited. Manchester, Glasgow, and Aberdeen each provided two, as did the small Staffordshire town of Walsall. The midlands and northeastern industrial towns of Halifax, Burnley, Nottingham, Bradford, and Hull each supplied one, but a greater number came from small regional towns, where Congregationalism was traditionally stronger.[4] Of the three Australian LMS missionaries, one was from Richmond, Melbourne, another from Balmain, Sydney, and the third from Milton, Brisbane.

The Methodist missionaries were drawn most heavily from New Zealand and the southeastern states of Australia. Thirteen were born or brought up in New Zealand, twelve in Victoria, eleven in New South Wales, and six in South Australia. Western Australia and Tasmania provided two missionaries each, and Queensland one. Besides being colonial rather than English, the Methodist missionaries differed from those of the LMS in more frequently having rural backgrounds. Of the thirteen recruited in New Zealand, all but two or three came from farming regions such as Blenheim, Lower Hutt, Willowby, Napier, Howick, and Waitara. The Australian Methodist missionaries were more commonly from country towns. Of the twelve Victorians, for example, four were from Geelong, a notably strong Methodist area, two from Ballarat, two from Bendigo, and one from another goldfields town, Clunes. Two of the Victorians, however, were from metropolitan Melbourne, and among the eleven Methodists from New South Wales, five were from the suburbs of Sydney.

Like the Methodist Mission, the Anglican Mission had a strong Australian component, again mainly from the eastern states. Of the sixty-six Anglican missionaries recruited in Australia, twenty-six came from New South Wales and fifteen from Victoria. But whereas the Methodist workers were drawn almost entirely from the southeastern states, the Anglican Mission recruited thirteen workers from Queensland, three of them English priests working in the colonial church. Three Anglicans came from Western Australia and two from Tasmania. Australian Anglicans also more frequently came from the capital cities of the eastern states than their Methodist colleagues. Nine of the thirteen Queenslanders were from Brisbane, eleven of the fifteen Victorians from Melbourne, and at least sixteen among the twenty-six recruits from New South Wales were from Sydney.[5]

Social Background

While much is known of the social origins of a few missionaries who achieved eminence in their careers, the backgrounds of many rank-and-file missionaries, some of them distinguished only by the fact that they served for a few months or years in the mission field, remains obscure. Inferences must be drawn from such indicators as their own occupations and those of their fathers (Table 2); their educational experience, where such information is available; and from such general allusions to their background as have been made by the missionaries themselves, their contemporaries, or their descendants. Some elude even such a loosely woven, widely cast net, to remain shadowy figures until their arrival in the field.

In the Sacred Heart Mission, this problem is compounded by the fact that the majority of priests went into holy orders without first engaging in secular employment. Their backgrounds can only be deduced from their fathers' occupations where known (see Table 2), or from vaguer, more general references to their families. Two of the best known priests were men from eminent families. Alain de Boismenu, who served in the mission from 1898 to 1945, becoming in 1900 the youngest bishop in the Roman Catholic hierarchy, was the son of a shipowner, of an "old and noble" Breton seafaring family, in whose veins, it was said, the blood of the corsairs of St. Malo mingled with that of medieval Irish princes.[6] André Jullien, an introverted, highly intelligent priest who served as superior of the mission from 1895 to 1909, was the son of a "rich and honourable" family from Marseilles.[7] But there were also men of humble birth among the mission's leaders. Archbishop Louis-André Navarre, first vicar apostolic of Melanesia, was the son of a peasant vine-grower of Bourgogne, near Auxerre.[8] His "right arm," Henri Verjus, founder of the mission, a man whose intense mystical faith and premature death were to make him the best known of all Sacred Heart missionaries, was also of modest origins. His father was a Savoyard soldier (and in peacetime, rural constable) who married an Italian peasant woman while serving in Piedmont, where Verjus was born.[9] Louis Couppé, who achieved eminence after his years in Papua as vicar apostolic of New Britain, was the son of a locksmith in the small French town of Romorantin.[10]

What is known of the backgrounds of other priests within the SHM suggests that many were men whose families were of modest socioeconomic status. Father Jean Genocchi, whom Sir Hubert Murray regarded as "a most enlightened man" and "perhaps the greatest scholar" he had ever known, was the son of an unsuccessful small-businessman in Ravenna.[11] Several had artisan fathers. Henri Eschlimann was the son of a housepainter; Edmond Joindreau the son of a blacksmith; Bernard van Riel the son of a builder; and Maximilian Branger the son of a tilemaker.[12] The fathers of three priests were engaged in skilled or semi-skilled industrial work, two as machinists and one as an iron-molder.[13] Father Gsell himself, later Bishop of Darwin, worked as an apprentice

Table 2. Socioeconomic origins of missionaries by occupational status of fathers

Socioeconomic grouping*	LMS		Methodist		Anglican		SHM† Priests		SHM† Sisters		Total	
	No.	%	No.	%	No.	%	No.	%	No.	%	No.	%
I Large employers, merchants, bankers, high officials in shipping and insurance, liberal professions, private means			2	4	11	15	4	7	4	6	21	8
II Small employers, small dealers, wholesalers, retailers, local government officials, teachers, subordinate officers in insurance and church, clerical occupations	14	42	9	19	11	15	1	2			35	13
III Artisan crafts, skilled labor, lower class traders	5	15	7	14	4	5	8	13	3	5	27	10
IV Small farmers, peasant farmers	2	6	8	17	5	7	8	13	23	35	46	16
V Semi-skilled workers, sailors, soldiers, subordinate government service, police, miners			6	12	6	8	8	13	3	5	23	8
VI General unskilled labor, unskilled work in transport, municipal labor									4	6	4	1
Unknown	12	36	16	33	37	50	32	52	28	43	125	44
Total	33		48		74		61		65		281	

Notes: Percentages may not add up to 100 due to rounding.
The occupational status of the fathers of missionaries can often only be gleaned from the missionaries' birth certificates. Because of the difficulty of obtaining such data, this table is no more than suggestive.

*Socioeconomic groupings are based on those constructed by G. Stedman Jones (1971, 355–356). He stressed that the classification does not purport to be a class analysis. His table has been modified to include a rural component. In my study, because of the difficulty of making cross-cultural comparisons, it should be regarded as a categorizing rather than a ranking classification.

†Because of the difficulty of discovering the origins of the brothers of the SHM, they have been omitted from this table.

in a cotton-spinning factory.[14] But more were from rural backgrounds. Theophile Dontenwill's father was a farmer, Joseph Caspar's a gardener, Jean-Pierre Lang's, like Navarre's, a vine-grower, and Joseph Chabot's, steward of an old castle.[15] Fathers Fastré, Norin, Cramaille, and Rossier, all of whom had distinguished careers, were the sons of peasant farmers, trained and ordained at a time when the aristocracy had given way to the peasantry as the main recruiting ground for the French clergy.[16] Other fathers whose stated occupations are more ambiguous—boatman, sea captain, storekeeper, oilman and "splintman"—were probably also of working class origins.[17] The only priests known to be from the *haute-bourgeoisie* were Fernard Hartzer, whose father was director-general of prisons in Alsace, and Vincenzo Ėgidi, the son of an Italian civil servant.[18]

The brothers of the SHM were all, despite their range of nationalities, men of modest origins.[19] Many were artisans, the Dutch brothers being traditional masters of three trades. Among their ranks were three blacksmiths, two carpenters and cabinetmakers, two clockmakers, two bakers, a pastrycook, a printer, a spinner, and a clogmaker. Another seven were sailors and fishermen, five of them from the small Dutch fishing village of Volendam. Most of the remaining brothers, especially those of France and Italy, were peasants.

Like the priests, the Daughters of Our Lady of the Sacred Heart were of more diverse origin (Table 2). Sister Kostka Duflôt was a Parisian French aristocrat;[20] Mother Liguori Debroux, born into an affluent Belgian family, had assisted in her father's prosperous grocery and drapery business before deciding that she was called to a different destiny; Mother Thérèse Jean was the daughter of a lawyer and Mother Paule Perdrix was the cultured and much-traveled daughter of a solid Strasbourg family. Many others were women of modest origin. Until the early years of the twentieth century the congregation retained a division, common at the time, between choir sisters and lay sisters, which reflected the accepted stratification of society on the basis of birth and the resultant distinctions in "education and refinement of manners."[21] Choir sisters were expected to furnish a dowry on entering the congregation. Most of the European sisters who went to New Guinea before the turn of the century were lay sisters and hence of humble family,[22] the daughters of peasant farmers and artisans. Raphael Suramy sewed in a workshop, Eusebia Dedierjean worked in a silk factory, and Madeleine Masselin served in a small Parisian shop before entering the congregation.[23] The European sisters were supplemented, in the decade before the Great War, by women whose fathers were skilled tradesmen, farmers, or unskilled laborers in Australia.[24]

In 1906 Bishop Stone-Wigg drew the attention of readers of the

Anglican Mission's annual report to the fact that during the eight years of his episcopacy, the "professional classes" of Australia had given no recruits to the mission. And yet, he reminded them, "the Church of England has a preponderating influence among these classes."[25] The Anglican Mission in New Guinea did not have the same aristocratic ethos as its counterpart in central Africa, nor even the upper middle-class character of its neighbor, the Melanesian Mission, which, despite its failure to fulfil its founder's injunctions concerning the acceptable background for recruits, still drew heavily on the ranks of university-educated English gentlemen.[26]

There were a few such men in the New Guinea mission. Stone-Wigg himself was the son of a "fine old English gentleman," a justice of the peace, alderman, benefactor, and pillar of the community of the elegant town of Tunbridge Wells.[27] His successor, Gerald Sharp, second bishop of New Guinea, was the son of Thomas Beatt Sharp, "gentleman" of Lowfields, Childer Thornton, in Cheshire.[28] Despite Stone-Wigg's protestations, a number of priests of professional background were recruited to the mission, though often before or after his episcopacy, and sometimes from England rather than Australia (Table 2). Copland King, cofounder of the mission with Maclaren, was a member of the Sydney elite, son of the Reverend (later Archdeacon) R. L. King, Principal of Moore Theological College, and great-grandson of Philip Gidley King, third governor of New South Wales.[29] His nephew, Frank Elder, was also the son of an Anglican priest, as was Romney Gill, whose father had moved from British nonconformity into the Church of England.[30] Another English priest, Ernest Wesley Taylor, was the son of a Methodist minister, a brilliant Oxford scholar and brother of a professor of philosophy at McGill.[31] Henry Newton, third Bishop of New Guinea, was brought up in Australia as the adopted son of a scholar and later priest, John Frederick Newton.[32]

But the mission also encompassed priests of humble origins. Albert Maclaren was a Scottish stonemason's son who had found employment, before ordination, with the Ordnance Survey.[33] His fellow pioneer, Samuel Tomlinson, ordained after serving the mission as carpenter for twelve years, was the son of a foreman patternmaker.[34] Percy Shaw and Frederick Ramsay, also ordained during their missionary careers, were of working class origins.[35] Like a number of their LMS counterparts, William Murray, Frank Elder, and John Hunt were clerks before seeking ordination.

In the Anglican Mission, the priests were a minority. Twenty-eight of the missionaries were laymen. Whereas the priests were men of varied social backgrounds, those laymen whose origins are known were nearly all of working-class or, occasionally, lower middle-class families.[36] They were the sons of small farmers, artisans and minor officials, among them a police magistrate and a postmaster. Before joining the mission, they worked as artisans (printer, carpenter, blacksmith, engineer, baker), as farm laborers or miners, or in white-collar employment as draper's assistant or architectural draftsman. The only three laymen known not to share these origins were Francis de Sales Buchanan, born of a wealthy propertied family in the southern United States and grandson of the fifteenth president;[37] Ernest Davies, son of a London physician;[38] and Eric Giblin, stepson of a station owner, whose family bore a good name in Tasmanian society.[39]

The twenty-eight women in the Anglican Mission were of less homogeneous origins. Many were women of middle-class or upper middle-class origin, to whom Bishop Stone-Wigg referred, probably with some acidity, as "lady-workers."[40] Two such women were Gertrude and Louise Robson, the former a teacher, the latter a nurse, both daughters of John Shield Robson, a shipbuilder from Durham, sisters to Ernest Iliff Robson, first headmaster of North Sydney Church of England Grammar School, and sisters also to Sir Robert Garran's wife, Hilda. They were a prominent family in Sydney and Garran described Gertrude, who ran a private school, as a "cultivated and much educated woman."[41] Several women had sufficient private means to be able to serve without claiming any allowance from the mission. But like the priests of the Anglican Mission, the women were of mixed origins. Women such as Elizabeth Tomlinson, diminutive and retiring migrant from working-class Manchester, or Alice Cottingham, daughter of an English farmer, or Ellen Combley, a yeoman's daughter who worked at Guy's Hospital and the Plague Hospital, London, before nursing massive dysentery epidemics in Papua and finally succumbing to the disease herself, were as much at home in the mission as the "lady-workers" from Sydney.[42]

Despite Stone-Wigg's disparaging remark, there was more professionalism among the Anglican women than among those of any other mission. Twelve of the twenty-eight women were certificated teachers, nine were fully trained and two were partly trained nurses. Their acceptance by the mission depended on the skills they had to offer as well as their commitment to the cause.

During the early nineteenth century, the London Missionary Society had recruited most of its missionaries from "pious congregations of artisans and tradesmen . . . from the lower middle and mechanic classes,"[43] a humbler stratum of society than was characteristic of the adherents of Congregationalism in general.[44] The century saw a general rise in the social status of LMS candidates, but this section of society remained its most fruitful recruiting ground for the Papuan mission.[45]

Among the thirty-three who came before the First World War, only four could be considered to have come from professional families. Fourteen were "black-coated workers": clerks, accountants, small retailers, shop assistants, and elementary school teachers who, although in Marxist terms proletarian, were often accorded honorary lower middle-class status because they were salaried and performed semiskilled nonmanual work with little supervision in clean and "respectable" surroundings.[46] Nine were clerks, one was a bookseller, one a warehouseman, and three were from that most fertile of LMS recruiting grounds, the draper's shop. The next largest group were the artisans or skilled tradesmen, from the section of society described by Kitson Clark as labor's aristocracy,[47] which although scarcely distinguishable from the black-coated work force in terms of income, was more likely to retain a proletarian identity and way of life. They included a printer, two shoemakers, a housepainter, an engineer, a shipbuilder, and an able seaman. Only two LMS missionaries were skilled or semiskilled employees in manufacturing industry, and three had jobs that required no particular skills.

During the forty years between 1874 and 1914, LMS recruitment in general was moving away from the artisans and skilled workers toward those of middle-class occupations. But this trend was not reflected in the Papuan mission. Over the four decades there was no appreciable difference in the occupational status of those recruited. Of the pioneer missionaries of the first decade, Samuel McFarlane was an archetypal "godly mechanic" born of a large and poor family and employed in a railway machine shop; William Lawes, a tailor's son, and James Chalmers, a stonemason's son, had both joined the black-coated work force, the former as a draper, the latter as a clerk; and William Turner, a medical student and son of a missionary, was one of the four to come to Papua from a professional family. Each subsequent decade saw the arrival of one missionary from a professional background: another student and missionary's son, and two chemists and druggists, one of them also a medical student. In each decade the largest recruitment was from the black-coated workers, the next largest group the artisans, with only a few skilled or semiskilled industrial workers, or unskilled laborers.

The occupational status of the LMS missionaries was at times, however, a misleading indicator of their background. Most were only at the outset of their careers, often in apprenticeships or lowly positions from which they might aspire to rise. For others, intent on a career in the ministry, a secular occupation was seen as only a temporary necessity. One of the three missionaries working in an unskilled job had a father who was a clerk, and the father of another was managing director of a firm of scale makers. These were not proletarians. The third unskilled worker, Ben Butcher, whose father was liveryman in the Clockmakers'

Guild and who helped other members of his family sell fish at the big wholesale market at Billingsgate, also asserted a middle-class identity. Theirs was a very old London family and Butcher was, by patrimony, a Freeman of the City.[48] Similarly, two of the clerks had fathers from the greater middle class, one the owner of a successful paint factory, the other headmaster of a private school.[49] The social backgrounds of the LMS missionaries may not always have been, then, as modest as their occupations suggested. Nevertheless, recruits for work in Papua remained, throughout the period, overwhelmingly lower middle class or artisan in origin.

The early Methodist missionaries in Papua came from occupations basically similar to those of their LMS contemporaries. Four of the five members of the pioneer party were white-collar workers or artisans. William Bromilow, leader of the group, was a carpenter's son who had been a schoolteacher before ordination.[50] John Field, the son of a customshouse agent, was an architect and builder.[51] James Watson, whose father was an engineer, was himself an engineer and blacksmith, and George Bardsley, the only layman in the group, was a carpenter.[52] The fifth member of the party, Samuel Fellows, had worked in rolling mills in Derbyshire before emigrating with his family and studying for the Wesleyan ministry in New Zealand.[53]

Where the occupations of the fathers of Methodist missionaries are known, they suggest a greater diversity of social backgrounds and a lower concentration of clerical employment than in the LMS. Whereas the urban black-coated work force was the main recruiting ground of the latter, that of the Methodists was the farm. Of the thirty-two Methodist missionaries whose fathers' occupations are known (Table 2), eight were the sons or daughters of farmers. The fathers of seven were semiskilled workers and of seven, artisans or skilled workers. A further seven had fathers in white-collar employment.[54] Only two belonged to the families of professionals or large property owners: Ambrose Fletcher was the son of a schoolmaster who was the third member of his family to be principal of Wesley College, New Zealand, and James Williams' father was a "gentleman" of private means.[55]

Unlike those of the Sacred Heart and Anglican missions, the backgrounds of the ordained Methodist missionaries showed no apparent variation from those of the lay men and women. Almost all, regardless of status within the mission, were drawn from families of farmers, artisans, small business operators, and clerical employees, which was consistent with the social composition of colonial Methodism in general.[56] While numbers of the male missionaries moved into the middle classes through ordination into the Methodist ministry, several of the women also rose in status, five by becoming qualified teachers and two by becoming certificated nurses.

Family Backgrounds

Differences in nationality, rank, period, and family history ensured that the domestic experience of the missionaries varied considerably. Glimpses of this diversity are captured in the recollections of the small minority who have committed their memories of childhood to paper, or allowed others to do so.

Even among the British missionaries there were appreciable differences in home environment. The settled early Victorian childhood of William Lawes, centered on the chapel, the school, and his modest, godly home at Aldermaston,[57] was a different experience from that of his colleague and friend, James Chalmers, who tasted the freedom of Scottish lochs and glens as his family moved from place to place according to his father's work.[58] Ben Butcher, born in late-Victorian London, remembered a childhood of horse-drawn buses, weekly baths before the kitchen fire in tubs filled from huge cast-iron kettles, candlelit bedrooms, and naked gas-jets in the best rooms.[59] Charles Abel, also born in London, but a decade earlier, recalled genteel evenings with his lower middle-class family gathered around the piano in their suburban home.[60] Romney Gill's brother, sculptor Eric Gill, wrote of the childhood they shared with their eleven brothers and sisters in Brighton and Chichester, sometimes with a maidservant but often not, because their strong-willed mother, an opera singer before her marriage, "was not good at keeping servants." Their father painted "quite well" and read Tennyson, Carlyle, Maurice, Robertson, Farrar, George McDonald, and Kingsley, naming his children after them and their characters.[61]

Although few of the missionaries referred to the political affiliations of their families, it can be assumed that the British nonconformists, like most of their kind, would have been more or less actively Liberal. This would also probably have been true of those Anglicans such as Gill, Taylor, and Stirrat, whose heritage was that of Dissent. Some families may have joined the large-scale nonconformist defection from Gladstonian liberalism to Liberal Unionism in the 1880s as did Romney Gill's;[62] others, like those of Charles Abel and Oliver Tomkins, would have remained loyal to Mr. Gladstone.[63]

Looking back on his childhood, wrote Eric Gill, was like looking back on a different world, and "the chief thing about that world was this, that . . . we believed the world of England was divinely guided, the British Empire a divinely ordained institution, Religion the mainspring of political and social structures."[64] Such confidence was probably shared by all the British missionaries, irrespective of their differences in background. Ben Butcher, of humbler birth, reflected similarly on growing up in the "heyday of the Victorian era, when Britain ruled the waves and boasted of an Empire on which the sun never set. . . . It was a whiteman's world and the British thought themselves in charge of it, and for lads like myself it was a world full of boundless possibilities with vast areas unknown and waiting to be explored."[65]

There was as much diversity in the family backgrounds of the French missionaries. Louis-André Navarre, in old age recalled his romantic, youthful delight in the beauty of the fields, the forests, the flowers, and the vines of Auxerre, and the chagrin of growing up, motherless, under the control of a shrewd, pragmatic peasant father to whom religion mattered little.[66] Alain de Boismenu, whose mother died after his birth, grew up in a comfortable family home in the old maritime town of St. Malo, submitting to a strict paternal discipline and the even less welcome discipline of his eldest sister.[67] His pupil and friend, Paul Fastré, experienced the rough childhood of a peasant born on the poor, arid soil of the Pyrenees, where, as a youth, he grazed his father's two or three cows.[68] André Jullien, only son of a wealthy widowed mother, passed a different childhood, with winters spent in the town of Marseilles and summers at the family's country estate, Château Gombert, surrounded by a wide circle of rich and cultured relatives.[69]

Although the French missionaries seldom referred to the political allegiances of their families, these can be inferred with a fair degree of certainty from pioneering psephological studies of nineteenth-century France.[70] In general terms, the French church, although a supporter of Napoleon III in the early days of the Second Empire, was, during the Third Republic, an ally of legitimism, whose traditionalist values were closely associated with Catholicism. There is a close, though not complete, correlation in the map of the strength of religious adherence with that of the strength of the Right in 1876 and 1914.[71]

The majority of French missionaries came from areas noted both for religious observance and for the strength of the vote for the Right. They were mostly in the west of France, stronghold of the Right, and included Brittany, Normandy, and the lower Loire in the northwest, and the Aveyron, the Lozère, and the higher Loire in the Massif Central. In the northwest, from where more than two-thirds of the French missionaries originated, the conservative influence of the church was reinforced by that of the *château*, for through the system of *fermage* (use of land for a cash rent) common in that region, the landlords exerted control over the peasantry. In the Massif Central, where peasant proprietorship was prevalent and hence, it has been suggested, more independence could be expected of the peasantry, the clergy retained unusually strong political influence.

A third area that supplied a number of missionaries, French Lorraine, Franche-Comté, and Burgundy, was a region of peasant proprietorship with a long democratic tradition. But like the other areas from which the missionaries came in strength, it was a Catholic area, and during the first decade of the twentieth century, it rejected radicalism to join the vote for the Right. Conversely, few of the missionaries came from either the middle classes or the regions where republicanism was strong, such as the Midi, several departments of central France, Paris, and the northern industrial areas.

Born of loyal Catholic peasant families, deferential to both priest and landlord, many of them in the strongholds of legitimism, most French missionaries grew up amid conservative political influences. Father Bodet of the Vendée was proud of his Chouan heritage and all his life, "like all good Chouans," remained loyal to the king of France.[72] Father Norin, of Breton peasant stock, was also a self-proclaimed monarchist.[73] The few whose families were notables were likely to have grown up in a similar political milieu, for the provincial landed gentry—Catholic, patriotic, and conservative—had also, after 1883, thrown itself solidly behind the legitimist cause. Although loyal Catholic families were bound, in the nineties, to heed Leo XIII's policy of *Ralliement*, it is doubtful whether it had much appeal, especially after the assault on the religious orders.

For many of the French missionaries, childhood was less tranquil than for their English contemporaries. About half of them, born during the Second Empire, experienced the dislocation caused by the Franco-Prussian War and the establishment of the Third Republic. Sister Madeline was probably the missionary most directly touched by the war—a cannonball lodged itself in the linen press that she was sorting.[74] During the bombardment of Strasbourg, Fernand Hartzer, his mother and brother, with other women and children, were evacuated to Switzerland.[75] After the war his family, like those of other Alsatian missionaries, had to choose between German citizenship and exile. Joseph Poupenay saw his father, mayor of a village in Franche-Comté, taken prisoner by the Germans for refusing to pay war contributions.[76]

The colonial childhood of the Australian and New Zealand missionaries has scarcely been documented. Surviving family records generally suggest only its outlines. For some it included the long voyage by sailing ship with their migrating family and the struggle and adventure of settlement in a new land. Several, like William Bromilow, had fathers who felt the "lure of the goldfields" and tried their luck before returning to their trades or settling on the land.[77] Margaret Jamieson, a Methodist sister and later wife of fellow missionary Arthur Scrivin, grew up on the forty-acre farm that her father, an immigrant from the Shetland Isles, had carved out of the bush at Marawatu, New Zealand. Her father died when she was a child and she and her six brothers and sisters were brought up by their mother, also a Shetland Islander, who had taught herself to read.[78] Another missionary sister, Maisie Lill, growing up in a large and happy New Zealand farming family, counted riding a cow among the accomplishments of childhood.[79] Such experiences were far removed from those of Copland King, whose intellectual interests were fostered by scholarly private tuition in his family's Sydney home.[80]

Families from which the missionaries came were of all sizes. Those of Romney Gill and Alphonse Clauser, each with thirteen living children, were the largest whose size is known. Other missionaries also came from the large families typical of the period: of the fifty families whose exact size is known, ten contained ten or more living children, and another ten between seven and nine. But a slightly greater number were from families of medium size. Ten missionaries are known to have come from families of five or six children, and twelve from families of three or four. A few families were very small—six with two children, and two where the missionary was the only child. In all these eight cases, the smallness of the family could be attributed to the death of either the father or the mother during the missionary's childhood. As was common in the period, family size in general was frequently curtailed because of infant deaths. Surviving records document the deaths of up to five children in families to which missionaries belonged. The position of the missionary in the family, where known, shows great variation and no significant pattern, except perhaps a tendency for the missionary to be about the middle of the family more frequently than eldest or youngest.

Even more difficult than discovering the external contours of the missionaries' families is to uncover the nature of the relationships within them. Although evidence is necessarily fragmentary and impressionistic, two motifs recur. The first is testimony to the overriding influence of the mother in the life of the male missionary as a child, especially in his spiritual formation. Missionaries recall hearing bible stories at their mothers' knee or claim that they owe everything to the prayers of their mothers who "prayed as only a mother can pray" for their spiritual welfare.[81] "All I am or ever will be is owing to her everyday Christian life," declared Methodist missionary, Ernest Johns.[82] The second motif is the close relationship that frequently existed between mother and son and was attested to by the missionary himself, either explicitly or through the tenor of the letters written to his mother from the field, or by the observations of contemporaries. "Oh mother, see how I love you," wrote Henri Verjus, "all I do, I do it first for the love of God and then for the love of my dearest mother."[83] André Jullien, whose mother, on her husband's death, had resolved to devote herself solely to God and her son, said a Magnificat whenever he received her letters.[84]

These observations may simply reflect a basic fact of nineteenth-century family life: the upbringing of children and especially the inculcation of religion was almost exclusively the concern of the mother.[85] This was as true for the French peasantry as for the English middle classes. Louis-André Navarre lamented the deprivation of religious understanding that the death of his mother caused him: "It is the mother, if she is really Christian, who conveys [such things]."[86] In this context the close bond of affection between mother and son may be seen as no more than the response of those children who were, for whatever reason, predisposed to be sympathetic to what their mothers, frequently devout women, stood for and the gratified response of a mother to a child who fulfils her expectations.

But in many of the families in which the missionaries grew up, the strong positive influence of the mother appears to have been counterbalanced by the exceptionally negative influence of the father, through death, absence, or failure of sympathy. This characteristic is most apparent among the families of the priests of the Sacred Heart Mission, possibly only because more evidence is available. Of the eminent SHM missionaries, about whose childhood most is known, Navarre lost his mother at age twelve, Henri Verjus lost his father at age ten, Fernand Hartzer's father died when he was eleven, and André Jullien's when he was four. Alain de Boismenu, whose mother had died soon after his birth, lost his father at thirteen. Another eminent MSC priest, Jean Genocchi, had a father whose "irresponsible and ruinous habits" alienated him from his family, which was sustained by his mother, a "pious and strong character."[87] Of the sixty priests in the SHM, seventeen are known to have lost their fathers during childhood or adolescence; others may have.[88]

Indications of similar patterns are present in the less comprehensive records of the other missionary societies. Of the thirty-three LMS missionaries, seven are known to have lost their fathers early,[89] eighteen are known to have had living fathers, and of the fathers of eight nothing is known. There is evidence that some missionaries had very limited or inadequate relationships with their living fathers. James Chalmers recalled in his autobiography that his father was often away from home and that it was his devout highlander mother who raised the family.[90] Charles Abel's son wrote of his father's childhood that "there was little real understanding and no intimacy between the father and his sons in those early days, for William Abel led his life apart."[91] One missionary had a father who was a drunkard, and another, whose father was a "ne'er-do-well," had a "saintly" mother to whom he was "devoted."[92] Ben Butcher, who as a young man had little contact with either parent, adopted a substitute mother, a wealthy patroness, to whom he wrote daily letters, addressing her as Mater II.[93]

Insights into the familial relationships of the Anglican and Methodist missionaries are even more scarce, but there are glimpses of comparable patterns. Albert Maclaren remembered his father as a remote, dour, and punitive man, of whom he was in awe.[94] Montagu Stone-Wigg's father, ostensibly a model Christian gentleman, had little sympathy for and no intimacy with his son.[95] After his death, Stone-Wigg's uncle wrote to him: "He would have been more to *me* and possibly to *you* if he had been less interested in public engagements and had given up a little more time to *family* interests."[96] Henry Newton was fatherless, although he did have a strong substitute in his adoptive father. Francis de Sales Buchanan, deprived of his father at the age of four by his death in the American Civil War, had a "very tender relationship" with his mother.[97] Nine of the seventy-four Anglicans are known to have lost their fathers during childhood or youth.[98] Among the Methodist missionaries, for whom information is most scant, five of the forty-eight suffered the death of their father while young.[99] Conversely, of only ten Anglican missionaries and twelve Methodist missionaries is it known with certainty that their fathers did not die during their childhood or adolescence.

Although the evidence available is too fragmentary, subjective, and uneven to afford any firm generalizations about the patterns of relationships in the missionaries' families, it does seem that an exceptional proportion of them experienced the death of their father during childhood or adolescence.[100] Despite the scarcity of the data, 28 percent of the priests of the Sacred Heart Mission, 21 percent of LMS missionaries, 12 percent of Anglican missionaries, and 10 percent of the Methodists are known to have lost their fathers in this period.

But maternal dominance must not be overemphasized. The majority of missionaries grew up with both a mother and a father, and several of them acknowledge the influence of and their gratitude to their "godly parents" rather than singling out their mother for special comment.[101] A few spoke with special appreciation of their fathers: Brother Rintz Bosma, in the last letter he wrote before his death, recalled for his "beloved father" the time when seated on his knee he learned to make the sign of the Cross and repeat the "Our Father"; LMS missionary James Clark attributed his "conversion" to the solicitous concern of his father; and Harry Dauncey regarded his father as his "greatest chum."[102] But such tributes are rare.

The loss, by so many missionaries, of their fathers during childhood may have been part of a more general experience of bereavement that is harder to quantify. As well as the seventeen priests of the SHM who lost their fathers, at least five had lost their mothers. Three of the forty-eight Methodist missionaries were known to be orphans, as were two of the LMS missionaries, one of the Anglicans, and four of the Sacred Heart missionaries.

Education

What education the missionaries received before their formal theological training depended on both the socioeconomic status of their parents, and the time and place of their early years. The earliest missionaries in New Guinea, who had grown up in England and Scotland before the establishment of a national system and the provision in 1876 for compulsory education, had very little schooling. They were dependent on the village schools established by such voluntary bodies as the National Society for Promoting the Education of the Poor and the British and Foreign School Society, which received grants-in-aid from the government, or, in Scotland, on the parish schools. Those educated after the institution of Robert Lowe's Revised Code in 1862, with its "payment by results" received an education which concentrated on routine drilling in the three Rs.

When applying to the LMS, these early missionaries were generally unspecific about the education they had received.[103] Lawes described his as "a very partial one at a village school," Savage described himself as having had the "ordinary educational advantages of childhood and youth," and Sharpe referred to his education even more vaguely as "an ordinary one." Samuel McFarlane admitted that his "advantages at school" had not been "very great," and Hunt confessed that his education was "not all it should be," while Pearse referred to his simply as "limited." Such statements, where translated into more concrete information, suggest that most of the early LMS missionaries left school at about eleven or twelve, or even at ten, which was to become the minimum school-leaving age in 1876.

James Chalmers, who, to the age of thirteen, attended Scottish parish schools, generally regarded as superior to those in England, and briefly, a grammar school, received an education that was marginally more diverse than that of his English colleagues. He learned a little Greek, elementary Latin, and mathematics "up to Euclid."[104] William Young Turner, also a product of the Scottish system, completed his education with a Scottish medical degree, as did one of the early English missionaries, Thomas Ridgley, who had been educated at Cowpers School House, Huntingdon.

Among the LMS missionaries who arrived after 1888 and who had been at school in the seventies or later, there was a marked increase in the amount of schooling they had received. While only three of the twelve who arrived before 1888 had received anything beyond elementary education, of the twelve who came to New Guinea between 1888 and 1902, all but three had probably had some taste of secondary education. One had passed the Cambridge Junior with first class honors and another qualified for the Victorian Intermediate Certificate. The three who had not received any secondary education—Holmes, Rich, and Schlencker—had, like many of their predecessors, left school at the age of eleven or twelve. The nine missionaries who arrived between 1902 and 1914 were, on average, better educated again. Two had completed only an elementary education, one in a board school, the other in a Scottish parish school, but the other seven had received a partial or complete secondary education. Three had gone on to tertiary studies, one of them finishing as a Master of Arts from Glasgow and another a Bachelor of Arts from Melbourne. They brought to four the total number of graduates serving with the LMS in Papua during this period. This proportion (13 percent) was small compared with that of LMS graduates in other places. In India, for instance, between 1850 and 1900, 27 percent of LMS missionaries were graduates.[105]

After an elementary education in a National School, or an English school, or one of the newer board schools set up after 1870, the LMS missionaries had received their secondary schooling at a variety of institutions, few of them in the mainstream of the English educational tradition. Two received an endowed school education, Reginald Bartlett at Winchester House School and Caleb Beharell at Stepney Grammar School, and two attended high schools. But most went to small private schools run by religious groups, individuals, or proprietary companies. Will Saville, for example, spent five years at Caterham Congregational School; James Cullen went to a Moravian boarding school; Oliver Tomkins attended Great Yarmouth College, run by his father; and Ben Butcher was educated at Aske's, the school of the Haberdashers' Company, which, Sidney Webb considered, provided a "very efficient education of an excellent modern type."[106]

Whatever the amount or quality of the schooling received by the LMS missionaries, the outstanding characteristic of their educational experience throughout the period was their dedication to "self-improvement" after their formal education ended. Like many of their generation and rank, they were earnest disciples of Samuel Smiles, whose *Self-Help*, published in 1859, sold 150,000 copies over the next three decades.[107] Samuel McFarlane, an operative who worked from six in the morning to six at night, spent his evenings "endeavouring to improve" himself in English grammar. At least twelve other LMS missionaries, intent on self-improvement, devoted part of their leisure to private study or to classes held by mechanics institutes, working men's colleges or institutes set up by the Congregationalists for the training of home missionaries.

The Australasian Wesleyan Methodist Missionary Society were the heirs of a missionary tradition in which educational qualifications were not rated as highly as in the Puritan heritage of the LMS.[108] Although a "fair English education" was one of the attributes expected of even lay recruits to the Wesleyan mission, it was a requirement thoroughly subordinate to godliness, moral probity, and zeal. A typical candidate's "character" stated that while his education had not gone beyond the public school, he had read Wesley's sermons and works on the New Testament, he had "no matrimonial engagement," was "a total abstainer," did not smoke, and had no debts.[109] It may be a comment on the attitude of the Wesleyan Methodists to the place of education in the formation of the missionary that surviving information on the attainments of its missionaries in Papua is scant.

Where such information exists, it suggests that the education of the Methodist missionaries was generally more limited than that of their LMS contemporaries. Although there were four university graduates among the LMS missionaries, the Methodist mission had none. Most highly educated of the Wesleyan workers was the chairman, William Bromilow, who, after completing a colonial education, attempted a Bachelor of Arts at Melbourne University, until the strain of study combined with schoolteaching precipitated a breakdown in his health.[110] One or two of the other ministers, like Bromilow, had gained a colonial matriculation, but others had left school at or near the completion of their elementary education.[111] A few had improved their qualifications through adult education, but a preoccupation with self-improvement is not as apparent as among the LMS missionaries. Most of the lay workers whose educational experience is known had received only a primary schooling, or less—George Bardsley, the carpenter, left school at the age of eight.[112] One exception was Keith Chapman who arrived just before the outbreak of war, having completed two years at Hawkesbury Agricultural College. The best educated group among the Methodist missionaries may well have been not the ordained ministers but the schoolteachers, all women, several of whom had matriculated through the universities of Australia and New Zealand.[113]

The educational experience of the Anglican missionaries was as diverse as their backgrounds. A number of the priests of the Anglican Mission were the products of a public school education, though unlike the clergy of the UMCA and the Melanesian Mission, only one was educated at a "great" English public school. Bishop Stone-Wigg received his education in one of the four commoners' houses of Winchester.[114] Throughout his life he remained a loyal Wykehamist and a committed supporter of the "public school" system. Writing to his father at the time of the Winchester Quincentenary in 1893, he remarked, "It almost makes one's eyes water to read about the dear old place—one does not realise the hold it has on one after these years until it is brought home to one in this way. . . . What a terrible blow to Australia to have no public school system of this kind."[115] Gerald Sharp was educated at Manchester Grammar School which had, by the late nineteenth century, established an excellent reputation, especially for its science teaching. It won more Oxford and Cambridge scholarships than most of the "great" public schools, and, although a day school, was widely regarded as one of the elite band of "public schools."[116] Other priests attended less eminent British grammar schools, or their colonial counterparts.

Eight of the Anglican priests were university graduates: Stone-Wigg, Abbot, Newton, and Taylor from Oxford; Sharp from Cambridge; Maclaren from Durham; King from Sydney; and Chignell from Adelaide. Unlike the others, whose university courses were the final stage of an uninterrupted academic career, Albert Maclaren had left school at fourteen and enrolled at Wrexham Grammar School as an adult to equip himself for further study. He subsequently took his degree at Durham supported by donations from the parishioners among whom he had worked in Queensland.[117] Several of the priests ordained while in the mission field were men much more limited in education, Samuel Tomlinson, for instance, having received only an elementary schooling.[118]

Among the lay men of the mission were some who were the counterparts of the LMS and Methodist missionaries, who came to Papua with only an elementary education, gained in the government schools of England or Australia. But others, such as Eric Giblin and George Downton, had matriculated after an education in a colonial grammar school.[119] The women missionaries, mostly teachers and nurses, were generally well educated, two of them being university graduates, and several matriculants.

Although the Anglican Mission had a leadership whose education, both in duration and in kind, set it apart from the Protestant missions, it was not, by Anglican standards, a highly educated community. The eight priests who had degrees constituted 16 percent of the total male staff. By contrast, almost half the male staff of the Melanesian Mission recruited up to 1920 were graduates, and "probably more the average for Church of England missions," one quarter of the male missionaries of the UMCA had degrees.[120]

The education received by the clergy of the Sacred Heart Mission is not readily comparable with that of the non–Roman Catholic missionaries. While clerical and lay members of the Anglican and Protestant missions had a secular education that was quite distinct from whatever vocational training they received after deciding to become ministers or missionaries, the education of most priests of the Sacred Heart Mission from the age of twelve was devoted above all else to the formation of the religious, the priest, and the missionary. Under the benign provisions of the *loi Falloux* of 1850, the minor seminaries of France had been able to reestablish themselves as the purveyors of a traditional Catholic secondary education instead of being, as since 1828, merely schools for potential seminarists.[121] However the *Petit-Oeuvre* of the MSC, their apostolic school or minor seminary, at which the great majority of the priests of the SHM were educated, although equipping them for the baccalaureate, was fundamentally vocational. It was not, wrote a superior-general of the congregation, "an ordinary school." It welcomed only "chosen children whom God [had] marked with the double seal of the priestly and the apostolic vocation."[122] It is thus more convenient to discuss the education of the MSC priests within the context of their religious formation.

The lay brothers of the MSC came to their novitiates at Issoudun or the other houses of the congregation with a very limited education. At a time when many priests were recruited from the peasantry, educational attainment and potential rather than birth was probably the chief distinction between novice priests and novice brothers. Brother Alexis Henkelmann, who had received a "good elementary instruction" was considered potential material for the priesthood,[123] but generally the brothers were unambiguously marked by their inferior education. Many, the sons of peasants, had received only a partial or seasonal education, their school attendance being dictated by the demands of the fields. The pioneer Italian brothers Nicolas, Salvatore, and Mariano were illiterate.[124]

Consistent with the greater diversity of background of the sisters in Papua was their greater range of educational achievement. The distinction between choir and lay sisters reflected differences in education as well as birth.[125] Choir sisters such as Mother Liguori and Mother Paule were said to be well educated, as was also Sister Kostka.[126] But like the coadjutor brothers, many of the sisters had received only a limited education in parish schools. Sister Jeanne from Nantes, for example, was recorded as having "scant reading ability."[127] As among the other missionary groups, there was probably a progressive general improvement in the amount of education received. Observers commented on the difference between the usually poorly educated older sisters from France and the better-educated younger sisters from Australia.[128] But even during the two years preceding the war, the sisters who arrived from France were women whose rural backgrounds included only a simple elementary education.[129]

Conclusion

There were considerable differences in the social backgrounds of the missionaries who served in Papua before the Great War. These differences existed not only between the personnel of the various missionary bodies, but also among the members of any one mission. Nevertheless it is possible to identify amid the diversity Weberian "ideal types"[130] for each of the four missions.

The priest or sister of the Sacred Heart Mission was most likely to be French, and like the majority of his or her compatriots, of rural origins, the son or daughter of a peasant or artisan, born in one of those regions of France where Catholicism had most successfully withstood the assault of anticlericalism. The MSC brother was more likely to be Dutch, and a skilled artisan, recruited from one of those areas where the congregation was established. Alternatively he may have been of the European peasantry. The LMS missionary was almost certainly British and urban in origin, a black-coated worker or perhaps an artisan, who had compensated for his limited social and educational advantages by an earnest program of self-improvement. The Methodist missionaries were more likely to be from a rural background, though possibly of English origin, brought up on a farm in New Zealand or in one of the provincial towns of southeastern Australia where Methodism was strong. Like their LMS colleagues, their families were lower middle class or artisan, though their fathers were more likely to be farmers than clerical workers. Most elusive is the identity of the Anglican missionary. A university-educated English gentleman, a lady-worker from Sydney, a poorly educated working man or woman of English origin, or a more highly educated colonial from one of the capital cities of eastern Australia—all were represented in the Anglican Mission.

Despite these differences in "ideal types" and the much vaster differences in the reality that lay behind the ideal, several general statements can be made about the backgrounds of the missionaries. Nineteen centuries ago, one of the first Christian missionaries, Paul of Tarsus, wrote to his colleagues at Corinth: "My brothers, think what sort of people you are whom God has called; . . . few are powerful or highly born."[131] The same might have been said of the missionaries who worked in Papua before 1914. Despite the differences in the socioeconomic origins of the missionaries of the various bodies and, indeed, within each mission, most were men and women of the lower ranks of nineteenth-century society. The great majority were drawn from the semiskilled, white-collared work force of the lower middle class, or from labor's aristocracy, the artisans. From these two sections of society came most of the LMS missionaries, many of the Methodists, and a high proportion of the nonordained members of the Sacred Heart and Anglican missions. Small farming families, of comparable social status, supplied the Methodist and Sacred Heart missions with most of their other workers. The only missionaries in Papua during that period who were of higher social rank were the few "highly born" members of the Sacred Heart and Anglican missions, and the small minority of middle-class men and women from professional backgrounds, mostly concentrated in the Anglican Mission and scattered lightly in the other three.

But if the very highest ranks of nineteenth-century society were thinly represented in the Papuan mission field, so were the very lowest. Observers of nineteenth-century British society remarked on the gulf that existed, not between the lower middle-class clerical workers and the proletarian artisans, but between the artisans and the unskilled workers. To cross that gulf, wrote Henry Mayhew, was to move "among another race."[132] The race of unskilled laborers provided few recruits for the mission field. Domestic servants and unskilled workers, two of the largest sectors of the unskilled work force after agricultural laborers, were totally unrepresented, a pattern common throughout the mission fields of the late nineteenth century.

Less can be said with certainty about the domestic backgrounds of the missionaries. Despite the great diversity of home environments and the relative paucity of evidence about them, it can nevertheless be concluded that for many individual missionaries, during childhood and adolescence, a strong and close maternal influence was counterbalanced by a much more remote paternal influence, frequently severed completely by the death of the father.

Although the amount and type of education received by those who became missionaries in Papua varied with their socioeconomic backgrounds, they were not men or women of great learning, apart from the priests of the Sacred Heart Mission—whose extensive formal education was an integral part of their religious formation—and the few graduates in the Anglican Mission and the LMS. But nor were many of them the equivalents of the unlettered missionaries who had staffed the evangelical missions of the late eighteenth and early nineteenth centuries. They were fairly typical products of their class and their generation, distinguished neither by their birth nor by their education, but by their common conviction of a particular call from God.

CHAPTER 2

"Whom God Has Called"

Religious Influences

"I COULD as easily relate circumstances connected with the dawn of my conscious life as tell of my first religious awakenings," wrote Charles Cribb, applying in 1892 to become an LMS missionary.[1] This was typical. Future missionaries grew up in homes that were permeated with religion. Most Roman Catholic missionaries were raised by pious parents and brought up within the protective arms of parish church and school. A faithful Catholic background, together with legitimate birth, was required of those who joined the Sacred Heart congregation.[2] LMS missionaries came most frequently from devout Congregational homes, two of the three Australians, for instance, being from families that were "standards of Independency" in Queensland.[3] Four were the sons of ministers, three of them LMS missionaries.[4] Wesleyan missionaries were almost universally of staunch Methodist stock, two of them being from leading colonial Methodist families, the Fletchers and the Waterhouses, and one the proud descendant of Yorkshire preacher, Dicky Birdsall.[5] The religious antecedents of the Anglican missionaries were more diverse, at least seven being of Protestant families,[6] but numbers of them experienced steady, if not fervent, religious influences in childhood. "Religion, in the world of our childhood, was the fundamental basis of life," recalled Romney Gill's brother, Eric.[7] Six Anglicans were the children of clergy, and although there were no offspring of clerical families among the Methodists, a number had fathers who were lay preachers.[8]

Church going and other religious observances were a major part of most childhoods. Ben Butcher recalled trooping into Marlborough Chapel each Sunday with his seven brothers and sisters and reflected that, though they rarely understood the sermon, it was on the whole a pleasurable experience.[9] Protestant children attended Sunday schools and class meetings, joined Bands of Hope and other church-associated groups, and participated in family prayers and Bible readings. Some recalled, years afterward, reading *Pilgrim's Progress*, poring over the colored pictures in the great Family Bible, or learning to sing "Rock of Ages" on a Sunday afternoon.[10] Those who became Sacred Heart missionaries passed through the rites of a Catholic childhood—confirmation and first communion—frequently at an early age. Louis-André Navarre, who drifted away from the church after his father's failure to pay his mother's burial fee, was humiliated because he still had not made his first communion when conscripted into the army.[11] Most fervent of all Sacred Heart missionaries, Henri Verjus, was confirmed when six years old.[12]

Several of the leading missionaries were precociously pious. At the age of five, Verjus celebrated Mass on his mother's chest of drawers, and at ten Alain de Boismenu, having decided that he wanted to be a priest, asked for an altar.[13] Jean Genocchi built himself an altar and pressed his sisters to join him in prayer.[14] As a child, Albert Maclaren, founder of the Anglican Mission, gathered his brothers and sisters together on Sunday evenings to preach to them.[15] In childhood, Verjus felt the stirrings of more intense religious desires: "There was, at St. Maurice at Annecy, a picture representing a martyr burned by tormentors. The picture always pleased me and whenever I looked at it I longed to be a martyr."[16]

More frequently, religion was an intrinsic but not dominant part of childhood. There was little place for the sudden, cataclysmic conversion experience often associated with the popular stereotype of the nineteenth-century missionary who, having seen the light himself, hurried out to impart it to others. Only two of the LMS missionaries claimed this kind of experience; thanks to the thorough selection procedures of the Society, their religious history is most fully documented. Samuel McFarlane testified to a change of desires away from "the ballroom, the billiard table and other such fruitless and destructive pleasures" to things of the spirit. James Chalmers' description of his own conversion during the 1859 Revival was an archetypal account, which alluded to a sinful youth, a casual encounter with God's word—which he had come to jeer at—the moment of conviction, and the ensuing ordeal through abasement and despair to deliverance:[17]

> I was pierced through and through with conviction of sin, and felt lost beyond all hope of salvation. On the Monday, Mr. Meickle came to my help and . . . as he quoted "The blood of Jesus Christ his Son cleanseth us from all sin" I felt that this salvation was possible for me, and some glad-

ness came into my heart. After a time light increased, and I felt that God
was speaking to me in His Word, and I believed unto salvation.[18]

McFarlane and Chalmers were children of the early Victorian era. In
both their accounts, the sinfulness of their life before conversion was
probably painted blacker than the reality to heighten the significance of
the experience, a common tendency among Evangelicals of the time.[19]
Without doubting the genuineness of the experience, one may suggest
that their accounts were cast in terms designed to meet contemporary
expectations of what constituted a true conversion.

Neither those of their colleagues who belonged to the same era nor
those who followed them into the LMS field in Papua claimed an
equally dramatic experience. All except McFarlane and Chalmers were
nurtured Christians who had grown up in the faith. If they used the
word conversion in their spiritual biographies, they used it to indicate
"the culmination, in a sense of spiritual rebirth of a lengthy and largely
subconscious process of self-examination."[20] They alluded to a stage, or
stages, in their life when, perhaps after a period of indifference, their
faith took on a heightened significance and a greater compulsion. Like
those who experienced a sudden conversion, they made a token reference to past sinfulness, but unlike the dramatically converted, they gave
little evidence of emotional stress in the making of their commitment. It
was generally prompted by conversation with parents or other mentors,
by reading devotional books such as Angell James' *The Anxious
Inquirer*, or by listening to particularly challenging sermons—occasionally by eminent revivalists like Moody, but more commonly in local
churches—and in most cases it did little to disturb the even tenor of a
steady spiritual growth that had its origins in infancy.

Urged by the LMS to pinpoint special circumstances associated with
their Christian commitment, less than half the candidates could identify any. Nine of the fourteen alleged this commitment to have been
made at the age of fourteen, fifteen, or sixteen, reputed to be the most
common age for male conversion.[21] Two believed themselves to have
been converted between seventeen and twenty, and three as early as
eleven. For them, as for most Evangelicals, conversion was an adoles-
cent experience, which frequently took place soon after puberty. Studies
have suggested a link between conversion and the sexual confusion and
tension of adolescence, and although no aspiring missionary admitted
this link, if indeed he was conscious of it, the language used by some
was compatible with it. Reflecting in his diary on his conversion, one
missionary wrote:

Repeated failure had led me to doubt whether I should ever get the mastery of sin. Romans VI seems now to mean that . . . Christ's powers will

be so manifested in my life as to lead me to reason thus before yielding—:
This is a temptation to gratify my old nature. . . . [God's] claims are superior and [as] I cannot obey both I forego the lower claims as not worthy of
my consideration i.e. I treat my old "self" as dead.[22]

In this confession, guilt about masturbation, still regarded as both sinful
and a source of degeneracy and ultimately insanity,[23] may have been
especially critical.

Seventeen of the thirty-three LMS missionaries claimed no conversion
experience of either kind, half of them explicitly denying its occurrence,
asserting that there were no "particular events," no "definite time," or
"no special experience that I can distinctly call conversion." These missionaries reiterated the influence of godly parents or a devout mother
and described their spiritual development as a "slow and steady
progress" from infancy to the time of their candidature for the mission
field. Contrary to what might be expected, there was not a progressive
decline in the use of the term or concept of conversion in the testimonies
of candidates through the years. The terminology employed seemed to
depend more on the religious subculture with which the candidate identified than the era in which he applied. As early as 1880 Thomas
Ridgley denied that there were any "memorable circumstances" in his
Christian commitment, while Oliver Tomkins, applying in 1899, im-
bued with the spirit of the Keswick holiness movement, could name the
day on which he was saved with the same certainty as any eighteenth-
century convert.[24]

Although conversion was a standard part of Methodist and evangelical Anglican religious experience, it does not feature prominently in the
known religious histories of missionaries of those persuasions. Like most
of the LMS missionaries they testified to a steady growth of faith from
childhood, with moments of intensified commitment. William Bromilow, for instance, although raised in a strong Wesleyan evangelical tradition, referred in his autobiography only to the growth of a "deepened,
more personal religious experience."[25] The "characters" of missionaries,
submitted when they were seeking candidature to the ministry, suggest
a pattern of close childhood involvement in church and Sunday school,
culminating in a commitment conventionally called conversion. Frederick Winn's "character," for example, read: "His home training was of
the highest order. From early childhood he attended a Methodist church
and Sunday School. He was converted during a special session held in
the church . . . in 1904, being then 16 years of age."[26]

All missionaries, having made a commitment to Christ, made a second commitment to the missionary vocation. There was generally an
interval of years between the two, but, like the profession of faith, the

decision to become a missionary frequently had its roots far back in childhood. Missionaries Bromilow, Tomkins, Bartlett, and Beharell all claimed to have been dedicated to the missionary cause by their parents at birth.[27] As a child, Albert Maclaren was held and kissed by a black missionary who was reputed to have said: "There, your son has been kissed by a black missionary, if he lives he will be a great missionary himself one day."[28]

The LMS Candidates' Papers, which provide the most thorough insight into the making of a Protestant missionary, reveal that of the thirty-three who went to Papua before 1914, sixteen claimed their wish to be a missionary to have originated in early childhood. While allowing for an obvious concern to impress the directors with the maturity of their decision, the emphatic phrases used—"almost as long as I can remember," "from my earliest recollections," "ever since I can remember"—suggest that they at least believed themselves to have cherished a lifelong desire. Of those who did not claim a childhood decision, most alleged an aspiration of about seven or eight years' standing.

Less is known of the awakening of the missionary vocation among members of the other missions, but fragmentary evidence suggests similar experiences for some. Henri Verjus, at the age of three, joined the French Catholic children's missionary organization, the Holy Childhood, becoming "godfather" to a Chinese child. At five he told his mother that he wanted to be not a priest but a missionary.[29] Joseph Chabot, as a boy, read the life of the martyred missionary Theophane Venard and dreamt of mission work in Indochina.[30] Anglican missionary Romney Gill, explaining to his father his decision to become a missionary, wrote:

> I received this call, not at some public meeting, or when listening to some emotion-stirring sermon, or at . . . some particular date and moment fixed in my memory, as the Salvation Army people, who can tell you the exact date, place and moment when and where they were "saved" but YEARS ago when a very young child. . . . Sometimes I wanted to be an engineer, sometimes a sailor, sometimes a "cowboy"—and all the time something pointed to the Divine Life.[31]

After the death of Mary Alicia Newton in the Anglican Mission, her sister wrote to Stone-Wigg that it had been "her one wish from quite a young girl to go out as a Missionary."[32] Although one Methodist minister and one sister testified to a similar childhood ambition,[33] it seems that for the ordained Methodist missionaries on the whole, with their concept of a world parish, there was a less clearly defined distinction between the vocation of minister and that of missionary. Service in the mission field was seen as one phase in an uninterrupted clerical career, rather than a separate commitment.

The childhood desire to be a missionary was frequently a romantic response to heroic mission literature and sometimes cooled; even if it remained fervent, it had to be converted into a hard-headed and mature decision. This was often effected by the vast apparatus of the missionary societies, which also generally prompted the adult decisions of those without a childhood commitment behind them. By far the most potent influence was personal contact with a working missionary which seemed at times to work as a type of apostolic succession. W. G. Lawes, hearing William Gill and Isaiah Papehia, a Rarotongan, speak in 1858, "there and then gave his life to God for missionary service."[34] Chalmers, whose boyhood resolve had lapsed, had his interest rekindled by a conversation with George Turner of Samoa.[35] Chalmers himself, with his homespun eloquence and intense conviction, inspired a whole generation of missionaries from deputation platforms. Among those who responded to his appeal for New Guinea were James Cullen, Will Saville, Oliver Tomkins, and Reginald Bartlett.[36] His less flamboyant but equally dedicated colleague, Lawes, turned the boyhood wishes of Charles Cribb and Percy Schlencker into a commitment to the LMS.[37]

The same lines of personal communication are discernible in the vocations of members of the other missions. The persuasive enthusiasm of Albert Maclaren convinced Copland King, as they shared a train ride through the dusty outback of New South Wales, that he should join Maclaren in the foundation of the Anglican Mission.[38] The other pioneers were recruited after hearing Maclaren preach at St. Mark's, Fitzroy. Henry Newton was invited by Stone-Wigg to join the staff, and a number of the men and women who came to the mission around the turn of the century offered as a result of hearing Stone-Wigg's appeals for staff in sermons given in local churches.[39] Invited to become third bishop of New Guinea, Gerald Sharp recalled that he had first been asked to join the mission by Stone-Wigg, just as Stone-Wigg had first been invited to New Guinea by Maclaren.[40] William Bromilow's missionary career began when he heard an "inspiring" call for staff of the Methodist missions of Fiji and Tonga, and others in turn responded to his appeals for missionaries for New Guinea.[41]

Among the Sacred Heart missionaries, some had been impressed by the single-minded zeal of Henri Verjus, even before he reached the mission field. Navarre, Genocchi, and Jullien all turned from actual or proposed careers as secular priests to the apostolate partly as a result of his influence.[42] Many other young students and scholastics at Issoudun were inspired by the visits of missionary priests, especially Verjus and Genocchi, to make a commitment to the New Guinea field.[43]

Mission literature was perhaps the second most important mechanism for arousing a missionary vocation. Missionary tracts and periodicals and biographies of missionaries influenced Catholics and Protestants

alike. Among the latter, books by and about David Livingstone probably outweighed all the other print devoted to the Protestant missionary
cause in that generation.[44] The lives of Richard Knill of India, Gilmour
of Mongolia, John Williams, and Chalmers himself were also influential.[45] Young Catholics were similarly inspired by the biographical
accounts of martyred missionaries, Chanel, Marchand, and Venard.[46]

A third influence on potential missionaries, especially Protestants,
was the missionary meeting. Even without the dramatic presence of the
missionary on deputation, the meeting could be an enticing influence
which, perhaps aided by lantern slides, brought excitement and romance into the drabness of a small town or the tedium of a village. John
Henry Holmes, at the age of ten, heard an illustrated lecture on India in
his small Devon village, and from that time dreamed of being a missionary.[47]

A more diffuse but no less pervasive influence in the making of a missionary was the general mission-mindedness of the community to which
the individual belonged. Parents, priests, ministers, and mentors were
frequently people with a strong mission commitment. LMS missionaries
often attended chapels which, without any institutional links, were
keen supporters of the Society. From his childhood Ben Butcher remembered collection boxes adorned with a picture of a "well-dressed missionary standing under a coconut tree with crowds of very respectable
brown people" around him, and book prizes illustrated with mission
scenes, won by collecting for the mission ship, the *John Williams*.[48]
Oliver Tomkins found the influence of a devout mother reinforced by
Keswick Conventions and by the strongly missionary church at Princes
Street, Norwich, associated with the Congregational Forward Movement.[49] Other LMS missionaries besides Tomkins may have been influenced in the last decade of the century by the Forward Movement, a
brave attempt at a time of dwindling resources, to put a hundred new
missionaries in the field, through an appeal to the "intertwined con-
sciences of countless chapel communities."[50] Although most LMS missionaries sought ordination with the intention of going to the mission
field, a few trained for the home ministry and found their missionary
interest kindled while at college.[51]

Many Anglican missionaries grew up in Queensland parishes whose
members, besides being Anglo-Catholic and thus in sympathy with the
prevailing ethos in the Anglican Mission, were on the frontier themselves and probably had a greater awareness of the need for pioneering
church work than was evident in the more established parishes of the
south. Of the Anglicans from New South Wales and Victoria, a dispro-
portionate number were from Anglo-Catholic parishes such as Christ
Church St. Laurence in Sydney, and St. Peter's, Eastern Hill, and St.

Mark's, Fitzroy,[52] in Melbourne. In a generally apathetic ecclesiastical environment, the personal influence of sympathetic bishops like Montgomery, Webber, and White was an important factor in the making of Anglican missionaries.

A similar network of communal influence is discernible among the Roman Catholic missionaries, especially those of France. Many of the priests and sisters belonged to families that supported the two congregations (MSC and FDNSC) through membership of the Archconfraternity of Our Lady of the Sacred Heart. Nine of the priests and at least four of the sisters were from families with other members in orders, usually the MSC and FDNSC. Some of the families of missionaries, particularly those of Brittany and Savoy, were interrelated.[53] Although evidence is scant, it seems that many of the French missionaries belonged to a close-knit and strongly committed subculture that had firm bonds with the two congregations. For others, the links were less direct. As was common at the time, many MSC priests took their first steps toward a clerical career when their exceptional piety or ability was noted by the parish priest; he directed them toward the institutions of the MSC, with whose founder, Jules Chevalier, he might have had personal ties. Canon Robert of Nantes, a loyal supporter of the congregations, was responsible for a large proportion of that diocese's remarkable contribution to the mission.[54] Other potential MSC missionaries were recruited by visiting representatives who toured the countryside in search of vocations. Paul Fastré, for instance, declined the invitations of a Franciscan, a Jesuit, and an Assumptionist, before agreeing to join the MSC.[55] In one notable episode in Holland, a recruiting priest, told of the pious village of Volendam, gained the support of the parish priest who, in true Galilean fashion, strode among the returning fishermen and enlisted six volunteers to serve as brothers in New Guinea.[56]

All Missionaries of the Sacred Heart, however recruited, chose to join the MSC out of the vast proliferation of orders and congregations of the nineteenth century, because of their attraction to its distinctive features: its stress on the apostolic life, its devotion to the Sacred Heart of Jesus, and its worship of Our Lady of the Sacred Heart. These emphases were characteristic of the warmer form of piety that had grown up earlier in the century in reaction to the austerities of Jansenism.

Motivation

Missionary organizations were generally careful to scrutinize the motives of those who offered for the mission field. Aware of the array of considerations that might inspire such a decision, the LMS asked a series of searching questions of its candidates, including for some years the pointed query: "How long have you entertained the desire to become a missionary and what motivated you to form that desire?" In the Anglican and Methodist missions, selection procedures appear to have been less exhaustive, but in both cases applicants were personally interviewed either by the staffs of the missionary bodies or by trusted agents. The large file of rejected applicants for the Anglican Mission suggests that even if their selection procedures were more random than those of the LMS, they were not entirely undiscriminating.[57] In the Sacred Heart Mission it was recognized that the long training for the priesthood and the intensive novitiate that preceded the taking of vows did not necessarily make a missionary, and the decision had to be made by mutual agreement between the religious and his superiors.

The prime motive for all Christian missionary endeavor was obedience to the divine command, "Go ye into all the world and preach the gospel to every creature." Confronted with this command, many earnest Christians felt it a matter of "plain duty" to obey.[58] Some asked themselves, as Hudson Taylor urged supporters of the CIM, not why they should go, but why they should stay at home.[59] "Possessing a strong constitution and being free of any obligations to stay in England, I feel myself marked out to go," explained Frederick Walker to the LMS and concluded: "Lastly, but above all, the simple command of Christ to preach the gospel to all nations personally outweighs all considerations which might otherwise lead *me* to remain at home."[60]

A number of missionaries of all persuasions claimed the conviction that the general command had been translated into a personal call from God. "I have felt all along . . . that were I to stay at home while the way is open for me to go abroad would be a deliberate neglect on my part of what I feel to be God's will for me," wrote James Birkett Clark, applying to the LMS.[61] Anglican missionary, Mary Alicia Newton explained to Bishop Stone-Wigg: "My Lord, I came out to New Guinea in answer to a command from God which I dared not disobey."[62] Other religious convictions that had moved an earlier generation of missionaries—the desire to work for the greater glory of God and gratitude for one's own salvation—were only occasionally listed in conjunction with Christ's command. Despite a revival in premillennial teaching during the nineteenth century, eschatological anxiety was not an apparent motive.

Among the LMS missionaries, response to the divine command was frequently reinforced by a realistic appraisal of need. Believing that the gospel was for all people, they were impressed by the "greater need of the heathen" and the scarcity of laborers to meet it. Their response was to the Macedonian cry. Some added candidly that the home churches were already oversupplied; others recognized that their talents and training fitted them for mission work rather than service in the home churches.

John Wear Burton, going out to the Methodist field of Fiji in 1903 gave his interpretation of the needs of the heathen to a missionary audience before his departure. He told them that it was not the belief that the heathen was destined for hell that impelled him to go forth but the "unhappy condition of people deprived of the joy of the gospel." His statement provoked a violent response from one of his audience, the venerable Presbyterian missionary, John G. Paton:

> Then the grand old warrior rose, shook his leonine head and in his down-right manner, and with the weight of his great personality, and with his record of long and sacrificial service behind him, hurled his burning indignation at the view I expressed. "Young man," he almost roared, "do you think I would have risked my life amongst the savages and cannibals of the New Hebrides if I had not believed that every man, woman and child I met was going to hell?"[63]

Changes in contemporary theological belief, which were themselves influenced by the missionary movement, led to a decline in the importance of the "perishing heathen" motive as the nineteenth century progressed. Information afforded by the evangelization of distant lands led to an increased awareness of the immense numbers condemned to eternal torment by the current theory of everlasting punishment of the wicked. This was challenged by F. D. Maurice in 1853 in *Theological Essays* and more fully by Dr. Samuel Cox in 1877 in a series of essays published as *Salvator Mundi*. Their doctrine of universalism, or the "larger hope" that inspired Tennyson's influential poem "In Memoriam," was taken up in the theological debate that gathered momentum in the late seventies and the eighties. Another theory was supplied by the Congregational theologian Edward White in his *Life in Christ*, 1875. While attacking the grounding of missionary activity in the belief in hell, White nevertheless felt that universalism reduced the urgency of the missionary task. To universalism he posed as an alternative the doctrine of "conditional immortality," which, he believed, resolved the conflict between the love of God and eternal torment. According to White's conditionalism, God created humans mortal but with a capacity for immortality that may be achieved through Christ. For those without faith in Christ, mortal life is followed not by eternal torment but by annihilation.

This evolution of belief is reflected in the papers of the LMS candidates who came to the Papuan mission field during this period.[64] A few of the older missionaries claimed that for them, as for Paton, their apprehension of the needs of the heathen included the conviction that, unsaved, he was destined for hell. "I consider there are plenty of labourers at home while thousands of my heathen brethren are perishing for want of knowledge concerning that Saviour by which alone they can be saved, and therefore while few respond to the cry, 'Come over and help us,' I am constrained to say, . . . 'Lord send me,' " wrote James Chalmers in 1862. The last of the LMS missionaries to Papua to state this motive explicitly was Albert Pearse who, in 1866, told the directors that his heart burned to "save the perishing heathen." Those who followed him preferred to allude more generally to the "need of the heathen" or, like Burton, more specifically to their entitlement to share in the good news of the gospel. In his exposition of conditionalism, *Life in Christ*, published in 1875, Edward White claimed that the doctrine of everlasting punishment of the heathen was doubted by missionaries; in 1882 one of their number, T. E. Slater, declared that it had been abandoned.[65]

Toward the end of the century, concern for the afterlife of the heathens was largely replaced by a concern to ameliorate the conditions of their life in this world. They became "suffering" rather than "perishing" heathens. This concern was sometimes allied to a sense of moral trusteeship that urged aspiring missionaries to introduce the unconverted to the best while protecting them from the worst of European civilization. James Cullen, who had been a sailor, wrote that his missionary commitment was strengthened by the knowledge that "the first effect of civilisation upon savage races was to impart to them all the vices and none of the virtues of our own country," and a longing "to counteract the injuries being done to such lands."

The changes in Protestant belief that were reflected in the statements of the LMS candidates took place within the context of larger shifts of emphasis in contemporary theology—from the wrath of God to the fatherhood of God, from atonement to incarnation, and hence to a more socially oriented gospel. The "perishing heathen" slipped so effortlessly from the candidates' declarations of motivation that by the sixties the concept had become rhetorical rather than the motivating power that Paton had found it in the fifties.

How much and for how long the doctrine of the "perishing heathen" motivated Methodist missionaries is difficult to tell because no statements comparable to the LMS Candidates' Papers have survived. It seems likely that the doctrine persisted longer among Wesleyans than among the LMS missionaries.[66] Samuel Fellows, training for the ministry in 1886, heard a colleague point out in a sermon that "there were some in hell because of our faithlessness" and, much impressed, reconsecrated himself to the salvation of souls.[67] Pioneer Wesleyan missionaries who preached hell to unbelievers[68] presumably believed the doctrine they taught, but it is likely that some later Methodists such as Matthew Gilmour, possessed of a more liberal, humanitarian theology, would have shared the convictions of their contemporary, John Wear Burton, rather than those of Paton.

For Anglo-Catholic missionaries, who accepted the Catholic doctrine of purgatory, the problem was not so acute as for the Evangelicals who had only the alternatives of salvation and damnation. Educated and enlightened men, some of the Anglican priests may have accepted the universalist convictions espoused by broad churchmen. "It was no grim feeling, such as had moved our forefathers, that the heathens should be damned if they were not converted that inspired [us] to spread abroad the religion of Jesus Christ," asserted Bishop Stone-Wigg.[69]

Roman Catholic missionaries experienced no comparable challenge to the motivating power of this belief. Like their Methodist counterparts, pioneer priests threatened unbelievers with hell.[70] The salvation of souls remained the proclaimed *raison d'être* of their apostolate. It was, however, closely tied to a second motive, which at times seemed to become dominant in their commitment to the missionary task—the desire for the achievement of personal sanctity through suffering and sacrifice, the ultimate manifestation of which was martyrdom. "The only authentic missionaries," wrote Henri Verjus, "are those who aspire to the missions for one sole reason—to suffer and sacrifice themselves totally for the salvation of souls."[71] A common conviction at the time, it was for Verjus an obsession. While at the apostolic school of the MSC, he organized a sodality dedicated to suffering for the Sacred Heart. Its act of consecration, signed in blood, stated: "Oh Sacred Heart, we desire to be Thy victims. . . . Make martyrs of us."[72] During his novitiate he prayed for "Sufferings! sufferings! and more sufferings still! then death, the most ignominious, hidden and cruel!" and begged for grace to be "a saintly missionary and a holy martyr."[73] Reading a graphic account of the torture and martyrdom of Joseph Marchand of Indochina, he prayed for "as cruel a martyrdom as that."[74] By the time of his ordination, the missionary vocation and martyrdom were synonymous: "I do and wish everything in view of my dear missions. This is my vocation, my *raison d'être*, my object, what I have been created for. . . . My longing for the missions and martyrdom is maturing in a way that is a puzzle to myself."[75]

Other Sacred Heart missionaries expressed a similar aspiration. Jean Genocchi, in his first as in all subsequent Masses, "begged of God the grace to die for Him in the Missions."[76] Sailing with a large contingent of priests, brothers, and sisters for the Papuan mission field, he reported them unanimous in their conviction that those of them who died in the field would be "greatly blessed."[77] This preoccupation with the attainment of personal holiness was criticized by those of other religious persuasions. William Crosfield, member of a deputation of the LMS, reacted to a visit to Yule Island with the terse observation that "by a course of privation and hardship they were all engaged in saving their own souls."[78]

Yet despite traditional evangelical suspicion of asceticism, a similar orientation was found among evangelical Protestants. A Wesleyan preoccupation with entire sanctification could inspire acts of dedication such as a commitment to the missionary vocation.[79] The growth of a holiness movement within evangelicalism in the eighties, with its stress on a life of sacrificial discipline, gave added impetus.[80] Those influenced by the Student Volunteer Missionary Union or by Keswick Conventions learned to see suffering as a source of spiritual growth, as well as a proof of spiritual vitality. "I cannot describe to you exactly what prompted me to do this," Oliver Tomkins wrote to his brother after applying to the LMS, "It may only be possibly to try my faith and lead me to further consecration."[81]

Just as it would be naive to assume that most missionary commitments were inspired by purely altruistic considerations, it would be cynical to assume that they were wholly self-interested.[82] Like most major decisions, the decision to become a missionary was, for most, prompted by a complex of motives, some conscious and articulated, some recognized but unconfessed, and others subconscious. Obedience to Christ's command, the needs of the heathen—whether "perishing" or "suffering"—and, in a milieu where it was acceptable, the desire to achieve spiritual growth through sacrifice, were the most commonly declared motives. Those that missionaries kept to themselves or of which they were barely conscious must be inferred from their behavior, from statements made in unguarded moments, or, with caution, from the observations of contemporaries.

The modest social background of the majority of missionaries in Papua prompts the question whether for them the missionary vocation was an attractive avenue of upward mobility. Missionaries who had been regarded as "the dregs of humanity" at the end of the eighteenth century and who were still "not quite gentlemen" in the 1850s, were by the last quarter of the nineteenth century respected and esteemed.[83] In England, eminent missionaries on furlough were lionized by the church-and-chapel-going public, featured by the press, consulted by academics and civil servants, and occasionally received by royalty. The romantic saga of David Livingstone's life and death turned the missionary into a modern-day folk hero. In deputation speeches, missionaries gave glimpses of a different world, where they ruled like kings over their domains, surrounded by black subjects to whom their word was law.

All this was apparent to the young men and women who attended mission meetings and read mission literature. For those of artisan or lower middle-class origins, an attempt to better their social position would have been perfectly consistent with the prevailing philosophy of self-improvement. An immediate enticement for prospective LMS candidates would have been the free theological education that all received till 1881 or even the partly free training offered after that date.

The astute administrator of British New Guinea, Sir William Mac-Gregor, discerned ambition in the pioneer, Albert Maclaren. "He was ambitious. . . . He hoped to be a bishop and had he lived he would have done so."[84] Anglican layman William McMullan, finding the missionary vocation intolerable, confessed to Bishop Stone-Wigg that social advancement had been his motive in joining the mission.[85] The social may have been mixed with the spiritual in the ingenuous account given of the decision of a Breton clogmaker, Auguste Lainé, to become a brother with the MSC: "He thought his life mediocre. Would it not become more marvellous if he gave it to God?"[86] Years later Brother Lainé recalled the past, when "in the world" he had been "only a clog-maker in a little lane of his village."[87] For peasant boys, selection by their parish priest for a seminarian education and ordination was an obvious channel of upward mobility, and was accepted as such.[88] Eric Gill recognized in his autobiography that the move of his father, himself the son of an evangelical artisan missionary, from nonconformity into the Church of England, was prompted partly by his parents' social ambitions,[89] and it is conceivable that their missionary son's espousal of Anglo-Catholicism was also fed partly by the same ambition. Certainly, in his missionary career, Romney Gill derived innocent pleasure from his close association with gentlemen like Gerald Sharp, bishop of New Guinea, and Sir Hubert Murray, lieutenant-governor of Papua.[90] The other six Anglican missionaries known to have moved from their Protestant origins into the Church of England may well have been similarly influenced by social ambition.

While the prospect of status may have been, to some, an additional enticement to the mission field, there is little evidence of wealth being a consideration. Although no one could accuse the Sacred Heart missionary of trying to get rich on 40 francs per year, or an Anglican on £20, Protestant stipends were sufficiently large to have been an attraction.[91] LMS missionaries received between £144 and £240, Methodist missionaries between £160 and £180. In 1906 the average annual wage of a British manual worker was £72.[92] The average salary of a commercial clerk was £80, with 75 percent of them receiving less than £150.[93] The salary of an artisan was comparable. Stipends of nonconformist ministers varied widely, but probably only a minority could have hoped for £200.[94] *The Methodist Magazine* of 1860 noted that in some districts the average was less than £70 per year.[95] The missionaries received other material advantages as well—a house, which was generally spacious and comfortable, servants, and provision for the education of their children and for their own old age.

The four decades in which the missionaries arrived spanned periods of severe economic stress in both England and Australia. Whether the desire to escape economic hardship or seek economic security entered into the consideration of any missionary is difficult to judge. Most LMS missionaries stressed in their applications that they were leaving good prospects in their present employment to go to the mission field. The only New Guinea missionary whose subsequent behavior raises the question whether he saw the mission field as a source of financial gain was Samuel McFarlane, whose amassing of wealth on Lifu was notorious. Declaring that he had "never been troubled with the feeling that because we are missionaries we ought to deny ourselves of easily acquired conveniences and comforts," he, with one other missionary, made a large personal fortune from trading and, when forced to leave the Loyalty Islands, "abandoned acres of property and houses and workshops which would have been the delight of many an English squire."[96] New Guinea provided him with more modest worldly prospects, but Archbishop Navarre, admittedly a partial witness, reported him in 1885 as saying that he was only there to make a fortune and would return to England as soon as possible.[97] The raw, uneducated operative from the railway machine shop had come a long way, but whether the possibility of wealth was even a subconscious consideration in his decision to become a missionary, or whether he merely succumbed to opportunities in the field, is impossible to tell.

Diametrically opposed to those whose attraction to the mission field included some consideration of enhancement of prospects in the world they knew were those who were lured by the enchantment of an unknown and exotic world. Nurtured frequently by the literature they read as children, a romantic element remained in the decision to become a missionary for some. Ben Butcher admitted that for him "the idea of travel and adventure had a lot to do with it,"[98] and James Cullen remembered having "pictured a life full of romance and adventure" in his boyhood imagination.[99] The love of adventure was recognized as a strong motive among MSC missionaries,[100] many of whom came from villages of Brittany and Normandy that faced out across the sea. Toward the end of the century, the prevailing romance of imperialism colored attitudes as—largely owing to Livingstone's influence—Christianity, commerce, civilization, colonization, and imperial expansion became increasingly associated, and missionaries could feel the attraction of serving a patriotic as well as a spiritual mission.[101]

Missionary work had a romance of its own that was nourished by stirring tales of great deeds of missionary heroes. Romney Gill's turning from his dreams of being a cowboy or a sailor to become a missionary was not solely a move from fantasy to reality, but from one romantic career to another. Bromilow recognized romance in his response to the call to the Methodist mission field: "The call was an inspiring one; the glory of the first triumphs of these missions had only recently thrilled the Christian world, and to follow in the steps of the heroic pioneers . . . might well appeal to a young ministerial candidate."[102] Among Roman Catholic missionaries the romance of missions was particularly strong, associated as it was with their aspirations for holiness through suffering and their attraction to martyrdom. The historian of the Sacred Heart Mission in Papua, André Dupeyrat, wrote of the late nineteenth century as an era of "religious romanticism" when Joseph Chabot, like many of his contemporaries, longed to "cross the seas, win souls and die."[103]

Besides those who were drawn to the mission field partly by the prospect of status, the glamor of the missionary career, or the lure of the unknown, there were others whose decision was in some degree influenced by a desire to escape from various pressures in their home environment. Some may have looked clear-sightedly at the mission field as providing an opportunity for social betterment, but it seems likely that others perceived it in a more intuitive way simply as an escape from the anonymity and constraints of a lowly position in a complex and hierarchical society. "I know well in England I am nobody—lost, unknown—here I am Tamate—a king with great power . . . ," wrote James Chalmers from New Guinea, declining to even visit his native land.[104] Many, like Chalmers, were people of initiative and energy, to whom the constraints of lower middle-class or working-class expectations would have been particularly irksome. Romney Gill, working in Bognor, recoiled from the pressure to "settle down in business and make a home for myself and perhaps become 'Town Clerk.' What fun!!!"[105] One writer has drawn attention to the number of men who committed themselves to the LMS during their apprenticeship, a time of notable restlessness and insecurity.[106] Others took their first steps toward the mission field at particular moments of frustration. Bromilow, for example, applied for the ministry after his failure to combine schoolteaching with attempting a university degree,[107] and Navarre, humiliated at his rejection for the teaching service, heard a voice tell him, "You will be a priest."[108]

For some, the escape might have been from the complexities of modern industrial society. Anglo-Catholic missionaries with a romantic, neomedieval abhorrence of industrialism, may have been especially susceptible to this pressure. Departing for the mission field, Chignell reflected, "It was very good indeed to feel that I was going at last on foreign service, and to look forward to a 'solitude cure' after living too long in cities and crowds."[109] Others, it has been suggested, may have sought escape from the complexities of theological debate and the atmosphere of increasing doubt in the late nineteenth century.[110] If this was a factor in their decision, it was one they were unlikely to admit to.

Some sought escape from difficult or unsatisfactory personal relationships. Sydney Ford volunteered for the Anglican Mission after a quarrel with his brother.[111] Four LMS missionaries left broken engagements behind them.[112] Natalie Debroux joined the Daughters of Our Lady of the Sacred Heart when she was about to be married,[113] and Hélène Duflôt, while laundering the clothes of the priests in New Guinea, was heard to lament that she had come to the mission field to get away from one man and now she was washing for a dozen of them.[114] Eleanor Walker applied to the Methodist missionary society after her fiancé died on the eve of their wedding,[115] and James Williams, after the death of his wife and child.[116] Montagu Stone-Wigg probably left England for the other side of the earth, like all but one of his brothers and sisters, partly to escape from an unsympathetic father.[117] For others, was the influence of a solicitous and overprotective mother a trifle oppressive?

While missionary societies could test the strength and authenticity of the approved religious motives, the underlying motives mostly remained locked within the individuals, who sometimes scarcely recognized them themselves. Inferences about unacknowledged or subconscious motivation must be tentative; nevertheless it seems that the prospect of enhanced status, the romance of the missionary profession, the lure of foreign lands, and the desire to escape from the pressures of their present lives joined the professed motives of obedience to Christ's command, need, and the desire for sanctification in providing the dynamic for the missionary service of some individuals. Indeed, it may have been the nexus of self-interest and idealism that generated a motivation strong enough to withstand the inevitable privations, frustrations, and failures of a missionary career.

Apart from the greater Catholic stress on sanctification through sacrifice, and the shift among Protestants from concern for the salvation of the perishing heathen to a more temporal and humanitarian interest, these motives varied little from mission to mission, and scarcely altered through time. For the majority of missionaries of all persuasions, commitment was based on strong theological conviction, reinforced in varying degrees by a range of social and psychological compulsions.

Training and Formation

The policy on which the London Missionary Society based the training of recruits for the mission field during the last quarter of the nineteenth century and the early years of the twentieth century was framed at meetings of its Funds and Agency Committee in 1867.[118] The committee reaffirmed the necessity, recognized since the 1830s, for a "sound and complete education," but resolved that it should be acquired through the existing Independent [Congregational] colleges rather than through any institution of their own. Gosport Academy, which, under the direction of Dr. Bogue, had trained most of the LMS missionaries of the early nineteenth century, had been closed soon after his death because of the expense incurred by the LMS in running it. Bedford College, an institution offering more elementary training, at which W. G. Lawes and Samuel McFarlane studied under Jukes and Alliott, closed in 1867 on the death of the latter. Farquhar House, in Highgate, established by the LMS in 1861 to give candidates a year's training in linguistics, comparative history, mission history, and other subjects related to their prospective career, closed in 1872, again on the grounds of cost. James Chalmers was the only New Guinea missionary to study there, after an abbreviated course at Cheshunt College.

From the 1870s missionaries were trained for New Guinea, as for the other LMS fields, in such colleges as Cheshunt, Hackney, Western, Lancashire, Airedale, and Rotherham. Most influential upon the New Guinea field was Cheshunt College, which trained eight of the thirty-three prewar missionaries (Figure 7). Situated in a quiet village near Bishop's Stortford, with the New River flowing through its grounds, and in 1905 transferred to Cambridge, it was originally established for the training of ministers by the Countess of Huntingdon.[119] By the mid-nineteenth century it was predominantly Congregational, but still characterized by a rigid, conservative, and uncritical Calvinism, under which William Hale White (Mark Rutherford) suffered.[120] But the coming to Cheshunt of those destined for the New Guinea field coincided with the transformation which followed the appointment of the Reverend Henry Reynolds, a renowned scholar and preacher, as president. Under his guidance, the students were delivered from the "narrower confines of evangelical theology."[121] Scholars from London University were invited to give lectures, senior students were encouraged to become "deans" to rural parishes, and the syllabus was modified.[122]

Subjects studied included Hebrew, Old Testament and New Testament exegesis, homiletics, ecclesiastical history, theology, mental and moral philosophy (later called psychology), and political economy.[123]

Figure 7. Cheshunt College students, including (back row, 2nd from left) Charles Abel; (2nd from right) Harry Dauncey; (front row, 2nd from left) Fred Walker. (Council for World Mission)

New theological emphases were reflected in content. Although one term of theology concentrated on "the doctrine of sin treated biblically, doctrinally and historically," another was devoted to "the person and work of Christ." By the opening of the twentieth century the syllabus had broadened to include the "comparative science of religion," the "philosophy of theism," natural philosophy, and modern languages.

The formation of those attending other Congregational colleges was similarly influenced by the tone of the college and the leading personalities within it. Six missionaries received their training at Western College, most of them under the guidance of Dr. Charles Chapman.[124] Courses were comparable to those at Cheshunt. After 1895, when LMS missionary training was extended from four to six years to bring it into line with that of the home ministry, it comprised three years of arts and three of theology, which included Hebrew, Greek Testament, apologetics, theology, and church history and polity. By the turn of the century, comparative religion, philosophy, and the history of religion had been introduced.[125]

The five missionaries who attended Hackney College, although taking similar courses, were subject to more conservative theological influences. Originally designated the Village Itinerancy of the Evangelical Association for the Propagation of the Gospel, its evangelical tone was maintained in the late nineteenth century by its principal, Alfred Cave, foremost champion of conservative Congregationalism in the maelstrom of theological debate of the seventies and eighties.[126]

A minority of the missionaries were exposed to more liberal theological and intellectual influences. Watson Sharpe studied at Rotherham under Elkanah Armitage, a man of "broad social sympathies" who required his students to read Henry George.[127] William Lawrence, who attended Airedale Independent College, studied under A. M. Fairbairn, the "father of liberal Evangelicalism among Congregationalists."[128] Familiar with biblical criticism and aware of the importance of comparative religious study, Fairbairn was instrumental in introducing a broader theological viewpoint into ministerial education.[129] Lancashire Independent College, which trained two New Guinea missionaries, also had a strong intellectual tradition,[130] and the four missionaries who studied at theological halls associated with Glasgow and Edinburgh universities may also have received a broader theological education.

Few of the candidates who found their way to New Guinea were distinguished scholars. Handicapped by their limited schooling, many probably fell short of the level of educational attainment regarded by the Society as desirable in their candidates. However, a conviction seems to have persisted within the LMS that work among the preliterate societies of "savages" required less intellectual equipment than work among "barbarians" possessed of a written language and a "higher" culture. Men of limited education such as Holmes, Bartlett, Abel, Schlencker, and Cullen were accepted and trained on the tacit understanding that they would become "pioneer missionaries" among "backward races."[131] In college examinations all but a few of the New Guinea candidates appeared regularly near the bottom of their class lists, and tutors' reports habitually made glancing references to their "slender" attainments before passing on to reassurances about their earnestness, piety, and consecration.

Aspiring missionaries were accepted by the LMS at various stages of their training. Until 1881 they could apply before commencing their courses, which were then financed by the Society. In the years that followed they were expected to complete half their training before the LMS accepted financial responsibility for them, although most had made informal approaches to the LMS and undertaken training with the sole intention of becoming a missionary. In 1897 the LMS resolved not to take any financial responsibility until the completion of training. Acceptance by the Society, whenever it occurred, depended on interviews with the examinations committee, satisfactory performance in college, and acceptable responses to a series of questions to candidates.

Through these procedures the Society ensured the theological ortho-
doxy of its candidates. Although the Calvinism of early nineteenth century Congregationalism had crumbled by the last quarter of the century, and a greater tolerance of divergent theological positions was
acceptable, what the LMS expected of its candidates was still essentially
a statement of evangelical faith. Asked to name the principal distinguishing doctrines of the gospel, all repeated, with limited variation, a
formula that was an encapsulation of basic evangelical theology.[132]
Grounded in belief in one God, in the Trinity and in the divinity of
Christ, it included the creation of man in God's image, the fall and subsequent depravity of man, redemption through Christ, justification by
faith and regeneration through the Holy Spirit. Some added the second
coming.

While the main contours of belief remained the same throughout the
period, there were some shifts of emphasis, themselves pale reflections
of changes in contemporary Protestant theology. Early missionaries
either stated or implied an endorsement of the substitutionary theory of
the atonement. From around the turn of the century, candidates preferred to subscribe to no particular theory but contented themselves
with alluding to it in general terms. Many had been influenced by
Robert Dale's study of the atonement, published in 1875, which sought
to reassert its centrality without resorting to the offensive substitutionary theory.[133] A few of the twentieth-century candidates were
uneasy with the whole concept of atonement and employed instead such
terms as restoration or reconciliation. "The word Reconciliation rather
than Atonement seems to me to expess more accurately my belief concerning it," wrote Ben Butcher in one of a series of answers which, for
their lack of "evangelical insight," almost earned him rejection by the
Society.[134]

A decreasing emphasis on the atonement was counterbalanced by a
new appreciation of the importance of the incarnation and the life of
Christ as a "pattern" or "perfect example."[135] The Calvinist conception
of the wrath of God received no expression in the papers of the candidates, many of whom stressed that salvation was available for all. Conversely, the love of God, advanced by some individuals throughout the
period as one of the principal doctrines of the gospel, was mentioned
increasingly as time passed. The penultimate missionary to arrive in
Papua before the Great War reflected a contemporary attraction
toward the social gospel in his reference to the fatherhood of God and
the brotherhood of man.[136]

Candidates trained in the eighties and early nineties frequently
volunteered a belief in the infallibility, or at least the divine inspiration,
of the Scriptures. Of the fifteen who applied to join after 1895, only two

expressed a similar conviction. Absence of comment does not necessarily imply disbelief, but it does suggest a sensitivity to the effects of biblical criticism on fundamentalist faith. Butcher, expressing doubts on this subject, was championed by Owen Whitehouse, Reynolds' successor at Cheshunt, who told the LMS secretary that he sympathized with Butcher's hesitation on the question, "if infallibility implied inerrancy."[137]

Intending missionaries were also asked from time to time to name the books they had read.[138] The lists they supplied were generally modest, some of the earlier candidates, especially, demurring that they had done no serious reading. Predictably, considering the purpose for which the list was intended, theological and devotional books were the largest category. The books of this nature most frequently listed were Henry Drummond's *Natural Law in the Spiritual World* (1883), William Paley's *Evidences of Christianity* (1794), and F. W. Farrar's *Life of Christ* (1874), three books which, though exceedingly popular, were not in the vanguard of nineteenth-century scholarship.[139]

Frequent reading of Bible commentaries by the candidates revealed the influence of textual criticism,[140] but the authors whom they read, such as Westcott, Farrar, and Godet, were among the more conservative of such scholars.[141] Their appreciation of homiletics was enriched by the works of eminent preachers such as Beecher and Spurgeon. Other theological and devotional books they read were also written by respected nonconformists such as Henry Reynolds, Joseph Parker, Robert Dale, Alfred Cave, and R. F. Horton.

Their reading lists are as interesting for what they omit as for what they include. If any had read F. D. Maurice, whose challenges to prevailing ideas of the atonement and of everlasting punishment had profoundly influenced contemporary thought, they did not mention it. Nor did they admit having read other eminent scholars and critics such as Jowett or Baden Powell. None mentioned the influential *Essays and Reviews* (1860), a controversial series of essays by seven authors who believed in the necessity for free inquiry in religious matters. The missionaries read Farrar's *Life of Christ* (1874), but not more contentious studies like David F. Strauss' *Das Leben Jesu* (1835), which applied the "myth theory" to the life of Christ and denied the historical foundations for the supernatural elements in the Gospels; or Joseph E. Renan's *The Life of Jesus* (1864), which provoked great controversy by demythologizing the life of Jesus. Only one missionary listed Samuel Cox's universalist *Salvator Mundi*.

The amount of secular literature listed increased throughout the period. Most often mentioned were the works of Tennyson, which, according to the historian Owen Chadwick, embodied "Victorian hesitation and its reverence before a perhaps divine mystery."[142] Next most popular were the poetry of Shakespeare, Milton, and Wordsworth, and the novels of George MacDonald who, by the late nineteenth century, had abandoned his earlier religious radicalism. Dickens, the most popular writer of his time with society at large, was listed by the candidates slightly less frequently, and only as often as Charles Kingsley, George Eliot, Walter Scott, and Macaulay. Almost as popular were the essays of Charles Lamb and the works of Ruskin and Carlyle.

The third large category of reading that the candidates mentioned was missionary biography. Most often listed were biographies of Livingstone, followed closely by books by or about Robert Moffat, James Chalmers, John Williams, J. G. Paton, and Bishop Hannington. They also read biographies of Richard Knill, James Gilmour, and William Carey.

One category of reading that was notably slight in the candidates' bibliographies was that of the sciences and the newly emerging social sciences of anthropology and sociology. Only one missionary, Charles Abel, listed Darwin's *Origin of Species*. Even the great contemporary debate between science and religion was scarcely reflected in their reading. Apart from Drummond, only one other writer on the subject was mentioned, by one missionary. One had read on astronomy, one on physiology, and one on engineering. No LMS missionary listed any anthropological or ethnographic works, and only one a study of comparative religion.

The Society sought in other ways to test the suitability of the applicants through their candidates' papers. The first was to ensure that they had had some type of home missionary experience, the second to test their expectations of the missionary career. Missionary candidates could generally furnish an impressive list of the Christian works with which they had been associated. Almost all had taught Sunday school, and many had participated in local missions, which frequently demanded open-air preaching. Two had worked with the North Sea Fisherman's Crusade, and three had been employed as home missionaries, working in Glasgow and Bristol. Three had worked with the YMCA, and one with a temperance society. Others had conducted prayer meetings and Bible classes, or distributed religious tracts. Most exotic was the experience of Charles Abel, who had combined trading with preaching to the Maoris.

Asked what they considered the most important qualities for a missionary and the severest trials and temptations he would endure, most showed a realistic appreciation of the missionary career. A strong faith, love of God, wholehearted commitment, and personal piety were the qualities considered most essential. Good health and physical strength were frequently mentioned. Eight believed love and understanding of people to be important and four of the later missionaries stressed the need for adaptability to the thought of the people. Willingness to work and sacrifice were frequently listed, and occasionally, patience, perseverance, courage, geniality, enthusiasm, humility, sound judgment, and a good education.

By far the greatest trial foreseen by the aspiring missionaries was separation from their families and from the spiritual refreshment of Christian society. The effort of learning a new language and adjusting to a foreign culture was mentioned by some and several anticipated the trial of being surrounded, as one bluntly put it, by "dull, dead heathenism."[143] Several listed the rigors of climate or other physical privations. Only two apprehended physical danger and one of the two LMS missionaries to die violently in New Guinea, James Chalmers, foresaw the possibility of "bloodshed and death."[144] Lack of success was realistically expected by several, but only one foresaw what was to become the bane of many of their lives—monotony.

Confronted with the prospect of such trials, most candidates felt, not surprisingly, that despondency and discouragement would be their greatest temptations. These would result from the enormity of the work and their lack of success in it. The second greatest temptation they foresaw was to spiritual, mental, and physical slackness, the effect of the lack of spiritual and social support, and from the "degradation" of their new environment. They feared "sinking" to the level of those around them. Others anticipated the temptation to abuse freedom and become autocratic, impatient, or irritable. Two feared becoming self-satisfied.

When a candidate had completed his college course and satisfied the examining committee, both personally and through his answers to the questions for candidates, that he was acceptable, he looked forward to ordination and his overseas posting. Most missionaries of the early twentieth century crammed into their last few months in England a short course of medicine at Livingstone College, founded to teach missionaries and missionary candidates how to care for their own health and to offer rudimentary treatment to the people they would work among.[145] Earlier missionaries had frequently gained similar experience through private arrangements with doctors or medical lecturers.

Although all mission candidates agreed to leave choice of their sphere of work to the Society, they were permitted to express a preference, which was accommodated if possible. Hence the appointments of Dauncey, Bartlett, Tomkins, Cullen, Clark, Harries, and R. L. Turner to New Guinea were a fulfilment of an "earnest hope," while J. T. Scott, Ridgley, W. Y. Turner, Beharell, Holmes, and Riley went reluctantly, the last three having requested service in Africa. Of Thomas Ridgley, who decamped after only six weeks in New Guinea, an exas-

perated Lawes wrote that it was "the one place to which he did not
want to go."[146] The final stage in the making of the LMS missionary was
his ordination, which often took place in the church or chapel where he
had grown up, with representatives of the congregation and the Society
in attendance.

Candidates for the ministry of the Methodist church in Australia,
whether destined for the mission field or the home ministry, went
through a minutely regulated process of selection, training, and assessment.[147] The superintendent of the district in which he worshipped
nominated a candidate to the quarterly meeting, after ascertaining his
knowledge of Wesley's works and Methodist polity and his general suitability for the work. Like their LMS counterparts, most had already
demonstrated their earnestness through Sunday school teaching, open
air preaching, and home mission work. All were fully accredited local
preachers. Approved by the quarterly meeting, the candidate appeared
before the examining committee and the district synod to give an
account of his "conversion," to reply to an oral theological examination,
and to preach a trial sermon. If accepted, he was, where possible, given
three years' theological training, or else appointed to a circuit.

Of the Wesleyan ministers who served in New Guinea, the majority
had no formal theological training, but were appointed directly to a district.[148] For many it was the New Guinea district. The beginning of
their missionary career coincided with the mandatory four-year probationary period that followed their acceptance as a candidate, whether
or not they had attended a theological institution. For a minority of the
older missionaries, this apprenticeship had been served in circuits of
Australia or New Zealand, or, in Bromilow's case, Fiji.

For those who came to the mission field as probationers, as for all
other ministers on trial, the probationary period was committed to a
prescribed course of private study, on which they were tested by annual
examinations. The course was purely theological and in structure similar to that taken by LMS missionaries after the completion of their
humanities.[149] But it was more distinctly denominational in content.
The first fifty-three of Wesley's sermons were studied over the first two
years, and although Watson's *Theological Institutes* (1829), "the greatest textbook of Methodism after Wesley,"[150] had been dropped from the
course by 1891, it had been replaced by an equally classic statement of
Methodist Arminianism, William Burt Pope's three-volume *A Compen-
dium of Christian Theology* (1873), which was studied over three years.
Probationers were also examined on Gregory's *History and Polity of
Methodism* and on the laws of Australasian Methodism. Other parts of
the course were less distinctively Methodist. Each year probationers
studied portions of the Old and the New Testaments, George Park Fish-

er's *History of the Christian Church* (1887), and part of Butler's *The Analogy of Religion* (1736). It was a conservative theological education. In 1913 students at Newington College, Sydney, pleaded with the Examining Committee for "modern theological thought" to be put alongside Pope's theology in the syllabus: "We feel that the age to which we shall minister is one which thinks of theological problems . . . in new terms. . . . Furthermore it is an age stirred to the depths by social problems. . . . The present curriculum makes little provision to meet either of these needs."[151]

While the course prescribed varied little from 1890 to 1914, the list of recommended readings that accompanied it lengthened, broadened, and to some extent changed in content.[152] By 1895 it had expanded to include over seventy texts organized into five categories: biblical criticism and exegesis, theology, apologetics, church history and polity, and pastoral theology (homiletics). The isolationism that had characterized Methodism in its more sect-like days[153] had broken down, and probationers were encouraged to read selectively, not only from the works of such eminent nonconformists as Dale, Cave, Fairbairn, and Drummond, but also among Anglican theologians, from Bishop Butler and William Paley to Farrar, Liddon, Westcott, and Lightfoot. Probationers from 1895 were also urged to "acquaint themselves with the best classics of English and other literatures," a new trend in Methodism, which had, at least since the death of Wesley, eschewed secular literature.[154] In 1901 a new category of miscellaneous reading was introduced. Initially it included only two books on temperance and one on the physical sciences, but in 1904, Black's *Culture and Restraint* was listed, and in 1907 A. R. Wallace's *Darwinism* (1889) and four texts on the issue of science and religion were added. A new category of books, sociology, was also introduced, and in 1913 an eighth category, comparative religion. The 1913 General Conference also gave missionary probationers the opportunity of substituting some missionary subjects for those prescribed.

Despite the breadth of the reading list, there was no danger of studies of Methodist belief and practice being submerged. John Wesley's *A Plain Account of Christian Perfection* (1770) and John Hunt's *Entire Sanctification* (1853) introduced probationers to this essentially Methodist doctrine. After 1907 probationers were encouraged to read the theology of John Scott Lidgett who, drawing attention to Wesley's stress on the love as well as the omnipotence of God, outlined an immanentist theology which, like F. D. Maurice's, stressed the fatherhood of God and pointed to the social implications of such a gospel, which were in strong contrast with the individualistic theology of nineteenth-century Methodism.[155]

The oral examination to which candidates were subjected further ensured their understanding of evangelical doctrine in general and Wesley's works in particular. It tested their belief in scriptural infallibility, the Trinity, and the divinity of Christ, and their understanding of original sin, repentance, the atonement (without endorsement of any particular theory), justification, regeneration, and entire sanctification. Their views on the afterlife, the Sabbath, and the sacraments were sought, and they were asked finally for a submission to Methodist discipline and an unrestricted commitment to the church.[156] Preaching a trial sermon, the last stage of probation, was an ordeal dreaded by young candidates and one that several of the missionaries initially failed.[157] Most chose to preach on fundamental tenets of evangelical faith.[158]

After passing these tests, the candidate was recommended to the annual conference to be received into "full connexion." He was examined by the president and senior ministers on "his personal experience, his acquaintance with the Laws and Regulations of the Church and his determination to give himself fully to the work of the Ministry," after which he made a public statement to the conference, which then voted for his acceptance, rejection, or continued probation. Admitted into full connexion, he was ordained by the imposition of hands.[159]

Although given the opportunity through their courses and bibliographies to read widely, especially in the realm of evangelical theology, most Methodist missionaries scarcely availed themselves of it. Their theological studies coincided with the diverting, difficult, and busy phase of adjusting to a new language, a new culture, and a new career. Reading of the prescribed texts was crammed into evenings at the end of long and often tiring days, and it was not uncommon for missionaries to be passed in their year without successful completion of the examination, on the grounds that study of the language or other work had placed undue demands on them.[160] Compared with the LMS candidates, their training was essentially practical, an apprenticeship that allowed little time for sustained intellectual effort.

Anglican priests who came from England to the mission field had mostly received what was still in the late nineteenth century the traditional preparation for Holy Orders, a degree from Oxford or Cambridge.[161] In this, theological learning frequently played a minor part. Although an honors school of theology was established at Oxford in 1870 and a theological tripos at Cambridge in 1871, most ordinands continued to study for Greats, which they regarded as providing a more exacting discipline. While Ernest Taylor took a first class theology degree at Oxford, Stone-Wigg and Newton studied classics, as did Sharp, at Cambridge. Like most Anglican graduate ordinands, and unlike their Protestant counterparts, they received no financial support during their training, the assumption until the end of the century being that a clergyman was a gentleman and thus a person of means.

As the supply of gentlemen recruits dwindled, at the same time as the Church of England was awakening to a sense of responsibility toward the masses,[162] the sources of the Anglican ministry in England necessarily became more varied in the last three decades of the century. Despite resistance from a substantial element within the church, theological colleges were founded with the intention of preparing ordinands without a degree. Albert Maclaren received his training at St. Augustine's, Canterbury, a college founded in 1848 especially for the preparation of missionary priests, and only some years after ordination took a degree at Durham. Another priest, John Hunt, also studied at St. Augustine's, as did Ernest Davies, a lay missionary who failed to qualify for the priesthood. Acceptance at St. Augustine's depended on "satisfactory testimonials [as to] moral and religious character [and] special promise for missionary service."[163] Completion of the matriculation examination was followed by a probationary period, at the end of which the student had to "declare his intention of devoting himself to the service of God, in the ministry of the Church of England, in the distant dependencies of the British Empire." The three-year course was designed with this object in mind. Besides studying Latin and Greek classics, mathematics, and physical science, the Scriptures in English and Greek, evidences of Christianity, the standard Anglican divines, the Prayer Book, and the Thirty-nine Articles, students also learned oriental languages, if "intended for the East," undertook a short medical course, and studied mission history. Experience in preaching, pastoral work, and mechanical arts was also provided.

Three missionaries, Romney Gill, John Hunt, and James Fisher, studied at Burgh, another missionary college founded in 1878 to prepare candidates both for the field and for higher training at St. Augustine's.[164] Studies included English, Latin, Greek, the Scriptures and the Prayer Book, manual arts, and pastoral work. A bursary fund gave assistance to a limited number of applicants.

Several of those educated at Oxford or Cambridge completed their training with a brief period at a theological college, this, according to Anglo-Catholic opinion, aiding "the formation of clerical character" in the graduate, while ensuring a grounding in the received theological tradition.[165] Stone-Wigg and Wilfred Abbot spent a year at Ely, a Tractarian college designed for graduates, while Sharp went to Lincoln, which offered a one-year course for graduates and two years to nongraduates.[166] Others prepared independently for the Preliminary Examination of Candidates for Holy Orders, which was in many dioceses a prerequisite for ordination of nongraduate candidates.[167] Candidates were examined on parts of the Old and New Testaments (the latter in Greek); the creeds, the Thirty-nine Articles, and the Prayer Book; ecclesiastical history, and a translation from an ecclesiastical Latin author. Besides passing the preliminary, they had to satisfy various diocesan requirements. Although some dioceses accepted only graduates of Oxford, Cambridge, or Dublin, most, by the 1880s, also took applicants who had completed two years at theological college. Most required testimonial letters from three beneficed clergymen and from their college, a baptismal certificate, and a nomination to a curacy, and many subjected candidates to further examination, frequently in the works of Anglican divines such as Butler, Hooker, Paley, and Pearson.[168]

The Anglican priests trained in Australia were prepared for ordination on similar lines. Copland King took a Bachelor of Arts degree at Sydney University, but most who came from Australia to the mission field or who went from the mission field to Australia for clerical training, studied at Australian theological colleges. Despite the Anglo-Catholic orientation of the mission, several of the staff had trained at the evangelical Moore Theological College. Others studied at St. Francis' College, Brisbane; St. John's College, Armidale; Trinity College, Melbourne; St. Barnabas' College, Adelaide; or St. Alban's, Ballarat.[169]

After being "tried" and "examined" according to the dictates of the preface of the ordinal in the Book of Common Prayer, candidates were ordained deacon by the bishop as prescribed by the ordinal. A "Declaration of Assent" to the Thirty-nine Articles, an oath of allegiance to the sovereign, and one of canonical obedience to the bishop were required of the ordinand.[170]

Like their LMS and Methodist counterparts, most Anglican priests had some pastoral experience before departing for the mission field. Albert Maclaren, during vacations from St. Augustine's, worked in a poor district of Canterbury, and in London and Gravesend dockside missions; Wilfred Abbot worked among factory workers at Kettering. Most had served curacies, often in urban parishes. Stone-Wigg confessed himself less at home among the "swells" of Brisbane than among the artisans of Hammersmith, but preferred both to "feeding on the luxuriant pastures of some English country living."[171] Gerald Sharp also served part of his curacy at Holy Innocents' Mission, Hammersmith, while James Fisher came from St. Alphage's, Southwark. Some had colonial experience as curates, Maclaren among the "Kanakas" of Mackay; Abbot, Stone-Wigg, and Hunt in Brisbane; Chignell, Elder, and King in parishes of Sydney; and Ernest Taylor on the Western Australian goldfields.

Lay men and women of the Anglican and Methodist churches could expect no training before their departure for the mission field. Most had participated in those forms of good works expected of a devout laity. Several of the Anglican men were lay readers and most of the nonordained Methodists were lay preachers. Several of the women had worked in Methodist or Anglican sisterhoods in Australia.

The Missionaries of the Sacred Heart mostly began their training for the priesthood and the apostolate at the congregation's apostolic school, the Petit-Oeuvre du Sacré-Coeur, so named because it financed the education of its poor students from an annual donation, from numerous benefactors, of one sou.[172] Young boys of eleven or twelve, frequently the sons of peasants, entered the Petit-Oeuvre, originally housed in a former Benedictine monastery near Issoudun, France. They progressed through the school studying Greek, Latin, mathematics, physics, history, geography, liturgy, music, and religion, finally reaching the first class, where they were introduced to rhetoric, in preparation for the baccalaureate.

Priding itself on being a school with a special purpose, the Petit-Oeuvre fostered a simple and affectionate family environment. Punishments were not employed, and the only sanctions were term and monthly reports from teachers. The atmosphere was pious but robust. Sports and recreation were encouraged, "special friendships" among the pupils discouraged. Father Marie, the superior, became a true father to the fatherless Verjus, as to the other pupils, permitting him his Society of Victims but checking his more ardent attempts at mortification. Verjus expressed his delight in the regime of the school: "Frequent communion, Mass every day, instruction regularly, excellent teachers, a superior who is to us a father. . . . Safe from the world, we labour to become saints and *savants*."[173]

After completing their humanities in the relatively benign atmosphere of the Petit-Oeuvre, most prospective MSC spent a much more demanding year as novices.[174] In the words of one member of the congregation, the novitiate was "the crucible where gold is purified and shines forth."[175] It was an austere regime, much of it spent in silence and segregation. The novice-masters, such as Father Ramot at St. Gerand-le-Puy and Father Piperon at Tilburg, men of unfaltering faith and profound devotion to the Sacred Heart, imposed a rigid rule.[176]

Commencing with a short retreat and the taking of the habit, the novitiate had as its central feature the thirty-day retreat devoted to the complete practice of the *Spiritual Exercises* of St. Ignatius, a series of meditations and rules designed to lead novices to "conquer their passions and give themselves to God."[177] It was an extraordinarily effective and influential manual on Christian perfection. "With this book I will become a saint," declared Henri Verjus, who left a detailed record of his progression through the Exercises.[178] Other influential texts for the novitiate were Thomas à Kempis' *The Imitation of Christ* (1418), and Rodriguez' *The Practice of Perfection of Christian Virtues* (1609). The novitiate ended, after another retreat, with the taking of temporary vows, the three simple vows of poverty, chastity, and obedience.

Their novitiate completed, most prospective missionary priests returned to their studies for the priesthood. As scholastics they embarked on the required courses of philosophy and theology. The congregation had established its own scholasticate with the novitiate in the large château of St. Gerand-le-Puy, but as the anticlerical persecutions intensified, many scholastics of the eighties undertook their studies in exile, in Barcelona or Rome. At times of crisis in the mission, young scholastics completed their theology in Australia or in the field, under the supervision of Genocchi, Jullien, and de Boismenu. When the persecution relaxed toward the end of the century, a scholasticate was reestablished in France, only to be driven into exile again with the Waldeck-Rousseau laws of the new century.

Like most seminarian education of the period, the courses offered to MSC scholastics were probably conservative and outdated.[179] The only students to be exposed to intellectual and theological ferment were those who studied in Rome. The MSC scholastics at the Pontifical Seminary of the Apollinare were taught by a series of eminent theologians.[180] Those who were students in the eighties plunged into the turmoil that followed Leo XIII's endorsement of Thomism, through the bull *Aeterni Patris* (1879), to which the Apollinare was resistant.[181] Genocchi, studying at the Seminario Pio, and already a gifted scholar, threw himself into the debate as a pro-Thomist.[182] There was also some opportunity for the study of biblical criticism, seized by Genocchi and resisted by the theologically able but more conservative Jullien.[183]

After the conclusion of their courses, students looked forward to ordination, first as subdeacon, then deacon, and finally as priest. Their appointment to the mission field was in the hands of their superiors. Verjus, obsessed with his desire for the missions and martyrdom, chafed at the delay in his appointment as he watched two contingents of missionaries set out without him.[184] Navarre, who had joined the congregation after a period as a secular priest, never sought the apostolate, and joined the pioneer expedition reluctantly.[185] De Boisemenu and Jullien were needed for teaching in the rapidly growing apostolic schools, and Gsell was obliged to teach scholastics in Sydney for three years before being appointed to Papua. But the chronic shortage of staff in the field, exacerbated by the high death rate, meant that sooner or later most who desired missionary service found themselves embarking from Marseilles for distant Oceania.

Diverse as the range of training was for the missionaries of the various persuasions, one factor was common to all. Almost nobody was prepared specifically for the mission field. Few encountered any language other than Greek, Latin, or Hebrew during their studies; few had read texts in anthropology or comparative religion. More mundane but no less important, many had received no medical training, and most, no training in manual skills. Their training was scarcely differentiated from that of the home ministry. LMS missionaries studied essentially the same courses at the same colleges as Congregational ministers; Methodist missionaries passed through the same theological education and probation as their brethren in the colonial churches, with a token gesture toward reading for the mission. Anglican priests at Oxford or Cambridge, or in theological colleges, received an education that fitted them for a rural English benefice; only the few at the missionary training colleges received a training in any way tailored for the mission field. Training for the Roman Catholic priesthood was shaped by the universal dictates of Canon Law, and although the MSC superiors discussed the desirability of a distinctive novitiate for prospective missionaries,[186] it remained essentially a classical novitiate molded more by the objectives of the congregation than the needs of the mission field. The best preparation that all could hope for was the contact with active or retired missionaries that association with the congregation or society provided.

Embarkation

The final trial for the missionary eager to begin service was the sea voyage to New Guinea. Roman Catholic missionaries sailed from Marseilles to Australia in ships of the Messageries Maritimes Line. As they traveled in large contingents, they could maintain their communal life, using the six weeks on the sea for study, preparation, and their religious offices.[187] British missionaries sailed individually from England, frequently in P&O steamers, some joining in the social activities of shipboard life,[188] while the more pious dissociated themselves from its levity, participating only in the Sunday services, at which they were often invited to preach.[189] All persisted in their reading and devotions, despite, frequently, the presence of "godless" cabin mates, and the more enterprising took lessons in navigation.[190]

Arriving in Australia they, like the colonial missionaries, looked for coastal shipping, frequently that of Burns, Philp & Company, or sailed in boats owned or chartered by the missions themselves. The pioneering Methodist party, sailing in the chartered three-masted vessel, *Lord of the Isles* was, according to a later missionary, the "largest missionary expedition in modern times [and] surely the best equipped."[191] Into the small schooner were packed eight Europeans, six Fijian ministers and their wives, twelve assorted children, material for three houses, a cutter, two whaleboats, stores, tools, a complete outfit for a blacksmith's shop, medicines, instruments, furniture, a cow, and several dogs, as well as the trunks of the Europeans and the bundles and mats of the Islanders. The missionaries on the deck watched the tearful crowd of well-wishers on the Sydney wharf receding while their own "choking throats refused to sing . . . 'God be with you till we meet again'."[192] Subsequent Methodist missionaries traveled with less drama, but usually, like the pioneers, in small, cramped ships, optimistically trying the latest remedies for seasickness, braving coarse meals in stifling saloons, trying not to notice the cockroaches that invaded deck and cabin, and scanning the seas for the first sight of land.[193] All were pleased to leave behind the "tedium" or "slackness" of shipboard life, though neither the correct British nor the laconic colonials expressed quite such exuberant delight as the ardent French missionaries who, on reaching the "Promised Land," threw themselves on their knees and kissed the soil.[194]

CHAPTER 3

"The Object Lesson of a Civilized Christian Home"

Protestant Domesticity

WHEN THE TWO young missionaries, Harry Dauncey and Frederick Walker, arrived in 1888 to work in New Guinea, their first taste of mission life was, as for most LMS missionaries, at the Port Moresby station. The small weatherboard cottage in which William and Fanny Lawes had spent their first years (Figure 8) had been replaced by a substantial timber building raised on piles and covered with a corrugated iron roof. Walker and Dauncey were enchanted by their introduction to the mission:

> Dinner was served at Mrs. Lawes's house—a long, narrow building, containing four small rooms, but furnished all round with a verandah, either side of which could be used as a dining place, according to the direction of the wind. I often found myself looking over the bay or watching the children, or gazing at the changing loveliness of the sky. . . . We were waited on by three bright looking native boys. . . . They seemed very proud of their duties and really did remarkably well.[1]

After dinner Lawes escorted them round the station, pointing out the twelve bush material houses of the married student teachers, guiding them past the cooking house, domestic quarters, and Chalmers' small cottage, through a picket gate down the hill to the house of veteran Rarotongan missionary, Ruatoka, and to the long corrugated iron mission store (Figure 9). At the foot of the hill were clustered the villages of Hanuabada.

The first glimpse of mission life for the Methodist missionaries, who disembarked at Samarai, was frequently on the nearby island of Kwato, where they were received by the LMS missionary, Charles Abel. This too was a gentle introduction to the mission field. Sister Minnie Billing described her arrival in 1895, in a letter to friends:

Figure 8. The first mission house at Port Moresby, built 1874. (Council for World Mission)

Figure 9. The mission settlement, Port Moresby. (Council for World Mission)

Envy me now as you read this. The beauty of the place surpasses anything I have ever dreamed of. . . . The house occupied by Mr Abel is a native one, but furnished in English fashion. The sitting-room . . . is such a pretty room, beautifully furnished. The table at tea-time was lovely—the china and silver, serviettes etc. of the best. The native boys waited on the table very cleverly. It was like getting into perfect Paradise after the rough life of the "Zephyr."[2]

From Kwato, most Methodist missionaries went to their own district headquarters at Dobu, another orderly station that by the turn of the century resembled a small village of about forty houses, dominated by the mission house. Raised on sturdy piles, framed by a shady verandah, and surrounded by a neatly fenced garden, it was regarded by Sir William MacGregor as the best house in New Guinea (Figure 10).[3]

Other Protestant mission stations were more rudimentary and their housing more primitive, but most shared the general features of Port Moresby, Kwato, and Dobu. Most were coastal, frequently built on a ridge or hill with the mission house commanding a view across the rooftops of a village and its palm-fringed beach and out to sea. High ground was allegedly chosen because it was healthy, caught the breeze, and allowed warning of approaching ships, but considerations of supremacy may also have been involved. Villages were not chosen as sites in part because they were often low-lying and unhealthy; but more importantly, the missionaries argued that the mission should become "a model village in itself" to draw the people from their pagan surroundings to a "higher" way of life. Moreover, when neighboring tribes were frequently at enmity, it was important to choose neutral ground.[4]

Figure 10. Methodist mission house, Dobu. (Uniting Church)

On any Protestant station, the focal point was the mission house. By the turn of the century most, like those at Port Moresby and Dobu, were large, simple, substantial houses of sawn timber with corrugated iron roofs, built on piles, and surrounded by a verandah. Some replaced earlier bush material houses, the missionaries arguing not only that European-style houses were more conducive to health and comfort, but also that they were ultimately more economical, as "native" houses had to be replaced every three or four years.[5] Most houses were prefabricated in Sydney and shipped to New Guinea. In the early years such a house could be purchased for about £100,[6] but costs rose steeply and by the end of the century Archibald Hunt did not consider £600 excessive for a newly erected mission house at Port Moresby.[7] By 1914, the Methodist Mission could anticipate spending £1000 on a new European-style house.[8]

Some individuals within both missions, including Chalmers, Schlencker, and Holmes of the LMS and the Methodist Ambrose Fletcher, remained committed to housing of local materials.[9] But these were the exceptions. Most Protestant missionaries lived comfortably in their spacious, pleasantly furnished houses—a scandal in the eyes of the ascetic James Chalmers. In an autobiography found among his papers after his death, he castigated all his LMS colleagues except Holmes and Schlencker for their "luxurious habits" and their "palatial residences," far finer than that of the governor.[10] Stung into reply, Hunt agreed that he and his colleagues did live in good houses: "Better far to spend a few extra pounds on the houses than to spend it in necessary sick furloughs and constant breakdowns." The charge that their houses were better than the governor's residence signified little, since this was a poor cottage that the governor himself referred to as a "biscuit box."[11]

Whatever the style, the mission house was the pivot of Protestant missionary endeavor. In this situation, it was agreed, "the best of men was only a poor helpless creature" without a good wife.[12] Having learned from its initial endeavors of the pitfalls of sending single male missionaries to the South Seas, the LMS urged its candidates to marry before embarking on missionary service. The AWMMS did not have such clear-cut expectations, and indeed forbade marriage to probationers going into the field, but generally marriage was approved for ministers in full connexion. For many aspiring Protestant missionaries, therefore, acquiring a wife became an essential part of the preparation for missionary service, along with packing, vaccination, and ordination. For some, marriage and ordination took place in a breathless few days before embarkation.

The missionaries went about their wife-getting in a practical, businesslike way. William Bromilow described his courtship of Lily Thomson, a lively young woman whom he had met while preaching in the country in Victoria. "I offered myself [to the mission] and was accepted. But for these posts an occupant must be married, a qualifcation I was prepared . . . to assume." He sent a telegram to Lily's parents and, receiving a positive answer, married, and "at once proceeded to Sydney where I was ordained. Four days later we sailed."[13]

The wives chosen by the missionaries were generally from backgrounds similar to their own. Those of the LMS were, like their husbands, frequently from British towns; six were Australians. Most had no professional qualifications; of the thirty LMS wives, five were trained as teachers and three as nurses. They were loyal church members; all except three of Congregational churches in which they might have taught Sunday school or participated in other parish works. One was a former missionary, three had close relatives who had served with the LMS, and two others were related to LMS directors.

A number of the LMS missionaries chose wives who, while of similar origins, were of higher social status than themselves. Samuel McFarlane, the former factory operative, married Elizabeth Joyce, daughter of John Joyce, "gentleman." James Chalmers, an artisan's son, married Jane Hercus, of a family eminent in the scholarly tradition of Scottish Presbyterianism. J. T. Scott's wife, Eliza Mitchell, was "a lady of high culture" while the wife of Harry Scott, former clerk, was the daughter of Professor Todhunter of Cheshunt. Riley, Rich, and Harries, of artisan or small-farming backgrounds, married well-qualified schoolteachers, and in all cases were considered fortunate in their choice. Charles Abel, the knockabout trader, married Beatrice Moxon, a brewer's daughter who had completed her education in a Belgian finishing school, while Ben Butcher, from Billingsgate Fish Market, married Ena Davidson, whose family was prominent in the Bank of New South Wales. These discrepancies in social status may have been an indication of the esteem in which the vocation of missionary was held by godly Protestants, as well as a reflection of the desire for "self-improvement" on the part of the missionaries themselves.

The Methodist wives were, like their husbands, more commonly from Australia or New Zealand. More were from rural backgrounds while others were daughters of clerks or small businessmen. Three had trained as teachers and two as nurses, and two had earned a living in trade, one as a tailoress, the other as a milliner. All were from staunch Methodist families and one had a sister, another a brother, in mission service.

If the LMS missionaries were not prepared to be hard-headed in their choice of a wife, the board of directors was quite unsentimental. A "lover's testimony" was not sufficient evidence of a suitable choice, the board admonished one missionary.[14] Others were advised that "satisfactory evidence of the lady's suitability for the position of missionary wife, as well as a favourable medical certificate" had to be furnished, if the directors' sanction were to be given.[15] Generally they received a testimonial from the local minister and other character references, besides a detailed medical report from a doctor designated by the Society. On one occasion they refused to sanction a marriage, leaving their candidate Thomas Beswick with the dilemma of whether to dishonor an engagement or withdraw from the work that he felt called by God to do.[16]

The Methodist mission secretary, George Brown, initially took no more than a paternal interest in the matrimonial maneuvers of his missionaries. He wrote approvingly of Samuel Fellows having "fallen a victim to a nice able-bodied widow" on his first furlough.[17] But the disastrous health record of the first five Methodist wives into the field convinced him of the need for a change in policy. "It seems a thousand pities that Missionaries should choose wives as unfitted for Mission Work as many do," he complained to Bromilow in 1895, adding, "We require a medical certificate now."[18]

Of all the Protestant male missionaries, only four LMS and five Methodists remained unmarried during their missionary service. For those who, from inclination or necessity, came to the field as bachelors, finding a wife became a major preoccupation. Some LMS missionaries succumbed to pressure from the Society to marry; most, of both societies, became convinced of the advantages of having a wife. These were usually explained in functional terms; romantic or sexual needs were rarely intimated. Baxter Riley, describing his new house to the LMS directors, added, "Now it is absolutely necessary I should be in a position to keep that house in a fit and proper manner. There is only one way this can be done . . . and that is by getting married, a business which I am afraid will be a difficult matter."[19] Others stressed the contribution a wife could make to the work.

New Guinea provided few opportunities to find a wife. Four Methodist missionaries availed themselves of an option their LMS colleagues did not have and married missionary sisters from their own staff. But most went "wife-seeking" in the colonies. Many, like Riley, found it a difficult matter. Some of the LMS missionaries were hostile to the thought of a colonial wife and self-conscious about the whole enterprise.[20] Saville reproved Wardlaw Thompson, the foreign secretary of the LMS, for the levity of his comments on the subject, while Robert Lister Turner, defending himself against Thompson's charges of becoming "morbid" on the marriage question, explained most earnestly that he was awaiting the guidance of God.[21] All agreed that a three-month furlough was too short for their objective. "Deputation work opens many opportunities, but of a fleeting character," observed James Wil-

Figure 11. Polly Dauncey at home at Delena. (Council for World Mission)

liams. "I am going about open-eyed and praying continually for direction."[22]

Sooner or later most Protestant missionary homes were presided over by wives (Figures 11, 12). Many transformed austerely functional houses into gracious suburban bungalows. Lizzie Chalmers described with pride the comfortable, cluttered parlor she had created in her "semi-native" house on the mud-banks of the Fly River.

> All my curios, and old glass and china, are on the corner shelves. Four small tables under the shelves hold photos etc., and books. My big likenesses on the walls. . . . The centre table is 3 ft. wide and 4 ft. long, and two pretty and very comfortable large chairs and a delightful tête-à-tête lounge are all from Hong Kong. . . . Six ordinary chairs and one arm chair and couch of Australian bentwood. . . . My portable piano on a stand. . . . Photos wherever there is room to put them of all my dearest and nearest . . . with one or two oil paintings—plenty of cushions, covered, some in gold silk, some in green.[23]

Figure 12. First mission house at Dirimu, and missionary's wife. (Council for World Mission)

At Kwato, the comfortable, partly bush material house that Minnie Billing had admired in 1895 was replaced soon after by an imposing European-style house, the only home in Papua to boast a grand piano and a marble fireplace.[24] Some wives found comfort in surrounding their houses with gardens full of "gay English flowers."[25]

Within their homes most wives employed servants, usually young boys and girls who lived in the mission compound. They were trained by the wives, not all of whom had come from homes where servants were employed. The amount of skill and tact they exercised in this task varied. Many complained of the patience required to train their staff, but some succeeded admirably, as the comments of visitors on the competence and cleanliness of their servants indicated. Domestic staff waited at table, cleaned, laundered, and helped prepare meals. Many wore a simple uniform—for the Kwato boys, a blue loincloth and white top.[26] Bromilow paid his house- and table-boys 5 shillings per quarter, considerable less than the wage of an unskilled plantation laborer who earned 10 shillings per month.[27] For many such youths domestic service was the first step into a new Papuan elite. Lawes boasted that some of his best teacher trainees had begun their education in his wife's kitchen.[28]

Although the influence of many missionaries' wives extended well beyond the confines of their homes, their accepted role was that of "help-meet" to their husbands. They were expected to support them in their work, run the household, bear and raise the children, and together provide the "object lesson of a civilized Christian home."[29] This was the role that LMS and Methodist wives had been accustomed to in other parts of the Pacific and elsewhere. Samuel McFarlane, one of New Guinea's pioneer missionaries, wrote floridly:

> And whilst the missionary is forming Christian churches, his wife is forming (what is equally important) Christian homes. . . . In the South Seas there are multitudes of homes which are centres of refinement, culture, happiness and intelligence, presided over by women, officiating in those offices recognised as her sphere of duty. In these abodes it is no mockery . . . to sing "Home, Sweet Home."[30]

A female contemporary, the novelist Ada Cambridge (Mrs. George Cross), wrote of the "killing strain" imposed on clerical wives in Australia at the time. There was, she wrote, "no doubt, as to which of the clerical pair is in the shafts and which is in the lead. It is not the parson who . . . bears the burden . . . but the uncompromising drudge who backs him up at all points."[31] The comment is applicable to the New Guinea mission field. Lacking the status of their husbands, and, in some cases, without their whole-hearted missionary commitment, the wives often bore the heavier part of the burden. For many, the transition from provincial city, town, or farm to a remote station on the Papuan coast was harsh, and they were perhaps less prepared than their husbands for the trials that were inevitably encountered as part of mission life. Some of the hardships, trivial or serious, affected the women especially.

Many grieved over the destruction of their household possessions by climate, porterage, and pests. Contemplating their leaky thatched roof, Holmes reflected: "poor, dear Ally, she is a woman and to see her few, very few, household goods spoiling must be a serious trial to her woman's heart, but never a complaint."[32] His colleague, Ben Butcher, wrote of the plight of Lizzie Chalmers who, a widow when she married James Chalmers, "had been used to all the comforts of a lovely English home." It hurt to think of her at Saguane, he wrote, "for it was a dreadful place." There, she "faced loneliness and fever and watched the destruction of all the things she treasured as reminders of her English home."[33]

Tied to their stations by domestic responsibilities, most wives suffered more from isolation than did their husbands. Many especially craved the companionship of another white woman. "I should much enjoy a lady friend," wrote Chalmers' first wife, Jane, from Suau.[34] Sister Edith Lloyd of the Methodist Mission described in a letter the pleasure of Bertha Williams, wife of the missionary of Panaeati, at her visit, the first she had received from a white woman in twelve months.[35] Frequently wives were deprived for weeks at a time even of the companionship of their husbands, whose work generally involved supervision of outstations as well as administration of a head station. "If I ever stop to think, I feel as if I can't live another day in this loneliness," Lizzie Chalmers confessed to an English friend during one of her husband's frequent absences.[36]

Whether or not women had weaker constitutions and less capacity to withstand the climate, as many male contemporaries believed, their lives were haunted by illness. Besides the constant malaria, intestinal diseases, and other ailments common to all missionaries, the women in the mission field were believed to suffer also from nervous complaints to which it was assumed men were more immune. Without doubt, the psychological well-being of many wives was affected by the stress of missionary service, resulting in some hypochondria, psychosomatic illness, and, in a few sad cases, insanity. But many, perhaps most, of the illnesses suffered by the wives were unmistakably organic, ranging from tuberculosis, blackwater fever, typhoid, and peritonitis to gallstones, dysentery, and malaria. Despite acerbic comments about the frequent trips south by missionary ladies, many wives battled against chronic ill-health and critical illness at their stations, only leaving at the insistence of husbands or colleagues when their lives were in jeopardy. In 1912 Harry Dauncey gave the LMS directors a list of twelve wives who had been "literally carried out of the country," two of them twice, since his arrival in 1888. It was doubtful whether any of them would have recovered had they stayed, he added.[37] Four of the Protestant missionaries' wives—Jane Chalmers, Mary Turner, Lizzie Chalmers, and Bertha Williams—died in the field.

Childbirth was a recurrent source of stress and anxiety. Thirty-nine children were born to LMS parents and twenty-six to Methodists during their mission service (see Appendix 3). Although mission families were not excessively large, most of the wives spent their main childbearing years in the field. In the early days of the LMS mission, most wives followed Fanny Lawes' example and gave birth within their own home, attended by their husband or an experienced colleague. As the mission developed, Lawes became critical of an increasing tendency for wives to go to Australia for their confinements. To expect them to stay in New Guinea demanded no undue heroism; five nonmission wives had recently given birth at Port Moresby, he wrote in 1904.[38] A doctor was based at Port Moresby from 1895 and another at Samarai from 1900. Concerned that a number of the younger missionaries had no knowledge of midwifery, Lawes recommended that it should be an essential part of training.[39] But even in 1914, all four confinements of LMS wives were in Australia.[40] Within the Methodist Mission it was more common for births to take place in New Guinea. Some Methodist wives, as well as some of the LMS, gave birth in the gracious surroundings of Kwato Mission, to which the doctor could be fetched quickly from Samarai. Others were attended on their stations by nurses who were part of their own mission staff.

Infant deaths were frequent. Of the sixty-five children born during the parents' service, fifteen died (see Appendix 3). Ten died during their first year of life and another five, all girls, during their childhood, one from blackwater fever or kidney failure, one from whooping cough, one probably from sunstroke, and two from unspecified illnesses. Deaths were spread evenly. Of the twenty-nine women who bore children during their missionary term, eleven experienced one bereavement and two lost two children. Although the numbers involved are too small to have any statistical significance, it seems that the infant mortality rate was considerably higher in the mission field than in Britain or Australia. In England during the second half of the nineteenth century the average remained fairly constant at about 150 infant deaths during the first year out of 1000 live births, and by 1914 it had dropped to 105. By 1871, sixteen out of twenty children could expect to reach the age of twenty.[41]

When a child died, the missionary frequently made the coffin and conducted the burial service himself. He and his wife found comfort in their faith, seeing their loss as part of the cost of being coworkers with Christ. "We reckon it one of our sacrifices for having to live in New Guinea, and cheerfully submit to it for Christ's sake," wrote Ambrose Fletcher after the death of his six-week-old son.[42] Some prayed for the fuller understanding and greater devotion that such a trial might bring.[43] Firm believers in the afterlife, they were comforted by the thought that all was "well with the child" and sustained by the hope of a reunion in Heaven.[44]

But despite the brave words uttered for the benefit of mission boards or supporters, or for personal reassurance, faith did not render the missionary or his wife immune to the grief and pain of such an experience. "The awful blank in our lives is beyond telling, for Nancy was the brightest spirit among all our children," wrote Charles Rich after the death of his two-year-old daughter. "We try to trust and stay ourselves on the promises of Christ, and with Him, we know that all must be well with our treasure. . . ."[45] Some missionaries looked beyond their own pain to the suffering of their wives. Ben Butcher wrote of the death of his seven-year-old daughter, Phyllis, "So many hopes centred on our little daughter and now they were shattered and my heart went out to my weeping wife who, in that dark hour, had no friends or neighbours to help or comfort her."[46]

Most missionaries chose to avoid the risk of possible bereavement and the hazard of child rearing in such an environment by not bringing their children into the field, or by having them there for the shortest possible time. Many were billeted in England, Australia, and New Zealand, usually with relatives, or boarded at denominational schools that offered special places or reduced fees to the children of missionaries. Separation was another of the sacrifices made for their calling. Albert Pearse who, with his wife, served the LMS in New Guinea for twenty years, had four of his six children with relatives in England, and the youngest two—small girls when he began his service—billeted in Sydney.[47] Many of his colleagues shared his conviction that New Guinea was "no place for children" and chose instead the "heartbreak" of separation.[48] "The worst of it is one doesn't get over it," wrote Pryce Jones commiserating with his wife at her impending separation from her children.[49] For some of the LMS missionaries, it was a cross to be borne for many years. Harry Dauncey, pleading for furlough, reminded the directors that during his youngest child's fourteen years he had spent only nineteen months in the same country as she, and that mostly on deputation.[50] "I hardly know my children," he complained.[51] In the Methodist Mission the problem was not so acute. Shorter terms of service entailed briefer separations and moreover, the Methodists, having missed out on the pioneering years of white settlement were, by the turn of the century, more willing to have their children in the field with them for the few years that most of their careers involved.

Missionaries who did risk having their children with them found them to be a powerful asset in the task of evangelization. Within months of his arrival, Lawes noted that his son Charley "jabbers away in native as fast as he does in English."[52] Overburdened missionary parents frequently left the rearing of their children to trusty Papuan servants. Free of the prejudices and assumptions that their parents had brought with them, the children became a cultural bridge able to enter into the idiom, the thought forms, and the lives of the local people in ways that their parents could never achieve. Among people for whom love of children was universal, the frequently fair-haired, blue-eyed sons and daughters of missionaries became magnets that drew fearful, suspicious, or otherwise reluctant Papuans into the orbit of the missionary's influence.[53]

Of all the Protestant missionary families, only the Abels of Kwato managed to establish a permanent home for their children in New Guinea. For the others, a carefree childhood playing on Papuan beaches was a prelude to a life lived remote from parents in boarding school and lodgings. The LMS paid an annual allowance of between £10 and £25, depending on age, for each child up to eighteen, later twenty, years.[54] Methodist missionaries were paid at the same rate as ministers of the New South Wales Conference, receiving a children's allowance of £12.12s.0d. for each child.[55]

In New Guinea it was not usually, as in Polynesia and Africa, fear of contamination by a primitive environment that prompted mission parents to send their children away.[56] Generally, before the age when they would have been considered susceptible to such corruption, parental concern for health or education had forced the decision. White children in New Guinea were generally regarded as pallid, listless, and weakly.[57] The only opportunities for education were those provided in the missionary's home, and frequently the missionary and his wife, struggling to cope with the running of a head station and the supervision of outstations, had little time or inclination for this task beyond a rudimentary level.

With their children away in England, Australia, or New Zealand, missionary wives experienced the pain of divided loyalties. How they coped with it was largely a personal decision, although the tacit assumption in both mission societies was that the wife's place was beside her husband. The disruption caused to a missionary's "domestic comfort" by an absent wife was regretted, especially if the solitary husband was left in a place where the local women had a dubious reputation.[58] Nevertheless, it was common for missionary wives to spend months and even years at a time caring for their children thousands of miles from their husbands. For some missionaries, such as Dauncey and Walker, this situation resulted in the virtual breakdown of their marriages.[59] For others it was a constant source of pain, sometimes only revealed in their letters to their distant wives. "It is so long since . . . I left you behind and I'm hungering for your nearness," Ben Butcher wrote to his wife. "I wonder to myself if I'm going again to see the love that has looked on me out of your eyes and whether I'm again going to know that you really care as I feel your arms round me. Love can make this place so rich and so companionable."[60] Samuel Fellows poured out his loneliness in love letters to his wife, Sallie, and "cried like a child" on receiving her first letter.[61] Pryce Jones wrote to his wife of his dream of a "long, loving embrace" he had shared with her. "I felt your arms round me and we clung to one another, Oh! it was nice, then I awoke!!!"[62] Later he confessed to her, "Dear old sweetheart . . . I find the absence harder to bear now than in the days of our courtship. I love you, old woman, more than I ought to tell you."[63]

Godly domesticity remained the ideal in the Protestant missions, but in New Guinea reality played havoc with the ideal. For most missionaries, it was at best only a sporadic experience. The unresolved tensions of this existence caused Ben Butcher to ask a question that other married missionaries may have pondered:

> I read this call to forsake wife and children for the sake of the Kingdom of heaven and I wonder whether it really means the sort of things we are doing. . . . I'm much troubled about that for it does not seem fair to bring children into the world and then deny those children a proper chance.[64]

In anguished letters to his wife he debated the central dilemma of his life—the conflicting claims of his family and of his Papuan flock.

> I don't moan to you all but at times I just dare not think of all I'm losing and the price I'm paying. I may be losing you all. . . . I know the children need you—I know I'm losing touch. I know they will grow away from me. I'm not blind to all this but at present I see other needs. . . . I see a few beginnings of a Christian church and thousands who look to me for help and guidance.[65]

The answer for Butcher, as for most of his colleagues, was to resign and leave Papua to rejoin his family, though in his case not until he had put in thirty-five years of service.

The missionary bodies that sent the married missionaries to New Guinea came to doubt the wisdom of their policy, as did many missionaries in the field. Lawes was firm in his conviction that only one woman in a thousand was a true missionary (and he was married to that one), and both he and Chalmers were adamant that newly married wives should not come to the mission field because of the likelihood of pregnancy, "the natural result of marriage. . . ."[66] Lawes' experiences led him to wonder whether a celibate mission was not the answer, a possibility that had also occurred to Ralph Wardlaw Thompson, the Society's foreign secretary in London.[67] George Brown, general secretary of the Methodist Missionary Society, was similarly disheartened.[68] But neither society changed its policy, modifying it only to the extent, in the case of the AWMMS, of insisting on a doctor's certificate as the LMS always had, and in the case of the LMS, of putting less pressure on missionaries to marry, especially at the outset of their careers.

The creation of the "civilized Christian home" on the New Guinea mission field was to some extent a dream that failed. Whether the missionaries saw any alternative to the disruption, uncertainty, and anxiety caused by childbirth in the field is an open question. By the 1880s contraception was widely practiced among the middle classes of England. Improvements in synthetic rubber molding in the 1870s led to the manufacture of cheap sheaths, and spermicides were available by 1885.[69] Ideas about birth control promulgated by Place, Bentham, and Mill were given widespread publicity by the Bradlaugh-Besant trial of 1877–1878. After the trial, birth-control propaganda became less liable to prosecution.

But it is doubtful whether the missionaries availed themselves of either the literature or the products advocated. Most belonged to the lower middle class, bastion of respectability, and even by the end of the century, contraceptives had a tainted reputation. Moreover the churches to which they gave their allegiance continued to oppose birth control, although in 1893 the influential *Christian World* gave its approval to the use of the "safe period," alluding to "certain easily understood physiological laws" that could provide a mode of limitation free of the "doubtful morality" of other methods.[70]

As would be expected, the missionaries were discreetly silent on the subject, but the *Christian World*, read in the mission field, may have influenced their thinking. It is not known whether any of the missionaries followed Jane Austen's advice about the "simple regimen of separate rooms,"[71] but it seems likely that "prudential restraint" or at most use of the safe period were the only forms of birth control that they would have contemplated. One of the most enlightened and resourceful of the Protestant missionaries, Ben Butcher, wrote to his wife in 1920 of his longing for her as he anticipated her return:

> Yet when I most long there comes a chilling remembrance that you will wish to deny me the loving intimacy of married love even when you are near. . . . I don't know which is harder, being apart like this or being together and yet obsessed with that ceaseless injunction to "Take care."[72]

It seems that in Butcher's case it was his wife's fear of the unwanted child rather than the many other trials of their missionary life that turned their marriage from one of lighthearted, loving companionship to the "broken, fettered thing" that Butcher later felt it to be.[73]

For many, perhaps most, missionaries the only forms of limitation were involuntary ones such as frequent absences, the debilitating effects of malaria and other diseases, and miscarriages whose incidence may have been increased by the liberal use of quinine. Many would have seen any conscious attempt at contraception as an impious tampering with the will of God.

Some observers compared the family-based Protestant missions unfavorably with their celibate Catholic counterparts. An Australian who visited New Guinea in 1899 commented, on his return, on the greater preoccupation of the Protestants with salaries and material welfare.[74] Others objected to the inhibiting and constricting influence of the wife and family on the missionary. James McAuley argued this case most sweepingly, not of missionaries only, but of all Europeans in the colonial situation. Why, he mused, did the "great enterprise of European colonialism" breed rejection among its subjects?

> Perhaps the simplest answer is: the white woman. While European men went out, without wife and family, they entered into a different sort of relationship, socially and sexually, with the people. When the white woman came out, it was all very different. It was not the woman's fault if her urge to create and defend a home and bring up children by the standards of her own community, made her wish to draw a circle of exclusion round her domain.[75]

McAuley's criticisms had some validity. It was no accident that the missionary's move from his original simple bush-material house to his large European-style home frequently coincided with the arrival of his wife. Concern about salaries and allowances, furnishings, transport, and health facilities also followed her coming and the birth of children. With a wife and children at home, some missionaries became less willing to spend time away from their stations: "when one is married one cannot run round quite as much," Butcher explained, describing an unusually unadventurous year.[76] Chalmers, one of the few missionaries who made little concession for the comfort of his wives, castigated his colleagues for "living a life of ease at head stations."[77] The only two whom he excepted, J. H. Holmes and Percy Schlencker, were both then still bachelors. It is true, too, that many wives were the cause of their husbands' temporary absences from New Guinea and that twenty-two of the forty-nine married Protestant missionaries resigned on the grounds of the wife's ill-health or other domestic pressure.

But other aspects of McAuley's attack applied less to missionaries than to other colonial groups. Rather than constricting the missionary's relationships with the people, the missionary's wife augmented them. Not only did the Protestant missionaries generally eschew any sexual relationships with Papuan women or girls, but they also avoided any real contact with them at all. The coming of a missionary's wife meant that social relationships could be established with female as well as male Papuans. It is doubtful too whether the missionary's wife drew the rigid circle of exclusion around her domain that McAuley envisaged. The mission house was generally part of a large compound and was, in varying degrees, accessible to the hundred or so Papuans who lived within its confines. Insofar as there was a boundary between the compound and the village, it was one that was frequently crossed, at least by the missionary's children.

Against McAuley's criticisms must be set the positive features of godly domesticity as it existed in the New Guinea mission field. Despite the practical, unromantic beginnings of many, a number of mission marriages embodied close, loving relationships. Lawes remained devoted to his "dear Fan" until his death in 1907; Holmes believed he and his wife, Alice, whom he had fetched from a Devon farm to the mud-swamps of the Papuan Gulf, to be "about the happiest couple in the whole world."[78] Lizzie Chalmers, a middle-aged and ailing woman awaiting her husband's return was "more unsettled and fidgety than if I expected a young lover."[79] To a close friend she confided, "I feel only half-alive without him."[80] Charles Abel's letters to his wife reflect a romantic love that did not abate with time.[81] Edith Turner, a former missionary from China whose marriage to R. L. Turner was the outcome of his anxious wife-seeking expeditions, believed herself to have "the best husband in the world."[82] It is impossible to doubt the comfort, strength, and stability that these relationships must have given the missionaries. Despite the conventional helpmeet image in which they acquiesced, women such as sturdy, forthright Fanny Lawes, bustling, energetic Norah Gilmour, or forceful, indomitable Lily Bromilow were arguably the stronger partner in the relationship.

Others besides their husbands felt their lives to be enriched by the presence of these women. Lonely, uncertain young missionaries of the LMS regarded Mrs. Lawes as the mother of the mission, Holmes comparing her to Mary Moffat in Africa.[83] Similarly, Mrs. Bromilow, though a more formidable person, was *Marama* to the Methodist Mission. Even traders, who generally had little time for missionaries, paid tribute to the gracious and comforting presence of some of their wives. Jack McLaren described Mrs. Riley at Daru as "a dear old lady who made much of me, and mothered me, and gave me tea in dainty china cups at her beautiful home which was manned by trained servants and delightful with the touches that only a woman can give."[84] Andrew Goldie, trader and naturalist at Port Moresby, marveled at the indefatigable ministrations of Fanny Lawes, "one of the Florence Nightingale heroines."[85] Sir William MacGregor testified to the contribution of Fanny Lawes to the missionary cause: "A skilful and industrious housekeeper, a devoted wife, and an affectionate and sensible mother, Mrs Lawes put before the natives of the country an object lesson of a model home, and of pure and happy family life."[86] Elsewhere he declared: "Perhaps no missionary did more good in New Guinea than Mrs Lawes and Mrs Bromilow."[87] In such women at least, the Protestant ideal of the help-meet in the civilized Christian home was vindicated.

Catholic Communality

The way of life in the celibate Sacred Heart Mission and in the Anglican Mission, which was celibate in ideal if not entirely in practice, was necessarily different from that of the Protestant missionaries. Whereas so much of Protestant mission life revolved around the individual and his family in their Christian home, the emphasis among the Roman Catholics and Anglicans was on the community, the total mission family. Sir William MacGregor compared the Sacred Heart missionaries unfavorably with their Protestant counterparts: "They cannot, like the married ministers of the Protestant mission, put before the natives the example of family life, after the European model."[88] In a spirited and ironic defense of the celibate mission, Archbishop Navarre reproved Mac-Gregor:

> If your Excellency is so anxious that the natives should have before their eyes the example of family life . . . why does not your Excellency set the example? . . . But surely your Excellency must know that it is the celibate missionaries of the Catholic Church that have . . . given the world the true idea of the Christian home.[89]

Navarre objected to an allegation made by MacGregor that the communal life of the mission involved its members in spending too much time at Yule Island in "ceremonial observances," replying that only for the eight-day annual retreat was the presence of all missionaries at Yule Island mandatory.[90]

Nevertheless Yule Island remained the heart of the mission. It was the station through which new Roman Catholic missionaries were introduced to the mission field; to which they came for retreats, conferences, festivals; and to which the infirm and old were brought to convalesce or await death. The story of its foundation by the heroic Henri Verjus continued to grip the imagination and the hearts of later missionaries.[91]

By 1889 the buildings that Henri Verjus and the Italian brothers had erected four years earlier, on the windswept hill that crowned the island, were in ruins. Those added since—"imitations of poor European barns"[92]—were in little better condition. The eight brothers slept in a common dormitory with an earth floor. The sisters' house, built of native materials only two years earlier, was disintegrating. The missionaries resolved to replace these huts of reeds and grass with houses of sawn-timber and corrugated iron raised on stilts; at the same time they would move the station down the hill onto a sheltered plateau overlooking the jetty and more accessible to it. Lacking funds to import wood from Australia, the missionaries sawed their own from timber they cut on the mainland and floated across to Yule Island. Visiting the Sacred Heart missionaries on his tour of inspection a year later, Albert Maclaren found them still living in their "most primitive native buildings" but engaged in the construction of a presbytery, a chapel, and a sisters' house.[93] At the end of 1890, MacGregor noted that added to these buildings were a leathery, a blacksmith's forge, a carpenter's shop, and a sawmill.[94] By 1896 it was a beautiful and imposing station, its main street lined by scarlet hibiscus and framed by coconut palms.[95]

Unlike the other missions, whose stations were mostly scattered along the Papuan coasts, the SHM, constrained by the "spheres of influence" agreement (see chapter 9), founded most of its stations inland, on either side of the St. Joseph River, on the marshy, humid Mekeo Plain, and, after the turn of the century, in the mountainous interior, accessible only by the roads surveyed and built by the missionaries themselves. Numbers of these stations were simply a few buildings grafted on to existing villages, rather than separate compounds like the Protestant stations. Sometimes the mission buildings were situated in the heart of the village, but more often the missionaries built at one end to preserve the traditional symmetry. In a typical Sacred Heart village, an avenue led from the village center to the church. The father's house and the boys' school were at the right, the sisters' house and a girls' school to the left. Vegetable gardens and orchards surrounded the buildings.

Most stations were, initially, unprepossessing. Beatrice Grimshaw described Waima as she saw it in 1911:

> A church, partly or wholly corrugated iron, with a few rude seats, a home-made communion rail, and an altar decorated by the hands of the missionaries themselves, . . . pitiful, brave shifts to hide the barest poverty—jam jars and bottles cunningly disguised in gilt paper and cardboard . . . candlesticks out of tin. A house for the Fathers and Brothers—built of wattle sticks, with chairs, tables and beds all carpentered roughly from the nearest bush material. . . . A house for the Sisters much the same. . . . A tiny plot of garden ground, where some handfuls of carrots, half a score of aubergines, a couple of bean plants, struggle feebly in the sandy ground.[96]

Other stations were similar. The first living quarters were always of bush materials.[97] On most stations fathers and brothers lived in one functional, sparsely furnished house, sisters in another, frequently sleeping in rooms that served also as storeroom, dispensary, or library.

But as the stations became better established, bush-material huts gave way to timber-and-iron houses, built always from wood cut and sawn by the brothers. A large sawmill at Aropokina provided timber for Mekeo and Yule Island while resourceful priests and brothers in the precipitous mountain districts built water-powered mills to serve their own areas. A team of brothers trained in carpentry was based at Yule Island and sent to stations as needed. Skilled artisans, the brothers and sometimes the priests built houses that, if simple, were solid and durable, and sometimes graced with furnishings that were the product of a craftsman's delight in his work. Visiting Father Fastré at Dilava in 1921, the photographer Frank Hurley observed, "His houses are adorned with aesthetic embellishments all made in his own workshop from local timbers. In a place so remote it seems incongruous to see such excellent buildings and so much learning."[98] Hurley saw in these sturdy, well-constructed buildings evidence of the strength and permanence of the SHM's commitment to the country. "The fathers have made everything here to last, like their work and faith. They are here for their lives. . . ."[99]

Besides the church, school, and living quarters common to all mission stations, those of the SHM had features that Protestant stations rarely shared. The forge, tannery, carpentry shop, and sawmill observed by MacGregor at Yule Island were repeated at other stations, most of which also had a farmyard and a garden. Confronted with dwindling resources and almost insuperable problems in getting supplies, Navarre had early enjoined the mission to the greatest possible self-sufficiency.[100] These efforts met with qualified success, but in the attempt alone they were distinctive. Father Hartzer, visiting New Guinea from Thursday Island in 1893, described the pleasant hum of activity at Yule Island:

> The sonorous and regular noise of a hammer striking an anvil came from Brother Simon's forge and mingled its merry village note with the distant bellows of the cattle. In front of us . . . Brother Rintz and Brother Gabriel drove a flock of goat and sheep to the mountain. Further away, at the Sisters' house, a murmur of children's voices chattering in the classroom. . . . Finally Brother Moorees kept the press clattering with a new catechism in Roro.[101]

The poverty of the Sacred Heart stations in the early days was in stark contrast to the comfortable, well-equipped Protestant stations. But through the craftsmanship of their staff, most stations reached a standard not far short of their Protestant counterparts, for considerably smaller cost. Critics believed that they paid for their road- and station-building with their lives,[102] but despite the high death rate, the missionaries continued to take responsibility for the creation and maintenance of their stations. Unlike the Protestants they employed no servants and hired no labor, contenting themselves with accepting the services offered them by their parishioners. Constraints imposed by poverty joined with a conviction that they had come to give, not to take from the Papuans. The coadjutor brothers were responsible for most of the manual work on the station, the sisters taking charge of the farmyard, the garden, and domestic chores.

On these stations, the missionaries lived in communities ordered and regulated by the constitutions of their congregations. When Navarre's parochial organization gave way to de Boismenu's concept of centers of influence, it was possible for the mission to become more communally concentrated. Priests, brothers, and sisters lived at one of six, later eight, district centers from which, in their work, they radiated out into the surrounding countryside. The life of a celibate community has its problems no less than that of godly domesticity, but whatever the underlying crises or tensions, the overwhelming impression they gave to strangers was that of a united and happy family. Traveling through the Sacred Heart district, Frank Hurley was impressed by the camaraderie and good-natured banter of the priests and brothers, and the graciousness of the sisters. Departing, he let his "unreligious" pen conclude: "in all my travels I have never met a family so contented and united."[103]

The Anglican Mission strove to create the same communal atmosphere. Its founder, Albert Maclaren, inspired by Anglo-Catholic communities in England, had dreamed of creating a similar celibate community in New Guinea.[104] Although forced to abandon his scheme, celibacy remained for him and his successors the norm in the Anglican Mission. Stone-Wigg, equally devoted to Anglo-Catholic principles was indignant to find that the writer of a *Penny Post* article contrasting Catholic communality with Protestant domesticity credited "only one mission with the use of methods which two out of the four have adopted."[105]

Only ten of the forty-six male Anglican missionaries were married for any part of their missionary service, two of them only for a short final phase. Of the remaining eight, five married fellow missionaries during their service, a practice regarded as, if not desirable, at least acceptable, as it brought no extra expense to the impoverished mission. When Frederick Ramsay, a muscular Christian layman later ordained, requested permission to marry a prominent church worker from Melbourne, to whom he had been engaged for three years, Stone-Wigg refused: "I hope some way may be found by which your engagement . . . may be honorably terminated for . . . the work in New Guinea needs men without ties."[106] Later the bishop relented, perhaps recognizing that at Samarai, with its large white population more a parish than a mission, a rector's wife could be useful. So entrenched was the celibate ideal that when Stone-Wigg's own engagement to Elsie Mort, a voluntary church worker in Sydney, was announced in the year before his retirement, it provoked much surprise, some discomfort, and an inquiry from Mrs. Tomlinson as to whether it was not a sin for a bishop to marry.[107]

For the thirty-six unmarried men and the twenty-one single women who had joined the mission by 1914, their family was the Anglican community. Stone-Wigg especially nurtured this concept. In his farewell letter to his staff, he exhorted them to "maintain the family character of mission life," and continued, "I trust all will guard this family feeling and brotherly harmony. It secures a much-needed atmosphere of warmth and brotherhood for all."[108]

Living arrangements reflected the communal ideal as far as possible. At Dogura, the male and female missionaries attached to the station all lived in the house slowly and painfully erected by the pioneers, Maclaren and Tomlinson. A large, airy building raised on ten-foot piles and surrounded by a wide verandah, it was built in the shape of a cross, with a chapel at its heart, and rooms for the staff in the arms.[109] It was rebuilt in 1903, the chapel becoming a separate building, but Dogura House remained the home of the staff. Later, when small cottages were built on the station for various staff members, all still ate communally in the mission house, a tradition that continued into the 1970s. A missionary who arrived at Dogura in 1955 has left a memorable description of dinner, a ritual that could have changed little since the days before the Great War. The priest-in-charge sat at the head of the table, the bishop at his right, with the other members of staff, in order of seniority, ranged down each side of the big refectory table:

> The meal was a solemn one, formally served, with the dean carving while plates and dishes of vegetables were passed around. However he was not carving a roast of beef . . . or even a leg of mutton. He was carefully slicing up the contents of several tins of camp-pie, and the vegetable dishes contained yams, sweet potato, taro and boiled pumpkin leaves. Glasses were filled, but the beverage provided was water.[110]

Numerically smaller than the SHM, the Anglican Mission could not provide the same opportunity for all its missionaries to live in communities. Many, like their Protestant counterparts, were scattered singly or in pairs through a series of coastal stations from Mukawa, where the Tomlinsons lived, to the Mamba River, where Copland King had his remote station. Conscious of the isolation of these missionaries, Stone-Wigg and his successor, Gerald Sharp, spent much of their time traveling from station to station, providing a link between them and reinforcing the sense of community.

Apart from Dogura House, the rectory at Samarai, and the Tomlinson's large white house with a gold cross on its gable at Mukawa, Anglican mission houses were made from bush materials. Belief in the virtue as well as the necessity of poverty, romantic idealism, and perhaps a desire to identify as closely as possible with their Papuan flock led to a preference, on most parts, for "native" housing. Describing a typical mission house with its thatched roof of sago palm leaf, floor of strips of pliant wood, and walls of coconut fronds, Stone-Wigg assured his mother, "Two ladies live very pleasantly in one of these."[111] Anglican missionaries deplored the necessity of later replacing their aesthetically pleasing thatch with roofs of corrugated iron. "Utility has conquered art," lamented Henry Newton.[112]

In 1906, after the mission had been shaken by the deaths in rapid succession of three of the white staff, it resolved that it was "desirable in future to use European buildings wherever white missionaries are placed."[113] The following year, a project to improve the houses of all European missionaries was initiated, but the use of bush materials persisted till well after the First World War, even the bishop's "palace" remaining a building with walls of coconut leaf.[114]

Some of the women, like their counterparts in other missions, created beautiful gardens around their houses, but the houses themselves were severe and poorly furnished, often lacking the personal touches and embellishments that the Protestant wives, or the Catholic sisters and brothers, had provided. Personal effects were few. Laura Oliver's will contained an inventory of her possessions after twenty-five years of missionary service: "a cupboard, small organ, gramophone, bread-mixer, blackboard, china tea-pot, twelve pieces of cutlery, nine bits of china (two with pieces broken out), one cheap watch (no glass), several pieces of tortoiseshell, a small silver jug, an ornamental clock (works damaged), thirty-one books, four iron travelling trunks and one suitcase."[115] The sole possessions of Francis de Sales Buchanan, most ascetic of Anglican missionaries, were said to be a gramophone, a set of patched clothes, and a small library.[116]

The poverty and austerity of the Anglican stations was similar to that of the Sacred Heart Mission in the early days. But unlike those of the SHM, Anglican stations remained little improved up to and beyond the First World War. Visiting the mission in 1921, Frank Hurley contrasted unfavorably its shabby, impermanent housing with that he had admired on the Sacred Heart stations.[117] Employing only one or two carpenters at a time, the Anglican Mission was as dependent on hired labor as were the Methodists and LMS. Its stations showed few of the marks of self-sufficiency that characterized those of the SHM. As in the Protestant fields, young Papuans were employed as domestic servants, receiving in return board, schooling, and a little pocket money. Laymen looked after the few cattle and coconuts belonging to the mission, and for a time the station of Hioge was a modestly successful agricultural center. But in general Anglican stations were modest clusters of buildings, almost engulfed in the lush vegetation of the north coast, and bearing evidence of neither the diversity of activity of the Sacred Heart Mission nor the orderly domesticity of the Methodist and LMS stations.

CHAPTER 4

"Books and Quinine"

Mission Lifestyles

DESPITE THE notable differences between the domesticity of the Protestant missionaries and the communality of the Roman Catholics and Anglicans, there were marked similarities in the way of life of all missionaries in Papua. All were guided by similar objectives and ideals; all were constrained by the same physical and social environment.

One of the dominant considerations affecting the missionaries' way of life was that they had not come to Papua for financial gain. Their mission societies forbade them to trade or to take remunerated public positions. For the Sacred Heart missionaries, the vow of poverty was one of three simple vows made on entering the congregation.[1] Anglican missionaries were warned to expect no "salary . . . or temporal advantage of any kind" in mission service;[2] the Wesleyans, molded by their founder's strictures against "softness and needless self-indulgence" were advised by the AWMMS to "regulate [their] expenses by as much conscientious regard to economy as may be consistent with . . . health and comfort."[3] Missionaries of the LMS were similarly exhorted to "avoid display and self-indulgence in your style of life; in your dress; in the food and furniture of your house; and in your personal habits."[4] A modest, self-denying life was enjoined on all.

The salaries or allowances they were paid ensured that their way of life would be modest, to a greater or lesser extent. Most highly paid were the LMS missionaries. The Society, while stressing that stipends could not be commensurate with the value of the missionaries' service, undertook "to make such provision for their support as, under the different circumstances of their missionary life, may secure to each an equal amount of comfort."[5] There were three scales of personal allowance. An unmarried missionary was paid £155 per year, a newly arrived married missionary, £206, and a married missionary of more than three years' standing, having passed the language qualification, £240. Allowances for children and for minor expenses were additional.[6]

Although these salaries compared well with those that their backgrounds and education might have led them to expect had they remained in the British work force, most felt that they were barely sufficient for New Guinea. When a salary reduction was proposed during a financial crisis in the LMS in 1889, most of the missionaries objected vehemently. Some compared their salaries adversely with those of government employees, Dauncey pointing out that his equaled "two-thirds of that paid to the government cow-keeper," while Lawes maintained that his £240 was "the same as that given to a single man who looks after houses for the government."[7] Married missionaries with growing children claimed the greatest hardship, finding it difficult to meet their children's expenses for board and education, and the cost of their wives' frequent trips from the mission field.[8]

The Methodist Missionary Society assured its workers that it was pledged "to pay an affectionate attention" to all their wants and to "afford them every reasonable and necessary supply."[9] It offered its married missionaries in New Guinea £160 per year for the first two years of probation, £170 for the third and fourth years, and £180 when received into full connexion. In 1913 these stipends were raised to £190, £200, and £210 respectively. When the new category of lay missionary was introduced, those thus employed received initially £100 per year, increased in 1903 by £20 for married laymen. By the end of the period a married layman's salary could rise by annual increments of £5 from £150 to £170.[10] Although there is less evidence of discontent with salaries in the AWMMS than in the LMS, Bromilow complained in terms similar to those used by the married LMS missionaries, prompting the board, when threatened by his resignation on the grounds of financial stress, to vote him an extra allowance.[11]

Allowances paid to the Sacred Heart and Anglican missionaries bore no comparison to the stipends of the Protestants, nor were they expected to serve the same purpose, as these two missions provided their workers with food, furnishings, and other material requirements. The Sacred Heart Mission paid its workers no salary, but permitted them a small allowance furnished by the Society for the Propagation of the Faith. Each priest received approximately £40 (F 1000), the brothers and sisters slightly less (F 900).[12] In the Anglican Mission, although Maclaren originally intended paying his workers £300 a year, and indeed employed the first workers on high salaries,[13] circumstances soon forced his successor to a change in policy. Stone-Wigg offered Anglican missionaries £20 a year, an allowance less than a quarter of that paid by their

Anglo-Catholic neighbors in the Melanesian Mission,[14] and one that remained unchanged till the Second World War.

Dress

The simplicity and frugality enjoined on the missionaries was reflected in their dress, which was casual and functional. The part of the stereotype of the nineteenth-century Protestant missionary that portrayed him in somber, formal, black frock coat and top hat, or his Catholic counterpart in "impeccable soutane and starched surplice"[15] never fitted the reality in New Guinea. Soon after his arrival, Lawes paused to wonder what his English supporters would think of his preaching in white trousers and collarless check flannel shirt.[16] Khaki or white drill trousers with flannel shirt remained standard missionary dress, differentiating them little from the other Europeans in the colony. Pith helmets were occasionally worn, but felt or straw hats were more common.

Sometimes dress might reflect individual tastes or idiosyncrasies. The eccentric Anglican, Wilfred Abbot, who was wont to impress his congregation by donning his "gaudy Oxford hood," also had in his wardrobe riding breeches and gaiters, three black coats, two gross of collars, linen-faced, four dozen cuffs, one biretta and two surplices.[17] His colleague Francis de Sales Buchanan embellished his outfit of white shirt and khaki trousers with a bright red silk scarf tied at the waist, as did also the sturdy veteran of the LMS, James Chalmers.[18] LMS pioneer Percy Schlencker wore a garb "suggestive of a Texan cowboy," while his Methodist contemporary, Ambrose Fletcher, wore a similarly rugged outfit of "blue dungaree trousers and a Crimea shirt."[19] Their dress, always simple, was frequently shabby. Ben Butcher described himself working in a "very old shirt, . . . pair of paint-marked khaki pants tucked into socks that need darning and a pair of burst out boots."[20] A government officer was taken aback to be welcomed to the Anglican Mission by a priest, Copland King, dressed in "flannel shirt and dirty trousers."[21]

In the Sacred Heart Mission, poverty in dress was even more noticeable. "The Fathers and Brothers have barely enough common shirts and trousers (of the kind worn by miners and railwaymen) to keep them clad," Beatrice Grimshaw observed. "The habits of the nuns are patched and darned and faded; their veils are a wonder of stitchery. Boots and shoes are freely lent from one to another, patched, re-made, worked out to the last shred of leather."[22] During one of the mission's worst financial crises the sisters resorted to making shoes from discarded goatskins.[23] Visitors to Mekeo and Roro were moved by the sight of gaunt, bearded priests, their eyes burning with fever, dressed in the patched khaki trousers and shirt of navvies.[24]

Diet

The same frugality was apparent in the diet of the missionaries. Their commitment to simplicity was in this respect reinforced by the necessity, in an environment that yielded them only a limited variety and amount of food, of importing most of what they ate. The missionary's staple was tinned beef. A. K. Chignell's observations on the food served at Anglican stations described the regimen, not only of most missionaries, but of most Europeans in Papua at that time:

> The ordinary food on most of the stations . . . is tinned meat and biscuits three times a day at the conventional Australian hours. There may be a dish or two of badly cooked . . . native vegetables . . . and there is sure to be a big pot of . . . overdrawn tea, . . . but bulumukau [beef] and biscuits, biscuits and bulumukau seem to be the staple food.[25]

A typical grocery list sent to Messrs. Burns, Philp & Company in Cooktown in 1891 included also tins of soup, honey, coffee, lard, and butter; potted meats; two hams; and bottles of chutney, herbs, oil, capers, and sauce.[26] "I live largely on tins from morning to night and seem to flourish on these strange articles," Ben Butcher informed a friend in England.[27]

After the early years, scarcity was rarely a problem, but there are numerous feeling testimonies to the lack of variety in the diet. Visiting the Anglican Mission as Metropolitan in 1908, the Archbishop of Brisbane listed the "intolerably nauseous monotony of tinned beef and milkless tea" as one of the missionary's greatest privations.[28] It was, said Henry Newton, "deadly monotonous, the sameness of taste, or lack of taste."[29] Confronted with this dreary diet, missionaries dreamed of grilled chops and begged friends to send delicacies.[30] Albert Maclaren wrote to a lady supporter for a Christmas box, which he did not live to receive. He asked for currants, raisins, and French plums. "Don't be offended at my asking for sweets," he wrote. "I often long for luxuries, perhaps it's wrong."[31]

Fresh meat and dairy foods were rare treats in the Protestant and Anglican missions. At Dogura, a beast was killed on festive occasions, but fresh meat was unknown at most other stations. The Methodist missionaries at Dobu, receiving a breast of mutton from the *Merrie England* at the same time as Mrs. Bromilow brought a sheep from Samarai, ate "more fresh meat in one week than . . . we ever had in a year."[32] Another Methodist missionary, J. R. Williams, visiting Rossel

Island where a resident kept cattle, marveled: "Fresh beef, fresh butter, new milk and cream. . . . When did I last have them?" The answer was, two years earlier on furlough, but at other times, added Williams, "I've been four or more years without."[33]

As they became established, missionaries supplemented their diet with indigenous and cultivated foods. Most learned to substitute sweet potato, yams, and taro for English potatoes, bananas for bread, and wallaby and pigeons for fresh meat. Buchanan's diet, consistent with his whole life-style, comprised mainly local foods.[34] But only the most resourceful of the Protestant and Anglican missionaries wholeheartedly exploited their environment for foodstuffs. By 1914, Butcher could boast that at Aird Hill he was successfully growing oranges, limes, mangoes, macadamia nuts, pineapples, pumpkins, taro, sweet potato, banana, Indian corn, sugar cane, and yams.[35] Several years later, he assured his absent wife that for a weekly food bill of 15 shillings he had a balanced and varied diet: eggs for breakfast, a small tin of soup for lunch, and for dinner he would "kill a tin of meat" and make an Irish stew, finishing with fresh oranges and bananas.[36]

Despite the initial poverty of the Sacred Heart Mission and the chronic shortages that brought its pioneer missionaries close to starvation, later Sacred Heart missionaries managed, through their energetic self-help program, to eat better than their Protestant contemporaries. Like them they depended partly on imported foods, turning on MacGregor's advice from salted beef, which was indigestible and frequently tainted, to tinned meat;[37] but with a large herd of cattle at Yule Island and small herds at other stations, they could more readily vary their diet with fresh meat.[38] They also exploited local food sources, eating crocodile and parrot as well as a wide range of fruit and vegetables.[39] The French sisters, schooled in domestic excellence, and the brothers, among whom were butchers, bakers, and pastrycooks, were able to make the most of the resources at their disposal. They baked their own bread, made their own butter and cheese, grew and roasted their own coffee. Dining at Yule Island in 1891, Sir William MacGregor was served "soup, a fowl, claret, cheese and one or two other dishes."[40] A few years later another visitor to Yule Island described a five-course dinner that included an entrée of bacon-cabbage croquettes; poultry, mutton, and kid; dessert of pressed curds and cream; fruit, coffee, wine, and brandy.[41]

One of the major differences in diet between the Sacred Heart Mission and the others was in their consumption of alcohol. In the Methodist Mission, where all were "temperance enthusiasts," the only alcohol was a small amount of brandy locked in the medicine cupboard;[42] at the impoverished Anglican Mission, a bottle of claret might be opened for a special occasion such as the bishop's birthday;[43] and in the LMS, although Chalmers had his whiskey, Rich his beer, and Holmes and his wife, a "nightcap," most were teetotalers.[44] But in the Sacred Heart Mission, alcohol was a standard part of the diet. The LMS boatbuilder, Robert Bruce, having enjoyed a "splendid" dinner while visiting Yule Island commented, no doubt with some satisfaction, "They do not spare the wine at meal-times."[45] In the cold, damp, mountain stations, missionaries laced their tea with rum.[46] The presence at Yule Island of a copper still for distilling rum led to a lively correspondence between the missionaries and the government, ending in the former reluctantly handing over to the government agent "one worm—part of a distilling machine."[47] MacGregor explained that he thought it best for "the moral and physical health of the mission" to confiscate it.[48]

But despite their more varied and interesting diet, the daily fare of the Sacred Heart missionaries was as frugal as that of the Protestants. Hospitable to a fault, the fathers pressed wine and good food on guests, or celebrated their own feast days with fresh meat, wine, and home-cooked *gâteaux*, but generally meals were modest and simple. Genocchi noted in 1894 that wine was only served on Sundays.[49] Priests and brothers on remote stations often had makeshift cooking arrangements. Father Eschlimann's diet was simple: French fries for breakfast, lunch, and dinner. Father Dubuy at Ononghe "just opened a tin of meat and with a hunk of bread, washed down with a substitute for tea, made a frugal meal."[50]

The diet of the missionaries, while only in exceptional cases leading to malnutrition, probably did little to maintain their health, and still less their sense of psychological well-being. Most ate too little fresh food, especially green vegetables and dairy foods, were too dependent on carbohydrates, and had too little variety.

Health

The missionaries' health was most influenced, however, not by their poor diet, but by the ubiquitous presence of the anopheles mosquito. Like all their contemporaries, the missionaries in New Guinea were ignorant of its malignant influence till the end of the nineteenth century, attributing their sufferings instead to the noxious gas emanating from decayed vegetable matter in swamps, a theory almost universally accepted since Roman times.[51]

Malaria, or fever as it was commonly called, dominated their lives. It was "the inescapable companion of the inhabitants of New Guinea."[52] Old hands nursed newcomers through their first bouts, hoping that early attacks would give them some immunity. Father Cochard described the period of acclimatization of a group of newcomers to Yule Island:

> Father Coltée was down with fever, Father Bouellat trembled like a leaf.
> . . . The next day I had fever; it gripped me for eight days then left me,
> but in a state of weakness that one could not imagine without experiencing
> it. I have not suffered the most. Brother Edmond raved for three days.
> . . . Father Claudius has been the only victim claimed for heaven, after
> six days of almost continual delirium. We have been in New Guinea for
> only a month.[53]

Early attacks were often more acute, but for most missionaries, fevers were a continuing experience. Archbishop Navarre reckoned on half of his staff being ill at any time. Attacks were borne stoically. The Archbishop of Brisbane noted that at the annual conference of the Anglican Mission at Dogura in 1907, not once did the whole company sit down to a meal. "Fever invariably seemed to claim a victim, but the matter, by a sort of tacit etiquette, was not referred to in conversation; it was accepted as the normal condition of things, to be borne without complaint."[54] Father Genocchi, reporting four or five stricken with fever added, "but one knows it is transitory, and therefore little notice is taken of a malady to which we are so accustomed that we hardly take it into account at all."[55]

Despite such overt stoicism, some missionaries confided to diaries, memoirs, and letters accounts of their intense sufferings. Ben Butcher wrote:

> It is a miserable experience and the first time it hit me I hardly knew what
> was happening. I had found life full of excitement . . . and then suddenly
> the zest of it all went from me and the days seemed heavy. . . . My head
> ached terribly and I shivered under blankets, while my skin was burning
> hot. I shivered so much that the bed shook and then the shivering gave
> place to heat and I would perspire . . . profusely. Then the attack would
> pass, leaving me exhausted. . . .[56]

"Yesterday I felt brave and well; today I am as useless as a piece of wet blotting paper," reported Matthew Gilmour.[57]

Worse than the burning fever, the aching limbs, the vomiting, occasional delirium, or unconsciousness was, for many missionaries, the condition in which a malaria attack left them. Charles Abel, among the strongest and most resilient of the missionaries, described the aftereffects as "most depressed spirits and an indescribable feeling of utter prostration."[58] One of the "most miserable looking wretches" to be seen in the mission field, wrote Henry Newton, was "a man sitting on a verandah after . . . fever, looking gloomy, surly, inwardly wondering why he had been such a fool as to come to such a place."[59] It is impossible to understand the tensions, failures, and breakdowns in the mission field without taking into account the lassitude and deep depression that pervaded the bodies and spirits of chronic malaria sufferers.

Even the earliest missionaries in New Guinea, while not knowing the cause of malaria, were familiar with the use of quinine in its treatment. Lawes noted that he was taking fifteen grains daily,[60] a larger and more systematic dose than that generally taken by later missionaries. Methodist missionaries were prudent in using quinine prophylactically; a few others took regular doses of fifteen grains at the end of a ten-day cycle, but it seems that, most commonly, missionaries simply dosed themselves at the onset of and during an attack.[61] A bitter-tasting drug, taken in liquid form or later in five-grain tablets, quinine could produce unpleasant side effects ranging from headache, nausea, vomiting, diarrhea, and skin rashes to deafness, ringing in the ears, dizziness, and disturbance of vision. Some could not tolerate it at all. MacGregor believed it was Maclaren's allergy to quinine that caused his premature death.[62] Arsenic was another approved form of treatment in all four missions.[63] Veteran missionaries had their own remedies. Chalmers earnestly advised Sir Peter Scratchley to drink champagne,[64] while his colleague, Lawes, placed sober faith in Warburg's tincture, "far and away the best medicine for New Guinea fever,"[65] Maclaren favored a bottle of stout, while the trusted remedy of teetotaler William Bromilow was one tablespoon of rum or brandy, one-quarter teaspoon of black pepper, and a few drops of laudanum, ammonia, and nutmeg. "The first two alone may effect the cure," commented Stone-Wigg.[66]

Although there is no evidence of speculation by the missionaries as to the mode of infection, the more scientifically minded charted the course of their attacks. Lawes published a paper in the *Australasian Medical Gazette* of 1887 based on more than a decade of careful observation.[67] Besides the simple intermittent fever and the remittent type recognized by medical science, he identified another type which seemed "to partake of the character of both intermittent and remittent" with violent symptoms and premature recurrences.

In August 1897 Major Ronald Ross proved, after three years' investigation in India, that, as he and other scientists had long suspected, malaria was caused by parasites transmitted by a mosquito, which he identified as the anopheles. The following year he established the mode of infection.[68] The new century brought to the missionaries in the remote New Guinea fields, details of these discoveries. "I have read a splendid lecture in *Nature* on Malarial Fever," George Brown wrote from Sydney to his nephew, Ambrose Fletcher. "It seems clearly established now that the infection is by mosquitoes."[69] Later in the year, they read of these discoveries for themselves. "There has been much in the paper lately about the malarial fever being caused by the mosquitoes," a Methodist sister noted in her journal in November 1900, adding that there was some skepticism about the theory among the Methodist missionaries.[70]

It is difficult to tell to what extent increased understanding led to the reduction in the incidence of malaria among the missionaries. The observation of the Archbishop of Brisbane as to its prevalence among the Anglican staff was made as late as 1907; but four years later it was reported of that same staff that its health was "uniformly good." The report added, "The increased knowledge of malaria and how to avoid it has done wonders."[71] However, the practice of using quinine to cure rather than to prevent malaria seems to have persisted well into the twentieth century—among missionaries as among other white residents.[72] Consequently, malaria remained a major problem.

The handbook compiled for present and prospective residents in the first decade of the twentieth century assured its readers that Papua was free of most of the deadly contagious tropical diseases.[73] The three diseases listed as causing death in Papua were malaria, blackwater fever, and dysentery. Blackwater fever, a reaction to falciparum malaria probably precipitated by incorrect and inadequate treatment with quinine,[74] but then regarded as a separate disease, wrought havoc in the Sacred Heart Mission. In one year, 1898, Navarre reported four deaths from this disease, known in the mission as hematuric fever *(la fièvre hématurique)*, and in total at least ten Sacred Heart missionaries died from it. Numerous others survived attacks. By contrast, only one non–Roman Catholic missionary died of blackwater fever,[75] and only five others are known to have suffered attacks.

Dysentery, a disease capable of decimating the Papuan population of this period, especially those concentrated on the goldfields of the Mamba and Lakekamu rivers, threatened Europeans less. Among the missionaries, those who suffered most were single males living under primitive conditions on remote stations. One Sacred Heart priest died from it, and a number of priests and brothers suffered attacks, a fact attributed by some observers to lack of care in selection of drinking water and to their tolerance of burials, within both mission and village, in close proximity to housing.[76] One Anglican layman, also living a spartan life on an isolated station, died from dysentery.[77]

Minor stomach ailments plagued the missionaries, one of whom ranked them as a health problem second only to malaria.[78] The missionaries suffered from biliousness, diarrhea, "Indigestion and Constipation and other kindred diseases of the Bowels,"[79] complaints undoubtedly related to their poor diet and, in some cases, to fever remedies. Other minor maladies endured were various skin complaints. Many suffered the misery of boils or watched small scratches spread into gaping tropical ulcers. Besides the host of tropical ailments the missionaries suffered from the same range of diseases as they might have incurred in a temperate climate—respiratory infections, influenza, pneumonia, rheumatic fever, and tuberculosis—the only difference being that in the chronically anemic state to which malaria reduced them, they had less resistance than they might have had elsewhere.

Given the continued prevalence of such a range of ills—major and minor—in the mission field, it is extraordinary that the mission societies themselves had so few qualified medical workers. In the SHM, where ill health was so widespread, there was not a single qualified doctor or nurse, though a few of the priests had gained some practical experience in European hospitals, and many of the sisters had developed considerable nursing skill through years of devoted practice. In the Anglican Mission, eight of the women were trained nurses, but there was no doctor on the staff until the arrival of Cecil Gill in 1926. The Methodist Mission staff included two nurses but no doctors. In the LMS, after the abortive careers of Drs. Ridgley and Turner, no further doctors were appointed before the First World War, although a number of missionaries took brief courses in tropical medicine in preparation for mission work, as did a few of the Anglicans. Several mission wives were qualified nurses. But in general the missionaries were dependent for medical treatment on the two government doctors, or, between 1888 and 1898, on the kindly ministrations of Sir William MacGregor, himself a qualified physician, or, in the overwhelming majority of cases, on the trial and error procedures of home treatment, an experience common to all in frontier situations. In all four missions it was accepted that critical cases could be taken off the field, and probably many lives were thus saved, but frequently isolation, poor communications, and erratic shipping made this little more than a hypothetical expedient.

Despite the increased understanding of malaria, lack of proper medical attention and poor diet ensured that chronic poor health remained a fact of life for many missionaries. Through the period up to the First World War, many faced their work anemic from malaria, debilitated by intestinal ailments, and irritated by a host of minor complaints. This was especially true of the Sacred Heart missionaries, a factor that contemporaries related to their more austere and arduous life. "They half starve themselves so they soon fall victims to fever; they work at manual labour in the heat of the day and don't take care of their bodies," noted Albert Maclaren.[80] Sir William MacGregor reported Father Vitale as saying that they were "never well and never very ill," while Navarre explained to colleagues in Europe that when they said they were well, they meant they were not utterly prostrated by fever.[81] If the Protestant missionaries suffered less, their problems were compounded by the ill health of wives, children, and the South Sea Island teachers in their care. Archibald Hunt wrote of returning to Port Moresby "weak as a rat," after being attacked by fever while traveling, to find "Mrs. Hunt semi-delirious, Ruatoka down with pneumonia, a Samoan teacher's wife bad with blackwater fever, and more than half my large family here down with colds and fever."[82]

Recreation

Solicitude for the health of their workers led all the mission societies to stress the need for recreation as an intrinsic part of mission life. It was part of the rule regulating the lives of the Sacred Heart missionaries; it was constantly urged upon the LMS missionaries by their paternal foreign secretary, Ralph Wardlaw Thompson; and it was encouraged in the Anglican and Methodist fields by the bishop and chairman respectively.

A number of missionaries devoted their leisure to developing and mastering hobbies and skills. For some, exploration or linguistics became a passion rather than simply an evangelistic tool. Hobbies frequently reflected contemporary interests. LMS missionaries Holmes and Saville plunged with enthusiasm into the new science of anthropology; others such as Father Guis and Bishop Stone-Wigg became competent ethnographers. The scholarly Father Genocchi found that contemplation of the star-filled tropical sky impelled him to a more profound study of science and the universe.[83] Copland King pursued his lifelong interest in botany, and Ben Butcher collected butterflies, hoping to become a "second-class entymologist."[84] Young missionaries like Dauncey, Walker, Butcher, and Giblin became fascinated by photography, occasionally earning rebukes for letting the hobby become too absorbing. J. H. Holmes revealed a typically Protestant concern to justify the use of leisure and the pursuit of science in his observation that working with his microscope reminded him of God's "infinite skill in all his works."[85]

Sport was regarded as a proper part of life of a muscular Christian. LMS, Methodist, and Anglican missionaries played tennis with government officials at "Port," or on the grass courts of the Anglican Mission at Dogura, and participated in games of cricket on pitches prepared under their own supervision. Some enjoyed riding, hunting, and shooting; some played badminton and billiards. The Methodist sisters played decorous games of croquet and swam on Saturday mornings. When it was too wet for outdoor sport, they tried the "new game of ping-pong."[86] At Dogura, Bishop Stone-Wigg escorted the lady missionaries on evening strolls to Ganuganuana, about half a mile away. There is not the same evidence of organized sport in the Sacred Heart Mission, perhaps because European Catholic missionaries did not share the same convictions about its character-building properties or perhaps because in their vigorous, outdoor lives there was not the same need for additional physical activity.

In the evenings, missionaries at the larger stations gathered for parlor games and music. It seems that even the traditionally austere attitude of the Methodists toward such amusements relaxed as the century drew to a close. "Are we not frivolous?" a Methodist sister asked a former colleague in a letter detailing their recreation.[87] There is no evidence of missionaries playing cards, but the anthropologist Alfred Haddon played ludo with Archbishop Navarre; Ben Butcher learned to play chess, and other LMS missionaries played "Bobs" and "Up Jenkins."[88] Haddon delighted the Sacred Heart missionaries in 1898 by giving them their first experience of a phonograph, and Methodist missionaries at Dobu welcomed visits from the resident magistrate, Campbell, for the same reason.[89] During the early years of the twentieth century some stations acquired their own gramophones, but more often missionaries made their own music, usually by gathering for communal singing around an organ or a harmonium. Several of the Sacred Heart missionaries were accomplished musicians. A colleague painted a memorable pen portrait of Bishop de Boismenu spending an evening in the mission hut on the high mountain station of Oba Oba, leaning back, eyes closed, and smiling as Father Fastré, a gifted flautist, played his repertoire of airs from opera and comic opera, old French songs, and religious music.[90]

One mode of relaxation that was important in the lives of the Sacred Heart missionaries and notably less in the lives of the others was the use of tobacco. In the Anglican and LMS missions some individuals indulged in a pipe or even a cigarette, but in the Sacred Heart Mission smoking was almost a universal habit among the male missionaries.[91] The ascetic Father Chabot, at first nauseated by his companions' smoking, became a devotee of the pipe. Brother Lainé smoked a long tube of newspaper containing native tobacco, Father Guilbaud a bamboo pipe that stained his white beard orange, and after his death Father Norin was always remembered with an "eternal cigarette."[92] In a revealing comment in a letter to his sisters, de Boismenu wrote, "I must chat a little with you, a humble cigarette on the corner of the table. Don't open your eyes wide. It substitutes for so many things. . . ."[93]

For missionaries of all persuasions, reading was a favorite leisure activity. "Books, books, books—there is nothing as good out here. . . . Books and letters are as valuable as quinine," wrote Romney Gill from

his lonely station on the Mamba River.[94] What books, and how many
the missionaries read, depended—as in any community—on their background, education, and personality. There is little evidence in the available records of the reading habits of the majority of the missionaries,
but the diaries and letters of a small minority give some idea of what
was read and enjoyed in the mission field.

Much of the reading matter was "improving" rather than entertain-
ing. Missionaries read devotional books and theology, biography, reference books, and some modern classical literature. Arriving at Aird Hill
after her marriage, Ben Butcher's wife was pleased to find that her husband possessed "all Dickens, Thackeray and Shakespeare in nice handy
little volumes, a lot of Ruskin and Walter Scott." Of course, she added,
there were also "lots of religious books and various sundries on carpentering and Mechanical Things."[95] Like many of her contemporaries, in
the mission field as elsewhere, she sat down with her husband in the
evenings to laugh with Mr. Pickwick or to cry over *Little Dorrit*.[96]

The only author as frequently mentioned as Dickens was Thomas
Carlyle. George Bardsley and J. H. Holmes both recorded reading his
great spiritual autobiography *Sartor Resartus*, Holmes considering it
"next to the Bible in fascination."[97] Other missionaries read *Past and
Present*, *The French Revolution*, and *On Heroes*.[98] Works by Longfel-
low, Thackeray, Tennyson, Ruskin, and Whittier were also read. In the
Anglican Mission, Bishop Sharp read Jane Austen while traveling, and
Romney Gill enjoyed Herman Melville's *Moby Dick* (1851).[99] Ben
Butcher and Romney Gill are the only missionaries known to have read
a popular love story.[100]

A visitor to the LMS station at Kalaigolo was impressed by the size of
the library of devotional books owned by its evangelical missionary,
Percy Schlencker.[101] Other missionaries' libraries were more modest,
but in most, religious books were preponderant.[102] Much of the religious
literature read in the Methodist and LMS missions seems to have been
evangelical theology. Methodist probationers were given so extensive a
reading list of such items that they would have had little time for any
other reading. Even the biographies read in all four missions were
mostly lives of great religious figures.[103]

Only faint echoes of theological controversies then agitating British
religious circles were heard in the New Guinea mission fields. LMS missionary Thomas Beswick read Renan's *Life of Jesus*, still regarded as
dangerously radical for its portrayal of Jesus as a man, but he read also
Mozley's conservative book, *On Miracles*, which, although published in
1865, was pre-Darwinian in its argument from design.[104] In the first
decade of the twentieth century Ben Butcher devoured the new theology of J. R. Campbell, whom he admired.[105] Anglo-Catholics such as

Maclaren and Stone-Wigg read *Lux Mundi* in New Guinea, the former only a year after its publication and at the time when the controversy it provoked in the debate on biblical criticism was at its peak.[106]

Whenever the mail arrived, missionaries received chunky packets of newspapers and periodicals, frequently months out of date. Anglican missionaries enjoyed reading *The Times* and *Punch*.[107] French missionaries practiced their English with Australian dailies, and Ben Butcher received the British *Daily News* and the *Examiner*.[108] Describing the hunger of LMS missionaries for such literature, Lawes appealed to supporters for copies of the *British Quarterly, Nineteenth Century, Contemporary Review*, and Cassell's magazines.[109] Religious periodicals such as the *Christian World*, the *British Weekly*, and denominational and mission magazines were received and circulated.[110] Father Verjus wrote of the "almost childish joy" experienced by the Sacred Heart missionaries on the arrival of the *Annales* of their Society.[111] For at least one Sacred Heart brother, the only publication to reach his remote mountain station was a missionary magazine, *Le Petit Messager des Missions*, from his home town of Nantes.[112]

Communications and Transport

The arrival of the mail was one of the high points in a missionary's life. New missionaries tried to hide their longing for the first mail from home; old missionaries never ceased to feel the excitement, anticipation, and nostalgia that its arrival evoked. "The mail means so much to us poor missionaries," wrote Nurse Combley from the Mamba River. "One almost dreads it sometimes."[113] An Anglican missionary, Arthur Chignell, devoted a whole chapter of his memoirs to the mail, describing the impatience and restlessness of the missionaries as they awaited it, the "frequent disappointments"—worst of all the missionaries' disappointments—the excitement of its arrival, and the transformation it wrought in their ordered, uneventful lives.

> I have tried as usual—and as usual I have failed—to be reasonable and take it calmly . . . and what with the tangle of string and newspaper wrappers on the table, and the dregs of the mailbag all over the floor, and one's amazement at the latest matrimonial engagements and episcopal appointments and one's deep, deep thankfulness that once again all is well "at home"—it is no longer a steady-going missionary priest in his quiet room at the end of another day of happy, methodical, plodding work, but an excited, over-stimulated and uncontrollably effusive creature. . . .[114]

Mails were infrequent and erratic. At the beginning of the 1880s letters from London took about six weeks to reach Thursday Island,[115] but delivery from there depended on local shipping. Missionaries, traders, and government officials cooperated in an effort to carry the mails to their destinations as speedily as possible. In 1911 Charles Abel reported that a letter from London had reached him in record time—thirty-nine days.[116] Letters from Australia were little faster. One might take sixty days, the next nineteen, but rarely did they arrive in less than a month. It was not uncommon for missionaries to wait two or three months for mail, and services did not necessarily improve with time.[117] Anglican missionaries who had received mail from England in two months when the mission had its own schooner, later had to wait up to a month longer because of their dependence on commercial shipping.[118]

Missionaries awaiting mail or supplies were well aware of their limited means of transport and communication. All missions had their own small fleet of boats, mostly for traveling round their own field. In the early days there were schooners, cutters, and whaleboats. By the early 1890s the missionaries of the Sacred Heart and the LMS were begging for steamboats to enable them to ascend the fast-flowing rivers—the "roads" to the interior. Henri Verjus brought a steamer back from Australia in 1890 and James Chalmers' eloquent pleading resulted in the arrival in 1893 of the *Miro*, a steam launch for the Fly River (Figure 13).[119] To the chagrin of the missionaries, neither performed satisfactorily on the log-strewn and at times shallow rivers. In the first decade of the twentieth century, motor launches were added to the mission fleets,

Figure 13. The LMS steam launch, *Miro*. (Council for World Mission)

their cantankerous engines invariably causing much grief to missionaries who depended on them.[120] Short journeys were most commonly
undertaken in canoes or in whaleboats rowed by crews of four, six, or
eight Papuans—either mission employees or villagers engaged for the
trip. A mast and sail were carried in the whaleboat in the hope of a
favorable wind.

The names of the mission boats reflected their owners' Christian concerns and objectives. The Sacred Heart Mission, purchasing Yankee
Ned's lugger, the *Gordon*, rechristened it the *Pius IX* and soon after supplemented it with a 35-ton schooner, *l'Annonciade*, and smaller boat,
l'Ange Gardien. Their steamer was named the *Saint-Michel* and a yacht
that ran between Port Moresby, Yule, and Thursday Island, the *Saint
Andrew* after the patron saint of Archbishop Navarre.[121] The Methodists received years of sterling service from their ketch, the *Dove*, purchased from Sunday school subscriptions, and a yacht belonging to the
LMS, which generated much controversy because of its luxuriousness,
was christened the *Olive Branch*.[122] The Anglican Mission remembered
its founder with its 14-ton schooner, the *Albert Maclaren*, and one of its
church's ancient seats with its cutter, *Canterbury*. Many of the boats
were provided through public subscription or the generosity of individual patrons. The *Ellangowan*, a small schooner with auxiliary steam
sailed by the LMS from 1874 to 1898, was given the name of the Scottish
home of its benefactress, Miss Baxter.[123] The *Abiel Abbott Low*, a motor
launch that served the Anglican Mission from 1903 till it was lost in a
hurricane in 1912, was named after its American donor.[124]

Although the missionaries provided their own local transport, they
were largely dependent on commercial shipping for links with the rest
of the world. Sacred Heart missionaries traveling from Europe paid
Messageries Maritimes 1200 francs (£48) for each fare to Australia and
then paid another 550 francs (£22) for a passage on an Australian boat
bound for New Guinea.[125] Although the LMS's Pacific ship, the *John
Williams*, called once or twice yearly at New Guinea stations, the LMS
missionaries were as dependent as their colleagues on regular and chartered commercial services for the transport of supplies and additional
travel.

The company with whom the missionaries had most dealings was
Burns, Philp & Company, who began a regular service in alternate
months from Cooktown to New Guinea in 1892,[126] and signed comprehensive contracts with all the mission societies. In 1893 they offered to
supply the LMS with "all necessaries" for 15 percent commission on
landed cost in bond at Thursday Island. Two sailing vessels, the *Myrtle*
and the *Wanganui*, were fitted out to carry passengers and cargo on this
service.[127] Contracts drawn up with the Wesleyan and Sacred Heart

missions in 1902 offered a regular steam ship service to Samarai and Yule Island in return for a guarantee that all their work be given to the company.[128] Each mission was given one free passage per year, and rebates were offered on freights and fares. In deference to universal missionary opinion, the company agreed that no work would be done at mission stations on Sundays. By the end of the century, Burns Philp still provided the only regular sea link with the outside world. A schooner, the *Alice May*, still made the six-to-twelve-day journey to Thursday Island, but in addition a steamer, the *Titus*, offered a fifteen-to-twenty-day trip to Sydney once every three months.[129] Missionaries of all denominations grumbled at the monopoly enjoyed by Burns Philp and the "exorbitant" prices they were able to charge.[130]

Besides traveling by sea, many missionaries tramped vast distances on foot, usually in parties that were small and modestly equipped compared with government patrols. In the Sacred Heart Mission most of the staff, priests, brothers, and sisters, were accomplished horseback riders. Individuals tried other modes of travel. Reginald Bartlett of the LMS traversed Papuan beaches in true colonial style in a rickshaw,[131] while Wilfred Abbot terrified his Anglican parishioners by hurtling around Wanigela on a bicycle.[132]

But for most, the sea remained their chief route to the world beyond their station, a cause of joy to some, of regret to many. An observer noted that James Chalmers visibly expanded with a deck beneath his feet.[133] Alexis Henkelmann, a Dutch brother who had begun his working life as a pastrycook's apprentice, found his niche in the SHM as "admiral" of the mission fleet.[134] Mechanically minded missionaries like Matthew Gilmour or Ben Butcher spent happy hours tinkering with the motors of their launches, the latter succeeding, after the war, in building two motor launches on his station (Figure 14).[135] But many missionaries never came to terms with sea travel, and for them the frequent journeys on capricious seas in cramped boats infested with cockroaches and often permeated with the stench of copra, were a necessary but dreaded ordeal.[136] Each of the missions had its sagas of perilous journeys and shipwrecks.

Despite the network of local and Australian shipping around the Papuan coast, services were often sporadic and unpredictable. Missionaries frequently experienced the failure of a boat to arrive on schedule, sometimes with unhappy results. In his diary for June 1892, Archbishop Navarre noted that while they awaited the overdue *Wanganui*, which was bringing them a case of medicine and other supplies, one brother and one sister lay gravely ill. On 18 June, Brother Rintz died. On 29 June, as the ship appeared on the horizon, Navarre wrote, "Sister Berchmans is dying. She will not profit from the medicines that the

Figure 14. Ben Butcher's launch, *Moana*. (Council for World Mission)

Wanganui is bringing." The following day, Sister Berchmans was buried, and the *Wanganui* anchored at the jetty.[137]

Young missionaries had to learn to tolerate the tedium and frustration of awaiting an overdue boat. "Anxiously waiting for the *Harrier*," noted Walker in his journal soon after his arrival in New Guinea. "It seems very strange not to be able to telegraph or write and enquire about her."[138] After three more days of fruitlessly scanning the horizon, he commented, "Looking for a ship which never comes might, I can readily believe, develop into a sort of madness. We are all very restless and unsettled."[139] On all coastal mission stations, the cry of "Sail, oh!" as a white speck first appeared on the horizon signified one of the high moments of mission life.

At Port Moresby in 1887 a telephone was set up between the mission house and the government bungalow, and the following year another line joined the mission to Andrew Goldie's store.[140] At Ubuia in 1908 the first telephone in a Wesleyan South Seas station linked the mission house to the wharf.[141] But no such communication was possible over a distance. The missionaries' only contacts with the outside world were through mail and shipping services. Even the use of the electric telegraph at Cooktown depended on their having a boat to carry a message from New Guinea to Cooktown.[142] As late as 1915, when Methodist missionary Andrew Ballantyne died at Kiriwina on 7 June, news of his death did not reach his colleagues at Ubuia till 25 June, or his relatives in New Zealand till 24 July.[143]

Isolation was one of the chief characteristics of mission life. Links with the world beyond the mission were tenuous and difficult. This could cause anguish if there were a sick missionary to evacuate, an absent family, a colleague or urgent supplies to await, or simply mail to anticipate. But, except perhaps at times of crisis, the missionaries did not spend their time "gazing pensively over the sea in the direction of home."[144] In June 1899 Methodist sister Edith Lloyd noted in her diary, "Not many or important events break the quietude of life at Dobu, not that there is any dullness in the place, . . . only that our little world goes round almost independently absorbed in its own interests, with plenty to do."[145] The mission station was a world of its own, small, enclosed, and absorbing. In this world the missionaries lived.

CHAPTER 5

"Though Every Prospect Pleases"

Perceptions of the Papuan

THE *Encyclopaedia Britannica* assured its late nineteenth century readers that the Papuan was among the lowest forms of humanity, "lower even" than the average Polynesian in intellect or character.[1] This opinion was expressed by many of the early Protestant missionaries as they first confronted the Papuans and their culture.[2] Steeped in the evangelical literature that since the end of the eighteenth century had promulgated the image of the "ignoble savage" in opposition to the "noble savage" of the Enlightenment, they saw the degradation that they expected to find.[3] Lawes, likening the vices of civilization to "weeds in a cultivated garden," contrasted them to the vice of heathenism, which, he said, was "one wilderness of little but weeds." New Guinea was a land of "moral degradation and spiritual darkness," he told LMS supporters when he returned to England on furlough.[4]

Many of the Protestant missionaries who followed Lawes into the LMS and Methodist fields expressed similar initial responses, propagandist intent probably reinforcing strong personal reactions. Thomas Beswick, who joined the LMS in 1879, found the people of Hula "very low and degraded."[5] Arriving in 1894, J. H. Holmes declared that he could almost feel "the darkness of heathendom" in the atmosphere.[6] In the Methodist field, Bromilow, settling at Dobu in 1891, saw only "sullen savages, brutal cannibals and merciless women."[7] Samuel Fellows, first missionary at Kiriwina, found its inhabitants a "dark and degraded people."[8] Gordon Burgess, arriving at Bunama in 1910, noted the "awful degradation of the multitude," and Walter Enticott, pioneer missionary to the Rossel Islanders, wrote of the "settled gloom" with which their faces were stamped by the "iron of heathenism and darkness."[9]

Some regretted the contrast between the natural beauty of their envi-

ronment and the degradation they professed to see among its inhabitants. "If only the people were in accord with their surroundings, this
place would be a second garden of Eden," lamented Sister Julia Benjamin in 1897.[10] Others, reacting in the same way, fell back on the
words of Bishop Heber's well-known missionary hymn, "From Greenland's icy mountains":

> Though every prospect pleases
> And only man is vile.[11]

A few Protestant missionaries, prepared to find the darkest degradation, were relieved to discover "redeeming traits" or features that were
"lovable" among the people.[12] Even Lawes found amid the wilderness
of heathenism characteristics to admire—the domestic affection of the
Papuans, their industriousness, the absence of drunkenness, and the relatively superior status of women.[13] Frederick Walker, arriving in 1888,
gave a conventional description of the "naked savages" who greeted him
at Toaripi (Uritai Mirihea), their hair "fantastic and wild," their bodies
tattooed, and their teeth "red as blood" from betel chewing. Yet at the
same time he wrote, "the people at home little understand how much
there is that is lovable and good amongst these people."[14] His colleague,
J. H. Holmes, commenting on the "depravity" of the Torres Strait
Islanders, added: "I like the natives immensely, there is so much about
even the hardest and fiercest . . . that is loveable."[15] One missionary,
the Christian Socialist carpenter of the Wesleyan mission, George
Bardsley, found his preconceptions about primitive society shattered by
his observations. "All my thoughts of these men as cannibals are dispersed. They are exceedingly smart men," he wrote a month after his
arrival. He found them intelligent, musical, sensitive, and affectionate.
"I like these Dobuans very well," he concluded.[16]

The Sacred Heart missionaries expressed their first responses in terms
similar to those used by the Protestants. Archbishop Navarre's severe
verdict on the Papuan recalls that of W. G. Lawes, "Our Kanakas are
like wasteland which has never been cultivated—all weeds grow there
. . . their hearts are hardened by vicious habits, their spirits which do
not rise above earthly joys, are little able to receive supernatural
impressions."[17] Henri Verjus believed the culture of his "dear savages" to
be the "most obscure of paganisms ever invented by the devil."[18] Father
Hubert made a typical assessment when he wrote in 1893 of "these poor
souls, so degraded and so low."[19] Like some of the Protestant missionaries, some Sacred Heart priests found characteristics to admire. Father
Couppé was impressed by their intelligence, Father Coltée by their
morality: "What strikes us first is their morality. . . . It is clear that the
Savage is other than a brute."[20]

Such judgments abounded in the writings of Protestant and Roman Catholic missionaries, but fell less readily from the pens of Anglicans, for whom the "ignoble savage" was less a part of their thoughts and experience. Their impressions of Papuan culture were generally warm and appreciative and unclouded by the metaphors of darkness and degradation in which Protestant responses were soaked. Albert Maclaren, arriving among the Massim in 1891, found them a "very social, kind-hearted, contented lot of folk, and very affectionate."[21] Bishop Gerald Sharp wrote even more appreciatively of the "great attractiveness of the Papuan people . . . Affectionate, confiding, sunny tempered, polite in manner, attentive to one's wants, very graceful and winning in their manners, most distinctly good-looking, with a wealth of intelligence . . . they are people for whom one can easily conceive a very strong personal affection."[22] Bishop Stone-Wigg, in contrast with his Protestant counterparts, concluded a report on one Anglican district with the observation, "Every prospect pleases, and man is by no means vile."[23]

Missionaries of all persuasions found their preconceptions modified by experience. For some, close acquaintance with Papuan cultures only reinforced their opinions. William Bromilow, for nearly two decades the guiding spirit of the Methodist Mission, wrote of the people of Dobu, "As we learn their manners and customs and get an insight into their village life . . . we are brought face to face with the terrible sin prevailing in the heart." All his years as a missionary served only to convince him of the "essential vileness" of this "ignorant and barbarous race."[24] More commonly though, increased contact led to growing understanding and appreciation. Even the pioneer missionaries of the LMS, who had only their own observations to mold their impressions, made thorough and not wholly unsympathetic assessments of the culture of the Motu and their coastal neighbors. Lawes, visiting the village of Kerepunu, found a new "respect for the stone period," extolling its technology, its social organization and its "cleanliness, order and industry."[25] In 1878 his colleague W. Y. Turner read a paper to the Anthropological Institute of Great Britain, on the ethnology of the Motu, the first such study of mainland Papua.[26] Although some of his observations perpetuated stereotyped beliefs about the "native," many were careful and objective. He believed the Motu to be moral, affectionate to their children, and peaceable, but conservative, deceitful, and dirty in their habits. His colleagues Lawes and Chalmers followed his lead in writing ethnographical papers, as did pioneers of the other missions, among them Fathers Jullien and Guis, MSC, Methodist missionaries J. T. Field and Samuel Fellows, and the Anglican bishop, Stone-Wigg.[27] Different writers found different features to praise in the various societies they observed, but there was general approval of some aspects that were shared—the simplicity and self-sufficiency of Papuan life, the closeness of familial relationships, and the communality and cohesiveness of the social system.

Not all of the pioneer missionaries had the intellectual curiosity or the moral flexibility to adapt their preconceptions to reality. After more than a decade of service, Albert Pearse of Kerepunu wrote unsympathetically and uncomprehendingly of the continual feasting of the people and "all their stupid ceremonies."[28] The same blind complacency is apparent in Methodist sister Edith Lloyd's diary jottings in 1901: "It is impossible to really understand the native mind. . . . What ridiculous creatures they are for the sake of custom."[29] For others, the conflict between preconceptions and reality led to an unresolved ambivalence. After leaving the LMS mission field in 1886, Samuel McFarlane published a book characteristically entitled *Among the Cannibals of New Guinea*. In it, standard evangelical phraseology abounds. The Papuans are "howling savages," the "debased savage," "degraded savages."[30] Yet the book also contains a lyrical outburst on the archetypal "noble savage" as he existed in New Guinea, "where the native are found in their primitive simplicty, the undisputed lords of the soil, displaying a proud independence, their lives void of care, and with little to excite either ambition or jealousy."[31]

The Influence of Anthropology

The new science of anthropology was crucial in helping the missionaries to shake themselves free of their initial cultural assumptions and in giving them a conceptual framework for their observations. Although none of the missionaries of the late nineteenth and early twentieth centuries had much exposure to anthropological theory during their training, some found, when in the field, that intellectual curiosity or contact with practicing anthropologists guided them toward it.

For a small minority this led to close involvement with the discipline. An example was LMS missionary, J. H. Holmes. A poorly educated Devonshire house painter, he arrived in New Guinea with the same prejudices as most of his colleagues. He found the nakedness of the Gulf men "repulsive," the Maipua *dubu* 'sacred house' "too horrid to describe," and the New Guinean generally avaricious and insensitive.[32] In 1898 the anthropologist Seligman visited Holmes' station at Moru, and toward the end of the year Holmes started reading Tylor's *Anthropology*. From that time on, a change is apparent in his writings. His diary for January 1899 recorded his reactions to a cannibal raid he witnessed at Maipua, where "the whole night was given up to debauchery and revellings of the most immoral and base kind."[33] Juxtaposed with this judgment, however, are scholarly and dispassionate notes describing the feast and the associated sexual ceremonies. His subsequent writings, which culminated in his large study, *In Primitive New Guinea,* are marked by an attempt to see the Gulf peoples on their own terms. In the preface to his book he wrote: "Their views of life do not lack a philosophy which was intelligible to them. I do not endorse them, neither do I condemn them. I have set them down as I got to know them."[34]

No other missionary was so obviously influenced by an exposure to anthropology, but in each of the mission societies there was a handful of workers whose understanding of the people was enriched by some contact with the discipline. In turn, they themselves, by their unsurpassed knowledge of the language and their familiarity with the culture, enhanced the understanding of the anthropologist. Holmes' colleague Will Saville, while on furlough, attended a course of lectures given by Malinowski, and afterward published a study of the Mailu, *In Unknown New Guinea.* Malinowski's personal opinion of Saville was typically acerbic—"a petty greengrocer blown up by his own sense of importance"[35]—but he wrote a sedate appreciation of his work in the foreword of the book, depicting Saville as "the modern type of missionary who has been able to fashion himself into an anthropologist."[36] A. C. Haddon paid a similar tribute to the "valuable contribution" of Baxter Riley to the "ethnography of the Kiwai" by his book, *Among Papuan Headhunters,*[37] and wrote appreciatively of Reginald Bartlett, "a bright attractive youth" who attended his lectures before embarking for the New Guinea field.[38] In the Methodist Mission, J. T. Field's careful studies of totemism, exogamy, and burial customs showed familiarity with the theories of Tylor and Morgan.[39] Haddon acknowledged his indebtedness to Field's notebooks.[40]

The willingness of some of the Protestant missionaries to embrace the new science of anthropology may have been a reflection of the Samuel Smiles self-improvement philosophy, which had greatly influenced lower middle-class evangelical thought. Among the Anglican missionaries, King, Stone-Wigg, and Giblin all collaborated with anthropologists in ethnographic studies, but in general the Anglicans' appreciation of the Papuans was more romantic than scientific. In the Sacred Heart Mission there was some skepticism about ethnography, a skepticism shared, incidentally, by one LMS missionary, Charles Abel.[41] Nevertheless, an Italian priest of the SHM, Father Egidi, published a series of studies of the Kuni that were well regarded by anthropologists,[42] and a German priest, Father Clauser, earned the gratitude of the anthropologist R. W. Williamson for his meticulous assistance in his study of the Mafulu.[43] Father Gsell, who went from Papua to work among the Australian Aborigines, regretted that anthropology was only in its infancy during his early career as, had it been more advanced, he might have avoided many mistakes.[44]

In a more diffuse way anthropological thought influenced all but the most rigid and inflexible of the missionaries after the turn of the century. Wholesale condemnation of practices such as infanticide and polygamy gave way to attempts to explain them.[45] Many missionaries stressed the need for understanding, and at the annual conferences of the various missions, members read papers and discussed aspects of traditional cultures. The terms used to describe the people softened. Throughout the first decade of the twentieth century there were a decreasing number of references to "savages" and "degradation" from the English-speaking missionaries—doubtless partly a reflection of the changes that had taken place at the missionaries' instigation, but an indication, too, of a growth in sensitivity and understanding. Among the French-speaking missionaries, terminology was more complex. From the beginning, the Sacred Heart missionaries used five words to describe the Papuans: *sauvage, canaque* (sometimes *kanak*), *noir, indigène,* and *naturel.* Henri Verjus invariably referred to the Papuans as *mes chers sauvages,* Archbishop Navarre favored the term *canaques,* and Father Couppé never used any word but *naturels.* But most frequently the words were used interchangeably, although, like its English counterpart, the term *sauvage* became less common. André Dupeyrat, describing Father Hubert's love for his *sauvages,* found it necessary to explain that he did not use the word pejoratively.[46] Father Norin, writing in 1913 of the still-unconverted mountain people of Jebel ul Enda, used none of the words employed previously, referring to them simply as *gens.*[47]

The influence of anthropology on missionary thought is best illustrated by the evolution of attitudes toward Papuan religion. "Religiously all is a blank," declared W. G. Lawes after five years residence in New Guinea.[48] Pioneers of the Methodist and Sacred Heart missions endorsed this opinion, as did his own colleagues. They saw only a "slavish fear of evil spirits" and a "deep and terrifying belief in magic."[49] The Papuans had no "religious enthusiasm," no "devotional instinct," no "notion of prayer," and no "true penitence."[50]

The Anglican missionaries seem to have been more agnostic about the lack of Papuan spirituality from the outset; their writings avoid the confident assertions made by their colleagues. The first sustained appreciation of Papuan religion was shown by Bishop Stone-Wigg, in his essay, "The Papuans: A People of the South Pacific," in which he defined and analyzed a "religious instinct"[51] among the Papuans, the lack of which had been asserted by many of his counterparts. Addressing himself to the question "How far can traces be discovered of anything that may be called a religion?" Stone-Wigg answered that "the Papuan lives in daily and hourly realisation of an immaterial world in which he believes intensely."[52] He saw the whole of Papuan life as regulated by totemism. With a wealth of illustrative detail, he analyzed the features of Papuan belief and observance, concluding that they embraced "all the elements of a religious system," an openness to the supernatural, the use of propitiation, incantation, and sacrifice, and a belief in the immortality of the soul.[53] While Stone-Wigg's perceptiveness depended in part on his own learned and flexible mind, it was also stimulated by an acquaintance with anthropology. In 1902 his sympathetic observations had combined with the theoretical understanding of A. C. Haddon to produce a joint lecture at Cambridge on the similarities of Papuan religion and Christianity.[54]

The writings of two anthropologists especially were important in opening the shuttered minds of the missionaries to the presence of the spiritual in Papuan culture. They were E. B. Tylor and Sir James Frazer. Although Tylor's *Primitive Culture* was published in 1871, there is no evidence of missionaries in New Guinea reading it until the late nineties, and it was Frazer's more popular work, *The Golden Bough*, published in 1890, that was frequently the missionary's introduction to the concept of "primitive" religion. Missionaries who came to Papua in the early twentieth century often came with a knowledge of Tylor's axiom that all people had a religion, an insight of which the pioneers had not been aware. They looked at Papuan culture guided by Tylor's comprehensive definition of religion as "the belief in spiritual things" or by Frazer's alternative definition, "A propitiation or conciliation of powers superior to man, which are believed to direct and control the course of nature and of human life."[55] It is not surprising that they found evidence of religion that their precursors failed to see. Ben Butcher, arriving in 1904, could assert, albeit with hindsight, that he never felt himself to be among "an irreligious people."[56] Longer established missionaries, originally dismissive of Papuan religion, revised their opinions. Holmes, for example, used animism, Tylor's minimum definition of religion, to organize his thoughts about the religion of the Papuan Delta, which he compared to the totemism of the Elema.[57]

With their growing appreciation of Papuan religion, some missionaries recognized that Christianity could build on foundations already existing, as Stone-Wigg had already: "What a basis is here for the building up of the Christian faith and the Christian life!"[58] In succeeding years, the Anglicans sought to use traditional ceremonies for Christian purposes, hoping eventually to link the two great rituals of initiation and confirmation. Sacred Heart missionaries also used Papuan religion as a preparation for belief, and incorporated traditional practices into worship. In the LMS mission, Ben Butcher wrote, "Quite early in my missionary career I sensed that if I were to get anywhere with the Papuan, I had to begin where I found the people and from there try to lead them on to that larger conception of God. . . ."[59] Charles Abel, despite his derogatory opinion of Papuan religion, also believed that there was a common substratum of belief—in a spirit world and in a future life—on which Christianity could build.[60] But among Protestant missionaries generally, recognition of Papuan religion was more likely to consist of token gestures such as incorporating Papuan music into worship.

Increased understanding of the complexity and coherence of Papuan culture and religion led to a growth in humility on the part of the missionaries. Holmes later regretted his brash condemnation of the *eravo* system, and his colleague Edwin Pryce Jones, rereading his own diary, made marginal comments such as, "Observations due to ignorance and conceit."[61] The veteran missionary W. G. Lawes, consulted in 1906 by Bishop Stone-Wigg about Papuan culture, was modest and tentative in his answer. William Bromilow believed it took him four years to "penetrate the mind"[62] of Papuans; Henry Newton was far less complacent: "The worst of it is the longer one lives among them the less one seems to know of their customs; you think you know everything in twelve months; you doubt whether you know anything in twelve years. . . ."[63]

Several missionaries—Anglican, LMS, and Sacred Heart—compared Papuan society favorably with that of the "civilized" world. Anglican missionary Arthur Chignell put forward a catalog of ways in which Papuan life, as exemplified at Wanigela, was superior: the Papuans were not overfed or degraded by alcohol, they breathed unpolluted air, had plenty of exercise, their work was "interesting and sensible labour to supply [their] actual needs," in fact their whole life was "a glorified picnic."[64] Chignell's analysis suggests a Ruskinian, neomedieval attachment to preindustrial society and a corresponding rejection of modern technological culture. There is a nostalgia in his description of Wanigela society, which he declared to be in its Golden Age.[65]

Such sentiments are latent in statements made by other missionaries, who may have shared in the "colonial vocation," described by Mannoni, that impelled its possessors to reject the civilized society in which they had been raised, to seek a more pristine world.[66] "These savages, as we call them, are perhaps less savage after all than many Europeans," Henri Verjus reflected after living among the Roro for two years.[67] Archbishop Navarre compared them favorably to the peasants of Berry and assured Pope Leo XIII that they were in their ways "more pure than those of many cities in civilised countries."[68] Father Coltée told French mission supporters that "the civilised could come to these blacks

of an inferior race . . . for a lesson in modesty, good taste and morality."[69] LMS missionaries Holmes and Butcher, and Anglicans Maclaren
and Chignell, also compared Papuan and European morality—to the
detriment of the latter.[70] Lawes noted that Papuan society was free of
that "abject squalor" noticeable in British society.[71] Admiring the artistry of the Massim people, Anglican missionary Isobel Robertson mused
in 1911, "indeed they constantly make us feel that there is much in our
civilisation which we should be ashamed to have them know of, while
there is much we could learn from them."[72]

Such challenges to a complacent belief in the superiority of their own
culture led a few missionaries to question the incursion of the Europeans
with their gift of "civilization." "Sometimes I am half-inclined to think
it would have been better if a white man had never become acquainted
with these shores," wrote Holmes in 1899.[73] When one sees a dying
native, wrote Chignell, one "cries out for civilisation [but then] one
remembers that the gifts of civilisation are of many kinds and that along
with what is good and merciful would come much that the natives are
better without."[74]

Cultural Evolutionism

Paradoxically, as anthropology encouraged in the missionaries a greater
flexibility toward aspects of Papuan cultures, it also stimulated a
greater rigidity in their overall assessments of them. As the doctrines of
cultural evolutionism gained popular currency in the early years of the
twentieth century, the missionaries' vague metaphors of darkness and
degradation gave way to confident pseudo-scientific statements. "Poor
New Guinea, it is awfully low in the scale of mankind," wrote LMS missionary Will Saville in 1902.[75] Archbishop de Boismenu told the Second
Australasian Catholic Congress of 1904 that the Papuans were "near to
the lowest type," while one of his colleagues found them "incontestably
at the lowest level of humanity."[76] Most believed them to be "below" the
African negro, the American Indian, and the Polynesian; some held
them to be "above" the Australian Aboriginal. As they became familiar
with the various peoples of Papua, some of the missionaries were
tempted to arrange them on the scale. J. H. Holmes found the people of
Maiva "higher" than those further west; Percy Schlencker believed the
"awful drop" occurred at Orokolo.[77] In both cases they reflected a
belief, widespread among missionaries and consistent with popular
opinion, that the "black" Papuans of the west were inferior to their
lighter-skinned neighbors in the east. The only known dissenter from
the ubiquitous hierarchical model was the Anglican bishop, Stone-
Wigg, who, in a letter to the lieutenant-governor, castigated govern-

ment officers for regarding the Papuans as an "inferior type of humanity."[78]

At one with most of their contemporaries in their belief that the Papuans were a degraded people "low in the scale of humanity," the missionaries were at odds with many of them in their conviction that they could be "raised" from this lowly position. Their belief was based on the Christian doctrine of the spiritual unity and equality of all humankind, a source of optimism not necessarily available to nonbelievers. In cultural terms, this was translated into a firm adherence to the doctrine of monogenism, which asserted the unity of the human race as descendants of Adam. Despite an almost universal acceptance of the alternate theory of polygenism by the end of the nineteenth century, the missionaries' respect for the Scriptures ensured their adherence to the Adamite interpretation.[79] Believers in the unity of humankind, they were therefore believers in the modifiability of human nature. Racial differences were seen not as innate—a logical corollary of the polygenist position—but as the result of "an evolutionary process involving more or less rapid environmental feedback."[80]

These assumptions are reflected in the comments of even the earliest missionaries to New Guinea. The term almost universally used to describe the condition of the Papuans was "degradation," a term that implies a decline from a higher to a lower state rather than an innate lowness or inferiority. Moreover the missionaries generally described the Papuans as having been exposed "for generations" to the corrupting influence of a heathen environment. This qualification again suggests that they did not see their condition as permanent and immutable. Heathenism was seen as an environmental influence, like a disease to which the people had succumbed and from which they could be retrieved. J. H. Holmes stated explicitly in his preface to *In Primitive New Guinea*, "The savage is soul-sick, and we cannot help him satisfactorily till we can diagnose his disease of heathenism."

The conception of a fall from a higher state may have been loosely related to the biblical doctrine of the fall, but it seems to have been more directly influenced by theories of degeneracy that had been current since the eighteenth century and were given new significance as a concomitant of cultural evolutionism. According to such theories, the unilinear progress of certain groups was arrested at particular points by hostile or difficult environmental factors, often encountered through migration. Under pressure from these influences, the people slipped backward while other races continued along the path of progress. Although only implicit in most missionary writings, theories of degeneracy were explicitly stated by a few. Samuel McFarlane believed that the Papuans had "fallen from a higher civilisation," that their progress was "downwards" and that they were merely "remnants of a worn-out race."[81] William Bromilow saw the dignified dancing of the Dobuans as "a vestige, probably, of better days."[82] Father Jullien, MSC, glimpsed in the death rites of the Roro and Mekeo "vestiges of a higher civilisation, of a primitive religion, of which these poor people, across numbers of migrations, have preserved the practice while forgetting the meaning."[83] Father Hartzer wondered if they were the lost tribe of Israel.

The doctrine of cultural evolution was attractive to the missionaries because it gave a conceptual framework to their belief in the unity of humankind and a "scientific" imprimatur to their attempt to "raise" the Papuans. It gave coherence to another of their assumptions—that they had the right and the ability to "raise" the Papuans. Like most of their contemporaries, many missionaries believed in a triangular hierarchy of races with, in H. A. C. Cairns' words, "the white race, western civilisation and Christianity" at the apex, then the "complex but stagnant" cultures of the east, and a broad base of the "non-literate, technologically backward cultures" of Africa, America, and the Pacific.[84] With unshaken complacency about their own position at the pinnacle of the racial hierarchy, many European missionaries reached out to give the Papuans, whom some saw as "contemporary ancestor[s]," a "guiding hand" along the evolutionary path. Seen from the "giddy heights of modern civilisation," the Papuan may seem "a sorry type of manhood," wrote Holmes. "He is nevertheless a man following the trail the rest of mankind has trod."[85]

With the Papuans firmly fixed on the evolutionary scale, a number of missionaries speculated as to their intelligence and ability. Some saw the intellectual backwardness to be expected among a people seen as low even on the scale of savagery. Charles Abel found the children "bright" but felt that there was a definite limit to their receptivity to learning;[86] Edwin Pryce Jones found them "intellectually lower" than the Malagasy among whom he had worked previously.[87] Holmes found them intelligent only "so far as intelligence goes with Natives."[88] But more often the missionaries paid tribute to the Papuans' intelligence. W. G. Lawes asserted that all the Papuans he knew had "good intellectual capacity" and that some were capable of being "trained and educated."[89] William Bromilow, generally dismissive of Papuan culture, wrote that as to "the intellectual capacity of the Papuan" he could not agree that he should have "a low classification."[90] Sydney Burrows, who joined the LMS in 1913, was so impressed with the Papuans that he wrote that where education was concerned, he refused "to set any limits whatever."[91] Those engaged in education were especially positive in their assessments. Archbishop de Boismenu thought young Papuans "fairly intelligent, sometimes even quite quick."[92] Bishop Sharp told the

Anglican children that Papuan boys and girls could learn "nearly as well" as Australian or English children;[93] Archibald Hunt of the LMS wrote that the intelligence of their children compared "very favourably" with that of Australians;[94] and Matthew Gilmour of the Methodist Mission stated that he believed the children of Kiriwina to be "quicker at learning" than white children.[95] Such assessments were made in the first decade of the twentieth century, nearly three decades before the cautious but much publicized statement of Sir Hubert Murray, who ventured to suggest that there was "some overlap" between the "best Papuan" and the "worst European," but that in general the European was innately more intelligent than the Papuan.[96]

The capacity of the European missionaries to form a realistic assessment of the Papuans was inhibited by their adherence, in varying degrees, to the prevailing belief in the existence of the "native character." According to the stereotype the "natives" were emotional, impulsive, and volatile, capable only of superficial affection and transitory grief. It was commonly, though not universally, believed that Papuans were lazy, untruthful, and lacking in gratitude.[97] Herbert Spencer, in his *Principles of Sociology* (1896), gave a pseudoscientific authority to these prejudices by his concept of the "biocultural specialities" of "inferior" races—"natives" are lazy; they suffer moral and spiritual ills if educated beyond primary level; they are insensitive to physical discomfort and injury; they hold life less dear than Europeans.[98]

As late as 1902, Charles Abel maintained that the Papuans were "slow and lazy" and "seldom thorough"; they were "guided in [their] conduct by nothing but [their] instincts and propensities" and "governed by unchecked passions." Latent in their hearts was a "capacity for unspeakable cruelty." Occasionally when "unbridled passion" seized and mastered them, they became "fiend[s]." They were incapable of love, even parental love. "I know of no animal except perhaps the duck, which is more careless in attending its young than the average Papuan mother."[99]

Few missionaries retained the stereotype image as intact as did Charles Abel. Even those who came with it entrenched in their thoughts found their prejudices modified to a greater or lesser extent by experience. Archbishop Navarre perpetuated the stereotype of the Papuans as "eminently lazy" as did also, in the next generation, Father Peeters and Will Saville.[100] But from the first, W. G. Lawes denied their laziness.[101] Newton, Stone-Wigg, and Chignell in the Anglican Mission, Butcher and Holmes of the LMS, and Ballantyne and Bromilow of the Methodists all followed Lawes' lead in denying this preeminent "native" characteristic. "There has probably never been a more unjust charge," wrote Stone-Wigg.[102]

Abel's conviction that the Papuans were incapable of genuine love or grief was endorsed by Sacred Heart fathers Guis and Chabot,[103] but repudiated by a number of missionaries. "It is very hard to see the grief of the people who love their children," wrote Ben Butcher after only a few months in the country.[104] His colleague Holmes, like Abel, believed initially that grief was feigned, but time convinced him of its genuineness.[105] Anglicans Stone-Wigg and Newton, Methodist sisters Walker and Billing and their male colleagues Field, Bardsley, and Bromilow, LMS missionaries Lawes and Turner, and SHM Father Hartzer all remarked on the intensity of domestic affection among the Papuans.[106]

Other elements of the "native character" were less challenged by the observations of the missionaries. Andrew Ballantyne told the 1906 Royal Commission that the Papuans were "frightful liars,"[107] an opinion almost universally endorsed by the missionaries. Both Archbishop de Boismenu and Bishop Stone-Wigg described them as "fickle," and various other missionaries commented on their "avariciousness" and "lack of gratitude."[108] But a number of missionaries, especially Anglicans, characterized the Papuans in ways that modified or offset the conventional stereotype. Stone-Wigg commented on their strong sense of justice and on their generosity, an attribute also praised by Methodist sister Ethel Prisk and by LMS missionary Samuel McFarlane.[109] Newton appreciated their sense of beauty and their good manners, as did also Father Hartzer.[110] Chignell found them "loyal, fair and faithful," an opinion to be echoed by those of his successors who were to owe their lives to them under Japanese occupation three decades later.[111] Matthew Gilmour of the Methodist Mission described the Kiriwinans among whom he worked as a "bright, clever, industrious, dear people." To him they were like the Methodists of Cornwall, "excitable, brave and revengeful" but "deeply emotional and loving."[112]

However the missionaries weighed the Papuans in the scale of virtue and vice, there was one characteristic on which they all agreed. They were children—albeit children with the passions of adults. "Poor things, they are only grown-up children," observed Albert Maclaren when first confronted with the Massim of Bartle Bay.[113] Bromilow and Stone-Wigg both referred to the Papuans as a "child-race."[114] Bishop Verjus saw them as "big, badly brought-up children."[115] Even to J. H. Holmes in 1915, after all his years of anthropological study, the Papuan was still "a child, a precocious child, an indolent child."[116]

The child-image had a number of different connotations. In the eyes of the cultural evolutionists the child was taking the first steps along the path toward the adulthood of civilization. The Papuans were the survivors of the childhood days of the human race. Insofar as the missionaries believed in the existence of such immature traits of the "native character" as fickleness, impressionability, volatility, and transitory grief, these also reinforced the analogy of the Papuans as children. Commonly used in all four missions, the child image was most prevalent among the Roman Catholic and Anglican missionaries, for whom the concept had an additional theological dimension. As the priest was the "father," so were his flock his "children"—whether white or brown.

The child analogy guided the policy of the missionaries toward the Papuans, as did also the doctrine of cultural evolution. Whether they viewed the Papuans as "child[ren]," "contemporary ancestor[s]" or both, most missionaries held an unquestioned belief that it was their duty to "raise" them. Lawes warned mission supporters in England in 1879 that "these races will never themselves struggle into light, and will never raise themselves, unless help comes to them from without, unless a saving hand is extended."[117] Charles Abel defined the missionary's role as being to lead the Papuans "onward and upwards" and J. H. Holmes wrote that during their "climb of the steep ascent" the Papuans would "need the wise and sympathetic guidance of people of our race."[118] In the Sacred Heart Mission, Archbishop Navarre spoke of the missionary's responsibility to "raise" the Papuans from "moral degradation" and in the Methodist Mission, Bromilow believed that cannibalism revealed "the deeper depths from which these people had to be lifted."[119] Only in the Anglican Mission, where the image of the degraded being low on the scale of humanity had never had much currency, was the concept of raising the Papuans not a common part of the rhetoric.

"Raising" the Papuans

Missionaries differed in their understanding of what it meant to "raise" the Papuans. All were committed to some degree of change—a metanoia[120]—in the lives as well as in the hearts of their converts. All assumed the need to introduce education and medicine; all agreed to oppose such practices as cannibalism, head-hunting, malign sorcery, and infanticide—objectives in which they supported and were supported by government policy. Although each of the four missions proclaimed its intention of retaining all native customs compatible with Christianity, the decision as to what was or was not compatible was a unilateral one. In their choice of what to oppose, what to retain, and what to introduce, the missionaries most clearly revealed beliefs and underlying values that were a product of their own origins.

Earlier in the century, missionaries had debated whether they should first civilize or Christianize. Samuel Marsden in the Pacific and the Moravian missionaries in Greenland had chosen the former. By the 1870s Protestant missionaries were inclined to assume that civilization without Christianity was meaningless; that "a savage in a shirt is no better than one without."[121] This axiom reflects what the missionaries meant by civilization. It was associated in their minds with the externals of Western culture, especially the adoption of clothing. Most Protestant missionaries, although skeptical about attempts to civilize before converting, still saw the two as inextricably intertwined. Their goal, as one of them explained, was the "Christian civilisation of the Papuan people."[122] Only a small minority expressed any doubts about the necessity of their civilizing role.

In their efforts to "civilize" the Papuans, the Protestant missionaries showed a concern for the minutiae of behavior that was less characteristic of their Anglican and Sacred Heart counterparts. All but a few were free of the inhibitions about traditional dress, or the lack of it, associated with their predecessors in the Pacific. A common feature of the stereotype of missionaries is that they were obsessed with swathing their converts in ungainly Victorian garments in the attempt to "civilize" them. But by the time the missionaries reached New Guinea, this obsession was far less apparent than it had been a generation earlier. The elderly missionary at Kerepunu, Albert Pearse, noting his pleasure at seeing his congregation "clothed with European garments," revealed the prejudices of an earlier generation, a legacy perhaps of his service in the Pacific. The same explanation can be given for Lawes' lament, "Civilisation is not advancing. The people wear less clothes than they used." But influenced by Chalmers, Lawes' attitude broadened. At the end of his career he wondered whether he and Chalmers had erred in discouraging the wearing of clothes and explained, "We both had a horror of Brummagen or Manchester Christians." Their fellow pioneer Samuel McFarlane also believed that a "simple girdle of leaves" was more suitable than European clothing. The only two LMS missionaries to complain about their naked flock were the young single men, Beswick and Holmes, their discomfort probably revealing as much about their own psychological state as about any Protestant doctrine as to the virtue of clothing. As time passed, Holmes' growth in understanding included a recognition of the need to shed his cultural assumptions about the "dignity of clothes." Most of his colleagues joined Chalmers in opposing clothing, on grounds of both aesthetics and health.[123]

Missionaries interfered with numerous other aspects of Papuan cultures. Bishop Stone-Wigg, visiting the Methodist head-station of Dobu in 1901, noted the "very persistent opposition given by the Mission to many native ways."[124] These included the chewing of tobacco, the marking of the face with black gum, the use of impure language, the observation of traditional funeral rites, and the beating of the drum on Saturday nights. Strict Sabbath observance was imposed. That other great hallmark of late Victorian Methodism, teetotalism, was less prominent, because of effective government enforcement of the regulations prohibiting alcohol to Papuans. In the LMS, which, consistent with its Congregational tradition, was less unified than the Methodist Mission, there was greater diversity of practice. Some of the staff earned the respect of anthropologists for their tolerance and restraint, while others adopted prohibitions comparable to those of the Methodist Mission. The bitter campaign waged by W. G. Lawes and some of his colleagues against the traditional Motu dance, the *mavaru*, was the most noteworthy example.[125]

The Sacred Heart Mission adopted, in theory, a position close to that of the Protestants. Archbishop Navarre stated, for the benefit of the government, that their object in coming was to "civilize" as well as "convert."[126] But in practice, for the Sacred Heart missionaries, civilizing seems to have been a concomitant of conversion rather than an intrinsic part of a two-pronged objective. Unlike many Protestant missionaries, they encouraged traditional dancing until 1908, when a review of mission policy suggested that it was interfering too severely with church attendance. Their attitude toward other aspects of traditional cultures was tolerant and pragmatic. Early denunciations of sorcery gave way to attempts at understanding and some accommodation, and in Mekeo, opposition to mortuary ceremonies was withdrawn when church attendance plummeted.[127]

The link between Christianity and civilization was most firmly repudiated by the Anglican missionaries. Bishop Stone-Wigg drew on the tradition, exemplified by Bishop Tozer and his successors in the Universities Mission to Central Africa and endorsed by the Melanesian Mission, of divorcing Christianity from its Western context and integrating it with village life. Less convinced of the superiority of Europeans or the degradation of Papuans, the Anglicans in New Guinea did not want "a parody of European or Australian civilisation." Aware of the limits to their understanding and knowledge of Papuan cultures, they remained "conservative in dealing with native customs" except those universally condemned.[128] They debated what attitude to adopt toward death feasts until 1929, when they decided they should be opposed. They encouraged dancing and they looked at the possibility of synthesizing initiation ceremonies—usually opposed by their Protestant counterparts —with their own confirmation ceremony.

Despite their unanimously expressed policy of minimum interference, and their varying degrees of tolerance toward Papuan cultures, there were aspects of traditional social organization, apart from those also controlled by government regulation, that all the missionaries remained opposed to. Many of these related, not surprisingly, to marriage and sexual mores. Preeminent among them, as in all mission fields where it existed, was the issue of polygamy. Although they recognized that polygamy in Papua was not such a problem as in other places, missionaries, especially those of the SHM, defined it as one of the major challenges confronting them. All four missions allowed polygamists to become "candidates under Christian instruction"—or, in Anglican terminology, hearers—but within the Sacred Heart, Anglican, and Methodist missions no polygamist could become a catechumen until the polygamous union was renounced.[129] This involved the banishment of all but one wife, a practice that may have caused other missionaries the disquiet voiced by Methodist Andrew Ballantyne: "It seems too hard to put wives and families away. . . . If we could allow these old marriages to stand, much possible hardship might be avoided. . . ."[130] In the LMS, early workers followed the compassionate lead of James Chalmers in rejecting this requirement. Recalling that some members of the early Christian church had more than one wife, Chalmers claimed that interference in such matters was "only man's device, a requirement our Lord Jesus had not laid down."[131] The same compassion was present in Holmes' conviction that under existing circumstances, polygamy was a "necessity" in Namau.[132] However, although preexisting polygamous unions were accepted in the LMS, it was expected that Christian converts would abstain from such marriages after baptism.

While Roman Catholics, Anglicans, and Methodists all debarred polygamists from church membership, the intensity of their general opposition to polygamy varied. The attitude of Anglican missionaries seems to have been fairly relaxed. Copland King wrote, in retrospect, "Polygamy itself did not . . . concern us much, although we stopped it when we could."[133] Methodists were less yielding, opposing it from the early days when Samuel Fellows "bashed polygamy" with vigor.[134] Danks assured the uneasy Ballantyne that opposition was "the shortest way to a reform that is absolutely necessary."[135] In the Sacred Heart Mission, opposition was even more thoroughgoing, Archbishop Navarre threatening polygamists with the fires of hell.[136] The anthropologist Pitt-Rivers, admittedly not an impartial witness, alleged three instances in which interference in traditional polygamous marriages extended to the abduction, by priest, teacher, or convert, of second wives, and their subsequent remarriage to Christians.[137] Sir Hubert Murray admitted knowledge of only one of these cases.[138] After the introduction of Archbishop de Boismenu's new program in 1908, opposition to polygamy intensified. Christians who had lapsed into polygamy were expelled from the church, a policy that was revoked in 1929 with the realization that the "road to repentance" was thus cut off.[139] Archbishop de Boismenu told the Royal Commission of 1906 that the government should discourage polygamy as had Sir William MacGregor.[140] When the Marriage Ordinance was passed in 1912, the Sacred Heart Mission, while generally approving it, regretted that by recognizing all native marriages as legal, the government thereby "protected" polygamy.[141]

On the general issue of sexual mores, there was more consensus. All missionaries opposed "licentiousness" in any form, their main concerns being "fornication" and adultery. In their opposition to the latter they were joined by the government, which made adultery among Papuans a crime punishable by six months' imprisonment. Their attitude toward sexual morality led the missionaries to oppose numbers of traditional customs and ceremonies. Chalmers energetically attacked the Kiwai *moguru*, which he described as "abominably filthy," and Butcher opposed the *buguru* of the delta region.[142] After some hesitation, the Anglican missionaries decided that they must oppose *numagwaru*, the custom of sleeping together without sexual intercourse.[143] But opposition was not always, as their opponents liked to think, based solely on a negative and repressive attitude to sexuality. Butcher's anxiety about the promiscuity associated with the *buguru* was prompted by his observation of the ravages of venereal disease among participants.[144] Much of the missionaries' opposition to polygamy was based on their conviction that it exploited women, turning them into "concubines" or "slaves."[145]

One of the most persistent elements in the stereotype of the missionaries is that they were iconoclasts. Dominated by prudery, ignorance, and complacency, they set out to destroy mores and customs that they found offensive, incomprehensible, or different from their own. In the period after the First World War, the dominance of the functionalist school of anthropology over evolutionism and diffusionism caused increased sensitivity to the interdependence of the various parts of a culture and the damage done to the whole fabric by an assault on any part. The prevailing philosophy of cultural relativism deplored the missionaries' espousal of particular value judgments. Anthropologists, formerly the "intellectual partners" of missionaries, joined popular writers in stereotyping them as dangerously destructive. Pitt-Rivers, for example, alleged that the missionaries' influence in Papua had

> destroyed the native's tribal life, the prestige of his chiefs, his morality, his pleasures, his beliefs, his hopes, the cement of his society and the very meaning of his life. It has, with clumsy dogmatism, meddled with his sex life, destroyed his *tapu* system, and freed him only from the old fears which made him loyal to his corporate group. It has left him with new fears . . . and a helpless incapacity to control his own destiny, while it bids him mimic the culture forms he can never make his own.[146]

In assessing the validity of the image of the missionaries as "iconoclasts" as it applied in Papua, several points must be considered. First,
the missionaries were concerned almost exclusively with the behavior of
converts. Prohibitions on dancing, feasting, polygamy, and sexual
license were directed toward those within the Christian community, not
toward the society at large, though of course the whole society was indirectly influenced by missionary opposition. Second, missionaries in
Papua seem to have been more tolerant not only than most of their
predecessors—a product of the growth in anthropological understanding—but also than many of their contemporaries. It seems that the Society of the Divine Word Mission and the Lutheran missions in New
Guinea were more destructive of traditional culture than their Catholic
and Protestant counterparts in Papua. Even Pitt-Rivers admitted that
missionaries in Papua were less guilty of "wilful destruction of native
culture" than those in other parts of the Pacific.[147] J. H. Holmes and his
colleagues in the Gulf earned a tribute from the anthropologist F. E.
Williams for the "broad-minded attitude which they adopted towards
native institutions."[148] Remarking that none of the white missionaries
adopted any direct measures against the *hevehe* festival of Elema, Williams went on to say, however, that the same sympathetic, tolerant attitude was not characteristic of native teachers associated with the mission. The third point that can be made in defense of the European
missionaries is that much of the destructiveness identified with the missions originated in the zeal of Papuan and Polynesian teachers and of
converts from among the Papuan people.

Finally it must be recognized that missionary interference was only
one of the influences tending toward the disintegration of traditional
cultures. Missionaries' stands on many issues were reinforced by government policy. In more subtle ways, too, colonization was forcing change.
Men who moved from the village in search of wage employment no
longer had the leisure to build majestic *eravo*, carve elaborate masks, or
prepare for and participate in cycles of feasting and dancing. Nevertheless, the missionaries cannot be absolved from the charge that they participated in a large-scale destruction of many aspects of traditional culture. Their commitment to effecting change was their *raison d'être*. Not
only through repression of the old ways, but also through the conflicting
demands imposed on their converts, they destroyed much of the basis
for traditional socioeconomic activity.

Paternalism

The influence of the missionary over the convert was exercised through
a personal relationship more intimate and directive that those that gen-

erally existed between Europeans and Papuans at the time. The child analogy that dominated responses to the Papuans in all four missions acted as a sanction and a rationale for this relationship. "Poor things, they need a father to guide them," observed Albert Maclaren.[149] This compassionate but arrogant statement, which set the tone for the relationship between the Anglican missionary and his flock, was echoed in the other missions. "They are children and need much patience, love and leading," wrote Reginald Bartlett from Orokolo.[150] Archbishop Navarre advised his staff, "The father of a family watches over his children constantly. The Missionary must be like a father even to the old people, for all, young and old, are big children."[151]

The type of relationship established was the paternalistic one common among well-intentioned colonialists of the period. The dominant group, the missionaries, exercised a benevolent despotism over their subordinates, the Papuans, whom they saw as inferior, childish, immature, and irresponsible. Roles and status were "sharply divided along race lines" and the social distance between the two groups was so unambiguous as to allow "distant intimacy."[152] Within this relationship, love for the subordinate group was not impossible so long as they "stayed in their place." Among the subordinate group there was "accommodation to their inferior status."

The paternalism of the late nineteenth and early twentieth centuries has been much criticized by those of a later age. One of its worst manifestations was a failure to treat those of the subordinate group as if they were fully human and of equal significance to members of the dominant group. The missionaries were, in some degree, insulated from this temptation by their belief in the spiritual equality of all humankind, but in some of their responses there is a condescension that comes close to a negation of full humanity. Charles Abel dismissed the Massim's belief system with the observation that it took "great patience to enter into all his little ideas."[153] Arthur Chignell alluded to the Papuans as "these comical brown fellows."[154] The Anglican Mission seems to have been particularly prone to this form of condescension. The photographer Frank Hurley was repelled by the dinnertime conversation at Dogura: "They seem to regard the native as a pet or prize puppy dog. Mark do this—Peter did this—John is quite rude and such inanities float across the table. . . ."[155]

In the missionary literature of the period, Papuans rarely emerge as individuals. In the memoirs of the early missionaries they generally form a shadowy, black background to the exploits of heroic white men; in the writings of later missionaries they become objects of scholarly study. Chignell drew some memorable pen-portraits of the Papuans and Melanesians he had worked with, but in each case the portrait was composed to show endearing but inferior characteristics such as laziness or amiable foolishness.[156] One of the few missionary publications to present appreciative portraits of individual Papuans was James Chalmers' *Pioneer Life and Work in New Guinea*, from which the powerful Koapena, the devoted Kone, and the exuberant "Queen" Koloka emerge as distinctive and memorable people.[157]

The depersonalizing tendency that the missionaries were prone to was probably even more prevalent among secular contemporaries. Speaking of the Papuans to a mixed audience in Melbourne, W. G. Lawes pleaded, "I ask you to accept them as fellow-subjects and fellow-men. Don't talk about them as 'niggers' or 'black-fellows' but . . . let them be treated as men, weak, ignorant and childish, but still members of the human family."[158]

A second and related aspect of paternalism was the authoritarian control exercised by the missionaries over the Papuans. Bishop Verjus, the esteemed *Mitsinari* of Roro and Mekeo, was, despite his great affection for his "dear savages," autocratic and sometimes harsh in his dealings with them. "One has to be savage with savages," he explained.[159] Other much-loved missionaries, such as James Chalmers and Albert Maclaren, were also remembered for the peremptory manner they adopted at times.[160] J. H. Holmes found himself becoming increasingly authoritarian at the same time as his understanding of the Papuans was growing. "There is only one way to treat the Papuans," he wrote in 1900, "and that is to be arbitrary and commanding in all our dealings with them."[161] In these missionaries, authoritarianism was tempered by a genuine love for the people. In the regime of a minority of other missionaries, such as the impetuous Wilfred Abbot of Wanigela, the element of fear dominated over that of love.[162] Like a father with his children, the missionary interfered in the lives of the Papuans, watching over their behavior, controlling their environment so as to remove temptations and dangers, frequently putting pressure on them to adopt what they saw as the right way of life, and punishing them when they deviated from it.

Missionaries believed that they had a right to punish, as with a wayward child. Punishment could range, according to the heinousness of the offense in the eyes of the missionary, from the cutting of a tobacco allowance to corporal punishment. Missionaries in Papua did not share the convictions as to the virtues of flogging held by their Lutheran brethren in New Guinea, nor did they resort to it as frequently. But there is evidence that it was used occasionally in all missions. Caleb Beharell of the LMS threatened to "thrash" any man who prostituted his daughter, and the redoubtable Mrs. Bromilow made the same promise to any woman who attempted infanticide.[163] George Brown, large-hearted secretary of the Methodist Missionary Society, was disturbed by reports of the use of force by Samuel Fellows and John Andrews. "Try to remember that love is the greatest power in the world," he advised the missionaries. "Let the people feel that you love them and your work will be easy."[164] In the Anglican Mission a layman, Charlie Sage, inflicted a "punishment with a rope's end" after a sexual lapse by a convert, and Henry Newton flogged male students for breaking through the fence of the girls' quarters.[165] Another Anglican, Charles Kennedy, was brought before the government on an assault charge, as was also the domineering LMS missionary Edward Baxter Riley. Both were reprimanded but acquitted.[166]

Aloofness derived from an unassailable sense of superiority was a third feature of paternalism, which the missionaries exhibited in varying degrees. Archbishop Navarre warned his staff against the danger of "a too great familiarity with the natives."[167] Bishop Sharp advised Anglicans to adopt a middle course between "familiarity" and the accepted white colonial status of *bada*, adding, however, "I sometimes think we ought to be 'badas' much more than we are."[168] Methodist missionaries were told that it was "not wise to fondle natives."[169] When in 1915 the board of the LMS asked its missionaries to describe their social relations with Papuans, typical responses were "no social relations with the natives" and "kept in their place."[170] Will Saville of the LMS devised a set of laws to regulate his interaction with the Papuans that forms an archetypal statement of the paternalistic relationship. They included:

1. Never play the fool with a native.
2. Never speak to a native for the sake of speaking.
3. Never call a native, send someone for him.
4. Never touch a native, except to shake hands or thrash him.
5. Never let a native see you believe his word right away, he never speaks the truth.
6. Rarely agree with a native, and then only when he is alone.
7. Warn once, afterwards proceed to action.[171]

In their aloofness, the missionaries only reflected the convention of the time. Indeed, they deviated sufficiently far from the norm to be frequently criticized by secular contemporaries for encouraging a familiarity that "lowered the white man's prestige" and encouraged "indolence" and "bumptiousness" among the "natives."[172]

Beside these negative aspects must be set one positive feature that was as much a part of paternalism as were condescension, domination, and aloofness. This was the element of trusteeship. Pioneer missionaries Chalmers and Lawes set a fine precedent with their lusty battle against exploitation of Papuan lives, land, and labor by white settlers. Many of their successors self-consciously adopted the role of "native protector" and were thus seen, with varying degrees of pleasure, by settlers and traders, government officials and observers, and by the Papuans themselves (see chapter 9). Ben Butcher reported that the people spoke of him as "their man," different from the trader and the government official.[173]

Criticism of paternalism has often obscured the fact that it was a relationship that could be exploited by both sides. From the first, Papuans manipulated the missionaries to obtain such benefits as tobacco and hoop iron; protection, not only from foreigners but also from intertribal enemies; learning; and the status that derived from close association with a white man. The old Roro chief, Raouma, who first welcomed Verjus to New Guinea, expressed at his death a Papuan perception of the paternalistic relationship: "He was good to us, he loved us well, he defended us, he gave us tobacco, he scolded us only when we deserved it. And he is dead!"[174]

Diverse Missionary Responses

Responses by the European missionaries to the Papuans and their culture ranged along several different spectrums, from condemnation to admiration, from incomprehension to understanding, from intolerance to acceptance, and from reticence to aggressive interference. How individual missionaries responded depended on the interplay of the personal convictions, preconceptions, attitudes, and prejudices that they brought to New Guinea and their own experiences in the field.

The times at which the missionaries arrived were an important factor. Those who served in the last years before the First World War came out with a degree of anthropological awareness that could not have been expected of Lawes, Chalmers, and the other pioneers. They came, moreover, to a people who had already experienced up to three decades of the restraining influence of mission and government. Ben Butcher, describing his own interest in Papuan culture, cast his imagination back to the experiences of the pioneers and concluded: "It is not surprising that early missionaries, coming up against the cruelty and bestiality associated with primitive religion, saw nothing good in it."[175]

Equally important were the places to which the missionaries came. Not all Papuan cultures were equally reprehensible to the eyes of a nineteenth-century Christian European. In the cultures of the Motu, the Roro, the Elema, or the Mailu there was little to tax the tolerance of the missionary, while those working among the Namau, the Kiwai, or the Goaribari experienced much greater strains on their capacity for understanding. Ben Butcher's cry of despair that the more he learned the

"more revolting" everything was,[176] reflected not a narrow, uncomprehending bigotry but a struggle to come to terms with a culture that
allowed ten-year-old girls to be "raped" by elderly men. Different cultures, moreover, taxed the understanding of the missionaries in different
ways. Those working among the Namau, the Goaribari, and the Massim were confronted with cannibalism; those working among the Roro,
the Mekeo, the Elema, and the Motu were not. Missionaries who lived
among the D'Entrecasteaux Islanders and the Elema were distressed at
the prevalence of infanticide; Holmes, working among the poorly
regarded Namau, found no evidence of it. The relaxed attitude of the
Anglicans toward polygamy was partly a reflection of the fact that it
was not widely practiced among "their" people. The Kiriwinans,
admired for their artistry and industry, were censured for their licentiousness, a feature much less apparent among, for instance, the Roro
and the Mekeo.

Yet time and place are not sufficient to explain the different responses
of the missionaries. The people Charles Abel had referred to as "fiends"
were of the same Massim stock as those Gerald Sharp wrote about
warmly. The Motu dance that caused W. G. Lawes such anguish was
defended equally strongly by some of his colleagues. Even in identical
experiences, individual missionaries brought with them attitudes derived from their social background, their religious formation, and their
own personality that ensured that their reactions would rarely be identical to those of any other.

The anthropologist Kenelm Burridge has hypothesized that missionaries from southern and Mediterranean Europe, where "diverse cultural forms and moralities exist in some profusion," were prepared to
allow a greater variety of cultural expression than those from the more
monocultural countries of northern Europe.[177] This may have been a
factor in the tolerance of the French and Italian fathers of the Sacred
Heart Mission, in contrast with, for example, the predominantly British
LMS missionaries.

The socioeconomic background of the missionaries, including the
amount of education they had received, doubtless also molded their
responses. Mostly from the lower middle or artisan classes, the Protestant missionaries in Papua reflected as they had in other places, the
mores of that section of society—in their greater preoccupation with
dress, decent language, and sabbatarianism and in their condemnation
of secular pleasures like dancing and feasting. In contrast, the priests of
the Sacred Heart and Anglican missions, often well-educated members
of the upper middle class, exhibited on most issues other than that of
sexual license, a greater broadmindedness, flexibility, and tolerance
that very likely were derived in part from their education and experi-

ence. Conversely, the censorious judgments of some of the Sacred Heart brothers, or of the Anglican carpenter Samuel Tomlinson, suggest an outlook closer to that of some Protestant missionaries than to that of the educated leaders of their own missions. Where understanding and tolerance of magic and ritual was required, however, Sacred Heart brothers, many of them products of peasant cultures of Brittany, Berry, or Italy, may well have had greater intuitive understanding than their better-educated colleagues or counterparts in the other missions.

The greater acceptance of traditional cultures on the part of Catholic missionaries was closely tied to their Natural Theology, which held that while sin had brought about a certain perversion of human nature, by their surviving powers of reason, individuals could comprehend God through the reality of creation. A partial manifestation of God could be sought and found in all cultures, and thus a greater measure of accommodation and assimilation could be allowed. By contrast, Protestant missionaries, influenced by the Reformation doctrine of total corruption, which rejected the competence of fallen human reason to engage in Natural Theology, saw a greater need for a total break with heathenism.[178]

Differing conceptions of the church also influenced the relationships of the missionaries to the Papuans and their culture.[179] For both Roman Catholics and Anglo-Catholics, the church was a universal, divinely ordained institution that for centuries had embraced all manner of people. Insofar as it rested on human endeavor at all, its preservation depended on the fidelity of its clergy, rather than its members. From the convert was expected assent to a formal theology and a faithful observation of the sacraments. But the evangelical Protestants' understanding was totally different. For them the church was not an institution that derived its strength from divine ordination and historical continuity, but was the body of believers. With a lower view of the sacraments and the ministry and a less formal theology, the Protestant church defined itself in terms of its members, and was impelled to a much greater concern for the ethics and morality of each individual convert. Moreover, unlike the Roman Catholic and Anglican missionaries who were encouraged to think of their service as lasting a lifetime, and of that of their successors as lasting for centuries, Protestant missionaries envisaged shorter careers and an independent church. This may have lent a greater urgency to their attempted reforms.

Differences in social and religious background cannot totally explain the differences in responses of the missionaries any more than can the time and place at which they served. The aristocratic, learned, and urbane Frenchman, Alain de Boismenu, was capable of as harsh a judgment on the Papuans as was the most ill-educated Protestant, whereas the LMS missionary James Chalmers, or the Methodist carpenter George Bardsley, both of modest origins, were capable of a spontaneous appreciation as warm as that of any highly educated Roman Catholic or Anglican.

Some missionaries came to Papua with an innate affection for the Papuans; others did not. Copland King regretted that it was duty that brought him to the Anglican mission field rather than the love that inspired his leader, Albert Maclaren.[180] Another Anglican, Arthur Chignell, at first felt revulsion at the touch of a brown skin, but later his warm-hearted, enthusiastic nature guided him to a genuine, albeit paternalistic, affection for the Papuans.[181] In contrast, Charles Abel continued to feel "nausea" in their presence throughout his long career.[182] Despite his autocratic manner, James Chalmers was motivated by a deep affection for the people that enabled him to fling his arms around their necks as unself-consciously as he stamped his foot at them. Such an appreciative response was not dependent on any theoretical understanding. Chalmers himself was completely unlettered in anthropology—unlike his colleague Will Saville, for instance, who combined a solid theoretical knowledge with a cold, remote personal style.

While the missionaries were unquestionably influenced by their racial and class origins, their education and experience, and the intellectual climate to which they were exposed, at the heart of the their responses to the Papuans lay the mysteries of their own personalities. Fundamental differences in personality ensured that missionary responses ranged through a broad spectrum that makes any stereotyping impossible. At one extreme, some missionaries closely matched the stereotype of the cold, judgmental and iconoclastic killjoy, but at the other extreme were those who showed a spontaneous affection and a tolerance that far outstripped that of most of their contemporaries.

CHAPTER 6

"Preaching, Teaching and Knocking Around"

Contact and Communication

IN A PENCILED diary entry written the day before his death, LMS missionary Oliver Tomkins recalled one of his earliest impressions of mission work. It was "gathered from a picture of the missionary jumping ashore, with a book, presumably the Bible in his hand, from which the picture leads one to suppose that he is forthwith going to instruct the natives who are to be seen gathering around."[1] Tomkins' childhood impressions evoke a stereotype of mission work that was probably shared by many of his own and subsequent generations. Black-coated, the missionary of the imagination stands, Bible in hand, and preaches before a dark-skinned, attentive crowd. Pervasive as this image may have been, it bore scant relation to the experience of most missionaries. Despite the fond illusions of mission supporters at home, there was no initial demand for the gospel.[2] A pioneer missionary, wanting to preach, found it necessary to coax, cajole, and even bribe to get a congregation —and was more likely to preach in flannel shirt and cotton trousers than in the somber black garb beloved of satirists. Overt evangelism was only a fraction of the work of the missionary and in the pioneering days was a negligible part of the daily routine. "How do we preach the Gospel?" James Chalmers asked an audience at Exeter Hall, and answered, dispelling the illusion Tomkins had shared, "No we do not go with a black coat and white neck-tie, standing in the boat with a Bible in our hand. We go as man to man to try to live the Gospel."[3]

All missionaries claimed their fundamental objective to be conversion of the heathen, but all recognized as necessary prerequisites the threefold task of winning the confidence of the people, establishing themselves among them, and learning the language. Much of the work of the pioneer missionaries, as distinct from those who came to established stations, was devoted to these three objectives.

For a minority of missionaries in New Guinea, mostly of the LMS and the SHM, their task required making contact with peoples previously unvisited by Europeans. W. G. Lawes, the first European to settle on the Papuan mainland, traveled from his base at Port Moresby eastward along the coast and inland, his arrival at villages heralded, as word of him spread, by the cry "Misi Lao," which, a later observer remarked, became a talisman in that area.[4] His indefatigable colleague Chalmers worked first from the east and along the southern coast, claiming in one expedition alone to have visited ninety previously uncontacted villages, and later pressed into the Papuan Gulf, the Delta, and, in the months before his death, into the distant reaches of the Fly River.[5] Sacred Heart missionaries worked first among the Roro, who were accustomed to white intruders, and the Mekeo, who had had less experience of them. Finding themselves constrained by the spheres of influence agreement, they pushed inland, becoming the first Europeans to visit the almost inaccessible mountainous interior.[6] Anglican and Wesleyan missionaries, arriving three years after the commencement of Sir William MacGregor's energetic administration, had neither the same necessity nor the same opportunity for first contact.

Mission literature is full of accounts of expeditions of exploration and contact.[7] Mission supporters read narratives of perilous voyages in small craft, of landings on palm-fringed beaches observed by wary villagers, of cautious offerings of gifts, and the first tentative gestures of friendship. Although the style of making contact varied to some extent with the individual, most missionaries worked to a similar formula, which had elements that distinguished it from the style of traders and even government officials. Unlike their secular contemporaries, most missionaries traveled unarmed. Although the pioneer Wesleyans were issued two rifles, one for bird-shooting and one, should it be needed, "for nobler game,"[8] most missionaries rejected the use or even display of weapons as incompatible with their intention of gaining the trust of the people. Jane Chalmers boasted to a friend in England that her husband did not possess "a firearm or fighting weapon of any description."[9] Entering a village, the missionaries displayed their empty hands.[10] Unlike government officers who traveled on patrol with contingents of police and carriers, European missionaries traveled in small parties with perhaps a South Sea Islander and several Papuans to act as interpreters, guides, carriers, or crew. Like others engaged in first contact expeditions, they made intelligent use of previously contacted people, working through their normal trading relationships with the uncontacted. While government officials camped in tents guarded by native police, missionaries sought accommodation from villagers, stoically enduring the mosquito-filled air of coastal houses or the smoke of mountain dwellings, the grunting of pigs, and the cacophony of human sounds, in their efforts to win acceptance by the people.[11]

Most first meetings opened with the presentation of gifts—stock trade articles such as axes, hoop iron, turkey red cloth, knives, tobacco, and beads. The recipients were often selective in what they accepted. As soon as initial suspicion was allayed, the missionary tried to explain his presence, either directly or through an interpreter, assuring the people that he was their friend and that he was not a trader or government official. Often the people subjected him to a nonverbal inquisition, prodding and patting him, and minutely examining his clothes and equipment. First meetings were generally brief. "My plan for a first visit is to arrive, make friends and get away again before the people realise what has happened,"[12] wrote James Chalmers, pioneer missionary par excellence, who also developed an impressive repertoire of acts for dealing with situations he believed to have become menacing.[13]

The response of the Papuan people to the white intruders varied from place to place. There were instances of hostility. The first expedition of de Boismenu and his colleagues to Fuyughe ended in flight as they saw themselves threatened by local carriers who coveted their trade goods.[14] But such incidents occurred more often among people with previous experience of Europeans than among the newly contacted, a fact that led missionaries confronted with inexplicable hostility or threatened violence to conclude that it was retaliation for wrongs committed by earlier European visitors, frequently traders.[15] This frequent Eurocentric assumption, which credited Papuans with the capacity merely to react to European intrusion rather than to initiate action, may have explained some unfriendly encounters, but more often the answer probably lay in aspects of the diverse cultures of the Papuans themselves.

Most initial responses were peaceful. Accustomed to intervention in their society by humans or spirits, the Papuans accepted the European missionaries on their own terms. Many saw them first as spirits, often those of returned ancestors.[16] When they recognized the newcomers as human beings, the Papuans were quick to see the advantages in accepting them. Trade goods were a persuasive argument for tolerance, and glimpses of European technology, even without firearms, impressed them. Reports of the missionaries from earlier contacted neighbors made Papuan communities eager to exploit their presence, not only as providers of material goods, but as status symbols, as protectors, and as allies in the prevalent local warfare. Having decided to accept a missionary, the people often became possessive, and a common feature of missionaries' accounts of contact was the ostensibly disinterested assurances of those contacted that the missionary's life would be imperiled if he ventured among their neighbors—advice that he usually chose to ignore.

Most missionaries were clear-eyed about the reasons for their accept-ance. They realized that they were welcome for the material benefits they brought, but remained optimistic that this response could be trans-formed in time. "Today's Gospel with the natives is one of tomahawks and tobacco," wrote Chalmers. "We are received by them because of these. By that door we enter to preach the Gospel of Love and I wish it could be done now."[17]

Whether or not the people to whom the missionaries came had been previously contacted, the first phase of mission work was always devoted primarily to winning their acceptance.[18] Most pioneer mission-aries believed that such a program required their living among the peo-ple, so their first task was to acquire land and establish a base. Before the imposition of colonial rule, land was bought by direct negotiation with the people; afterward, protection of native land being a declared aim of government policy, it was obtained through the government. Payment was in trade goods. Henri Verjus bought land on Yule Island from the Roro "chief" Raouma, for 3 singlets, 3 pocket-knives, 3 neck-laces, 2 mirrors, 2 musical boxes, and a little tobacco.[19] The Anglican pioneers obtained 260 acres of the grassy Dogura plateau from the vil-lagers of Wedau for 10 tomahawks, 10 big and 10 small knives, 24 look-ing glasses, 112 pounds of tobacco, 5 shirts, cloth, beads, pipes, and matches.[20] Panaeati station in the Louisiades was acquired by the Methodists, through the government, for trade goods worth 2 guineas.[21] The months that followed the purchase of a site were largely absorbed by the material work of station building. Such work, as James Chalmers observed, enabled the missionary to establish a relationship with the people that would be the foundation for evangelism:

> Day after day in duty's routine, not in hymn-singing, praying or preaching in public, as some imagine that missionaries spend their days, the work was ever going on. The Gospel was working its way in bush-clearing, fenc-ing, planting, house-building and many other forms of work, through fun, play, feasting, travelling, joking, laughing, and along the ordinary experi-ences of everyday life.[22]

These activities provided the missionaries with the opportunity to begin to learn the language. Sacred Heart missionaries were urged by their superiors and by the Sacred Congregation for the Propagation of the Faith (commonly known as Propaganda) to make it their principal occupation: "A missionary who has good command of their language is all-powerful."[23] Early methods of acquiring the language were simple— the missionaries questioned, pointed, listened, scribbled the answers in notebooks, and by a painstaking process of deduction and testing mas-tered the syntax and idiom. However, among the pioneers were able lin-guists such as Lawes, Verjus, King, Tomlinson, Bromilow, and Fellows, on whose compilations subsequent linguistic work was based. Later missionaries were tutored by the veterans, those of the Anglican Mission, for instance, learning from King or Tomlinson by the Gouin method.[24]

Pioneer missionaries also sought to build up trust by involving themselves in the lives of the people. Most went daily to nearby villages where they tested and improved their limited vocabulary in simple teaching and conversation and practiced basic medicine. Their ability to heal sores and dispel fever was a powerful agency in winning acceptance. "They always come to us in sickness, and in death send for me to comfort their mourners," noted Albert Maclaren three months after his arrival at Dogura.[25] Many missionaries won trust by mediating in the intertribal warfare that plagued Papuan society, helping to achieve the peace to which they exhorted the people. "We preach the Gospel in many ways," observed Chalmers, "one of our best at present is making peace between tribes."[26]

Although direct evangelism was recognized as having limited value in such new and tenuous relationships, it was never neglected. As soon as a pioneer missionary had acquired a few stumbling words of the language, he sought to share his faith with his flock. Early sermons were basic, prescriptive, and sometimes theologically crude. "When I reach a village, I get the people together and give them an address," wrote Copland King from the Mamba. "I tell them they are to be friendly with the white man, and that fighting is to stop. I tell them about the Father in the sky, what his words are to us, and about His Son, Who came to earth."[27] Often the first lesson taught was of the "one true God" depicted as the Father or the God of Love.[28] Shortly after his arrival at Suau, Chalmers preached to the people under a leafy *tamano* tree. "We have begun speaking of God's love to the people in very broken language, yet sufficient I hope to make them think a little," he reported.[29] Albert Maclaren, fortunate in the presence of an interpreter who had learned English on a Queensland plantation, preached a similar message under the shade trees of Wedau: "They listened to the singing and I got Abrahama to interpret a few words to them about God the Great Father and his love and care for them."[30] Ben Butcher, on his first visit to the villages of the mud flats of the Bamu River spoke of the "Good Father," the "Life Beyond," and the "Friend of Man," concepts that he described as "the first letters of the gospel alphabet."[31]

Methodist and Roman Catholic pioneer missionaries, while preaching the same doctrine of the God of Love, were more likely to be moved to balance it with warnings of eternal punishment for unbelievers. "By the terrors of the law we persuade men and it is only from fear of the consequences of . . . depravity that the love of Christ can be shown,"[32] wrote a Wesleyan pioneer. Samuel Fellows recorded preaching at Panaeati on the love of God and on his "dealings with the ungodly" at the Day of Judgment, "One woman shrieked when I described the thrusting down of sinners into a prison of fire."[33] Verjus advised his colleagues to preach first the doctrine of hell, as "these poor people cannot initially understand Divine Love."[34]

With only a sketchy and sometimes inaccurate knowledge of the language, and mostly without the services of an interpreter, pioneer missionaries found their early attempts at worship greeted with indifference, incomprehension, and sometimes derision.[35] Congregations were noisy and inattentive, though some courteously imitated the preacher in bowing their heads in prayer. Missionaries were resourceful in exploiting devices to attract the people to their teachings. Samuel Fellows found his harmonium an asset as he landed on the beaches of Panaeati to bring the first words of the gospel.[36] Henri Verjus fascinated the villagers of Roro with the brightly colored pictures of heaven and hell, the creation, and the fall, in the picture catechism he had compiled as a student and with the medallions of Mary and the pictures of the Sacred Heart that he distributed among them.[37] Most enticing of all were magic lantern shows. Missionaries leavened their representations of biblical subjects with comic slides that proved universally popular.[38] After the first experiences, which occasionally inspired listeners to flight, singing proved an attraction, and before long Papuans of Dobu were learning to sing "Pull for the shore" and "What a friend we have in Jesus," while those at Tsiria (Yule Island) learned the Our Father and Hail Mary, and those at Dogura, more mysteriously, "Home, sweet home."[39]

If the pioneer missionaries had had to judge their first months or even years in terms of the conventional image of their work, they would have had to admit failure. Many would have recognized the experience of Lawes, who reported after fourteen months at Port Moresby that the Motu were more apathetic and indifferent to his teaching than they had been a year before. The first curiosity had been satisfied, attendances at services were smaller, and "if possible, the spirit of enquiry less." But, he added, the missionaries had "won the confidence of the people," who now better understood the object of their coming.[40]

Gaining the acceptance of the people, building a station, learning the language, and, for the earliest missionaries, the sheer struggle for survival, absorbed most of the time and energy of the pioneers. Lawes and his wife in their "poor little shanty" at Port Moresby nursed their large contingent of South Sea Island teachers during recurrent attacks of fever, saw their own baby son die, and watched "hearts sick with hopes deferred" for the boats on which they had to depend for supplies when

Port Moresby proved to yield none of the abundance they had been accustomed to in Polynesia.[41] The pioneering phase of the Sacred Heart Mission was even more precarious. Alain de Boismenu, reflecting on the period, reckoned that it was more than a decade before the work of evangelism really started. The first ten years were "heroic times during which a handful of missionaries, exhausted by privation and fever, ruined their strength in the preliminaries of establishing the mission, learning the language and exploring the country."[42] The Anglican pioneers, who were deprived of their leader four months after arrival by the death of Albert Maclaren, were capable of no more than a holding operation for the next few years, while observers in Australia predicted that the mission would be abandoned.[43]

Only the carefully prepared, solidly staffed and prudently equipped Methodist pioneer expedition avoided a phase when its very survival was in doubt. But despite their businesslike approach, their experience of the initial phase of mission work was similar to that of the other pioneers. Taking stock of his first year at Panaeati, Samuel Fellows wrote:

> Just a year ago today . . . we landed first time at Panaeti. A year of hard work. . . . Not at all an unhappy year tho' much sickness and first experience of loneliness. Not altogether resultless either tho' not the spiritual fruits I have longed . . . for. Still there is a great change in the people and in the mission station. After great toil I have got the bush cleared for 350 palms to be planted and a road to be made. . . . Many days of toil and sweat and tired limbs . . . but the worst is now over.[44]

The Daily Routine

In all four missions the work of extension and that of consolidation was held in continual, if sometimes uneasy, balance. Rather than pioneering work being replaced in time by the work of the settled mission station, both types were undertaken concurrently. Many missionaries' work was a combination of the two; others with strong preferences opted for one or the other insofar as the mission structure would allow. Thus, twenty-five years after the establishment of the LMS in Papua, while its founder, Lawes, taught and translated at Vatorata station, his pioneering partner, Chalmers, was still tramping beaches and sailing rivers, tasting the "strangely wonderful charm" of being the first to preach the gospel in a new place.[45] As late as 1916, J. H. Holmes, another inveterate pioneer, traveled 866 miles in six months among the people of the delta region.[46] In the SHM, Archbishop Navarre confined his attention to the work of the settled stations of Roro and Mekeo, while young and energetic missionaries de Boismenu, Jullien, and Hubert lifted their eyes to the towering blue mountain range that could be seen from Yule Island and, at the turn of the century, led the first expeditions among the Kuni and Fuyughe.[47]

As the country was explored, the people contacted, stations established, and churches and schools built, the opportunities for pioneering work diminished, and more and more missionaries found themselves living the orderly life of a settled station. The daily routine varied from mission to mission and, to some extent, according to the needs and personnel of the particular station, but most missionaries worked long and demanding hours.[48]

For most, the day began with the ringing of the station bell at 6:00 AM and ended with "lights out" at 9:00 PM.[49] For all, it began in prayer. Sacred Heart missionaries with more elaborate devotional exercises gathered in the chapel at 5:30 AM—for prayer, meditation, and, if sufficient were present, mass. Some Anglican stations, also working to a timetable of "monastic regularity and precision,"[50] held a morning service at the same time; others said morning prayer at 6:00 or 6:30 AM, a common time also for the Wesleyan prayer meeting and the family prayers or service on LMS stations. After prayers, while the air was still cool, missionaries supervised work sessions in which students and teachers undertook manual work and domestic chores necessary for the efficient running of the station. Some, including the idealistic Anglican bishop, Stone-Wigg, believing in the virtue of manual labor, participated in the digging, planting, fencing, and other chores.

Breakfast followed (Figure 15), after which the missionary might put in a busy half hour or so in his dispensary before ringing the station bell for school at about nine o'clock. On many stations, school was only held three or four mornings a week, to allow the students time to participate in the village routine of hunting, fishing, and gardening. Midday was dinnertime, and a lucky missionary might have time for a rest before resuming school at two o'clock. But frequently other obligations intervened. Anglican missionaries at Dogura attended language lessons; some were called on for consultations with teachers or villagers; others returned to their dispensaries. When school ended, missionaries often set out on pastoral visits to nearby villages (Figure 16), after which there might be time for a game of cricket or a stroll along the beach or around the station before the evening meal.

Evenings were put to equally good use. On LMS stations, night classes were often held—a legacy, perhaps, of Samuel Smiles—and the evening concluded with prayer. Methodist missionaries held class meetings, singing classes, and prayer meetings. Sacred Heart missionaries said compline, the last of the offices that regulated their day, and Angli-

Figure 15. Breakfast on the beach for the Daunceys. (Council for World Mission)

can missionaries held two services, *taparoro* or "native" prayers for the unbaptized and evensong for church members, followed on some of the larger stations by compline. Free of their responsibilities, the missionaries enjoyed a brief period of leisure, Protestant missionaries to read, write letters, and relax with their families, Sacred Heart missionaries to gather and chat on their verandah in a companionable cloud of smoke, and Anglican missionaries to assemble for supper, to discuss and plan, or, during Stone-Wigg's episcopacy, to listen to the bishop giving an account of his travels, "mimicking, as only he could, those whom he had met, white, brown or black."[51]

Although almost all the missionaries were ardent sabbatarians, Sunday was, for them, no day of rest. Most reproduced, in the moist heat of the Papuan coast, the sabbath routine they had grown up with in the midlands of England, the west of France, or colonial Australia. After an arduous day in the company of James Chalmers, a weary Holmes recorded in his diary, "Tamate is very happy tonight, he has had a Sabbath . . . after his own heart—services from day-break to well past sunset."[52] It was a routine, he felt, better suited to the highlands of Scotland.[53] On most Protestant stations, after early morning prayers for family, staff, and boarders, the main service of the day was held in the

Figure 16. Pioneer missionary Henry Schlencker and his wife, Mary. (Council for World Mission)

large station church and attended by people from nearby villages as well as station people. Besides hymns, prayer, Bible readings and a sermon, it generally included a catechism session or other religious instruction, and was commonly followed by Sunday school. In the afternoon the missionary often conducted services at more distant villages, returning in time for supper and evening prayers.

In the Sacred Heart Mission, services were held for large and orderly congregations at Yule Island and other head stations. After the service the priest received in turn the various groups from the congregation—the ill, the children, the chiefs, and those seeking baptism or confession. Because many secondary stations were in the care of brothers, sisters, or catechists, priests often spent much of Sunday traveling from head station to outstations to celebrate mass and sometimes to administer baptism.[54]

Outside this common and fairly constant routine, missionaries fulfilled a variety of roles. Some found that translation absorbed an increasing amount of their time; others threw their energy into the upkeep and improvement of station and plant. Methodist missionary J. T. Field estimated, for instance, that in four years he had invested 555 hours on launch maintenance.[55] All missionaries were called on from time to time to intervene in village crises—epidemics, deaths, brawls, fights, negotiations with the government, or the intrusion of strangers. And even the most settled missionary spent some time visiting the outstations under his care, checking on their progress and encouraging the teachers, brothers, or catechists in whose charge they were. Reflecting on the work of an Anglican missionary, Henry Newton wrote:

> To be a butcher and a baker and a cook, carpenter, house-builder, fencer and painter, adviser in moral and legal difficulties, settler of matrimonial disputes . . . , schoolmaster, housekeeper, referee in case of sorcery, linguist, pastor, priest, sailor would surely be enough for variety, and then on top of all, doctor and nurse.

The missionary, Newton concluded, had to be "Jack of all trades" and consequently ended up "master of none."[56]

Despite Newton's complaints, in the missions of Papua medical work never assumed the prominent place it held in other mission fields. As has already been noted, apart from the fleeting presence of Ridgley and W. Y. Turner in the LMS, there were no doctors in the Papuan mission fields till well after the First World War (see chapter 4). In these circumstances, as the missionaries themselves readily admitted, the medicine practiced was inevitably amateur. All missionaries learned to apply simple remedies to simple ailments, often picking up "a little about bandaging and boracic acid, and vaseline and soap and water" from older missionaries.[57] They dressed ulcers and sores with picric acid or Condy's fluid, treated fever with quinine, and dosed minor internal ailments with Epsom salts or castor oil.[58] Arthur Chignell recalled that on his second or third morning at Wanigela, he was invited to "have a shot at ministering to the sick."[59] Perhaps two, perhaps twenty, cases were treated each morning except Sunday. At the dispensary at Dobu one day in 1896, the missionary treated eleven people—one each for dog-bite, neuralgia, teething, ophthalmia, and fever; two for burns, two for ulcers, and two for unspecified illnesses.[60]

Common sense and experience were generally sufficient to guide the missionary in the dispensary, except when an epidemic swept through the station. Baxter Riley reported treating seventeen cases of dysentery simultaneously at Daru, and Chignell described the anguish of watching helplessly as children died of whooping cough.[61] Several missionaries criticized the lack of medical expertise in their mission.[62]

Within the broad range of duties listed by Newton, missionaries usually had a clear conception of what were the essential aspects of their work. These James Chalmers defined as "preaching, teaching and knocking around," a laconic but concise definition of the missionary role.[63] Lawes saw his work a little differently, as to "teach, preach and translate," and Holmes divided his into church work, school work, and industrial work.[64] All were agreed on the primacy of their role as evangelist and educator.

Preaching and Conversion

Preaching, which had necessarily been played down in the pioneering phase of mission work, assumed a dominant place in the lives of the settled missionaries. Once the immediate objective of winning the confidence of the people was accomplished, they could devote their energies to the fundamental goal of conversion.

Each of the four missions divided its flock into distinct groups. The largest, most amorphous group were the adherents who attended services but had made no commitment. These were known by Roman Catholic missionaries as neophytes and by Protestants as hearers; however, the Anglicans reserved the latter term for those among them who had expressed a wish to be baptized. Hearers or neophytes who, having acquired an elementary understanding of the faith, sought church membership, became catechumens. In the catechumenate, they undertook more intensive instruction in preparation for baptism. At the apex of the indigenous Christian hierarchy were the church members.

Much of the work of the established missionaries was devoted to leading the people through these stages into the church. This was accomplished by a variety of means, the chief of which were preaching, catechizing, and storytelling, often with the use of visual aids. Education, although increasingly conceived as a separate obligation, was also essentially an evangelistic device, as was medical work. All these modes of evangelism were employed in all missions, but the emphasis placed on them varied.

Consistent with their tradition, Protestant missionaries relied on direct preaching. The rudimentary messages preached by the pioneers were expanded into more comprehensive and subtle religious teaching as each missionary gained mastery of the language and the people gained greater understanding of the new cosmology. Early missionaries of the LMS preached from the Old Testament, making use especially of the Decalogue, to discourage fighting, dancing, promiscuity, and pagan ceremonial. Lawes found that the Motu readily identified with Old Testament worthies. "They know all about Adam and Eve, but it was a

New Guinea garden in which the Fall took place. . . . Themselves
hunters and agriculturalists, they make Esau hunt the wallaby and
Jacob plant yams and bananas."[65] But Lawes' teaching was also strongly
Christocentric, as his younger colleague J. H. Holmes observed with
approval.[66] Holmes himself, of a generation exposed to the immanentist
theology of the last decades of the nineteenth century, found himself
confining his preaching almost exclusively to the gospels.[67] His contemporary Ben Butcher also drew inspiration from the gospels, preaching
the ethical teachings of Jesus and the Christian message of "enduring
and eternal love," a conviction that permeated his being and that he
subsequently wrote about.[68]

In their wholehearted presentation of the God of Love, the European
missionaries of the LMS were often at variance with their Polynesian
pastors, whose God was the Old Testament Jehovah. The anthropologist A. C. Haddon quoted the opinion of a boatbuilder who worked for
the LMS, Robert Bruce, that the latter image was more influential:
"Really the South Seas teacher knows the kind of God to depict to the
natives far better than the white missionary does; his God of love is
beyond their comprehension. They look as if they believe in Him, but
converse with them and you find the God of wrath is their ideal of what
God is."[69] Holmes lamented the impact of the "bullying sermons" of the
South Sea Islanders as did his colleague Dauncey, who regretted that
many Papuans saw God as the "Big Policeman."[70]

Methodist missionaries threw themselves into their preaching, frequently reporting that they had "had a good time" with their sermons,
although the volatile, red-haired Samuel Fellows habitually took himself to task for too much "bashing."[71] Methodist sermons from the beginning had a strong moral content and often involved a direct attack on
local custom and traditions. "Had a good service and showed picture of
Queen," Fellows noted in his diary a few months after his arrival at
Panaeati: "Spoke of duties of natives as subjects—honor placed by
Britishers on Queen and pleaded for lightening of labours of women.
. . . I then went on to speak of Albert the Good as having only one wife,
and bashed polygamy."[72] This mode of address became a characteristic
Wesleyan style. "One's utterances to the heathen hearers have sometimes reached a "red-hot" pitch, evidently making an impression on sin-
hardened ones," Samuel Fellows told his supporters. "Plain speaking is
our preaching."[73] Uninhibited by the doubts about hell that constrained
their LMS counterparts, Methodist missionaries continued, at least to
the turn of the century, to draw graphic pictures of "prisons of fire" in
their sermons.[74]

The emphasis on rigid moral principles that dominated Wesleyan
preaching was characteristic, to a lesser extent, of all mission preaching.

Concerned to effect a change in the way of life as well as in the hearts of their hearers, missionaries used their sermons to give clear-cut moral imperatives. Probably only a minority of the later missionaries shared Holmes' repugnance at preaching precepts and prohibitions. "It is so much easier to tell the old story that Jesus died to save sinners than to drum away at laws and rules of conduct," he confided to his diary in 1900.[75]

Protestant missionaries found that their preaching met with varied responses. Whether they preached the love of God or the terrors of hell, all were attempting to arouse in their hearers a sense of sin from which they could be led, according to the well-tried evangelical formula, through repentance to salvation in Christ. But many were disconcerted to find that they could evoke no sense of sin. "One did not expect to find among these savages a self-satisfied objection to the evangelical doctrines of the necessity for pardon and a new heart," complained a perplexed William Bromilow.[76] Many consoled themselves with the belief that the conviction of sin was the work of the Holy Spirit, their "co-worker."[77] But sometimes the Holy Spirit seemed slow to act. Dispirited LMS workers, especially, continued to report "indifference" and "irregular attendance" among their people. "They were frank with us to the point of cruelty," Holmes wrote of the Namau. "They told us that if we did not pay them in tobacco to listen to our Message, they did not want us in their villages."[78] Holmes explained the resistance of the Namau in cultural terms: their whole approach to life was characterized by a wariness that was not so typical, for example, of the Orokolo, who had been more receptive to his preaching.[79]

Methodist missionaries met with less sustained initial resistance. Scarcely eighteen months after their arrival, nearly six thousand "heathen hearers" were attending public worship.[80] It was a remarkable response and one that earned the admiration of Sir William MacGregor who, at the end of his term of office in 1898, declared publicly that there was "perhaps no more successful mission than theirs."[81] Nondoctrinal factors clearly contributed to their success (see chapter 8), but it is tempting to speculate on the influence of their confident hellfire preaching. One of the early Methodist missionaries, J. T. Field, believed that it was the fear of "eternal punishment for sin" that prompted "the majority if not all" to make a commitment.[82]

Missionaries of all persuasions found the Papuans selective in their response to Christian teachings. Just as their acceptance of trade goods had varied from place to place, so did their acceptance of particular doctrines. Gerald Sharp believed the Massim of the Anglican district to be especially impressed by the doctrine of the resurrection which, according to Chalmers, the Gulf people found incomprehensible. Sacred

Heart missionaries found the Roro and Mekeo particularly susceptible to the story of the passion, which Sharp thought made little impact on his people. Even within the same mission such disparities occurred, Copland King believing that the people to whom he preached responded well to the doctrine of the atonement, while Gerald Sharp found it ineffective.[83]

Sacred Heart missionaries were advised by Archbishop Navarre not to place too great reliance on preaching as a mode of conversion, it being better suited to those who already had some understanding of the faith. Instead he urged them to evangelize through the use of stories accompanied by picture charts.[84] In a small missionary manual, he instructed his community in pedagogical techniques, many of which anticipated the precepts of modern educationists.[85] Move from the known to the unknown, he advised them, involve the neophytes by questioning them, teach them in short sessions, reinforce by repetition, and reward achievement.

With painstaking care, he discussed two of the stories and pictures to be thus employed.[86] The first dealt with the creation and fall. The missionary was to hang the picture beside him and tell the story it depicted, introducing his neophytes to the doctrines of the six days of creation, of Adam and Eve and the Garden of Eden, of the creation of the invisible world of angels, and of rebellion in heaven. They were to be encouraged to identify the protagonists in the picture. The missionary was to conclude his story with some general remarks about the goodness of God, the disobedience of humans, and the existence of guardian angels, and with the more specific observations that Adam had only one wife and that God did not want them to work on Sundays. The second story, that of Cain and Abel, was to be introduced with the observation that Cain was, like themselves, a cultivator, and Abel a shepherd who minded sheep like the missionaries' flock at Yule Island. From the story and picture the people were to learn that God was present in all things, that He saw all they did, punished those who killed, and forgave those who admitted their faults.

After their neophytes had become familiar with the main elements of Christian doctrine and practice, the missionaries could introduce them to the catechism, to be learned in the traditional fashion of question and response. For the children this exercise was part of the daily school routine; the women were instructed by the sisters, and the men by a priest or brother. While parish priest at Tsiria, Father Jullien walked through the village at about four o'clock, when the men had returned from gardening and fishing, calling them to catechism with the aid of the station bell.[87]

Navarre warned his staff that teaching the catechism to their neophytes was difficult and arid work, and some complained in turn of the difficulty of "dinning into their perverse brains the elementary notions of our holy faith."[88] But, in general, after initial resistance had been overcome, most found their work straightforward. Comparing the conversion process in 1892 with the struggle of the pioneering days, Father Hartzer wrote:

> In New Guinea the mode of conversion of our savages is not complicated. We tell them first to learn the prayers and the catechism. Then comes the practice—don't steal, etc.—a little more difficult, but they obey. They understand already that the good God sees them and rewards and punishes. They learn to confess and when they have adopted Christian ways, are baptised.[89]

Tridentine theology taught Roman Catholics that baptism was the instrument used by God for the justification of infidels.[90] For the early Sacred Heart missionaries, with their zeal for souls, it was of supreme importance. Soon after his arrival, Verjus made a census of the people of Yule Island, that none might die unbaptized.[91] He and his colleagues baptized dying children, explaining to their parents that baptism prevented their going to hell. If they encountered intransigent opposition, they baptized surreptitiously.[92] By the end of 1887, fifty Roro, mostly children under five and those in danger of death, had been baptized, each receiving from the priest a little tobacco and cloth.[93] At the end of 1891, after two or three years' instruction, almost all the people of Yule Island were baptized by Verjus in large groups in a series of Sunday ceremonies.[94]

Such wholesale baptism was rejected by Alain de Boismenu, who, on becoming bishop, expressed a "firm determination to baptise none but the thoroughly disposed."[95] He urged his staff repeatedly to caution, "They are a race so lazy, so fickle, our poor natives, that it would be imprudent to accord them baptism without having tested the seriousness of their desire."[96] In a pastoral letter of 1908, devoted to the "instruction and discipline of infidels," de Boismenu signaled a withdrawal from the old methods of conversion employed by the early missionaries.[97] The catechumenate was given greater formal recognition as a distinct stage in Christian life, governed by definite rules, according to which any adult in good health could only receive baptism after one year's testing as a catechumen. Previously this requirement had only been characteristic of the newer mountain stations; now it was to be universally applied.

Within the other three missions, the need for caution in baptizing was constantly reiterated, and the desirability of mass baptism repudiated. In the Anglican Mission, after regular attendance at Sunday services, which included *giu* 'religious instruction', those who sought baptism entered hearers' classes and received instruction for up to two years, often based on Stock's *Steps to Truth*.[98] After this elementary instruction, they entered the catechumenate and studied Gardner's *Gradual Catechism*, which was translated into Wedau.[99] Catechumens received instruction once or twice weekly and, in the weeks just preceding baptism, daily.[100] The customary two-year catechumenate was later shortened as the people became more familiar with Christian doctrine.[101] Nevertheless it was an exacting preparation and many dropped out along the way. Anglican policy was always to proceed slowly and a priest showing an inclination to baptize precipitately was admonished.[102] The first baptisms, of two young men, Samuel Aigeri and Pilipo Agabadi, took place at Easter in 1896, five years after the establishment of the mission. Later baptismal services saw larger groups, of thirty or forty, wade into the river and emerge to join the church members on the opposite bank, but these, Gerald Sharp assured the Archbishop of Canterbury, were hardly "mass movements."[103] They were the result of a group passing at an even pace through services, hearers' classes, and the catechumenate.

Preparation for baptism was no less thorough in the Protestant missions. In nonchiefly and relatively nonhierarchical societies, it depended on the decision of the individual. Missionaries often expected a public confession of faith from a convert.[104] Preparation required generally twelve months' instruction as catechumens and, for Methodist converts, another twelve months as members on trial. Protestant missionaries were wary about ostensible conversion.[105] Some retained misgivings even after baptizing people, recognizing the difficulty in gauging a "change of heart."[106] The first Papuan to be baptized by the LMS, Aruadaera, was not baptized until 1881, nearly a decade after the commencement of the mission, and the first Methodists in 1894, three years after the arrival of the Wesleyan missionaries.

For the LMS missionaries the main emphasis in the conversion process was not so much on the sacrament of baptism as on admission into church membership. Their aim was to create "a strong church in every village."[107] Defining the church in terms of the believers, LMS missionaries devoted much of their working time to the nurture of members, recognizing that "back-sliding" inevitably weakened the church. Sunday schools, church meetings, religious instruction, and later such moral agencies as Girls' Improvement Societies, Boys' Brigades, and Boy Scouts were all means of attempting to ensure the continuous moral and spiritual development of the people.

In the Methodist Mission, the doctrine of entire sanctification reinforced concern for the nurture of the community of believers in encouraging the missionary to vigilance about the spiritual and moral well-being of converts. Sir William MacGregor remarked on the autocratic style of Samuel Fellows, whose methods he found "in some respects, peculiar." Questions of conduct were freely discussed in his congregation and offenders were "had up, interrogated and admonished."[108] The traditional institution of the class meeting was employed for instruction, confession, remonstrance, and encouragement and a "White Flag Society" established to foster "social purity" through a pledge to daily prayer and abstinence from "bad words" and impurity of thought and deed.[109]

Anglican missionaries, like their Protestant counterparts, found pastoral care of their converts a major aspect of their work. Besides showing a general concern for religious observance, they showed a particular concern for sexual morality. Ecclesiastical discipline was exercised over those who committed offenses against God's law, of which the most common were "offences against the seventh or eighth commandment." Those living "in a state of mortal sin" were severely censured and excluded from all church services and, in the last resort, excommunicated.[110]

Although baptism was of central importance to the Sacred Heart missionaries, Archbishop Navarre reminded them that their object was to see the people "not only baptised, but true Christians." It was not sufficient to "preach, teach the catechism and administer the sacraments"; the missionary must watch over "the spiritual and temporal interests of his flock," giving advice "in all things and at all times." He should question the people in their faith, urge them to confess, ensure their attendance at worship and their reception of the sacraments. Men, women, boys, and girls should be organized into separate congregations, under particular patron saints, in which they could meet and receive further instruction.[111]

Despite Navarre's pastoral concern, the work of nurture fared poorly in the SHM compared with that of conversion. In 1902 Propaganda questioned the disproportion between the number of Catholics and the number of Easter communicants.[112] When Navarre finally relinquished control of the mission in 1908, his successor, de Boismenu, analyzed the condition of Papuan Catholicism in a pastoral letter.[113] He found it "puny" and scarcely differentiated from its pagan surroundings. For fear of asking too much of their converts, they had asked too little. "And this has given us indifferent Christians, slack . . . and refractory in their Christian duties . . . ." De Boismenu outlined a vigorous and exacting program to infuse Papuan Catholicism with life. Doctrine was to become standardized and accessible to the Papuans through the translation into Roro, and later other languages, of Monsignor Leroy's

Table 3. Growth of SHM by number of
converts and Easter communicants,
1895–1914

YEAR	CATHOLIC CONVERTS	EASTER COMMUNICANTS
1895	1,000	?
1900	3,400	500
1905	4,593	864
1910	5,574	1,188
1912	6,010	1,555
1913	6,390	2,089
1914	6,693	2,431

SOURCE: Dupeyrat 1934, 382.

catechism; priests were to ensure that their people received regular and ordered religious instruction; Sabbath observance was to be enforced, and disciplinary measures taken against dancing and irregular marriages. The importance of village visiting, which had become sporadic and perfunctory, was reaffirmed. To ensure that intention was translated into action, annual reports were instituted, in which missionaries had to supply statistics for each district and to answer a series of detailed questions on all aspects of apostolic activity.

The effects of de Boismenu's program were reflected in the statistics, which showed a steady increase in the number of converts and, by 1912, a notable increase in the proportion of Easter communicants (Table 3).

If evangelistic success could be measured in terms of church membership and attendance, the missionaries had some cause for a sense of achievement by the early years of the twentieth century. All of them could look down each Sunday on large, orderly congregations who listened attentively to the sermon and conformed to the devotional practices.[114] In 1914 the Wesleyan mission had more than 1000 members, 600 members on trial, 2000 catechumens and over 24,000 attending public worship.[115] The Anglicans had 2000 Papuan church members by 1912 and 500 catechumens.[116] LMS statistics in Papua are, according to the Society's historian, "elusive" but by 1920 it had between 2000 and 3000 members.[117] By 1914 members of the three non–Roman Catholic missions could look also to the beginnings of churches indigenous in leadership as well as in membership (see chapter 8).

Education and Evangelism

The missionaries made no secret of the fact that their prime motivation for education was evangelistic. Education was a technique for the conversion and nurture of the Papuans no less than preaching, a "valuable ally in the strenuous endeavour to win them to the faith and service of our Lord."[118] Its aim was the "Christianisation" of the people.[119] A secondary objective was the training of a Christian elite, from whom pastors, teachers, and catechists could be drawn.[120]

Because of their concern for the access of every individual to the Scriptures, the Protestant missionaries placed a strong emphasis on literacy. Their immediate objective was to enable the children to read the Scriptures, and especially the New Testament, in their own tongue.[121] Anglican missionaries, many of them products of the public school system, while not neglecting literacy, saw education as a "character-strengthening" exercise, an attitude also shared by some Protestants.[122] The Sacred Heart missionaries, impelled to undertake secular education partly by a concern not to be outpaced by the other missions, saw it as an extension and enrichment of religious instruction.[123]

All were encouraged in their work by their recognition that children, the future generation, were more receptive and malleable than adults. Navarre constantly reminded his staff to concentrate on the children and Stone-Wigg told the Anglican missionaries that they were "as plastic under our hands and we can mould them at will."[124] Though Protestant missionaries were less inclined to make this observation, the same conviction was the basis for the settlement schemes espoused by many of them.

Despite the minor differences in their conception of education, the four missions developed similar structures, procedures, and curricula. Each head station had its school, generally run by a European missionary, and there were besides village or outstation schools, commonly staffed in the Protestant and Anglican missions by South Sea Islands teachers and in the Sacred Heart Mission by sisters or Filipino catechists. Missionaries had no illusions about the quality of education in the village schools. Lawes lamented not only the limited attainments of the Polynesian teachers of the LMS, but also their autocratic style: "The teacher shouts and storms, scolds and whacks the desk with his stick, until the poor little mortals are half-frightened out of their wits."[125] If the regime of the Melanesian teacher, Peter, at the Anglican station at Wanigela was more mellow, his learning was even more slender, and the missionary-in-charge, Arthur Chignell, could not help wondering as to the value of his class chanting with him "four fundle one penny, ten fardles t'ree penny . . ." ten and twelve times over.[126] After making a tour of inspection of Anglican schools, Chignell concluded that, while there were exceptions, on the whole, the Melanesian teachers were "probably as ill-instructed and incapable as any body of men who ever handled a piece of chalk."[127] His colleague, Henry Newton, agreed that "any educationist would pronounce most of our out-station schools a hopeless failure," yet, like Chignell, he believed them to be valuable in moral and spiritual formation.[128]

In the head-station schools, as in the village schools, most emphasis was placed on religious instruction. Protestant and Catholic pupils learned the cathechism, Bible stories, and prayers.[129] Apart from the religious emphasis, the curriculum was similar to those of the government schools of the Australian colonies, the three R's being its main component. There was much rote learning of the alphabet, numbers, addition and multiplication tables, currency, and weights and measures. Pupils also learned to identify countries on brightly colored maps and to sing hymns and choruses. Official visitors to head stations were impressed by the children's copperplate handwriting, their obedience and orderliness, the sweetness of their singing, and, sometimes, their agility with mental arithmetic.[130]

It was a curriculum without obvious attraction or relevance to Papuan village life, but from the beginning there were missionaries who taught with imagination. Walker and Dauncey at Hanuabada introduced painted alphabet letters, mechanical toys, and "three hearty British cheers" into the classroom and did much of their teaching through "object lessons," a technique learned from Chalmers.[131] Convinced of the need to make education "look more like play," Chalmers devised programs that a visiting government officer said would have "horrified an English School Board Inspector." Standing in line, hands on the shoulders of the one in front, the children "pranced round the room in high glee singing the multiplication table. A little elementary drill followed and distribution of lollies."[132] Anglican missionaries had some success in teaching English by the Gouin method.[133]

Besides the religious instruction given in all mission schools, there was a strong emphasis on moral teaching. At Kwato, as well as educating his pupils against "filthy speaking, indecent symbols, and open, unchecked immorality" and toward "cleanliness,"[134] Charles Abel issued them with a catechism of government laws to instruct them in the "duties of citizenship."[135] While Abel's zeal was extreme, most missionaries taught the gospel of "cleanliness, order and industry."[136] To this end, missionaries of all persuasions gave a prominent place to drill in their curriculum as a means of teaching "self-control and obedience."[137] Sir William MacGregor was impressed by the "admirable order and discipline" at the Dobu school. "The class rises, sits down, turns, half turns, halts etc. to the words of command."[138] Frank Lenwood, visiting Mailu station on deputation for the LMS, praised the precision of the children's drill but wondered whether the use of toy wooden bayonets was really necessary.[139] Even the Sacred Heart missionaries, though immune from the contemporary British enthusiasm for drill and "Swedish" exercises, marched their children in and out of school and stood them at attention to inculcate discipline and obedience.[140]

Missionaries were aware that their morality was in constant competition with that of the village, their authority in conflict with that of parents. The solution for some was to form settlements. All mission compounds were, to some extent, settlements, the product of almost inadvertent growth as converts and students were drawn into the station routine. But beyond this there was, on the part of some missionaries, a deliberate policy of attracting children, and sometimes adults, from the "dirt and filth and immorality and lamentable ignorance" of the village and influencing them through "daily living in a Christian atmosphere."[141] The compound, with one hundred or so inhabitants, was also seen as an object lesson to its heathen environment.[142]

Settlements appealed especially to the Sacred Heart missionaries and to evangelical Protestants. Most remarkable was Charles Abel's Christian settlement at Kwato, where children, totally cut off from the "heathen habits and ugly practices" of their home villages, submitted to a rigid discipline, with Abel and his wife "directing them in the common affairs of their daily life."[143] An island settlement, it had elements of a theocracy. Abel's colleague, Henry Percy Schlencker (Figure 17), another ardent evangelical, was converted to the settlement principle

Figure 17. The Reverend Henry Schlencker (LMS) and mission students. (Council for World Mission)

by a visit to Kwato, as were Abel's missionary neighbors, Rich and Saville. Holmes, in the Gulf and Delta, fostered the growth of settlements and, in a more modified form, so did his neighbors Butcher, Pryce Jones, and Dauncey. But within the ranks of the LMS, a sturdy band of individualists, there were others who totally opposed settlements as "hot-houses," destructive in alienating the people from their culture and unrealistic in the environment that they substituted.[144] Lawes, Turner, and Lawrence opposed settlements on these grounds and so, in time, did Rich, Pryce Jones, Butcher, and Dauncey. After the 1915 deputation reported negatively on the policy, it survived only on a reduced scale.[145]

Methodist missionaries, who were neighbors of the most fervent LMS proponents, pursued a similar settlement policy. As at Kwato, the aim was "to get some of the young people entirely under the influence of the Mission" rather than that of their parents.[146] To win them from heathenism, "a settlement is indispensible" declared one Methodist missionary and his colleagues echoed his judgment without any dissenting voices.[147] Besides a boarding school, the settlement at Dobu comprised an orphanage and a "reformatory" for children mandated to Bromilow under a "Neglected Children's Act" to save them from "living in awful sin."[148]

In the Sacred Heart Mission, one of Verjus' earliest works was to establish on Yule Island a new village for Christian converts and their families, to protect them from the temptation of village life.[149] As stations developed, it became common for priests to have a group of young boys boarding with them (Figure 18). Father Fastré had a dozen students in his house at Popole, and Father Dubuy of Ononghe had forty students living under his roof.[150] "These children are the hope of our district," wrote Father Chabot of Kuni to a benefactor, "better educated than the others, shielded as far as possible from the superstitious ways of the country, they will be able to form Christian households."[151] Anglican missionaries, consistent with the Anglo-Catholic orientation of most, saw their stations as "communities"[152] rather than settlements, and were generally less committed to weaning their converts away from their own culture, but the difference was only one of degree. Like their Methodist neighbors they provided homes for orphaned children and also for mixed-race children mandated to the bishop by the government.

Few missionaries found their schools welcomed by the local people. Papuan children, not surprisingly, preferred the freedom of beach and bush to sitting cross-legged on the floor nursing a slate, and generally their parents saw little reason to encourage their attendance. Many missionaries resorted to a reward of tobacco for attendance and prizes of

Figure 18. Sacred Heart priests, brothers, and students. (Mitchell Library)

cloth, knives, toys, and mirrors for performance. But most continued to be frustrated by irregular attendance. Following a proposal made by Charles Abel, Sir William MacGregor in 1897 introduced legislation making attendance compulsory for all children within a two-mile radius of any school teaching English.[153] The district committee of the LMS, apart from Abel, felt that it was premature and in fact it was often ignored by the resident magistrate whose responsibility it was to enforce it.[154]

The question of whether to teach in English or in the vernacular exercised the minds of the missionaries. Because their initial objective was evangelistic, most saw their prime task as being to make the people literate in their own language. Skeptical outsiders believed that vernacular teaching was also a device for preserving mission hegemony and resisting the influence of other Europeans.[155] Sacred Heart missionaries had an additional incentive to teach in the vernacular in that until the turn of the century few of them spoke English.[156] When confronted with a diversity of languages each of the missions opted for one to become its literary language. Copland King advocated the use of Wedau, understood for only forty miles of the Anglican Mission's three-hundred-mile coastline,[157] and W. G. Lawes provoked one of the most bitter controversies in the LMS by urging the use of Motu for the whole southeast coast.

As time passed there was a growing acceptance of the need to teach English, at least in the head-station schools. Strenuously encouraged by Sir William MacGregor, who publicly praised those who taught English and admonished those who failed to,[158] this change in policy was symptomatic of a general broadening of the missionaries' conception of education. Among Protestant and Anglican missionaries in particular there was an increasing conviction that it should be "for life." It should "uplift" as well as "convert" and enable the Papuans to take their "proper place in the country" or, as Abel described it, their "place as a British subject under British rule and in touch with civilization."[159] Recognizing that the Papuans would not be able to lead their lives untouched by outside influences, missionaries felt a growing sense of responsibility to equip them to communicate with and compete against foreigners, to prepare them, in short, for the "altered conditions of Papuan life."[160] The prevailing neo-Darwinian pessimism about the survival of the "backward races" gave added impetus to their concern to provide them with a corrective to apathy, skills to compete in a secular world, and training in the "necessary habits of thrift and industry."[161]

Within the LMS the growth of these convictions coincided with a sensitivity to criticism of proselytization.[162] Conceiving of their schools initially as agents of conversion and for the nurture of the converted, the LMS, during the last decades of the nineteenth century, viewed them increasingly as services to the community at large.[163] While they believed education to be the responsibility of the government, those in Papua were forced to recognize that for some time it would continue to depend solely on the initiative of the missions.

These changing perceptions led to reappraisals of the type of education offered. One superficial change was the increasing emphasis placed on sport in Protestant and Anglican schools. Abel believed football taught "tenacity of purpose"; others saw it as banishing apathy in lives deprived by missionary prohibition of many of their traditional activities.[164] A far more profound change, in the Protestant missions especially, was the embracing of the concept of industrial education.

Industrial Mission

Manual training had, from the beginning, formed a modest part of the work of all missions.[165] While W. G. Lawes was instructing the Motu in the first letters of the alphabet, Samuel McFarlane was training young LMS converts in boatbuilding and house construction at Murray Island in the Torres Strait. Two years after the inception of the SHM, Navarre spoke of their intention to "civilize" the Papuans through "social and industrial training."[166] Brothers of the mission, originally farmers and artisans themselves, instructed the Roro and Mekeo in new forms of agriculture and elementary manual arts. Even in the Anglican Mission, sometimes depicted as holding itself aloof from such activities, the founder called for "practical men" to initiate the "practical training of the natives in as many useful arts as possible."[167] But all these activities were kept in strict subordination to the traditional missionary tasks of preaching and teaching. While the SHM continued with learning of this kind, formalizing it into an apprenticeship system just before the First World War, what happened in the Protestant, and to a lesser extent in the Anglican, missions at the end of the nineteenth century was so far-reaching as to suggest a new vision of mission work.

Throughout Protestant mission fields of the period there was a strong move toward industrial mission, prompted in part by changing perceptions of the future of the "backward races" and in part by the "social gospel" of the period, which provided both a model in the carpenter of Nazareth and an imperative in its concern for the whole being—body, mind, and spirit.[168] Belief in the "dignity of work" reinforced their conviction. Advocates of industrial training looked to the Basle Mission in India and Africa, which had involved its people in the successful production of tiles and khaki cloth.[169]

The chief evangelist of this new gospel in Papua was Charles Abel, LMS missionary at Kwato. To the arguments usually adduced in favor of industrial missions, Abel added one that he felt to be particularly compelling in Papua—"the poverty of the material we have to work on in a country like this." The Papuan was so benighted, he claimed, that a purely spiritual gospel made little impact. Missionaries should reexamine their methods in the light of this knowledge rather than mindlessly applying techniques that had succeeded in Polynesia. Could not the time spent teaching children to "write copper-plate" be put to better use "industrially"?[170] Despite periodic opposition from an ambivalent and sometimes hostile district committee, Abel plunged headlong into a program that took him through copra plantations, boatbuilding yards, and workshops to, in 1918, rupture with the LMS and the formation of an autonomous Kwato Extension Association.[171]

Visitors to Kwato workshops were impressed by the "whizzing wheels and hissing straps and circular and vertical saws, besides a planing machine and lathe—all this machinery as well as the engine and boiler being conducted by Papuan youths without any help from Europeans.[172] Abel's neighbor Charles Rich was inspired to develop industrial work at Isuleilei and Abel's close colleague, Fred Walker, sharing his enthusiasm, eventually resigned from the LMS and set up another autonomous scheme, a Christian trading company, Papuan Industries Pty. Ltd. Among the visitors to Kwato were the Anglican bishop, Stone-Wigg, and the Methodist missionary who succeeded Bromilow as chairman, Matthew Gilmour. In both of them a belief in the value of industrial work was probably reinforced by what they saw. Bishop Stone-Wigg told his staff in 1901 that, their concern being for the souls, minds, and bodies of the Papuans, they should divide their work into spiritual, educational, and industrial components.[173] He recruited a printer, a boatbuilder, and a layman to care for stock and establish a model plantation at Hioge. For a variety of reasons these schemes did not flourish, and in 1913 Bishop Sharp, convinced that the mission had insufficient capital for a viable experiment, signaled, in his address to the mission's annual conference, a withdrawal from industrial activities.[174] The projects initiated in the Methodist Mission under Matthew Gilmour, a practical man with great mechanical ability, fared better. Successful plantations were established, and by 1913 students at the workshops of Ubuia had helped Gilmour build two launches, a jetty, and several houses and schools.

Some missionaries were converted to industrial mission independently of Kwato's example. Although impressed by what he saw there, J. H. Holmes found his starting point in the unresponsiveness of the Namau to traditional forms of evangelism: "Our work here has resolved itself into a strictly industrial mission. In brief it has been our business to find out what appeals to our people that they may become amenable to our Message."[175] Where Holmes' motivation remained wholeheartedly evangelistic, his neighbor at Aird Hill, Ben Butcher, was prompted to industrial work by a concern similar to Abel's to "uplift" the Papuans and provide them with a viable future.[176] Missionaries wearied or discouraged by the problems inherent in direct evangelism found comfort in the tangible results of industrial work.[177] For all those who practiced a settlement policy, it had the added attraction of keeping converts within the orbit of the mission's influence by providing them with employment as an alternative to recruitment to plantations or reabsorption into the village.

As with the settlement policy, to which it was closely allied, industrial work was opposed consistently by individuals within each of the four missions. Most adamant of its opponents in the LMS were those with lower middle-class rather than artisan backgrounds—Lawes, R. L. Turner, Lawrence, Riley, Dauncey, Pryce Jones, and Saville. Their argument was simple: industrial work deflected too much time and energy from evangelism and education. "Workshops obscure the Cross," wrote Lawes.[178] After more than a decade of dissent in the LMS in Papua, a visiting delegation came in 1915 to assess the situation. "Industrial work has received its death warrant," wrote Will Saville after reading their report,[179] though, in fact, it persisted in a modified form as part of LMS mission work.

Missionary Self-images

As missionaries became absorbed in the administration of large settlements and the supervision of industrial schemes, the black-coated, Bible-wielding preacher of Tomkins' imagination receded even further from the reality. Although there were exceptions in each mission, the majority of Protestant and Anglican missionaries became increasingly tied to their stations. The Protestant preacher who stood before most Papuan congregations every Sunday was not the European missionary but the South Sea Islands teacher—and, incongruously, in the LMS he *did* wear a black coat. In the Sacred Heart Mission, the necessity for Mass to be said by a priest ensured the fathers' greater involvement in outstation and village worship, and the fulfilment of this obligation probably increased rather than diminished with time, as de Boismenu's reforms of 1908 were implemented.

Although Newton had complained that the missionary was a jack-of-all-trades, there was increasing scope for role-specialization as the missions became established. Besides those whose time was largely absorbed by administration, some in each mission came to devote a vast amount of time to translation. Even Holmes, a fervent evangelist, grumbled at being diverted from translating.[180] Beginning first, generally, with St. Mark's Gospel, missionary translators set themselves to translate the other gospels, then other books of the New Testament, parts of the Old Testament, hymns, and catechisms. W. G. Lawes completed a Motu New Testament in 1890, a work that MacGregor described as "monumental."[181] Bromilow completed a Dobu New Testament in 1908.[182] The work of these two missionaries—as of King, Tomlinson, and Cottingham in Wedau, King in Binandere, Fellows in Panaeatian and Kavatarian (Kiriwina), Holmes in Namau, Butcher in Kerawa (Goaribari) and Norin in Fuyughe and other languages of the SHM—made a lasting contribution that went far beyond the bounds of the mission field. But it was made at the expense of removing them even further from daily contact with the Papuan people.

At no stage in the development of mission work in Papua was Tomkins' stereotype an accurate relection of reality. The pioneer missionary was too absorbed in the preliminaries of gaining acceptance, establishing a station, and learning the language to have much scope for formal evangelism and what was attempted was often the least fruitful part of his apostolate. Although they gave preaching first place in their work, settled missionaries were also engaged in a myriad of other activities, mostly motivated by evangelistic objectives initially, but increasingly prompted by a concern for the total well-being of the Papuans. When the missions became thoroughly established, as the numbers of missionaries involved in specialized tasks grew, so did their contact with their flocks diminish—whether that contact was through preaching or any other activity. Moreover, the stereotype took no account of the work of more than one-third of the missionaries in Papua—who happened to be women.

CHAPTER 7

"The Gracious Influence of Wise and Thoughtful Womanhood"

Women—A Neglected Force

OF THE 327 MISSIONARIES who served in Papua up to 1914, 115 were women (Table 4). The Sacred Heart Mission, which employed more than half the missionaries during that period, also had the largest number of women. More than one-third of the Anglican missionaries were women, and almost half of the Methodists. The LMS had none. However, there were 29 wives of LMS missionaries and an additional 18 Methodist wives.

Missionary literature gives little indication that more than one-third of the missionaries in Papua during this period were women. Absence of comment is justified on the grounds that recognition of the women and their contribution is implicit in all general accounts of mission activity. "We are asked sometimes why in our books and *Annales* we speak so little of the Daughters of Our Lady of the Sacred Heart," noted Father Bachelier, MSC. He replied, "We do speak of them, without naming them. Wherever we are, they are there too."[1] As the women missionaries participated in the general life and work of the mission, they can to a large extent be considered in the context of the mission as a whole. Nevertheless, certain aspects of their experience were distinctive, or different in some degree from that of the male missionaries. These include

Table 4. European missionaries, male and female

	LMS	SHM	METHODIST	ANGLICAN	TOTAL
Male	33	107	26	46	212
Female	0	65	22	28	115
Total	33	172	48	74	327

163

the status and role of the women in the mission field, the particular contributions they made, as women, through their work, and the effects of missionary service on them.

Perceptions of Women's Roles

In the last quarter of the nineteenth century, a period noted in Britain for its female surplus,[2] the employment of women became a recognized part of Protestant missionary endeavor, previously thought of largely as a male preserve. Mrs. Emma Pitman, in her *Heroines of the Mission Field*, noted that in 1879 the LMS employed 12 English women, the China Inland Mission, 10, and the Baptist Missionary Society, 9. Other British missionary bodies employed a further 120 women, and about 200 women worked under the auspices of various American societies. And, concluded Mrs. Pitman, "of the success of this new missionary agency, there can be no doubt."[3]

The London Missionary Society took pride in being in the vanguard of the movement to give women an independent status in the mission field. At a meeting of the directors held in 1875, it was resolved "that it is desirable that suitable English and native Christian women should be employed . . . in connection with our missions in India and China . . . to promote the educational and spiritual enlightenment of the female population."[4] By 1895 there were sixty-five women missionaries in the LMS.

But not one of them was in Papua. The LMS board and the male missionaries in the field were unanimous in their belief that Papua was not a suitable country for a single white woman, and it was not until the 1920s that women were first appointed there. William Lawes once went against his convictions to the extent of proposing to his brethren that they request the appointment of a missionary sister in order to avoid the expensive trips to the colonies necessitated by their wives' frequent confinements, but his proposal was unanimously rejected. During this period the only European women associated with the LMS in Papua were the missionaries' wives, who had never had separate status in the eyes of the Society. Furthermore, a single woman missionary was required to resign if she married another missionary with the intent of sharing his work. This, wrote the LMS historian, "does not betoken ingratitude on the part of the Society; . . . it registers the fact that the continuing service which she may render is offered by her without any contractual obligation."[5]

Accordingly, the LMS was circumspect in its expectations of wives. Its foreign secretary, Wardlaw Thompson, wrote carefully to the newly married missionary Charles Abel:

I do not know whether your wife is one of those who are fitted by nature to take an active part in the general work and life of the station. If she can do this she will . . . be a constant blessing among the women of the place. But it is not essential that a missionary's wife should be an energetic worker in the general Mission to make her a blessing to all around.[6]

Like most of his contemporaries, Thompson saw the woman's role as that of helpmeet to her husband. Her most fruitful contribution to the missionary cause was "the gracious influence of wise and thoughtful womanhood."[7]

Some LMS wives envisaged for themselves a role broader than simply exemplar of domestic propriety, and the structure of the LMS helped them achieve it. The male missionary, responsible for both running the head station and supervising numerous outstations manned by Polynesian or Papuan pastors, was often forced to leave the maintenance of the home base to his wife. Most wives taught at the station schools, and many held clinics as well as sharing in the administration of the station. They saw their special responsibility as being to the women. At women's classes they taught a range of subjects—reading, writing, arithmetic, geography, Scripture, and domestic skills such as sewing, washing, and ironing. Some wives introduced the simple cottage industries of lace making and mat plaiting. Younger wives sometimes traveled widely within their husbands' districts, but most concentrated their energies on the people of the settlement—the pastors' and students' wives and the children who lived within the mission compound (Figure 19).

Figure 19. Mission students with Mrs. Butcher. (Council for World Mission)

Many wives had the enthusiastic support of their husbands. "It is our wives who are saving Papua," declared Will Saville, describing his wife's successes with the settlement children.[8] So appreciative was Lawes that he proposed to his colleagues that wives be admitted as voting members of annual committee meetings. His colleagues opposed the idea, but his strongest opponent was his wife. "Mrs. Lawes is dead against the whole thing," he reported.[9]

Later wives were less content with the self-effacing role chosen by Mrs. Lawes. In 1910, Robert Lister Turner married Edith Calvert, who had served for ten years as a missionary in China. Although she was obliged on marrying to renounce her missionary status, she refused to relinquish the responsibilities of a missionary. She threw herself into the work on Vatorata station, making shrewd observations about the weaknesses in the LMS system of organization and tackling intelligently the task of gaining understanding of people different from those she had previously worked among. She apologized for sending much of this information in a report enclosed with her husband's. "After all, though women missionaries who marry are reported as 'retired', I believe you do regard us as missionaries all the same," she concluded.[10] The following year, one of her neighbors, Margaret Beharell, wrote to Thompson describing her husband's work at Hula and her own. "A Missionary's wife although not accounted for much by the Board at home, still has much to do," she reminded him. Asserting that much of the medical work could be left to the common sense of the wife, she concluded, however, "Still it is nice to have a man who *does know* at one's back."[11] Four years later, disappointed at the scant attention paid to women's work by a visiting deputation, she was stung into writing, "I should like you to know that a wife and mother can also burn with missionary enthusiasm."[12]

Meanwhile, the Papuan District Committee of 1915 had resolved that a committee of wives should be set up to consider work among women in Papua, and the minutes of 1917 reported that such a committee had met, that the district reports had been read, and that "one or two of the ladies . . . spoke about the work that is being done amongst the women."[13] But throughout the period, the role of the LMS wives remained essentially unchanged. They were auxiliaries, or helpmeets, accorded some recognition but no official status.

The first women to come to Papua with formal missionary status were the Daughters of Our Lady of the Sacred Heart, sister order to the Missionaries of the Sacred Heart. Their congregation was a new one, founded at Issoudun, France, in 1874 by Jules Chevalier, as a special tribute to the Virgin Mary, for whom he conceived the title, Our Lady of the Sacred Heart.[14] Once the Missionaries of the Sacred Heart committed themselves to foreign mission work, it was inevitable that the sisters, with the same founder, the same motto, and a parallel constitution, should do likewise. In this they were encouraged by their Superior General Marie-Louise Hartzer, a widow whose son, Fernand, was one of the first Sacred Heart missionaries in Papua. Moreover, the anticlerical laws of the 1880s, directed especially against teaching orders, had frustrated their original intention of devoting themselves to education within France, and the prospect of unfettered missionary work overseas became doubly compelling.

The pioneer group left in 1884, accompanied by Father Henri Verjus, who shortly afterward made his first quixotic attempt to carry the Catholic faith to the mainland of New Guinea. Arriving in Sydney, the sisters opened schools in the parishes of Botany Bay and Randwick, entrusted to the Missionaries of the Sacred Heart by Cardinal Moran. The following year several sisters moved to Thursday Island, where the order had established a foothold, and on 1 August 1887 the first of them arrived at Yule Island, where Father Verjus, three other priests, and two brothers were precariously settled.

The conditions under which the sisters came were governed by their constitution. All had completed the novitiate before their arrival and had made at least their temporary vows—the three simple vows of poverty, chastity, and obedience. Some made their final vows during their missionary service. Overseas service was voluntary, but for a time an optional fourth vow was allowed to those making their profession "to give [their] life to the missions at the will of the superiors." The 1881 constitution explained:

> The third degree is composed of those . . . sisters who, after perpetual profession may be disposed in a generous contempt of even life itself, to make for love of the Heart of Jesus, the vow to go to the foreign missions at the command of the Superiors of the Congregation and that notwithstanding the perils, sacrifices of all kinds and even death itself which may await them.[15]

As religious, they received no remuneration for their service, which was expected to be for life. They wore a distinctive habit, described by the novelist Beatrice Grimshaw as "a dark blue cotton robe, forget-me-not coloured veil streaming out under a huge convent hat [and] strong-nailed miners' boots."[16]

Although the congregation was a new one, it could draw on centuries of experience among Roman Catholic institutes. For these early missionary sisters, there was no ambiguity or uncertainty in their prescribed role, which had three main aspects. The first was devotional—they were "to render through Our Lady of the Sacred Heart devotion to the Sacred Heart of Jesus . . . [and] to make reparation for the outrages of which the Divine Heart is the object by reason of the ingratitude of man."[17] The second was to provide for the spiritual and physical needs of women and children. And the third was to be responsible for the mission's material needs, an all-encompassing objective that saw them serving as cooks, laundresses, seamstresses, cowhands, farmers, gardeners, and keepers of the sacristy.

Despite their independent status and their clearly defined role, the sisters were seen as auxiliaries in the mission field, no less than the LMS wives. Theirs would be the tasks that were too humble for the priest, who was preoccupied with the larger claims of evangelism. In terms that echo those used by Thompson to describe the contribution of the LMS wives, Bishop Navarre wrote in his first pastoral letter:

> It is the sisters who give the stamp of sweetness, order and good management to newly-converted families. . . . The care given to the ill is more assiduous, more tender. . . . The Missionary cannot take responsibility for everything. The Sisters, besides instructing the young girls, take care of the church, the chapel, the linen and altar ornaments . . . all things that the numerous occupations of the Missionary do not allow him to do.[18]

The second group of women missionaries to arrive in Papua were the Methodist sisters. For the Australasian Wesleyan Methodist Missionary Society this was an innovation, largely the inspiration of their general secretary, George Brown, who first raised the possibility of employing women in 1890. The following year, the missionaries of the newly established New Guinea field approved the idea, recognizing the influential position of women in the Massim society that confronted them. Lily Bromilow, wife of the chairman of the mission, pressed for the appointments to be made. "There is nothing here to shock any right-minded woman," she assured the board.[19] In April 1892, the first two sisters of the AWMMS, Eleanor Walker and Jeannie Tinney, sailed for New Guinea.

Most of the rules and regulations affecting the status and role of the Methodist sisters were drawn up in the field. The Australasian Conference of the church stipulated only that they were to work under the direction of the superintendent of their circuit, and that they were to be members of the circuit meetings (Figure 20). Like male lay missionaries they were to have one year's probation. The New Guinea district meeting resolved that the work of the sisters was to be solely among the women and girls; that they were to plan and report on their work at weekly meetings; that each sister was to be left free to carry on the work in her section, as approved by the weekly meeting; that they should train girls from the boarding school in housework; and that a "Lady

Figure 20. Methodist missionary sisters with William Bromilow. (Uniting Church)

Superintendent" of sisters could be appointed by district synod if necessary.[20]

At the instigation of Mrs. Bromilow, the sisters adopted a uniform: "a
blue-grey zephyr dress, collars and cuffs, black coat and black bon-
net."[21] Their salary was £50 a year, increased in 1908 to £70 a year. In
addition they received an outfit allowance of £10 at the beginning of
their service. Ladies' Auxiliaries, which sprang up in Australia and New
Zealand to support the new venture, supplied much of the furnishings
and equipment needed and paid for the Sister's Home at Kiriwina.

The first task of the Methodist sisters was, as for all missionaries, to
learn the language, and several reported preaching in faltering Dobuan
within weeks of their arrival. That accomplished, their permanent
work fell into three parts—school-work, village visiting, and the training of girls in the home.[22] In the schools, the sisters taught reading,
arithmetic, writing, dictation, geography, Scripture, and—most popular of all—sewing.[23] Village visiting included holding services, giving
religious instruction, and providing simple medical and welfare services. Domestic training had the dual purpose of providing the sisters
with household help and initiating the settlement girls into the skills of
European housewifery. In addition to these specifically womanly tasks,
on Sundays they participated with the male missionaries in all the obligations of that day—preaching, leading prayers, playing the organ, and
conducting Sunday schools and village services.

The sisters made use of the authority given them to plan thorough
programs of work. Jeannie Tinney noted in her diary the timetable
drawn up by the two sisters at Kiriwina villages in April 1898.[24] School
was to be conducted by both at Kavataria on Tuesdays and Thursdays,
9:30 to 10:30 and 3:30 to 4:30; by Sister Emily at Gumilababa on Fri-
days, 10:30 to 12:00 and 2:00 to 3:00; and by Sister Jeannie at Tukauka
on Wednesdays at the same times. Settlement girls were to be taught
sewing on Wednesday and Friday mornings; Sunday schools were to be
held at Kavataria, Tukauka, and Gumilababa. Village visiting was to
take Sister Emily to Kavataria on Wednesdays and Sister Jeannie on Fri-
days. The other villages would be visited when school was held. A
Workers' Meeting would be held on Sunday evenings. Sunday was no
day of rest. Sister Eleanor described a typical Sabbath in her diary:
"Sun mg. prayer-meeting 7 AM. Morning service 10 AM. Sunday School
2 PM to nearly 3 then Miss T. and I went in a canoe to Piasia, Iai-iai, and
Taroborena to hold services, getting home about 20 to 7."[25] Rendering
account of the week's activities, she noted: "This week I have made 36
visits to villages; school 5 times; teachers' meeting 1; class meeting 1;
Dobuan lesson 1; Sunday School 1 and 2 services."[26]

Bromilow testified to the contribution of the sisters in terms reminis-
cent of those used about the LMS wives and the Sacred Heart sisters:

> They create an atmosphere of grace incomprehensible to the Dobuan
> mind, yet permeating it and making possible the culture of better things;
> while the personal knowledge of Jesus Christ is ever the end they have in
> view, whatever they teach—simple domestic arts, household hygiene,
> child nurture, sewing or school-work.[27]

Working in close partnership with the sisters were the Methodist wives.
Like those of the LMS they had no independent status, and the four
Methodist sisters who married fellow missionaries had to resign, although their work was scarcely interrupted by marriage. As in the
LMS, the home was seen as the principal domain of the wives, but
strong women such as Lily Bromilow and Norah Gilmour carved out for
themselves careers that extended far beyond its confines. A special contribution of these two childless women[28] was the establishment and
maintenance of a home for motherless Dobuan babies, many of whom
would otherwise have been buried alive, bound to the bodies of their
dead mothers. Some of the sisters and single women in the other missions also found an outlet for their maternal instincts in lavishing affection on orphaned Papuan children.

The final group of women to serve as missionaries in Papua were the
Anglicans, who came under the auspices of the Australian Board of Missions. Although Albert Maclaren abandoned his scheme to establish a
celibate community, which was to include a sisterhood, twenty-six single women joined the Anglican Mission before 1914. Only two married
women were recruited, and four of the single women subsequently married male colleagues. Unlike the wives of the LMS and Methodist missionaries, married women in the Anglican Mission came with, and
retained, the same independent status as the male missionaries or the
single women. Women did not form a separate order, as in the Sacred
Heart Mission, nor a separate branch, as did the Methodist sisters. Their
status was much less clearly differentiated from that of their male colleagues; they were recruited as individuals rather than as women, and
they took their place with the male missionaries in the close-knit Anglican community. After a discussion with an Anglican woman missionary,
a Methodist sister noted with some surprise that "the Bishop, clergymen
and Sisters all live in the one home."[29]

The "paper of conditions to those who desire to join the mission" was
directed at all prospective missionaries, male and female. It appealed
especially to "clergymen, medical men, certificated school teachers
[and] ex–pupil teachers."[30] The only specific qualification required of a
woman was that she be at least twenty-five years old. The same conditions of service were offered to all. Like the male missionaries, the
women were encouraged to see their vocation as a life service, for
which, like priests and laymen, they would receive an allowance of £20
a year, should they need it.

The role of the Anglican women was also less strictly differentiated. Like the Methodists, many were engaged in teaching, but, as a Methodist sister observed, they "teach the boys as well as the girls whilst here we have simply nothing to do with them."[31] Annie Ker made her main contribution to the mission through translation work, a task generally assumed by male missionaries. A few Anglican women took charge of stations, which involved an exercise of authority over men and boys as well as women and girls. Apart from the differences dependent on clerical or lay status, what role differentiation there was in the Anglican Mission depended on the particular skills of individuals rather than on their gender.

By the end of the nineteenth century there were in Papua four separate groups of missionary women, each with distinctive status—the blue-robed Roman Catholic sisters, confident in their vocation and their identity; the Methodist sisters, self-conscious in their new gray uniforms and their newly created organization; the Anglican women, with a status akin to that of their male counterparts, their identity absorbed into that of the general Anglican community; and the LMS and Methodist wives, given no independent status but often achieving independent identity through force of personality and conviction. Despite these differences in status, it is clear that there were basic similarities in the roles of all the missionary women in Papua. All were, to quote Sir William MacGregor, "occupied in the duties of their own sphere,"[32] a phrase that fell readily from the lips of male contemporaries.

Missionary Women and Papuans

Apart from the obvious contributions that the women missionaries made through teaching, nursing, village visiting, and welfare work, there were less direct benefits from their work among the women and children. Perhaps the most important of these was the improvement in the status of women. This concern was shared by a number of the male missionaries, but the women were in a position to translate concern into action. Mrs. Beharell of the LMS lamented the plight of the Hula woman:

> heathen, without ambition, merely the slave of men, the drudge made to carry his loads of food, firewood, etc. . . . The married woman's head shorn and made to look ugly. . . . The girl was neglected as an infant, later tattooed in order to enhance her market value and then given whilst still a child to the highest bidder. . . . [33]

She rejoiced when the Hula women, emboldened by her encouragement, ceased shaving their heads at marriage.[34] Similarly, Mrs. Bromilow, at the outset of her service in New Guinea, recalled the time in Fiji when women had been "mere beasts of burden" and resolved to wage war on this custom in New Guinea as she had in Fiji.[35]

Different customs loomed large according to the different cultures that the women confronted. On Dobu, where strong able-bodied women had considerable status, the plight of the widow touched Sister Minnie Billing. Seeing one such woman in prolonged seclusion, dirty, unkempt, and neglected, she wrote in her diary, "Her face is before me all the time. It would be worthwhile coming to New Guinea if only to make the people more comfortable."[36]

The destiny that the women missionaries saw for Papuan women was a modest one. They were to become clean and godly wives for the men who had become part of the Christian community—"clean and helpful wives for our boys," as one LMS wife put it.[37] A few saw their work among the women as having broader significance. Moved by a contemporary debate on depopulation, Methodist sisters Corfield and Gibb reported in 1912: "Feeling that the saving of the race depended largely on our women, we have added to our curriculum . . . a series of talks on Physiology and Hygiene."[38]

In their work among the Papuans, the women often established relationships of greater intimacy than those contracted by male missionaries. Social convention forbade the male missionary any close contact with the Papuan women, and generally made him self-conscious about any intimacy with men. A few extroverts like James Chalmers submitted cheerfully to nose-rubbing and hugging, but for most male missionaries, physical distance was commensurate with assumed social distance. Among some of the younger women especially, there was not the same aloofness. The diaries of the Methodist sisters record their walking hand in hand with the women, putting their arms round the girls as they read to them, or dancing a Scottish reel with them from sheer exuberance when the oppressive presence of the Bromilows was removed.[39] Many of the sisters had village mothers who adopted them. The sisters of the Sacred Heart Mission describe women and children clinging to their hands, their robes, and their veils, kissing them, and rubbing noses with them.[40] After hugging a tall youth whom she had known since infancy, Sister Kostka, an aristocratic French woman, explained with a gesture of her hand, "To me, he is still that high."[41]

But essentially the nature of their work brought the women into closer touch with the people. While the male Methodist missionaries preached, taught, translated, and administered at the head stations, the missionary sisters went out two by two, grafting their activities onto the normal routine of village life. Some, finding their daily expeditions inadequate, had small bush houses built, enabling them to stay in the village from Monday to Friday.[42] Sisters in the Sacred Heart Mission lived in simple houses among the people, sometimes remaining in one village for decades, absorbed in its dramas of life and death. The more resourceful of them learned much about the culture of the people. "I begin to find my work in the villages more interesting as the language becomes more familiar and [I] can understand more of what the people tell me of their customs," wrote Methodist sister Edith Lloyd.[43] Annie Ker of the Anglican Mission used some of the information thus gleaned to publish the first collection of Papuan fairy tales.[44] Especially as mission work became more routinized, many male missionaries found few opportunities for such prolonged and intimate contact with the people.

Moreover, the relationship of the women with the people was not so obviously one of domination as that of the male missionary. The Papuans saw them in a serving role: they dressed their sores, nurtured their children, nursed their sick, and comforted their dying. "They became the humble servants of those whom others regard as the dregs of humanity" was the fulsome opinion of one visitor to the Sacred Heart Mission.[45] While some of the same authority was vested in them simply by virtue of their being white, their status as auxiliaries within the mission structure was apparent: "They just 'try it on' as the boys say . . . as we are women, to see how far they can go," complained Sister Eleanor.[46]

In their responses to the Papuans and their culture, the women missionaries showed the same range of attitudes as their male colleagues. Sister Agnès admired the "ability and good taste" of the people as she watched them dance,[47] and Sister Madeline, observing the gentle features of recently contacted mountain people, asked herself "why we call them savages. They are as susceptible to civilisation as certain people who were far from possessing it formerly, and who today are proud of it."[48] But some of the women of all missions exhibited evidence of the same ignorance, prejudice, and sense of superiority as was found among the men.

Not through any more enlightened attitude was the relationship of the women to the people different from that of the men, but simply through the opportunity for closer contact and a more profound involvement in the mundane and personal aspects of their lives. Some women never availed themselves of this opportunity; others responded to it magnificently. At the death of Sister Gabriel, a short, stout French woman who had spent sixty-two of her eighty-nine years in Mekeo, her body was drummed to the grave with all the honors usually only accorded the great men of the village. The chief who gave the funeral oration spoke of her as "Sister Gabriel, beloved woman, Mekeo woman."[49] On her grave was a wreath from the people of Veifa'a, inscribed "Mother of the Mekeos."[50]

Pioneer Lives

The lives of the women missionaries, especially those of the Sacred Heart Mission, were demanding and filled with physical activity. The hobnailed boots were as much a part of the sisters' working dress as their forget-me-not-blue veils. There is some truth behind the hyberbole of Beatrice Grimshaw's account of their lives: "A Sister of the Mission when she is not praying, or tending native babies rescued from murderous cannibal parents, or making clothes, or cooking, or mending fences or carpentering, or milking cows, is usually engaged in some form of athletic exercise," such as swimming across rivers, walking ten to twenty miles a day, or riding precipitous bridle tracks.[51]

Father Eugene Meyer, MSC, who knew the backgrounds from which they came, marveled to see the life led by the sisters in the field:

> For these are women, often young girls, who have been raised in the middle of the care and tender attentiveness with which Christian families surround their children; who have grown up with the comfort and abundance with which our civilisation provides us . . . and here they are, all of a sudden transported to a torrid zone, devoured by mosquitoes, periodically visited by malaria, sheltered in rough huts, sleeping on board, if not on the bare ground, . . . condemned often to solitude, . . . forced to walk through high grass, . . . to cross creeks, rivers and marshes, and on top of all that perform all the ordinary ministries of a nun.[52]

The sisters shared fully in the general austerity that characterized the Sacred Heart Mission, especially in its early days. Reflecting on Navarre's first call for sisters to join the hungry, debilitated community at Yule Island in 1887, a later Sacred Heart missionary insisted, "It was inconceivably imprudent, pure madness, contrary to good sense and reason."[53] On six separate occasions in the first decade, the mission was reduced to total dependence on local food, the supply of which was uncertain because the dry, impoverished soil of Yule Island could scarcely provide the needs of its indigenous population. In 1890, Archbishop Navarre gave first the sisters and then the priests and brothers the option of withdrawing temporarily to Sydney, or dispersing among the villages to live off the land. All chose the latter.[54]

Accommodation for the sisters was no less primitive than that for the other Sacred Heart missionaries. Sister Madeline described their first convent at Yule Island:

> All the walls are leaves bound with vines . . . the flooring is wood but all the planks are convex and retain the shape of a tree trunk split in two; . . . the roof is also of leaves, the external doors are made of wood and the windows are only bamboo shutters through which we can see out. For fur-

niture, a table, a what-not, three wooden stools and one chair for receiving visitors.[55]

Their sleeping quarters were often simply a palliasse tucked away in a
convenient corner. At Veifa'a, Sister Antoinette's room was also the dispensary and library, while Sister Ange shared her room with tins of
meat and fish, hands of bananas, and bags of rice.[56] Beatrice Grimshaw
captured the almost medieval atmosphere of the sisters' house at Inawi,
with its "tall, arched doorway, . . . the rough bare table with benches
set beside, the brown walls and floor, the amber glow of evening,
stabbed with high colour where the red clay water jar stood on the
table."[57]

How different this was from the Adelaide Sisters' Home at Kiriwina,
a replica of a comfortably furnished suburban house, donated to the
Methodist sisters by the South Australian Ladies' Auxiliary. "We have a
nice little home here and when we get our nick-nacks etc. out, we will
be able to make it pretty as well," noted Sister Jeannie. "We have such a
pretty Vienna suite for the dining-room. . . . There are 6 chairs, 1 arm-
chair, a most comfortable rocker and a settee, a dining and side table
and enough Chinese matting to cover the floor. We each have our own
bedroom furniture."[58]

Life generally was probably less arduous for the Protestant and
Anglican women than for the Roman Catholic sisters, but it was only a
matter of degree. In none of the missions were they regarded as delicate
creatures to be cosseted and protected. In a brisk letter to Bishop Stone-
Wigg, Ellen Combley described a week's work on the Mamba goldfield
that included, beside the constant nursing of dysentery patients, two
operations, one the opening of a child's abdominal wall, the other,
amputation of a gangrenous hand.[59] Her colleague, Maud Nowland, a
partly trained nurse, wrote of a nine-mile journey, the last part of it
made on all fours up a mountainside, to see a youth with an infected
leg: "He was lying in a small room with only a hole . . . for the door.
. . . I crawled in and my first impulse was to crawl out again, the smell
was so bad. His leg was in a dreadful state, the matter running down his
feet from a dreadful sore. . . . I was able to clean and dress it."[60]

One LMS missionary, Reginald Bartlett, watching the *hevehe* festival
of the Papuan Gulf, thought of his English fiancée, who was shortly to
join him: "Poor Alice! Whatever will she think of such 'shows' when she
comes out here?" but concluded comfortably, "She's a sensible sort and
will see the reason for such things better and quicker than most."[61]
There is little evidence of attempts to shield the missionary women from
the harsher realities of Papuan life. Some wives may have been insulated by their preoccupation with home and family, but Mrs. Bromi-

low, for one, along with the Methodist sisters, encountered cannibalism, the digging up and eating of corpses, and the burying alive of
infants with dead mothers, and in the last case was responsible for
bringing it to an end on Dobu. Never was there any hint of the fear of
sexual assault that was to become a hysteria among the white women of
Papua thirty or forty years later. LMS wives remained on stations for six
or eight weeks at a time while their husbands were absent; because of
chronic shortages caused by illness and death, Roman Catholic sisters
often found themselves alone in recently contacted villages; and in the
Anglican Mission, Ellen Combley's and Maud Nowland's hospital on
the Mamba goldfield was hundreds of miles from the head station at
Dogura.

Despite the genteel, cultured backgrounds of some of the women missionaries, the image of the frail, languid, and over-refined Victorian
"lady" does not fit well with the reality in Papua. Many of the women
seem to have been closer in type to the robust, resourceful, and resilient
pioneer women who were their contemporaries in the Australian outback.

Stresses, Failures, and Successes

Nevertheless, many of the women failed to survive the stress of missionary service. Many died, and many others retired, their health and
morale, and occasionally their sanity, shattered. Contemporaries
believed them less able to withstand the rigors of missionary life than
their male colleagues, a conviction that reflected contemporary opinion
as to the susceptibility of women to nervous conditions. A woman,
observed Dr. Corlette, medical adviser to the Anglican Mission, was
commonly regarded as "a uterus surrounded by protoplasm."[62] Hysteria, believed to be a consequence of uterine problems, was seen as an
exclusively female complaint.[63] During the nineties, the newly named
disease, neurasthenia (nervous exhaustion), became fashionable.[64] Although it was conceded that both men and women were vulnerable to
it, in the mission field it was invoked much more frequently in relation
to women. Yet, whether or not women were in fact more susceptible to
such conditions, an examination of the records of their service suggests
that their stamina was little different from that of their male counterparts.

In the Methodist Mission, where the average length of service for all
missionaries was shorter than in the other missions, the mean service of
the women missionaries was appreciably shorter than that of the men—
4.7 against 7.7 years. This difference was partly a reflection of the fact
that missionary sisters were required to resign on marriage although

remaining in the field, but even so the careers of many Methodist women were exceptionally brief. The first two mission sisters each gave more than ten years of service, but only two others managed a decade of work (Table 5). By the turn of the century, George Brown was brooding on whether his idea had failed.[65] If he was thinking of abandoning the idea, he was restrained by the knowledge that the vigorous Ladies' Auxiliaries would divert their zeal to other missions, such as the China Inland Mission, if thwarted in their recruiting for the Methodist fields.[66]

Among the reasons given for the resignations of the missionary sisters, ill health was the most frequent, ten women resigning on these grounds. There were cases of acute distress. All suffered more or less severely from malaria. Sister Minnie Billing survived typhoid and the early stages of tuberculosis before withdrawing to the milder climate of Fiji, and finally to Melbourne to die. At least one other sister retired with tuberculosis. Eight Methodist sisters resigned for "domestic reasons," of which the most socially acceptable was marriage. Other domestic reasons given were the need to care for ill or aged parents or to return home when one parent was left alone.

Ill health and family pressure were two socially acceptable explanations that sometimes masked other reasons for resignation such as emotional, psychological, or mental stress. "Nerves" were as common an ailment among the Methodist sisters as among the married women. Malaria was frequently blamed for their distress. Nurse Speers was refused permission to return to New Guinea because of what were delicately referred to as "head symptoms" consequent upon malaria,[67] and when Sister Julia threatened suicide in 1913, the missionary in charge attributed her overwrought condition to fever.[68] The saddest case was that of Maisie Lill, a lively sister from New Zealand who, three months after her marriage to fellow missionary, Ernest Harrison, collapsed with what was believed to be gastritis and was carried by her husband

Table 5. Length of service of women missionaries, 1874–1914

Length of Service	SHM	Methodist	Anglican
Less than 1 year	0	3	2
Between 1 and 3 years	2	6	4
3–5 years	4	6	8
6–10 years	13	6	3
11–20 years	14	1	6
21–40 years	14	0	4
More than 40 years	15	0	1
Unknown	3	0	0
Total women missionaries	65	22	28

aboard a trader's small boat, to be taken to the doctor at Samarai, 180 miles away. After a week's abortive tossing on stormy seas, they found themselves back at their starting-point. She was subsequently taken by steamer to Sydney, from where, after a period in hospital, she returned to her family in New Zealand. For the rest of her life she was as "helpless as a child," unable to recognize her husband or recall her life in Papua. What part marriage, pregnancy, illness, or the hazardous boat trip played in her mental collapse is not clear. Her family ascribed it to cerebral malaria.[69]

The depressive effects of malaria, fatigue, isolation, and the climate undoubtedly affected the psychological health of the Methodist women as they did that of the men. But in an outburst to the General Secretary written at the time of her alleged suicidal tendencies, Julia Benjamin testified to another source of stress peculiar to the women:

> Your question concerning our Synod gatherings shows that you consider that a Missionary Sister's voice should be heard there. Unfortunately I have proved that in Papua a Sister's opinion has no more weight than the opinion of a Papuan.

Describing constant curtailment of the sisters' authority, she concluded:

> Sir, are you surprised that though I love my Papuans with all my heart, yet it would be a relief if for health reasons I could resign? . . . This may enable you to see why so many Sisters remain only a short time.[70]

Instead of being directly responsible to the chairman, the sisters found that their only access to him was through his wife, who had been appointed lady superintendent. Instead of the autonomy promised them in the planning of their programs, they found that Mrs. Bromilow, with all the authority of a married woman over single, supervised them like recalcitrant schoolgirls. A dominating woman, immensely aware of her own status (she once upbraided Brown for publishing a sister's letter ahead of hers in the *Missionary Review*),[71] she would tolerate no opposition to her wishes. Other sisters resented Mrs. Bromilow's "iron hand covered with a velvet glove."[72] One, Miss Thomas, stayed long enough only to assess the situation, abuse the Bromilows, and catch the next boat back to Australia where she told George Brown that she "objected to the position they occupied."[73] Eleanor Walker, despite her ten years of loyal service, left a diary that was a record of constant conflict with Mrs. Bromilow. Like Julia Benjamin, she was a woman of thirty, and she resented being peremptorily cut off in the middle of a sermon, or scolded for holding a divergent opinion.[74] An orphan craving affection, she was particularly vulnerable to Mrs. Bromilow's harshness. Samuel Fellows, a dispassionate observer, concluded that there was "too much dignity and not enough milk of human kindness" on the Bromilows' part.[75]

The real status of the Methodist sisters, as distinct from the theoretical status outlined by the regulations, was a widespread cause of frustration and resentment among the sisters and perhaps, as Julia Benjamin alleged, a major cause of their premature resignations. It was at least a hidden factor that should be set beside ostensible reasons such as ill health and domestic pressure.

In marked contrast to the Methodist sisters, many of the Sacred Heart sisters served until their missionary career was terminated by death. Of the nineteen who served for ten years or less, fifteen died in service. Excluding all those who died prematurely (arbitrarily designated as under forty-five years), of the remaining forty-six sisters, twenty-nine served for more than twenty years, fifteen of them for over forty years, of whom eight celebrated their Golden Jubilee in the mission (Table 5). The longest serving of all the missionaries to come to Papua before the First World War was Sister Clothilde Caroll, who arrived in 1900 and remained till her death, at the age of ninety, in 1966. The average length of service for the Daughters of Our Lady of the Sacred Heart was 23.9 years, while that of the Missionaries of the Sacred Heart was 17.4 years. The most obvious explanation for these extraordinarily long careers is that they were a life service. Especially in the early days, those who sailed from Marseilles to distant Oceania did not expect to see their homelands again. Father Meyer, MSC, wrote a moving description of one such departure, recalling to a friend:

> You remember that beautiful evening of May 1900, when standing on the platform of the station of Issoudun we witnessed, astonished, the departure of seven Sisters: all were Bretons: around them pressed old women and young girls whose sobs shook their white coifs like sea-gulls wings; it was their mothers and sisters come from Brittany to say good-bye: they, on the contrary, laughed and joyfully promised a meeting in heaven.[76]

It is tempting to ask whether these joyful young sisters became trapped in a commitment of which they could have had little prior understanding, despite their dedicated preparation by Mother Marie Louise. Undoubtedly, the pressure for them to remain at their post was stronger than for the Methodist sisters who had not made the same total commitment. When Sister Claire begged in 1888 to be sent to Sydney after three months' constant illness, Father Couppé, acting head of the mission, advised her that she should "resign herself to staying at Yule."[77] Nevertheless many sisters did leave freely over the years, most of them transferring to other mission fields, the convent at Kensington, or other houses of the congregation.

Letters written by members of the mission and by visitors do not give evidence of disillusionment or depression among the sisters. On the contrary there is continual and ample testimony to their "gaiety." Complaining to Navarre of the low morale of the coadjutor brothers, Father Couppé added, "The Sisters show a good spirit. They suffer more than us but are alway gay, in good humour, and work well with a great spirit of faith."[78] At about the same time Sister Madeline, writing to Mother Marie Louise about the exhaustion of their provisions, reassured her, "despite these trials, do not believe that we are sad. Thank God, fever attacks only the body, the soul is free. If you listen carefully from Issoudun, you will hear us laughing."[79] Father Meyer, visiting the mission in 1902, was relieved to find that "the joy which radiated on their faces at their departure from France is not veiled in a cloud of sadness; the disillusionment which we suspected has not come."[80]

The Daughters of Our Lady of the Sacred Heart found strength and security not only in their faith, but in their total commitment to the congregation. "All the earth being the Lord's, I am everywhere at ease," wrote one in 1887, "I have in my Superior a mother, and in my companions, sisters. My rule guides me. Our fathers sustain me. . . . Who could be happier than a Daughter of Our Lady of the Sacred Heart?"[81]

For a time their identity was threatened by interference from some of the younger priests who, in their immature zeal, exceeded their authority in relation to the sisters. "The poor sisters, above all, Sister Joachim, have suffered too much from this régime," wrote Navarre, implying that Sister Joachim's death was at least partly the result of the impossible demands placed on her by the authoritarian young Father Vitale.[82] To put an end to the constant conflict, Navarre resolved in 1899 to sever the close working relationship that since the beginning had existed between the priests and the sisters, and to make a "complete separation according to canonical law."[83] Henceforth the sisters were to have the status of religious in a French parish, responsible to their own Superior, and through her to the vicar apostolic. They were to live farther away from the priests and to order their own economy. They were not to be held responsible for the daily care of the priests though they could, and did, continue voluntarily to cook and launder for them.[84] Such service was not incompatible with the sisters' view of their own status and role in the mission field.

Other stresses occurred as in any community. Sometimes there was conflict among the women themselves. Mother Paul had herself removed to a mainland station after conflict with Mother Liguori.[85] But the organization of the SHM seems to have been flexible enough to contain these stresses and strains. Perhaps their total commitment gave the sisters a freedom which transcended the privations and irritations that were a necessary part of everyday mission life, and which their Protestant colleagues, for whom every day in the mission was effectively a new decision, did not have. "To live away from the mission is to live like a fish out of water," observed Sister Madeline, sympathizing with Sister Agnès, who had been exiled through illness.[86]

The Anglician Mission was distinguished by both the very long and the very short careers of its staff, male and female. Several of the women were outstanding for their length of service. Mrs. Tomlinson, who had arrived with Maclaren's pioneering party in 1891, died at Mukawa after forty-eight years in the country; Alice Cottingham, Maud Nowland, and Laura Oliver died in the mission after thirty-seven, thirty-three, and twenty-five years respectively. But the Anglican Mission, like the Methodist Mission, was also dogged by the problem of women missionaries who came and stayed scarcely long enough to justify the expense of their fare. Six of the twenty-eight served less than the required three years, and another six just saw three years' service. Bishop Stone-Wigg felt something of the same despondency about his women workers as did George Brown. He wrote of "the risk of friends dragging them away, of their getting engaged to be married, of their lack of vocation to a life-long work" and contemplated, as had his predecessor, Maclaren, the possibility of introducing an Anglican sisterhood to the mission.[87]

The reasons given for the resignations of the Anglican women missionaries were similar to those of the Methodists. Six left because of ill-health, two to marry outside the mission, four because, having married male colleagues, their departure was determined by their husbands' careers, and two left for family reasons. As in the Methodist Mission, resignations for ill health or for family reasons were sometimes pretexts masking more basic causes. Dr. Corlette wrote to Stone-Wigg of the "nervous troubles that have disabled so many of the Mission ladies."[88] Florence Thomson left the mission fearing that she was "going out of her mind";[89] Ellen Combley withdrew from her exhausting work on the Mamba goldfield with hysterical paralysis,[90] and Harriette Murray, after living alone for some years at Wamira, was reduced to a nervous condition in which she "could not stand the sight of a Wamira man."[91] All three left the mission but subsequently, their health restored, begged to be taken back. "All I desire is to return to live and if it please God, to die in his service there," Florence Thomson pleaded with Stone-Wigg.[92] Harriette Murray and Ellen Combley returned, but Florence Thomson remained in Sydney, to die two years later.

Debilitated by malaria, overworked, and poorly nourished, the women, as in any community, experienced conflict with each other. The resident magistrate, C. A. W. Monckton, recollected analyzing Stone-

Wigg's problems for him, "Your second worry is that you have half a dozen or more spinster ladies, . . . and in their spare time they quarrel like hell among themselves and keep on appealing to you to settle their differences, which you find an impossible thing to do."[93] The fact that the bishop was a handsome and extremely eligible bachelor may have aggravated the tension.[94]

As in the other missions, threats to their status and identity added to the stresses experienced by the women. These, as in the SHM, came especially from the young celibate men. Eric Giblin, dismissing the women missionaries as "a necessary source of trouble,"[95] proposed that the mission be staffed by a brotherhood.[96] Copland King complained of the behavior of another young bachelor who did not "understand how to allow the ladies to have due authority over the girls. . . . He interfered unnecessarily. . . . The ladies had also to submit to . . . personal rudeness."[97] Other male missionaries simply refused to cooperate with the women. Lacking Archbishop Navarre's option of making a total separation between the status and roles of men and those of women, the bishop could only mediate in each case.

Although Stone-Wigg was particularly aware of the failures among the women workers, their pattern of service reflected that of the mission as a whole. Of the total Anglican personnel, one-third (twenty-four) failed to complete the required three years. And the male missionaries were worse offenders than the female: 39 percent of Anglican males, against 32.5 percent of Anglican females, left without completing the minimum three years of service. The average length of service for Anglican males was nine years; for women it was eleven.

Besides the normal stresses of missionary service, the women missionaries had to contend with pressures to which their male colleagues were immune. They had no share in the exalted status that was accorded male missionaries by admiring contemporaries in the last quarter of the nineteenth century, and to a lesser extent, up to the Great War. Their work received less recognition, both from colleagues and from the world at large. Although most acquiesced in the designated role of auxiliary, it was bound to create tensions, especially when threatened by the expectations of superiors or colleagues. The Daughters of Our Lady of the Sacred Heart, with their clearly defined identity and mutually supportive community, probably suffered least from such threats, especially after Archbishop Navarre acted to reduce their occurrence. The LMS and Methodist wives, though lacking formal missionary status, had the clearly defined and publicly recognized role of missionary wife to provide a context for their activity. But both the Methodist sisters and the Anglican women were very vulnerable to encroachments on their more tenuous status and less clearly defined role.

Nevertheless, despite the convictions of male contemporaries, the length of service of the women missionaries was comparable to that of the men. Methodist women gave slightly shorter, Anglican women slightly longer periods of service, while the sisters of the SHM outdistanced all other missionaries in the field, including even their own long-serving male colleagues. In each mission there was a dedicated body of women who served quietly, and for the most part unspectacularly, in careers that spanned several decades. In 1913, after thirty-two years of service, Fanny Lawes, the first white woman to settle in Papua, was still mothering lonely young missionaries as they passed through Sydney and visited her in her one-room lodgings crammed with Papuan mementoes. On the north coast of Papua, Elizabeth Tomlinson outlived her husband by two years, to die in 1939, the longest-serving Anglican missionary. At the Methodist Mission, Lily Bromilow and Norah Gilmour served beside their chairman husbands for twenty-one and thirty-two years respectively, and no one doubted the influence of those two formidable women. At Yule Island a growing number of sisters, having spent their whole working lives in Papua, retired to await death and burial in the mission graveyard. Sister Madeline, one of the first group to arrive, in 1887, remained at Yule Island till she died, frail and blind, in 1927; Sister Marthe, another pioneer, died in 1931 after forty-four years' service; and Sister Claire, whose life was feared for in 1888, died in 1930, aged seventy-three years. The "gracious influence of wise and thoughtful womanhood" had proved more durable and more pervasive than many contemporaries would have dared to hope.

CHAPTER 8

"Brothers in the Faith"

ALL THE MISSIONARIES who worked in Papua before the First World War were members of one of four missions, each of which was in turn associated with a larger organization—a society or church. There were fundamental differences in the nature of the metropolitan organizations, the type of relationships that existed between home and field, and the internal structures of the missions themselves. The life and work of the missionaries must be seen within the context of the organizations to which they belonged, for their successes and failures depended not only on their own individual strengths and weaknesses, but equally on the distinctive structures that supported them, constrained them, and to some extent molded them.[1]

The London Missionary Society

The London Missionary Society, the first to commence work on the mainland of New Guinea, was also the oldest of the missionary organizations to work there. Established in 1795 with the "sole object [of] spreading the knowledge of Christ among heathen and unenlightened nations," its "fundamental principle" asserted its nondenominational character.[2] Although the fundamental principle continued to be upheld, by the time the LMS reached New Guinea the predominant influence within it was Congregationalism, with its individualistic conception of Christianity and emphasis on local autonomy.

By the 1870s, when LMS missionaries reached New Guinea on the last wave of their great westward expansion through the Pacific, the Society was an experienced and successful missionary organization. Free of institutional links with any church, it was controlled by a board of up to three hundred directors chosen from its membership (subscribers of one guinea or more, or representatives of congregations donating

£5 or more). Clerical and lay representation was kept in balance, and women could and did become directors. Besides controlling the finances of the Society, the directors were empowered to "select and manage Mission Stations, to appoint and send forth and fittingly sustain Missionaries, . . . to make, alter and amend by-laws for the general conduct of business, and otherwise to carry out . . . the object of the Society."[3]

The chief link between the missionaries in the field and the directors to whom they were responsible was the Society's foreign secretary, who had charge of "all matters connnected with the Society's mission in foreign countries and the same matters requiring attention at home." The missionaries who came to New Guinea before 1914 were fortunate that, for most, their ministry coincided with the term of office of the most enlightened of the Society's foreign secretaries, Ralph Wardlaw Thompson. For their first five years in the field, the New Guinea pioneers were subject to the domineering administration of Thompson's predecessor, Joseph Mullens, who had responded to the rapid growth and diversification of the mission fields by imposing autocratic control and rigid organization. Thompson, described by contemporaries as a man of spirituality, sympathy, and statesmanlike vision, ushered in a new era with his appointment in 1880, following Mullens' death.[4]

Resolving to be the friend and champion of missionaries in the field, he wrote them frequent letters that were, in Will Saville's words, "full of inspiration and help and personal interest."[5] With great empathy and tact, he sympathized with their frustrations and loneliness, encouraged their efforts, praised their achievements, and, when necessary, rebuked their waywardness. "The lapse of years has never turned you into a purely official leader," wrote the missionaries from Papua upon his retirement, "and we have found pleasure and strength in the personal and friendly . . . relations which have existed between us."[6] A closer link was established through deputations. Thompson visited New Guinea in 1897, and his successor, Frank Lenwood, in 1916.

Thompson, while still asserting the directors' control over the general lines of development within the LMS, gave increased freedom of action in the field, to be exercised through its chief executive authority, the district committee. Composed of all the missionaries, it had "joint charge and control over the whole range of labours carried on by its individual members."[7] Each missionary was responsible to the whole committee, which was expected to meet annually for business and devotions. Finances were controlled by the district committee, which provided the directors annually with an estimate of probable income and expenditure for each station and received in return a warrant authorizing the outlay.

Contact between the board and the field was maintained through the foreign secretary, and through the annual reports and letters that missionaries were required to send. The board urged them in their letters to detail "their personal and family experience, the progress of their labours and the difficulties which they meet [since] all things which affect the happiness and usefulness of the missionaries are to the Directors matters of interest."[8] In their reports they were to be "honest and candid," not exaggerating the good or concealing the bad. Closer periodic contact was ensured through a system of regular furloughs, which also enabled the directors to put the missionary before the wider constituency and the general public through an energetic program of deputation work.

The advantages of the organization of the LMS to the missionaries are apparent. They had behind them the support of a large and powerful mission society, along with almost unfettered freedom in the field. They had the foreign secretary as champion and counselor and their colleagues in the district committee for consultation and support.

At the same time, however, some of the greatest tensions, conflicts, and failures were caused or exacerbated by defects in the structure and organization. Relationships between the missionaries and the board were frequently clouded by misunderstandings, sometimes unavoidable because of the vast distances that separated them and the consequent delays in communication. Despite the great measure of autonomy accorded the district committee, the directors retained some powers that provoked conflict. One was their right to send missionaries "ticketed and labelled" to a specific part of the field.[9] Missionaries believed that the directors in London, ignorant of the nature of the field and the sometimes rapid changes in needs and personnel, were incapable of such decisions. "You can't know the South Cape from the South Pole," Lawes rebuked Thompson.[10] Finances were often a source of conflict, missionaries in New Guinea believing that the directors refused to recognize the peculiar nature of their field with its heavy reliance on imported goods, and the directors for their part finding the missionaries careless and cavalier in their production of estimates.[11] The serious financial crisis experienced by the Society in the eighties and most of the nineties aggravated this tension.

Occasionally the missionaries felt themselves misjudged by the board. Dependent on the reports they received from the field, the directors at times put too much faith in those who presented a glowing picture, while censuring those who attempted a more sober estimate. The first decade of the mission's existence was dogged by a misconception of this kind as the directors were taken in by the rosy reports written by Samuel McFarlane of his work in the "Western Branch" of the mission from his base in Torres Strait; with these, he, and the directors, unfavorably compared Chalmers' and Lawes' work in the east.[12] They were disconcerted to find after McFarlane's retirement from the mission in 1886 that the Western Branch was in "total collapse," while the Eastern Branch, about which Lawes and Chalmers had written more judiciously, was well established.[13] The same misunderstanding blighted the board's relationship with McFarlane's successor in the west, Edwin Savage, ultimately resulting in his resignation.[14] A young and inexperienced missionary, he failed to cope with the chaos that was McFarlane's legacy and was censured by the directors for his failure. When an officious young missionary, Archibald Hunt, joined him in the west and reported adversely on Savage, the directors accepted Hunt's assessment unquestioningly. Stung by their criticisms, Savage resigned. "If I had written . . . glowing reports you would have thought better of me," he remarked.[15] With his departure, Harry Dauncey told Thompson, the mission lost "a thoroughly good man."[16]

Aware of the ambiguities and the possibilities for deception in report writing, many missionaries shared Dauncey's "rooted objection" to it.[17] Commencing his report from Moru in 1898, Holmes asked, "Shall I simply give statistics of Church and school work? or on the other hand: Shall I speak out forcibly . . . suppress nothing?"[18] Holmes decided on the latter course, but among the missionaries were others who, like McFarlane, were known to put on "rose-coloured glasses" when assessing their work for the directors.[19] It was a problem common to all fields. Lawes was sickened by the stale triumphalism of mission reports: "Thirty years ago we were told that Hindooism was shaking to its foundations. I see it is reported to be shaking still. But would it not have fallen long ago if the Church, instead of shouting victory, had marshalled her strength for the siege?"[20]

A further source of tension between the board and the missionaries in New Guinea derived from furlough and deputation work. The missionaries argued that the trying climate, the prevalence of malaria, and their frequent enforced separation from their families necessitated furloughs more often than every ten, later eight, years as was customary.[21] They resented too that such furloughs as they had were largely committed to deputation work. "Rest is not for a missionary at home," complained Holmes from Exeter. "I seem to have had no time for myself . . . but just had to run about all over England and God knows where it will be next."[22] Some made fine platform speakers, but many shared Chalmers' distaste for the "grand speeches, lying reports and salted statistics" that the work demanded.[23] "Hearing myself talk was simply rushing me into a lunatic asylum," he complained.[24] For a missionary's wife, alone in rented lodging in a country where she was no longer at home, the prospect was little more inviting, as Lawes pointed out to the board.

Thompson was able to smooth over many of the tensions between the board and the missionaries, but his ability to do so depended on his exceptional personal skills. The brusque manner of his predecessor, Mullens, and the more forbidding personality of his successsor, Frank Lenwood,[25] at times further alienated the missionaries from the home base. "The new Foreign Secretary . . . is a man out of sympathetic touch altogether with the methods which have produced the finest results in Papua," wrote Will Saville after Lenwood's 1916 deputation.[26]

The problems provoked by misunderstandings and conflicts between home and field were nothing compared to the deficiencies of the Society's organization in the field. All missionaries of the LMS were appointed on a basis of absolute equality.[27] There were obvious virtues in such an arrangement, but the mission suffered from a lack of leadership. There was no one with pastoral responsibility for young and inexperienced missionaries, no one to arbitrate and conciliate in disputes, and no one to encourage cooperation among the collection of headstrong individuals who made up the mission's staff. Holmes, at his lonely and difficult station in the Gulf, complained to Thompson of the "isolation and lack of sympathy" from his colleagues, while at Port Moresby, where Dauncey struggled alone to cope with the head station of the mission, MacGregor noted a "complete breakdown of discipline."[28] Observing the difficulties of South Sea Island missionaries at the East End, MacGregor reported, "The truth is that their organization is defective. There is a great want of proper supervision and inspection."[29]

Personal antipathies, exacerbated by proximity, isolation, and the strains imposed by heat and malaria, might have been defused by the intervention of a wise counselor and confessor. When the partnership in the west between Hunt and Savage drifted from mistrust into hostility, the situation could have been redeemed by judicious arbitration. It was "six of one and half a dozen of another," Lawes reported.[30] In fact Lawes, the recognized "patriarch" of the mission, did assume an achieved leadership role, as did the veteran missionary William Lawrence after him, but their leadership carried no authority except that derived from their own personalities. "In a young church like this . . . a Bishop is needed," wrote Schlencker from Orokolo in 1915. "In fact taking our Mission as a whole in Papua there seems a sad lack in the fact that we have no head."[31]

Jealous of their own autonomy and equality, missionaries looked askance at any suggested cooperation that seemed to threaten them. The refusal of Chalmers, Lawes, and William Turner to cooperate with

McFarlane was based partly on his assumption of the role of senior partner. "The MacFarlanes are simply unbearable," wrote the outspoken
Fanny Lawes. "Mcfarlane assumes a most over-bearing manner and
treates George and Dr Turner as if they were his inferiors and subordinates."[32] Much of Savage's distrust of Hunt sprang from his suspicion
that Hunt had come to "lord it over" him.[33] At times assertions of independence were allied to sensitivity about social status. Looking around
the 1915 district meeting at his lower middle-class colleagues who
opposed his industrial schemes, Abel, the ex-trader, burst out, "Our
Society has no use for a man of my class. It's because I've been of a different class."[34]

A serious failure in cooperation was the establishment of the Vatorata
Training College for the preparation of teachers and pastors, which
foundered and was almost wrecked on the individualism of the missionaries.[35] Some felt genuine misgivings about Lawes' insistence that it
should educate in Motu, spoken along only a fraction of the Papuan
coastline, but their reluctance to support it was closely tied to their wish
to train their own pastors and retain them exclusively for the use of their
own district. Although the college was established in 1894, it was crip-
pled by only token support from some of the missionaries up to the First
World War. Reporting on its problems in 1915, Robert Lister Turner,
Lawes' successor as principal, observed that "an individualistic spirit
. . . has been, and still is, the bane of our mission in Papua."[36]

Many of these problems could have been overcome had the district
committee fulfilled the role ascribed to it by the Society. But in Papua
the district committee was ineffectual. For the first decade, Chalmers
and Lawes believed that the differences between themselves and
McFarlane—evangelizing from among the people rather than from a
"city of refuge" in the Torres Strait, using tobacco as currency, and, in
Chalmers' case, consuming alcohol—were so great that a district committee was "useless"; it scarcely ever met, despite constant rebukes from
Thompson.[37] He warned Lawes in 1886:

> The fact is our present method of working our Missions depends for its con-
> tinuance upon the fidelity with which the Missionaries carry out such
> arrangements as this. . . . The Board are very unwilling to attempt any
> individual control of the Missions direct from England such as is exercised
> by other Societies. . . . If however the rules of the Society relating to
> meetings of District Com^ees are disregarded by the missionaries, it will be
> necessary for the Board to make some fresh arrangements.[38]

Despite his admonishments, meetings, though held only once a year,
continued to be poorly attended. Some missionaries—particularly
Charles Abel—were notorious for ignoring them completely. "We are in

danger of falling to pieces for want of cohesion," lamented Lawes in 1892, contrasting their weakness due to an excess of "Independency" with the strength of the Wesleyan mission.[39] Our committee is "little but a farce," reported the secretary in 1911.[40] The following year the missionaries "heartily and willingly" resolved to "submit to the ruling of the Committee with reference to its control over the whole range of labours carried on by its individual members,"[41] but for all that the mission remained essentially a "chain of isolated almost independent units."[42]

Because the district committee failed to provide "that measure of mutual supervision and control" for which it was intended, missionaries had almost absolute power in their own districts. The most notable case was that of Charles Abel, who infringed regulations, ignored requests, and made special demands on the Society in his energetic and ambitious attempt to build up his industrial mission at Kwato and on nearby plantations. " 'The New Guinea and Kwato Mission' would be a good new title," commented Lawes bitterly in 1903, foreshadowing by fifteen years the rupture between the two.[43] Although Abel's theocracy was an extreme, there were elements of the same situation in all the other mission districts, where the missionaries were rulers not only over their Papuan flocks but also over the South Sea Islanders under their supervision. Their personal relationships with the Polynesian pastors varied in the same ways as those they established with Papuans, yet their official relationship to the pastors was inevitably authoritarian and their power absolute. Asked by the board in 1915 to define their status in their district, most compared it to that of a bishop. It is "like episcopal government," Clark explained. "All power is vested in the missionary."[44]

The Methodist Mission

The LMS was the only mission in Papua organized through a missionary society independent of any church. Nearest to it in structure was the Methodist Mission which was also administered by a society, the Australasian Wesleyan Methodist Missionary Society, which, following the independence of the Australasian Conference of the Wesleyan Methodist Church from the British church, was established as the organizing body of the missions for which the new church took responsibility. "The object of the Society is to excite and combine the exertions of the Methodist Churches and Congregations . . . in the support and enlargement of that branch of the Foreign Missions . . . which is now carried on under the direction of the General Conference of the Methodist Church of Australasia."[45] New Guinea was added to the existing fields—Fiji (1835), Samoa (1835), and New Britain (1875)—in response to a request from Sir William MacGregor. Seeking some special way of commemo-rating the centenary of Wesley's death, Australian Wesleyans saw the call to this difficult and relatively untouched field as the call of God.[46]

Unlike the LMS, the AWMMS was integrally tied to its parent church, the Wesleyan Methodist Church of Australasia (after union in 1902, the Australasian Methodist Church). Its mission board was made up of the president and secretary of the General Conference of the Aus-tralian church, to which it was responsible; the president and secretary of the New South Wales Conference (under whose supervision it remained in the intervals between General Conferences); and repre-sentatives from the other conferences of Australia and New Zealand, and from the mission districts.[47]

The main contact of the Methodist missionaries in the field with the home administration, like that of their LMS counterparts, was through the secretary of the board. And like the LMS missionaries, they were fortunate in the man who filled the role of general secretary for most of the period before the First World War—former missionary George Brown. Brown was for the Methodist missionaries, as Thompson was for those of the LMS, a father, a counselor, and often a friend who spoke to them as "the old Missionary who had known the joys and sorrows of Missionary life."[48] His successor, Benjamin Danks, appointed in 1907, was more official and formal in his relations with the missionaries. Andrew Ballantyne wrote in 1910 to tell him of the "feeling of a lack of sympathy on the part of the Mission Office" among the missionaries in the New Guinea field. "There has been a feeling of separateness which has been fatal to any attempt at unity. If the Field and Office are one then you will be greatly helped."[49]

In other ways too, the contact between the Methodist missionaries and the home administration was similar to that of their LMS counter-parts. They received the district's annual financial grant from the AWMMS; they sent home, as requested, "copious extracts"[50] from the journals they were required to keep, some of which were edited and published in the monthly *Australasian Methodist Missionary Review*, just as the letters and reports of the LMS missionaries appeared, edited, in the *Chronicle*. Like their LMS colleagues, they argued the "pecu-liarly trying nature of the New Guinea climate" to persuade the board to reduce the period between furloughs from ten to six, and finally, three years.[51] As in the LMS, much of furlough was taken up with depu-tation work, "doing the dancing bear business" in George Brown's elo-quent phrase.[52] Throughout their missionary service they were subject to the agreement that each of them signed with the AWMMS and to its "Instructions to Missionaries."[53]

The great difference between the LMS and the Methodist Mission, as

Lawes was aware, was their government in the field. The Wesleyans imported into New Guinea, as into their other fields, the whole complex, hierarchical organization that characterized Wesleyan Methodism. Accordingly, New Guinea was administered as one district of the Methodist Church, over which presided a chairman. His position was analogous to that of a bishop, although his authority was more limited, being subject to the sanction of the synod, the annual meeting of the mission district.[54] Within the New Guinea district five circuits were established, each in the charge of a superintendent. The circuit was composed of a series of churches, mostly run by South Sea Island teachers, within which operated the traditional local organization of society meetings, class meetings, prayer meetings, and services.

In marked contrast to the almost anarchic individualism of the LMS was the tightly controlled, unified, and cohesive polity of Methodism. The Wesleyans entered New Guinea as an invading army, a disciplined, united cadre of Christianity. That they saw themselves in this light is apparent in their rhetoric, which rings with battle imagery. Their impressive initial landing was "an attack in force"; extensions into heathen villages were incursions into "the enemy's camp."[55] Reports sent home to be published in the *Missionary Review* were headed "News from the Front," while a missionary on deputation could delight his listeners with firsthand news "from the seat of war."[56] This self-confident, aggressive onslaught won the admiration of Sir Willam MacGregor.

Methodist missionaries derived comfort, support, and inspiration from the mission's structure. But, like the very different organization of the LMS, it was at times a source of conflict. Its greatest inherent danger was the temptation of those at the head of district and circuits to arrogate powers not legally theirs. In the circuits, where even the chairman was not permitted to intervene except through persuasion, a superintendent could assume almost unbridled power. "You will do well to give Mr Fellows a little good advice," George Brown told Bromilow. "I am afraid he is in danger of being too overbearing with the natives. . . . He is a very energetic man and certainly magnifies his office."[57] As in the LMS, authoritarian control was exerted not only over the Papuans of the circuit but also over its South Sea Island teachers. "Right royal devotion do we get from most of the teachers," reported the missionary at Bunama, James Osborne. "The travels of a white missionary here are like the visitations of a colonial governor, so enthusiastically is he received."[58]

But while the superintendent ruled supreme within his circuit, the position of chairman was potentially the most powerful in the district. William Bromilow was a strong and authoritarian chairman in the New Guinea district, as were his contemporaries Langham in Fiji and Goldie in the Solomon Islands. "Bromilow seems to be autocratic and to be doing things of all kinds without consulting his colleagues," observed MacGregor.[59] Those who suffered most from Bromilow's regime were members of the two new orders introduced through New Guinea into the missionary structure of Australasian Methodism—the missionary sisters and the lay missionaries. Although accorded full missionary status after the customary year's probation, they found themselves in fact forced to occupy an inferior position in the hierarchy of the mission. This led to the resignation of the first lay missionary, George Bardsley, and of several of the missionary sisters, whose status was probably further diminished by virtue of their being women.[60]

Among the Papuans, Bromilow's authority was absolute (Figure 21). "Who rules over us?" he interrogated a class of children at Dobu. "You," they replied in unison.[61] The effect on them of the concentration of power in Bromilow's hands was apparent after his retirement in 1908. "Very deeply do we feel the loss of Mr and Mrs Bromilow," wrote his successor, Matthew Gilmour, likening their departure to "the taking away of training poles from young plants."[62] Their departure coincided with a time of crisis in Australian Methodism. The generous contributions inspired by the Wesleyan Centenary Fund, which had launched the mission, had not been maintained, and by 1909 the Society had a deficit of £10,000. In 1914 the allocation for Papua was reduced by more than a thousand pounds to £7,640 instead of being increased by two thousand pounds as had been anticipated.[63] At the same time, the supply of teachers was diminishing rapidly, and it was becoming apparent that the policy of employing a small white staff augmented by a large support staff of South Sea Islanders was inoperable.[64] By 1914 there were few echoes of the brash and energetic self-confidence that had characterized the Methodists who first invaded New Guinea.

The Anglican Mission

Addressing the annual anniversary conference of the Anglican Mission in 1902, Henry Newton told his colleagues that "it is almost impossible to get the official mind and that of the public to realise that we Anglicans are not members of a Mission Society, but are an integral part, one diocese, of the Anglican Church," whose task happened to be preaching the gospel to the heathen. "There is no Anglican mission society and there never has been one in New Guinea," he added.[65]

The Anglican Mission in New Guinea had its origins in the catholic conviction that mission work was the duty "not of societies within the Church, but of the Church itself—of the Church as a whole."[66] This belief had inspired the Anglican bishops of Australia and New Zealand

Figure 21. Mr. and Mrs. Bromilow with Papuan converts. (Uniting Church)

to establish in 1850 the Australasian Board of Missions as the sole missionary agency of the colonial church. Its object was "the Propagation of the Gospel among the heathen races in the provinces of Australasia, New Caledonia, the Loyalty Islands, New Hanover, New Ireland and the other islands in the Western Pacific" among which, by implication, was New Guinea.[67] But it was not until 1891 that its successor, the Australian Board of Missions (ABM), established in 1872 by the newly constituted General Synod of the Dioceses in Australia and Tasmania and consisting of "the Bishops forming the House of Bishops in the General Synod," launched the Anglican Mission to New Guinea. First constituted as a missionary diocese, after 1904 it was attached to the newly reorganized Queensland province of the Anglican Church.

Although the first leader of the mission, Albert Maclaren, was only a priest, the majority of the prelates who constituted the ABM held a strong conviction that "a Bishop is the Church's natural leader of a great missionary enterprise."[68] However, their attempts to establish a bishopric were for a time thwarted by the primate, Archbishop Saumarez Smith, president of the ABM, who, in the words of Bishop Webber of Brisbane, was "dead against the whole thing."[69] A rigid Evangelical, he opposed the High Church enthusiasm for an episcopal mission as unbiblical and sought to resist the increase of Tractarianism that a missionary bishopric would encourage. But despite his opposition, the movement for the establishment of a see in New Guinea gathered momentum, encouraged by receipt of a dispatch from Sir William MacGregor that stressed the "imperative urgency for the sending as soon as possible of a strong Bishop to take charge of the Mission," while paying tribute to Copland King's "gallant struggle" to maintain it after Maclaren's death.[70] Two courses were open to them, Bishop Webber told the bishops of Australia and Tasmania. Either they must advise MacGregor that they were "too impotent a body to be entrusted with a work requiring so much missionary zeal," or they must appoint "the Church's natural leader—a bishop" as head of the mission.[71] In October 1896 he reported triumphantly the resolution of the Australian Church to appoint "forthwith" a bishop to New Guinea—despite "the wet blanket with which our well-meaning but disastrous Primate has endeavoured to smother the movement."[72] At the same time he put forward his own candidate, Montagu John Stone-Wigg, canon of the Brisbane cathedral, to the vicar of Windsor, who had been entrusted with the selection, in consultation with the archbishop of Canterbury.

After Stone-Wigg's consecration in 1898, the nature of the Anglican Mission changed. Not only did the establishment of the see give spiritual and psychological encouragement to the handful of missionaries who had struggled to keep the mission alive, but in Stone-Wigg they found a leader who assumed almost total control of the mission. The ABM had never emulated the Protestant mission societies in their fund-raising and supportive role, and in the months before his departure for New Guinea Maclaren had exhausted himself traveling the Australian colonies in search of money and men.[73] But after Stone-Wigg was consecrated, the ABM formally transferred to him the whole responsibility for raising funds, recruiting staff, and even finding his own stipend. A group of businessmen promised him an annual grant of £450 for five years, but he never drew on it, living and to some extent financing the mission from his own private means. Before taking up his appointment, Stone-Wigg spent eight months touring Australia, lecturing and fund-raising, and reduced the diocesan debt of £1400 by £600.[74]

With episcopal authority, complete organizational and financial control, and the self-confidence inherent in his gentleman's birth and education, Stone-Wigg became the pivot of the Anglican Mission. Like the bishops of the Universities Mission to Central Africa, which provided a model for the New Guinea mission, he was supreme in his diocese.[75] All but one of the missionaries who came to New Guinea during his episcopacy were recruited by him personally, and all signed a paper of conditions that declared them to be "in the service of the Right Reverend the Lord Bishop of New Guinea."[76] Many felt strongly that their allegiance was to him. "It has been my affection and admiration for yourself more than the work which has kept me," confessed a turbulent young layman, Robert Dakers, as he contemplated resignation.[77]

A staunch Anglo-Catholic with a high conception of the spiritual and pastoral role of the bishop as father-in-God, Stone-Wigg kept a close personal watch over his staff, visiting all his diocese once every three months. "The Bishop, who is the centre of unity, should also act as the cement which makes the unity of the Staff a real thing," he believed.[78] His wistful attachment to the ideal of community was frustrated by the sprawling nature of his diocese, but he nevertheless strove to inculcate in his staff the spiritual discipline and order characteristic of a community. "I think they regard me as very exacting, but they very loyally carry out what I put before them," he wrote.[79] By the end of his episcopacy, he could report, "We seem to have got rid of, or absorbed, our undisciplined elements and to have such a loyal set of workers."[80] Criticized by some for his failure to make allowances for frailer mortals,[81] Stone-Wigg always demanded more of himself than of his staff. Copland King, a man of very different theological outlook and temperament, wrote to him, "I can only repeat what we have all said before, that your example has been the greatest help to us in our efforts to live the life of self-denial and devotion."[82]

Despite his intense pastoral concern, much of Stone-Wigg's episcopacy was necessarily spent in the organizational tasks of recruiting and fund-raising. By 1908, when he was forced to retire through ill health, the see was endowed, a fund for clergy established, and one for lay-workers' pensions begun.[83] After an interregnum of two years, when the see was administered by Archbishop Donaldson, the metropolitan of Queensland, Gerald Sharp was consecrated as the second bishop of New Guinea in 1910. His relationship to the see was different from that of Stone-Wigg. Although his episcopal authority was completely sup-ported by his predominantly Anglo-Catholic staff, Sharp was an unas-suming man who encouraged a more participatory form of government than was characteristic of either his predecessor or his successor, Bishop Henry Newton. The ABM had taken over the finances of the mission after Stone-Wigg's retirement, leaving Sharp free of that area of respon-sibility and control and permitting him to devote more time to his pasto-ral role.

Henry Newton pointed out to the Anglican staff the advantages of mis-sion being the responsibility of the whole church. "It means that we do not represent—and therefore, are not hindered by the opinions of a sec-tor, no matter how worthy. . . . We are catholic, not sectional."[84] This meant that the mission could look to the whole Anglican church in Aus-tralia for support and for recruits. To a large extent, it was successful in encompassing both Evangelicals and Anglo-Catholics, it being the boast of the ABM that "no man had been refused work on party grounds."[85]

The Anglican Mission's freedom from the control of an established society enabled it to enter New Guinea with fewer preconceptions about the nature of mission work than the Protestant societies. Both the LMS and the Methodist missionaries came to New Guinea influenced by the heritage of their societies' work in other parts of the Pacific. Among the veterans who had themselves served in other Pacific fields—Lawes, McFarlane, Chalmers, Pearse, and Bromilow—as well as among those in the home administration, this encouraged some rigidity of outlook and a failure to see the peculiar characteristics of the New Guinea field. The Anglican Mission, on the other hand, was cheerfully pragmatic:

> It is doubtful whether the Anglican Mission to New Guinea had any defi-nite theory as to how mission-work should be carried on. . . . We have been content to do just what seemed the obvious duty, clinging to certain Catholic principles of truth and order. . . . The absence of any theory lays us open to the charge of being rather hugger-mugger in our work, but at least it means we were open to conviction as to what was best to be done.[86]

This advantage was offset to some extent by the lack of experience of the Anglican missionaries compared with the Protestants.

There were some disadvantages in the Anglican Mission's attachment to the church rather than a society. A mission of the whole church was free of the taint of sectarianism, but it inherited the tensions and conflicts of that church. Although Anglo-Catholic and Evangelical Anglicans generally worked harmoniously in the field, the mission was handicapped—at times paralyzed—by the division within the church that nominally supported it. Albert Maclaren, seeking support for the proposed mission, was so "worried and anxious" about his reception in New South Wales that he contemplated resignation.[87] The delay over the appointment of his successor and the establishment of the see was prompted by the same conflict, and even when the bishops were seeking a replacement for Stone-Wigg, they were constrained by the same considerations. "He must be a High Churchman but not a ritualist. He must remember what New South Wales and Sydney are and he ought to get more aid there than in the past."[88] The Australian Church wanted "a less extreme man than Stone-Wigg," Montgomery advised the Archbishop of Canterbury, to whom they had entrusted the selection in their effort to secure an "unexceptionable appointment."[89] In more minor ways, too, the mission was irritated by the "carping criticism" of the Low Church Anglicans of the Sydney diocese, who objected to the use of the term "altar" in the mission, attacked the appointment of a Tractarian bishop, and implied a lack of spirituality in Stone-Wigg's report of the mission's activities.[90] Ironically, the mission's leading Evangelical, Copland King, leapt to the defense of his bishop.[91]

The absence of an administrative machine to mobilize a church that was not only divided, but also largely apathetic and characterized by diocesanism, meant that an enormous burden was placed on Bishop Stone-Wigg. The task of persuading bishops to release clergy from their own dioceses and of encouraging the laity to support a mission that was competing for funds with the better-known Melanesian Mission[92] was an onerous one for a man in indifferent health. Bishop Montgomery recalled that at the 1901 general synod, Stone-Wigg's "spare and wasted frame was one of the most notable memories for Churchmen."[93] After his trying fund-raising campaign in England, Stone-Wigg complained to his staff:

> It is an experience that a Missionary Bishop may well be spared. . . . He has to beat up relatives, hunt up school and college friends, make personal calls . . . on leading incumbents and use every device possible to . . . make known the needs of his Diocese. . . . Should it be left to the personal influence or the importunity of the individual Bishop to rescue an unendowed see from extinction? Is not the whole Church committed to its preservation?[94]

Stone-Wigg's unease was increased by the knowledge that such activities deprived his staff of "his leadership, his sympathy and his presence."[95] The effects of this were particularly acute because of the concentration of authority in Stone-Wigg's hands. "I do so hate going away, for so much seems to go queer in my absence," he wrote.[96] During his periods away from the mission, he was bombarded with letters from his staff, chronicling their problems and lamenting his absence. "I cannot tell you how much we miss you—there is a void . . . which none but yourself can fill," Dakers wrote to him in 1902.[97] Eric Giblin wrote to him in 1906, "I do wish it had not been necessary for you to go; in your absence skeins tangle at once . . ."[98]

The intensely personal style of administration that Stone-Wigg adopted gave the Anglican missionaries leadership and support, the lack of which in their own mission had been regretted by their colleagues in the LMS. Resigning from the mission, the layman Eric Giblin thanked Stone-Wigg for his "kindness and sympathy," for which, during six years of service, he had never "asked in vain."[99] But apart from the problem of dependence that Stone-Wigg's style created, it exposed the mission to the danger of personality conflict. When the impetuous Wilfred Abbot was rebuked by the bishop for overspending, he reacted with personal animosity, flinging at Stone-Wigg as he resigned, "I have quite lost any feeling of respect for you as a man, much less as a Bishop. . . ."[100] Stone-Wigg's strong leadership was probably suited to a mission struggling for survival. Through his "devotion and statesmanship" he raised the New Guinea mission from "insignificance to one of the foremost places in the church," wrote Bishop Montgomery.[101] The more democratic style of leadership his successor introduced in 1912 may have been better suited to a mission that was by then well established. Both would have been better served had they been able to draw more effectively on their constituency, the Anglican Church.

The Sacred Heart Mission

The Missionaires du Sacré-Coeur (MSC) came to New Guinea, like the Anglicans, as a mission of the church rather than of a missionary society. But unlike the Anglicans, who had to rely on desultory and haphazard support from the Church of England, the MSC came as part of the powerful and experienced missionary structure of the Roman Catholic church. Like all its overseas missionary orders and congregations, they came under the direction of the Sacra Congregation de Propaganda Fide (Propaganda), established by Gregory XV in 1622 and directly responsible to the Pope.[102]

In 1881, Father Jules Chevalier, founder and superior general of the

congregation of the MSC, received a letter from Cardinal Simeoni, prefect of Propaganda, written in the name of Leo XIII and drawing his
attention to the Vicariate of Melanesia and Micronesia, established in
1844, and vacant since the withdrawal of the Marists and the Milan
Foreign Mission in the 1850s.[103] Renewal of interest in Melanesia by the
Holy See had been stimulated by the establishment of the Marquis de
Rays' free Catholic colony of Nouvelle France at Port Breton on the
southern tip of New Ireland in 1880. Not knowing what a fiasco that
expedition had become, Simeoni had acquiesced in the Marquis' request
for missionaries, while ensuring that the Vicariate of Melanesia and
Micronesia was not too closely identified with the colony.[104]

Founded at Issoudun in 1854, the congregation of the MSC had been
conceived not for foreign mission work but for the revitalization of the
faith, through dedication to the Sacred Heart of Jesus, in Issoudun and
throughout France. In 1881 it had only sixty members, most of them
exiled by the anticlerical Ferry Laws. Nevertheless Chevalier recognized the aptness of his motto, "May the Sacred Heart of Jesus be everywhere loved," to foreign mission work.[105]

Navarre, who was named superior in the first mission party after the
breakdown in health and morale of its designated leader, Father Durin,
established stations on New Britain and Thursday Island and, in
response to requests from Archbishop Moran of Sydney to Propaganda,
ordered his young priest Henri Verjus to establish a station on New
Guinea.[106] In May 1887, Navarre was named vicar apostolic of Melanesia and administrator of Micronesia (except the Carolines), and titular
bishop of Pentacomia. The following year he was designated titular
archbishop of Cyr, and his vast vicariate apostolic was divided into the
first two of seven ecclesiastical districts of Melanesia and Micronesia—
the vicariates of New Guinea and New Britain. German New Guinea,
which was originally attached to Navarre's vicariate of New Guinea,
was in 1890 transferred to New Britain, leaving Navarre's vicariate
coterminous with the boundaries of British New Guinea. Henri Verjus
was first named vicar apostolic of New Britain but, acquiescing to pressure from the ailing Archbishop Navarre, Propaganda appointed instead Father Louis Couppé, retaining Verjus in New Guinea as Navarre's coadjutor bishop. Following Verjus' death in 1892, ecclesiastical
authority rested with Archbishop Navarre alone until 1900, when Alain
de Boismenu was raised to the episcopacy. As titular bishop of Gabala,
de Boismenu served as coadjutor until Navarre's retirement in 1908,
after which he was named vicar apostolic.

Parallel to the ecclesiastical hierarchy that passed from the Pope
through Propaganda to the vicar apostolic and his coadjutor bishop,
was the hierarchy of the congregation to which all belonged. As reli-

gious who had made the three ordinary vows for perpetuity, they were bound in obedience to their superior general in Europe and to his representative in the field, the religious superior of the mission. Under his jurisdiction were all matters affecting the religious life of both the priests and the brothers of the congregation. Navarre and then Verjus fulfilled this role in the pioneer years of the mission. In 1894, the mission received as superior the scholarly and ascetic Father Jean Genocchi. He was succeeded in 1896 by Father André Jullien who, except during his absences from the mission, served as superior until 1909, when Father Chabot took over from him.

The missionaries of the Sacred Heart in New Guinea gained spiritual and moral support from their direct attachment to the church. The early missionaries were sustained through their many adversities by the knowledge that they were emissaries of the Pope. Receiving the pioneers before their departure from Europe, Leo XIII had blessed their banner saying: "Fear nothing! It is the Church which sends you."[107] During an audience with Bishop Verjus in 1892, he ordered that thirty more missionaries be sent to the mission, which was then struggling for survival.[108] Convulsed by internal dissension at the time, the MSC nevertheless fulfilled his command, sending for the first time scholastics, young men who had completed their novitiate but not their theological studies.[109]

While the Sacred Heart Mission (SHM) could draw strength from the church, it obtained from it only a fraction of the financial aid that the Protestant missionaries drew from their supporting societies. Apart from donations from individual benefactors, small annual allocations from the Society for the Propagation of the Faith and from the Holy Childhood were its only income. In 1887, the mission received twenty thousand francs (£800) from the former and six hundred francs (£240) from the latter. Donations brought their income for the year to the equivalent of £1300 of which £800 was spent on the fares of missionaries to the field.[110] The £500 that remained to feed and clothe the twenty-five missionaries of New Guinea and New Britain was equivalent to the salaries of two Protestant missionaries. Like his Protestant counterparts, Verjus argued the "peculiar difficulties" of New Guinea—the loss in real value of the franc when converted to the English pound, the high cost of provisions (ordinary mass wine £5 per bottle instead of fifty centimes as in France), formidable transport costs, and double customs duties—in appealing for a special allocation.[111] By 1908 their income had increased to F58,000 (£2320),[112] but the mission remained painfully impoverished and, especially when poor transport and communications caused delays in the arrival of funds, embarrassed by debt.

The organizational links between the metropolitan authorities and those in the field were more tenuous than their spiritual links. Poverty, distance, poor transport, and a commitment to life service meant that personal contact with the home administrations was less frequent than for the Protestant missionaries. The vicar apostolic sent annual reports to Propaganda and to his benefactors, the Society for the Propagation of the Faith, and the Holy Childhood, but because these organizations directed or supported all Roman Catholic mission activity, their involvement with any one mission was necessarily perfunctory. Sacred Heart missionaries corresponded with members of their congregation, their letters reaching the wider circle of the archconfraternity through publication in the monthly *Annales de Nôtre-Dame du Sacré-Coeur.*

The organization of the MSC in the field was based on the fundamental principle of the obedience of the religious to their superiors. "A missionary does not calculate. For him the orders of his superiors are divine," wrote Brother Lainé to his supporters in Brittany.[113] Priests and brothers were subject to the vicar apostolic and his coadjutor in ecclesiastical affairs and in the ordering of the mission, and to their superior in all matters affecting their religious life.[114] Although the vicar apostolic was subject to Propaganda and the superior to his superior general, their authority was absolute in the field. Much of the experience of the Sacred Heart missionaries is illuminated by an understanding of the interplay between these roles and the men who filled them.

Two men more different than the first two leaders of the SHM would be difficult to imagine. Navarre was cautious, shrewd, and pragmatic, Verjus impetuous, ardent, and romantic. Verjus chafed at his archbishop's slowness to take initiatives, his refusal to cooperate with government officers or other missionaries, and his reluctance to extend the mission.[115] In 1891 Sir William MacGregor observed that Verjus found Navarre "a nuisance and a hindrance."[116] Yet his vow of obedience required submission to Navarre's will. After one difference between them, he recorded in his diary "I was wrong to tell His Grace this morning that he had no experience on the subject in question," and begged Navarre's forgiveness.[117]

Navarre's chronic ill-health, lapses of memory, and frequent absences from the field meant, however, that Verjus was the effective leader of the mission. His passionate zeal for the salvation of souls and his obsessive desire for martyrdom left their mark on all missionaries who came to the field before his death in 1892. Navarre depended on him increasingly and was desolated when Verjus was named vicar apostolic of New Britain in 1891. "It is the death of the Mission," he warned his superiors in Europe. "I could disappear without the Mission suffering much but the departure of Verjus . . . is ruin."[118] He was relieved when Verjus, his "right arm,"[119] was named his coadjutor bishop instead, but shattered by his death little more than a year later. Oppressed by anxiety and perhaps paranoiac in his illness, he sailed for Europe, intending to resign, leaving in New Guinea three exhausted priests and a small group of brothers and sisters whose numbers were steadily reduced by the extraordinarily high death rate of the mission.

The mission was revitalized in 1893 and 1894 by the arrival of the thirty missionaries commanded by the Pope, and by the appointment of Father Genocchi as its superior. Finding the mission in disorder, chaotic in its religious observances, and subject to the sometimes arbitrary authority of the vicar apostolic, Genocchi imposed a firm discipline on its members.[120] But constant conflict with Archbishop Navarre impeded him. He was opposed to Navarre's old-fashioned catechetical approach to conversion, preferring to incorporate the teaching of the catechism into a broader program.[121] Navarre, supported by most of the older missionaries, resisted Genocchi's exacting religious regime, believing it unsuitable for a tropical climate.[122] The problem was intensified by Navarre's illness, which Genocchi described to his superior general in Europe, "He forgets, he takes shadows for realities, he dreams and fabricates facts which have never existed."[123]

Conflicts of personality and style were entangled with a larger conflict between the roles of vicar apostolic and superior. Areas of overlap of authority, such as that of the well-being of a missionary (who was also a religious), required tactful negotiation and often compromise. Navarre, who, ignorant of canonical procedure, had been raised from missionary priest to vicar apostolic in the field, acted as if his authority were absolute in all spheres.[124] The conflict between the two rival authorities polarized the mission,[125] and in 1896 Genocchi resigned. Before departing he prepared statutes concerning the exercise of supreme ecclesiastical authority and that of the congregation as it affected subjects, the superior, and the vicar apostolic.[126] Conflict between the two roles was reduced but not vanquished by their definition. Bishop de Boismenu, who was appointed superior during Father Jullien's absence, resigned from the latter position because he found the two incompatible.[127]

From 1900, authority in the field rested with Navarre as vicar apostolic, de Boismenu as coadjutor bishop, and Jullien as superior. Navarre, "old and broken," declared that he wished to "leave everything" to his coadjutor.[128] But in fact the two younger men, de Boismenu and Jullien, found their plans frustrated by their vicar apostolic's conservatism, as had Verjus and Genocchi. The main point at issue was the organization of the mission field. De Boismenu opposed Navarre's impossible dream, inspired by rural France, of a parish priest in every village, favoring instead Father Jullien's proposal to place missionaries in communities at centers from which their influence could radiate out into the surrounding countryside.[129] This would facilitate the expansion into the mountains of which the two men, barred from further coastal expansion, dreamed. The Europe-bound vision of Navarre, a man of the Berry plains, could not accommodate the vast, sparsely settled, and almost inaccessible interior.[130]

Navarre's retirement in 1908, after years of virtual incapacity and frequent absence, gave de Boismenu greater freedom of action. In the same year he set out in his pastoral letters the elaborate and thorough program that was to give the mission a new sense of direction and a renewed commitment (see chapter 6). In January 1912 Navarre died. De Boismenu wrote gracefully of him. Archbishop Navarre, former soldier of France was the perfect "soldier of the Church," proud of his mission, utterly dedicated, and faithful at his post to death. He had remained, despite ill health, a "reminder of the mission's harsh beginnings," a symbol of continuity amidst insecurity and change.[131] The three decades that followed his death were characterized by the leadership of Alain de Boismenu.

"Routinization" and Indigenization

Despite such significant differences in structure and organization among the four missions, some aspects of their administrative experience were common to all. Two of the most significant were the "routinization" of mission administration and the preliminary steps toward indigenization of mission structures.

The first generation of missionaries in Papua shared some of the characteristics of Weber's "charismatic" leader in their relations with the Papuans.[132] They were "men set apart from ordinary men." The Papuans saw them as "endowed with supernatural, superhuman or . . . exceptional powers or qualities." Their white skins, often associated with the spirit world, the paraphernalia of Western technology that accompanied them, and, not least, the fact that the pioneers Lawes, Chalmers, Maclaren, Stone-Wigg, Bromilow, Navarre, and Verjus were all tall men of imposing appearance, encouraged their belief. The missionaries were "outside the realm of everyday routine," into which they broke with new demands and new obligations, setting up their authority against that of the established order. Their authority was derived from their person, not their status. There was at first little structure in the missionaries' interaction with the Papuans, reward was by booty (to use Weber's phrase), and roles and activities were fluid and ever changing.

Charismatic authority, according to Weber, exists only in the "process of originating."[133] Its survival depends on its "routinization," that is, its transformation into rational-legal leadership whose authority is vested not in the person but in the position.[134] Such a process occurred in all the missions. The early missionaries were accepted and obeyed because they were perceived as extraordinary beings. Those who followed them were accepted because of their status—that is, because they were missionaries. Their individual attributes mattered little.

The transition from charismatic to rational-legal authority caused problems in the mission field, as elsewhere. The distancing of the missionary leader from the people has already been noted (see chapter 6). A second difficulty was the creation of false expectations among the missionaries themselves. Nurtured on the writings of the pioneers, the second generation arrived eager for the life of the charismatic leader. Instead they found well-established routines, complex administrative structures, and often several layers of personnel between themselves and the village Papuans. This caused some disillusionment. Sister Edith Lloyd wrote from the Methodist field in 1899: "The path is already opened up and the routine of work arranged for me. . . . How seldom reality is rightly pictured by imagination."[135] Her colleague Gordon Burgess wrote similarly from Bunama, "The days of romance have gone from this Circuit. . . . It is a time now of steady plodding."[136] The more humble missionaries were inclined to depreciate their own role in contrast with that of the pioneers. Reading of the early missionaries of the LMS, J. H. Holmes reflected that "they were giants in those days. We of the present day are a puny, weak-kneed, colourless lot when compared with them."[137] Young missionaries found it difficult to take the place of the pioneers. William Avery, who followed Bromilow at Dobu, gave vent to his frustration: "The people think there is only one right way to do things and that is the way in which 'Saragigi' used to do them"; Oliver Tomkins, Chalmers' colleague, declared that it was "impossible for *anyone* to take Tamate's place."[138]

In the years before the First World War, there was little evidence of a place for Papuans in the structures of the churches that the mission bodies had come to establish. Although all acknowledged the indigenization of the church as a long-term objective, by 1914 only the first steps had been taken in its direction.

Most explicit in their articulation of this objective and most energetic in its prosecution was the LMS. From the outset its missionaries in Papua, as in its other fields, looked to the creation of a "self-supporting, self-governing and self-propagating church"[139] that was to be a thoroughly indigenous institution. Practical difficulties reinforced conviction in their determination to replace the Polynesian pastors as quickly as possible with Papuans. From the first years of the mission's existence, missionaries trained the most promising of their students as pastor-teachers, and in 1884 the first Papuan, Rarua, was ordained to that position.[140] In 1894, despite opposition from some of his colleagues, Lawes established Vatorata Training College as a central institution for the preparation of a Papuan pastorate.[141] Taking students who had received a preliminary education in their own districts, it gave them a modest training in reading, writing, and simple arithmetic as well as in theological subjects. Sir William MacGregor, visiting the college, found its education "so suitable . . . to the character and condition of the natives" that he could suggest no improvement.[142] Students, many of whom were married, grew their own food, and their wives were instructed in domestic skills by Fanny Lawes. They emerged prepared to fulfill the dual role of pastor-teacher and, after a satisfactory probation, were ordained. By 1920 there were fifty ordained pastors in the LMS.

At the village level, the churches of the LMS were, by the time of the First World War, to some extent indigenous institutions. Many were run by Papuan pastors or teachers, assisted by a Papuan diaconate. After 1915 church councils were set up in most districts,[143] but all remained subject to the authority of the white missionary and the district committee. The Papuan ministry remained dependent on grants from the LMS, although by 1920 more than one-third of the sum required for this purpose was raised by local contributions.[144]

The Methodist missionaries, while acknowledging the same objective as the LMS,[145] were much slower in implementing it. The first chairman, Bromilow, made only tentative gestures toward the raising of an indigenous elite at Dobu, believing that Papuans lacked the necessary authority to become pastors. His successor, Matthew Gilmour, supervised the establishment in 1906 of a central training institution at Ubuia that provided further education for a small minority who had passed successfully through the village and circuit schools. Its curriculum included reading, geography, arithmetic, writing, scripture, history, general knowledge, and mechanical work.[146] But unlike Lawes' college at Vatorata, the institution did not equip its graduates for ordination. They were appointed, unordained, to the position of teacher. By 1914 there were sixty Papuan teachers who, like the LMS pastors, combined the supervision of village worship with schoolteaching.[147] In the same period, fifty-five Papuans had been licensed as local preachers.[148] But as late as the beginning of the Second World War, not a single Papuan had been ordained to the indigenous ministry, which was a subsection of the Australian Methodist ministry.[149]

In the Anglican Mission, Bishop Stone-Wigg, at his consecration in 1898, stated his intention of working toward a "Native Church manned by a native ministry and self-supporting."[150] In 1903 St. Aidan's training college was established at Dogura with Henry Newton as principal. It gave a three-to-five-year training in the Bible, the Book of Common Prayer, sermon preparation and delivery, teaching, preparation of candidates for the sacraments, devotional life, English, and the three R's.[151] Despite this ambitious program, the Anglican Mission proceeded cautiously toward its objective. In 1914 Peter Rautamara and Edwin Nuagoro were ordained as deacons. Three other Papuans, Francis Tutuana, John Regita, and Aidan Vivedo were admitted to Holy Orders before the end of Sharp's episcopate in 1921. As a further step toward indigenizing the church, Bishop Sharp in 1913 introduced village councils to encourage a sense of independence and responsibility.[152] But the mission came nowhere near Stone-Wigg's objective of self-supporting local churches. Disliking the commercialism and competitiveness that characterized the fund-raising campaigns of the Protestants among their converts, the Anglican Mission remained reluctant to exact contributions from its local congregations and, to the end of Sharp's episcopate, relied heavily on funds raised from overseas.[153]

Almost from the beginning, the Sacred Heart missionaries sought to use Papuans within the church in the lay role of catechist. Plans made in 1889 for the foundation of a school for catechists came into effect in 1896 at Thursday Island, where young Papuans were instructed by Father Guis.[154] The school failed, as did its successor on the mainland at Maea'era, which closed in 1902.[155] For the following period, missionaries trained their own catechists in their districts and by 1915 there were twenty-two of them. The next decade saw a great increase in their numbers, as missionaries, urged by a series of de Boismenu's pastoral letters, looked to their parish schools as seminaries for catechists.[156] By 1928 there were more than a hundred, and those in the mountain districts especially played a key role in the processes of conversion and nurture.

Progress toward an indigenous priesthood was predictably slower. The year 1914, which saw the first ordination to the Anglican priesthood, also saw the first vocation in the SHM. Joseph Taurino, a fourteen-year-old student of St. Patrick's School, Yule Island, expressed a wish to become a priest and was entrusted to Father Norin for preliminary training.[157] In 1918 he was sent to study at the congregation's apostolic school in Switzerland, but died in France. Three years later another young Papuan, Louis Vangeke, offered for the priesthood. Ordained priest in 1937, he lived to become a bishop of the Roman Catholic church of Papua New Guinea.

There were several reasons for the absence of Papuans in all but the lowest positions in the structures of the Methodist, Anglican, and

Sacred Heart missions before the First World War. First, while the LMS by 1914 had been established in New Guinea for forty years, the Sacred Heart Mission was less than thirty years old, and the Anglican and Methodist missions only twenty-three. As has already been shown, during this period most energy was expended on the preliminary tasks of conversion and the nurture of the new Christian community as a whole, rather than the creation of an elite. Second, for the Roman Catholic and Anglican missionaries, with their high view of the priesthood and, in the case of the Roman Catholics, the extremely rigorous training it required, there was doubt as to the ability of these recently Christianized people to meet its demands. The Sacred Heart missionaries were cautioned by the notable failures of missionaries in other parts of Oceania to establish an indigenous priesthood[158] and by the performance of the Protestant pastors, of whom they were scathingly critical (see chapter 9). Furthermore, although Rome, and Propaganda especially, had held firm to the apostolic commitment to a local priesthood, the concept had declined in favor throughout the church since the sixteenth century. It was only Benedict XV's encyclical of 1919, *Maximum Illud*, and more particularly Pius XI's *Rerum Ecclesiae* of 1926 that restored the idea of an indigenous clergy as one of the prime objectives of mission.[159] The Methodists' failure to create an indigenous ministry was probably in part because, unlike the Catholic missions, they did not need a large clergy for the regular administration of the sacraments. Most of the daily and weekly tasks of the Methodist Mission could as easily be accomplished by the lay village teacher.

The slowness of the missions to create indigenous churches must be attributed at least in part to the racial prejudice that hampered their vision—as it did that of their secular contemporaries. Their low estimation of the Papuan character and culture gave them little faith in Papuan ability. Their essentially Western conception of the church seemed to demand a leadership with Western skills to run it. And the whole conception of devolution of even limited authority to Papuans was quite foreign to the colonial atmosphere of the era before the First World War. Another twenty-three years would pass before (Sir) Hubert Murray ventured to suggest that Papuans could conceivably "be educated to the standard of an ordinary professional career," an insight stimulated by the ordination of the first Roman Catholic priest.[160]

For the Europeans who dominated the structures of the missions and the emerging churches until well beyond 1914, being a missionary was an experience that varied according to which organization they belonged to. The LMS missionaries had the satisfaction of a large degree of autonomy and were supported, at a convenient distance, by a powerful society. But they faced the pressures of working in isolation without the support and cooperation of their colleagues. The Methodist missionaries had the confidence derived from a recognized status and role within a close-knit, cohesive organization, but they ran the risk, if high in the hierarchy, of augmenting that status unwarrantedly or, if low, of suffering because of the overinflated status of others. The Anglican missionaries derived security from a sense of community and strong pastoral leadership, but suffered the frustration of weak support from an apathetic and divided church. The religious in the Sacred Heart Mission found strength in their papal commission, their congregation, and their vow of obedience, but their apostolate was at times circumscribed or misdirected because of the poverty of the mission and the limitations of their all-powerful superiors.

CHAPTER 9

"The Sinister Trio"

LMS Missionaries and Annexation

FROM TIME TO TIME, the affairs of the larger world broke in on the missionaries' small, enclosed domains. The frequency with which this happened depended on the degree of isolation of the mission station. Asked, for instance, to describe their interaction with government officers of Papua in 1915, LMS missionaries gave varied responses. Lawrence at Port Moresby and Saville at Mailu claimed frequent and cordial contact, while Rich at Isuleilei saw no officials except "when a passing ship anchors in the Bay for a few hours," and Schlencker at Orokolo saw them "once in a blue moon."[1] However remote their stations, though, all missionaries were involved in a complex and delicately balanced set of interrelationships with government officers, with missionaries of other persuasions, and with the motley collection of settlers, traders, and miners who made up the remainder of the expatriate population of Papua. These intricate relationships of missionary, trader, and official fostered the image of the missionary as one of the "sinister trio of capitalist imperialism."[2]

In the years following Lawes' settlement at Port Moresby, there was a steady incursion of traders into southeastern New Guinea. Some, such as Lawes' neighbor at Port Moresby, the naturalist and trader Andrew Goldie, settled peacefully; others Lawes and Chalmers saw as a grave threat to the precarious peace they had encouraged among the coastal Papuans. A gold rush to the Laloki River, inland from Port Moresby, caused them particular concern, but their fears were ill founded. The rush was small, and the diggers' presence brief. However, subsequent violent encounters between traders and villagers led Chalmers and Lawes to define for themselves the role commonly adopted by missionaries confronted with a perceived threat to their flock—that of protector. "The natives have from the beginning looked upon us as their friends and defenders and . . . we shall never give them occasion to doubt it."[3]

Visits to the East End from the "man-stealers" of the labor trade in 1883 and 1884, and the Kabadi land swindle of 1883,[4] prompted Lawes and Chalmers into vigorous campaigns against the exploitation of Papuan labor and land. Recognizing that there was no indigenous government capable of controlling threats to Papuan life, labor, and land, they reluctantly acknowledged the need for "foreign jurisdiction."[5] LMS missionaries had traditionally adopted an isolationist, anti-imperialist stance, and Lawes and Chalmers, consistent with this tradition, insisted that they "would much rather not be annexed by anybody."[6] But once they realized that intervention of some kind was inevitable, as both a means of protection for the Papuan people and a response to the clamors of the Australian annexationists, they threw themselves into a campaign in favor of control by their own country, Britain, rather than Queensland.[7] "Nowhere in the world," wrote Lawes to the LMS foreign secretary, "have aborigines been so basely and cruelly treated as in Queensland—the half has never been told, and are the natives of New Guinea to be handed over to their tender mercies?"[8]

Lawes and Chalmers were disconcerted when, in April 1883, Henry Chester, police magistrate at Thursday Island, arrived in Port Moresby to annex southeastern New Guinea for the Queensland government. After examining his instructions they had no course but to cooperate, their readiness to act as interpreters strengthened by their concern to give the Papuans an understanding of what was taking place. But Lawes despised himself for "the meanness of the whole transaction."[9] Privately he confided to the LMS secretary his unease at the annexation of "the largest island in the world" by "a Police Magistrate . . . in a little tub of a cutter" and his relief when the annexation was disallowed.[10]

Lawes envisaged that British jurisdiction might be imposed through a protectorate, or simply through extension of the powers of the high commissioner of the Western Pacific so as to provide a deputy or British resident in New Guinea.[11] When the protectorate was announced, he was cautiously optimistic, seeing it as embodying the concept of trusteeship, which had been a long-standing element of LMS policy.

> Much will depend on the character of the man who may be chosen as Resident Commissioner. Almost anything, however, will be better than leaving the people and their lands at the mercy of lawless and mad adventurers. We must welcome the Protectorate as a good and hope that it will protect the weak and defenceless.[12]

Renowned for their influence over the coastal peoples and their mastery of the local languages, Lawes and Chalmers were widely involved in the series of flag-raising ceremonies that proclaimed the extension of Queen Victoria's protection to the peoples of southeastern New Guinea. In an effort to disarm the disapproval of the LMS directors and other potential critics, Lawes stressed that their "prominent position in the ceremonies [was] owing simply to the fact that we alone were able to act as interpreters, and make the people understand the meaning of the proclamation."[13] The directors were mollified by the fulsome tributes paid to their missionaries by the eminent men associated with the proceedings.[14]

The close cooperation between mission and government was maintained by Acting Special Commissioner Hugh Hastings Romilly, who lived with Chalmers and found him "a capital fellow . . . utterly unlike a missionary,"[15] and by General Sir Peter Scratchley, when he arrived as special commissioner in August 1885. "No better fortune could be desired for a Special Commissioner than to have Mr Chalmers as his 'Prime Minister'," Captain Cyprian Bridge assured Scratchley.[16] "I feel that without him I could do nothing," Scratchley confided to his wife.[17] A proposal that Chalmers should be offered a government appointment was considered seriously at the Colonial Office.[18]

Relations between the traders and the missionaries were further estranged by the identification of the latter with the government. A correspondent to the *Townsville Bulletin* warned its readers that "Mr Chalmers has, I understand, been admitted to the position of confidential adviser to His Excellency, so we can form a pretty fair estimation of what the ruling principles of His Excellency's policy will be."[19] Traders in New Guinea muttered of "mission rule."[20] In their hostility they had the support of the government secretary, Anthony Musgrave, who disagreed with the missionaries' belief that the proclamation precluded the acquisition of land for settlement, resented their interference in government affairs, and suspected their general orientation to the future of the country.[21] Musgrave reported after conversation with Chalmers that his views were "utterly one-sided" and that it would be useless to expect from him "any sympathy with the objects of the white man."[22] After Scratchley's death in December 1885, the greater independence of his successor, John Douglas, and the continuing opposition of Musgrave (whose attitude to the mission, according to Lawes, was best characterized by "a big sneer")[23] led to a decrease in mission influence for the remainder of the protectorate period.

A persistent element in the stereotype of the nineteenth-century missionaries has been their close association with imperialism. Writers of an earlier generation paid tribute to the contribution of missionaries to empire, acknowledging especially their "civilising role." C. Brunsdon Fletcher, writing at the time of the First World War, included Chalmers in his list of great imperialists in the Pacific in the late nineteenth century.[24] Critics of empire have, since Hobson's pioneering study of 1902, attacked missionaries for their association with "aggressive imperialism."[25] Most trenchant has been the criticism of Marxist historians who see missionaries as an intrinsic part of colonial exploitation and mission activity as "an inseparable part of imperialist politics."[26] The remarkably close identification of Lawes and Chalmers with the establishment of imperial rule in New Guinea should be examined in the light of this stereotype.

In a general sense, the missionaries' introduction of Western civilization foreshadowed the coming of British rule, in New Guinea as elsewhere.[27] There is no doubt that once Lawes and Chalmers became convinced of the necessity for foreign intervention, they lobbied energetically and effectively to have Britain assume the responsibility. Both believed their representations to have had influence at the Colonial Office.[28] Moreover, if the role of imperial adviser was thrust on them rather than sought, there is no evidence that they tried to avoid it. On the contrary, they used it to full effect to ensure that the policies they advocated were embodied in government policy.[29]

The influence of Chalmers and Lawes in bringing about colonial rule and molding its character cannot be denied. But they differed from the jingoistic imperialist in their lack of enthusiasm for imperial rule as an end in itself. They accepted a measure of it, finally, as the only alternative to interracial anarchy and the exploitation of the Papuan people. Their attitudes to the declaration of the protectorate were ambivalent, those of the ebullient Chalmers expressing greater extremes than the cautious statements of Lawes. Recalling the ceremony in the mission compound at Port Moresby, Chalmers wrote, "We felt that we were citizens of the greatest Empire the world had ever seen."[30] But as he watched the pomp and ceremony of one flag-raising after another, he reflected sardonically, "Some Britons think the world was made for the Anglo-Saxon."[31] Because his concern was for the protection of the Papuans and not the expansion of empire, he opposed the transformation of the protectorate into a colony. "Annexation would, I fear, render just treatment almost impossible; . . . the young, pushing, daring Anglo-Saxon colonist would look upon the 'nigger' as something to be got rid of."[32] Chalmers and Lawes, while approving some degree of imperial control, did not see it as synonymous with colonization. In his early days in New Guinea, Chalmers had dashed off letters and reports extolling the virtues of the country with the impetuous enthusiasm that characterized all his undertakings. But as they grew to fear the havoc wrought by the incursion of Europeans, both missionaries wrote to discourage white settlement, publicizing the shortcomings of the climate and the lack of resources.[33]

The community of interests between mission and government, as Roland Oliver has written of East Africa, was never regarded by either as more than "a happy accident."[34] Neither side deviated from its own natural course in order to form a more powerful combination. The same could be said of the coming of British rule to New Guinea. The missionaries in their self-styled role of protector used the imperial authorities to achieve their stated aim, the protection of the Papuan people. The government officials used the missionaries to ensure the Papuans' acceptance of imperial rule.

SHM versus Government

The missionaries of the Sacred Heart, who reached New Guinea in the year following the proclamation of the protectorate, experienced a very different relationship with the government from that enjoyed by the LMS. Inaugurated amid political controversy because of its association with the Marquis de Rays' expedition, the mission's first years in New Guinea were marked by continual conflict with officials and the Protestant mission.

From the time the Sacred Heart missionaries planned to embark for New Guinea from their base on Thursday Island, their efforts were frustrated by government policy. Navarre had visited Scratchley in February 1885 and received, he said, spoken assurances that his mission would be welcome in New Guinea. But Henry Chester, police magistrate at Thursday Island, in the absence of official papers refused to sanction their entry, invoking a recently passed law that forbade all shipping to New Guinea. Navarre, with some justification believing Chester to be a "fanatical friend" of the LMS, interpreted his intransigence as part of a Protestant plot to exclude them.[35] This embargo prompted Verjus and his colleagues to make their first voyage to New Guinea illegally, on the lugger of a sympathetic trader.

Before their departure, Navarre had also talked with Samuel McFarlane, whom he understood to be the "chief missionary" of the LMS.[36] Despite McFarlane's history of anti-Catholicism, which had resulted in his removal from Lifu for the alleged desecration of a chapel,[37] the meeting was harmonious. Although Navarre refused to consider McFarlane's suggestion that they settle on the northeast coast, he assured him that their intention was not to go where the LMS was already established and agreed specifically not to settle at Port Moresby as Propaganda had suggested.

Accordingly, Navarre decided to send his missionaries to Yule Island. But his concession did not avert conflict.[38] After three months' precarious existence, Verjus and his companions were visited by the government secretary, Musgrave, empowered by Scratchley to negotiate their settlement in New Guinea. Following Verjus' refusal to take any decision without consulting Navarre, the missionaries were taken in the LMS boat *Ellangowan* to await Scratchley at Thursday Island—an episode subsequently known within the congregation as "the expulsion." Interpreting, probably rightly, Scratchley's changed attitude as a response to pressure from the LMS, who claimed Yule Island, Navarre refused his written proposal that they should move to the northeast coast or the Louisiades, but agreed to an interview with him on 8 December. After Scratchley's death on 2 December, Navarre believed himself free to send his missionaries back to New Guinea.

Verjus' return to Yule Island and the subsequent arrival of Navarre brought to a head the conflict with the LMS over rights to the island. Verjus found that during his absence Lawes had placed a teacher at Yule, a station that they had previously occupied but abandoned. Lawes and Navarre bombarded the government with memoranda arguing their claims.[39] Verjus, whose conciliatory spirit was far removed from the intransigent ultramontanism of his superior, sought an interview with Lawes at Port Moresby, which gained him little but the disapproval of Navarre, who saw it as a "compromise."[40] Lawes finally conceded defeat and removed the teacher. During Douglas' term of office, Scratchley's fear of sectarian rivalry and his belief in the "prescriptive right of the L.M.S. to certain districts" was replaced by a policy of "a fair field and no favour shown."[41]

Auxiliaries to Government?

The arrival of Sir William MacGregor in 1888 as first administrator of the new colony introduced an era when the "happy accident" of community of interest between the government and the three non–Roman Catholic missions was exploited to the utmost. After his retirement MacGregor reflected that the two best institutions he had left behind him were the missions and the native constabulary.[42] It was no accident that he linked the two. In MacGregor's eyes the missions were, like the police force, an auxiliary, a "necessary adjunct to the work of government,"[43] devoted to the same ends—the imposition of peace and the promotion of the well-being of the Papuan peoples. The missionaries were under no illusions about being thus used. After an interview with MacGregor, the visiting LMS director, William Crosfield, reported, "He makes no mystery about his object being to have influential helpers of the civil power. . . ."[44] Father Dupeyrat condemned that "narrowness of spirit which considers religion as a kind of police force";[45] William Bromilow more charitably attributed his patronage not only to statesmanship but to the convictions of "a Christian believer."[46]

MacGregor spared no effort to facilitate the missions' operations. After inviting in the Wesleyans, who had so impressed him in Fiji, and conducting their secretary, George Brown, and the Anglican founder, Albert Maclaren, on a tour of inspection, he encouraged a meeting held at Port Moresby on 17 June 1890. There Brown, Maclaren, and the LMS representatives Lawes, Chalmers, Dauncey, and Walker agreed to the partitioning of the colony into "spheres of influence" within each of which one of the three missions would work exclusively. The whole southeast coast except for a small stretch opposite Yule Island was to remain the sphere of the LMS, while the northeast coast from Cape Ducie to Mitre Rock at the German border was entrusted to the Anglicans, and all the islands at the eastern end of Papua (except two to which the LMS had a prior claim) were allotted to the Methodists, who were also given a small strip of the mainland from East Cape to Cape Ducie (Figure 22). Although MacGregor subsequently disclaimed responsibility for the agreement, Lawes' report shows that the initiative was his. "The Merrie England came in and with her . . . the Rev. A. A. Maclaren. We waited on Sir Wm. He disclaimed any wish to dictate etc. But he is in a little fix because both Mr Maclaren and the Wesleyans are coming for the same field."[47]

MacGregor praised the "generous spirit" of the agreement and the "remarkable group of men" who were its authors—the "scholarly, accomplished, devoted and experienced" Lawes, the "courageous, indefatigable" Chalmers, the "large-hearted, brave veteran" Brown, and the "tactful and courteous" Maclaren.[48] He ensured its implementation by the simple device of granting land to only one mission in any one village, a policy subsequently approved by Secretary of State for Colonies Joseph Chamberlain and published in the government gazette.[49] So scrupulously was it observed that many, including some of MacGregor's field officers, assumed it to have the authority of law.

MacGregor's attention to the missions was constant and vigilant. He visited stations, inspected schools, praised translation work and other achievements, prodded missions into further expansion and rebuked their tardiness, advised them on station sites, and warned newly contacted villagers that any disrespect to the mission was tantamount to disrespect to him. With a number of missionaries, especially the Wesleyans, for whom he never lost his high esteem, he had a warm paternal relationship, casting a fatherly eye over the new mission sisters and sending to Samuel Fellows' daughter, "the forget-me-not-baby," a bottle of Mamba gold.[50] He used his medical skills to advise fever-stricken missionaries of all persuasions, comforting some with gifts of champagne and food and carrying others off in the *Merrie England* to convalescence in Australia.[51]

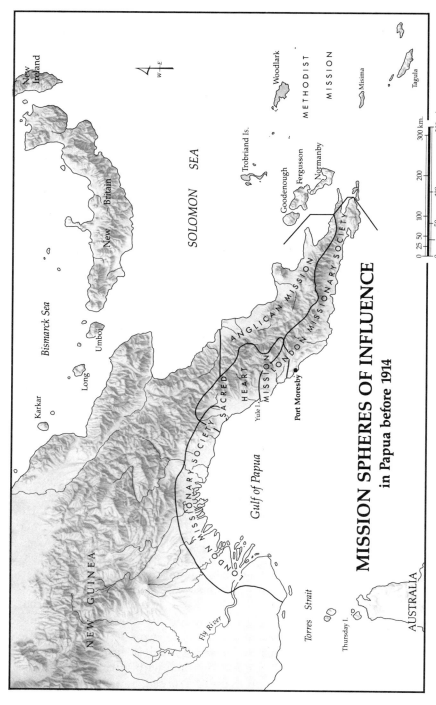

MISSION SPHERES OF INFLUENCE
in Papua before 1914

Figure 22.

In return the missionaries were to continue their work of peace-making, evangelizing and "civilizing," paying particular attention to the inculcation of loyalty to the imperial government. MacGregor praised missionaries whose efforts made the Queen's name a "household word" throughout British New Guinea.[52] Missionaries who shared MacGregor's passion for exploration accompanied him on patrol, Verjus, for instance, introducing him to the fertile and populous Mekeo Plain and Chalmers joining him in expeditions in search of the Tugeri headhunters of west New Guinea.

MacGregor was, declared Bishop Stone-Wigg, "the best friend the Papuan ever had."[53] Because they saw in him one who shared their concern for the well-being of the Papuans, the Anglican and Protestant missionaries cooperated readily with his policies. It was a close partnership, but different from the one of the early protectorate period. Then, inexperienced and uncertain officers had deferred constantly to the authority and experience of the missionaries, who thus exerted considerable influence on government policy. During MacGregor's period, missionaries were consulted on aspects of policy within their province, such as regulations on marriage and education, but they were discouraged from playing politics. MacGregor rebuked missionaries who intervened on behalf of their charges against prosecution and after his retirement praised them for their general abstention from politics.[54]

Declaring his readiness to "take his chance under any creed,"[55] MacGregor asserted as his policy that "all Christian churches are exactly alike and that which does the best work will be most appreciated."[56] Despite his pragmatic approach, he harbored some of the prejudices of a Protestant sectarian. He admired Albert Maclaren, of whom he wrote, "I have known few more lovable men,"[57] but retained a distaste for the ritualism of Anglicanism—"Dang it all, it's bob up and bob down etc. etc.," he confided to Samuel Fellows[58]—and resisted Maclaren's attempt to have the Church of England recognized as a national church.[59] His private observations on the Sacred Heart Mission, with its "bloodless brothers" and their quarters that had "the musty smell . . . almost peculiar to lunatic asylums"[60] also betrayed the prejudices of a son of John Knox.

The close coalescence of interest between MacGregor and the three non–Roman Catholic missions was not reflected in his relationship with the SHM. Although MacGregor assured Navarre, as he had the other missionaries, that whichever mission taught the catechism was "a matter of complete indifference"[61] to him, the archbishop persisted in his belief that the outlook of MacGregor, a "Presbyterian Scot and a freemason," prejudiced his treatment of the Roman Catholic mission.[62]

At the heart of the tension between the lieutenant governor and the

Sacred Heart missionaries was his endorsement of the "spheres of influence" policy. The SHM, with the approval of Propaganda, refused to be party to the agreement, seeing such a "compromise" as "a denial of her claim to be the only true church of God."[63] The expansion of the SHM through Roro and Mekeo caused no conflict as these districts were tacitly accepted as being their domain, but in 1896 and 1897 the Roman Catholic mission issued a direct challenge to the spheres by establishing themselves in the Pokao village of Vanamai, claimed by the LMS, and at Waima, where LMS teachers were actually at work.[64] Navarre justified their actions on the grounds that they were in response to repeated requests from the people for *popi* missionaries, asserting their right and responsibility to go wherever they were called.[65] The SHM earned a public censure from MacGregor,[66] who reiterated his determination to grant no land to any mission in a village where another mission was already at work or had signified its intention to work by applying for land, implied that Navarre had tacitly accepted the spheres by agreeing not to go to Port Moresby, criticized the SHM for making no formal application before entering Vanamai and Waima, and pointed out that much of Roro and Mekeo was still unevangelized.[67]

Navarre made a spirited defense of his mission's actions.[68] Denying that he had ever accepted the spheres of influence policy, he argued that it unfairly excluded the SHM from most of the colony, that its rigid enforcement along the lines proposed by MacGregor would incite jealousy and lead to a scramble for occupation, that it forced them into the position of having to disobey either the government or their ecclesiastical superiors, and that the Papuans should have freedom of choice in religion. He concluded with a plea for religious liberty: "Give us the consolation in the midst of our work of enjoying that full freedom which missionaries have always had under the English flag."[69]

The confrontation between MacGregor and Navarre over incursions into Protestant territory was the culmination of a series of conflicts based on mutual mistrust. MacGregor had been angered to discover that Navarre had bypassed him and appealed to the Queensland government for favorable terms in the retrospective recognition of their rights to land on Yule Island. "I am now firmly convinced these Roman Catholic dignitaries lie," he wrote in his diary after an interview at Yule Island.[70] He was further incensed to discover that Navarre had accused him of being the perpetrator of a conspiracy to have them expelled from the island, a charge that MacGregor denounced as "utterly fictitious," challenging Navarre to produce evidence and unsuccessfully demanding a retraction.[71] Navarre, likening MacGregor to a crocodile,[72] continued to find evidence of discrimination against his mission, interpreting the colony's customs regulations thus despite the fact the the duties were equally burdensome to the LMS, who had invited him to join in protest against them.[73] When Navarre's allegations of discrimination were embodied, at Propaganda's instigation, in a formal complaint from Cardinal Vaughan of Westminster to the Colonial Office, MacGregor's reply was uncompromising:

> Physically he is totally unfit for this climate. . . . He has remained a foreigner, with only a slight acquaintance with our language, and he in no degree understands our institutions. It is perfectly natural therefore that he should be querulous and suspicious: but it is greatly to be regretted that he should think that there is any field in this administration for the intrigues of Protestant ministers.[74]

MacGregor's unease about Navarre, "a French man of the ultra antiEnglish type"[75] was heightened by the prospect of a visit of a French warship to Yule Island, which he successfully opposed.[76]

In the struggles that marked MacGregor's relationship with the SHM, it seems that despite his prejudices he generally acted with fairness and consistency. Their conflicting attitudes to the spheres of influence were based on premises so fundamentally opposed as to allow of no accommodation. In this situation, the uncompromising, old-fashioned ultramontanism and anglophobia of Navarre exacerbated the tension. Delusions induced by illness, which Genocchi had noted, may also have impaired his judgment. Henri Verjus fretted when he failed to see the evil designs that Navarre perceived: "The Governor has been charming and yet Mgr. Navarre told me to be mistrustful. I am very foolish that I see only what is in front of me."[77] Later both Verjus and Hartzer intimated to MacGregor their embarrassment at the stance taken by their archbishop.[78] MacGregor, for his part, praised Verjus as "a broadminded man free from bigotry or sectarianism in any form."[79] The same mutal esteem existed between MacGregor and Father Genocchi during the latter's brief period in the mission field. After MacGregor had transported him, delirious with blackwater fever, to Thursday Island, Genocchi wrote:

> As for Sir William MacGregor . . . he certainly cannot have the hatred of the Catholic religion typical of malevolent people. He does his duty, heedless of fatigue . . . consecrating his life to the good of the savages. He . . . admits readily that the missionary is his best auxiliary, and in his reports, he speaks of us with almost too much praise.[80]

A letter Navarre received from Propaganda in 1889, urging him to end his struggle with MacGregor, suggests some concern in Rome about his policies.[81]

In Sir George Le Hunte, appointed lieutenant governor in 1898, the

Protestant missionaries believed New Guinea had a "worthy successor"[82] to MacGregor. William Bromilow, who prided himself on being on "intimate terms" with Le Hunte, believed that like MacGregor he exemplified the "highest qualities of British rule."[83] The missionaries saw him as one who, unlike the down-to-earth and frequently dusty and disheveled MacGregor, "upheld the dignity of his office,"[84] but they found in him the same sympathy and readiness to cooperate for common goals. Like his predecessor, he held that "one Mission body is the same as another—absolutely" and asserted it to be the "duty and privilege" of the government to give them all possible assistance.[85]

Unfortunately, the missionaries could not always expect the same sympathy and community of interest among Le Hunte's field officers. "The Governor has not a single officer like minded with himself," observed Lawes in 1901. "The magistrates and administrative officers are for the most part uneducated men from the same class as those who are bound to be hostile to the natives and the mission."[86] MacGregor had kept his small band of officers under close supervision, even persuading Musgrave to restrain his hostility to the LMS,[87] yet even under that vigilant and energetic administrator, officers had from time to time strained mission–government relations. It seems likely, for instance, that the tensions between the SHM and MacGregor were aggravated by the hostility of the resident magistrate for the central division, Frank Lawes, son of W. G. Lawes, who fomented anti-Catholic feeling among the Papuans, provoked the mission by tearing down the flag from the *marea* 'ceremonial house' at Vanamai and probably spread the rumor that fed Navarre's fears of expulsion.[88]

When the missionaries believed the interests or well-being of the Papuans threatened by the actions of field officers, they abandoned their customary alliance with the government. They protested at violence, pillage, and rape committed by indigenous policemen and at coercion and exploitation by government officers.[89] In 1901, for instance, Henry Newton was responsible for forcing the resignation of Yaldwyn, a young assistant resident magistrate, after the magistrate C. A. W. Monckton had acquitted him of the rape of a Papuan girl.[90] The same year Abel and Walker uncovered complicity between magistrates and miners in a series of incidents that included the murder of three Papuans and one European storekeeper.[91] Hostility toward Abel from the expatriate community was so intense that for a time he could only travel unmolested with an armed Papuan escort. To the distress of the missionaries, Judge Winter, chief judicial officer, acquitted the miners of murder on the remarkable grounds that "racial feeling was so general and so strong" that he could not consider them morally culpable.[92] The missionaries' fears that Winter's judgment augured ill for the future of the Papuans seemed justified soon after, when another miner boasted publicly that he had "done for another of the d[amne]d niggers."[93] They were jubilant when Le Hunte intervened, and the two magistrates, Moreton and Symons, were demoted, while Judge Winter resigned. Commenting on the sordid episode, Will Saville of Mailu reflected that pure heathenism was like "an oasis in a desert" compared with the corrupting influence of some officials.[94]

Relations between missionaries and field officers were often strained by rivalry. They were two competing sources of authority and influence in village life. Government officers, obliged to use missionaries as interpreters, guides, and mediators, were aware that the people frequently deferred to their missionary before responding to government regulations. As was common in mission fields, opposition or hostility from officials was interpreted as jealousy.[95]

Occasionally genuine differences in policy occurred. District officers in Roro and Mekeo became exasperated at the refusal of the Sacred Heart missionaries to oppose burials within the village.[96] Missionaries at times objected to the greater permissiveness of government officers on questions of morality. Anglican missionary Ernest Taylor, noting the laxity of the resident magistrate of the northern division toward marriage and divorce, reflected, "What are we coming to when the British Empire gives us representatives who cannot behave with the common decency of gentlemen," and wondered what benefit the Union Jack had conferred on the people of New Guinea.[97] In 1898 the encouragement given by Dr. Joseph Blayney, resident magistrate for the central division, to the revival of traditional dancing provoked the opposition of the LMS. "It is an entirely new departure for our Government Officer to defend what we condemn . . . as immoral and thus put himself in the eyes of the people in direct opposition to the Mission," Lawes admonished Blayney.[98] Relations between the LMS and the government remained strained over this issue, particularly after the revival received the encouragement of the administrator, Captain Barton. Lawes had always seen the relationship between the missions and the government as "a form of contract, under which we . . . work in New Guinea for the benefit of the natives."[99] Now, he believed, the contract was dishonored. Missionaries of all persuasions deplored the gratuitous violence of government officers who accompanied the acting administrator, Christopher Stansfeld Robinson, on his ill-conceived voyage to Goaribari in 1904.[100]

Such friction and occasional confrontations took place within a generally harmonious relationship. Most mission stations enjoyed visits from government officers. " 'Government' has been here twice lately. It was very nice having them," reported an Anglican missionary in

1916.[101] Missionaries nursed government officers when they were injured or ill; officials carried supplies to hungry missionaries. Both cooperated to reduce the loneliness and isolation of a mission or government station by transporting personnel and mail. Each went to the help of the other in shipwrecks or other crises. Missionaries accompanied officials on patrol in areas they were familiar with and joined them in exploration.[102] Magistrates and missionaries commonly joined to impose peace, identify sorcery, and suppress cannibalism.[103] Senior missionaries for a time acted as recruiting officers for the government, and two LMS missionaries in the Torres Strait served as justices of the peace until it was recognized that such an appointment contravened the Society's instructions.[104]

Responses to Australian Rule

The close cooperation that had characterized the relationship of the government with the Anglican and Protestant missions throughout most of the period of British rule in New Guinea was weakened in the years marking the assumption of Australian power, shattered by the report of the royal commission appointed in 1906 to inquire into the affairs of the colony, and only painstakingly restored by the long-serving lieutenant governor, J. H. P. (Sir Hubert) Murray.

Lawes, whose poor opinion of Australian rule had led him to campaign for a British protectorate in the 1880s, viewed with equal apprehension the prospect of Australian rule in the 1900s. Fearing for the treatment of the Papuans, he, with the full support of the Papuan district committee, called for the appointment of a "Protector of the natives." He explained, "We are their only friends. I am afraid there are not half a dozen men in all New Guinea outside the Mission who care anything about the natives except as they can be utilised to promote British interests."[105] Lawes was also concerned that the "non-religious character" of the Australian Commonwealth might prevent their incorporating into the Papua Act any equivalent to clause *xxxi* in the Royal Instructions, which required the administrator "to the utmost of his power to promote religion and education among the native inhabitants of the Possession."[106]

The first trial of strength between the missionaries and the federal government was over an issue whose connection with the protection of the Papuans was not immediately apparent. Nor was it consistent with the wowser image of the nineteenth-century missionary. In 1903 Stone-Wigg and Abel were in the vanguard of the widespread opposition of the European residents of Papua to a proposed prohibition clause in the Papua Bill.[107] Their stand was supported by the Anglican and Sacred

Heart missions, by the district committee of the LMS, and even by the traditional crusaders for prohibition, the Methodists,[108] among whom doubts as to its effectiveness had been sown by an influential book, *Temperance Problems and Social Reform.*[109] A circular sent to all missionaries individually, as to other expatriates, showed them almost unanimous in sharing the conviction that prohibition was undesirable.[110] The missionaries may be suspected of a degree of self-interest in their opposition to prohibition, but in fact the two chief protagonists, Abel and Stone-Wigg, were teetotallers, as indeed were their strongest supporters, Lawes, Schlencker, Cullen, and Saville. The Anglicans admitted that they were concerned about the availability of wine for sacramental purposes and as a remedy for fever, but their main contention, like that of their Protestant counterparts, was that prohibition in Papua "would not be for the good . . . of the native population."[111] Most believed that it was "unworkable," "impracticable," and that the Papuans, hitherto protected by the laws of the colony from access to alcohol, would be at the mercy of illicit traders.[112] Despite the opprobrium of the temperance movement in Australia,[113] Abel and Stone-Wigg persisted in their campaign, writing and speaking to the press and interviewing politicians. The Act was passed without the prohibition clause.

In the closing months of 1906, the commissioners appointed to inquire into the government of the colony[114] traveled through Papua collecting evidence. Six missionaries appeared before them: Charles Abel and E. Baxter Riley (LMS), Andrew Ballantyne (Methodist), Copland King (Anglican), and Alain de Boismenu and Alexander Fillodeau (SHM). Consistent with their self-image as "native protectors" they spoke most on issues concerning the Papuans—recruiting, cultivation, education, justice in the law courts, and the conduct of the police. As well as hearing evidence from the mission representatives, the commissioners briefly visited several mission stations.

When the missionaries read the commissioners' report, many believed their fears about the changeover to Australian rule confirmed. It marked, reported Stone-Wigg, a complete change of attitude. "It is thoroughly 'Australian'. The country must be made to pay, the natives must not obstruct the white man, the Missions will be tolerated if they make as their *chief objective* the teaching of English (the Gospel is evidently to be a very poor second)."[115] Like Stone-Wigg, many missionaries objected to the report on the grounds that it was "anti-native" and "anti-missionary."[116] Some objected too that it was unfairly anti-Barton, seeing the attacks on the administrator, an Englishman, as an assertion of "Australia for the Australians" and a rejection of his policy of protection of the Papuans in favor of one of exploitation.[117] Several Anglican and Protestant missionaries shared the widespread criticism of Judge Hubert Murray's role in the proceedings; he "practically impeached Barton," reported Stone-Wigg.[118]

The recommendations of the commissioners regarding missions provoked strong opposition on a number of grounds.[119] Many missionaries were aggrieved that no credit was given for their work, especially as much of it was supportive of government policy. Others, like Stone-Wigg, objected to the utilitarian emphasis on the teaching of English. Some, proud of their pioneering record, resented the implication that the missions were dependent on the government for their safety. Copland King believed that the commissioners' survey of missions had been too perfunctory and beyond their brief. Protestant and Anglican missionaries, above all, feared for the future of the spheres of influence agreement, which the report described as a "purely private arrangement."[120]

Entangled with the missionaries' objections to the "anti-missionary" recommendations of the report was their opposition to its "anti-native" tone. Recognizing that the report advocated the commercial exploitation of Papua, they feared its effect upon the Papuans. Of particular concern was a proposal for compulsory purchase by the government of "such of the native's land as is not reasonably required by him."[121] Will Saville expressed a typical missionary reaction to this proposal:

> Papua has always been governed for the natives; it has always been considered the Papuan's country and its lands were held sacred. . . . Australia says no, land must be compulsorily sold to us. . . . I really believe Australia would not mind smudging another page of its history by shooting the natives off.[122]

Confronted with such a threat, missionaries of the LMS, Anglican, and Methodist missions fought their most concerted battle as protectors of the Papuans. "Of course we loyally recognise that we are under Commonwealth Government," wrote Dauncey, "but we recognise also that we must not stand by and see the native helped out of existence as he has been in Australia."[123] Abel, Bromilow, and Stone-Wigg, deputized by their respective missions, strove to influence press, politicians, and public opinion in Australia. Their joint letter of protest, juxtaposing Erskine's promise of 1884, "Your lands will be secured to you," with the compulsory purchase clause, drew sympathetic editorials and articles from most of the leading daily papers to which it was sent.[124] Bromilow mobilized opinion through the missionary board, which entreated Methodists throughout the commonwealth to "use their influence to prevent any injustice being done to the natives of Papua."[125] Abel worked through the Society's influential agent, Joseph King, and through that pioneer protector of the Papuans, W. G. Lawes, who had recently retired to Sydney.[126] The missionaries counted it a personal victory when they received an assurance from Acting Prime Minister Sir John Forrest that the Papuans' land would not be taken.[127]

The hostility of the Protestant missionaries toward the Royal Commission was strengthened by their suspicion of Roman Catholic influence, especially that of Cardinal Moran, which they believed to have been exercised through the Australian Natives' Association.[128] They interpreted the appointment of J. H. P. Murray, a Roman Catholic, as lieutenant governor in the same light. "The hand making the changes may be the hand of Esau (Labor Party) but the voice directing the changes is the voice of Jacob (Cardinal Moran) and there are dark days ahead of us," predicted Harry Dauncey.[129]

Other Protestant missionaries shared Dauncey's misgivings. Even the Methodist secretary, Benjamin Danks, referred to Murray with unbecoming bigotry as a person to whom "one would scarcely look for a criterion of Christian character."[130] Anglican wariness of Murray dated from 1904 when he, as chief judicial officer, acceded to a request from the SHM that it be known as "The Catholic Mission." Bishop Stone-Wigg responded, "As there are four Missions working in the Possession, and at least two claim to be Catholic missions . . . may I ask you . . . to which of the four Missions reference is made?"[131] After protracted correspondence between the Anglican bishop and the government secretary, it was agreed in 1908 that the SHM be designated the "Roman Catholic Mission."[132]

But the dominant source of mistrust between the three non–Roman Catholic missions and the new Australian regime was their fear that, owing to Roman Catholic influence, the mission spheres would be dismantled. Representatives Stone-Wigg, Bromilow, and Abel wrote to Prime Minister Alfred Deakin in December 1907, protesting at the opinion of the commissioners and arguing for the maintenance of the spheres.[133] Their letter was sent in January 1908 to the new lieutenant governor, Murray, who, with his executive council, sought the opinion of the Sacred Heart Mission.

In the years since the departure of MacGregor, the SHM had gained, in the person of Alain de Boismenu, an impressive champion. More conciliatory than Navarre and more political than Verjus, he had campaigned consistently against the spheres, "a wretched piece of political Erastianism,"[134] which he saw as a fundamental violation of religious liberty. At the Second Australasian Catholic Congress held in Melbourne in 1904 he condemned the agreement as "intolerable . . . perni-

cious [and] alien to the British sense of 'fair play'."[135] Although some of
the intensity of the conflict between the SHM and the government had
been defused after the turn of the century by the redirecting of much of
the mission's expansion toward the mountains, and by their removal, in
Waima, to land obtained from European traders and thus exempt from
the need for government ratification, the Sacred Heart missionaries
remained uncompromising in their determination to win freedom of
movement. Invited by Hubert Murray to state their case, de Boismenu
launched a cogent, ironic, and persuasive attack on the spheres.[136] The
executive council of Papua referred the issue back to the federal government, which, without pronouncing on the policy in general, contented
itself with upholding the practice of having only one mission in each village.

Although their challenge to the spheres had not succeeded, the Sacred
Heart missionaries received from Murray more personal sympathy than
they had experienced from his non–Roman Catholic predecessors. They
found in the Australian government, wrote de Boismenu in 1911, "a
benevolent fairness that our missionaries do not always find in our
French colonies."[137] Anglican opposition to Murray was softened by the
influence of Henry Newton, an old school friend who, after his en-
thronement in 1921, insisted on total cooperation with the government.
Protestant missionaries were slower to shed their anti-Catholic suspicions. But as the years passed, growing recognition of Murray's impar-
tiality and his support, and above all the realization that protection of
the Papuans was as much a cornerstone of his policy as of their own,
encouraged increasing respect.[138] Missions and government worked
together, wrote Murray in 1907, "towards a common end—that end
being the amelioration of the native races of Papua."[139] Murray actively
courted the missionaries' support as he became embroiled in a struggle,
culminating in the twenties, against settler interests, which he saw as
incompatible with the interests of the Papuans.[140]

Of course, there was occasional friction. Ben Butcher became an
adversary of the government in 1919 through his condemnation of an
unnecessarily violent government raid on the small village of Kumu-
kumu, near Aird Hill.[141] LMS and Methodist missionaries fought
against laxness in the recruiting system and the proposed introduction of
"coolie labour."[142] Methodist missionaries maintained for decades a running debate with Murray on the extent of depopulation.[143] But in general Murray's policy, and his ability, like MacGregor's, to impose it on
his field officers, won increasing approval from the missionaries in the
interwar years. The period of cooperation was heralded in 1914 when
representatives of the non–Roman Catholic missions waited on Murray
in Melbourne to express their approval of his "native policy."[144]

Missionaries and Imperialism

It is an oversimplification to see the British missionaries in New Guinea as manipulated by "selfish forces" of imperialism who took "protective colour" from their idealism,[145] or to see them simply as one of the "sinister trio of capitalist imperialism," in league with traders and officials.[146] Missionaries saw themselves as distinct from government officers and to a large extent—and in the case of the Protestant missionaries, on the instructions of their societies—held themselves aloof from politics. The absence of a hereditary chieftainship or any form of strong, centralized, indigenous government removed the temptation of becoming *éminences grises* to which some missionaries had succumbed in Polynesia.[147] Insofar as missionaries did enter the political arena, it was most commonly in their role as "the native's watchdog," a role recognized as theirs by government officials.[148] This did not make them inevitable allies of government. When they saw Papuan interests advanced by official policy, they cooperated with the government; when they saw it threatened, they opposed it. And because of the influence they exerted on both the local peoples and public opinion in Britain and Australia, they negotiated from a position of strength. They were not puppets, nor tools of government; their cooperation was always conditional on their objectives being fulfilled. That they lent support to the call for foreign intervention in New Guinea and that they were such close allies for much of the period before the First World War, was due to the "happy accident" of perceived community of interest.

Yet if it is fallacious to see the missionaries simply in their stereotyped image as one of the sinister trio, it is equally misleading to view their involvement with imperialism solely in terms of their self-promoted image as champions of Papuan rights. While they strove, consistently and conscientiously, to curb the exploitation inherent in imperial rule, they were nevertheless fundamentally implicated in the whole process. Most held the common assumption of European superiority and supported its corollary of "the white man's burden," the civilizing mission to the "backward races."[149] Methodist and Anglican missionaries especially, many of British stock, shared to a greater or lesser extent their contemporaries' enthusiasm for British imperial rule. They celebrated the queen's birthdays and jubilees, mourned her death, commemorated the coronation of her son, and in turn mourned his passing. "We are doing our best out here to keep loyal feelings alive and I think we shall get quite enthusiastically British Empire," Bishop Stone-Wigg wrote to his mother in the Jubilee Year of 1897.[150] Few would have disclaimed their association with empire. "I suppose the missionaries of all denominations are considerable factors in spreading the Imperial idea?" a journalist asked Stone-Wigg. "Undoubtedly," replied the bishop. "Of course the natives don't understand Imperialism as we understand it. . . ."[151] For advocates of industrial mission, who supported the nexus between Christianity, colonialism, civilization, and commerce expounded by Livingstone, the bonds were particularly close. To most of their contemporaries, imperial rule was of unquestioned value.

In a country where they were surrounded by largely unknown peoples of a different race, the similarities between missionaries and officials inevitably appeared greater than the differences. Despite their protests of independence, some missionaries were comforted by the security of imperial rule. Some, of humble birth, were flattered by their association with senior officials, while others, more highly born and frequently of similar social origins, felt affinity with them.[152] Such association, while not nullifying their protector role, embroiled them more deeply, at least in the eyes of others, in the processes of imperialism.

The great irony of the missionaries' role in New Guinea, as in other colonial situations, was that the distinction between missionary and official, which they strove so carefully to maintain, was not always perceived by the people. Papuans often successfully exploited the differences between missionaries and government officers, using the former as mediators or intercessors with the latter, or playing one off against the other, but at other times, in their eyes, the distinction became blurred. Even the Sacred Heart missionaries, who by virtue of their non-British origins were less intimately associated with the imperial government, found that the Papuans were prone to confuse the two. "We have told the natives we have nothing in common with the government; they only half believe it," observed Navarre.[153] The Motu who identified the gunboats in Moresby Harbour at the declaration of the protectorate as "Tamate's canoes" or the Massim who watched the *Merrie England* tow the pioneer Methodist party ashore, or the Kiriwinans marched to church by the commandant of the "native constabulary," could not be blamed for failing to distinguish between missionaries and officials.

Missionaries were compromised in other ways. Their attitude to punishment was ambivalent and at times inconsistent. Most deplored punitive expeditions. Before his expedition to Goaribari, the LMS begged Le Hunte not to seek vengeance for the death of Chalmers and his companions, and the SHM pleaded similarly for the Fuyughe after their attack on de Boismenu and his party in 1900.[154] "Our system of revenge is thoroughly savage," Chalmers had reflected early in his career,[155] yet that great champion of the Papuans had himself taken part in a punitive expedition in 1881 after the people of Kalo had killed several Polynesian teachers and their families.[156] That he did so reluctantly, and only to prevent unnecessary bloodshed, was unlikely to have been apparent to the people whose village was shelled. On other occasions missionaries kept strangely silent in the face of violence by officials.

The Roro, threatened by Verjus for the theft of an axe with the words: "Don't you know that I have only to say a word and the man-of-war at Port Moresby will come to punish you?"[157] or the Mekeo, to whom Verjus introduced MacGregor as "the big chief,"[158] might well have failed to see much difference between mission and government. For the Mekeo of Inawaia, subjugated by MacGregor after Verjus' representations to him and reconciled to the government through Verjus' mediations, the difference between missionary and official must have been especially elusive.[159] Sir William MacGregor, not one to be indecisive when action was required, reported when urged by Copland King to take reprisals for cannibalism that he did not always "concur with King's use of violence."[160] Papuans, like government officers, may have been confused by the tendency of some missionaries to report misdemeanors but not to press charges.[161] Such collusion between missionaries and officials, while generally consistent with the missionaries' paternalistic understanding of the Papuans' best interests, in the eyes of the people compromised them in their role of protector. The Papuans could be pardoned for believing, like the Nigerians under colonial rule, that missionary and official were "birds of a feather."[162]

Relations between the Missions

Official relations between the three non–Roman Catholic missions remained generally harmonious before the First World War. The highest possible standards for cooperation had been established at their first meeting in 1890. There was a natural sympathy between the two Protestant bodies, and Albert Maclaren, of an era and a tradition not known for its ecumenism, had won their esteem for his flexibility, "largeheartedness," and "broad sympathies."[163] Had he only come earlier, wrote Lawes, "I might have joined him and become the first bishop of New Guinea!"[164] Despite a private distaste for Protestant worship, which he found "too flippant" and "not dignified enough,"[165] Maclaren joined LMS missionaries in family prayers and in a service to open the new "European" church at Port Moresby, and received communion from the hands of the Protestant missionaries.[166] "Am I not right?" he reflected. "Surely in a heathen country we don't want to shock the poor natives with our unhappy divisions. . . . I trust I am none the less a Catholic in its deepest meaning."[167] Missionaries of all persuasions mourned his death.[168]

The Evangelical, Copland King, who became leader of the Anglican

Mission after Maclaren, found no difficulty in cooperating with his Protestant colleagues. In 1893 a second meeting of representatives of the three missions discussed, at the government's request, "native marriage" and, for their own benefit, the definition of the Sabbath and the adaptation of biblical names to local languages.[169]

Bishop Stone-Wigg's uncompromising Anglo-Catholicism placed some strain on relations with the Protestant missions. The Anglicans' tendency to style themselves "The New Guinea Mission" was, wrote Lawes, "a piece of cool sacerdotal cheek."[170] LMS and Methodist missionaries resented the building of an Anglican church at Samarai, regarded as within the LMS district of Charles Abel.[171] It was, remarked George Brown to Bromilow, "a monstrous piece of sacerdotalism."[172] Stone-Wigg's refusal to give communion to Protestants or to allow into his pulpit any nonconformists save, as a special concession, Charles Abel, provoked further indignation.[173]

But despite the friction caused by Stone-Wigg's activities at Samarai, personal relations remained civil and cooperative. The representatives of the LMS and Anglican missions at Samarai, Charles Abel and Frederick Ramsay, both muscular Christians, met harmoniously; Stone-Wigg visited Kwato and Dobu, two Anglican women missionaries also visited Dobu to discuss their work with the Methodist sisters, and a Methodist Fijian taught mat-making at Dogura.[174] Doctrinal differences were put aside for joint protests against government policy and practice.[175]

It is not surprising that Archbishop Navarre suspected a powerful coalition of Protestant (in which he included Anglican) interests. Albert Maclaren had established friendly relations with the SHM by visiting Verjus when he was ill, drinking wine with him, and worshipping in the Yule Island chapel.[176] Later Verjus remarked to MacGregor that Maclaren was said to be "more Catholic than him."[177] De Boismenu was impressed by Stone-Wigg, whom he found "admirably cultured, well-raised and sincere." After meeting him, he lamented, "They are so close, so close to us!"[178] But the Anglicans shared their Protestant colleagues' suspicions of the intentions of the SHM, and Stone-Wigg, seeing the church of Rome as "the implacable enemy of all other forms of Christian endeavour," pressed into the Mamba district for fear of encroachments.[179] The Anglican Mission was, however, distant from the SHM, and the sole encounter of any substance between the two was over the right to the title The Catholic Mission.

The only major conflict between Protestants and Roman Catholics in Papua was the struggle between the LMS and the SHM over the disputed territory of Waima. Although it avoided the violence of similar encounters in other colonies, it was a form of sectarian warfare, perhaps exacerbated but not caused by the spheres of influence. As was common in that period, each side acted in profound ignorance of the other, relying upon the stereotyped prejudices of its own religious subculture. Navarre embellished his image of the Protestant missionaries with the allegations of the trader, Edward Guise, that Lawes was a drunkard and that Chalmers had two native mistresses at Port Moresby.[180] There was more basis for his criticism of the Polynesian teachers of the LMS, but scarcely sufficient to justify the contempt with which he and his priests wrote of them.[181] On the other side, Lawes manifested an uncompromising anti-Catholicism, an attitude in which he was encouraged by the Society. "Roman Catholic missions may be better than nothing," Thompson told him, "but I have little hesitation in trying to keep them out."[182] The subsequent scramble to fill in the gaps in their coastline, while the SHM extended itself beyond its resources through Roro and Mekeo, was motivated primarily by the desire of each to exclude the other.[183]

Although the Sacred Heart missionaries' decision to move into Protestant territory was based on their "duty" to distribute the "good bread of God" among the "false doctrines" of Protestantism,[184] their manner of taking occupation was undeniably provocative. The missionaries galloped into Waima like conquerors, their horses' bridles garlanded with plumes and flowers,[185] and when the priests and brothers gathered there to rejoice at "the splendid rout inflicted upon the Protestants," it was a victory celebration.[186]

That the confrontation was not more violent was due in part to the forbearance of some of the main antagonists and the personal relationships that developed among them. Chalmers, despite his Scottish Presbyterian heritage, extended his vast sympathy to the Roman Catholic missionaries. "If any of the New Guineans are benefitted and blessed, and Jesus glorified, I don't care who may be the instruments," he wrote in 1893.[187] Brother Alexis Henkelmann, after receiving from Chalmers "saxon hospitality in all its splendour," regretted that "a strength such as his was not Catholic."[188] Pryce Jones won similar respect from Father Clauser for the "free and cordial" welcome he offered at Iokea.[189] But above all others, Harry Dauncey, LMS missionary at Delena, strove to keep the peace between the two missions. In the face of criticism from some of his colleagues, he withdrew the LMS claim to Vanamai and, despite Navarre's conviction that "sooner or later there must come a crash," sought to make their joint occupation of Waima as free of conflict as possible.[190] Father Genocchi, superior of the SHM when the crisis began, described Dauncey to his confrères in Europe as "a perfect gentleman full of good faith [who] would not for all the world give pain to us Catholic missionaries, whom he loves and esteems sincerely."[191]

The Sacred Heart missionaries were fortunate to have as neighbors the more liberal and tolerant members of the LMS rather than the Methodists whose traditional antipopery, judging from the violence of their protests at Cardinal Moran's perspective on missions,[192] had not mellowed with time.

But despite the conciliatory attitude of men such as Dauncey and Genocchi, relations between the two missions deteriorated following the SHM's incursion into Waima. Conflict at village level became common as Samoan pastors competed with European priests and brothers for the allegiance of the people.[193] LMS missionaries resented the enticements offered by the SHM in the form of material rewards for attendance and the imposition of only a "continental sabbath."[194] Each side made slanderous allegations about the other.[195] By 1911 there were occasional skirmishes between priests and the headstrong Samoan pastors. "Striking, kicking, biting and any amount of strong language," reported Dauncey after one such incident.[196] "It is now an open fight," he told the LMS directors.[197] Hostility and sporadic violence continued to blight the relationship of the two missions throughout the interwar years.[198]

Because of the operation of the spheres of influence policy, contact between the personnel of the various missions was limited, except at the frontier. When it did occur, missionaries were generally courteous and cooperative, despite official tensions, offering members of all other persuasions hospitality, transport, resources, medical aid, and even comfort in bereavement.[199] Faced with the challenges of a strange and sometimes hostile land, the differences between them appeared fewer than the bonds that united them. Besides their common commitment to Christ, they shared their commitment to the protection of the Papuans, which threw them together, sometimes with, sometimes against the government, and almost invariably in opposition to the third major expatriate group in the colony, the traders, miners, and planters.

Missionaries, Traders, and Settlers

Throughout the years before the First World War, the commercial population of Papua outnumbered both missionaries and government employees. In 1907–1908, for instance, miners alone constituted 27 percent of the working European population, while planters, traders, storekeepers and hotelkeepers accounted for 21 percent, government officials and employees 15 percent, and missionaries 14.5 percent (Table 6). The commercial community consisted of a small solid core and a large floating population of traders and diggers who shifted according to gold strikes and the commercial prospects of a particular area.

Table 6. Census of European work force—year ended 30 June 1908

Occupation or profession	Central Division	Eastern Division	Western Division	Gulf Division	Northeastern Division	Northern Division	Southeastern Division	Total Papua
Government officials and employees	55	10	2	1	2	5	3	78
Missionaries	47	16	1	3	4	1	3	75
Planters	23	6	1	3			8	41
Storekeepers	1	18	4			7	4	34
Traders	4	10	1	3	1	2	11	32
Mariners	23	3				1		27
Hotelkeepers	1	3						4
Miners	15	4				77	41	137
Native labor recruiters		10					3	13
Carpenters, ship-builders, and boat-builders	3	14					4	21
Other occupations	19	18	1			1	15	54
Total	191	112	10	10	7	94	92	516

Source: Adapted from Papua *Annual Report 1907–08*, 25.

Throughout the period the number of traders decreased and the number of planters increased, although the change was partly one of definition as settlers with small landholdings and trade stores chose to identify themselves by the more prestigious title. None fitted the image of the large-scale, wealthy tropical planter.

The general antipathy between missionaries and traders was, in Papua as elsewhere, mutual. Each was prone to a false stereotype of the other, observed their contemporary, C. A. W. Monckton. The traders saw the missionary as "a measly, psalm-singing hypocrite"; the missionary regarded traders as "drunken, debauched, pyjama-clad ruffians."[200] Most missionaries continued to make the simple equation that had motivated Chalmers' and Lawes' attack on the early traders: commercial exploitation of the country was synonymous with the exploitation of the Papuans. In their self-appointed role of protector, they opposed the exploitation of Papuan resources, labor, and women.[201]

Their attitude to sexual exploitation by the traders was based not only on its disruptive effect on Papuan society, but also on the affront it presented to their own strict morality, which anathematized "loose living."[202] Cohabitation or casual liaisons became a symbol, especially to the Anglican missionaries, of the immorality that the traders represented.[203] Stone-Wigg was gleeful when the report of the Royal Commission recommended deportation for any Europeans suffering from venereal disease or "interfering with immoral purpose" with native women. "This is the great fight I have waged for nine years," he wrote, "But I am out-Heroded by the Commissioners for I have never gone so far as to suggest deportation . . ."[204]

Opposition to the presence of the traders was reinforced by the awareness that they represented a rival, and at times more attractive, influence on village life. The impotent fury of James Chalmers when the traders Guise and Currie enticed the people of Hula away from his services with lavish payments of tobacco and lessons in rifle-shooting and swearing,[205] or the frustration of Samuel Fellows when Nicholas the Greek arranged a conch-shell-blowing demonstration to compete with his first service on Kiriwina,[206] were not entirely disinterested.

While the missionaries lamented the immorality of the traders, the traders mocked the self-righteous wowserism of the missionaries. But their antagonism was often based on more than a false image of them. The missionaries' unofficial but always vigilant protection of Papuan interests frustrated the sharper practices of some of the traders. Others felt that the missionaries betrayed their color by identifying with the interests of the "native" against those of the "white man." Intransigent mission opposition to Sunday trading was a constant source of irritation. And from the protectorate period on, traders suspected mission influence on government policy.[207]

But the greatest source of resentment was over the question of trading. Traders objected to missionaries who set up trade stores on their stations and undercut their prices. Although mission societies forbade their members to engage in trade, all missions owned plantations on a modest scale. The tensions caused by such practices became more acute at the turn of the century, when the concept of industrial mission lent respectability to a measure of trading. The arch-exponent of industrial mission, Charles Abel, argued that rather than hold themselves aloof from the world of commerce, the missionaries should compete with the traders, thereby providing the Papuans with the option of a Christian commercial activity. Such a philosophy, and his energetic and successful prosecution of it, earned him, and to a lesser extent other missionaries, the intense hostility of the traders whose interests were threatened.[208] Abel's personal attitude toward the traders, of whom he wrote to the LMS directors, "I'll sweep the Bay clean of these blackguards in three years,"[209] did nothing to reduce the conflict. In him the traders saw an embodiment of all they loathed in the missionary—the puritanical opponent of their way of life, the aggressive protector of the Papuans against all exploitation, and above all the successful competitor (Figure 23).

From the time of the Laloki gold rush, missionaries had feared the influence of miners. Stone-Wigg incurred their anger at statements allegedly made by him and reported in the *North Queensland Register*, denouncing their drunkenness, their "vicious traffic with native women," the introduction of venereal disease, and their "disastrous counteracting influence to the civilizing . . . influence of missionaries and Government officials."[210] Perhaps contrite at the offense his comments gave, Stone-Wigg visited the diggers, and, although unable to agree on questions of morality—the diggers answering his charges with the assertion that the missionaries' celibacy was unnatural—they parted amicably.[211] Later Stone-Wigg confessed himself "an admirer of the digger, with all his faults" and reminded his staff that although "the profanity, the drunkenness, the immorality, the coarseness" disgusted them, "just as much wickedness" could exist under a quiet exterior.[212]

Attitudes to settlers were more diverse. Most missionaries shared the fears of the pioneers that settlement would lead to the dispossession of the Papuans, and perhaps genocide. But while some missionaries expressed total opposition to white settlement, others supported controlled colonization. Both Copland King and Charles Abel declared themselves before the Royal Commission in favor of some European settlement,[213] and Stone-Wigg reflected the prejudices of his class in advocating "settlement on a big scale."[214] Believing that the "small man" was the "mean man," he urged controlled immigration to ensure the presence of a "good class of men."[215]

Figure 23. "The cocoa-nut religion." (*Bulletin*, 14 August 1886, 22)

Whatever their personal prejudices, missionaries of all bodies working in Papua recognized a responsibility to its settlers as well as its indigenous population. For those placed near concentrations of settlers, as at Port Moresby and Samarai, that responsibility became a substantial part of their work.[216] But the two missions most broadly affected by the presence of Europeans were the Anglicans and the Methodists, in whose spheres much of the mining and other commercial activity of the colony occurred. Both missions took their responsibilities seriously. Stone-Wigg built a church and a school for the settlers of Samarai, and the mission station on the Mamba, established by Ernest Hines in 1899 and taken over by King, ministered to the large population of diggers in that district. When quartz mining brought a large incursion of miners to Murua, the Methodists stationed a series of missionaries on the island, each of whose careers was cut short by illness or death.[217]

Such personal contact between the missionaries and the traders, miners, and settlers went some way toward modifying the attitudes of each to the other. W. H. Gors, manager of Burns, Philp & Company and a friend of Stone-Wigg and other missionaries, paid public tribute to their work and influence.[218] Some missionaries won admiration even from the traders. One unidentified trader, attending the memorial service for Chalmers and Tomkins, remarked that although not a churchgoer, he "would walk one hundred miles to church to do honour to the memory of Tamate."[219] Another, recalling kindness from Tomkins, observed, "they never made anybody nearer a saint."[220] Samuel Fellows, subjected to continual harassment by the traders on his arrival at Kiriwina, won their affection by his good-natured readiness to offer assistance.[221] Copland King earned respect though not affection for his dedicated service on the Mamba,[222] while his colleague Frederick Ramsay, a "real man" with a "dirty left" was universally esteemed on the Mamba and in Samarai.[223] In 1903 the Yodda diggers collected £31 as a testimonial to the nurses Cottingham and Nowland, insisting, however, that the money go to the women and not to the Anglican Mission.[224] Throughout Papua, settlers, miners, and traders remembered care received from missionaries or their wives in illness, injury, or other crises.[225] For their part, many missionaries probably discovered, as did A. K. Chignell, that such people were "just ordinary men—like the missionaries themselves."[226]

Nevertheless, relations between the missionaries and the Europeans with commercial interests in New Guinea remained at best, distant and at worst, hostile. In the triangular relationship between missionary, settler, and official, the distance between the missionary and the settler was always greater than that between the missionary and the official. Missionary objectives were always distinct from, and frequently at odds with, those of the planters, diggers, and traders. These objectives were an intricate mixture of the philanthropic and the self-interested, but, as in their relations with the government, a significant element was their commitment to the protection of the Papuan people.

Despite fundamental differences in outlook and objective, the missionaries and the traders were, to a degree, unwitting collaborators. The economic activity of the missionaries of this period was minuscule, but the acculturation process that their arrival initiated had economic as well as social implications. For some Papuans living close to mission stations, their first experience of working for European employers was not in the labor lines of plantations, nor in the compulsory village labor exacted by government officers, but in the mission compound. Contact with the mission station introduced Papuans—if not to the cash economy (for payment was commonly by stick tobacco or other trade goods) —to the consumption of Western goods through the agency of the mission store. And, more fundamentally, the demands imposed on villagers by missionaries, as well as by traders and officials, and the opportunities their world provided, conflicted with and radically altered the old socioeconomic order.

Through their role as champion of Papuan rights, the missionaries sought to prevent economic exploitation. But their effect was to soften the impact of the introduction of a capitalist system rather than to challenge its foundations. While many missionaries opposed European settlement and the recruitment of Papuan labor, others sought only to regulate the process and curb abuses. Despite their concern for the Papuan people, most were as culturally bound in their conception of social and economic organization as the majority of their contemporaries. Neither stereotype of the missionaries, either as one of the sinister trio or as champion of Papuan rights, allows for the inevitable ambiguities of their position as mediators between two cultures.

CHAPTER 10

"A Peculiar People"

Public and Personal Crises

ON 24 AUGUST 1914, Ben Butcher, at his Gulf station, Aird Hill, heard rumors of a war among the European powers. "It is too dreadful to contemplate what it may mean for the world," he wrote. "We shall all suffer and no country will be better off at the end of it all."[1] Then followed an anxious fortnight while he awaited confirmation. On 8 September, he heard definite news of the war and by 16 September, had received "one ragged paper" bearing reports.[2] For other missionaries the experience was similar, the delay being greater or less according to the state of communication with their stations.[3]

The months that followed were marked by suspense as the missionaries "read and re-read" papers that were invariably a month old.[4] "We feel that all the news is on your side of the world," Butcher wrote to a confidant in England. "On this side we just live from day to day looking for the next boat and trying to get along with our duties, though all the time wondering what is happening in the great struggle."[5] Butcher could not recall a year when he had felt "such strain."[6] The installation of wireless at Port Moresby enabled the government to circulate items from cables in Australian newspapers, which meant that missionaries close to shipping routes could receive news that was only four or five days old. But, lamented one, it was "woefully tantalising" in its brevity.[7]

Few missionaries spoke against the war. Charles Abel did so as a pacifist and Ben Butcher denounced as "wickedly insane" the recourse of "civilised nations" to arms.[8] But as the war progressed, perhaps influenced by the patriotic press, Butcher's faith in Divine Providence and his hope that war might lead to disarmament reconciled him to it, and while on furlough he served as a chaplain in France. Some missionaries responded to the war with the same patriotic fervor as many of their compatriots. Will Saville exulted in the "oneness of Empire."[9] A few manifested in their enthusiasm a jingoistic excess scarcely compatible with Christian charity. LMS missionary Charles Rich urged that the "wily Hun" be completely crushed, while his colleague Saville advocated that German soldiers be killed, since "prisoners live to fight another day."[10]

Several left the mission field for the battlefield. Norman Fettell left the Anglican Mission to fight for "liberty, freedom and indirectly the spread of the Gospel,"[11] as did another Anglican, Ernest Owen Davies, who died in the trenches in 1918. Their colleague, A. K. Chignell, leaving the Papuan field for an administrative post with the mission in London, regretted that he too could not take part in the "dreadful, splendid things" that were going to be "the re-making of England and the next generation of Englishmen."[12] Thirteen French missionaries of the Sacred Heart presented themselves for enlistment but, worn and debilitated by chronic malaria, all were judged unfit for service. Two MSC from Papua, recruited elsewhere, served as chaplains, one of them, Father van Neck, winning high military honors, including the Croix de Guerre. Methodist missionary F. J. Winn, who served with the Australian Expeditionary Forces, was at first advised by the missionary board that he would "do better service both for the British Empire and the Greater Empire" through his mission work.[13] A similar conviction may have influenced other eligible missionaries, who believed themselves to be fighting a battle greater than the temporal.

The leaders of the Methodist, Anglican, and Sacred Heart missions were moved to address their staffs on the war. Matthew Gilmour simply urged the Methodists to greater sacrifice.[14] Bishop Sharp explored the attitude of Christianity toward war and assured the Anglicans that it was necessary as a way of settling disputes between nations. "It is this judicial character of war as a mode of obtaining justice that gives it its morality," he concluded.[15] Bishop de Boismenu, addressing his scattered staff through an episcopal letter, described the war as the "great school of the supernatural."[16] Faith enabled the Christian to see beyond the explosion of human hatred and ambition to an omnipotent God who could "turn even these excesses to his own good and merciful ends." For believers, the war provided an opportunity for sacrifice, suffering, and expiation. For unbelievers, it was a "call to order." Confident of its "eminent place in the divine plan," the missionaries could pass through it, "not without suffering but without mistrust."

Although remote, the war did engender considerable suffering among the missionaries. In material terms it meant disruption of shipping, shortage of provisions, inflated prices, and reduction in personnel.

But for most, these privations were probably negligible compared with the emotional dislocation it caused. Missionaries suffered the frustration of lack of involvement, the anguish of wondering whether they had made the right decision, and the demoralization of doubt as to the significance and usefulness of their work. Sacred Heart missionaries, whose emotional and organizational ties with Europe were strongest, suffered intensely.

No previous event that occurred beyond the shores of New Guinea had affected the missionaries so profoundly or so universally. British and Australian missionaries had followed the progress of the Boer War, their various reactions to it reflecting those of their compatriots.[17] Many felt a personal loss in the death of Queen Victoria, which they saw as the end of an era.[18] LMS missionaries mourned their colleagues who were victims of the Boxer Rebellion, and French Catholic missionaries grieved at the rupture of the concordat and the persecution of their congregations and other religious in the France of the Third Republic.[19] But generally the missionaries' sense of involvement in world affairs was slight.

Absorbed in the routine and occasional drama of mission life, isolated from all information save that gleaned from out-of-date papers, letters, and periodicals, and encouraged, moreover, in an apolitical stance, missionaries commented little on current issues. Some nonconformists followed the education struggle that dominated British politics at the beginning of the twentieth century, and rejoiced in the Liberal victory of 1906,[20] but declaration of party allegiance is rare in the missionaries' writings. Where political comment is ventured, it is generally conservative—the French Catholic missionaries expressed a nostalgia for royalist France, and British and Australian Protestants, an approval of the *status quo*. William Bromilow infuriated one of the few politically committed Methodist missionaries, the Christian Socialist carpenter George Bardsley, by his complacent belief that poverty was a necessity intended by God, a reflection of an attitude then still prevalent in colonial Methodism.[21] Will Saville of the LMS hated and feared the growth of socialism and trade unionism in Britain. "It is not drink, Alfred, that is going to ruin our land, it is Trade Unionism," he warned his brother.[22] He expressed a similar hostility to the "low-down rabble" of the suffragette movement.[23] But such comment is scant in missionary writings. It took an event as cataclysmic as the First World War, and perhaps the sense of immediacy fostered by the introduction of wireless, to jolt the missionaries out of their "isolation" and "out-of-the worldness" and into vicarious participation in the events of "the outside world."[24]

But, as with most of their fellow mortals, the crises that impinged most on the missionaries were not the great and distant events, but the smaller personal, domestic, and professional crises of their own life and work. These determined the balance for each missionary between hope and despair, faith and doubt, and, in some cases, life and death.

One of the most pervasive crises of the mission field was ill health. Missionaries who suffered not only from the endemic diseases such as malaria and gastroenteritis, but also from the nagging discomfort of decayed teeth, ear infections, and skin complaints, or the "New Guinea tiredness" due to poor nutrition and a trying climate, rightly attributed their depression or low morale in part to their physical condition. In many cases, men and women alike traced "a nervous breakdown" or "nervous derangement" to chronic ill health.[25]

For some missionaries, bereavement caused a crisis of faith or morale. Many who stoically accepted the death of a child or spouse were, at the death of a colleague, mystified that God should allow reduction in the ranks of his sorely needed workers. W. G. Lawes, who had fretted at the high death rate of his Polynesian staff, reacted in "silent bewilderment" to the death of a promising young missionary, Watson Sharpe, shortly after his arrival in New Guinea. "I cannot tell you how depressed and sad we feel," he wrote to Wardlaw Thompson. "All our hopes are dashed. It seems as if we were never to have any help. I can't ask you to send any more young men now. I can't take any responsibility for bringing out young men to die here."[26]

Personal conflict between missionaries, or stresses provoked by the structure of the mission, caused considerable suffering for some. Hostilities or antipathies, often exacerbated by poor health, low morale, and unavoidable propinquity, were endemic in all missions. Domination of subordinates by superiors, of women by men, and of lay by ordained, led to demoralization among those subjected to it. This was a source of particular stress in the Anglican Mission where, because of an exalted view of the priesthood, lay workers perceived themselves as relegated to a markedly inferior position. A young layman, Robert Dakers, wondered whether it was "the layman's fault that the average years of his missionary life are so short." The lay worker came to the field with "as much enthusiasm and earnestness" as the priest, he told Stone-Wigg. "A priest's dignity, authority and peculiarities must be upheld . . . even at the expense of the layman."[27] Periodic demoralization among the brothers of the SHM can be similarly explained.[28]

Loneliness was a constant trial to some missionaries, especially Protestants, who lacked the comfort of community. Particularly vulnerable were single, young missionaries or men separated from their wives. "Eh man!" wrote Will Saville to his brother, "did you but know the battles one has to fight here and that all alone, none to encourage you, none to advise you, none to whom you can speak, waiting and waiting and waiting for mails."[29] For such isolated, embattled missionaries, visits from sympathetic colleagues were "red-letter days,"[30] dispelling for a time the loneliness which, confessed one, was so intense as to be "almost unbearable."[31] Homesickness struck even seasoned missionaries, especially on the festival days of their own society. "Separation from a home such as mine at this time is more than I can bear to think about," wrote Fred Walker on Christmas Day, 1888.[32] Beyond their personal loneliness was a "cultural and racial loneliness"[33] derived from being isolated representatives of European culture in an alien society. This encouraged missionaries to reproduce features of their own society and to attach sentimental significance to minor aspects of their own culture.

One of the crises of isolation for young bachelors, or even for married men deprived for long periods of the company of their wives, was sexual temptation. All four missions placed great emphasis on sexual purity, the Anglican Mission favoring the chastity of celibacy practiced by their Roman Catholic brethren or, as a poor second, the restriction of sex to marriage enjoined on their Protestant colleagues. All would have supported the stand taken by Stone-Wigg who, urged by the administrator, C. S. Robinson, to allow his staff "liaisons with native women," insisted that sexual purity was as much a plank of Christian life as were the incarnation or atonement of Christian belief.[34] "Immorality," which invariably meant, in mission parlance, falling short of the approved sexual standards, was one of the most heinous sins a missionary could be guilty of.

Celibacy posed problems in the Anglican Mission especially, where it lacked the supportive institutional framework that was provided in the Roman Catholic church. It caused particular stress in young laymen who had neither priestly status nor religious vows to constrain them. Percy Money, a dedicated layman, confessed to his bishop the "wicked, lustful thoughts" that often filled his mind.[35] Stone-Wigg eventually acquiesced in his marriage, as he did also in that of Frederick Ramsay, whose behavior with the Samarai barmaids had created scandal.[36] But two laymen were forced to leave the mission after casual sexual encounters with Papuan women, and rumors of the immorality of three others probably reinforced Stone-Wigg's willingness to let them go.[37] "Single missionaries in New Guinea are a dead failure," declared one as he departed.[38] The only priest about whom allegations of immorality were made was Copland King, whom the diggers accused of fathering a child in a Mamba village.[39] Subsequent investigation by Monckton showed the baby to be an "ordinary native child," whose mother, a "most unmitigated whore," admitted a native policeman to be the father.[40] But even the devoted King had apparently felt some of the pressures of celibacy. He admitted to Stone-Wigg that he had once "erred grievously, morally."[41]

Within the other three missions, there was less evidence of immorality. The Sacred Heart fathers, protected by both their priestly status and
their vows, seem to have resisted whatever temptations beset them, but
two lay brothers, who had made only temporary vows, were required
to leave the congregation and marry after being discovered in liaisons
with Papuan girls.[42] One became a planter and loyal supporter of the
mission. Most Protestant missionaries had the double protection of ordination and marriage, although the frequent and long absences of so
many wives weakened the efficacy of the latter. Writing to his absent
wife of his loneliness, Ben Butcher confessed, "I doubt if I should have
kept straight had I not been a missionary."[43] Against only one Protestant
missionary, J. R. Osborne, ordained but alone in the field, were
charges of a relationship with a Papuan woman substantiated.[44]

Sexual lapses among the missionaries in Papua were considerably
fewer than among, for instance, the pioneer missionaries to the South
Seas.[45] This may be explained by the higher self-esteem of missionaries
of the later period and perhaps to some extent too by their generally low
estimation of the Papuan people. But for some, especially those who
lacked the support of marriage, ordination, or religious vows, "the climate and the passions excited by seeing women near naked"[46] were the
cause of considerable stress.

While most of the missionaries avoided the stigma of moral failure,
many felt a deep sense of failure in their work. "It would break my
heart to give up the work, though it is often broken in the attempt to
execute it," wrote Will Saville.[47] Evidence of progress was often scant,
and backsliding was common. At times their very presence was openly
resented or, at best, treated with stolid indifference. "The people don't
want us," admitted Saville. "We have constantly to overlook this or be
lost in despair."[48] LMS missionaries, upon whom fell the responsbility of
organizing their own programs, were plagued by fundamental doubts
as to whether their work was on the right lines. "What if my work is not
sound?" Holmes asked himself, confessing "a desperate leaning to the
blues."[49]

It is difficult to gauge what happened to the beliefs of the missionaries
during the course of their careers. Their faith was so bound up with
their identity that any doubts or loss of faith could not be lightly admitted. For only two lay missionaries, both Anglicans, it is clear that loss of
faith was the final crisis endured in the mission field. Eric Giblin, a
gifted linguist whom Stone-Wigg had encouraged to seek ordination,
confessed to the bishop his "doubts and disbelievings" on the "vital
issues" of the cross, the atonement, and the hereafter, and declared himself a "semi-agnostic." His loss of faith was accompanied by a period of
emotional turmoil during which he was rebuked for drinking, taking

"indecent" photographs of naked girls, and alleged relationships with Papuan women.[50] George Morris labeled himself a rationalist. The main stumbling blocks to his belief were the virgin birth and the resurrection. Embroiled in conflict with a number of his fellow missionaries, he saw himself as the "black sheep" of the mission.[51]

Missionaries were largely insulated from the turmoil of theological debate. This, C. P. Williams and others have suggested,[52] was one of the attractions of the mission field. Exposed to little but devotional literature and religious periodicals, most probably retained intact the beliefs they brought with them, or else assimilated new concepts so gradually that they experienced no stress. Only in two intellectually lively missionaries is a marked evolution of belief discernible. Ben Butcher, whose initial theology had disturbed the LMS directors, jettisoned many of his beliefs "in the light of modern knowledge," rejecting especially the virgin birth and the atonement. In old age, he found his faith reduced to "one essential," belief in God as the spirit of love.[53] Father Jean Genocchi was influenced by the liberalizing of theology in late nineteenth-century Rome and, on his retirement from the mission, threw himself into biblical criticism and the reconciliation of science and religion, thereby becoming identified with the cause of the modernists whose beliefs were attacked by Pope Pius X in the encyclical *Pascendi* and the decree *Lamentabili san Exitu* of 1907.[54]

For many missionaries, if there was no loss of faith, there was a steady process of attrition whereby things of the spirit were increasingly crowded out by the temporal demands of missionary life. "Too much work and too little prayer" was Ben Butcher's assessment of 1905.[55] The diaries of new missionaries, especially Roman Catholics or Methodists on the path to sanctification, were often filled with spiritual self-examination and prayerful aspirations. In 1891, soon after his arrival, Samuel Fellows wrote in his diary of "much searching of the heart" and declared his constant need for "the atoning-cleansing blood" of his Savior.[56] In the diaries of all but such ardent souls as Henri Verjus, spiritual introspection usually became less frequent with time.[57]

In their self-examinations, many missionaries confessed a tendency to spiritual coldness. The chief temptations, wrote Archibald Hunt, "are negative. Our prayers lack vitality and our words lack enthusiasm."[58] They had no doubt what caused their loss of ardor. They were "beset by the low and sensual and degraded."[59] "One breathes a loathesome atmosphere the whole time," Saville observed.[60] "One needs so much more help to live near the Cross out here," concluded Anglican missionary, Mary Newton.[61] Protestant missionaries especially lamented that at the same time as they were exposed to the contaminating influences of heathenism, they were deprived of the "means of grace through mutual encouragement."[62] Those whose faith had been stirred in Keswick conventions or suburban churches or chapels found their ardor cooling when dependent on their own resources. Oliver Tomkins advised his brother, who was preparing for the mission field, to cultivate spiritual discipline "independent of outside aids," for the temptations were "many and strong."[63] Missionaries deprived of a Christian community for long periods felt themselves depleted and spiritually arid. Ben Butcher in 1914 confessed his relief at the prospect of furlough: "I've reached the limit and want to get among my own people and . . . Christian surroundings."[64] Even Catholic missionaries, who found renewal in community and sacraments, suffered from the "solitude of the soul"[65] in a "heathen" land.

Ill health, bereavement, interpersonal conflict, loneliness, a sense of failure and the cooling of spiritual ardor—and frequently the interaction of two or more of these factors—together with the privations of a harsh climate and poor nutrition, caused frequent depression among missionaries, and sometimes despair. A few sought solace in alcohol;[66] some pleaded their health or "shattered nerves" as a reason for resignation, but the majority plodded on, clinging to the explanations their faith provided for the sufferings they endured.

The comforts the missionaries found in their faith varied little from mission to mission, although the rhetoric was sometimes different. The overriding solace for all was the belief that they were there at God's command. Missionaries of all persuasions spoke of the "privilege" of being "co-workers," "partners," or "collaborators" with God, or, more modestly, "messengers" or "servants" of the King.[67] There was "no happier calling than that of a foreign missionary," proclaimed Robert Turner.[68] Those confronted with failure consoled themselves with the conviction of ultimate triumph. With God all things were possible, and it was the convicting power of the Holy Spirit, not they, who were merely its "instruments," that would bring about "the victory of truth and righteousness."[69]

A very real belief in the presence of Christ animated the lives of many missionaries. For evangelical Protestants and Roman Catholics alike, a literal belief in Divine Providence cast out fear. There was "no danger to God's servant," asserted Samuel Fellows.[70] As Protestant theology became more liberal, however, faith in divine intervention became less common. "Is the old-fashioned belief that if we trust in God He will protect us . . . a delusion?" Lawes wondered, as he reported the resignation of a new missionary after a bout of fever.[71] In the Sacred Heart Mission, the unquenchable belief that God would "supply" their "insufficiency" underlay the "imprudence" of starvation, exhaustion, illness, and death that marked its early years.[72]

From the missionaries' faith in the presence and intervention of God sprang a belief in the efficacy of prayer and the sacraments. Missionaries of all persuasions valued the opportunity for private and corporate prayer, and some isolated Protestant missionaries found a growing appreciation of Holy Communion as they gathered with their colleagues.[73] Many drew comfort and strength from the support given through prayer by families, communities, and, for those of Catholic belief, their intercessors in paradise.[74]

Missionaries answered their own sufferings with the faith that the universe was purposive, that although God's ways were inscrutable, all that happened was part of the divine plan. The resident magistrate, C. A. W. Monckton, confessed himself moved by Sacred Heart missionaries who faced adversity with the affirmation: "Courage, my friend, it is the will of the good God."[75] Some suggested that their sufferings were God's way of testing and tempering them. God was "putting them through the mill," straightening "a crooked stick," or wielding "the pruning knife," as part of their spiritual growth.[76] Others saw their suffering as designed to make them more dependent on God.[77]

Some found comfort in the belief that they were sharing the sufferings of Christ.[78] A solace to missionaries of all persuasions, this belief became a central motif of service in the Sacred Heart Mission. While Protestant missionaries tried to explain away their suffering, Roman Catholics embraced it as an integral part of their apostolate. In their suffering, they believed, they not only shared the suffering of Christ, but they became co-redemptors with Him. Henri Verjus, a living embodiment of this belief, explained his conviction to a French priest, "It seems to me that for the redemption of . . . souls, . . . we must continue the work of Our Lord Jesus Christ across the centuries and that the best way . . . is to become ourselves another Jesus . . . and to go right to the end. . . . Without shedding of blood, no pardon, no redemption."[79]

In this belief, Verjus found a rationalization for the desire for suffering that had obsessed him since his seminarian years. He declared it to be especially important for missionaries to imitate "the last part of Our Saviour's life: the Passion," which had particular significance for him. "The thought of the passion of the Lord transports me," he confided to his spiritual diary. "Good Jesus. . . . Oh! how I love you broken under the whips and nailed on your Cross."[80]

His conviction that the redemption of New Guinea would be won through the suffering of its missionaries inspired not only his own incessant pleas for suffering and martyrdom, but the foundation in 1891 of a Society of Victims, which drew to itself a select group of fathers, brothers, and sisters who wished to immolate themselves for the salvation of

New Guinea. They were to be victims, who were to continue the work of reparation begun on the cross. Their supreme objective was martyrdom but short of that they were to suffer, and to suffer cheerfully. Hunger, thirst, heat, danger, poverty, fever, and mosquitoes—all the normal privations of mission life—were to be joyfully accepted as part of the redemptive process. For those ardent souls for whom this was not sufficient, there were self-imposed disciplines and programs of mortification. "It is a pleasure to see how all these dear souls rejoice to imitate Jesus in the flagellation and crown of thorns," recorded Verjus, who inflicted sufferings on himself with a whip, spiked iron chains for arms and legs, and an iron belt fashioned for him by Mother Liguori.[81] Other mortificatory exercises, which Verjus himself described as "holy follies,"[82] included sculpting with a knife a way of the cross into his flesh, stretching himself on a spiked iron cross, and rubbing vinegar and salt into his wounds.

For a time suffering became the *raison d'être* of the SHM. "Tell them that it is to suffer that one comes here," Verjus instructed a Belgian novice-master.[83] The letters of Fathers Chabot and Hubert, both of whom had a variety of instruments of penance, as well as those of Jullien, Genocchi, Vedère, and several of the sisters, show a conviction similar to that of Verjus. "It is by suffering more than all other means that we will procure the glory of God and the salvation of souls," wrote Father Hubert to the superior general.[84] "To suffer is nothing; to love souls and save them, that is happiness," affirmed one of the sisters.[85] Verjus' society was suppressed in 1893 by the more earth-bound Archbishop Navarre, who feared that the "exuberance of sacrifices"[86] might deflect the missionaries from the more orthodox methods of the apostolate. But the influence of Verjus outlasted his death in 1892, and suffering remained a significant, though probably diminishing, part of the apostolate. "I admire those who love suffering," mused Archbishop de Boismenu on his deathbed in 1953. "It is not for poor men like us."[87]

Length of Service

The length of service of missionaries who came to Papua up to 1914 varied considerably. The longest serving missionary was, as has already been noted, Sister Clothilde, FDNSC, who spent sixty-six years in the country (see chapter 7). The briefest career was that of Dr. Ridgley, who gave the LMS six weeks' service. The average missionary career was, in the SHM 19.8 years, in the LMS 10.1, in the Anglican Mission 10.0, and in the Methodist Mission 6.2 years.

There were notable variations in the pattern of service within the four missions. In the SHM, despite the constant loss of dedicated missionaries through premature death, almost half the total gave more than twenty years of service. In the LMS, which lost fewer missionaries through death, almost 40 percent gave over twenty years of service. In contrast, only 17.5 percent of Anglicans, and in even more marked contrast, only 4 percent of Methodists remained for more than twenty years (Table 7).

These variations were not simply a reflection of the tenacity of the members of the various missions, nor of the effectiveness of their rationale for mission service. Their patterns of service were to some extent molded by the differing expectations of the respective missionary bodies they served.

Members of the SHM came to the mission, as has already been noted, not expecting to return home. Although there was no inflexible rule, poverty, the remoteness of their homeland, and the expectations of their congregations ensured that many who might otherwise have returned to European or Australian houses of the congregation to convalesce or to grow old and die, remained instead in the mission that in many cases had been their home for several decades.

The LMS which, like the SHM, had invested a considerable amount in preparing the missionaries, expected a good term of service from them in return. Unlike the SHM, however, it required its staff to retire and return home in old age, and for some of its workers, the last crisis of missionary service was accepting the need to give up their life's work and return to a land where they no longer felt at home.[88] Apart from the 24 percent who failed to give three years of service (see Table 7), most LMS workers conformed to the Society's expectations.

The markedly shorter service of the Methodist missionaries was, in part, a reflection of the Wesleyan ideal of itinerancy. Methodist missionaries saw their service as one posting in Wesley's "world parish," from which they were expected to move on to another. But even such an interpretation of mission service could not justify the extremely brief

Table 7. Length of service of missionaries

Years of Service	LMS	Methodist	Anglican	SHM	Total
Less than 3	8	12	24	16	60
3–5	4	18	16	23	61
6–10	3	10	12	31	56
11–20	5	6	9	36	56
21–40	13	2	9	36	60
More than 40	—	—	4	27	31
Unknown	—	—	—	3	3
Total	33	48	74	172	327

careers of a vast number of Methodist missionaries, whose premature departures were constantly lamented at the mission office.[89]

Members of the Anglican Mission, which espoused the Catholic ideal of life service, failed most signally to live up to the expectations of the organization. A small minority of men and women lived and died in the mission, but most fell far short of life service. Both Maclaren and Stone-Wigg suspected that individuals whose commitment was based solely on an agreement with their leader were less likely to see a lifetime of service than those under vows. Yet a number of LMS missionaries gave virtually a lifetime of service without religious vows to sustain them. It seems likely that the higher proportion of medium and long careers in the LMS was related to the Society's more professional selection and preparation procedures.

Despite the differing expectations of the missionary bodies, there were a number of workers in all missions who failed to fulfill the hopes of the organizations that put them into the field. Their decision to resign was a personal choice that their employers opposed, or acceded to only reluctantly. Most notable was the large group of Anglican and Protestant missionaries who failed to stay for three years.

All missions deplored the investment of effort and money in staff who stayed in the field for only a short period. The Anglican Mission set a minimum of three years for initial service, after which a missionary could leave without dishonor, but assumed that its members would stay unless there were pressing reasons for leaving. The other three missions had higher expectations. Yet almost one-quarter of the Protestant missionaries and one-third of the Anglicans failed to give three years of service. If five years is regarded as a reasonable period for a missionary to learn the language, gain some familiarity with local people and cultures, and master the manifold skills of mission work, 62.5 percent of the Methodists and 54 percent of the Anglicans failed to survive their apprenticeship.

To gauge the reasons for the resignations of missionaries is no easier than to judge any human motivation. Unsuccessful missionaries often slipped off the pages of mission records, their departure scarcely acknowledged. When an official reason for resignation was given, it must be treated as the explanation the mission wished to present to the world. Consideration for the individuals involved and concern for the effect of failure on the mission-supporting public ensured that a discreet silence was often maintained, or a euphemism employed to disarm suspicion. Bishop Stone-Wigg, for instance, protected some of his most spectacular failures with the explanation that they were "quite unequal to the climate."[90] Ill health was a convenient and acceptable explanation that at times masked disillusionment, depression, conflict, mental disturbance, and, occasionally, moral failure. Sometimes, though probably not often, missionaries managed to conceal their basic motives for resignation from the mission authorities and perhaps even from themselves.

Recognizing the problems inherent in deducing motivation, the following analysis offers some probable reasons for resignations, drawing on stated and implied explanations and indications inferred from personal records. Where more than one explanation for resignation is given, I have tried to select the essential from the ephemeral, or the sufficient from the necessary conditions.

Among the forty-four Anglican and Protestant missionaries who survived less than three years were six whose careers were terminated by death. Of the remainder, the greatest number (thirteen) gave breakdown of health as the reason for their premature departure. Another four resigned because of dissatisfaction with the work, disillusionment, or generally low morale, and six were deemed unsuitable by the missions, being unable to adjust to life in the field. For a further six, conflict with other members of the mission was the key factor in the decision to resign. Of the rest, two were dismissed; one claimed family pressures, one loss of faith, and one his wife's poor health; two women resigned at marriage; one was a temporary appointment and one left for reasons unknown.

The factors prompting the resignations of missionaries who served for less than three years were similar to those of missionaries who stayed longer (see Table 8). For all the missionaries, apart from those whose careers ended in death (who will be considered separately), poor health was the chief cause of departure, 18 percent resigning on these grounds. It is impossible to judge how much illness was psychosomatic, illusory, or invented. Some malingering was suspected in all missions. But records testify that for at least some, retirement was probably the only alternative to the early death experienced by many of the Sacred Heart missionaries. As well as Methodist sister Maisie Lill, whose case has already been described (chapter 7), five men and four women left the field because they feared insanity, or others feared it for them. At least two of them died in psychiatric hospitals.[91]

Breakdown of morale, which accounted for 8 percent of resignations, was of various kinds, and surviving records do not always indicate its underlying causes. It frequently accompanied physical illness, particularly the depressive effects of malaria. For some it was associated with recognizing a mistaken vocation, for others, with conviction of failure. Several attributed it to false expectations of the nature of the work; for others it resulted from inability to cope with the challenges presented by mission life. In three cases it was a reaction to the constant presence of "black faces," though in each case this repugnance seems to have been a

Table 8. Reasons for termination of missionary careers

	LMS	METHODIST	ANGLICAN	SHM	TOTAL
Ill-health	6	16	16	21	59
Ill-health of spouse or child	7	7	1		15
Maladjustment or demoralization	1	4	7	16	28
Loss of faith			2		2
Interpersonal conflict	4	4	6	1	15
Marriage or departure of spouse		5	8	2	15
Family pressure		3	2		5
Transfer to other duties			1	26	27
Dismissal		1	2		3
Old age	10	2			12
Death	5	4	16	99	124
Other			2		2
Unknown		2	11	7	20
Total	33	48	74	172	327

symptom of a more deep-seated nervous problem.[92] Those who experienced demoralization also included a small number of MSC who, deciding before taking final vows that they had no religious vocation, left both mission and congregation.

Transfers to other duties accounted for the largest number of departures from the SHM. Sometimes these were arranged on compassionate grounds—ailing sisters were sent to Kensington, NSW, while a number of priests were repatriated to enjoy the benign climate of Provence. Some were transferred to other mission fields of the MSC, especially Port Darwin and the Gilbert Islands (now part of Kiribati). Four priests were raised to the episcopacy in other fields—Louis Couppé in New Britain, François-Xavier Gsell in Port Darwin, Joseph Bach in the Gilberts, and Edouard van Goethem in the Belgian Congo—and several priests and sisters were called away to senior administrative positions within their congregations.

For the Protestant missionaries, various domestic pressures were the other substantial cause of resignation. The poor health of wife or child prompted the departures of 4.6 percent, while a further 4.6 percent —all women—resigned to marry or left because their missionary husbands were leaving the field. A small proportion claimed the needs of parents or other dependent relatives as the reason for departure.

Death

The largest single factor terminating missionary careers in Papua before the First World War was death (see Table 8). Of the 327 missionaries who served in this period, 124 (38 percent) died in service. Of those, 99 (80 percent) died in the SHM. The extraordinarily high death rate in this mission can be explained, in part, by the deaths in old age of a number of Roman Catholic missionaries. But a large number of those who died in the Sacred Heart Mission died from other causes (Table 9).

A final flourish of the missionary stereotype, especially as perpetuated in cartoon and music-hall comedy, suggested that the hapless missionary ended his days in the cannibal's cooking pot (Figure 24).[93] But parody was forgotten when in April 1901 news was received in Britain and Australia that the veteran LMS missionary James Chalmers, with his young colleague Oliver Tomkins and eleven Papuans, had been killed by cannibals in the Papuan Gulf.[94] Provoked by the taunt of a government officer that he was dependent on government protection, the pioneer missionary had met the challenge by taking his party to one of the few remaining parts of the southeast coast with only limited experience of Europeans—and that unfavorable. They had been invited ashore at Dopima village on Goaribari Island, led into the *ravi* 'ceremonial house', and clubbed to death. Their bodies were cooked, mixed with sago, and eaten. A public much wider than that of normal mission supporters mourned the death of Chalmers, who was to many the archetypal missionary, and of Tomkins, a twenty-eight-year-old who had shown much promise.

No other European missionary in Papua died at the hands of its people. Indeed, death by misadventure of any kind was rare. Only among the Sacred Heart missionaries, with their more rugged way of life, were there any deaths as the result of accident. Father Bouellat died after a fall from his horse, and Brother Joseph Caron after an accident with a horse and cart. Father Dubuy died from a fractured skull after being hit by a flying rock. The deaths of Brothers Stanislas and Edmond followed boating mishaps, and Brother Nicholas died of pneumonia after being

Table 9. Deaths in the missions

	LMS	METHODIST	ANGLICAN	SHM
Aged 45 or younger	3	4	5	43
Aged over 45	2	—	11	56
Total deaths	5	4	16	99

FAITHFUL BEYOND DEATH.—THE STORY OF A MISSIONARY IN THREE CHAPTERS.

The Missionary.   The Reception Committee.   Voice from Within: "My friend, you forgot to say grace."

Figure 24. "Faithful beyond death." (*Bulletin*, 6 March 1886, 6)

rescued from drowning. For all but these few, premature death was the result of illness.

The two outstanding aspects of deaths from causes other than old age in the Papuan mission field were the low death rates in the Protestant missions and the high rate in the Sacred Heart Mission (Table 8). Some of the physical factors contributing to these mortality rates have been considered in chapters 3 and 4. Protestant missionaries lived in solid, well-equipped houses, generally with ample provisions and medication. Most used quinine prophylactically and heeded scientific discoveries as to the cause of malaria. All lived near the coast and a missionary who fell ill was readily evacuated in a mission ship. In contrast, especially in the early years, Sacred Heart missionaries lived in primitive bush material houses. Their lives were arduous, and their diet poor. Many of the sisters and brothers of the mission, among whom the death rate was highest, were little-educated peasants with small understanding of the dangers of contaminated water or the importance of quinine. Some of their stations were five or six days' walk from the coast, and the ill were more likely to be cared for at their own stations, or if necessary at Yule Island, than sent to Australia.

Commenting on the extraordinarily high mortality rate of the Sacred Heart sisters, Sir William MacGregor remarked that he could see no "physical cause" for its being so different from that of the other missionary women in Papua.[95] His observation raises the possibility of a non-physical explanation of the higher death rate in the SHM. Markedly different attitudes toward death may have had some bearing.

For LMS missionaries, there was no romance in death. They consoled themselves with the belief that a colleague who died was with Christ, but lamented the waste of human resources.[96] In the Methodist Mission, the bleak fact of death was masked by a euphemistic and sentimental rhetoric. Those who died were visited by "Death's angel" or "the reaping angel." In death, they were "promoted," they "exchanged earth for heaven," or went "home." A pious death was important, missionaries having great satisfaction in reporting that the deceased "died well."[97] But despite the rhetoric, Methodist missionaries did not glory in death. Pioneer Wesleyan J. T. Field probably expressed a typical attitude when he maintained that he was "no advocate of the heroic business" in mission work.[98] As with their LMS colleagues, the Methodists were encouraged to be prudent out of consideration for their families, a restraint that celibate Catholics did not have. Toward death, as toward other aspects of mission experience, the Methodists maintained a hard-headed realism.

Though their death rate was much lower than the Roman Catholics', if higher than the Protestants', Anglican missionaries shared not only the spartan life-style of the Sacred Heart missionaries but also something of their orientation toward death. "These damned churchmen are like the papists," grumbled the resident magistrate, H. G. Moreton. "Plenty of them willing to be martyrs."[99] Anglican missionary A. K. Chignell guessed that the mission's founder, Albert Maclaren, died as he would have wished, "a martyr in all but the strictly technical sense."[100] Sir William MacGregor, a seasoned practitioner of tropical medicine, was puzzled by Maclaren's death, because the malaria that preceded it did not seem unduly severe. According to Maclaren's biographer, Mac-Gregor thought "he seemed to give in to the fever and made no effort to struggle against it."[101] Similar comments had been made on other occasions about Polynesian pastors, who European observers believed succumbed to malaria simply because they did not have the will to fight it. Maclaren had been lonely and depressed during his four months at Dogura. He may have been drinking "inordinate quantities of brandy."[102] His last sermon was on the subject of death.[103] It is possible that the attraction of "martyrdom" reduced his will to fight for life, which was proving burdensome. Other Anglicans felt the lure of "martyrdom." Charles Cribb, of the LMS, reported traveling to New Guinea with a young Anglican who bought only a single ticket because he intended to die in the mission.[104] Annie Ker envied Mary Newton the "glorious end to her life" when she died at Dogura at the age of thirty-five.[105]

But the Anglicans did not emulate the single-minded enthusiasm for "martyrdom" of their Roman Catholic counterparts. On this as on other issues, they pursued a middle way, avoiding both the practicality of the Protestants and the mystical romanticism of the Roman Catholics. Henry Newton revealed the ambivalent attitude of the mission when he reminded the staff both that life was a precious gift from God and that "he who loseth his life for Christ's sake shall find it."[106]

Only in the Sacred Heart Mission did "martyrdom" become the supreme form of mission service. A philosophy of work built around the concept of suffering found its ultimate manifestation in death. Verjus, who had craved martyrdom since his student days, if not since childhood, cultivated the desire for it among his missionaries, as both the crowning achievement in the search for holiness and the means of winning the salvation of New Guinea. Observers remarked that they embraced death joyfully, offering their sufferings for their "dear savages" in an effort to win the conversion of New Guinea. "How could we be sad near her?" wrote Sister Madeline of the dying Sister Berchmans, "She burned with a desire for death."[107] How and to what degree such a predisposition could influence the mortality rate is impossible to assess. Much was clearly attributable to poor living standards and arduous work. Yet it is significant that no workers died in the mission in the pioneering phase, when accommodation was poor, provisions unprocurable, labor exhausting, and the missionaries unacclimatized. The first death occurred after the mission had been established six years, in 1891,[108] the year of the foundation of the Society of Victims. In the folllowing three years, twelve missionaries died, their average age thirty-five years. By 1905, Bishop de Boismenu reported, the mission had seen the death of twenty-eight "victims"—one-third of the total work force—all but three under forty years of age.[109] In the same period the average age at death for Roman Catholic missionaries in Africa was forty-eight years and in Asia, fifty-four.[110]

Missionaries who avoided premature death often lived to a good age. In each mission were some who retired to administrative positions within the home organization. LMS missionaries generally returned to Britain, either to service in the Congregational Church or to retirement. A few settled in Australia or New Zealand, with which they had become familiar during their service. Ordained Methodists were absorbed by the various conferences of Australia and New Zealand, and many gave long post-missionary service to them. Anglican priests who did not die in the field mostly returned to parishes in England or Australia. Lay missionaries commonly took up work for which their pre-missionary experience had fitted them, although some, especially women, retained close voluntary links with the missionary organizations.

Several missionaries were granted secular recognition for their work.

Five were awarded honorary doctorates—Lawes, Bromilow, Stone-Wigg, and Sharp in divinity, and McFarlane in law. Three long-serving missionaries, Alice Cottingham (Figure 25), Robert Turner, and Matthew Gilmour, received coronation medals in 1937. Archbishop de Bois-menu was made a Chevalier of the Legion of Honor in 1950, as was also Bishop Gsell in 1951, after each had given half a century of service in the mission fields of Papua and Australia.

Few of the missionaries who had struggled to make a home in the

Figure 25. Long-serving Anglican missionary Alice Cottingham. (Uniting Church)

mission field had the satisfaction of seeing their children follow them into the work. Charles Abel's sons took up his work after his accidental death in 1930, and Kwato, which had been independent of the LMS since 1917, remained a family concern until the sixties.[111] Harold Schlencker followed his father into service with the LMS in Papua for a short period, and two of McFarlane's sons became missionaries in China. But the other children of missionaries chose different careers, a number of them turning to medicine, perhaps as a secular channel for the same concern that had motivated their fathers. Some felt bitterness at the price they had paid for their parents' service,[112] and at least a few showed evidence of what might have been the results of parental deprivation. Ben Butcher's children cost him constant anxiety.[113] Pryce Jones' children grieved him by becoming Roman Catholic and Anglican.[114] W. G. Lawes suffered the pain of seeing his son, Frank, become a scandal for his sexual promiscuity and alcoholism before his early death.[115] But Lawes' other sons, like most of the sons and daughters of missionaries, settled into middle-class society in Australia, New Zealand, or Britain and, while not maintaining particularly close links with the missionary movement, continued to worship in the church their parents had served, and to retain a justifiable pride in their parents' work.

Uniformity, Diversity, and "Ideal Types"

A study of the missionaries who lived and worked in Papua up to 1914 reveals differences among them that were shaped by ethnic and social origin, by the denominational influences under which they grew up and worked, by the passage of time, and above all by the vagaries of individual personality and experience. It also reveals some common features that transcend those variables.

The ethnic and social origins of the missionaries were diverse, the majority being drawn from the lower (though not the lowest) ranks of European, British, and colonial society. Despite their social diversity, many experienced strong and consistent religious influences from childhood, often mediated through the mother. Their decisions to become missionaries, in most cases prompted by a genuine sense of vocation, were often reinforced by secular considerations that either repelled them from Western society or lured them to the mission field. Their religious formation varied in nature and scope, its one common feature being its failure to prepare them for much of what lay ahead. The liberalizing of theology, and especially the growth of the social gospel, led to changing conceptions of the missionary's role.

In their style of living the missionaries reproduced features of their own society. Protestants built their lives round middle-class ideals of the nuclear family and bourgeois domesticity; Roman Catholic missionaries recreated in New Guinea the communities of Europe; Anglicans strove for the latter, but to some extent acquiesced in the former. In other ways, similarities of lifestyle were determined by the constraints of a common social and physical environment.

Missionary perceptions of Papuan cultures revealed much of the complacent superiority, arrogance, and Eurocentrism of those who believed themselves to be at the pinnacle of the ethnic hierarchy. Unlike many of their secular contemporaries, however, the monogenist missionaries believed that the Papuans, equal in the eyes of God, could be "raised" from their lowly position. Acquaintance with Papuan cultures and, for some, exposure to the new science of anthropology, led to growing appreciation. Although some continued to fit the stereotype of the bigoted, uncomprehending wowser, many achieved a knowledge and understanding more profound than that of all but a few of their contemporaries. The extent to which missionaries attacked traditional cultures depended not only on their degree of appreciation, but also on assumptions shaped by their own cultural and theological backgrounds.

The missionaries' perceptions of their work were also molded by social origin, theological outlook, and perceptions of Papuan cultures. Few fitted the stereotype of the black-coated, bible-wielding preacher, or manifested the narrow obsession with the salvation of souls attributed to them. As theological outlooks broadened, so did their conception of their work, concern for the well-being of the whole person replacing a simple preoccupation with salvation. Education and welfare work became increasingly important, and the Protestant enthusiasm for industrial mission developed in the same context.

The performance of all missionaries was both supported and constrained by the distinctive structure and organization they belonged to. The experience of the isolated LMS missionary with sole responsibility for his sprawling district was very different from that of his counterpart in the tightly controlled, hierarchical Methodist force. The experience of each differed from that of the Roman Catholics working in community in total obedience to their superiors, or from the Anglicans working in personal allegiance to the bishop. For one group however the experience was comparable across mission boundaries. Despite their special contributions to mission service, women in all four organizations were regarded as second-class citizens, auxiliaries in the male-dominated structures.

Although inevitable accomplices in the processes of imperialism, the missionaries defined for themselves a distinctive role, that of protector of the Papuan people. At times compromised by their association with the imperial powers, they nevertheless succeeded, through this role, in ameliorating some of the more exploitative aspects of colonial rule.

The reality in the Papuan mission field was much richer and more multifaceted than any stereotype could capture. The predominant impression that emerges from a study of the 327 missionaries is of a host of individuals, many of them complex, strong, and memorable personalities. Yet amid such diversity it is possible to discern "ideal types" to which reality approximated. These are not personality types, nor do they correlate with denominational allegiance or socioeconomic factors. Transcending these and other variables that produced such diversity, they relate most closely to the individual's basic orientation to mission work. The four types may be called the mystic, the administrator, the humanitarian, and the romantic.

For the mystics, the central fact of their career was a personal relationship with God. They came to the mission field to seek fuller communion with God and to bring their souls into more perfect harmony with His will. The SHM was the most congenial home for this type of missionary and Henri Verjus or Mother Liguori its archetypes. Protestant examples are less apparent, although an Evangelical like Samuel Fellows, with his craving for sanctification, was a close approximation.

The administrators were rational, practical persons, whose attention was directed toward organization and structure. They brought to the mission field talents that might otherwise have been used in shop, office, or countinghouse. Although probably persons of strong faith, their attraction was to the status and role of the missionary. Bromilow, categorized by MacGregor as a man of exceptional organizational ability, was a good example of the administrator missionary. Less admirable was Samuel McFarlane, whose shrewd opportunism could have been deployed in commerce had not his humble origins precluded it. A more impressive example was Charles Abel, whose main preoccupation was the skilful creation and nurture of a personal missionary empire. If any women missionaries shared this orientation, they found little scope for expressing it in the male-dominated structures of the missions.

For the humanitarians, the chief focus of mission work was not their relationship with God, nor the organization of the mission, but concern for humankind. This concern was often accompanied by love of God, just as the mystics' love of God could overflow into love for humanity. Often touched by the social gospel, humanitarian missionaries concentrated their energies on teaching, healing, and welfare work, and on translation and the study of culture insofar as they facilitated fuller communication with the people. A large number of the women missionaries had a predominantly humanitarian outlook. Among the male missionaries, an archetypal humanitarian was Ben Butcher. Others included LMS missionaries Holmes and Riley, Anglicans Gill and Chignell, and Methodist Matthew Gilmour.

The fourth type of missionary, the romantic, was drawn to the mission field by the attraction of the unknown, the magic of the exotic, a quest for adventure. A missionary career provided the opportunity to shake off the fetters of a confined life and enter a world of infinite possibilities. The characteristic activities of the romantic missionary were the pioneer ones—exploration and first contact, building remote stations, collecting artifacts, and studying traditional cultures. James Chalmers, attacked by contemporaries for his passion for exploration and his inability to tolerate routine, was the romantic missionary *par excellence*.

These types were to some extent determined by the structure of the missions. Women found it difficult to be administrators but easy to fulfil the serving role of humanitarian. Mysticism was encouraged by the spiritual atmosphere of the SHM. Nevertheless in all missions there was some scope for role specialization, and in each there was evidence of individuals who found their métier within the structures, and equally of those who chafed under the burden of administration because they wanted to explore, or shrank from exploration because their inclination was to prayer or administration. If in part molded by circumstances, the missionaries' style was also the outcome of their conception of mission work, of whether their primary focus was God or their fellow beings, the fabric of the mission or the unknown horizons of the land they served in.

Missionaries as a Social Group

How representative the missionaries in Papua were of the Christian missionaries who were their predecessors or their contemporaries elsewhere could only be determined by a series of further case studies for, as was noted in the Preface, serious study of missionaries as a social group has been slight. Certain inferences can be drawn, however, from existing scholarship.

Compared with their counterparts of the late eighteenth and early nineteenth centuries,[116] the Protestant missionaries of a century later appeared as moderate and respectable men and women. Most were better educated and many of higher social status. An equally significant difference was that they were nurtured Christians, not converts. By the mid-nineteenth century, evangelical religion had been institutionalized in British society, and the passion of the Revival had cooled.[117] A second Evangelical Revival stirred some British souls in 1859—prompting, for instance, the conversion of James Chalmers—but most of the Protestant missionaries who came to Papua had grown up taking their religion for granted. If the ardor of a nurtured Christian is less than that of a convert, this tendency was reinforced by the disappearance of the "perishing heathen" motive and the consequent reduction in the sense of urgency of the missionary task (see chapter 2). Some found their zeal further curbed by the routinization of an established mode of work. Animated by the same faith as their predecessors, their expression of it in the field was more temperate and restrained.

The Sacred Heart missionaries, on the other hand, were stamped with more fervor than had been characteristic of their coreligionists a century earlier. A reflection of the warmer piety that marked the revival of French Catholicism in the nineteenth century, it was fanned to white heat in the New Guinea field by the driven passion of Henri Verjus. In their romantic and mystical piety the Sacred Heart missionaries were closer to their medieval forebears than to those of the Enlightenment.

The social origins of the missionaries in Papua, though higher than they would have been a century earlier, seem to have been more modest than was typical by the end of the nineteenth century. At a time when Protestant missions were recruiting increasingly from the greater middle class, workers in Papua continued to be drawn from that traditional recruiting ground, the borderland between the working classes and the lower middle class. The Anglican Mission, despite its articulate upper middle-class leadership, failed to draw on that section of society to the same extent as its mentor, the Universities' Mission to Central Africa (UMCA), or even its neighbor, the Melanesian Mission. While some French Catholic congregations attracted members primarily from the aristocracy and upper middle class, the SHM was staffed preponderantly by the children of peasants and artisans, one of the objectives of the MSC being to facilitate the vocations of the godly but poor.

A further difference, in part a corollary, was that the missionaries in Papua were, as a group, less highly educated than most missionaries of the period. It was said of the Church Missionary Society that candidates with a First at Oxford or Cambridge were sent to the East, while those with an A1 life at Lloyds went to Africa.[118] What was true of Africa was more true of New Guinea. Even in Africa, 17 percent of males in the CMS East Africa mission had university degrees, mostly from Oxford or Cambridge.[119] The proportion for the UMCA was predictably higher— 25 percent.[120] In Papua, 11 percent of Anglican and Protestant male missionaries had degrees. Priests of the MSC, while undergoing the mandatory tertiary training for the priesthood, found their place in the spectrum of Roman Catholic congregations and orders, not among those renowned for intellectual achievement such as the Jesuits, but among those distinguished by dedication and apostolic zeal. The relatively lower standard of education is reflected in the level of scholarship in the Papuan field. While Holmes, Saville, Stone-Wigg, and Field published creditably in anthropology, and King, Lawes, Fellows, Guis, and others made substantial contributions to linguistic knowledge, none produced a study of the quality of those, for instance, of Maurice Leenhardt or R. H. Codrington.

Visitors to Papua commented that its missionaries were of a distinctive kind.[121] They were strong, practical men and women, who dressed ruggedly and used their hands. Their style was in part molded by environment—Papua was one of the few remaining pioneer fields—but it was also a reflection of the fact that mission societies sent their more scholarly recruits to work among literate peoples with more "sophisticated" cultures. As with the missionaries sent to Africa, the qualities required in candidates for Papua were strength, stamina, and resourcefulness.

If the missionaries in Papua differed considerably from those in Asia and even, to some degree, from those in Africa, they resembled more closely their contemporaries in the Pacific, many of whom were recruited by the same or similar organizations. LMS missionaries who served in Samoa, the Gilbert and Ellice Islands, Niue, the Loyalties, and other small island groups, were recruited and trained in the same fashion as their colleagues in Papua. The AWMMS sent workers to Fiji, German New Guinea, and the Solomons, as well as Papua. In both of these mission societies there was some movement of personnel between fields as there was also among the missionaries of the Sacred Heart whose other fields included German New Guinea, northern Australia, and the Gilberts. In style and orientation, the MSC were similar to the Marists, who were at work in the Solomon Islands, the New Hebrides, and Fiji. The Anglican missionaries, although of more modest origins, were not dissimilar in outlook from their counterparts in the Melanesian Mission.

What difference there was between missionaries in Papua and those elsewhere in the Pacific was not related so much to differences of origin, attainment, or orientation, as to the nature of the country they served in. One notable feature of missionary service throughout the Pacific was the establishment of missionary dynasties.[122] Missionaries came to regard the land they served in as their home. They settled there, sometimes buying land and engaging in commercial activity, raised their children, and often retired and died there while a second generation took up the work. In Papua, a country then still regarded as inhospitable to white settlement, few missionaries made a permanent home. They were sojourners in a strange land and home was somewhere else, across the sea. Even for many of the dedicated, long-serving Sacred Heart missionaries, home was the provincial town of Issoudun on the misty Berry plains, or the small villages of rural France or the Low Countries, and they died in exile.

Nevertheless, missionaries in Papua before the Great War were to a large extent representative of the genre. The four missions covered the broad theological spectrum of mission activity in that period—Roman Catholic, Anglo-Catholic, liberal Protestant, and Evangelical. In the careers of the missionaries were reflected the major shifts of theological emphasis, the new anthropological insights, and the changing conceptions of mission work that shaped missionary service during that period. Above all, in their self-image, they were representative of their kind in the "golden age of mission"—a period when missionaries enjoyed an exalted social status. But more important to many than the esteem of contemporaries was the belief that they had been called by God for "the most sublime of all works."[123] In the words of Saint Peter, they were a "peculiar people" chosen to "show forth the praises" of the God who had chosen them.[124] This self-image encouraged their dedication and endurance—and at times their complacency and arrogance—and gave impetus and meaning to the lives and deaths of missionaries of the late nineteenth and early twentieth centuries, in Papua, as elsewhere.

Abbreviations

AA	Anglican Archives
AAAS	Australasian Association for the Advancement of Science
AAO	Australian Archives Office
ABM	Australian Board of Missions
ADB	*Australian Dictionary of Biography*
AIF	Australian Imperial Force
AMHS	Australasian Methodist Historical Society
ANGAU	Australian New Guinea Administrative Unit
ANU	Australian National University
AR	Annual report
arr.	arrived
AWMMS	Australasian Wesleyan Methodist Missionary Society
b.	born
BA	Bereina Archives (MSC)
BNG	British New Guinea
ch.	children
CC	Congregational Church
CIM	China Inland Mission
c.m.	church member
C of E	Church of England
coll.	college
Cong.	Congregational
d.	died
ed.	education
FDNSC	Fille de Nôtre-Dame du Sacré-Coeur/Filia Dominae Nostrae a Sacro Corde—Daughter of Our Lady of the Sacred Heart
GBCO	Great Britain Colonial Office
GS	grammar school
HS	high school

JEH	*Journal of Ecclesiastical History*
JICH	*Journal of Imperial and Commonwealth History*
JPH	*Journal of Pacific History*
JPNGS	*Journal of the Papua and New Guinea Society*
JRAHS	*Journal of the Royal Australian Historical Society*
JRAI	*Journal of the Royal Anthropological Institute*
JRH	*Journal of Religious History*
LMS	London Missionary Society
m.	married
MCP	Methodist Church Papers
ML	Mitchell Library
MMSA	Methodist Missionary Society of Australasia
MOM	Methodist Overseas Mission
MR	*Missionary Review (Australasian Methodist Missionary Review)*
MSC	Missionaires du Sacré-Coeur/Missionaris Sacratissimi Cordis —Missionaries of the Sacred Heart
NG	New Guinea
NLA	National Library of Australia
NSW	New South Wales
NT	Northern Territory (Australia)
NZ	New Zealand
o.	occupation
OP	Occasional Paper
ord.	ordained
PC	Presbyterian Church
PDC	Papua District Committee
PIM	*Pacific Islands Monthly*
PJ	Papua Journals
PL	Papua Letters
PMB	Pacific Manuscripts Bureau
PNG	Papua New Guinea
PR	Papua Reports
Qld	Queensland
r.	retired or resigned
RA	Rome Archives (MSC)
RC	Roman Catholic
RCI	Royal Colonial Institute
RGS	Royal Geographical Society
SA	South Australia
SHM	Sacred Heart Mission
SMH	*Sydney Morning Herald*
SSO	South Sea Odds

stn/s	station/s
Tas.	Tasmania
UCA	United Church Archives
UCR	United Church Records
UMCA	Universities' Mission to Central Africa
UPNG	University of Papua New Guinea
VAMM	Vicariat Apostolique de la Melanésie et de la Micronésie
VANG	Vicariat Apostolique de Nouvelle-Guinée
Vic.	Victoria (Australia)
WA	Western Australia
WOL	Western Outgoing Letters

Chronology of Missionary Activity in Papua, 1874–1914

1871 *June–July:* Murray and McFarlane located Polynesian teachers on Torres Strait islands for the LMS, and visited Redscar Bay

1872 *14 September:* Murray and Gill sailed from Lifu with second contingent of teachers
November: LMS teachers stationed in Torres Strait, and on mainland at Katau, Tureture, and Manumanu
December: Cape York chosen as headquarters for LMS mission to New Guinea

1873 *March:* Teachers murdered at Bampton Island; deaths among teachers at Manumanu
November: Surviving teachers from Manumanu transferred to Port Moresby

1874 *21 November:* W. G. Lawes (LMS) and family settled at Port Moresby

1876 *April:* Lawes and McFarlane explored southeast coast to China Strait

1877 *August–September:* Lawes' first inland expedition to Koiari
21 October: Arrival of James and Jane Chalmers (LMS).
13 December: Departure of Lawes for England

1878 Chalmers' exploration of southeast coast from Suau

1879 *29 February:* Death of Mrs. Chalmers
November: Chalmers' exploration of Papuan Gulf

1881 *7 March:* Kalo massacre
25 March: Vicariates of Melanesia and Micronesia offered to MSC
12 April: Return of William and Fanny Lawes

1 September: Embarkation of first MSC contingent for Oceania
First LMS baptism, Aruadaera of Port Moresby

1882   *5 June:* Father Navarre named superior, MSC, after breakdown
of Father Durin
29 September: Arrival of MSC at Matupi, New Britain

1884   Ordination of first Papuan pastor, Rarua, for LMS
24 October: Arrival of MSC at Thursday Island
6 November: Declaration of protectorate over British New
Guinea

1885   *1 July:* Verjus (MSC), and two brothers reached Yule Island after
illegal entry
September: MSC pioneers forced to return to Thursday Island to
await Sir Peter Scratchley
3 December: Death of Sir Peter Scratchley

1886   *9 February:* Return of Verjus to Yule Island
16 April: Arrival at Yule Island of Navarre and two brothers
October: Resolution of Anglican General Synod to take up
responsibility for New Guinea

1887   *May:* Exploration of Mekeo by Fathers Verjus and Couppé,
MSC.
4 August: Arrival of first sisters (FDNSC) at Yule Island
30 September: Consecration of Navarre as titular bishop of Pentacomie

1888   *17 August:* Navarre named titular archbishop of Cyr
4 September: Annexation of British New Guinea

1889   *7 April:* Pontifical decree dividing Roman Catholic Vicariate of
Melanesia into Vicariate of New Guinea and Vicariate of New
Britain

1890   *February:* Verjus retained as coadjutor bishop to Navarre and
Couppé named vicar apostolic of New Britain
May-August: Visits of Albert Maclaren (Anglican) and George
Brown (Methodist) to British New Guinea
17 June: "Gentleman's agreement" between LMS, Methodists,
and Anglicans to define missions' spheres of influence

1891   *27 May:* Departure from Sydney of pioneer Methodist party, led
by William Bromilow
19 June: Arrival of Methodists at Dobu
10 August: Arrival of Maclaren and King at Bartle Bay to establish Anglican mission
3 November: Departure of Verjus for consecration in Europe

10 November: King left Anglican mission, ill, for Sydney

24 December: Maclaren transported, ill, in government yacht, from Samarai to Cooktown

27 December: Death of Maclaren, off Cooktown

1892 *March:* Return of King as head of Anglican mission

April: Arrival in New Guinea of first missionary sisters to be employed by AWMMS

13 November: Death of Verjus at Oleggio, Italy; departure of Navarre for Europe

1893 *8 May:* Combined missionary conference of LMS, Methodists, and Anglicans at Kwato

24 June: Arrival at Yule Island of large contingent of MSC and FDNSC

1894 *22 July:* Baptism of first eight Methodist converts

1896 *April:* First Anglican baptisms—of Samuela Aigeri and Pilipo Agabadi

1898 *25 January:* Consecration of Montagu Stone-Wigg, first Anglican bishop

1899 MSC explorations of mountainous interior at Kuni and Mafulu (the northwest corner of Fuyughe)

1900 *March:* De Boismenu consecrated Roman Catholic titular bishop of Gabala, coadjutor to Navarre

1901 *8 April:* Death of Chalmers, Tomkins, and eleven Papuans at Goaribari

1906 *29 March:* Retirement of W. G. Lawes

1907 *21 December:* Retirement of Archbishop Navarre; succeeded as vicar apostolic by de Boismenu

1908 Retirement of Bishop Stone-Wigg; retirement of William Bromilow (succeeded by Matthew Gilmour as Chairman of New Guinea District)

1910 *25 April:* Consecration of Gerald Sharp as second Anglican bishop of New Guinea

1912 *16 January:* Death of Archbishop Navarre

1914 Papuan candidate, Joseph Taurino, commenced studies for Roman Catholic priesthood

20 September: Peter Rautamara and Edwin Nuagoro ordained Anglican deacons

LMS and Methodist Wives in the Papuan Mission Field, 1874–1914

Name	Née Birthdate	Husband Marriage date	Church allegiance	Death (* = in service)	Comments
		London Missionary Society			
Abel, Elizabeth Beatrice	Moxon 28 Mar. 1869	Charles Abel 22 Nov. 1892	Evangelical Anglican		Daughter of brewer
Bartlett, Alice Mary	Bennett	R. Bartlett 1 Jan. 1907	Evangelical Anglican		Daughter of farmer; schoolteacher
Beharell, Margaret James	Patterson	C. Beharell 20 Dec. 1910	Park Gate Congregational Church, England		Schoolteacher
Beswick, Clara	Coombs	Thomas Beswick 1881			Husband died 1883
Burrows, Charlotte Christine	Robertson	S. Burrows 25 Feb. 1913	West Hawthorn Presbyterian Church, Vic.		Daughter of Peter Robertson (marine engineer); milliner
Butcher, Lucy Georgina (Ena)	Davidson	B. T. Butcher 28 Dec. 1912	South Brisbane Congregational Church	1955	Daughter of J. M. Davidson (bank manager)
Chalmers, Jane	Hercus	James Chalmers 17 Oct. 1865		20 Feb. 1879 Sydney*	Schoolteacher
Chalmers, Sarah Eliza (Lizzie)	Large	James Chalmers 6 Oct. 1888		25 Oct. 1900 New Guinea*	Formerly named Harrison
Clark, Annie	Muir	J. B. Clark 19 Dec. 1906	Penrith Presbyterian Church, Cumberland, England		Daughter of farmer; nurse
Cribb, Elizabeth	McNab	C. J. Cribb 20 July 1898	Milton Congregational Church, Qld		Daughter of coach builder

Cullen, Mattie Burr	Simmons	J. H. Cullen 30 June 1890	Robertson St. Congregational Church Hastings, England			
Dauncey, Mary Ellen (Polly)	Hinton	H. M. Dauncey 16 Aug. 1894	Wesley Church, Walsall, Staffordshire	23 Mar. 1921		
Harries, Edith Lillian	Gayton	T. O. Harries 7 Mar. 1911	Castle Gate Congregational Church, Nottingham			Schoolteacher
Holmes, Alice	Middleton	J. H. Holmes 4 July 1901	Sherwell Congregational Church, Plymouth, Devon			
Hunt, Harriet Rebecca	Tizard	A. E. Hunt 26 July 1887			Wellington, NZ	
Ingram, Louisa	Gunn	T. W. Ingram 17 May 1894	Southend Congregational Church, Essex, England			
Jones, Minnie Pryce	Page	E. Pryce Jones 30 Mar. 1893				Dressmaker
Lawes, Fanny	Wickham 1840	W. G. Lawes 1860	Canterbury Congregational Church, England	27 Jan. 1913	Sydney	
Lawrence, Jessie	Leslie	W. N. Lawrence 22 Nov. 1883	Edinburgh			
McFarlane, Elizabeth	Joyce 1840	Samuel McFarlane 1858	Bedford Congregational Church, Bedfordshire, England	28 Oct. 1916		Daughter of John Joyce, gentleman; sister of Alfred Joyce, LMS

(continued)

Name	Nee Birthdate	Husband Marriage date	Church allegiance	Death (* = in service)	Comments
Pearse, Susan	Jefferies	A. Pearse 12 Oct. 1869	Wrington Congregational Church, Somerset, England		
Rich, Caroline	Bryant	C. F. Rich 5 May 1900	Percy Congregational Church, Bath, England		Teacher
Riley, Jessie Marian	Maclean	E. Baxter Riley 10 Jan. 1906			Daughter of John Maclean (civil servant); teacher
Saville, Frances	Lawes	W. J. V. Saville 6 June 1903	Point Piper Road Congregational Church, Sydney		Daughter of F. E. Lawes; niece of W. G. Lawes; nurse
Schlencker, Mary	Cribb	H. P. Schlencker 1 Feb. 1905	Milton Congregational Church, Qld		
Scott, Eliza Jessie	Mitchell	J. Tait Scott 6 July 1880	Montrose Congregational Church, Forfar, Scotland		Received "a first-class education"
Scott, Mary	Todhunter	Harry Scott 1883			Daughter of Professor Todhunter of Cheshunt, LMS director
Turner, Edith Emma	Calvert	R. L. Turner 28 July 1910			BA, University of Wales; nurse; missionary; Wuchang medical mission, China
Turner, Mary Amelia	Colville	W. Y. Turner 19 Aug. 1875		1876 New Guinea*	
Walker, Rosalie Caroline	Wilson	F. W. Walker 27 June 1903	Nether Congregational Church, England		Sister of LMS director, Talbot Wilson

Methodist Mission

Name		Spouse	Date	Notes
Andrews, ?		A. J. Andrews		Local preacher
Avery, Elizabeth	Belton 24 Sep. 1880 New Zealand	W. W. Avery 14 April 1910		
Ballantyne, May	Jenness 1875 Wellington, NZ	A. Ballantyne 9 Oct. 1906	1953	Daughter of George Lewis Jenness (jeweler); matriculated; became Methodist missionary sister, Papua, 1905–1906 (register no. 61); resigned to marry
Barnes, ?		F. J. Barnes		
Bromilow, Lily	Thompson	W. E. Bromilow April 1879		Daughter of railway inspector
Burgess, Minnie	Chambers	G. A. Burgess 18 Mar. 1910		
Enticott, Doris Pearl	Bembrick 5 Sep. 1898	W. J. Enticott 7 Feb. 1917	1944	Daughter of Thomas Bembrick (merchant); teacher; Methodist missionary sister, Papua 1913–1917 (register no. 39); resigned to marry
Fellows, Sara (Sallie)	Hanna	S. Fellows 1894	1930	
Field, Frances Mary	Harding 1861	J. T. Field May 1892		Daughter of William Harding (grazier)
Fletcher, Jessie Maud	Bavin	A. Fletcher 13 April 1894		Daughter of Rev. Rainsford Bavin (Methodist—NZ & Australia); niece of C. Bavin (missionary, Fiji)

(continued)

Name	Née Birthdate	Husband Marriage date	Church allegiance	Death (* = in service)	Comments
Francis, Annie Elizabeth	Fathers	W. C. Francis			Daughter of Thomas Fathers (footwear business); partial nurse training
Gatland, ?	Vipond	G. Gatland			Schoolteacher
Gilmour, Nora Lilian	Francis	M. K. Gilmour		Aug. 1948	Daughter of Henry
Glew, Fairleigh Lillie	Newell	E. J. Glew 11 June 1901			Vernon Newell (clerk); milliner
Harrison, Rose Mary	Lill	E. W. Harrison 8 Oct. 1910		1972	Daughter of William Thomas Lill (farmer, Willowby, NZ); draper's assistant; local preacher; Methodist missionary sister, Papua, 1908–1910 (register no. 63); resigned to marry
Holland, Anne		G. R. Holland			
Johns, Elsie Berenice	Buchanan 1892	E. S. Johns 1 June 1912			Daughter of John Carslow Buchanan (station owner); tailoress
Osborne, Nellie		J. R. Osborne			
Scrivin, Margaret	Jamieson 13 June 1883	A. H. Scrivin 1915		1921	Daughter of Lawrence Jamieson (farmer, NZ); schoolteacher; Methodist missionary sister, Papua 1911–1915 (register no. 60); resigned to marry

Williams, Bertha	Walsh, ?	Begelhole	J. A. Walsh	8 Nov. 1904*	Married at Dobu
Williams, Charlotte			J. R. Williams 23 June 1899		
		Mason	J. R. Williams 3 Aug. 1910		After husband's death (1913) became Methodist missionary sister, Fiji

Sources: For biographical information sources include birth, marriage, and death certificates (when available); information from descendants; Sibree 1923; and mission archives, diaries, published autobiographies, and biographies, which may be found in the bibliography.

Biographical Register

The register contains short biographical entries on each of the 327 European missionaries who served in Papua from 1874 to 1914. Within each mission, entries are arranged alphabetically. Numbers and deaths of children apply only to period of parents' missionary service.

London Missionary Society

1. **ABEL, Charles W.**, b. 25 September 1862, London; father: cashier at Mudie's Library; "Surrounded by Christian influences" and impressed by Moody and Sankey at 11 years of age; o. clerk. Migrated to New Zealand as cadet farmer, finally becoming a trader to the Maoris; applied to LMS after seeing "deplorable condition" of Maoris and success of his work among them; trained, Cheshunt; ord. 23 July 1890; arr. NG 1890, stn. Kwato; m. Elizabeth Beatrice Emma Moxon, 22 November 1892, Sydney; 5 ch. (1 d.); d. 10 April 1930, Surrey, England (result of accident).

2. **BARTLETT, Reginald**, b. 21 March 1878, Newcastle-on-Tyne; son of Charles Henry Bartlett, managing director, firm of scale-makers and shop-fitters; ed. Winchester House School; devout Cong. family; c.m. Redland Park Church, Bristol; one sister, Edith Murray, missionary in China; lifelong desire to be missionary, supported by parents; challenged by appeal of Chalmers; trained, Western Coll.; ord. 30 April 1905; arr. Papua 1905, stn. Orokolo; m. Alice Mary Bennett, 1 January 1907, Sydney; 1 ch.; r. 1912, ill-health; CC, Painswick; District Secretary, LMS 1919; Samoa 1929–1931; home missionary 1931–1938; Samoa 1939–1941; d. July 1948, England.

3. **BEHARELL, Caleb**, b. 1 June 1881, Ilford, Essex; father: owner of paint factory; ed. Stepney G.S., evening classes; Congregational

family; dedicated to mission work by parents; o: worked in paint factory, 5 years; trained, Harley and Livingstone; ord. 25 July 1906; arr. Papua 1906, stns. Kerepunu and Hula; m. Margaret James Patterson, 20 December 1910; 3 ch.; r. 1919, ill-health; transferred to Niue; d. 1952.

4. **BESWICK, Thomas,** b. 29 September 1850, Manchester; son of Thomas Beswick; c.m. Rusholme Rd, Manchester; trained: Western Coll.; ord. 23 September 1878; arr. NG 22 November 1879, stn. Hula; r. 1881, when directors refused to sanction marriage to Clara Coombs because of her ill-health. Married, reappointed, but died returning to NG 12 August 1883, Townsville.

5. **BURROWS, Sydney,** b. 9 December 1881, Richmond, Vic.; son of John George Burrows, journalist, and Hannah (Favel); ed. private school, Working Men's College, Melb. University (B.A., Dip. Ed.); c.m. Lennox St. CC; o. business; ord. 1907; influenced by Mission Study Movement; applied to LMS; m. Charlotte Robertson, 25 February 1913; 1 ch.; arr. Papua 1913, stn. Port Moresby; r. 1916, child ill.

6. **BUTCHER, Benjamin Thomas,** b. 13 July 1877, New Cross, London; son of Thomas Butcher, fish wholesaler, and Mary (Robbins); ed. Aske's School; o. Billingsgate Fish Market; c.m. Hanover CC, Peckham; missionary interest since childhood; applied to LMS following Chalmers' death; trained, Cheshunt and Livingstone; ord. 1 November 1904; arr. Papua 1904, stns. Torres Strait, Aird Hill; m. Lucy Georgina Davidson, 28 December 1912; 4 ch. (1 d.); r. 1938, family pressure; president, Cong. Union of Aust., 1948–1950; d. 29 July 1973, NSW.

7. **CHALMERS, James,** b. 4 August 1841, Ardrishaig, Argyllshire; father, stonemason; ed. parish school and Inveraray GS to age 14; o. lawyer's apprentice; c.m. United Pres. Church, "conversion" 1859; influenced by missionary from Samoa, applied to LMS; trained, Cheshunt and Highgate; ord. 19 October 1865; m. Jane Robertson Hercus, 17 October 1865; served Rarotonga 1866–1876; arr. NG 1877, stns. Suau, Port Moresby, Toaripi, Saguane; wife d. 1879; m. Sarah Eliza Harrison (née Large), 6 October 1888 (d. 1900); 0 ch.; killed 8 April 1901, Goaribari, NG.

8. **CLARK, James Birkett,** b. 13 September 1881, Cockermouth, Cumberland; ed. Board School, private sch., science sch., Edinburgh University; o. apprentice draper; c.m. Cockermouth CC; applied to LMS after reading pamphlet at YMCA; trained, Cong. Theological Hall and Edinburgh University; ord. 21 December 1906; m. Annie Muir, 19 December 1906; arr. Papua 1907, stns. Buhutu, Boku, Port Moresby; r. 1931, ill-health.

9. **CRIBB, Charles James,** b. 19 January 1866, Milton, Qld; son of John George Cribb, accountant, and Lucy (Foote); ed. Brisbane GS; o. bookseller and stationer; prominent Cong. family; c.m. Milton CC; childhood desire to be missionary quickened by contact with W. G. Lawes; trained, Hackney; ord. 1896; arr. NG 1896, stn. Mailu; m. Elizabeth McNab, 20 July 1898; 0 ch.; r. 1899, ill-health; d. 28 July 1932, Sydney.

10. **CULLEN, James H.,** b. 20 November 1864, Nottingham; ed. Moravian boarding school, Nottingham HS; o. able-bodied seaman and architects' apprentice; childhood desire to be missionary rekindled by Chalmers' appeal at Hastings; trained, Cheshunt; ord. 3 June 1891; m. Mattie Burr Simmons, 30 June 1890; 0 ch.; arr. Papua 1902, stn. Port Moresby; r. 1903, ill-health; missionary, South Africa, Niue; d. 14 September 1919, England.

11. **DAUNCEY, Henry Moore,** b. 3 January 1863, Walsall, Staffordshire; son of Henry Dauncey, newspaper reporter, and Elizabeth (Moore); o. 4 years in justice's clerk's office, then reporter; c.m. Wednesbury Rd. CC; lifelong desire to be missionary strengthened by watching ordination of two missionaries; trained, Cheshunt; ord. 2 July 1888; arr. NG 1888, stns. Port Moresby, Delena; m. Mary Ellen Hinton, 16 August 1894; 3 ch. (1 d.); r. 1928, ill-health; d. December 1931, England.

12. **HARRIES, Thomas Oliver,** b. 25 August 1879, Walwyn's Castle, Pembrokeshire; father, farmer; ed. Board School and Cong. Institute, Nottingham; o. 9 yrs. in ship-building trade; c.m. Hindpool CC, Barrow-in-Furness; trained, Paton Cong. Coll.; m. Edith Lillian Gayton, 7 March 1911; 1 ch.; arr. Papua 1912, stn. Torres Strait; r. 1915, ill-health of wife; minister, Stourbridge CC, 1916.

13. **HOLMES, John Henry,** b. 19 June 1861, Habertonford, Devon; father, farmer; ed. to 11 years; o. decorative painter; c.m. Sherwell CC, Plymouth; longed to be missionary since, aged 10, saw lantern lecture on India; trained, Western Coll.; ord. 7 June 1863; arr. NG 1893; stns. Iokea, Moru, Orokolo, Urika; m. Alice Middleton, 4 July 1910; 0 ch.; r. 1919, ill-health of wife; d. 19 April 1934, England.

14. **HUNT, Archibald Ernest,** b. 24 September 1861, St. Helen's, Jersey; father, minister; orphaned; ed. modest; o. draper's assistant; c.m. Trevor CC, Brompton, London; influenced toward ministry by fiancée; trained, Hackney; ord. 21 April 1887; m. Harriet Rebecca Tizard, 26 May 1887; 3 ch.; arr. NG 1887, stn. Murray I.; transferred Samoa 1889; returned NG 1895, stn. Port Moresby; r. 1902, ill-health of wife; minister, Timaru and Wellington CC, NZ.

15. **INGRAM, Thomas William,** b. 17 March 1866, Southend, En-

gland; o. mechanical engineer; c.m. Southend CC; trained, Cheshunt; ord. 12 June 1894; m. Louisa Gunn, 17 May 1894; 0 ch.; arr. NG 1894, stn. Port Moresby; r. 1895, ill-health of wife; minister, Broadstairs Vale, Farham, Clacton-on-Sea; d. 26 March 1914, England.

16. **JONES, Edwin Pryce,** b. 1 June 1864, Aberdare, South Wales; ed. a "fair classical education"; o. chemist and druggist; Christian family; c.m. Park CC, Camden Town; boyhood wish to be missionary; trained, Hackney; ord. 15 March 1893; m. Minnie Ellis Page, 30 March 1893; 5 ch.; served Madagascar 1893–1898; arr. NG 1899, stn. Iokea; r. 1926, old age; d. 27 July 1928.

17. **LAWES, William George,** b. 1 July 1839, Aldermaston, Berkshire; son of Richard Lawes, tailor, and Mary (Pickover); ed. elementary, at village school; o. draper; devout parents; c.m. Mortimer West CC; 1858 heard William Gill of Rarotonga preach; applied to LMS; trained, Bedford Coll.; ord. 8 November 1860; m. Fanny Wickham, 1860; 6 ch. (3 d.); served Niue, 1861–1872; arr. NG 1874, stns. Port Moresby, Vatorata; DD (honoris causa) Glasgow 1895; FRGS; r. 1906, old age; d. 6 August 1907.

18. **LAWRENCE, William Nicol,** b. 21 May 1859, Leaside, Aberdeen; ed. parish sch.; o. cardmaker; c.m. Woodside, Aberdeen; trained, Airedale Coll.; ord. 15 June 1883; m. Jessie Leslie, 22 November 1883; 0 ch.; served Aitutaki 1884–1905; arr. Papua 1906, stn. Port Moresby; r. 1917, old age.

19. **McFARLANE, Samuel,** b. 18 February 1837, Johnstone, Scotland; son of William McFarlane, engineer; o. mechanic; "Conversion," Sabbath School, Manchester; c.m. Oldham Rd. CC, Manchester; interest in missions aroused at missionary meeting; trained, Bedford Coll.; ord. 11 November 1858, Oldham Rd. Church; m. Elizabeth Joyce 1858; 5 ch. (1 d.); served Loyalty Islands, 1859–1870; arr. NG 1871, stns. Somerset, Murray I.; LL.D. (honoris causa) St. Andrew's 1877; FRGS; r. 1886, family pressures; officer of LMS, 1886–1894; d. 27 January 1911, England.

20. **PEARSE, Albert,** b. 26 April 1841, Bishop's Hull, Somerset; o. printer; pious parents; c.m. Bishop's Hull; desired from childhood to be missionary, as had his father; trained, Bristol Institution for Home Missionaries and Western Coll.; ord. 18 October 1869; m. Susan Jefferies, 1869; 6 ch.; served Borabora 1870–1874, Raiatea 1874–1887; arr. NG 1887, stn. Kerepunu; r. 1907, old age; d. 20 January 1911.

21. **RICH, Charles Fry,** b. 22 November 1872, Bath; ed. elementary; o. shoemaker; c.m. Percy Church, Bath; "claimed as a lad for mission work"; trained, Western Coll.; ord. 27 June 1900; m. Caroline

Bryant, 5 May 1900; 6 ch. (1 d.); arr. Papua 1900, stn. Isuleilei; r. 1939, old age; d. 1949.

22. **RIDGLEY, Thomas,** b. 21 August 1853, Huntingdon; ed. Cowper's School House, Edinburgh University (MB 1881); o. chemist and druggist; c.m. Wycliffe Church, Warrington; trained, Edinburgh University; arr. NG 1882, stn. Hula; r. 1882, dissatisfaction.

23. **RILEY, Edward Baxter,** b. 6 May 1868, Burnley, Lancashire; son of John Riley, manufacturer, and Sarah (Binns); ed. elementary sch., evening classes, Queen's Coll. to intermediate; o. clerk, weaver; missionary interest awakened by reading Livingstone, etc.; trained, Lancashire Coll.; ord. 19 December 1899; arr. NG 1900, stns. Vatorata, Fly R.; m. Jessie Marian Maclean, 10 January 1906; 3 ch. (2 d.); d. 1929, Papua.

24. **SAVAGE, Edwin Bentley,** b. 14 November 1854, Ringwood, Hampshire; father, boot and shoemaker; o. assistant in boot and shoe industry; c.m. Ringwood CC; trained, Hackney; ord. 8 July 1885; arr. NG 1891, stns. Murray I., Toaripi; r. 1891, criticized by LMS.

25. **SAVILLE, William James Viritahitemauvai,** b. 21 January 1873; son of A. T. Saville, missionary, and E. A. (Marston); ed. Catherham Cong. Sch.; o. draper's assistant; c.m. Rye CC; childhood desire to be missionary intensified; trained, Western Coll.; ord. 19 June 1900; arr. Papua 1900, stns. Mailu, Milport Harbour; m. Frances Lawes, 6 June 1903; 1 ch.; r. 1935, old age; d. 7 February 1948, England.

26. **SCHLENCKER, Henry Percy,** b. 21 September 1866, Balmain, NSW; son of William Happell Schlencker, writing clerk, and Mary Ann (Geard); o. hardware warehouseman; c.m. Grey St. CC, Brisbane; called by God in prayer meeting; trained, Hackney; arr. NG 1895, stns. Isuleilei, Kalaigolo, Orokolo; m. Mary Elizabeth Sarah Cribb, 1 February 1905; 3 ch.; r. 1927.

27. **SHARPE, Watson,** b. 30 November 1858, Halifax; o. employed in woollen shipping house; c.m. Horton Lane CC, Bradford; trained, Rotherham College; ord. 27 May 1885; arr. NG 1885; stn. Port Moresby; d. 20 March 1886, New Guinea.

28. **SCOTT, Harry,** b. 14 July 1858, Walsall, Staffordshire; o. clerk; Christian parents; c.m. Wednesbury Rd. CC; interest kindled by missionary appeal; trained, Cheshunt; ord. 1883; m. Mary Todhunter, 1883; 2 ch.; arr. NG 1883, stn. Murray I.; r. 1886, illhealth; pastor, Countess of Huntingdon's Church, Hereford; served with B. & F. Bible Society; d. 1939, England.

29. **SCOTT, James Tait,** b. 5 November 1852, Inverleithen, Scotland; ed. elementary; c.m. St. Paul's, Aberdeen; trained, Lancashire

Coll.; ord. 4 July 1880; m. Eliza Jessie Mitchell, 6 July 1880; 1 ch. (d.); arr. NG 1880, stn. Port Moresby; r. 1882, conflict and ill-health; pastor, Lymington CC, Hants; d. 1894, England.

30. **TOMKINS, Oliver Fellows**, b. 5 March 1873, Great Yarmouth; son of Daniel Tomkins, private schoolmaster, and Caroline Kate (Fellows), schoolmistress; ed. Yarmouth Coll. (1st class Cambridge Junior) and Switzerland; o. clerk; Leading Cong. family; c.m. Princess St., Norwich; influenced to become missionary by mission-minded church and Keswick Conventions; trained, Harley Coll.; ord. 6 December 1899; arr. NG 1900, stn. Torres Strait; killed 8 April 1901, Goaribari.

31. **TURNER, Robert Lister**, b. 4 February 1875, Apia, Samoa; son of George Alexander Turner, MD, missionary and Isabella (Nelson); ed. Glasgow HS, Glasgow University, (MA); o. student and tutor; c.m. Kelvingrove United Pres. Church, Glasgow; lifelong wish to be missionary; trained, United Pres. Theological Coll.; ord. November 1901; arr. Papua 1902, stns. Vatorata, Delena; m. Edith Emma Calvert, 28 July 1910; 0 ch.; awarded Coronation Medal, 1937; FRGS; member of Legislative Council, Papua; r. 1931, old age; d. 5 February 1949, England.

32. **TURNER, William Young**, b. 14 August 1851, Upolu, Samoa; son of Dr. George Turner, missionary, and Mary Ann (Dunn); o. student; c.m. Anderson United Pres. Church, Glasgow; trained, Glasgow University (MD); ord. 3 September 1874; m. Mary Amelia Colville, 19 August 1875 (d. 1876); 1 ch.; arr. NG 1876, stn. Murray I.; r. 1876, after death of wife and conflict with McFarlane; medical missionary, West Indies.

33. **WALKER, Frederick William**, b. 27 December 1860, Hull; father, lighter shipbuilder; o. deckhand, ironmonger's apprentice, cashier and bookkeeper, carpenter; c.m. Hope St. CC, Hull; influenced by reading Livingstone and hearing Chalmers; trained, Cheshunt; ord. 22 June 1888; arr. NG 1888, stns. Kwato, Torres Strait; r. 1896, conflict with LMS; managing director, Papuan Industries; further service with LMS 1902–1905, and with Kwato, 1925–1926; d. 1926, Papua.

Methodist Mission

34. **ANDREWS, A. John**, b. Scotland; o. carpenter; arr. NG 1 October 1893, stn. Vakuta; m.; 2 ch. (1 d.); r. 1897, ill-health of wife.

35. **AVERY, William Wesley**, b. 12 November 1877, Fairhall, Blenheim, NZ; father, farmer; ed. primary sch., Marlborough H.S. as adult; o. farm-worker; staunch six-generation Methodist family;

probationer 1906, Huntly; ord. February 1910; lifelong wish to be missionary; trained, Prince Albert Coll., Auckland; m. Lizzie Belton, 14 April 1910; 2 ch.; arr. Papua 1910, stn. Dobu; r. 1913, ill-health of self and wife; NZ ministry until 1946; d. 15 March 1954, New Zealand.

36. **BALLANTYNE, Andrew,** b. 1875, Buckingham, England; son of Andrew Ballantyne, coal-miner, and Ellen Elizabeth (Shepherd); migrated to Tasmania 1882; o. blacksmith's assistant; private, Boer War; Methodist family, father, lay-preacher; trained, Queen's College, Melbourne (1 year); ord. 1903; arr. Papua 1904, stns. Dobu, Bwaidoga; m. May Jenness, 9 October 1906; 4 ch. (2 d.); d. 7 June 1915, Papua.

37. **BARDSLEY, George Harry,** b. 1864, Cheshire, England; son of Isaac Bardsley, cashier, and Alice Ann (Ives); ed. primary to age 8; o. carpenter; family, Anglican; lay preacher; arr. NG 1891, stn. Dobu; r. 1892, conflict with Bromilow; d. 1929, Brisbane.

38. **BARNES, Frederick James,** b. 1881, Launceston; candidate for ministry, 1909; SA ministry 1909–1914; m.; arr. Papua 1914, stn. Panaeati; r. 1918, ill-health; SA ministry 1919–1951; d. 25 February 1967, SA.

39. **BEMBRICK, Doris Pearl,** b. 5 September 1888, Grenfell, NSW; daughter of Thomas Bembrick, merchant, and Emma (Fowler); ed. Grenfell Public Sch., Sydney Girls HS, Sydney Training Coll.; o. teacher; staunch Methodist family, father local preacher, sister missionary in Fiji; arr. Papua 1913, stn. Ubuia; r. 1917, to marry W. J. Enticott (no. 43).

40. **BENJAMIN, Julia,** b. Geelong, Vic.; applied to AWMMS "in obedience to unmistakable call of God"; arr. NG 1898, stn. Dobu; r. 1907; became missionary sister to Maoris; returned to Papua 1910; r. 1913, mental instability.

41. **BILLING, Minnie Mabel,** b. 27 November 1869, N. Adelaide; daughter of James Brooks Billing, warehouseman, and Adelina Tardiff (Harris); orphaned 1880, brought up by aunt, Elizabeth Nicholls, president WCTU (SA); ed. Glenelg Educational Establishment, completed secondary ed.; o. teacher; Methodist family, two cousins missionaries; arr. NG 1895, stn. Dobu; r. 1898, ill-health; missionary sister, Fiji 1900–1901; d. 15 April 1901, Adelaide.

42. **BROMILOW, William E.,** b. 15 January 1857, Geelong, Vic.; son of Thomas Bromilow, bricklayer and Jane (Owen); ed. Grenville Coll., Ballarat; o. teacher; strong Methodist family; ord. 1879; dedicated to mission work by mother before birth; responded to call for missionaries at Methodist Conference; m. Lily Thomson,

April 1879; 1 ch. (adopted); served Fiji 1879–1889; arr. NG 1891, chairman of NG Mission, stn. Dobu; r. 1907, ill-health of wife, DD (honoris causa), Aberdeen 1910, for translation of Bible into Dobu; chairman, NSW Conference 1911; returned to Papua 1920–1925; d. 24 June 1929, Sydney.

43. **BURGESS, Gordon Angelo,** b. 4 June 1882, Tasmania; son of Arthur Francis Burgess, contractor and builder, and Hannah (Lloyd); o. builder; accepted for ministry 1909; m. Minnie Chambers, 18 March 1910; 2 ch.; arr. Papua 1910, stn. Bunama; r. 1915, wife's ill-health; appointed to Aboriginal mission, NT; d. 20 March 1919.

44. **CHAPMAN, Harold Keith,** b. NSW; son of B. H. Chapman; ed. Hawkesbury Agricultural Coll.; o. agricultural officer, NSW; arr. Papua 1914, stn. Ubuia (plantation manager); r. 1917, ill-health.

45. **COLEBATCH, Annie,** b. 1 April 1869, Herefordshire, England; daughter of George Pateshall Colebatch, chemist, and Georgina (Gardiner); migrated to SA 1878; o. nurse; arr. NG 1898, stns. Dobu, Kiriwina; r. 1900, ill-health; m. Robert Vincent Butler, civil servant, 25 April 1905; d. 8 March 1958, SA.

46. **CORFIELD, Bessie,** b. Bury, England; daughter of William Corfield, bootmaker, and Alice (Bridge); migrated to NSW; arr. Papua 1904, stns. Kiriwina, Dobu; r. 1913 to marry Percy Waterhouse (no. 78), 11 April 1914.

47. **ENTICOTT, Walter,** b. 10 February 1880, Lewisham, England; son of George Enticott, coach-builder; ed. primary; o. coach-builder; father, C of E, mother RC, confirmed C of E; "converted" in mission, London; lay-missionary, South Africa and NZ; ord. NZ, 2 June 1913; arr. Papua 1913, stns. Panaeati, Rossel I.; m. (1) Doris Bembrick (no. 39), 7 February 1917 (d. 1944); 0 ch.; r. 1917, ill-health and disagreement with the church; NZ ministry until 1948; m. (2) Esther Rickard, 1950; d. 23 June 1969, NZ.

48. **FELLOWS, Samuel Benjamin,** b. 26 October 1858, Codnor Park, Derbyshire; son of Samuel and Mary Fellows; ed. National Sch., Codnor Park; o. employed in rolling-mills; strong Methodist family; father, local preacher; migrated to NZ, nominated for ministry, Dunedin; ord. 1888; invited by George Brown to become missionary; arr. Papua 1891, stns. Dobu, Panaeati, Kiriwina; m. Sarah Hanna, 1894; 4 ch.; r. 1901, wife's ill-health; Methodist ministry, Qld, WA; president of WA Conference 1912; d. 21 October 1933, WA.

49. **FERGUSON, Hilda,** b. Perth, WA; arr. Papua 1914, stn. Ubuia; r. 1914, inability to adjust.

50. **FIELD, John Thompson,** b. 1861, Geelong, Vic.; son of William

Field, customhouse agent, and Marian (Gillingham); o. architect, builder, and cabinetmaker; arr. NG 1891, stns. Dobu, Tubetube, Duau; m. (1) Frances Mary Harding, May 1892; 2 ch.; r. 1900, ill-health; Methodist ministry, Vic. and Tas.; returned to Papua 1913, stn. Ubuia; m. (2) Grace Lillburn; d. 20 October 1938, Vic.

51. **FLETCHER, Ambrose**, b. 3 July 1864, Auckland, NZ; son of John Fletcher, schoolmaster, and Eliza (Bale); ord. 1890; Methodist ministry, NSW; arr. NG 1893, stns. Panaeati, Bwaidoga, Dobu, Duau; m. Jessie Bavin, 13 April 1894; 3 ch. (1 d.); r. 1903, wife's ill-health; NSW ministry; returned to Papua 1922, Rabaul 1925–1927; d. 24 November 1957, NSW.

52. **FRANCIS, William Charles**, b. 6 March 1867, Dunedin, NZ; son of Robert Francis, music shop manager; ed. primary; o. wood-carver; m. Annie Elizabeth Fathers; 2 ch.; arr. Papua 1904, stns. Dobu, Bwaidoga; r. 1908, wife's ill-health.

53. **GATLAND, Gregory A.**, b. NSW; arr. Papua 1903, stn. Murua; m. Miss Vipond; 2 ch. (1 d.); r. 1908, ill-health of wife.

54. **GIBB, Jannett Catherine**, b. Sydney, 1879; daughter of W. T. Gibb, auctioneer, and Isabella (Baumann); arr. Papua 1909, stn. Ubuia; r. 1918, family pressure; member of Board of Missions, 12 years; d. 6 July 1957, NSW.

55. **GILMOUR, Matthew Kerr**, b. 1872, Inveraray, Argyllshire, Scotland; son of Hugh Kerr Gilmour, brush manufacturer, and Eliza (Templeton); migrated to NZ, settled Howick; ord. 23 April 1901; m. Nora Lilian Francis; 0 ch.; arr. Papua 1901, stns. Kiriwina, Dobu, Ubuia, Salamo; chairman, NG district, 1909–1919, 1923–1933; r. 1933, old age; NSW ministry 1933–1942; president of Conference, 1935; Coronation medal 1937; d. 22 July 1962, NSW.

56. **GLEW, Edward James**, b. December 1874, Brunswick, Vic.; son of Edward Paterson Glew, merchant, and Jane (Cornelius); arr. NG 1899, stns. Bwaidoga, Murua; m. Fairleigh Lillie Newell, 11 June 1901; 1 ch.; d. 25 June 1904, Samarai, Papua.

57. **GRIFFITHS, Laura**, b. Geelong, Vic.; o. nurse; trained, Blackwell's Missionary Training Home, Vic.; arr. Papua 1903, stns. Kiriwina, Dobu; r. 1913, ill-health.

58. **HARRISON, Ernest William**, b. 1883, Harnsfield, Nottinghamshire; son of George Henry Harrison, farmer, and Harriet (Cook); bugler in Boer War, 2 years in India with British forces; migrated to NZ, home missionary; arr. Papua 1909, stn. Murua; m. Maisie Lill (no. 63), 8 October 1910; r. 1913, after physical and mental collapse of wife; returned to Papua alone, settled as trader and planter Fergusson I.; served with AIF, World War I and ANGAU, World War II; d. 1961, Papua.

59. **HOLLAND, George Robert,** b. 6 September 1883, Tyagong Creek, Grenfell, NSW, son of Edward Holland, farmer, and Anne (McGrath); ed. public school (primary); Methodist upbringing, "conversion" at 18; trained Newington Coll.; ord. 1907; m. Anne (?); 2 ch.; arr. Papua 1908, stn. Kiriwina; r. 1912, nervous breakdown and ill-health; NSW ministry 1912–1949.

60. **JAMIESON, Margaret,** b. 13 June 1883, Palmerston North, NZ; daughter of Lawrence Jamieson, farmer, and Annie (Reid); ed. state sch. to grade 6; o. teacher; strong Methodist family; arr. Papua 1911, stn. Kiriwina; r. 1915 to marry A. H. Scrivin (no. 69); d. 1921, NZ.

61. **JENNESS, May,** b. 1875, Wellington, NZ; daughter of George Lewis Jenness, watch repairer and jeweller, and Hannah (Heaynes); ed. Wellington Girls' Coll. and home studies to matriculation; Loyal Methodist family; arr. Papua 1905, stn. Dobu; r. to marry A. Ballantyne (no. 36), 9 October 1906; returned to NZ 1916, after death of husband; d. 1953, NZ.

62. **JOHNS, Ernest Samuel,** b. 1881, Clunes, Vic.; son of John Johns, miner, and Emmeline (Radford); accepted for ministry 1911; arr. Papua 1911, stns. Dobu, Kiriwina; m. Elsie Buchanan 1 June 1912; 1 ch.; r. 1917, ill-health; Methodist ministry, WA; d. 5 May 1920, WA.

63. **LILL, Rose Mary (Maisie),** b. 31 January 1884, Newlands, Canterbury, NZ, daughter of William Thomas Lill, farmer, and Clara (Taylor); o. worked in draper's shop, Christchurch; primitive Methodist family, local preacher at age 17; arr. Papua 1908, stn. Kiriwina; r. 1910, to marry E. W. Harrison (no. 58), 8 October 1910; returned to NZ after physical and mental collapse; d. 1972.

64. **LLOYD, Edith,** father, miner, Burra, SA; arr. NG 1898, stn. Dobu; r. 1903, ill-health.

65. **McINTYRE, Sister,** from Strathfield, NSW; arr. Papua 1912, stn. Ubuia; r. 1912, inability to adjust.

66. **NEWELL, Emily A.,** b. Ballarat, Vic.; o. teacher; arr. NG 1896, stns. Kiriwina, Dobu; r. 1898, ill-health.

67. **OSBORNE, James R.,** from Vic.; m. Nellie (?); 1 ch. (Australia); ordained; arr. Papua 1904, stn. Bunama; r. 1910, trading interests and alleged immorality; became trader, Papua.

68. **PRISK, Ethel,** from Adelaide; arr. Papua 1910, stns. Ubuia, Kiriwina; r. 1916, domestic pressures.

69. **SCRIVIN, Arthur Henry,** b. London, 1 February 1883; son of John Scrivin, police sergeant, and Frances (Langdale); ed. elementary, adult matriculation; o. apprentice patternmaker, Woolwich Arsenal; migrated to NZ, 1907; ministerial candidate, 1909; trained,

Prince Albert College, Auckland; ord. 1912; arr. Papua 1914, stns. Dobu, Ubuia.; m. (1) Margaret Jamieson (no. 60), 1915 (d. 1921); 2 ch.; (2) Elsie Warner, missionary sister, 1926; 2 ch.; r. 1932, old age and retrenchment due to the depression; NZ ministry; President of Conference, 1945; d. 13 July 1969, NZ.

70. **SPEERS, Nurse E. E.**, from Melbourne; o. nurse; arr. NG 1894, stn. Dobu; r. 1895, mental instability.

71. **THOMAS, Sister**, from SA; arr. Papua 1902, stn. Dobu; r. February 1903, conflict with Bromilows.

72. **THOMPSON, Florence**, b. Stratford, Taranaki, NZ; ed. Stratford HS, matriculated 1899; o. teacher; staunch Methodist family; called to mission by sermon of Rev. S. T. Thomas of Dannevirke; arr. Papua 1907, stn. Ubuia; r. 1909, mother's illness.

73. **TINNEY, Jeannie**, b. 30 June 1867, Ballarat, Vic.; daughter of James Tinney, carter, and Annie (Landon); arr. NG 1892, stn. Dobu; r. 1902, ill-health and shattered nerves; mission work with Aborigines, NT.

74. **TRUSCOTT, Lise**, b. 1874, NSW; daughter of J. Truscott; arr. Papua 1903, stn. Dobu; d. 4 November 1908, Dobu.

75. **VOSPER, Janet**, b. Waitara, NZ; orphan; arr. Papua 1906, stn. Dobu; r. 1909, nervous breakdown.

76. **WALKER, Eleanor**, b. 1862, Harrowgate, Yorkshire; daughter of Thomas Walker, draper; historic Methodist family; orphaned, migrated to Sydney; applied to George Brown after fiancé died; arr. NG 1892, stn. Dobu; r. 1901; mission work with Aborigines, NSW; d. 29 April 1940, NSW.

77. **WALSH, James A.**, b. 6 June 1870, Berrima, NSW; son of James Alexander Walsh, farmer, and Jane (Wallace); Methodist family; father, local preacher; ord. 23 April 1901; m.; arr. Papua 1901, stn. Murua; r. 1904, disagreement with mission board.

78. **WATERHOUSE, Percy M.**, b. 1878, Glenelg, SA; son of William Towers Waterhouse, accountant, and Mary Ann (Padman); ed. to matriculation; eminent Methodist family; missionary teacher, Fiji, 1905; ord. 1909; arr. Papua 1912, stn. Rossel I.; r. 1913, ill-suited to work; m. Bessie Corfield (no. 46), 11 April 1914; NSW ministry 1913–1918; Fiji 1918–1923; d. 1 May 1958.

79. **WATSON, James**, b. 1865, Bendigo, Vic.; son of James Watson, engineer, and Margaret (Ryan); o. engineer and blacksmith; ministerial candidate 1890; arr. Papua 1891, stn. Panaeati; r. 1893, ill-health; m. Isabella Duncan Fraser, 21 July 1896; NSW ministry and Aboriginal mission, Goulburn I., NT; d. 27 September 1946.

80. **WILLIAMS, James R.**, b. 1869, California Gully, Bendigo; son of Joseph Webb Williams and Mary Anne (Roberts); m. (1) Annie

Worrall 1896 (d.); responded to Bromilow's appeal for recruits 1898; arr. NG 1898, stn. Panaeati; m. (2) Bertha Begelhole 1899 (d. 1904); 2 ch.; m. (3) Charlotte June Mason, 3 August 1910; ord. 1910; d. 1 October 1913, on sick leave.

81. **WINN, Frederick J.**, b. 2 October 1887, Lincoln, England; o. business; Methodist upbringing, "converted" at 16; called by missionary study class and address of George Brown; ord. 2 May 1912; arr. Papua 1912, stns. Ubuia, Guasopi; r. 1915, to join Expeditionary Forces; returned to Australia 1919.

Anglican Mission

82. **ABBOT, Wilfred Henry**, b. 7 June 1867, Dublin; son of Frederick James Abbott, priest; ed., matriculated 1888, MA 1897 Oxford, Keble College; trained, Ely Theological Coll.; ord. deacon, 18 December 1892, priest, 21 December 1894; minor canon, Brisbane pro-Cathedral, 1897; arr. NG 1898, stn. Wanigela; r. 1901, conflict with Stone-Wigg and debts; C of E priesthood, England, and Chaplain, Transvaal, 1914–1919; Military Cross 1915; d. 16 April 1941, England.

83. **ADAMS, Miss**, from Sydney; ed. to matriculation; o. teacher; ten-year wish to be missionary; arr. Papua 1903, stn. Dogura; r. 1903, unable to adjust.

84. **AMBROSE, Frederick**, from Sydney; o. sailor, packer; arr. NG 1899; r. 1899, ill-health.

85. **BARTLEMANN, Isobel Boyes**, from Sydney; o. nurse and governess (NZ); arr. Papua 1900; r. 1900, inability to cope.

86. **BATCHELOR, Albert James**, b. 18 February 1882, Reigate, England; son of Charles Barnard Batchelor, butcher, and Jane (Robinson); migrated to Melbourne 1908; c.m. St. Peter's Eastern Hill, Melbourne; arr. Papua 1912, stn. Dogura; r. 1914, ill-health; worked Defence Dept and ABM; m. Florence Ethel Jenkins, 1928; d. 5 July 1949, Melbourne.

87. **BAYLEY, Walter**, b. Bendigo, Vic.; father, RC; mother, Cong.; arr. NG 1898, stn. Dogura; r. 1898, after mission's discovery of criminal past.

88. **BECHERVAISE, Margaret**, b. Melbourne; o. teacher; c.m., St. Peter's Eastern Hill, Melbourne; arr. Papua 1914, stn. Dogura; r. 1915, family pressures; returned to Papua 1920–1941, 1948–1950.

89. **BUCHANAN, Francis de Sales**, b. 1 September 1854, USA; father, property owner; grandson of 15th president of USA; RC; ed. Jesuits; o. clerk; became Benedictine novice, Newbank, USA; remained oblate; came to Sydney, 1894; left RC Church over teach-

ings on miracles, became Anglican; home missionary; arr. NG 1899, stns. Boianai, Uga; d. 16 October 1921, Papua.

90. **BURNETT, T. A.**, from Sydney; o. carpenter; arr. Papua 1904, handyman; r. 1905, dissastisfaction and financial anxiety.

91. **CHALLMAN, Ella Florence**, from Victoria; ed. to matriculation; o. teacher; arr. Papua 1900, stn. Samarai; r. 1903, to marry R. S. Bunting, storekeeper, Samarai.

92. **CHIGNELL, Arthur Kent**, b. 9 March 1870, Bedfordshire; migrated to SA 1889; BA, University of Adelaide, 1900; trained, St. Barnabas Coll., Adelaide, 1893–1894; ord. deacon 27 December 1894, priest 22 December 1895; Anglican ministry, Adelaide and Sydney; arr. Papua 1907, stn. Wanigela; m. Elizabeth Rattigan (no. 136) 1914; r. 1914 for administrative post with ABM; Master, Charterhouse, Hull 1919; curate, Sculcoates, Yorkshire, 1920–1926.

93. **CLARKE, Edward Henry**, b. 1854; arr. NG 1896, stn. Taupota; d. 12 May 1899, Papua.

94. **COMBLEY, Ellen**, b. 7 April 1867, Erchfont, Wiltshire; daughter of James Edward Combley, yeoman, and Jane (Page); o. nurse; migrated to Perth, nursed on goldfields; arr. Papua 1900, stns. Dogura, Mamba, Lakekamu; d. 1912, Papua.

95. **COTTINGHAM, Alice Maud**, b. 21 June 1861, Dauningworth, Suffolk; daughter of Edward Cottingham, farmer, and Sarah (Ling); o. teacher; recruited WA; arr. Papua 1903, stns. Dogura, Mukawa; Coronation Medal 1937; d. 20 February 1940, Papua.

96. **DAKERS, Robert Hardy**, b. 1865, Byer's Green, Durham, England; son of Robert Dakers, mining overseer, and Margaret Maria (Hardy); o. business; longstanding desire for mission; arr. NG 1898, stns. Mukawa, Wanigela, Taupota, Hioge; r. 1907, discontent; worked on Burns Philp's coconut plantation, Solomons; d. 23 June 1920, Brisbane.

97. **DAVIES, Ernest Owen**, b. 21 May 1876, Kensington, London; son of Gomer Davies, physician, and Elizabeth Susan (Cropley); trained, St. Augustine's, but failed to gain ordination; arr. Papua 1909, stn. Hioge; m. Louise Robson (no. 140); r. 1916, to enlist; killed in action, 1918.

98. **DODDS, Norman**, b. 1882 (?), Collingwood, Vic.; o. engineer; c.m. St. Mark's, Fitzroy; applied to mission after hearing Stone-Wigg preach; arr. 1903, launch-driver; r. 1904, immorality.

99. **DOWNTON, George Edward**, b. 1885, Koroit, Vic.; son of George H. Downton; ed. Ballarat GS to matriculation; arr. Papua 1906, stn. Dogura; r. 1909, family reasons; d. 31 May 1927.

100. **DRURY, Leonard Bertram**, b. 1872, Ballarat, Vic.; son of Captain

Arthur Drury, police magistrate; ed. elementary; o. banking, prospector (WA), policeman, school-attendance officer; applied to mission as result of Stone-Wigg's appeal; arr. 1907; r. 1908, mental instability.

101. **ELDER, Frank Raymond,** b. 5 February 1888, Castle Hill, NSW; son of Rev. Francis Rowling Elder (C of E) and Aphrasia Catherine (King); ed. Sydney HS; o. clerk; trained, St. John's College, Armidale (ThL); ord. 1912; arr. Papua 1914, stn. Eroro; m. Julie Mary Cakebread, 12 June 1928; 4 ch.; r. 1934. C of E ministry, Sydney and Newcastle; d. 29 April 1962, NSW.

102. **ELWIN, Cyril,** arr. NG 1893, stns. Taupota, Boianai; r. 1893, ill-health; served Yarrabah Mission 1893–1895; returned to NG 1895; r. 1895, ill-health; returned to Yarrabah Mission.

103. **FETTELL, Norman Atkins,** b. 8 October 1884, Lincoln, Wellington, NSW; son of Robert George Fettell, farmer, and Isabella (Hayes); o. baker's assistant; arr. Papua 1906, stn. Hioge; began training for Holy Orders, St. Francis, Brisbane, 1913; r. 1915, to enlist.

104. **FERNEAU, Felix Albert,** Deacon; arr. Papua 1900, stn. Dogura; r. 1900, ill-health and inability to cope.

105. **FISHER, James Edward John,** from Southwark, England; trained, Burgh Missionary College, Durham University (ThL 1911); arr. Papua 1914, stn. Wanigela; m. Edith (?) 1916; 2 ch.; r. 1922, ill-health of ch.; C of E ministry, London and Oxford.

106. **FOOTT, Arthur Patrick,** from Brisbane; arr. NG 1898, stns. Taupota, Mamba; r. 1900, demoralized.

107. **FORD, Sydney Frederick,** b. February 1882, Sydney; son of Daniel Seazer Ford, compositor, and Jane Francis (Cooke); o. printer; joined mission after quarrel with brother; arr. Papua 1900, stn. Dogura; r. 1903, mistaken vocation; d. 17 June 1943, Sydney.

108. **GIBLIN, Eric Louis,** b. 30 April 1880, Hobart, Tas.; son of Louis Vincent Giblin, surveyor, and Elizabeth Eleanor (Sharpe); ed. GS, Hobart to matriculation; o. mining and farm work; applied to mission in response to address by Bishop Montgomery; arr. Papua 1900, stn. Hioge; r. 1906, moral and spiritual crisis.

109. **GILL, Stephen Romney Maurice,** b. 1886, Brighton, England; son of Rev. Arthur Tidman Gill (Countess of Huntingdon's Connexion —C of E); childhood desire to be missionary; arr. Papua 1908, stns. Boianai, Duvira, Dewade; ord. deacon 25 July 1909, priest 14 August 1910, archdeacon 1939, canon 1947; m. Olive Buckley, November 1949; r. 1952, ill-health; d. 26 March 1954, England.

110. **GRASBY, Kate,** from Tasmania; o. nurse; arr. Papua 1913; r. 1915.

111. **GRIFFITHS, Maud (Mrs. Percy Shaw),** b. 26 April 1881,

Faversham, England; daughter of George Griffiths, engineer, and Sarah Jane (Bobby); recruited NSW; arr. Papua 1906, stn. Samarai; m. Percy Shaw (no. 164), 20 November 1912; 1 ch.; r. 1921, with husband.

112. **HENRY, Beatrice M.**, from Qld; o. teacher; arr. Papua 1912, stn. Samarai; r. 1914, temporary appointment.

113. **HINES, Ernest William Mayman**, b. 19 September 1868, England; ord. deacon 1896, priest 1897, Grafton and Armidale; arr. NG 1899, stn. Mamba; r. 1900, ill-health; Anglican ministry, SA; m. Lucy Harriet Emily ?; d. 8 November 1927, SA.

114. **HOARE, Samuel**, from NSW; arr. NG 1896; r. 1897, conflict with High Church ethos of mission.

115. **HOLLAND, Henry**, b. Tyagong Creek, NSW; son of Edward Holland, farmer, and Anne (McGrath); Methodist family, brother of G. R. Holland (no. 59); arr. Papua 1910, stns. Ambasi, Isivita; ord. priest 1938; killed by Japanese, August 1942, Papua.

116. **HUNT, John**, b. 17 February 1861, N. Collingham, Nottinghamshire; son of Richard and Mary Hunt; ed. Collingham Wesleyan School; o. solicitor's clerk; Wesleyan baptism; 1887 conditional C of E baptism; trained, Burgh and St. Augustine's; migrated to Qld; ord. deacon 7 September 1884, priest 20 June 1886, Brisbane; Qld ministry 1884–1904; arr. Papua 1905, stn. Menapi; d. 7 September 1928, Papua.

117. **KENNEDY, Charles E.**, from England; recruited from Christchurch St. Laurence, Sydney; arr. NG 1891, stns. Dogura, Taupota; r. 1894 to become manager of clerical club, London, and planter, Mozambique.

118. **KER, Annie Caroline (Mrs. P. Money)**, b. 1874, Richmond, Vic.; daughter of Charles Ker, mine-manager, and Katherine (Cavanagh); o. nurse; c.m. St. Peter's, Eastern Hill; arr. NG 1899, stn. Wanigela; m. Percy Money (no. 123), 22 April 1909; r. 1910, with husband; d. 27 April 1945.

119. **KING, Copland**, b. 24 June 1863, Parramatta, NSW; son of Rev. Robert Lethbridge King (C of E); ed. Sydney GS and Sydney University (MA); ord. 1887, Sydney ministry; persuaded by Maclaren to join mission; arr. NG 1891, stns. Dogura, Ave, Ambasi; Fellow of Theology, Australian College of Theology, 1914; d. 1918, Sydney.

120. **MACLAREN, Albert Alexander**, b. 14 February 1853, Cowes, England; father, stone-mason; ed. to age 14, later night school, St. Ebbs, and Wrexham GS; o. clerk in Ordnance Survey; parents Presbyterian, confirmed by Bishop of Winchester 1885; trained, St. Augustine's, Canterbury; priest, Maitland, and Mackay, Qld;

Durham University (BA); chosen to lead pioneer expedition to NG; arr. 10 August 1891, stn. Dogura; d. 27 December 1891, at sea off Cooktown.

121. **McLAUGHLIN, Sophia,** from Sydney, NSW; o. teacher; arr. NG 1896, stn. Dogura; r. 1907, doctrinal conflict.

122. **McMULLAN, William,** b. 1878 (?), Tiaro, Qld, father, postmaster; o. worked on mother's farm; applied to mission "to better social position"; arr. Papua 1900, stn. Hioge; r. 1902, mistaken vocation.

123. **MONEY, Percy John,** b. 1877 (?), NSW, (?); o. architect; c.m. Enfield C of E; arr. Papua 1900, stn. Wanigela; m. Annie Ker (no. 118), 23 April 1909; r. 1910.

124. **MORRIS, George William,** b. 1872, Britain; o. soldier; recruited at Brisbane; arr. Papua 1905, stn. Buna; r. 1906, crisis of faith and interpersonal conflict.

125. **MURRAY, Harriet Alice,** b. Ballarat, Vic.; daughter of Patrick John Murray, commission agent, and Harriet (?); sister of W. H. Murray (no. 126); arr. NG 1895, stn. Wamira; r. 1903, ill-health; returned to Papua, 1912–1914.

126. **MURRAY, William Henry,** b. 28 October 1869, Ballarat, Vic.; son of Patrick John Murray, commission agent, and Harriet (?); o. clerk; Wesleyan baptism; trained, Moore Theological College; ord. deacon 11 June 1893, priest 19 March 1895; curate, St. John's Camden 1893–1895; arr. NG 1895, stn. Dogura; r. 1896, ill-health; priest-in-charge, Cressy, Tas.; d. 16 February 1902, Tasmania.

127. **NEWTON, Henry,** b. 1866, The Bucklands, Vic., as Henry Wilkinson, son of Thomas Wilkinson, engineer, and Annie (Magnay); adopted by John Frederick Newton, scholar and later priest; ed. BA Oxford (Merton College); curate, St. John's, Hackney; arr. NG 1898 after invitation from Stone-Wigg, stn. Dogura; m. Sarah Sully (no. 148), 29 May 1901; r. 1915, to become Bishop of Carpentaria; returned to Papua 1922, to become Bishop of New Guinea; d. 25 September 1947, Papua.

128. **NEWTON, Mary Alice,** b. 1869 (?); o. nurse (Prince Alfred, Sydney); childhood desire to be missionary rekindled by missionary meeting; arr. Papua 1902, stn. Ganuganuana; d. 23 April 1904, Papua.

129. **NOWLAND, Maud,** b. 1871 (?) England (?); o. nurse; recruited Rockhampton; influenced by George Halford, head of Bush Brotherhood; arr. Papua 1901, stns. Dogura, Mamba, Boianai, Hioge, Ganuganuana; d. 28 January 1934, Papua.

130. **OLIVER, Laura,** b. 1855, England; migrated to WA; arr. NG 1899, stns. Mukawa, Samarai, Watutu, Taupota; d. 25 July 1924, Papua.

131. **PARRISH, Edyth,** b. Brisbane; ed. St. John's Day School, Brisbane; o. teacher (C of EGS Brisbane); desire since schooldays to be missionary; arr. Papua 1912, stn. Ganuganuana; r. 1915.
132. **PEARCE, Joshua,** from Brisbane; o. carpenter, Sunday School Superintendent; arr. Papua 1907, stn. Dogura; r. 1910.
133. **PEUT, Maria Johanna,** b. 23 September 1881, The Springs, Qld; daughter of Henry Peut, carrier, and Annie (Peters); o. teacher; arr. Papua 1907, stn. Ganuganuana; r. 1912, home pressures.
134. **RAMSAY, Ann Ada** (née Armitage), b. 29 November 1877, Melbourne; daughter of Giles Armitage, cab-owner, and Eliza (Wilsmore); o. nurse (part-training); m. F. W. Ramsay (no. 135), 1906; 3 ch. (1 d.); arr. Papua 1906, stn. Samarai; r. 1919, with husband.
135. **RAMSAY, Frederick William,** arr. Papua 1900, stn. Samarai; trained, Brisbane Theological College, 1903; ord. deacon 1904, priest 1906; m. Annie Armitage (no. 134), 1906; 3 ch. (1 d.); r. 1909; C of E ministry, Ballarat, 1925–1936.
136. **RATTIGAN, Elizabeth (Mrs. A. K. Chignell),** from Melbourne; o. nurse (Royal Melbourne Hospital); c.m. St. Peter's, Eastern Hill; one sister missionary in China; arr. Papua 1912, stn. Wanigela; m. Arthur Kent Chignell (no. 92); r. 1914, with husband.
137. **REYNOLDS, Joseph Auburn,** b. 15 June 1871, Goulburn; son of Joseph Reynolds, dealer, and Jane Martha (Brightmore); trained, Moore Theological Coll. 1893–1894; ord. deacon, 8 March 1895, priest 22 December 1895; arr. NG 1896, stn. Dogura; r. 1897, ill-health; served in C of E ministry, NSW, SA, England, and Qld; chaplain, Boer War; d. 24 October 1946.
138. **ROBERTSON, Isobel,** from New Zealand; ed. MA (NZ); o. teacher (Girls' School, Nelson); arr. Papua 1909, stn. Dogura; r. 1912.
139. **ROBSON, Gertrude,** b. 1865, Monkwearmouth, Durham; daughter of John Shield Robson, shipbuilder, and Caroline (Iliff); sister of Louise Robson (no. 140); o. teacher (principal of Sydney Boys' Preparatory School); applied to mission after appeal from Gilbert White, Bishop of Carpentaria; previous missionary experience: Thursday I., Moa, and Mitchell R. (3 years); arr. Papua 1913, stn. Wanigela; d. 9 July 1917, Papua.
140. **ROBSON, Louise,** b. 1876, London; daughter of John Shield Robson, shipbuilder, and Caroline (Iliff); sister of Gertrude Robson (no. 139); o. nurse (Queen Charlotte's Hospital, London, and Royal Alexandra Hospital for Children); arr. Papua 1913, stn. Dogura; m. Ernest Owen Davies (no. 97); r. 1916, with husband; d. 1954.
141. **SAGE, Charles,** b. 1876, England; son of H. E. Sage, proprietor of carriage factory; o. blacksmith; c.m. St. Mark's Fitzroy; offered

for service at consecration of Stone-Wigg; arr. NG 1898, stn. Samarai; r. 1904, dissatisfaction with lay status; joined Melanesian Mission, ordained; drowned 1913, Solomon Islands.

142. **SCARTH, Elsie,** b. England; daughter of Canon Scarth of Bearsted, Kent; arr. Papua 1903, stn. Dogura; r. 1906, family pressure and ill-health; secretary to NG Association (Britain); d. 24 December 1917, England.

143. **SHARP, Gerald,** b. 27 October 1865, Lowfields, Childer Thornton, England; son of Thomas Beatt Sharp, gentleman, and Mary Anne (Lillie); ed. Manchester GS, St. John's, Cambridge (BA 1886); trained, Lincoln Theological Coll.; ord. deacon 1889, priest 1890; curate, Rowbarton, Leeds, 1889–1893, Holy Innocents, Hammersmith, 1893–1898; vicar, Whitkirk, Leeds 1898; consecrated Bishop of NG, 25 April 1910, Brisbane; arr. Papua 1910, stns. Dogura, Samarai; DD (honoris causa), 1 May 1914; r. 1921 to become Archbishop of Brisbane and Metropolitan for Qld; d. 30 August 1933, Brisbane.

144. **SHAW, Percy Charles,** b. 1880, Pyrmont, Sydney; son of Charles Shaw, engineer, and Christina (Peck); arr. Papua 1900, stns. Ambasi, Samarai, Taupota, Dogura; trained, St. John's Coll., Melbourne (ThL), 1908; ord. priest 1910; m. Maud Griffiths (no. 111), 20 November 1912; 1 ch.; r. 1921; C of E ministry, Brisbane, 1922–1923; d. 26 October 1943.

145. **SMITHSON, Frederick,** arr. Papua 1900; o. printer; r. 1900, dismissed for immorality.

146. **STIRRAT, James Baird,** b. 1853, Glasgow; migrated to NSW 1882; o. carpenter-joiner and shipwright; Presbyterian origin; c.m. Christchurch St. Laurence; arr. Papua 1900, stn. Dogura; d. 10 July 1903, Papua.

147. **STONE-WIGG, Montagu John,** b. 4 October 1862, Hungershill Park, Tunbridge Wells, Kent; son of John Stone-Wigg, gentleman, and Ellen Clements; ed. private school, Winchester 1875–1880, Oxford (University College), BA (1883), MA (1887); confirmed, Winchester Chapel 1877; trained, Ely Theological Coll.; ord. deacon 1885, priest 1887; curate, St. Andrews, Well St., Holy Innocents, Hammersmith, 1889; canon, St. John's pro-cathedral, Brisbane, 1891; consecrated Bishop of New Guinea, January 1898; arr. NG 1898, stn. Dogura; m. Elsie M. Mort, 21 August 1907; r. 1908, ill-health; DD (honoris causa); edited *Church Standard*, NSW 1908–1918; d. 1918, Sydney.

148. **SULLY, Sarah,** b. 1864, Brisbane; daughter of John Alfred Sully, master-mariner, and Lucy Ann (North); arr. NG 1898, stn. Dogura; m. Henry Newton (no. 127), 29 May 1901; r. 1915, with husband; d. 14 July 1919.

149. **SYNGE, Frances Mary,** b. 1867, Tabulam, Bullen, NSW; daughter of Richard Synge, gentleman, and Mary Jane (McElroy); arr. Papua 1900, stn. Dogura; r. 1903, ill-health; m. George Cecil Benson, 29 February 1908, Brisbane.

150. **TAYLOR, Ernest Wesley,** b. December 1871, N. Halsham, Norfolk; son of Alfred Taylor, Wesleyan minister, and Caroline Esther (Fox); ed. Oxford, BA (1st class hons. in Theology), MA; ord. deacon 1896, priest 1897; responded to bishop's appeal for staff in mission report; arr. 1901, stn. Dogura; d. 23 June 1903, Papua.

151. **TAYLOR, Joseph,** from Gayndah, Qld; o. carpenter, church warden and Sunday School superintendent, Gayndah; arr. Papua 1913, stn. Dogura; r. 1918.

152. **THOMSON, Florence Augusta,** b. 1867, Bega, NSW; daughter of William Thomson and Rose (Chila); o. nurse; arr. NG 1896, stn. Dogura; r. 1904, mental instability and ill-health; d. 26 May 1907, NSW.

153. **TOMLINSON, Elizabeth,** b. 14 January 1860, Manchester, England; daughter of John Wilkinson Paker and Sarah (Hackney); m. Samuel Tomlinson (no. 154); migrated to Melbourne, 1884; c.m. St. Mark's Fitzroy; arr. NG 1891, stns. Dogura, Mukawa; d. 17 September 1939, Papua.

154. **TOMLINSON, Samuel,** b. 25 September 1857, Manchester; son of James Tomlinson, foreman pattern-maker, and Amy (Poole); ed. elementary school; m. Elizabeth Paker (no. 153); migrated to Melbourne 1884; o. carpenter; c.m. St. Mark's Fitzroy; volunteered for pioneer mission party after hearing Maclaren preach; arr. NG 1891, stns. Dogura, Mukawa; ord. deacon 1903, priest 1904; canon of St. Peter and St. Paul's, Dogura 1927; Fellow, Australian College of Theology; d. 26 April 1937, Papua.

155. **WINTERBOTTOM, Honor Etta,** from Hay, NSW; o. teacher; arr. Papua 1910, stn. Wanigela; r. 1918 to marry Liston Blyth (resident magistrate, Kokoda), 13 August 1918.

Sacred Heart Mission

Missionaries of the Sacred Heart (MSC)

Priests

156. **ALLERA, Claudius,** b. 17 September 1871, Thônes, Savoy, France; son of Pierre Allera and Marie (Siegle); ed. Minor Seminary, Issoudun; devout family; MSC 1889; arr. NG 1893 as scholastic, stn. Yule I.; d. 24 July 1893, Papua.

157. **BACH, Joseph,** b. 1 September 1872, Urmatt, Alsace; son of Wendelin Bach and Marie Anne (Wick); ed. Minor Seminary, Issoudun; theological studies, Rome (DTh); MSC 1892; ord. priest 1896; impressed by missionary zeal of Verjus; arr. Papua 1902, stns. Thursday I., Dilava; r. 1927 to be vicar apostolic of Gilbert Is. (titular bishop of Eriza); r. 1934 to Bowral; d. 22 May 1943, NSW.

158. **BAILEY, Edward Albert,** b. 23 January 1880, Auckland, NZ; son of Edward Bailey, sea-captain, and Elizabeth Mary (Conway); MSC 1904; ord. priest 1912; arr. Papua 1912; r. 1917; d. 27 February 1943, Sydney.

159. **BODET, René,** b. 2 October 1882, Boissière-du-Doré, Brittany, France; "Honourable Christian family," nephew of Father Guilbaud (no. 187); ed. minor and major seminaries, Nantes; ord. priest, 29 June 1906; MSC 1908; attracted to Papua by letters of uncle, arr. Papua 1909, stns. Waima, Oba-Oba, Inawaia; r. 1932, ill-health; MSC France; d. 12 November 1971, Thiais, France.

160. **BONTEMPS, Edouard Eugene,** b. 12 October 1841, Niort, Deux-Sèvres, France; son of Désiré Bontemps, architect, and Elisabeth Joséphine (Nadler); ed. Lyceum Niort (BSc 1859), Polytechnic School, Paris 1860–1864, Seminary Poitiers 1864–1867; ord. priest 1867; MSC 1881; director of *Annales*, 1884–1885; superior Paris and Antwerp 1886; arr. mission January 1887, stn. Thursday I.; r. 1887 and transferred to Gilbert Is.; d. 24 November 1897, Nonouti, Gilbert Is. (Kiribati).

161. **BOUELLAT, Paul,** b. 2 October 1869, Coeuve, Jura, Switzerland; son of Simon Bouellat, machinist, and Louise (Ribeaud); one brother, MSC; MSC 1888; arr. NG 1893 as scholastic, ord. priest, 24 February 1894, stn. Veifa'a; d. 21 February 1902, Veifa'a, Papua.

162. **BRANGER, Maximilian,** b. 17 October 1876, Tours, France; son of Eugene Branger, tile-maker and machinist, and Madeleine (Proust); selected by parish priest; ed. minor seminary, MSC; theological studies, France and Spain; MSC 1896; ord. priest 1903; arr. Papua 1903, stns. Inawai and Inawaia; d. 18 July 1935, Yule I., Papua.

163. **BUISSON, Gilbert,** b. 31 July 1862, Magnet, Allier, France; son of Gilbert Buisson and Marie (Gaçon); MSC 1880; ord. priest 1885; arr. NG 1888, stn. Thursday I.; r. 1905, ill-health; d. 31 October 1927, NSW.

164. **BURKE, William,** b. 4 March 1872, Leeds, England; son of Edward Burke, iron-molder and Mary (Coogan); MSC 1892; ord. priest 1897; arr. NG 1898, stn. Mou; r. 1901, mental instability; d. 17 December 1924, Rome, Italy.

165. **CASPAR, Joseph,** b. 27 April 1875, Bernardswiller, Alsace; father, gardener; MSC 1897; ord. priest 1902; arr. Papua 1903, stn. Dilava; r. 1910; ex-MSC 1911; incardinated in diocese of Strasbourg; parish priest Sièges.

166. **CHABOT, Joseph,** b. 12 July 1873, Lésigny-sur-Creuse, France; father, steward of castle; pious parents; ed. priests' college to baccalaureate, major seminary, Poitiers; ord. priest 1896; MSC 1900; inspired as child by life of martyr, Theophane Venard; arr. Papua 1900, stns. Dilava, Oba-Oba; superior 1909–1912, 1924–1927; d. 5 March 1940, Kubuna, Papua.

167. **CLAUSER, Alphonse Marie,** b. 16 July 1877, Heidwiller, Alsace; son of Louis Clauser, splint-man, and Josephine (Meyer); deeply religious family; influenced as a child by Verjus; ed. minor seminary, Issoudun; MSC 1898; theological studies, Australia; ord. priest, 6 January 1904; arr. Papua 1902, stns. Mekeo, Mafulu; furlough 1919, stayed to help in Alsace; d. 17 November 1921, Heidwiller, Alsace.

168. **COCHARD, Louis,** b. 12 November 1870, St-Emilien, Loire, France; son of Jean Cochard and Anne (Pireaud); one brother, MSC; ed. minor seminary, Issoudun; military service; MSC 1890; arr. NG 1893, as scholastic, ord. priest 1895, stns. Mou, Bereina; r. 1904, ill-health; novice-master, Australia; d. 20 July 1933, Sydney.

169. **COLTEE, Jean-Gabriel,** b. 27 June 1867, Lisieux, Normandy, France; son of Léon Coltée and Eugénie (Coureul); MSC 1888; arr. NG 1893, as scholastic, ord. priest 1894, stn. Jesu-Baibua, Inawaia; r. 1902; bursar, MSC Kensington, NSW; d. 26 January 1945, Lamalou-les-Bains, France.

170. **COUPPÉ, Louis,** b. 26 August 1850, Romorantin, France; son of Charles Couppé, locksmith, and Adrienne (Cougnet), dressmaker; "Honourable Christian family"; ed. Jesuits, minor and major seminary, Blois; ord. priest 1874; influenced by Father Chevalier to join MSC 1881; met Verjus, Rome; arr. NG 1886, stn. Yule I.; r. 1888 to be vicar apostolic of New Britain (titular bishop of Lero); titular archbishop of Hieropolis, 1925; d. 20 July 1926, Douglas Park, NSW.

171. **CRAMAILLE, Théophile Magloire,** b. 18 October 1843, Villenauxe, Aube, France; o. shepherd; ed. minor seminary, Issoudun; MSC 1871; ord. priest 1875; served New Britain 1883–1889; arr. NG 1889, stns. Yule I., Bereina; d. 22 September 1896 in Red Sea on way to France.

172. **CROS, Louis,** b. 23 March 1871, Salles-de-Pradinas, Aveyron, France; son of Jean Louis Cros and Marie (Mazars); taught for 3 years in MSC scholasticate; arr. Papua 1902, stn. Yule I.; r. 1910,

transferred to Port Darwin; ex-MSC 1931; incardinated in diocese of Versailles, France, 1931.

173. **DE BOISMENU, Alain Guynot,** b. 27 December 1870, Saint Malo, Brittany; son of François Guynot de Boismenu, shipowner, and Augustine Marie (Desessarts); ed. St. Malo, Antwerp, Issoudun; MSC 1888; teacher in minor seminary and scholasticate, MSC; ord. priest 10 February 1895; arr. NG 1899, stn. Yule I.; consecrated titular bishop of Gabala coadjutor bishop to Navarre, 1900; vicar apostolic 1912; titular archbishop of Claudiopolis 1945; Chevalier of Legion of Honor 1950; d. 5 November 1953, Kubuna, Papua.

174. **DE RIJCKE, Victor,** b. 23 March 1871, Melsele, Belgium; ed. MSC minor seminary and scholasticate; arr. NG 1894 as scholastic, ord. priest 21 December 1895, stn. Vanamai; d. 5 January 1899, Yule I., Papua.

175. **DESNOES, Gustave,** b. 28 March 1878, Miré, Maine-et-Loire, France; son of Julien Desnoës, oilman, and Marie (Lemonçeau); MSC 1896; ord. priest 1903; arr. Papua 1906, stn. Yule I.; superior 1912–1919; r. 1927, ill-health, d. 1953, Marseilles.

176. **DONTENWILL, Théophile,** b. 1879, St. Marie-aux-Mines, Alsace; son of Nicholas Dontenwill, agriculturalist, and Marie (Reyss); pious family, one brother MSC, one sister FDNSC; childhood wish to be missionary; ed. minor seminary, Issoudun and Chezal-Benoît; MSC 1899; ord. priest 17 June 1905; arr. Papua 1906, stn. Mafulu; r. 1933, ill-health; chaplain at Girls' School, Lutterbach, then MSC house Strasbourg; d. 11 December 1967, Marseilles.

177. **DUBUY, Jules,** b. 10 April 1887, Coublanc, Saône-et-Loire, France; MSC 1905; ord. priest 1912; arr. Papua 1913, stn. Ononghe; d. 6 August 1952, Papua.

178. **DURIN, Fernand François,** b. 3 January 1836, Montmarault, Allier, France; son of Jacques Durin and Rose Anne (Mezier); ed. major seminary, Moulins; ord. priest 1859; MSC 1865; led pioneer expedition but returned to France after breakdown of health and morale; USA 1882–1886; arr. NG 1886, stn. Thursday I.; r. 1888, ill-health; MSC, USA; d. 1897, Chicago.

179. **EGIDI, Vincenzo,** b. 2 March 1875, Viterbo, Italy; son of Salvatore Egidi, pontifical gendarme officer and civil servant, and Eurosia (Giovannini); arr. Papua 1901, stns. Inawa, Dilava; r. 1911; left MSC 1916, probably with dispensation from vows; married.

180. **ELLIOTT, Denis Patrick** (secular priest trained by MSC), b. 17 February 1880, Carisbrooke, Vic.; father, cobbler who became miner; ed. MSC Kensington; temporary vows 1907; ex-MSC 1910;

arr. Papua 1912, accepted as student, ord. 25 March 1914; stn. Port Moresby; d. 11 September 1914, Port Moresby.

181. **ESCHLIMANN, Henri,** b. 27 September 1881, Rosheim, Alsace; father, house-painter; ed. minor seminary, Issoudun; MSC 30 September 1901; ord. priest 9 June 1906; arr. Papua 1906, stns. Oba-Oba, Kuni; r. 1946, ill-health; d. 5 January 1966, Marseilles.

182. **FASTRÉ, Paul,** b. 30 November 1880, Pradinas, Aveyron, France; son of Pierre Fastré, grocer, and Rosalie (Delmas); ed. Christian Brothers, Pradinas, and minor seminary, Issoudun; MSC 1898; theological studies, Algeria, Rome, Spain; ord. priest 1904; arr. Papua 1904, stns. Oba-Oba, Dilava, Popole; superior 1927–1936; r. 1939, became procurator, Marseilles; d. 3 July 1955, Marseilles.

183. **FILLODEAU, Alexandre-Marie,** b. 18 April 1868, Marans, Vendée, France; son of François Fillodeau, landowner, and Josephine (Coudrin); MSC 1890; ord. priest 1894; arr. NG 1896; r. 1902, demoralized and fearing insanity; returned to Papua 1905; r. 1909; dispensed from vows, ex-MSC; d. 28 October 1936, Sydney.

184. **GENOCCHI, Jean (Giovanni),** b. 30 July 1860, Ravenna, Italy; son of Frederico Genocchi, small businessman, and Celeste (Gori); ed. minor seminary, Ravenna, Seminario Pio, Rome; decided aged 12 to become priest; contact with MSC students, Rome, directed him to MSC; ord. priest 1883; MSC 1886; secretary of Apostolic Delegation in Syria (1886–1888); general vicar in Constantinople (1888–1892); arr. NG 1894, stn. Yule I.; r. 1896, conflict with Navarre; MSC teacher, Chezal-Benoît; worked with Holy See; d. 6 January 1926, Rome.

185. **GONZALEZ, José Velasco,** b. 24 April 1883, Llanazanes Oviedo, Spain; MSC 1901; ord. priest 25 May 1907; arr. Papua 1913, stn. Mekeo; r. 1923, ex-MSC 1931; incardinated in diocese of Assis, Brazil.

186. **GSELL, François-Xavier,** b. 27 October 1872, Benfeld, Strasbourg, Alsace; son of Laurent Gsell and Josephine (Jehl); o. apprentice in cotton factory; noticed by MSC priest; ed. minor seminary, Issoudun, Apolinarus University, Rome (DTh); MSC 1892; ord. priest 1896; professor of theology, Kensington, NSW, 1897–1900; arr. Papua 1900, stns. Tsiria, Mou, Inawi; r. 1906; apostolic administrator, Darwin, Bathurst I. 1911–1938; OBE 1936, Chevalier of Legion of Honor, 1951; d. 12 July 1960, Randwick NSW.

187. **GUILBAUD, Ernest,** b. 19 June 1870, Mouzillon, Loire M., France; ed. major seminary, Nantes and MSC; MSC 1893; arr. NG 1894 as scholastic, ord. priest 29 June 1896, stns. Tsiria, Maia-Era, Waima, Aropokina; d. 15 March 1937, Yule I.

188. **GUIS, Joseph Léon,** b. 13 December 1869, Marseilles; son of Joseph Léon Guis and Clemence Marie (Aubert); o. soldier; MSC 1888; arr. NG 1894, as scholastic, ord. priest 1895, stn. Thursday I.; r. 1906, to become procurator of mission, Sydney; d. 14 September 1913, Sydney.

189. **HARTZER, Fernand,** b. 24 November 1858, Ensisheim, Alsace; son of Victor Hartzer, public servant, and Marie-Louise (Mestmann), who became Mother Marie-Louise, FDNSC, after death of husband; only brother, MSC; ed. Ornans, Chezal-Benoît, and Rome (DTh); MSC 1877; ord. priest 1881; teacher at apostolic school, Watertown, USA; arr. NG 1884, stns. Mou, Thursday I.; r. 1894; superior, Glastonbury, England; d. 28 November 1932, Issoudun, France.

190. **HUBERT, Louis,** b. 25 February 1866, Bourges, France; son of Paul Hubert and Isabelle (Desmarquais); ed. major seminary, Bourges; influenced by Verjus; MSC 1889; ord. priest 1890; arr. NG 1891, stns. Inawabui, Bereina, Mou, Dilava; d. 26 December 1909, Bereina, Papua.

191. **JANET, Louis-Emmanuel,** b. 27 May 1861, Césarches, Savoy, France; son of Maurice Janet and Marie Jeanne (Milliex); ed. minor and major seminary, Moutiers; ord. priest 1887; MSC 1891; arr. NG 1891, stn. Mou; d. 15 April 1891, Yule I., Papua.

192. **JOINDREAU, Edmund,** b. 8 September 1882, Mont-sur-Guesnes, Deux-Sèvres, France; son of Jean Joindreau, blacksmith, and Elizabeth (Laverdin); arr. Papua 1902; r. 1913; incardinated in diocese of Bordeaux, France.

193. **JULLIEN, André,** b. 19 September 1861, Marseilles; son of Laurent François Jullien and Léonie Philomène; ed. Petit Sacré-Coeur Marseilles, and free school of M. Barnave; seminary, University of Rome (DTh); MSC 1882; ord. priest 24 April 1886; taught rhetoric at minor seminary, Issoudun; arr. NG 1894, stns. Tsiria, Yule I.; superior 1900–1909; r. 1911 to be assistant to superior general, MSC Rome; d. 15 December 1920, Marseilles.

194. **KARSSELEERS, Cornelius Joseph,** b. 23 March 1866, near Antwerp, Belgium; son of Pierre-Jean Karsseleers and Thérèse (Nagels); MSC 1881; ord. priest 1891; arr. NG 1893, stn. Mou; r. 1903, transferred to Europe; d. 5 March 1924, Borgerhout, Belgium.

195. **KÜTTER, Edward,** b. 12 February 1862, Rosheim, Alsace; son of Joseph Kütter and Thérèse (Eckert); MSC 1882; ord. priest 1886; arr. NG 1886, stn. Yule I.; r. 1888, demoralized; ex-MSC 1893; parish priest, Switzerland.

196. **LANG, Jean-Pierre,** b. 5 November 1879, Bernardswiller, Alsace; son of Alois Lang, vine-grower, and Thérèse Mosser; ed. minor

seminary, Issoudun; MSC 1899; arr. Papua 1902, as scholastic, ord. priest 1904, stns. Tsiria, Waima; d. 7 July 1951, Waima, Papua.

197. **MacCARTHY, Leonard,** b. 5 March 1884, Zeehan, Tasmania; son of Daniel MacCarthy, storekeeper, and Sarah Ann (Gory); MSC 1904; arr. Papua 1912, as scholastic, ord. priest 1912; r. 1913; d. 23 August 1950, Sydney.

198. **MARIE, Gustave,** b. 29 July 1862, Cherbourg, France; son of Gustave Nicolas Marie and Zélie (Levast); MSC 1890; arr. NG 1894, as scholastic, ord. priest 1895, stns. Oriropetana, Mou; d. 5 July 1900, Yule I.

199. **NAVARRE, Louis-André,** b. 2 February 1836, Burgundy, France; father, vine-grower; ed. elementary; o. vine-grower, art student, soldier, teacher; trained, Bourges seminary 1867; ord. priest 26 May 1872; influenced by Chevalier; MSC 1878; chosen for pioneering expedition to Melanesia, became leader after withdrawal of Durin; served in New Britain 1882–1884; established base, Thursday I., 1884; arr. NG 1886, stn. Yule I.; consecrated bishop (titular bishop of Pentacomie) and made vicar apostolic of Melanesia 1887 (titular archbishop of Cyr); d. 16 January 1912, Townsville, Qld.

200. **NORIN, Généreux,** b. 2 February 1887, Le Blanc, Indre, France; father, peasant farmer; ed. minor seminary, Issoudun, and Spain; MSC 1904; ord. priest 1911; arr. Papua 1911, stns. Mafulu, Yule I., Popole, Fane; d. 3 April 1945, Port Moresby.

201. **PAGÈS, Armand,** b. 10 June 1872, Sapet, Lozère, France; son of Jean Pierre and Sophie Pagès; very devout family, brothers and sisters in religious congregations; MSC 1892; ord. priest 1897; arr. NG 1898, stns. Rarai, Madiou; d. 19 August 1916, Yule I.

202. **PEETERS, Gustave,** b. 12 August 1867, Borgerhout, Belgium; son of David Louis Peeters and Marie Ann (Van den Bergh); MSC 1892; arr. NG 1894, as scholastic, ord. 1897, stns. Tsiria, Maia-Era; r. 1908, ill-health; d. 3 August 1930, Buggenhout, Belgium.

203. **PINEAU, André,** b. 2 December 1886, St. Hilaire-de-Clisson, Brittany; devout family including several religious; ed. minor seminary, Issoudun, Barcelona, and Fribourg; MSC 1904; ord. priest 1911; arr. Papua 1911, stn. Waima; d. 21 March 1965, Yule I.

204. **POUPENEY, Joseph,** b. 18 December 1870, Chamesol, Doubs; father, mayor of village; MSC 1894; ord. priest 1898; arr. NG 1899, stns. Bioto, Inawabui; d. 17 January 1918, Yule I.

205. **RIEGLER, François-Xavier,** b. 24 November 1882, Niedernai, Alsace; MSC 1902; ord. priest 1907; arr. Papua 1907, stns. Yule I., Kivori; d. 13 June 1945, Port Moresby.

206. **ROSSIER, Joseph,** b. 9 October 1881, Rue, Fribourg, Switzerland;

father, peasant farmer; ed. Jesuits, La Louvesc, Ardèche; called to priesthood by recruiter of vocations; chose MSC because they "worked in savage countries"; scholasticate: Spain and Switzerland; MSC 1902; ord. priest 25 July 1907; arr. Papua 1907, stns. Oba-Oba, Toaripi; d. 17 March 1966, Yule I.

207. **ROUSSEL, Eugène,** b. 28 February 1859, Fremesnil, Meurthe-et-Moselle, France; son of Auguste Roussel and Marie Elsa (Chatton); ed. minor seminary, Pont-à-Mousson, major seminary, Nancy; scholasticate, Rome; MSC 1880; taught at seminaries Tilburg and Issoudun, 1883–1887; ord. priest 1885; taught at Guayaquil, Ecuador; arr. NG 1893, stn. Yule I.; d. 11 April 1893, Yule I.

208. **SHAW, Archibald,** b. 16 December 1872, Adelong, NSW; son of Charles Shaw, publican, and Catherine (Scanlan); father Presbyterian, mother Irish Catholic; o. telegraphist in Post Office; Ex-Passionist novice (Br. Placide); MSC 1896; arr. NG 1894; r. 1897 to study for priesthood; ord. priest 1900; procurator for island missions, Sydney; d. 26 August 1916, Melbourne, after involvement in political bribery scandal.

209. **THOMAS, Eugène,** b. 7 October 1854, Tence, Haute-Loire, France; son of Etienne Jules Thomas and Adèle (Adibert); MSC 1876; ord. priest 1879; arr. NG 1888, stns. Yule I., Mou; r. 1889, demoralized; ex-MSC 1890; incardinated as secular priest.

210. **TOUBLANC, Athanase,** b. 21 March 1855, Nort, Loire M., France; son of Sebastien Toublanc and Madeleine (Graizeau); o. soldier; garrisoned at Bourges, met MSC priests; ed. minor seminary, Issoudun, 1880–1882; MSC 1883; ord. priest 1886; arr. NG 1886, stns. Tsiria, Mou; r. 1892, ill-health; transferred to Gilberts; d. 15 February 1917, Asserac, France.

211. **VAN GOETHEM, Edward,** b. 10 May 1873, Beveren Wass, Belgium; MSC 1894; ord. priest 1899; arr. Papua 1903, stns. Rarai, Veifa'a; superior 1919–1924; r. 1925; transferred to Belgian Congo; apostolic prefect 1924–1932; apostolic vicar of Coquilhatville 1932–1946; d. 26 May 1949, Borgerhout, Belgium.

212. **VAN NECK, Henri,** b. 6 December 1874, Tournai, Belgium; son of Auguste van Neck, boatman, and Marie (Lambaerts); one brother, secular priest; ed. MSC Borgerhout, Belgium; MSC 1895; ord. priest 1911; arr. Papua 1901, stns. Vanamai, Pokao, Yule I.; chaplain, World War I, Croix de Guerre, Order of Crown with palm, Croix de l'Yser; d. 18 June 1929, Antwerp, Belgium.

213. **VAN RIEL, Bernard,** b. 6 November 1877, Tilburg, Netherlands; son of Pierre van Riel, master-builder, and Maria (Pynenburg); MSC 1898; ord. priest 1903; arr. Papua 1903, stn. Waima; r. 1904; transferred to Manila; d. 31 August 1921, Manila, Philippines.

214. **VEDÈRE, Jean-Pierre,** b. 19 September 1859, Azereix, France; son of Jean Vedère and Jeanne (Gobert); ed. minor seminary, Issoudun, and Rome; MSC 1878; ord. priest 22 December 1883; director of MSC minor seminary, Rome; arr. Papua 1901, stn. Inawaia; r. 1905, ill-health; d. 28 August 1924, Rome.

215. **VERJUS, Henri,** b. 26 May 1860, Oleggio, Piedmont, Italy; son of Philippe Verjus, soldier, and Laura (Massara); ed. minor seminary, Chezal-Benoît; desire for missions since childhood; MSC 1878; ord. priest 1883; teacher of theology at Chezel-Benoît (France), Barcelona, and Apolinaris Seminary, Rome; arr. NG 1885, stn. Yule I.; consecrated titular bishop of Limyre, coadjutor to Navarre, 1889; d. 13 November 1892, Oleggio, Italy, while on episcopal visit; cause of beatification introduced in Rome.

216. **VITALE, Joseph,** b. 8 March 1866, Gildone, Italy; son of Jean and Benedetta Vitale; MSC 1886; ord. priest 1888; arr. NG 1888, stns. Tsiria, Veifaʻa, Inawai; d. 9 October 1947, Veifaʻa, Papua.

Brothers

217. **ADAN, Henri,** b. 30 August 1859, Oudenbosch, Netherlands; o. carpenter and cabinetmaker; MSC 1885; arr. NG 1887, stn. Yule I.; d. 7 November 1931, Yule I.

218. **ANTOINE, Jean-Joseph,** b. 27 March 1867, Ste. Croix-aux-Mines, Alsace; devout family, one brother MSC; o. printer; MSC 1889; arr. NG 1894, stns. Eboa, Oba-Oba, Yule I.; r. 1919 to France; d. 30 October 1938, Issoudun.

219. **ARNOULD, Fernand,** b. 3 August 1879, Jessains, Aube, France; MSC 1897; came to NSW 1897; secretary to Father Tréand; arr. Papua 1907, stn. Yule I.; r. 1910; ex-MSC 1912; settled King I., Tasmania, and probably married.

220. **BOSMA, Rintz,** b. 11 February 1858, Franeker, Netherlands; o. farmer; MSC 1885; arr. NG 1888, stn. Yule I.; d. 18 June 1892, Yule I.

221. **BRUNNERS, Georges,** b. 1885, Nandlstadt, Bavaria, Germany; MSC 1885; arr. NG 1887, stns. Abiara, Bereina, Babiko, Pinupaka; d. 28 September 1898, Yule I.

222. **CARLS, André,** b. 1866, Aix-la-Chapelle, Germany; MSC 1885; arr. NG 1893, stns. Aipeana, Pinupaka, Inawabui, Eboa, Veifaʻa; d. December 1903, Veifaʻa, Papua.

223. **CARON, Joseph,** b. 16 February 1887, St. Ferréol, Quebec; MSC 1906; arr. Papua 1912, stn. Kubuna; d. 14 February 1929, Maera-Era, Papua.

224. **DE MOOR, Pierre (Valentin),** b. 31 January 1869, Hoeven, Neth-

erlands; MSC 1894; arr. Papua 1907, stn. Yule I.; d. 11 March 1932, Yule I.

225. **DE SANCTIS, Giuseppe,** b. 19 November 1858, Castelnuovo, Italy; influenced by Father Verjus; MSC 1883; arr. NG 1884, stn. Yule I.; r. 1889, demoralized; ex-MSC 1894; dispensation from vows 1897.

226. **FEHRMANN, Lambert,** b. 18 December 1859, Wesuwe, Germany; US citizen; MSC 1898; arr. Papua 1900; r. 1915; transferred to Port Darwin; d. 2 July 1920, Sydney.

227. **FRIDEZ, Camille,** b. 21 November 1879, Boron, Franche-Comté; migrated to Switzerland; "profoundly Christian family," one brother, MSC (no. 228); o. clockmaker; MSC 1907; arr. Papua 1909, stn. Oba-Oba; d. 7 August 1964, Fane, Papua.

228. **FRIDEZ, Jules,** b. 23 February 1878, Boron, Franche-Comté; migrated to Switzerland; "profoundly Christian family," one brother, MSC (no. 227); o. clockmaker; novitiate, Glastonbury, England, 1902; arr. Papua 1907, stn. Dilava; d. 17 June 1935, Port Moresby, Papua.

229. **GASBARRA, Salvatore,** b. 1864, Ferentino, Rome, Italy; MSC 1885; arr. NG 1885, stns. Yule I., Oriropetana, Oba-Oba; d. 4 June 1945, Veifa'a, Papua.

230. **GRIPPA, Domenico,** b. 25 July 1865, Oppido Lucano, Calabria, Italy; MSC 1889; arr. NG 1894, stn. Yule I.; d. 13 August 1898, Yule I.

231. **HANSEN, Cornelius,** b. 30 March 1878, Volendam, Netherlands; o. sailor; MSC 1899; arr. Papua 1904, stn. Yule I.; d. 16 June 1911, Yule I.

232. **HENKELMAN, Jean-Baptiste (Alexis),** b. 17 July 1869, Bois-le-Duc, Netherlands; ed. elementary; o. pastrycook; family deeply religious; met MSC fathers, Tilburg; MSC 1890; arr. NG 1894, stns. Yule I., Mou, Thursday I.; captain of mission fleet; d. 21 June 1952, Yule I.

233. **HERAULT, Louis,** b. 15 June 1875, Treillères, Brittany, France; son of Louis Herault and Jean (Langlois); MSC 1895; arr. NG 1896, stn. Yule I.; d. 12 October 1897, Yule I.

234. **HEYSSE, Désiré Alois (Germain),** b. 24 February 1861, Eeklo, Belgium; MSC 1894; arr. Papua 1902; r. 1914, ill-health; MSC Europe; d. 5 April 1941, Borgerhout, Belgium.

235. **KOCKS, Hadrianus (Eduardus),** b. 13 May 1872, Oudenbosch, Netherlands; son of Cornelius Kocks and Regina (van Hock); MSC 1894; arr. Papua 1900; r. 1911; ex-MSC 1914, dispensation from vows.

236. **KOEWEIDE, Jean,** b. 27 March 1875, Gorsel, Netherlands; MSC

1899; arr. Papua 1906, stn. Kubuna; d. 13 March 1942, Arapo-kina, Papua.

237. **KUIJPERS, Johannes (Louis)**, b. 10 September 1866, Deurne, Netherlands; MSC 1895; arr. Papua 1898, stn. Maera-Era, Yule I., Thursday I.; r. 1924, ill-health; d. 1 December 1924, Gringerger-gen, Belgium.

238. **LACASSE, Jules (Felix)**, b. 12 November 1868, Alton, Moselle, France; MSC 1891; served New Britain, 1891–1898; arr. Papua 1900; r. 1904; Issoudun 1906–1908; ex-MSC 1908.

239. **LAINE, Augustus**, b. 1 October 1875, Le Cellier, Nantes, France; father, peasant farmer; o. clog-maker; heard sermon on needs of pagans; MSC 1897; arr. NG 1900, stns. Oba-Oba, Yule I.; d. 30 March 1952, Oba-Oba, Papua.

240. **MARCONI, Nicola**, b. 18 March 1866, Castelnuovo, Rome; influ-enced by Verjus; MSC 12 April 1885; arr. NG 1885, stns. Mou, Bereina, Jesu-Baibua; d. 20 November 1893, Inawi, Papua.

241. **MOOREES, Joseph**, b. 19 March 1862, Tilburg, Netherlands; son of Cornelius Moorees and Nicolasina van den Beck; arr. NG 1891, stn. Abiara; r. 1896; recalled for insubordination following liaison with Papuan woman; ex-MSC with dispensation from vows; mar-ried.

242. **MOREUX, Joseph (Marie-Joseph)**, b. 22 June 1867, Bué, Cher, France; son of Pierre Moreux and Solange Milleriaux (Gardiner); o. farm laborer; MSC 1893; arr. NG 1893, stns. Yule I., Oba-Oba, Dilava; d. 16 June 1906, Dilava, Papua.

243. **OBERLEUTER, Jean**, b. Obrienstädt, Germany; MSC 1886; arr. NG 1888, stn. Pinupaka; r. 1893, after liaison with Papuan woman; married, remained in Papua as planter; d. 1926.

244. **POIJER, Johannes (Alois)**, b. 5 November 1869, Volendam, Neth-erlands; son of Jacobus and Alide (Boer); recruited by visiting MSC, Father Peeters; MSC 1891; arr. NG 1897, stns. Veifa'a, Amo-Amo, Rarai, Maera-Era, Yule I.; d. December 1922, Yule I.

245. **PRIEM, Adrien**, b. 17 March 1872, Heikenszand, Volendam, Netherlands; o. sailor; MSC 1897; arr. NG 1899, stn. Yule I.; d. 10 April 1930, Yule I.

246. **SOMERS, François**, b. 15 November 1860, Koningshooikt, Bel-gium; father, farmer; o. milkman; influenced by sermon on St. Francis-Xavier and by singing in MSC house; MSC 1895; arr. Papua 1906, stn. Maera-Era; r. 1916, ill-health; became gardener MSC, Marseilles.

247. **STEYEART, Karel (Bonaventura)**, b. 28 December 1866, Melsele, Belgium; o. baker; MSC 1890; arr. NG 1894, stn. Yule I.; d. 11 April 1894, Inawi, Papua.

248. **STUDLER, Paul,** b. 28 June 1886, Sélestat, Alsace; father, artisan; orphaned; raised by nun and then by Father Eugene Meyer, MSC; wished to be priest, but advised to be brother; MSC 1904; arr. Papua 1909, stn. Ononghe; d. 11 July 1963, Port Moresby.

249. **TRAVAGLINI, Mariano,** b. 16 May 1863, Castelnuovo, Rome; MSC 1885; arr. NG 1886, stn. Thursday I.; r. 1901, demoralized; d. 5 January 1943, Florence, Italy.

250. **VAN BREUGEL, Theodore,** b. 23 September 1876, Bois-le-Duc, Netherlands; MSC 1900; arr. Papua 1904, stn. Yule I.; d. 27 April 1905, Yule I.

251. **VAN CAM, Constant,** b. 1 July 1858, Antwerp, Belgium; MSC 1890; arr. NG 1891, stns. Mou, Bereina, Yule I.; d. 27 September 1903, Thursday I.

252. **VAN DEN EIJKEN, Petrus (Modeste),** b. 25 January 1873, Ravenstein, Netherlands; o. sailor; MSC 1893; arr. NG 1899, stns. Maera-Era, Oba-Oba; d. 31 July 1917, Waima, Papua.

253. **VAN ERVEN, Petrus (Philippe),** b. 15 August 1866, Tilburg, Netherlands; son of Hubert van Erven and Kaf (van Benuden); o. blacksmith and carpenter; MSC 1889; arr. NG 1894, stn. Yule I.; d. 13 March 1918, Yule I.

254. **VAN HORENBECK, Stanislas,** b. 23 November 1858, Antwerp, Belgium; MSC 1896; arr. NG 1897, stn. Yule I.; r. 1902, ill-health; d. 7 December 1902, Sydney.

255. **VAN ROOIJ, Franciscus (Stanislas),** b. 15 November 1863, Enschot, Netherlands; son of Jacobus van Rooij and Wilhelmina (Smeyers); o. roof-thatcher and butcher; novitiate: Tilburg; MSC 1886; arr. NG 1888, stns. Babiko, Pinupaka, Maera-Era, Bereina; d. 24 April 1917, Maera-Era, Papua.

256. **VAN SPEIJK, Theodorus,** b. 31 December 1865, Drunen, Netherlands; o. blacksmith; MSC 1886; arr. NG 1894, boat-maker for mission; d. 21 March 1918, Yule I.

257. **VEREIJKEN, Johannes (Gabriel),** b. 16 November 1860, Beek en Donk, Netherlands; MSC 1889; arr. NG 1891, stns. Mou, Jesu-Baibua; d. 20 August 1911, Yule I.

258. **WAGEMANS, Simon,** b. 9 June 1861, Zevenbergen, Netherlands; son of Gabriel Wagemans, brewer, and Johanna (Thiel); o. blacksmith; MSC 1885; arr. NG 1888, stn. Yule I.; d. 3 July 1902, Sydney.

259. **WEBER, Conrad,** b. 5 November 1862, Grendelbruch, Alsace; o. spinner and woodcutter; novitiate: Tilburg; MSC 1886; arr. NG 1887, stn. Yule I.; r. 1887, ill-health; transferred to Gilbert Is.; d. 18 January 1955, Abaiang, Gilberts (Kiribati).

260. **WRIGHT, George,** from Australia, wanted to be priest but because of educational standard, advised to be brother; MSC 1900; arr. Papua 1900; r. 1901, ex-MSC; became priest in NZ; d. 16 May 1955.

261. **ZWARTHOED, Cornelius (Arnold),** b. 25 March 1869, Volendam, Netherlands; cousin of no. 262; o. sailor; MSC 1893, stn. Yule I.; d. 11 October 1908, Yule I.

262. **ZWARTHOED, Petrus (Edmond),** b. 1 November 1861, Volendam, Netherlands; cousin of no. 261; o. fisherman; called by Father Peeters, MSC; novitiate: Antwerp; MSC 1891; arr. NG 1893, stn. Yule I.; d. 9 July 1898, Yule I.

DAUGHTERS OF OUR LADY OF THE SACRED HEART (FDNSC)

263. **ALLERA, Henriette,** b. 1869, Thônes, Savoy, France; daughter of Pierre Allera and Marie (Siegle); devout family, friends of Verjus; one brother MSC (no. 156); arr. NG 1897, stn. Tsiria; d. 30 August 1935, Tsiria, Yule I.

264. **Sister André,** from Brittany, France; arr. Papua 1900, stn. Inawi; r. 1907, transferred to Sydney.

265. **ANNE, Clothilde (Joachim),** b. 1865 (or 1866), Verrebrock, Belgium; arr. NG 1887, stns. Mou, Inawi; d. 11 April 1894, Inawi, Papua.

266. **BACHELIER, Théodorine Valentine,** b. 1888, Le Bignon, Brittany, France; daughter of Benjamin Bachelier, farmer, and Léocadie (Guilbaud); arr. NG 1912, stns. Popole, Yule I.; d. 5 April 1943, Aropokina, Papua.

267. **BALUÇON, Rosalie,** b. 1867, Poilly, Ile-et-Vilaine, France; daughter of Ambroise Baluçon, farmer, and Jeanne (Laize); final vows, 1896; arr. NG 1893, stns. Inawaia, Yule I.; New Britain 1922–1924; d. 10 February 1946, Yule I.

268. **BATARD, Claudine,** b. 1869, St. Hilaire-du-Bois, Brittany, France; daughter of Alfred Batard, peasant farmer, and Marie (Boudaud); arr. NG 1897, stns. Veifa'a, Yule I.; d. 11 December 1942, Veifa'a, Papua.

269. **BELARBRE, Antoinette,** b. 1863, Monteux, France; arr. NG 1894, stns. Inawi, Veifa'a; r. 1907, transferred to Sydney; d. 23 October 1953, France.

270. **BONNARD, Mary Rose Constance (Rose),** b. 1863, Nantes, France; arr. NG 1893, stn. Tsiria; r. 1909 to Sydney; d. 3 March 1919.

271. **BOUFFORT, Françoise, (Léontine),** b. 1874, Lecousse, Fougères,

France; daughter of Jean Marie Bouffort, land-owner, and Françoise (Lepaurre); arr. NG 1892, stns. Waima, Inawaia; d. 10 September 1902, Inawaia, Papua.

272. **BRADY, Imelda (de Pazzi)**, b. Australia; arr. Papua 1904, stn. Thursday I.; d. 1909, Thursday I.

273. **BREEN, Honora (Leonard)**, b. 1880, Australia; arr. Papua 1914; r. ?; ex-FDNSC.

274. **BRIZAID, Bernadette**, b. 1864, Bonoron, Brittany, France; arr. NG 1887, stns. Yule I., Inawi; d. 17 September 1895, Inawi, Papua.

275. **CAILLAUD, Jeanne Marie**, b. 1866, St. Hilaire-du-Bois, Brittany, France; daughter of Jean Caillaud, farmer; arr. NG 1888, stns. Mou, Inawaia; d. 4 August 1913, Papua.

276. **CARROLL, Katie (Clothilde)**, b. 1876, Kiltealy, Ireland; daughter of William Carroll, farmer, and Ellen (Hayes); novitiate: Belgium; arr. Papua 1900, stns. Ivea, Yule I.; d. 12 March 1966, Yule I.

277. **CHATELLIER, Marie Melanie Valentine (Melanie)**, b. 1871, St. Hilaire-du-Bois, Brittany, France; father, farmer; one sister, FDNSC; arr. NG 1893, stns. Popole, Fane; d. 5 April 1943, Papua.

278. **DANIELS, Elizabeth Marie (Apolline)**, b. 7 March 1883, St. Helen's, Tas.; daughter of Walter Daniels, miner, and Margaret (O'Keefe); arr. Papua 1909, stn. Yule I.; r. 1919; d. 1932, Brisbane.

279. **DARCY, Hanna**, b. 1868, Newcastle, Australia; daughter of Patrick Darcy, laborer, and Johanna (Butler); arr. NG 1900, stn. Thursday I.; r. 1919; d. 1932, Brisbane.

280. **DEBROUX, Natalie (Mother Liguori)**, b. 1862, Overijse, Brabant, Belgium; father, proprietor, grocery and drapery business; well-educated; o. worked in father's business; solidly Catholic family, early recognition of vocation; FDNSC 1885; arr. NG 1887, stns. Inawi, Yule I.; r. 1908; became first superior, Port Darwin; returned to Papua 1915; r. 1921, for administration FDNSC, Europe; d. 18 December 1945, Rumst, Belgium.

281. **DEDIERJEAN, Marie (Eusebia)**, b. 1871, Orberg, Alsace; daughter of Sebastien Dedierjean, peasant farmer, and Rosalie (Batot); promised to become a religious if cured at Lourdes; arr. Papua 1900, stn. Waima; d. 10 February 1950, Yule I.

282. **DENIAUD, Augustine (Euphrasie)**, b. 1876, Montbert, Nantes, France; daughter of Joseph [? Augustin] Deniaud, farmer, and Mélanie [? Jeanne] (Hervouet); family prominent in church activities; one sister, FDNSC (no. 283); arr. Papua 1900, stn. Maiva; d. 8 May 1912, Maiva, Papua.

283. **DENIAUD, Marie (Julitte)**, b. 1881, Montbert, Nantes, France; daughter of Joseph [? Augustin] Deniaud, farmer, and Mélanie [?

Jeanne] (Hervouet); novitiate: 1911; first vows 1913; final vows 1918; arr. Papua 1914, stns. Veifa'a, Waima, Yule I.; d. 31 July 1973, Yule I.

284. **DERROZ, Florence (Adrienne)**, b. 1881, Cornesse, Belgium; FDNSC 1905; arr. Papua 1909, stn. Thursday I.; d. 22 December 1909, Thursday I.

285. **DESSAILLY, Claire**, b. 18 January 1853, Larbret, Pas de Calais, France; daughter of Philogene Dessailly, farmer, and Adelaide (Palt); entered Sisters of Holy Name of Jesus, Paris, 1873; transferred to FDNSC, Issoudun, 1884; arr. NG 1887, stn. Yule I. (cook); d. 14 March 1930, Yule I.

286. **DOUILLARD, Marthe**, b. 1 November 1852, St. Jean-de-Boiseau, Brittany, France; daughter of Louis Douillard, farmer, and Marie (Her); devout family; one sister, FDNSC; novitiate: Issoudun; arr. NG 1887, stns. Yule I., Thursday I.; d. 20 January 1931, Yule I.

287. **DUFLOT, Hélène (Kostka)**, b. 1880, Montmartre, Paris; daughter of Jean Baptist Duflôt and Mary Anne (Cousin); aristocratic family; well-educated; arr. Papua 1909, stn. Popole; d. 10 August 1955, Yule I.

288. **DUGAST, Marie (Anastasie)**, b. 1869, Trinité-de-Clisson, Brittany; daughter of Ferdinand Dugast, farmer, and Marie (Barre); arr. NG 1894, stn. Inawi; d. 31 August 1902, Inawi, Papua.

289. **FOUILLET, Celestine Josephine**, b. 1869, Combré, Maine-et-Loire, France; daughter of Pierre Fouillet, farmer; arr. NG 1893, stns. Yule I., Inawi, Inawaia; d. 21 August 1900, Yule I.

290. **FOURTER, Monica (Zita)**, b. 1883, Germany; migrated to Eden, NSW; arr. Papua 1909, stns. Inawaia, Bomana; d. 4 October 1955, Yule I.

291. **FOX, Brigid**, b. 1861, Ashfield, NSW; daughter of James Fox, prospector, and Sarah (Cahalan); arr. NG 1899; r. 1903, transferred to Sydney; d. 24 April 1943, Bowral, NSW.

292. **FOX, Mary Margaret (Finbar)**, b. 8 May 1881, Sydney; daughter of George Fox, laborer and Annie (Sullivan); arr. Papua 1905, stns. Yule I., Samarai, Trobriands; r. Sydney 1939; d. 1 January 1963, Sydney.

293. **GALLAGHER, Sarah (Patrick)**, b. 1863 (? 1861), Roskil, Ireland; daughter of Hugh Gallagher, farmer, and Hannah (MacFadden); arr. Papua 1900, stn. Yule I.; d. 2 February 1913, Yule I.

294. **GLEESON, Margaret (Kevin)**, b. 1875, Cashel, Ireland, daughter of Timothy Gleeson, farmer, and Mary (Tooby); sister of Bishop Gleeson, CSSR, Maitland, Australia; arr. Papua 1900, stn. Yule I.; d. 18 July 1932, Yule I.

295. **GUILLET, Clementine (Joachim II)**, b. 1887, Poire-sur-Vie, Ven-

dée, France; arr. NG 1914, stn. Yule I.; d. 26 November 1915, Yule I.

296. **HEFFERNAN, Honora (Aloisius)**, b. 11 September 1878, Wannon, Vic.; daughter of Denis Heffernan, farmer, and Johanna (Fitzgerald); arr. Papua 1904; d. 10 May 1923, Yule I.

297. **HERVOUET, Philomène (Alexis)**, b. 1878, St. Hilaire-du-Bois; peasant family, related to Sisters Julitte and Euphrasie (nos. 282 & 283); arr. Papua 1900, stn. Aipeana; d. 21 November 1919, Papua.

298. **HOUDMONT, Marie (Gabrielle)**, b. 17 January 1885, Renazé, France, baptized by Father Barbette, who saw Virgin Mary at Pontmain, 1871; first vows, 21 October 1907, arr. Papua 1912, stns. Pinupaka, Veifa'a; d. 1974, Yule I.; buried with full Mekeo ceremonial, Veifa'a, Papua.

299. **HULLIN, Camille Jean**, b. 1874, Clamecy, France, arr. NG 1897, stn. Maera-Era; r. 1923; d. 9 October 1946, Brazil.

300. **JANNOT, Hélène**, b. 1867, St. Hilaire-du-Bois, Brittany, France; arr. NG 1894, stn. Mou; d. 17 July 1901, Sydney.

301. **JEAN, Thérèse**, b. 1863, Au Puy, Haute-Loire, France; father, solicitor; came to Sydney 1886; established FDNSC house; arr. NG 1900, stn. Thursday I.; r. 1908; returned to Europe to serve on general administration FDNSC; d. 1945, France.

302. **JONES, Mary (Patricius)**, b. 1875 (? 1876), Bendigo, Vic.; arr. Papua 1904, stn. Yule I.; d. November 1930, Yule I.

303. **KELLY, Maria (Boniface)**, from Australia; arr. Papua 1913; r. 1924; ex-FDNSC.

304. **KEOGH, Mary (Thecla)**, b. 1878, Balmain, NSW; taught in FDNSC schools, Australia; arr. Papua 1910, stn. Thursday I.; r. 1929, to Sydney.

305. **KOOPMAN, Bernadette**, b. 1877, Nevershoof, Holland; arr. Papua 1902, stns. Inawaia, Kubuna; r. 1923, recalled to Europe to serve on general administration FDNSC.

306. **LECLAIR, Philomène (Eulalie)**, b. 1873, St. Hilaire, Brittany, France; daughter of François Leclair, farmer, and Marie (Poiroy); arr. NG 1897, stns. Inawaia, Waima; d. 4 September 1935, Yule I.

307. **LENEHAN, Maria (Hyacinth)**, b. 15 April 1862, Sydney; daughter of Patrick Lenehan, farmer, and Mary (Atkins); arr. NG 1893; r. 1909, transferred to Port Darwin; d. 16 November 1909, Port Darwin.

308. **LE ROUX, Yvonne**, b. 1863, Plomeur, Brittany, France; arr. NG 1887, stn. Thursday I.; d. 10 January 1893, Thursday I.

309. **McSWEENY, Margaret (Loyola)**, b. 1866, Wood's Point, Vic.; daughter of Morgan McSweeny, miner, and Hannah (Russell); r. 1914; d. 23 June 1953, Sydney.

310. **MAIRE, Marie (Agnès)**, b. 1866, Semur, Côte d'Or; arr. NG 1888, stns. Thursday I., Inawi, Tsiria; d. 1 February 1901.

311. **MASSELIN, Albertine Louise (Madeline)**, b. 18 March 1844, Bayeux, Normandy, France; daughter of Etienne Masselin, farmer, and Esther (?); raised by Sisters of Providence; worked in shop, Paris; joined Sisters of Holy Name of Jesus, Paris; transferred to FDNSC, Issoudun; arr. NG 1886, stn. Yule I.; d. 21 July 1927, Yule I.

312. **MAXWELL, Agnes (Ursula)**, b. 1872, Balmain, Sydney; arr. NG 1902; r. 1925.

313. **MERLET, Clothilde (Gonzague)**, b. 1878, St. Colombin, Brittany, France; daughter of Benjamin Merlet, blacksmith, and Françoise (Pichet); FDNSC 1898; arr. Papua 1902, stns. Toaripi, Popole; d. 15 December 1909, Yule I.

314. **ODE, Virginie (Ange)**, b. 1860, Valence, Drôme or Montauban, Brittany; peasant family; arr. NG 1887, stns. Inawi, Veifa'a, Inawui; d. 15 September 1895, Inawui, Papua.

315. **PARET, Julie (Marguerite II)**, b. 1875, Houthem, Belgium; daughter of Pierre Paret and Adele (Sesmedt); arr. NG 1902, stn. Oba-Oba; d. 22 May 1945, Yule I.

316. **PASTANT, Sebastienne Marie**, b. 1873, Beuzange, Lorraine, France; arr. NG 1897, stn. Tsiria; d. March 1924, Papua.

317. **PERDRIX, Pauline (Paule)**, b. 22 June 1864, Haguenau, Alsace; daughter of George Perdrix and Barbe (Keth); middle-class family; arr. NG 1887, stns. Thursday I., Yule I., Mou, Waima; r. 1926, ill-health; teacher, FDNSC, Sydney; d. 21 July 1931, Sydney.

318. **POIRON, Josephine**, b. 1864, St. Hilaire-du-Bois, Brittany, France; daughter of Joseph Jean Poiron, farmer, and Josephine (Raffegean); arr. NG 1887, stns. Inawui, Inawaia; d. 20 October 1905, Inawaia, Papua.

319. **RENAUD, Léontine**, b. 1886 (? 1884), La Marne, Brittany, France; daughter of August Renaud, farmer, and Jean (Templier); arr. Papua 1912, stn. Waima; d. 12 September 1967, Yule I.

320. **ROARTY, Ada (Lucy)**, b. 18 January 1867, Sydney; daughter of John Roarty, photographic artist, and Margaret (Woods); arr. NG 1893; r. ?; transferred to Sydney and Port Darwin.

321. **RYAN, Mary (Xavier)**, b. 1853 (? 1856), Tipperary, Ireland; daughter of Michael Ryan, farrier, and Bridget (Ryan); brought up by Brigidine Nuns; met Father Tierney, MSC, in Ireland; arr. Sydney 1887; established St. Bernard's School; arr. NG 1894, stn. Thursday I. (Mother Superior); r. 1900; transferred to Kensington and Mascot (Mother Superior); d. 23 December 1933, Sydney.

322. **SCHUTTE, Charlotte (Berchmans)**, b. 1856, Lildeshausen, Bavaria; arr. NG 1888, stn. Inawui; d. 28 June 1892, Yule I.
323. **SEPTVANTS, Angèle (St. Roch)**, b. 7 July 1874 (or 1876), Calvados, France; daughter of François Septvants, army-captain, and Desirée (Lacauve); arr. Papua 1900, stn. Mekeo; d. 13 November 1916, Yule I.
324. **SIMON, Jeanne (Albertine)**, b. 1887, Ile-et-Vilaine, Brittany, France; daughter of Jean Simon, farmer, and Marie Rose (Negris); arr. NG 1914; d. 14 February 1930, Yule I.
325. **SURAMY, Francine (Raphaël)**, b. 3 May 1868, Souvigny, Auvergne, France; daughter of Claude Suramy, gardener, and Marie (Nor); o. seamstress in workshop; recognized vocation at age of 21 and despite mother's opposition joined FDNSC 1892; arr. NG 1893, stns. Inawi, Maera-Era, Waima, Pinupaka, Inawaia, Yule I.; d. 18 June 1947, Yule I.
326. **SWEENY, Margaret (Margaret Mary)**, b. 5 March 1866, Ryde, Sydney; daughter of Daniel Sweeny, laborer, and Annie (Harkin); helped Marists at Villa Maria; met MSC on their arrival in Sydney; arr. NG 1887, stns. Tsiria, Bioto; d. 1 April 1896, Tsiria, Papua.
327. **THOMAS, Marie (Octavie)**, b. 1884, La Marne, Brittany, France; arr. Papua 1909, stn. Oba-Oba; r. 1936, ill-health; d. 23 August 1973, France.

Notes

Preface

1. E.g., 1890: 17 government officers, 28 missionaries; 1898: 21 government officers, 88 missionaries; 1912: 89 government officers, 82 missionaries (BNG-ARs; Papua ARs; mission archives).

2. Navarre var. *b*, 1: 1889, 42. Most of the source material for the Sacred Heart Mission was written in French. All translations are my own.

3. Cf. Ayandele 1966, xvii.

4. Knowles 1963, 13.

5. D. L. Oliver 1961.

6. K. R. Howe 1984.

7. Hezel 1983.

8. Macdonald 1982, viii.

9. Dening 1980.

10. Gilson 1980.

11. Gunson 1978.

12. Garrett 1982.

13. Latukefu 1974.

14. Wiltgen 1979.

15. Laracy 1976*a*, ix.

16. Hilliard 1978.

17. Wetherell 1977.

18. Gavan Daws 1973.

19. Lovett 1899.

20. Goodall 1954.

21. Findlay and Holdsworth 1921.

22. Burridge 1973, 207.

23. Beidelman 1974, 236–237. Since Beidelman wrote, the gap has been partly filled by a series of studies of the origins and motivations of particular groups of missionaries (Piggin 1978; Potter 1974; C. Peter Williams 1976; Oddie 1974). African mission history has also been enriched since 1974 by the studies of Strayer (1976 and 1978) and Ranger and Weller (1975).

24. McAuley 1955, 138–146. For other analyses of the stereotype see Warren (1967, 74) and Mobley (1970, 1–2).

25. Maugham 1956.
26. Mahood 1973, 190.
27. Ibid.
28. E.g., Pitt-Rivers 1930.
29. Clark 1965, 3.
30. E.g., Waiko 1972; Kiki 1968; Eri 1968.
31. Cairns 1965, xv.
32. Lovett 1899; Goodall 1954; Dupeyrat 1934; Bromilow 1914; Chignell 1913; Wetherell 1977.
33. Carruthers 1924, 65; R. Oliver 1952, 229.
34. Clark 1965, 14.
35. See, e.g., Strout 1968; Gavan Daws 1978; Dollard 1949.
36. Erikson 1972, 18.
37. Two useful critiques of prosopography are Lawrence Stone 1971 and Pyenson 1977.

Prologue

1. Chadwick 1966, 5.
2. The LMS was established in 1795 and the Wesleyan Methodist Missionary Society in 1818. See chapter 8.
3. The Church Missionary Society (1799) was an evangelical Anglican equivalent of the Protestant societies. Chadwick (1966, 387) contends, however, that the influence of the Evangelical Revival quickened not only the evangelical wing of the Church of England, but the whole church, including those who "carried their ardour of soul into Puseyism."
4. As used in this work, the term *Protestant* does not include Anglicans. The Anglican Mission in Papua identified itself strongly with the Anglo-Catholic wing of the Anglican Church in its stress on the dogmatic and sacramental aspects of Christianity, on the continuity of the church from the Middle Ages, and in its sympathy with the other churches of Catholic Christendom. Founded by a body of bishops mostly of High Church persuasion, it was led by individuals with a deep commitment to Tractarianism. Individual Evangelical (Low Church) Anglicans served within it, however. See chapter 8.
5. Chateaubriand 1802. See also Elliot-Binns 1936, 123; Latourette 1941, 23–26; Dansette 1961, 1:144–145.
6. Latourette 1941, 26–27.
7. Ibid., 60.
8. Missionaries had, in fact, worked previously off the coast of New Guinea on Murua (Woodlark Island). French Marists settled there in 1847, but, defeated by dissension and disease, were replaced in 1852 by missionary priests from Milan who, in turn, abandoned Murua in 1855 (see Laracy 1976 *b*).
9. Burton 1949, 44.
10. The name New Guinea is used here for the period before 1900, consistent with contemporary usage, and British New Guinea for the years of British rule, 1885–1900. The name Papua is used for the period after the assumption of Australian authority.
11. A more detailed analysis of the structure and organization of the four missions is given in chapter 8.
12. I use the term *European* as did (and do) the Papuans for all people of white skin, regardless of origin.
13. CEA-Australasian Board of Missions 1850.

Chapter 1: "Few Are Powerful or Highly Born"

1. For information on the national origins of individual missionaries and for biographical data that form the basis for many of the conclusions in this chapter, see Appendix 3.

2. Dansette 1961, 2:ii; see also Zeldin 1973, 2:988.

3. Zeldin 1973, 2:54–55. See also Dansette 1961, 2:12. Bishop de Boismenu wrote to one of the clergy of Nantes in 1902: "I know the Bretons, they will enlist in numbers for New Guinea . . . May God hear our call and choose for us . . . some of the sons of Brittany whose golden heart and iron heads will usually work marvels in the Mission." *Annales de Nôtre-Dame du Sacré-Coeur* (hereinafter *Annales*) 1903, 632.

4. R. T. Jones 1962, 247.

5. It is not known where in New South Wales five of the Anglican missionaries came from.

6. See Dupeyrat and de la Noë 1958; *Annales* 1948, 20; *Annales* 1953, 186–87.

7. Meyer 1922–1924.

8. Navarre, var. *c.*

9. Vaudon 1899, 1–5; Verjus 1910, 200.

10. ADB file: Louis Couppé.

11. Ceresi 1934, 4.

12. SMSC Personal files.

13. Ibid. and birth certificate: William Burke.

14. Gsell 1955, epilogue.

15. SMSC Personal files; Dupeyrat 1951.

16. SMSC Personal files; *Annales* 1897, 44; *Annales* 1955, 158–159. On changes in the social structure of the French clergy see Zeldin 1973, 2:995. For peasant origins of children educated by the MSC, see *Annales* 1955, 159.

17. SMSC var. *e*, and birth certificates.

18. Venard 1966, 10–18; *Annales* 1930, 13–15; SMSC var. *e*.

19. Dupeyrat 1934; Henkelmann 1928.

20. Sister Martha, 1979.

21. Venard 1966, 130.

22. See for example, fathers' occupations listed on death certificates of Leontine Renaud, Marie Dugast, Clothilde Merlet, Josephine Poiron, Rosalie Baluçon, Theodorine Bachelier, Françoise Bouffort, Augustine Deniaud.

23. *Annales* 1927, 341–44; *Annales* 1949, 22–25.

24. Birth certificates: Sisters Finbar Fox, Apoline Daniels, Lucy Roarty, Brigid Fox, Elizabeth Daniels, Margaret Sweeney, Mary Lenehan, Veronica Darcy, Honora Heffernan.

25. CEA-DNG *AR* 1906–1907.

26. Hilliard 1978, 31–33, 124–127. For the UMCA see Wilson 1936.

27. Stone-Wigg Papers.

28. Birth certificate: Gerald Sharp.

29. White 1929, 9.

30. Eric Gill 1940, 94.

31. *Guardian*, 9 Sept. 1903; Stone-Wigg Papers.

32. Newton 1938, 1–13.

33. E. Rogers 1920, 2–6; Synge 1908, 2–5.

34. Death certificate: Samuel Tomlinson.

35. Marriage certificates: Shaw/Griffiths, Ramsay/Armitage.

36. CEA-DNG var. *e:* boxes 20–23; birth certificates.
37. White 1923, 1–4.
38. Birth certificate: Ernest Owen Davies.
39. CEA-DNG var. *e:* Giblin, Bishop Montgomery to Stone-Wigg, 25 Nov. 1899.
40. Stone-Wigg Papers, Stone-Wigg to Montgomery 7 May 1904.
41. Garran 1958, 165.
42. CEA-DNG var. *e:* boxes 20 and 23; birth certificates.
43. Gunson 1958, 165.
44. Inglis 1963, 15. See also Chadwick 1970, 407–408.
45. LMS Candidates' Papers. All biographical information relating to LMS missionaries in this section is from this source unless otherwise stated.
46. Lockwood 1958, 27–34; McLeod 1974.
47. Clark 1965, 132.
48. B. T. Butcher 1963, 16.
49. Beharell 1978; O. F. Tomkins Papers.
50. Bromilow 1929, 15–20.
51. *MR*, June 1941, 5; death certificate: Field.
52. *MR*, June 1941, 5; death certificate: Watson; Bardsley Diary.
53. Fellows Diary; *MR*, June 1941, 4.
54. Information from family papers and biographical notes supplied by descendants of Colebatch, Gilmour, Ballantyne, Francis, Jenness, Lill, Jamieson, Scrivin, Bardsley; Billing var.; marriage certificates: Jenness/Ballantyne, Corfield/Waterhouse, Jamieson/Scrivin; death certificates: Glew, Ballantyne.
55. Death certificate: Fletcher; Fletcher 1933.
56. On the social background of colonial Methodism see Walker 1971; Renata Howe 1965, 1967.
57. Joseph King 1909, 1–10.
58. Chalmers n.d.
59. B. T. Butcher 1963, 14–15.
60. Russell Abel 1934, 9–12.
61. Gill 1940, 42–50.
62. Ibid., 94. On the defection to Liberal Unionism see R. T. Jones 1962, 275 and Richards 1977, 387–401.
63. Russell Abel 1934, 9; Binfield 1977, 223.
64. Gill 1940, 58.
65. B. T. Butcher 1963, 15.
66. Navarre var. *c*, 10–13.
67. Dupeyrat and de la Noë 1958, 1–10.
68. *Annales* 1955, 158–159.
69. *Annales* 1922.
70. This analysis is based on Anderson 1977, which synthesizes and analyzes the results of most of the available scholarship on the subject. See also Zeldin 1973, 1:365–392.
71. Anderson 1977, 54–55; Zeldin 1973, 2:988.
72. *Annales* 1961, 67. A Chouan was a royalist insurgent during the French Revolution.
73. *Annales* 1946, 29.
74. SMSC n.d. *c*.
75. Venard 1966, 1–18; *Annales* 1930, 1–14.
76. *Annales* 1918, 239.
77. Bromilow 1929, 15.

78. Notes on Scrivin family supplied by Dr. Lionel Scrivin.
79. Notes on Lill family supplied by Reverend George Carter.
80. White 1929, 9–10.
81. LMS Candidates' Papers.
82. MMSA 1911–1912: Johns to Danks, 21 April 1911.
83. *Annals of Our Lady of the Sacred Heart* (hereinafter Australian *Annals*), Aug. 1894, 199. See also Stone-Wigg Papers: letters of Stone-Wigg to mother; *Annales* 1922: letters of Jullien to mother; and Tomkins Papers: letters of Tomkins to mother.
84. *Annales* 1923, 387.
85. McLeod 1974, 56.
86. Navarre, var. *c*, 13.
87. SMSC var. *e*. For accounts of parentage of Verjus, Jullien, de Boismenu, and Genocchi, see biographies by Vaudon (1899), Meyer (1922–1924), Dupeyrat and de la Noë (1958), and Ceresi (1934), respectively. Hartzer's father's death is described in Venard 1966 and *Annales* 1930, 13–14. See also Verjus' account of his father's death in *Annales* 1910, 202.
88. It is impossible to ascertain whether or not the death of a father of a religious has always been recorded.
89. LMS Candidates' Papers.
90. Chalmers n.d.
91. Russell Abel 1934, 9.
92. LMS Candidates' Papers.
93. B. T. Butcher Papers.
94. Synge 1908, 4.
95. Beattie 1978. He was a hard man who disowned his daughter for an unsuitable marriage, an action which Stone-Wigg found difficult to forgive.
96. Stone-Wigg Papers: Clements to Stone-Wigg 1898.
97. White 1923, 9–10.
98. CEA-DNG var. *e*, boxes 20–23.
99. E. Walker Diary; Billing Papers; notes on Scrivin family enclosed in letter from L. Scrivin, 11 Sept. 1978; MMSA 1911–1912: Johns to Danks, 21 April 1911.
100. Cf. Iremonger 1970, 5.
101. See, for example, LMS Candidates Papers: Walker, Bartlett, Beharell.
102. *Annales* 1892, 636.
103. Information about education of LMS missionaries is from LMS Candidates Papers, unless otherwise stated.
104. Chalmers n.d.
105. Oddie 1974.
106. Sidney Webb 1904, 110.
107. Thomson 1950, 101–102; see also Briggs 1954.
108. Gunson 1978, 78–80; Gilbert 1976, 181.
109. MCA-NSW var.: Holland.
110. Bromilow 1929, 15–20.
111. Scrivin and Waterhouse gained an adult matriculation; Fletcher may have matriculated; Fellows, Francis, Holland, Watson, and Avery had an elementary education (MCA-NSW var.).
112. Personal communication, Howard Bardsley, 15 August 1978.
113. Among them, Minnie Billing, May Jenness, Florence Thompson, and Doris Bembrick.
114. Biographical note accompanying Stone-Wigg Papers.

115. Stone-Wigg Papers: Stone-Wigg to father, 4 Sept. 1893.

116. See Simon and Bradley 1975, 108; Archer 1921, 75, 186, 316; and Honey 1977, 143. The term public school is here used to denote all those endowed schools, originally grammar schools, that served the English public. The "public schools" are those of them, nine in number at the beginning of the nineteenth century and considerably more by the end, that had attained a reputation as elite, and generally boarding, institutions.

117. Rogers 1920, 6–11.

118. Personal communication, Canon Bodger, Alotau, PNG.

119. CEA-DNG var. *e:* Downton and Giblin.

120. Hilliard 1978, 125.

121. Anderson 1970, 51–52.

122. *Annales* 1923, 308.

123. *Annales* 1952, 134–136.

124. Navarre var. *b:* Journal 1 (1888): 19.

125. Venard 1966, 130.

126. Ibid., and Sister Paul-Marie 1979.

127. Navarre var. *b:* Journal, 12 Aug. 1888.

128. SMSC Correspondence: Couppé to Jouet, 23 Feb. 1885.

129. Sister Paul-Marie 1979.

130. For a definition and summary of this concept, see Sills 1968, 16:499.

131. I Corinthians 1: 27–28.

132. Quoted in Briggs 1960, 73.

Chapter 2: "Whom God Has Called"

1. LMS Candidates' Papers.

2. *Annales* 1921, 220.

3. Crosfield 1897, 49–50.

4. W. Y. Turner; Saville; R. L. Turner; Hunt. See Appendix 3.

5. Percy Waterhouse was a grandson of John Waterhouse, first General Superintendent of Wesleyan missions in Australasia; Ambrose Fletcher was one of seven sons of John Fletcher, all of whom became local preachers and four of whom were ordained. Ambrose Fletcher's grandfather was Methodist minister Joseph Fletcher, the son of W. Horner Fletcher who was called out and ordained by Wesley. For Eleanor Walker's descent from Dicky Birdsall, see the *Methodist*, 25 May 1940, 15.

6. Maclaren, Murray, Stirrat, Taylor, Hunt, Holland, and Gill were from Protestant families.

7. Eric Gill 1940, 59.

8. Fletcher, Walsh, Bembrick, Fellows, Bardsley, Ballantyne, and Lill were among the children of lay preachers.

9. B. T. Butcher 1963, 15.

10. E. Turner n.d.; B. T. Butcher Papers: Butcher to Mater II, 14 Jan. 1906; O. F. Tomkins Papers: Tomkins to parents, 21 Jan. 1900.

11. Navarre var. *c*, 5–12.

12. *Annales* 1910, 200.

13. Ibid.; Dupeyrat and de la Noë 1958, 10.

14. Ceresi 1934, 6.

15. Synge 1908, 3.

16. Verjus 1910, 202.

17. See Thompson 1968, 311.

18. Chalmers n.d.
19. Godwin 1951, 7; McLeod 1974, 70.
20. Godwin 1951, 2–4.
21. Ibid., 7.
22. Tomkins Diary, 12 Jan. 1898. See also Godwin 1951; E. D. Starbuck, *The Psychology of Religion* (London, 1889).
23. Eric Gill 1940, 42; see also Zeldin 1973, 1:306.
24. O. F. Tomkins Papers: Tomkins to Leo Tomkins, n.d. [1899].
25. Bromilow 1929, 19.
26. MCA-NSW var.: Francis, Waterhouse, Burgess, Holland.
27. *MR*, June 1920, 3; LMS Candidates' Papers: Tomkins, Bartlett, Beharell.
28. Synge 1908, 3.
29. *Annales* 1910, 200.
30. Dupeyrat 1951, 27.
31. Gill Letters: Gill to father 28 Jan. 1903.
32. CEA-DNG var. *e:* Newton—J. Newton to Stone-Wigg, 21 June 1904.
33. MCNZ Minutes, 8 Mar 1954, Obituary of Avery; Lloyd to Martha, 30 Sept. 1898, Letterbook 1.
34. Joseph King 1909, 9.
35. Chalmers n.d.
36. LMS Candidates' Papers.
37. Ibid.
38. Glencross 1949, 13.
39. See, for example, CEA-DNG var. *e:* Dodds, Downton, Sage.
40. CEA-*ABM Review*, May 1910, 32; Stone-Wigg Papers: Stone-Wigg to mother, 18 Feb. 1892, and Rattigan to Stone-Wigg, 5 July 1911.
41. Bromilow 1929, 22; *MR*, Nov. 1913, 5.
42. *Annales* 1893, 395; *Annales* 1921, 149; *Annales* 1926, 54.
43. Ceresi 1934, 186.
44. LMS Candidates' Papers.
45. Ibid.
46. Australian *Annals* 1894, 4–5; Dupeyrat 1951, 27.
47. LMS Candidates' Papers.
48. B. T. Butcher 1963, 15–16.
49. LMS Candidates' Papers. Keswick Conventions were annual gatherings of Evangelical Christians for prayer, Bible study, and addresses. They began in 1875 with the aim of "the promotion of practical holiness."
50. Binfield 1977, 219.
51. LMS Candidates' Papers: Hunt.
52. Of the 41 missionaries from NSW and Victoria, at least 10 were from these parishes (Appendix 3).
53. In Brittany the families of Father Guilbaud, Father Bodet, and Sister Theodorine Bachelier were related; in Savoy the family of Verjus was related to that of Father and Sister Allera.
54. *Annales* 1906, 591; *Annales* 1911, 15.
55. *Annales* 1955, 159.
56. Cuskelly 1975, 168.
57. CEA-DNG var. *e.*
58. See for example LMS Candidates' Papers: Schlencker and Ingram.
59. C. P. Williams 1976, 169.
60. LMS Candidates' Papers: Walker.
61. Ibid.

62. CEA-DNG var. *e:* (box 22), Newton to Stone-Wigg, n.d.

63. Burton 1949, 12.

64. The following analysis is based on LMS Candidates' Papers: Questions to Candidates, which is the source of all quotations unless otherwise acknowledged.

65. Oddie 1974; see also Rowell 1974, 131–215.

66. R. Howe 1965, 39.

67. Fellows Diary 1: 21 June 1886.

68. Ibid. See also Diary 5: 7 Aug. 1892; Bardsley Notebooks, 28 Nov. 1891; Tinney Diary, 19 April 1892.

69. CEA-DNG var. *f:* no. 51, 4.

70. *Annales* 1887, 228; *Annales* 1889, 26.

71. Venard 1966, 28.

72. Australian *Annals*, Aug. 1894, 198.

73. Ibid., Nov. 1894, 27.

74. Ibid., Dec. 1894, 5.

75. Ibid., Mar. 1896, 76.

76. Ceresi 1934, 186.

77. *Annales* 1893, 442–447.

78. Crosfield 1897, 107.

79. See, for example, Fellows Diary 1: 20 Feb. 1888.

80. Porter 1976, 5–33; also C. P. Williams 1976, 180–190.

81. O. F. Tomkins Papers: Tomkins to L. Tomkins, 31 Aug. 1895 Cf. Holmes Diary, 7 Aug. 1893.

82. For a useful assessment of missionary motivation see Piggin 1978, 327–337.

83. *Guardian Review*, July 1886, 143; C. P. Williams 1976, 235. See also LMS var. *g:* McFarlane to Thompson, 20 Feb. 1886.

84. MacGregor Diary 3: 6 Jan. 1892.

85. CEA-DNG var. *e:* McMullan (box 22), McMullan to Stone-Wigg, 22 Feb. 1901.

86. *Annales* 1952, 95.

87. Ibid., 1903, 32.

88. Dansette 1961, 1:3–7.

89. Eric Gill 1940, 65.

90. See S. R. M. Gill Papers: letters to family, e.g. 15 July 1943; Diary, 2 Nov. 1919.

91. For further information on missionary salaries see chapter 4.

92. Lockwood 1958, 27–28.

93. McLeod 1974, 20.

94. Chadwick 1966, 1:416–417, 522; Chadwick 1966, 2:168.

95. C. P. Williams 1976, 224.

96. K. R. Howe 1977, 43.

97. *Annales* 1885, 16.

98. LMS Candidates' Papers: Butcher.

99. Ibid.: Cullen.

100. Ceresi 1934, 190.

101. See C. P. Williams 1976, 238–240, for an interesting exploration of this theme.

102. Bromilow 1929, 22.

103. Dupeyrat 1951, 27.

104. LMS var. *i:* Chalmers to Hutchin, 25 April 1885.

105. S. R. M. Gill Papers: Gill to father, 28 Jan. 1903.

106. Potter 1974, 158–159.

107. Bromilow 1929, 19.

108. Navarre var. *c*, 136.

109. Chignell 1911, 128.

110. C. P. Williams 1976, 182.

111. CEA-DNG var. *e:* Ford to Stone-Wigg, 24 Oct. 1900.

112. See LMS Candidates' Papers: Tomkins, Butcher, Saville.

113. Vernard 1966, 59.

114. Sister Martha 1979.

115. *Methodist*, 25 May 1940.

116. Death certificate of Williams.

117. Beattie 1978.

118. Lovett 1899, 2:669.

119. Orchard n.d.

120. Maclean 1955, 59–62.

121. Orchard n.d., 12. Those who studied under Reynolds included Chalmers, Dauncey, Walker, and Abel.

122. Ibid., 13.

123. See LMS Candidates' Papers: reports of Cheshunt College students.

124. R. T. Jones 1962, 238.

125. See LMS Candidates' Papers: reports of Western College students.

126. R. T. Jones 1962, 236; Chadwick 1966, 2:105.

127. Binfield 1977, 221.

128. R. T. Jones 1962, 267.

129. Ibid.

130. Ibid. 237, 252–253.

131. See LMS Candidates' Papers: Holmes, Cribb, Bartlett.

132. Halèvy 1961, 347.

133. R. T. Jones 1962, 267.

134. LMS Candidates' Papers: Butcher, examiners' comments, 9 Sept. 1903.

135. See, for example, LMS Candidates' Papers: Bartlett, Butcher, Clark, Riley.

136. Ibid.: Harries.

137. LMS Candidates' Papers: Butcher, Whitehouse to Johnson, 12 Oct. 1903.

138. The following analysis is drawn from the lists supplied by candidates in their applications.

139. Paley's *Evidences*, a collection of illustrations that "proved" Christianity by use of external evidence such as in miracles, was both obsolete and irrelevant by the late nineteenth century. Drummond's *Natural Law* engaged superficially with the debate between science and religion, applying the laws of nature to the world of the spirit; although very successful, it did little to advance the debate, its contribution being limited by Drummond's confusion of the analogous with the identical. Farrar's *Life of Christ*, was "the best-selling biography of the late Victorian age"; it made use of the German critics but was nevertheless the work of "a man of faith for men of faith" (Chadwick 1966, 2:31).

140. Chadwick 1966, 2:67.

141. Ibid., 108.

142. Ibid., 129.

143. LMS Candidates' Papers: Clark.

144. Ibid.: Chalmers.

145. *Christian*, 1 Dec. 1904.

146. LMS var. *g:* Lawes to Thompson, 12 June 1882.

147. See Rigg 1872; Fitchett 1914.

148. Fellows studied at Three Kings, Auckland; Avery and Scrivin at Prince Alfred College, Auckland; and Burgess and Ballantyne at Queen's College, Melbourne, the latter for one year only.

149. See AWMMS-NSW 1890–1902 for prescribed content of courses.

150. Edwards 1943, 87.

151. MCA-NSW 1885–1914: Letter from students of Newington College, 22 Nov. 1913.

152. See prescribed reading lists, MCA-NSW 1902–1960.

153. Martin 1967, 78–80; Edwards 1943, 221.

154. Edwards 1943, 221.

155. Ibid., 93.

156. Rigg 1872, 150–153.

157. See, for example, MMSA 1913, Gilmour to Wheen, 9 Dec. 1913.

158. Fellows Diary 1: 5 Nov. 1885.

159. MCA-NSW 1902–1960.

160. MMSA-NGD 1891–1911*a:* Synod meeting, 10 Nov. 1891, 332. After 1900 probationers in their first year were not examined.

161. Chadwick 1966, 2:438–453.

162. K. S. Inglis 1963, 10.

163. CEA 1887, 282.

164. Ibid., 283.

165. Heeney 1976, 98.

166. CEA 1888, 4–5.

167. Ibid., 635–636.

168. Ibid., 636–652.

169. CEA-DNG var. *e:* Giblin, Ramsay, Tomlinson, Shaw.

170. *Book of Common Prayer;* Cross 1958.

171. Stone-Wigg Papers: Stone-Wigg to mother, 27 Apr. 1900.

172. *Annales* 1904, 741; 1955, 100; Rumble 1950, 8–9.

173. Australian *Annals*, June 1894, 151.

174. As in all orders and congregations, the novitiate was a mandatory period of preparation for the taking of vows, in which the novice reflected on his vocation, studied the constitutions and rules of the congregation, recognized the obligations imposed by the vows, adapted to an ordered communal existence, clarified his faith, and, by conquering himself, tried to regulate his life in accordance with the will of God.

175. *Annales* 1893, 11.

176. *Annales* 1955, 188–190; Dupeyrat 1951, 28.

177. Cross 1958.

178. Australian *Annals*, Oct. 1894, 247.

179. Dansette 1961, 1:6–7.

180. Among them professors Talamo, Sepiacci, Checchi, Ulbaldi, Turzi, Penacchi, and Satolli. (See Australian *Annals*, Feb. 1897, 55.)

181. Ceresi 1934, 36–40.

182. Ibid.

183. Ibid.; *Annales* 1921, 181.

184. *Annales* 1905, 648.

185. Navarre, var. *c*, 22.

186. SMSC var. *c:* Chevalier to Jouet, 27 May 1883.
187. Ceresi 1934, 190, 211; Dupeyrat 1951, 11–15.
188. F. Walker 1888.
189. LMS var. *g:* McFarlane to Whitehouse, 23 June 1874; Riley to Thompson, 18 July 1900.
190. Ibid.: Riley to Thompson, 18 Jan. 1900; F. Walker 1888.
191. *MR,* July 1941, 1.
192. Ibid., June 1902, 8.
193. E. Walker Dobu Diary, May 1892; Fellows Diary 3, July 1891; Beswick Diary, Oct. 1878–1879; Billing Diary 1; O. F. Tomkins Papers: Letters to parents, 1899–1900.
194. *Annales* 1895, 700; *Annales* 1899, 149; *Annales* 1911, 22.

Chapter 3: "The Object Lesson of a Civilized Christian Home"

1. F. Walker 1888, 18–19.
2. Billing Diary 1: 3 Jan. 1895, 60.
3. *MR,* Oct. 1891, 4.
4. B. T. Butcher, letter to *SMH,* 29 Mar. 1912.
5. See for instance, LMS var. *g:* Dauncey to Thompson, 6 Nov. 1900 and Lawes to Thompson, 3 Sept. 1888.
6. Ibid.: Lawes to Thompson, 3 Sept. 1888.
7. Ibid.: Hunt to Thompson, 23 Jan. 1900.
8. MMSA-NGD 1913–1914: Gilmour to Wheen, 1 July 1914.
9. See for example LMS var. *j:* Chalmers Report 1896; LMS var. *g:* Schlencker to Thompson, 1 May 1902; MMSA 1913: Williams to Danks, 28 Jan.
10. LMS var. *g:* Hunt to Thompson, 3 June 1901.
11. Ibid.
12. LMS var. *k:* Thompson to Dauncey, 9 Feb. 1904.
13. Bromilow 1929, 23.
14. LMS var. *k:* Thompson to Cribb, 1 Jan. 1897.
15. LMS 1873 *b;* LMS 1892, no. 10.
16. Beswick Diary, 2 Oct. 1880; LMS var. *k:* Whitehouse to Beswick, 4 July 1879. Beswick finally agreed reluctantly to serve the LMS for two years, after which he met and married his fiancée in Australia. Her health having been cleared, he set out with her to return to New Guinea, but died at Townsville from pneumonia.
17. George Brown, MOM Letterbooks: to Field, 3 May 1894.
18. Ibid.: to Bromilow, 8 May 1895.
19. LMS var. *g:* Riley to Thompson, 18 April 1904.
20. Ibid.: Saville to Thompson, 3 May 1902; Turner to Thompson, 4 Jan. 1908.
21. Ibid.: Saville to Thompson, 1 Jan. 1903; Turner to Thompson, 27 Dec. 1903.
22. MMSA 1909–1910: James Williams to Danks n.d. [1909].
23. LMS var. *i:* Lizzie Chalmers to Harrie Hill, 5 Apr. 1908.
24. Billing Diary 1:60; R. W. Abel 1934, 73.
25. *MR,* Sept. 1893, 4; see also Holmes Diary, 5 June 1908.
26. F. Walker Journal, 23 May 1892.
27. Stone-Wigg Diary 2:161.
28. LMS var. *g:* Lawes to Thompson, 1 Aug. 1903.
29. LMS var. *k:* Thompson to Abel, 6 Jan. 1893.
30. McFarlane 1888, 189.

31. Teale 1977, 119.
32. Holmes Diary, 18 Jan. 1908; see also LMS var. *g:* Riley to Thompson, 11 July 1912.
33. B. T. Butcher 1963, 63.
34. LMS var. *i:* Jane Chalmers to Harrie Hill, 26 July 1877.
35. Lloyd Letterbook, 23 July 1901.
36. LMS var. *i:* Lizzie Chalmers to Harrie Hill, 15 Mar. 1890.
37. LMS var. *g:* Dauncey, Notes on PDC Minutes, 1912.
38. Ibid.: Lawes to Thompson, 11 May 1904.
39. Ibid.: 28 Dec. 1903.
40. Ibid.: Harries, 10 Feb. 1914; Riley, 13 Apr. 1914; Butcher, 23 Apr. 1914; Burrows, 28 Oct. 1914.
41. Mitchell and Deane 1962, 36–37; Banks 1954, 194; F. B. Smith 1979, 65 & 122–123. Cf. Coghlan 1901, 85 & 92. In NSW the infant mortality rate was comparable to that of Britain. Over the years from 1895–1901, it averaged 110.9 deaths per 1000 live births.
42. *MR*, Aug. 1895, 2.
43. Ibid.; LMS var. *g:* Rich to Thompson, n.d. [July 1911] and 13 Oct. 1911.
44. Lawes Diary, 98.
45. Ibid., 97; LMS var. *g:* Rich to Thompson, n.d. [July 1911] and 13 Oct. 1911.
46. B. T. Butcher 1963, 184.
47. LMS var. *g:* Pearse to Thompson, 16 May 1899.
48. Ibid.
49. Pryce Jones Letter-diary 1900, 208.
50. LMS var. *g:* Dauncey to Thompson, 8 Oct. 1913.
51. Ibid., 9 Sept. 1914.
52. LMS var. *g:* Lawes to Thompson, 18 Mar. 1876.
53. See *MR*, Dec. 1915, 23, on Burgess children; Lloyd Letterbook 4, 11 July 1911, on golden-haired Ruve Bromilow; LMS var. *g:* Rich, 3 May 1902, on the influence of his blue-eyed baby; B. T. Butcher 1963, 141, on blue-eyed Phyllis; and LMS var. *g:* Mrs. Bartlett, 6 Nov. 1910, on her blue-eyed child, the first in the Delta region.
54. See LMS var. *k:* Missionaries' Warrants for each year.
55. MCA 1904, 55.
56. See, for example, Gunson 1978, 159–160.
57. See Green, letter of 27 Mar. 1895; Fellows Diary 5: 23 Aug. 1894; Pryce Jones Letter-diary 1900, 33.
58. Brown MOM Letterbook: to Bromilow, 6 Dec. 1895.
59. Pryce Jones Letter-diary 1900, 239; Cecil Abel 1978.
60. B. T. Butcher Papers: Butcher to wife, 8 Dec. 1920.
61. Fellows Diary 6: 29 Sept. 1899.
62. Pryce Jones Letter-diary 1900, 29.
63. Ibid., 44.
64. B. T. Butcher Papers: Butcher to wife, 12 Apr. 1920.
65. Ibid., 14 Nov. 1937.
66. LMS var. *g:* Lawes to Thompson, 22 May 1879, 29 June 1890; ibid.: Chalmers to Thompson, 11 Feb. 1884.
67. Ibid.: Lawes to Thompson, 28 Dec. 1903; LMS var. *k:* Thompson to Pearse, 13 Dec. 1891.
68. E.g. Brown Letterbook, 6 Dec. 1895.

69. Banks 1954, 3–10; McLeod 1974, 270; F. B. Smith 1979, 300–302.
70. Glass 1967, 427n.
71. Banks 1954, 144.
72. B. T. Butcher Papers: Butcher to wife, 17 Oct. 1920.
73. Ibid.: Diary letter to wife, 1920, 21.
74. C. Rogers 1900.
75. McAuley 1961.
76. B. T. Butcher Papers: Butcher to Mrs. Holtumm, 13 Dec. 1913.
77. LMS var. *g:* Quoted in Hunt to Thompson, 3 June 1901.
78. Ibid.: Holmes to Thompson, 29 June 1910.
79. LMS var. *i:* Lizzie Chalmers to Harrie Hill, 22 June 1891.
80. Ibid., 15 Jan. 1890.
81. Lutton 1979, 40.
82. LMS var. *g:* Edith Turner to Thompson, 29 June 1891.
83. Holmes Diary, 21 Nov. 1898.
84. McLaren 1946, 91.
85. Joseph King 1909, 77.
86. Ibid., 288.
87. J. H. P. Murray 1912, 27–28.
88. BNG *AR* 1895–1896, xxiv.
89. SMSC var. *d:* Navarre to MacGregor, 31 July 1897.
90. Ibid.
91. E.g. *Annales* 1906, 206.
92. Dupeyrat 1934, 168.
93. Maclaren 1890, 7 May.
94. MacGregor Diary 1: 14 Nov. 1890.
95. *Annales* 1895, 523.
96. Grimshaw 1913, 15–16.
97. *Annales* 1895, 452; *Annales* 1900, 567; *Annales* 1907, 83; *Annales* 1911, 458.
98. Hurley Diary, 12 July 1921, 17.
99. Ibid., 10 July 1921, 12.
100. Navarre var. *b:* Notes 1886.
101. *Annales* 1893, 92–93.
102. See, for instance, BNG *AR* 1890, 19–20.
103. Hurley 1924, 67; Hurley Diary D, 70; see also Maclaren Diary, 7 May 1890, 9; Grimshaw 1913, 55.
104. LMS var. *g:* Lawes to Thompson, 29 Sept. 1890.
105. CEA-DNG 1891–1914: *Ninth Anniversary Address* 1900, 5.
106. CEA-DNG var. *e:* Stone-Wigg to Ramsay, 5 May 1908.
107. Ibid.: E. Tomlinson to Stone-Wigg, 7 Sept. 1907.
108. Ibid.: Stone-Wigg, Farewell letter, 30 Sept. 1908.
109. Newton 1914, 49; Stone-Wigg Papers: letter to mother, 22 Jan. 1897.
110. Stuart 1970*a*, 78.
111. Stone-Wigg Papers, 22 Nov. 1897.
112. Newton 1914, 15; see also CEA-DNG var. *f:* Apr. 1912.
113. CEA-DNG var. *f:* Oct. 1906.
114. Ibid.: Jan. 1915.
115. CEA-DNG var. *e:* Laura Oliver, inventory.
116. Wetherell 1970, 191.
117. Hurley Diary D, 10 July 1921; cf. BNG *AR* 1899–1900, app. C.

Chapter 4: "Books and Quinine"

1. It was common for the congregations founded in the nineteenth century to require simple rather than solemn vows, because of the legal complexities of the latter.

2. CEA-DNG var. *e:* Paper of Conditions.

3. LMS 1873, 1892.

4. Ibid.

5. Ibid.

6. LMS var. *k:* WOL Missionaries' Warrants.

7. LMS var. *g:* Dauncey to Thompson, 27 May 1889. Government salaries were considerably higher. In 1889–1890, resident magistrates earned £300–£500, government agents £250. Lawes' salary was less than that of his son, a government agent.

8. E.g. LMS var. *g:* Hunt, 3 April 1889, and Lawes to Thompson, 5 July 1888.

9. Instructions to Missionaries, no. 10.

10. See MCA 1904, 55; 1913, 66.

11. MMSA-NGD: Journal of Synod 1902, Res. 5; George Brown, MOM Letterbooks: to Bromilow, 4 Feb. 1903.

12. Vaudon 1899, 83.

13. LMS var. *g:* Lawes to Thompson, 17 June 1890.

14. Hilliard 1978, 146.

15. Dupeyrat 1934, 385–386.

16. Lawes Diary, 22 Feb. 1876.

17. Chignell 1913, 105; CEA-DNG var. *e:* Abbot.

18. White 1923, 43.

19. Geil 1902, 211; *MR*, Nov. 1906, 10.

20. B. T. Butcher Papers: to Miss Holtumm, 10 Sept. 1912.

21. Green Letters, 18 Mar. 1895, 18.

22. Grimshaw 1913, 16.

23. *Annales* 1891, 452.

24. McLaren 1946, 121; *Annales* 1955, 217; Grimshaw 1913, 16.

25. Chignell 1911, 288.

26. Dauncey Letterbook: to Burns, Philp & Co., 19 Nov. 1891.

27. B. T. Butcher Papers: to Mrs. Holtumm, 22 Jan. 1905.

28. CEA-DNG var. *f:* 19 Sept. 1908, 4.

29. Newton 1914, 66.

30. LMS var. *g:* Riley to Thompson, 5 Jan. 1910, B. T. Butcher Papers: Ena Butcher to parents, 27 July 1913.

31. Maclaren 1891: to Mrs. Laidley, 9 Sept. 1891.

32. Tinney 1892–1902, 2:191.

33. *MR*, Oct. 1907, 13.

34. White 1923, 31.

35. B. T. Butcher Papers: to Mrs. Holtumm, 30 Jan. 1914.

36. Ibid.: to wife, 12 Apr. 1920; cf. Chignell 1911, 289.

37. BNG *AR* 1889, 19.

38. In 1906 the SHM had 100 head of cattle on Yule Island and 200 on the mainland.

39. Ceresi 1934, 204–205.

40. MacGregor 1890–1892, 3:9.

41. Green Letters: 21 Sept. 1892, 16.

42. Billing 1894–1898, 3:9.
43. Gill Diary, 3 Nov. 1914.
44. E.g. Lawes Diary, 8 Apr. 1882; Holmes 1900–1916: Holmes to Dauncey, 10 Sept. 1903.
45. LMS var. *g:* Bruce to Thompson, 30 Jan. 1894.
46. *Annales* 1905, 267; *Annales* 1945, 89.
47. SMSC var. *d:* Receipts and correspondence.
48. Ibid.: MacGregor to Navarre, 24 Nov. 1897.
49. Ceresi 1934, 239.
50. *Annales* 1911, 459; Hurley Diary D, 35.
51. *MR*, Aug. 1892, 8; Chignell 1911, 304; Ross 1923, 118ff.
52. *Annales* 1894, 273.
53. Ibid., 279.
54. CEA-DNG var. *f:* 17 Sept. 1908, 4.
55. *Annales* 1895, 22.
56. B. T. Butcher 1963, 49; Chignell 1913, 296–299.
57. *MR*, Feb. 1906, 3.
58. Charles Abel 1902, 168.
59. Newton 1914, 65.
60. Lawes 1887, 185.
61. George Brown, MOM Letterbooks: to Fellows, 15 Sept. 1902; Chignell 1913, 308–309; Lovett 1903, 346; *MR*, May 1898, 8.
62. MacGregor, Introduction to Synge 1908. However Maclaren mentions several times in his diary and letters that he had taken quinine, without alluding to adverse effects. In the Methodist Mission, after the death of Sister Lise Truscott, the sisters passed a resolution requiring that ability to tolerate quinine should be a prerequisite of missionary service.
63. E.g. George Brown, MOM Letterbooks: to Fellows, 15 Sept. 1902; Lawes 1887, 186; *Annales* 1905, 207.
64. MacGregor Diary 1: 25 Nov. 1890.
65. LMS var. *g:* Lawes to Thompson, 1 Nov. 1886.
66. Maclaren [1891]: to Primate, 10 Nov. 1891; Stone-Wigg var. *b*, 2:163.
67. Lawes 1887, 185–186.
68. R. Ross 1923, 201–291.
69. George Brown, MOM Letterbooks: to Fletcher, 19 July 1900.
70. Lloyd Journal 5, 4 Nov. 1900; *Annales* 1910, 500.
71. CEA-DNG 1891–1920 (1911): 14.
72. E.g. LMS var. *g:* Lawrence to Lenwood, 3 Dec. 1915.
73. M. S. Smith 1909, 12.
74. Adams and Magraith 1966, 48–49.
75. Andrew Ballantyne in *Methodist* 1915.
76. See Haddon 1901, 276; SMSC var. *d:* Kowald to MacGregor, 24 Sept. 1892.
77. Edward Clark, died 1899.
78. Chignell 1913, 292.
79. CEA-ABM, var.: Tomlinson to Hughes, 15 Oct. 1893.
80. Maclaren Diary, 20 May 1890; see also BNG *AR* 1890, 19.
81. MacGregor Diary 3: 14 Sept. 1892; *Annales* 1892, 333.
82. LMS var. *g:* Hunt to Thompson, 13 Jan. 1901.
83. Ceresi 1934, 252.
84. B. T. Butcher Papers: to wife, 12 Apr. 1906.
85. LMS var. *g:* Holmes to Thompson, 17 Apr. 1896.

86. *MR*, July 1902, 8.
87. Billing var.: Walker to Billing, 30 Aug. 1899.
88. Haddon 1901, 252.
89. Ibid.; *MR* Jan. 1902, 9.
90. *Annales* 1955, 193.
91. Dupeyrat 1951, 126; Hurley 1924, 157; *Annales* 1895, 221.
92. *Annales* 1937, 193; *Annales* 1946, 29; *Annales* 1952, 95.
93. Dupeyrat and de la Noë 1958, 61.
94. S. R. M. Gill var: letter to mother, 31 Aug. 1922.
95. B. T. Butcher Papers: to parents, 3 June 1913.
96. Ibid.
97. E.g. Bardsley Diary, 15 Sept. 1891; Holmes Diary, 20 Dec. 1894.
98. B. T. Butcher Papers: Ena Butcher to parents, 3 June 1913. *Sartor Resartus*, *On Heroes*, and *Past and Present* were published in 1888 as *Carlyle's Works* (London: G. Routledge & Sons). *The French Revolution: A history* was published in 1837 (London: James Frazer).
99. Lloyd Journal 5: 4 Nov. 1899; S. R. M. Gill var.: Diary, 22 Oct. 1916; Billing Diary 1.
100. B. T. Butcher Diary, 9 Sept. 1912; S. R. M. Gill var.: letter to mother, 1 Oct. 1922.
101. Lenwood 1917, 156.
102. See inventories of books owned by King (CEA-DNG var. *e:* King), Saville 1902–1930; Fellows 1883–1900: Diary; Bardsley 1892–1893; Billing var.
103. Stone-Wigg, var. *b*, 1:111–117; ibid., 2:26; Bardsley Diary, 28 Nov. 1891.
104. James B. Mozley, *Eight Lectures on Miracles* . . . (London, 1865). See also Chadwick 1966, 2:62, 131.
105. B. T. Butcher Papers: to Mrs. Holtumm, 9 Aug. 1914.
106. Synge 1908, 52; Stone-Wigg Diary 1:105; Chadwick 1966, 2:101. *Lux Mundi: A Series of Studies in the Religion of the Incarnation*, edited by Charles Gore, was published in 1889.
107. CEA-DNG var. *e:* Combley to Stone-Wigg, n.d. [1901]; Chignell 1913, 69.
108. B. T. Butcher Papers: to Holtumm, 3 Apr. 1906; cf. Saville 1902–1930: letter to brother, 21 Sept. 1906.
109. LMS var. *g:* Lawes to Thompson, 2 June 1883.
110. Saville 1902–1930: letter to brother, 20 July 1908; Danks 1900–1914: letter to Gilmour, 17 May 1910.
111. *Annales* 1893, 11.
112. *Annales* 1903, 29.
113. CEA-DNG var. *e:* Combley to Stone-Wigg, 10 June 1902; cf. *Annales* 1904, 275.
114. Chignell 1911, 259–263.
115. See Beswick 1878–1880 (cover): list of mail services.
116. LMS var. *g:* Abel to Thompson, 12 Jan. 1911.
117. Billing var.: to Lizzie (Nicholls), 1 July & 28 Dec. 1895.
118. Chignell 1911, 250.
119. Chalmers 1895, chapters 11 & 12; *Annales* 1890, 530–539.
120. E.g. Danks 1900–1914: letter to Gilmour, 4 Nov. 1910; B. T. Butcher 1963, 83.
121. For the best account of the boats of the SHM see Henkelmann 1949.
122. See LMS var. *g:* letters to Thompson from Walker, 1 May & 13 May 1896, 30 April 1897, and from Abel, 8 Sept. 1896.

123. Barradale n.d., 11.
124. Newton 1914, 37.
125. *Annales* 1887, 3⁻⁻.
126. *MR*, Dec. 1892, 2.
127. LMS var. *g:* Burns Philp to Chalmers, 11 Jan. 1893.
128. Burns Philp var.
129. Henkelmann 1949, 101.
130. Ibid., cf. *Annales* 1898, 264.
131. T. W. Reid 1960, 57.
132. Tomlin 1951, 50.
133. *Dundee Advertiser*, 25 Apr. 1901.
134. Henkelmann 1949.
135. B. T. Butcher 1963.
136. *Annales* 1889, 74 and 148; Butcher 1963, 52.
137. Navarre var. *b:* Journal 1892; see also *Annales* 1889, 414; *Annales* 1895, 221.
138. Frederick Walker Journal, 25 Jan. 1888.
139. Ibid., 28 Jan. 1888.
140. Ibid.; LMS var. *j:* Chalmers, Report 1897.
141. MMSA var. *a:* 1908, 138.
142. The electric telegraph was extended to Cooktown in 1874.
143. *MR*, Sept. 1915, 10; ibid.: Oct. 1915, 21.
144. CEA-DNG var. *f:* 36, 1913.
145. Lloyd Journal 2: 9 June 1899.

Chapter 5: "Though Every Prospect Pleases"

1. *Encyclopaedia Britannica*, 9th ed., s.v. "Papua."
2. This chapter does not enter the debate on the meaning and utility of the concept "culture." It uses the term in the sense employed by Geertz's definition: "an historically transmitted pattern of meanings embodied in symbols . . . by means of which men communicate, perpetuate and develop their knowledge about and attitudes towards life" (1966, 3).
3. For an elaboration of this concept see Bernard Smith 1960, 55ff.
4. Joseph King 1909, 136, 150.
5. Beswick Diary, 28 Feb. 1879.
6. LMS var. *g:* Holmes to Thompson, 29 Dec. 1894.
7. *MR*, Mar. 1908, 7.
8. AWMMS var. *a:* 1897, xxiii.
9. MMSA var. *a:* 1910, 114; *MR*, Aug. 1914, 21.
10. *MR*, Oct. 1897, 4.
11. Holmes Diary, 1 Jan. 1894; *MR*, June 1901, 2.
12. Joseph King 1909, 137.
13. Ibid.
14. Frederick Walker Journal, 18 Sept. 1888.
15. Holmes Diary, 2 Aug. 1893.
16. Bardsley Diary, 5, 17, and 20 July 1891.
17. *Annales* 1889, 455.
18. Ibid., 1893, 209.
19. Ibid., 1893, 209; ibid., 1901, 682; ibid., 1908, 326.
20. Ibid., 1888, 131; ibid., 1895, 584.
21. Maclaren var.: Letterbook 4:95.
22. CEA-ABM *Review*, 15 Nov. 1910, 169.

23. CEA-DNG 1891–1920 (1905): 204.

24. Bromilow 1914, 543; Bromilow 1929, 98; AWMMS var. *a:* 1897, lxvi.

25. Lawes Diary, 37.

26. Turner 1878, 470–475.

27. E.g. Lawes 1879, 69–77; Chalmers 1898, 326–342 and 1903*a;* Guis 1936; Fellows 1901, 47; see also J. T. Field 1898, 134; J. T. Field 1900.

28. LMS var. *j:* Pearse Report 1896.

29. Lloyd Journal 6: 18 May 1901.

30. McFarlane 1888, 34, 95.

31. Ibid., 131–132.

32. Holmes Diary, 3 Sept. 1893, 26 Nov. 1894, 29 Oct. 1897, 3 Nov. 1897.

33. Ibid., 10 Jan. 1899. For Holmes' anthropological studies, see bibliography. For a more detailed analysis of the evolution of Holmes' anthropological thought, see Reid 1978, 173–187.

34. Holmes 1924, preface.

35. Malinowski 1967, 16.

36. Saville 1926, foreword.

37. Haddon 1935, 1: 16; Riley 1925.

38. Holmes Papers: Haddon to Holmes, 21 July 1905.

39. J. T. Field 1898, 134; J. T. Field 1900.

40. Information from Dr. M. Macintyre, LaTrobe University, Melbourne.

41. *Annales* 1946, 29; R. W. Abel 1934, 214.

42. Egidi 1907, 107–115; Egidi 1913 *b,* 1914.

43. Williamson 1912, vii.

44. Gsell 1955, 173–174.

45. E.g. Prisk 1919, 61; *MR,* May 1907, 2–3; Stone-Wigg 1912, 37.

46. Dupeyrat 1951, 88.

47. *Annales* 1913, 138.

48. Joseph King 1909, 138.

49. Bromilow 1914, 594; see also Bromilow 1929, 87–90; William Y. Turner 1878, 492; LMS var. *g:* Chalmers to Thompson, 28 Oct. 1882; C. W. Abel 1902, 99; Navarre var. *b:* Journal 1887; *Annales* 1891, 451.

50. LMS var. *j:* Dauncey, Report 1896; Saville 1902–1930: letter to brother, 8 Oct. 1902; *MR* July 1892, 5.

51. Stone-Wigg 1912, 20–41.

52. Ibid., 11.

53. Ibid., 29.

54. Quiggan 1942, 124.

55. Saville 1931, 24.

56. B. T. Butcher 1963, 121.

57. Holmes 1924, 150–155, and Papers.

58. Stone-Wigg 1912, 30.

59. B. T. Butcher 1963, 121.

60. Charles Abel 1902, 87.

61. Holmes Diary, 30 June 1895; Pryce Jones Letter-diary, 19 Nov. 1900.

62. Bromilow 1929, 85.

63. Newton 1914, 72.

64. Chignell 1911, 190.

65. Ibid., 29.

66. Mannoni 1956, 108–109. The missionaries differed from Mannoni's stereotype in that they did not seek a world devoid of people.

67. *Annales* 1887, 187.

68. Ibid., 1890, 28; ibid., 1893, 2–3.

69. Ibid., 1895, 582.

70. Holmes Diary, 7 Mar. 1898; LMS var. *j:* Butcher, Report 1906; Maclaren Letterbook 4, 9 Sept. 1891; Chignell 1911, 30.

71. Joseph King 1909, 136.

72. CEA-DNG var. *f:* 26 Apr. 1911.

73. Holmes Diary, 17 June 1899.

74. Chignell 1911, 201.

75. Saville 1902–1930: letter to brother, 8 Oct. 1902.

76. De Boismenu 1905, 270; *Oeuvres Pontificales* 1911, 610.

77. Holmes Diary, 14 July 1898; LMS var. *j:* Schlencker, Report 1907.

78. Stone-Wigg Diary 2:169.

79. The monogenists believed that humankind sprang from a single pair of human beings, whose descendants gradually peopled the earth, and became divisible into "races" owing to changes wrought by climate and other external conditions. The polygenists maintained that humankind belonged to different stock derived from different species, repudiating the Mosaic account of creation. Monogenists found difficulty in explaining the diversity of humanity in the relatively short time span which they reckoned to have passed since Adam, and also in explaining different types in the same climatic conditions. Polygenists had to account for breeding across species. Although there was not a thorough correlation, polygenists tended to be racial determinists, while monogenists, with their belief in the unity and modifiability of humankind, were less prone to this conclusion, although in America monogenism was reconciled with racism.

80. Harris 1969, 84; Biddis 1979, 16.

81. McFarlane 1888, 96, 98.

82. Bromilow 1929, 93, 114.

83. *Annales* 1899, 86.

84. Cairns, 1965, 74. For a nineteenth-century exposition of this belief see Biddis 1979, 141–155.

85. Holmes Papers: "The schools of Namau."

86. LMS var. *g:* Abel to Thompson, 30 Apr. 1891.

87. Ibid., Pryce Jones to Thompson, 3 Dec. 1902.

88. Holmes Diary, 18 Apr. 1904.

89. Joseph King 1909, 338.

90. Bromilow 1929, 289–290.

91. LMS var. *g:* Burrows to Thompson, 3 Sept. 1913.

92. De Boismenu 1905, 272.

93. ABM *Herald* 1 (2): Oct. 1910.

94. *SMH,* 9 Apr. 1902.

95. J. H. P. Murray Diary, 18 June 1905, 45.

96. Papua *AR 1937–38,* 20–21.

97. Cairns 1965, 81–84; Van den Berghe 1967, 32.

98. Herbert Spencer, *The Principles of Sociology* (3 vols. London: Williams & Norgate, 1876–1896). See also Harris 1969, 134–136.

99. Charles Abel 1902, 42, 45, 128, and preface.

100. BNG *AR 1887,* 25; *Annales* 1895, 214; Saville 1902–1930: letter, 8 Oct. 1902.

101. Joseph King 1909, 338.

102. Stone-Wigg 1912, 39; Newton 1914, 97; Chignell 1911, 102.

103. Australian *Annals,* June 1908, 220; *Annales* 1904, 402.

104. B. T. Butcher Papers: Diary 1905.
105. Holmes Diary, 5 May 1894, 14 Nov. 1897; C. W. Abel 1902, 41.
106. Stone-Wigg 1912, 36–37; Newton 1914, 107; Eleanor Walker Diary 1892, 3; Billing Papers: letter, 17 Aug. 1895; *MR*, Sept. 1896, 5.
107. Australia . . . 1907: Ballantyne's evidence.
108. De Boismenu 1905, 270; Stone-Wigg 1933, 30–31.
109. Stone-Wigg 1912, 36, 40; Prisk 1919, 47; McFarlane 1888, 104.
110. Newton 1914, 48, 72; *Annales* 1898, 507–508.
111. Chignell 1911, 232.
112. AWMMS var. *a:* 1902, xlvii.
113. Maclaren 1891: letter, 9 Nov. 1891.
114. Stone-Wigg 1912, 46; Bromilow 1929, 83.
115. *Annales* 1886, 39.
116. LMS var. *g:* Holmes, Answers to questions 1915.
117. Joseph King 1909, 138.
118. Kwato Mission Papers: *Universal Brotherhood*, Jan. 1913.
119. Bromilow 1929, 97.
120. Burridge 1975, 10.
121. Joseph King 1909, 139.
122. LMS var. *g:* Beharell, Answers to questions, 1915.
123. See, for example, Joseph King 1909, 336; McFarlane 1873, 105; LMS var. *j:* Pearse, *Report* 1904; Beswick Diary; Holmes Diary. Cf. Pitt-Rivers, 1927*a*, 60, on effect of nudity on celibate clergy.
124. Stone-Wigg Diary 2:161.
125. LMS var. *j:* Lawes, Report 1893; LMS var. *g:* Lawes to Blayney, 14 July 1898.
126. SMSC var. *d:* Navarre to Douglas, 4 May 1887.
127. Hau'ofa 1975, 17.
128. Newton 1914, 251–252.
129. *MR*, Apr. 1912, 16; Copland King 1899, 26; Sharp 1917.
130. *MR*, Apr. 1912, 16.
131. C. Stuart Ross 1903, 467; see also LMS var. *g:* PDC Minutes 1914.
132. Holmes Diary, 9 Sept. 1899.
133. Copland King 1899, 26.
134. Fellows Diary, 15 Nov. 1891.
135. Danks Letterbook: to Ballantyne, 1 Feb. 1912.
136. Navarre var. *b:* Journal 1887, 21.
137. Pitt-Rivers 1927*a*, 138–140.
138. J. H. P. Murray 1930.
139. Dupeyrat 1934, 369.
140. Australia . . . 1907: evidence 2739.
141. Dupeyrat 1929, 370.
142. LMS var. *g:* Chalmers to Thompson, 31 May 1893; B. T. Butcher 1963, 181ff. It seems that Chalmers was probably mistaken in his belief that the *moguru* involved ritual sodomy (see Hely Journal, 19 Apr. 1893).
143. CEA-DNG var. *e:* Dakers, to Stone-Wigg, 7 June 1901; ibid.: Newton, to Stone-Wigg, 6 Jan. 1902 and 31 May 1902.
144. B. T. Butcher 1963, 186.
145. E.g. Holmes Diary, 14 June 1897; Navarre var. *b:* Journal, 1887, 22.
146. Pitt-Rivers 1930; see also Chinnery 1932, 163–175.
147. Pitt-Rivers 1930.
148. F. E. Williams 1940, 430–431.

149. E. Rogers 1920, 129.
150. T. W. Reid 1960, 70.
151. Navarre 1896, v–vii.
152. Van den Berghe 1967, 26ff. This analysis is based on his useful model of paternalism.
153. Charles Abel 1902, 99.
154. Chignell 1911, 212.
155. Hurley Diary 8, 114.
156. E.g. Chignell 1911, 40–41, 50–51, 55–57, 72–73.
157. Chalmers 1895, 146–186.
158. Joseph King 1909, 232.
159. Rumble 1950, 28; *Annales* 1901, 47.
160. Langmore 1974, 63; Synge 1908, 150.
161. Holmes Diary, 22 Oct. 1900.
162. CEA-DNG var. *e:* Abbot, to Stone-Wigg, 27 Mar. 1900; ibid.: King, to Stone-Wigg, 13 Feb. 1900.
163. Lenwood 1917, 167; Lloyd Journal 5: 13 Oct. 1900.
164. George Brown, MOM Letterbooks: to Bromilow, 10 Mar. 1896; ibid.: to Williams, 20 Dec. 1898.
165. CEA-DNG var. *g:* Minutes of meeting, 13 Jan. 1904.
166. BNG *AR* 1893–94, app. B, 5; J. H. P. Murray Diary, 27 Jan. 1909, 7.
167. Navarre 1896, 49.
168. CEA-DNG *Anniversary Address*, 1913. *Bada:* literally *big;* used as term of respect.
169. MMSA-NGD Synod Journal 1911, 443.
170. LMS var. *g:* answers to deputation questions 1915.
171. Saville 1902–1930: Letter to bro., 8 Oct. 1902.
172. See, for example, Australia . . . 1907: evidence 3; MacKay 1909, 40.
173. *SMH*, 29 Mar. 1912.
174. *Annales* 1893, 330.
175. B. T. Butcher 1963, 128.
176. B. T. Butcher Papers: letter fragment, n.d. [1928].
177. Burridge 1973, 205.
178. Luzbetak 1967, 148; Cairns 1965, 220–221.
179. Cairns 1965, 220–221; Burton 1949, 158.
180. White 1929, 11.
181. CEA-DNG var. *f:* 44, 3.
182. Abel 1902, 22.

Chapter 6: "Preaching, Teaching and Knocking Around"

1. O. F. Tomkins Diary, 7 April 1901.
2. E.g. Holmes Papers: "Stories of Namau," 6; LMS var. *g:* Pearse to Thompson, 14 Nov. 1891.
3. Lovett 1903, 212.
4. For Lawes' explorations see Joseph King 1909 and Lawes Diary.
5. For Chalmers' explorations see Chalmers and Gill 1885; Chalmers 1887*a;* also Lovett 1903; Langmore 1974.
6. Dupeyrat 1934, 300–321, 325–338.
7. See for example the literature based on Chalmers' pioneering expeditions in Lovett (n.d.); Seton (n.d.), Small (1923), and Nairne (1913).
8. Bardsley Diary, 9 June 1891.

9. LMS var. *i:* Jane Chalmers to Harrie Hill, 18 June 1897.

10. *Christian World*, 29 Mar. 1904.

11. Ibid.; Chalmers 1887.

12. Charles Abel 1902, 160.

13. See Chalmers and Gill, 1885.

14. Dupeyrat 1934, 300–321, 325–338; *Annales* 1911, 215–216; *Annales* 1923, 139.

15. Chalmers and Gill 1885, 83; Musgrave Papers: Confidential memo.

16. Stephen 1974, 84, 92n; also Langmore 1974, 58, 140n.

17. LMS var. *g:* Chalmers to Mullens, 25 Aug. 1880; Cf. *Annales* 1888, 131.

18. E.g. *Annales* 1901, 681; C. W. Abel 1902, 39.

19. *Annales* 1885, 322.

20. Maclaren 1891: 4 Sept.

21. Fellows Diary, 10 Nov. 1891.

22. LMS var. *g:* Chalmers to Mullens, Oct. 1882.

23. Navarre 1896, 31, also 23–30.

24. CEA-DNG 1898–1900: 30 May 1898.

25. Maclaren 1891: 8 Nov.; *Annales* 1887, 271.

26. Lovett 1903, 227; cf. *MR*, May 1909, 6; *Oeuvres Pontificales* . . . 1911, 607.

27. Chignell 1913, 123.

28. Lawes Diary, 25 June 1876.

29. LMS var. *g:* Chalmers to Mullens, 24 Jan. 1898.

30. Maclaren 1891: 25 Aug.

31. B. T. Butcher Papers: to Mrs. Holtumm, 7 Oct. 1909.

32. AWMMS var. *a:* 1897, lxvi.

33. Fellows Diary, 7 Aug. 1892.

34. Dupeyrat 1934, 200.

35. E.g. MacGregor Diary, 24 July 1892; CEA-ABM *Review*, 15 Apr. 1910, 7.

36. Fellows Diary 1892.

37. Australian *Annals*, Apr. 1899, 149; *Annales* 1887, 228.

38. CEA-DNG 1898–1900: 30 Aug. 1900; B. T. Butcher Papers: Diary, 1905.

39. Fellows Diary, 7 Aug., 11 Sept. 1892; *Annales* 1899, 23.

40. Lawes Diary, 3 Feb. 1876.

41. Ibid., 1874–1876.

42. *Annales* 1905, 514.

43. *Brisbane Daily Telegraph*, 31 Dec. 1891.

44. Fellows Diary, 4 Sept. 1891.

45. Lovett, n.d.

46. Holmes Diary, June 1916.

47. Dupeyrat 1934, 300–320, 325–338.

48. E.g. B. T. Butcher Papers: Diary, 1 July 1905.

49. This generalized description of the missionary routine is a synthesis of specific timetables. See, for example, Anglican timetables in CEA-DNG var. *f:* no. 16, June 1908; Stone-Wigg Diary 1: 27 June 1899; and Newton 1914, 61; Methodist timetables in *MR*, Nov. 1897, 8–9 and *MR*, Oct. 1902, 8–10; LMS timetables in Edwin Pryce Jones, Letter-diary; Ben Butcher Papers: to Mrs. Holtumm, 16 Aug. 1914; Tomkins Papers: to parents, 10 Oct. 1900; SHM timetables, *Annales* 1897, 500; *Annales* 1911, 63.

50. *Christian World*, 29 Mar. 1904.

51. Newton 1914, 64.

52. Holmes Diary, 3 Sept. 1893.

53. Ibid., 18 Oct. 1899.
54. *Annales* 1907, 268.
55. *MR*, Oct. 1896, 268.
56. Newton 1914, 273.
57. Ibid.
58. Ibid.; Chignell, n.d.; Holmes Papers: "Seeing Brown" chap. 9; Australian *Annals*, Feb. 1899, 81.
59. Chignell 1911, 187.
60. *MR*, May 1896, 1.
61. Chignell 1911, 188; LMS 1915.
62. *MR*, July 1912, 18; Chignell 1911, 188.
63. LMS var. *g:* Chalmers to Mullens, Oct. 1882.
64. Holmes Papers: 5 Sept. 1905.
65. *MR*, June 1892.
66. Holmes Diary, 17 Nov. 1898.
67. Ibid., 17 Nov. 1900.
68. B. T. Butcher Papers: to Miss Holtumm, 28 Apr. 1906; ibid.: Diary 1905.
69. Haddon 1901, 80.
70. Holmes Diary, 13 Aug. 1899; LMS var. *j:* Dauncey Report 1905.
71. Fellows Diary, 11 Oct. 1890.
72. Ibid., 15 Nov. 1891.
73. *MR*, Aug. 1895, 2.
74. Bardsley Diary, 2 Dec. 1890.
75. Holmes Diary, 2 Dec. 1900.
76. Bromilow 1929, 84; cf. LMS var. *j:* Lawrence and Holmes Reports, 1910.
77. LMS var. *j:* Pearse Report 1893.
78. LMS 1915: Holmes to Lenwood, 7 Oct.
79. LMS var. *j:* Holmes Report 1911.
80. *MR*, Jan. 1893, 3.
81. BNG *AR 1897–98*, xxviii.
82. AWMMS var. *a:* 1897, lxvi.
83. Davidson Papers: Sharp to Archbishop Davidson, 5 July 1912; CEA-ABM: *Review*, 1 Sept. 1912, 115.
84. Navarre 1896, 57; *Annales* 1887, 228.
85. Navarre 1896, 57.
86. Ibid., 58–74.
87. *Annales* 1922, 236.
88. *Oeuvres Pontificales* 1906, 329; cf. ibid., 1911, 149.
89. *Annales* 1892, 578.
90. Cross 1958.
91. Australian *Annals*, June 1897, 211.
92. *Annales* 1891, 577.
93. Dupeyrat 1934, 141.
94. Ibid., 218; *Annales* 1892, 402.
95. De Boismenu 1905, 270.
96. *Annales* 1905, 626; ibid., 1911, 218–220.
97. Dupeyrat 1934, 363–381.
98. Eugene and Sarah Geraldina Stock, *Steps to Truth* (London 1878); Tomlinson Papers, 18 Aug. 1894.
99. Sharp 1917, 22.
100. Ibid.
101. Ibid.

102. CEA-DNG var. *e:* Newton, to Stone-Wigg, 1 Sept. 1922.
103. Davidson Papers: Sharp to Archbishop Davidson, 5 July 1912.
104. Fellows Diary, 5 Sept. 1897; *MR*, Oct. 1895, 4; Chalmers 1887*a*, 243.
105. *MR*, Dec. 1894, 10; cf. Holmes Diary, 4 Apr. 1897.
106. LMS var. *j:* Hunt Report 1901; Edwin Pryce Jones, Report 1905.
107. LMS 1915: Dauncey, deputation question 37.
108. BNG *AR 1893–94*, app. C, 13.
109. George Brown, Journal 1897, 20.
110. Sharp 1917, 14–16. See also CEA-DNG var. *e:* letters of Newton, King, *et al.* to bishop, in which discussion of sexual lapses and the necessity for discipline is frequent.
111. Navarre 1896, 79–81.
112. Dupeyrat 1934, 377.
113. De Boismenu 1908.
114. E.g. *MR*, July 1902, 8.
115. Bromilow 1914, 554.
116. Davidson Papers: Sharp to Archbishop Davidson, 5 July 1912.
117. Goodall 1954, 435.
118. *MR*, Nov. 1912, 5–6; cf. LMS 1915: question 29; Navarre 1896, 83–84; CEA-DNG *Tenth Anniversary Address.*
119. LMS 1915: Schlencker, question 29.
120. Newton 1914, 259; LMS 1915: Butcher and Saville, question 29.
121. Lloyd Letterbook 3: 16 May 1899; LMS 1915: question 29.
122. Newton 1914, 258; CEA-DNG *Tenth Anniversary Address.*
123. Navarre 1896, 83; de Boismenu 1913.
124. Navarre var. *b*, 164; CEA-DNG *Tenth Anniversary Address.*
125. Lawes Diary, 23 July 1877.
126. Chignell 1911, 57.
127. Ibid., 104.
128. Newton 1914, 258–259.
129. *MR*, Nov. 1912, 5–6; LMS 1915: question 18; CEA-DNG *Tenth Anniversary Address;* Chignell 1911, 106; Navarre 1896, 74–75.
130. BNG *AR 1890*, 18; ibid., app. L, 86; BNG *AR 1893–94*, app. C, 18; BNG *AR 1897–98*, xxxi.
131. F. Walker Journal 1888, 35–36; Dauncey var.: Circular letter, 1888.
132. Queensland *Parliamentary Papers* 1883, Despatches relating to BNG 1.
133. BNG *AR 1897–98.*
134. LMS *Chronicle*, Apr. 1886, 181.
135. Crosfield Diary 1897.
136. LMS *Chronicle*, Apr. 1886, 161.
137. Russell Abel 1934, 43.
138. BNG *AR 1893–94*, app. C, 18.
139. LMS 1915: Lenwood to Saville, 25 Mar.
140. Navarre 1896, 74.
141. MMSA var. *a:* 1902, xcv.
142. LMS var. *g:* C. W. Abel to Thompson, 4 Apr. 1905.
143. Ibid., C. W. Abel: The aims and scope of the industrial branch . . . 1903.
144. Lenwood 1916: Mar.
145. Ibid.
146. Lloyd Letterbook 3: 16 May 1899.
147. MMSA var. *a:* 1902, xcv; ibid., 1913, 112.

148. *MR*, May 1898, 10.
149. *Annales* 1886, 52.
150. Ibid., 1956, 95–97; Hurley Diary D, 34; see also *Annales* 1892, 398.
151. *Annales* 1904, 401.
152. CEA-DNG *Tenth Anniversary Address*, 9.
153. BNG *AR 1895–96*, 49.
154. LMS var. *g:* Dauncey to Thompson, 26 May 1897.
155. *Brisbane Daily Mail*, 29 Oct. 1910.
156. BNG *AR 1897–98*, xxx.
157. CEA-DNG *Ninth Anniversary Address*, 6–11.
158. E.g. BNG *AR 1895–96*, xxxiii, 49, 51; BNG *AR 1897–98*, xxx, xxxi, 47, 49.
159. LMS 1915; CEA-DNG *Tenth Anniversary Address*, 6. In one of his *Pastoral Letters* (1913), de Boismenu revealed some of the same concern as the Protestant and Anglican missionaries to provide a relevant education. But his motivation was primarily to retain the influence of the church over converts and to maintain their esteem for it rather than equip them for secular life.
160. LMS 1915: Beharell, question 19.
161. See for example F. Walker, n.d., 4.
162. Goodall 1954, 459.
163. Ibid., 458–459.
164. LMS var. *j:* C. W. Abel, Report 1890; LMS 1915: Riley, question 33; Newton 1914, 63.
165. For a comprehensive account of the development of industrial training in the missions see Austin 1977.
166. BNG *AR 1887*, 25.
167. Maclaren 1891, 25 Aug. 1891.
168. See Thompson n.d.
169. Ibid., 3; *Times* (London), 9 Sept. 1905; Hallden 1968, 3–4.
170. LMS var. *g:* C. W. Abel, The aims and scope . . . 1903.
171. See Russell Abel 1934; Lutton 1979.
172. Papua *AR 1905–06*, 20.
173. CEA-DNG *Tenth Anniversary Address*, 6–7.
174. Ibid., 1913, 4–7.
175. LMS 1915: Holmes to Lenwood, 7 Oct.
176. LMS 1915: B. T. Butcher, question 29; Austin 1977.
177. Boutilier *et al.* 1978, 26.
178. LMS var. *g:* Lawes to Thompson, 8 Aug. 1913; Saville 1902–1930: letter to bro., 1 Aug. 1925.
179. Saville 1902–1930: letter to bro., 31 Mar. 1916.
180. LMS var. *j:* Holmes, Report 1911.
181. BNG *AR 1897–98*, xxxix.
182. *MR*, July 1911.

Chapter 7: "The Gracious Influence of Wise and Thoughtful Womanhood"

1. *Annales* 1950, 52.
2. Deacon and Hill, 1972.
3. Pitman 1880, 7–8.
4. Lovett 1899, 2:714.
5. Goodall 1954, 13.

6. LMS var. *k:* Thompson to Abel, 6 Jan. 1893.
7. Ibid.
8. LMS var. *g:* Saville to Thompson, 4 Jan. 1909.
9. Ibid., Lawes to Thompson, 10 June 1895.
10. Ibid., E. Turner to Thompson, 27 Jan. 1912.
11. Ibid., M. Beharell to Thompson, 13 Jan. 1913.
12. Ibid., 24 Jan. 1917.
13. LMS var. *g:* PDC Minutes 1913.
14. See Venard 1966; Venard 1979*a;* Cuskelly 1975.
15. Venard 1966, 160.
16. Grimshaw 1913, 13.
17. Venard 1966, 87.
18. Dupeyrat 1934, 133.
19. *MR,* July 1952, 1–2.
20. George Brown, MOM Letterbook 1903: Letter entitled Missionary Sisters (n.d.).
21. Billing Papers: By-laws affecting the sisters' work.
22. AWMMS var. *a:* 1897, i, xix.
23. *MR* 19 (12): 13.
24. Tinney Notebook 2: 5 Apr. 1898.
25. Eleanor Walker Diary, 14 Dec. 1892.
26. Ibid., 9 Dec. 1892.
27. Bromilow 1929, 2–3.
28. Mrs. Bromilow had one adopted daughter, Ruve, who spent most of her childhood at school in Sydney.
29. Lloyd Journal 2: 10 July 1899.
30. CEA-DNG var. *e.*
31. Lloyd Journal, 10 July 1899.
32. BNG *AR 1897–98,* xxxiii.
33. LMS var. *g:* M. Beharell to Thompson, 24 Jan. 1917.
34. Ibid., 13 Jan. 1913.
35. *MR,* June 1891, 6.
36. Billing Diary 1:96.
37. LMS var. *g:* Carrie Rich to Thompson, 4 May 1902.
38. MMSA var. *a:* 1912, 111.
39. See, for instance, Tinney Diary, entries of 12 May, 4 Aug., and 28 Sept. 1892; E. Walker Diary, 20 July 1892.
40. *Annales* 1896, 152.
41. Sister Martha 1979.
42. AWMMS var. *a:* 1898, lxxi.
43. Lloyd Diary 5: 25 Sept. 1899.
44. Ker 1910.
45. Dupeyrat 1934, 346.
46. E. Walker Diary, 5 Aug. 1892.
47. *Annales* 1897, 322.
48. Ibid., 1901, 396.
49. Sister Martha 1979.
50. SMSC n.d.*b.*
51. Grimshaw 1913, 13.
52. *Annales* 1904, 501–502.
53. Ibid., 1950, 52.
54. Navarre var. *b,* 26–27.

55. *Annales* 1887, 593.

56. Ibid., 1896, 153–154.

57. Grimshaw 1913, 27.

58. Tinney Notebook 2:7, 31 Dec. 1897.

59. CEA-DNG var. *e:* Combley, to Stone-Wigg, 2 Sept. 1903.

60. CEA-DNG 1902–1950: Nowland to Laura, 10 Aug. 1902.

61. T. W. Reid 1960, 34.

62. CEA-DNG var. *e:* Stone-Wigg, Corlette to Stone-Wigg, 23 Aug. 1903.

63. Zeldin 1973, 2:782.

64. Ibid., 840–843.

65. George Brown, MOM Letterbooks: to Bromilow, 9 May 1900.

66. Ibid., to Field, 3 Aug. 1893.

67. Ibid., to Speers, 29 Apr. 1896.

68. MMSA 1913: Avery to Danks, 8 Apr. 1913.

69. Lill Papers.

70. MMSA 1913: Benjamin to Danks, 7 Aug. 1913.

71. George Brown, MOM Letterbooks, to Field, 14 Apr. 1893.

72. E. Walker Diary, 9 July, 22 Nov. 1892.

73. George Brown, MOM Letterbooks: to Bromilow, 23 Feb. 1903.

74. E.g. E. Walker Diary, 9 July 1892.

75. Fellows Diary, 7 Sept. 1892.

76. Dupeyrat 1934, 345.

77. Couppé var. *a:* to Navarre, 12 Feb. 1888.

78. Ibid., 23 Apr. 1899.

79. *Annales* 1889, 25–26.

80. Ibid., 1904, 503.

81. Ibid., 1887, 436.

82. Navarre var. *b:* Journal 1894, 116.

83. Ibid., 1899, 145.

84. SMSC 1899.

85. Navarre var. *b:* Journal, 12–14 May 1892.

86. *Annales* 1901, 398.

87. Stone-Wigg Papers: to Bishop Montgomery, 7 May 1904.

88. CEA-DNG var. *e:* Stone-Wigg, Corlette to Stone-Wigg, 13 Apr. 1904.

89. Ibid.

90. Ibid.

91. CEA-DNG var. *e:* Newton, to Stone-Wigg, 1 Feb., 4 Mar., 20 Apr. 1902.

92. CEA-DNG var. *e:* Thomson to Stone-Wigg, 20 Mar. 1906.

93. Monckton 1934, 90.

94. CEA-DNG var. *e:* Letters to Stone-Wigg from Miss Adams (8 Feb. 1904), Mrs. Newton (9 June 1900), and Nurse Combley (21 Apr., 24 Aug. 1920).

95. CEA-DNG var. *e:* King, to Stone-Wigg, 7 Aug. 1903.

96. Ibid., Giblin, to Stone-Wigg, 1 Jan. 1906.

97. Ibid., King, to Stone-Wigg, 17 May 1907.

Chapter 8: "Brothers in the Faith"*

* Colossians 1:2.

1. For a general discussion of the polity of this period see World Missionary Conference 1910 no. 2.

2. LMS 1873 *a*.

3. Lovett 1899, 2:747–749.

4. For a succinct comparison of the styles of administration of Mullens and Thompson, see Mathews 1917, 43–50.

5. Saville 1902–1930: letter to A. Saville [1 Mar. 1924?].

6. LMS var. *g:* PDC Minutes, 1915.

7. LMS 1892.

8. Ibid.

9. LMS var. *g:* Lawes to Thompson, 29 Apr. 1887.

10. Ibid.

11. E.g. LMS var. *k:* Thompson to Lawes, 15 Feb. 1888; ibid.: to Abel, 20 Oct. 1893.

12. LMS var. *g:* McFarlane to Mullens, 27 Mar. 1875; ibid.: Chalmers to Whitehouse, 11 Dec. 1880.

13. LMS var. *k:* Thompson to Dauncey, 30 July 1890.

14. LMS var. *g:* Hunt to Thompson, 4 Mar., 20 July 1889; ibid.: Savage to Thompson, 29 July 1889, 3 Apr. 1891.

15. Ibid., Savage to Thompson, 9 Apr. 1891.

16. Ibid., Dauncey to Thompson, 7 May 1891.

17. Ibid., 29 Jan. 1905.

18. LMS var. *j:* Holmes, Report 1898.

19. LMS var. *i:* Lawes to Misses Burgess, 11 June 1876.

20. Joseph King 1909, 254.

21. See LMS 1892; also LMS var. *g:* Abel to Thompson, 3 Mar. 1906; ibid.: Dauncey to Thompson, 26 Mar. 1912 and 3 Jan. 1914.

22. Holmes 1900–1916: Holmes to Dauncey, 27 Mar. 1901.

23. LMS var. *i:* Chalmers to Hutchin, 25 Apr. 1884.

24. LMS var. *g:* Chalmers to Thompson, 10 Feb. 1885.

25. Lenwood succeeded Thompson as foreign secretary in 1915.

26. Saville 1902–1930: letter to bro., 31 Mar. 1916.

27. Roland Oliver 1952, 43.

28. Fellows Diary, 30 Jan. 1892.

29. Joyce 1971, 169–170.

30. LMS var. *g:* Lawes to Thompson, 20 May 1890.

31. LMS 1915: Schlencker, question 8.

32. LMS var. *i:* Fanny Lawes to Misses Burgess, 12 Nov. 1876.

33. LMS var. *g:* Hunt to Thompson, 4 Mar. 1889.

34. Lenwood 1916: 19 Mar.

35. E.g. LMS var. *g:* Pearse to Thompson, 20 July 1892; ibid.: Lawes to Thompson, 1 June 1894.

36. LMS 1915: Turner to Lenwood, 10 July.

37. LMS var. *g:* Chalmers to Thompson, 1 Dec. 1884. The bitter feud between Lawes and Chalmers and McFarlane can be followed in their correspondence with the foreign secretary, e.g. McFarlane, 27 Mar. 1875, 13 Aug. 1877, 13 May, 16 June 1882, 8 Apr. 1883, 21 Sept. 1884; Chalmers, 11 Dec. 1880, 20 Apr., 22 Oct. 1881, 14 Feb. 1883; and Lawes, 16 June 1882.

38. LMS var. *k:* Thompson to Lawes, 19 Mar. 1886.

39. LMS var. *g:* Lawes to Thompson, 15 June 1892.

40. Ibid., Letter with PDC Minutes, 1911.

41. Ibid., PDC Minutes 1912.

42. Ibid., Burrows to Lenwood, 28 Oct. 1914.

43. Ibid., Lawes to Thompson, 17 June 1903.

44. LMS 1915: question 12.

45. *MR*, May 1891, 2; *MR*, July 1914, 4.

46. MCA 1905, 72.
47. Fitchett 1914, 87.
48. George Brown 1897: Notebook 2.
49. MMSA 1909–1910: Ballantyne to Danks, 25 Oct. 1910.
50. MCA 1905, 130.
51. MMSA-NGD 1891–1911a: 1903.
52. George Brown, MOM Letterbooks: to Lawes, 17 Nov. 1893.
53. MCA 1905, 77, 128–130.
54. Grubb 1913, 67.
55. Bromilow 1929, 62; AWMMS var. *a:* 1896, xxxi.
56. *MR*, Feb. 1897; *MR* May 1903.
57. George Brown, MOM Letterbooks: to Bromilow, 2 May 1894.
58. *MR* May 1905, 4.
59. MacGregor Diary, 25 July 1892; cf. Thornley 1979, 27.
60. See Bardsley Diary 1891–1892 for record of constant conflict with Mr. and Mrs. Bromilow.
61. *MR*, Aug. 1908, 136.
62. MCA-MMSA var. *a:* 1908, 136.
63. *MR*, Mar. 1914; ibid.: 1916.
64. Ibid., Jan. 1913.
65. CEA-DNG *Conference Address* 1902, 3.
66. Ibid., 2.
67. CEA-ABM 1850.
68. Temple Papers 8/76: Bishop of Brisbane to Primate, 25 June 1896.
69. Ibid., 8/70: Bishop of Brisbane to Vicar of Windsor, 15 Oct. 1896.
70. Ibid., 8/76: encl. in Bishop of Brisbane to Primate, 25 June 1896.
71. Ibid., 8/71: Bishop of Brisbane to Australian bishops, 7 Apr. 1896.
72. Ibid., 8/70: Bishop of Brisbane to Vicar of Windsor, 15 Oct. 1896.
73. Tomlin 1951, 73.
74. Chignell 1913, 73.
75. Roland Oliver 1952, 12; cf. Hilliard 1978, 54.
76. CEA-DNG var. *e:* Paper of conditions.
77. Ibid.: Dakers, to Stone-Wigg, 27 Mar. 1905.
78. CEA-DNG 1891–1920: 1899, 7.
79. Stone-Wigg Papers: letter, 22 Dec. 1898.
80. Ibid., 6 Nov. 1907.
81. Stone-Wigg var. *c: Church Standard*, 25 Oct. 1918; *Carpentarian*, 1 Jan. 1919.
82. Stone-Wigg Papers: Copland King to Stone-Wigg, 5 Jan. 1909.
83. Newton n.d., 26–27.
84. CEA-DNG *Conference Address 1902*, 3.
85. CEA-DNG var. *e:* King, to Primate, 18 Apr. 1898. Only two missionaries in New Guinea, Reynolds, an Anglo-Catholic, and Hoare, an Evangelical, claimed party dissension as the cause of their resignation.
86. Newton 1914, 250.
87. Maclaren 1891: to Bishop of Brisbane, 2 June.
88. Davidson Papers: Memo from Bishop of Brisbane to Archbishop Davidson, 28 Aug. 1909.
89. Ibid., 22 Sept. 1909.
90. *Australian Churchman*, 1 Aug., and 14, 21, 28 Nov. 1903.
91. Ibid.
92. CEA-DNG var. *e:* Giblin, to Stone-Wigg, 25 June 1906. The Melanesian

Mission had been founded half a century earlier when the instructions of the newly appointed Bishop of New Zealand, George Selwyn, erroneously extended his diocese to 34°30' north instead of south. It was founded in New Zealand to work in the northern New Hebrides (Vanuatu), the Santa Cruz group, and the Solomon Islands.

93. *Church Times*, 1 Nov. 1918.

94. CEA-DNG *Address to Conference 1903*, 4–5.

95. Ibid.

96. Stone-Wigg Papers: letter fragment n.d. [1905?].

97. CEA-DNG var. *e:* Dakers, to Stone-Wigg, 18 Feb. 1906.

98. Ibid., Giblin, to Stone-Wigg, 18 Feb. 1906.

99. Ibid., Giblin, to Stone-Wigg, 1 Jan. 1906.

100. Ibid., Abbot, to Stone-Wigg, 9 July 1899.

101. Davidson Papers: Bishop Montgomery to Archbishop Davidson, 28 Aug. 1909.

102. See Hoffman 1967.

103. SMSC var. *c:* Simeoni to Chevalier, 29 Mar. 1881.

104. The supposed identification of the Congregation with the Marquis de Rays expedition, which the Marquis strove to foster, caused it some embarrassment. The archives of the MSC include a vast amount of documentation on the subject. Father Jouet, in Rome, was eager to support the Marquis, while Chevalier, the Superior-General, was more cautious. Simeoni stressed that New France was to be but one of many of the Congregation's responsibilities in Oceania.

105. The origins and objectives of the Missionaries of the Sacred Heart are described in Dupeyrat 1934, 32–35; *Annales* 1955, 1–21.

106. For the influence of Archbishop Moran, see SMSC var. *b:* Jouet to Chevalier, 9 Aug. 1881 and 21 Aug. 1884; ibid.: Simeoni to Chevalier, 7 Aug. 1884.

107. Jouet, n.d.

108. *Annales* 1892, 664–668.

109. Dupeyrat 1934, 234–236.

110. *Annales* 1887, 372; BNG *AR 1887*, app. E, 26.

111. *Annales* 1893, 85.

112. Dupeyrat 1934, 364–365.

113. *Annales* 1903, 30.

114. Ceresi 1934, 271–273.

115. Dupeyrat 1934, 30.

116. MacGregor Diary, 19 Sept. 1891.

117. *Annales* 1903, 523.

118. Navarre var. *a:* to Chevalier, 1 June 1889.

119. *Annales* 1892, 336.

120. Ceresi 1934, 276.

121. Ibid., 273.

122. Ibid., 273–274.

123. SMSC var. *d:* Genocchi to Chevalier, 31 Dec. 1895.

124. Ceresi 1934, 276.

125. Ibid., 273–274.

126. Ibid., 176.

127. SMSC var. *e:* Correspondence 1889–1922, 279.

128. Dupeyrat and de la Noë 1958, 52–53.

129. Ibid., 54; Dupeyrat 1934, 250–251; de Vaulx 1951, 510.

130. Dupeyrat 1934, 313.
131. De Boismenu 1912.
132. Weber 1947, 329. Weber defined charisma as a "certain quality of an individual personality by virtue of which he is set apart from ordinary men and treated as endowed with supernatural powers or qualities. These are such as are not accessible to the ordinary person, but are regarded as of divine origin and on the basis of them, the individual concerned is treated as a leader." The following analysis draws upon Weber's definition and his elaboration of the characteristics of charismatic authority (330–333).
133. Ibid., 334.
134. Ibid., 334–340.
135. *MR*, May 1899, 1.
136. Ibid., Dec. 1912, 22.
137. Holmes Diary, 16 Nov. 1908.
138. *MR*, July 1911, 16; Tomkins Papers: to parents, 13 Aug. 1900. "Saragigi" (the one who removes his teeth) was the name given by the Dobuans to Bromilow; "Tamate" was a Raratongan interpretation of Chalmers' name.
139. Goodall 1954, 7–9, 439–441.
140. LMS var. *g:* Lawes to Thompson, 30 Oct. 1884.
141. Ibid., Lawes to Thompson, 9 Apr. 1892 and 20 Nov. 1893.
142. LMS *Chronicle*, Oct. 1898, ii.
143. Goodall 1954, 441.
144. Ibid.
145. Burton 1949, 105–112.
146. *MR*, Nov. 1912, 6.
147. Bromilow 1914, 554.
148. Ibid.
149. Wetherell 1977, 316; cf. Hilliard 1966, 338–341.
150. CEA-DNG *Address to Conference 1900.*
151. CEA-DNG var. *e:* Newton, to Stone-Wigg, 24 Feb. 1904.
152. CEA-DNG *Address to Conference 1913.*
153. Wetherell 1977, 276–277.
154. Navarre var. *b:* Journal, 6 Jan. 1896 and 29 Oct. 1902.
155. Dupeyrat 1934, 435.
156. Ibid., 436–441.
157. Ibid., 452–454.
158. Attempts to establish seminaries in New Caledonia (1891) and Fiji (1912) both failed, as had earlier seminaries of the Picpus fathers in Hawaii (1842) and Gambier (1850), and Marist seminaries on Futuna (1845) and in Sydney.
159. See *New Catholic Encyclopaedia* 9, 1925.
160. Papua *AR 1937–38*, 20–21.

Chapter 9: "The Sinister Trio"

1. LMS 1915.
2. McAuley 1955, 138.
3. LMS var. *g:* Chalmers to Thompson, 11 Feb. 1884; cf. Burridge 1978, 25.
4. See Langmore 1974, 41–43; Lovett 1903, 240–243.
5. Joseph King 1909, 166.
6. E.g. LMS var. *g:* Lawes to Whitehouse, 7 Apr. 1883; ibid.: to Thompson, 8 May 1885. See also Gunson 1965, 307.

7. LMS var. *g:* Lawes to Thompson, 12 Sept. 1884; Joseph King 1909, 211.

8. LMS var. *g:* Lawes to Whitehouse, 7 Apr. 1883.

9. Lawes Diary, 3 Apr. 1883.

10. LMS var. *g:* Lawes to Whitehouse, 7 Apr. and 21 Sept. 1883.

11. Ibid., Lawes to Thompson, 21 Sept. 1883.

12. Ibid., Lawes to Thompson, 20 Oct. 1884.

13. *SMH*, 1 Dec. 1884.

14. Chalmers 1887*a*, 18.

15. Romilly 1886, 316.

16. GBCO 422/1, Bridge to Scratchley, 11 Feb. 1885.

17. Cooke 1887, 315.

18. GBCO 433/3/9760.

19. Musgrave Papers, newscutting, *Townsville Bulletin*, Nov. 1885.

20. Bevan 1890, 135.

21. BNG *AR 1886–87*, 29.

22. Musgrave n.d.

23. LMS var. *g:* Lawes to Thompson, 20 Nov. 1886.

24. Fletcher 1917, 108. Cf. Ogilvie 1923 and Pannikar 1959, 297.

25. Hobson 1902, 196–198, 200 and, e.g., Pannikar 1959, 297.

26. *Great Soviet Encyclopaedia:* Missions, quoted in Gunson 1969.

27. See Koskinen 1953; Roland Oliver 1952; Ayandele 1966; Temu 1972.

28. LMS var. *g:* Lawes to Thompson, 12 Sept. 1884.

29. See for example Chalmers 1887*a*.

30. LMS 1897.

31. Chalmers 1887*c*, 196.

32. Chalmers 1887*a*.

33. Ibid.; *Times* (London), 1 June 1887; *Brisbane Courier*, 30 Jan. 1886, 28 June 1888.

34. Roland Oliver 1952, 179.

35. Navarre var. *a:* to Chevalier, 18 Dec. 1884.

36. Navarre 1881–1886, 40–47; *Annales* 1886, 16.

37. K. R. Howe 1977, 63.

38. Dupeyrat 1934, 91–99, 101–102, 113–114; *Annales* 1886, 85–89.

39. SMSC var. *d:* Lawes to Musgrave, 2 Sept. 1885; Navarre var. *a:* to Douglas, 4 May 1887; BNG *AR 1886*, app. G, 46; BNG *AR 1887*, app. E, 25.

40. Verjus var. *a:* to Chevalier, 9 Aug. 1886.

41. BNG *AR 1888*, 7.

42. J. H. P. Murray 1912, intro.

43. *MR*, 1898, 7.

44. Crosfield Diary, 72.

45. Dupeyrat 1934, 256.

46. Bromilow 1929, 274.

47. LMS var. *g:* Lawes to Thompson, 20 May 1890.

48. MacGregor, intro. to Synge 1908.

49. See GBCO 442/11/4215; also GBCO 422/10/25985 and BNG *Gov. Gazette* 1897, no. 9.

50. Fellows Diary, 30 June 1898.

51. E.g. *Annales* 1892, 337; *Annales* 1895, 158; BNG *AR 1895–96*, app. L.

52. *Methodist*, 26 Feb. 1892, 10; *MR*, Nov. 1892, 2; BNG *AR 1895–96*, xxvii.

53. CEA-DNG var. *f:* 21 Jan. 1910, 2.

54. Monckton 1921, 90; BNG *AR 1895–96*, app. L, 58.

55. *Methodist*, 26 Feb. 1898, 10.

56. GBCO 422/5/15117.
57. Synge 1908, intro.
58. Fellows Diary, note facing 29 July 1892.
59. Ibid.
60. MacGregor Diary, 8 Sept. 1891.
61. SMSC var. *d:* MacGregor to Navarre, 6 Feb. 1897.
62. Navarre var. *b:* Notes 1889. This supports the hypothesis of Beidelman (1974) that mission-government antagonism was more likely when the two groups were of differing nationality.
63. De Boismenu 1905, 274.
64. See Dupeyrat 1934, 254–278; *Annales* 1896, 561; *Annales* 1897, 501; BNG *AR 1895–96*, app. L, 59–61.
65. SMSC var. *d:* Navarre to MacGregor, 9 Feb., 31 July 1897.
66. BNG *AR 1897–98*, xvi.
67. SMSC var. *d:* Musgrave to Navarre, 6 Feb. 1897.
68. Ibid., Navarre to MacGregor, 27 June 1896.
69. Ibid.
70. MacGregor Diary, 26 Apr. 1892. See also 7 Dec. 1890 and 17 Apr. 1892; also GBCO 422/6/3391 and 422/11/24125.
71. *Annales* 1891, 441; SMSC var. *d:* Navarre to Musgrave, 24 Apr. 1893; ibid.: MacGregor to Navarre, 22 Nov. 1893 and 4 Feb. 1897.
72. MacGregor Diary, 9 Sept. 1892.
73. SMSC var. *d:* Lawes to MSC, 20 Sept. 1888. See also ibid.: Musgrave to Navarre 29 July, 6 Nov. 1888; ibid.: Navarre to MacGregor, 10 Feb. 1889.
74. GBCO 422/11/24125.
75. Joyce 1971, 178.
76. Ibid., 177.
77. *Annales* 1902, 113.
78. MacGregor Diary, 19 Sept. 1891 and 5 Oct. 1892.
79. BNG *AR 1890*, 82.
80. *Annales* 1895, 334.
81. Dupeyrat 1934, 269.
82. LMS var. *g:* Lawes to Thompson, 31 Mar. 1889.
83. Bromilow 1929, 266, 279.
84. LMS var. *i:* Lizzie Chalmers to Harrie Hill, 27 Mar. 1900.
85. CEA-ABM n.d.*d*, 23.
86. LMS var. *g:* Lawes to Thompson, 21 Nov. 1901.
87. Joyce 1971, 192.
88. Navarre, var. *b:* Journal, 13 Apr. and 19–21 Apr. 1893; ibid.: Navarre to Musgrave, 24 Apr. 1893.
89. See for example, B. T. Butcher Papers: Letter-diary, 13 June 1914; *PIM* Apr. 1939, 26; LMS var. *g:* Walker to Thompson, 22 Jan. 1902; ibid.: Pryce Jones letter to Lenwood, 8 Feb. 1920; Stone-Wigg Diary 3: 2 Sept. 1903; BNG *AR 1895–96*, app. C, 9 and L, 58; BNG *AR 1900–01*, app. J, 49; Australia . . . 1907, para 2572.
90. Stone-Wigg Diary, 4 and 6 Dec. 1901.
91. LMS var. *g:* Abel to Thompson, 23 Nov. 1901 and 17 Mar. 1902.
92. Ibid., PDC Minutes 1902.
93. Ibid., Walker to Thompson, 22 Jan. 1902.
94. Ibid., Saville to Thompson, 10 Sept. 1902.
95. E.g. Ibid., Walker to Thompson, 5 Feb. 1895; Holmes to Thompson, 9 Feb. 1889. See also Stephen 1974, 78–79, 99–100.

96. SMSC var. *d:* Kowald to MacGregor, 24 Sept. 1892; BNG *AR 1892–93,* xiv.

97. CEA-DNG var. *e:* Taylor, to Stone-Wigg, 5 Jan. 1903.

98. LMS var. *g:* Lawes to Blayney, 14 July 1898.

99. Ibid., Lawes to Atlee Hunt, 11 Aug. 1905.

100. See Langmore 1972.

101. CEA-ABM *Review* Dec. 1916, 183.

102. E.g. Anglican missionary Percy Money accompanied C. A. W. Monckton on an expedition during which he named Mt. Stone-Wigg.

103. See, for example, BNG *AR 1895–96,* app. C, 6; BNG *AR 1899–1900,* app. B, 9–10; BNG *AR 1900–01,* app. M, 62; SMSC var. *d:* Wriford to Verjus, 15 Nov. 1891, and Kowald to Navarre, 11 Oct. 1897.

104. BNG *AR 1906–07,* 121.

105. LMS var. *g:* PDC Minutes 1903.

106. Ibid., Lawes to Atlee Hunt, 11 Aug., 14 Sept. 1905.

107. Stone-Wigg Diary 3: 5 Sept. 1903, 99; *Brisbane Daily Telegraph,* 21 Sept. 1903.

108. LMS var. *g:* PDC Minutes 1903; MMSA-NGD 1891–1911*a:* 1903, 286.

109. Renata Howe 1965, 83–84.

110. *Times* (weekly edition), 1 Sept. 1905.

111. LMS var. *g:* PDC Minutes, 1903.

112. Ibid.; and Lawes to Thompson, 10 Oct. 1903; *Australian Churchman,* Feb. 1904.

113. *Australian Temperance World,* Oct. 1903.

114. See Australia . . . 1907.

115. Stone-Wigg Papers: to Bishop [Montgomery], 18 Mar. 1907.

116. E.g. LMS var. *g:* Dauncey (27 Mar. 1907), Abel (4 Sept. 1907) to Thompson.

117. Ibid., Abel (4 Sept. 1907), Dauncey (28 June 1907) to Thompson.

118. Stone-Wigg Papers: to Bishop [Montgomery], 18 Mar. 1907.

119. Saville 1902–1930: letter to bro., 6 Apr. 1907; CEA-DNG *Report of the New Guinea Mission . . . 1907,* 15–17.

120. Australia . . . 1907, 40; see also 37–39.

121. *SMH,* 11 June 1907.

122. Saville 1902–1930: letter to bro., 6 Apr. 1907.

123. LMS var. *g:* Dauncey to Thompson, 27 Mar. 1907.

124. *Brisbane Courier,* 10 June 1907; *SMH,* 11 June 1907; Melbourne *Age,* 12 June 1907; Melbourne *Argus,* 14 June 1907; *Daily Telegraph,* 21 June 1907.

125. *MR,* July 1907, 1.

126. LMS var. *g:* PDC Minutes 1907; ibid.: Dauncey to Thompson, 27 Mar. 1907; Stone-Wigg Papers: to Bishop [Montgomery], 26 June 1907.

127. Stone-Wigg Papers: to Bishop [Montgomery], 26 June 1907. The Commonwealth Government subsequently tried to suggest that the missionaries' concern was unfounded, but it seems that a compulsory purchase clause had already been passed in Port Moresby before being suppressed in Melbourne in the face of the agitation (see LMS var. *g:* Abel to Thompson, 4 Sept. 1907).

128. LMS var. *g:* Abel to Thompson, 4 Sept. 1907.

129. Ibid., Dauncey to Thompson, 28 June 1907.

130. Danks Letterbooks: to Ballantyne, 19 Apr. 1912. Danks was rebuked by the Methodist missionary Andrew Ballantyne for his remark (MMSA Correspondence: Ballantyne to Danks, 18 June 1912).

131. CEA-DNG 1906–1925: Stone-Wigg to Musgrave, 18 Feb. 1905.

132. Ibid., 22 June 1905; ibid., Musgrave to Stone-Wigg, 19 Apr., and 6, 29 July 1905.

133. MMSA-NGD, 1903–1911: Bromilow, Stone-Wigg, and Abel to Deakin, 27 Dec. 1907.

134. Grimshaw 1911, intro.

135. De Boismenu 1905, 273–274.

136. Dupeyrat 1934, 283–286.

137. *Annales* 1911, 221.

138. The cooperation was formally recognized by the appointment in 1924 of a nonofficial member, elected from among all the missionaries, to the Legislative Council. LMS missionaries Dauncey, Clark, and Turner filled this post before World War II.

139. BNG *AR 1906–07*, 24.

140. West 1968, 177–203.

141. B. T. Butcher Papers: to Mrs. Holtumm, 18 Aug. 1914; ibid.: Ena Butcher to parents, 31 July 1914.

142. LMS var. *g:* PDC Minutes 1913; MMSA-NGD 1891–1911*a:* Synod Journal 1911, 441; Danks Letterbooks: to Ballantyne, 11 Jan., 19 Apr. 1912; ibid.: to Gilmour, 4 May 1912; Papua *AR 1908*, 94.

143. AAO 1942.

144. West 1968, 146.

145. Hobson 1902, 197.

146. McAuley 1955, 38. Cf. Temu 1972, 132.

147. Neill 1966, 239. But see also Gunson 1969, 263.

148. The phrase was coined by Judge Herbert, Chief Judicial Officer. See MMSA 1913: Burgess to Wheen, 25 Nov. For missionary perceptions of this role see, for example, Chignell 1911, 25; LMS var. *g:* Lawes, intro. to PDC Minutes 1903; ibid.: Chalmers to Thompson, 11 Feb. 1884; R. Turner Papers: History of the LMS, lecture 4; SMSC var. *d:* Navarre to Administrator, 18 Dec. 1903. Cf. Groves 1969, 475.

149. This was as much an article of faith among the French as among the British. See Zeldin 1970, 2:6–17. For some missionary doubts as to European superiority see chapter 5.

150. Stone-Wigg Papers: 11 June 1897; see also CEA-DNG 1898–1900: 24 May 1901; CEA-DNG var. *e:* King (10 Feb. 1901) and Ker (22 June 1902) to Stone-Wigg; Newton 1914, 242; Lloyd Journal, 10 Feb. 1901; Tinney Diary, 14 Mar. 1900.

151. *Brisbane Daily Telegraph*, 23 Mar. 1903.

152. See, for example, comments of Bromilow (1929, 266, 274) and Gill (Diary, 2 Nov. 1919). Stone-Wigg, for instance, traveled to New Guinea with Lord Lamington and Sir Henry Nelson, and on his arrival stayed at Government House. He was friendly with successive administrators, especially Sir George Le Hunte, an Anglican lay reader. Although critical of aspects of the policy of Le Hunte's successor, Christopher Stansfeld Robinson, son of an archdeacon of Christchurch, New Zealand, he maintained friendly social relations with him.

153. Navarre var. *b:* 1899, 149.

154. LMS var. *g:* Hunt to Thompson, 3 June 1901; Dupeyrat 1955, 74.

155. LMS var. *j:* Chalmers Report 1887.

156. Lawes Diary, 21 Aug. 1881. Eminent missionaries in other fields had been similarly implicated in punitive expeditions. See, for example, Adams 1977 on Paton and the Cucaçoa affair and Brown 1908, 252–261.

157. *Annales* 1889, 563. Cf. Tomlinson Diary, 14 Nov. 1891.

158. Stephen 1974, 68–69.

159. Ibid., 72–74; BNG *AR 1892–93*, app. D, 15–19, and app. E, 21; *Annales* 1896, 217.

160. BNG *AR 1895–96*, app. C, 6.

161. SMSC var. *d:* e.g. Wriford to MacGregor, 13 Sept. 1892, and Kowald to Winter, Sept. 1892.

162. Ayandele 1966, xvii; cf. Temu 1972, 2. See also Strayer 1976, 8–11.

163. LMS var. *g:* Lawes to Thompson, 17 June 1890.

164. Ibid.

165. Maclaren Diary, 15 June and 6 July 1890.

166. Dauncey var.: Diary, 10 May 1890; Maclaren Diary, 18 May 1890.

167. Maclaren Diary, 4 May 1890.

168. LMS var. *j:* Walker Report; *MR*, Jan. 1892, 2.

169. Bromilow 1914, 541; *MR*, Aug. 1893, 2.

170. LMS var. *g:* Lawes to Thompson, 20 June 1904.

171. Ibid.: Abel to Thompson, 3 Jan. 1899; AWMMS var. *b:* Bromilow to Brown, 14 Nov. 1899.

172. Brown, MOM Letterbooks: to Bromilow, 1 Jan. 1900.

173. Ibid. When in 1915 the Kikuyu controversy split the ranks of the Anglican clergy over the issue of admission of nonconformists to pulpit and sacrament, Bishop Sharp affirmed his commitment to Stone-Wigg's policy.

174. Stone-Wigg Diary 1897 and 1901; Lloyd Journal 2: 10 July 1899.

175. Beside those discussed above, the missions also cooperated to oppose Sunday labor and to request a reduction in the age of majority.

176. Maclaren Diary, 4 June 1890.

177. MacGregor, Diary 3: 6 Jan. 1892.

178. Dupeyrat and de la Noë, 1958, 64.

179. CEA-DNG *Address to Conference . . . 1904*, 2; Chignell 1913, 114.

180. Navarre, 1881–1886: 1885.

181. E.g. *Annales* 1896, 561.

182. LMS var. *k:* Thompson to Chalmers, 1 July 1881.

183. LMS var. *g:* Chalmers, 20 Apr. 1881; ibid.: Lawes, to Thompson, 27 Apr. 1881; *Annales* 1892, 395.

184. *Annales* 1923, 171.

185. Dupeyrat 1934, 267.

186. *Annales* 1899, 427.

187. LMS var. *j:* Chalmers Report 1893.

188. Henkelmann 1949, 161.

189. *Annales* 1914, 161.

190. LMS var. *g:* Dauncey to Thompson, 13 June 1896.

191. *Annales* 1895, 448.

192. *MR*, July 1895, 2–9; ibid., Aug. 1899, 1–4.

193. LMS var. *g:* Dauncey to Thompson, 27 Jan. and 31 May 1911.

194. Ibid., Edwin Pryce Jones to Thompson, 3 Feb. 1903; LMS var. *j:* Dauncey, Reports of 1897 and 1904; Holmes Diary, 13 Sept. 1897.

195. Holmes Diary, 13 Sept. 1897; LMS var. *g:* Dauncey to Thompson, 31 May 1911.

196. LMS var. *g:* Dauncey to Thompson, 31 May 1911.

197. Ibid., 27 Jan. 1911.

198. E.g. R. Turner Papers, 4 May 1932.

199. *Annales* 1895, 221; *MR*, Oct. 1899, 3; *MR*, Aug. 1904, 4; *MR*, Oct. 1913, 19; Tinney Diary 2: 28 June 1899.

200. Monckton 1921, 43.

201. E.g. LMS var. *g:* Savage, 7 Sept. 1880; ibid., Margaret Beharell, 13 Jan. 1913 to Thompson; LMS var. *j:* Holmes Report 1904; Maclaren Diary, 5 Aug. 1890; Stone-Wigg Papers: to Bishop [Montgomery], 18 Mar. 1907.

202. CEA-DNG *Anniversary Address 1901,* 9.

203. CEA-DNG var. *e:* Davis, to Stone-Wigg, 10 Feb. 1906.

204. Stone-Wigg Papers: to Bishop [Montgomery], 18 Mar. 1907.

205. LMS var. *j:* Chalmers, Report 1884.

206. Bromilow 1929, 191–192.

207. Stone-Wigg analyzes the reasons for trader hostility in his *Anniversary Address 1901* (CEA-DNG). See also Bevan 1890, 135.

208. Russell Abel 1934, 89; Lutton 1979. The hostility of a competing trader is embodied in a pamphlet: *Merchant missionaries. Trading teachers in New Guinea. The minister and the milk can. Parson's perquisites.* (Anon.)

209. LMS var. *g:* Abel to Thompson, 7 Feb. 1903.

210. *North Queensland Register,* 3 Sept. 1900.

211. Stuart 1970*a,* 12.

212. CEA-DNG *Anniversary Address 1901.*

213. Australia . . . 1907, evidence: 1206 and 1648.

214. *Sydney Daily Telegraph,* 9 Jan. 1902.

215. *Brisbane Daily Telegraph,* 21 June 1907.

216. LMS var. *g:* Abel to Thompson, 3 Jan. 1899; LMS var. *j:* Abel, Report 1897.

217. Gatland, Glew (d.), Harrison, Walsh.

218. *Sydney Daily Telegraph,* 6 Nov. 1902.

219. Hunt Letterbooks: to Pratt, 14 June 1901.

220. Tomkins Papers: Dauncey Report (Norwich, 1909).

221. Bromilow 1929, 193; see also Fellows Diary, 30 Aug. 1894.

222. *Brisbane Church Chronicle,* 1 Aug. 1903; Stone-Wigg Papers: 18 Apr. 1905.

223. *PIM,* June 1939, 4; MacKay 1909, 52.

224. CEA-DNG var. *e:* King, to Stone-Wigg, 31 Aug. 1903.

225. E.g. Lawes Diary, entries of 28 Mar., 3 Apr., and 8 Oct. 1876; LMS var. *g:* Lambert Loria to Thompson, 15 July 1896; F. Walker Diary, entries of 16, 18 Dec. 1888; R. Turner Papers: Edith Turner to Nora, 18 Sept. 1938.

226. Chignell 1913, 251.

Chapter 10: "A Peculiar People"

1. B. T. Butcher Papers: to Mrs. Holtumm, 24 Aug. 1914.

2. Ibid., 8, 16 Sept. 1914.

3. Sacred Heart missionaries at mountain stations heard of the war on 14 and 16 August and by 11 December they had caught up with the news to 5 November.

4. Saville 1902–1930: letter to bro., 23 June 1915.

5. B. T. Butcher Papers: to Mrs. Holtumm, 29 Oct. 1915.

6. Ibid.

7. Saville 1902–1930: letter to bro., 23 June 1915.

8. Lutton 1979, 176; B. T. Butcher Papers: to Mrs. Holtumm, 16 Sept. 1914.

9. Saville 1902–1930: letter to bro., 29 Sept. 1914.

10. LMS var. *g:* Rich to Lenwood, 3 Feb. 1919; Saville 1902–1930: letter to bro., 29 Sept. 1914.

11. CEA-DNG var. *e:* Fettell, to Sharp, 11 Sept. 1918.

12. CEA-DNG var. *f:* 41, Jan. 1915, 5.

13. MMSA-NGD 1913–1914: Wheen to Gilmour, 21 Aug. 1914.

14. CEA-DNG *Synod Report 1914; MR,* Dec. 1914.

15. CEA-DNG *Address to Conference 1914.*

16. De Boismenu 1915.

17. E.g. LMS var. *g:* 1900–1901.

18. Chalmers Journal, 26 Jan. 1901; E. Lloyd, Journal 6: 10 Feb. 1901; Tinney Diary, 14 Mar. and 4 Apr. 1901; CEA-DNG var. *e:* King, to Stone-Wigg, 10 Feb. 1901.

19. Tomkins Papers: to parents, 24 Nov. 1900; *Annales* 1904, 397; *Annales* 1906, 691; *Annales* 1907, 200.

20. B. T. Butcher Papers: to Mrs. Holtumm, 21 Jan. 1906; Saville 1902–1930: letter to bro., 29 Sept. 1915.

21. Bardsley Diary, 27 June 1891; cf. Renata Howe 1965, 96–97.

22. Saville 1902–1930: letter to bro., 29 Sept. 1915.

23. Ibid., 28 July 1914.

24. Ibid., 9 June and 14 Sept. 1914.

25. E.g. MMSA, 1909–1910: Osborne to Danks, 23 Feb. 1910; Stone-Wigg Papers: Letter to staff, 23 Aug. 1908; LMS var. *g:* Rich, 20 Feb. 1914; ibid.: Turner, 6 Mar. 1914; ibid.: Lawrence, 20 Dec. 1916, to Lenwood.

26. LMS var. *g:* Lawes to Thompson, 5 Apr. 1886.

27. CEA-DNG var. *e:* Dakers to Stone-Wigg, 27 Mar. 1905 and 21 Apr. 1906.

28. Navarre var. *b:* 1892; SMSC var. *e:* Couppé to Navarre, 24 Oct. 1887.

29. Saville 1902–1930: letter to bro., 2 Dec. 1901. Cf. Fellows Diary, 25 May 1892; Maclaren 1891: 9 Sept.

30. E.g. Holmes Diary, 21 Nov. 1907 and 24 June 1908.

31. CEA-DNG var. *e:* Newton, to Stone-Wigg, n.d.

32. F. Walker Journal, 25 Dec. 1888. Cf. Lawes Diary, 1 July 1877; Fellows Diary, 25 Dec. 1892.

33. Cairns 1965, 65.

34. Stone-Wigg Diary 2: 4 Aug. 1903.

35. CEA-DNG var. *e:* Money, to Stone-Wigg, 5 Apr. 1907.

36. Ibid.: Newton, 27 Apr. 1903; ibid., Giblin, 1 Jan. 1906, to Stone-Wigg.

37. Smithson was dismissed after "an indecent assault" (CEA-DNG var. *e:* Newton, to Stone-Wigg, 25 June 1900). Dodds, "little more than a boy," was sent home to Australia after confessing to three times inviting a girl onto the mission launch with the intention of sexual intercourse. Newton, who may have been consoled by Dodd's statement that he "failed to do anything to her," dealt kindly with him, allowing him three months' leave, from which he did not return. On the alleged associations of Ford, Dakers, and Giblin with Papuan women, see CEA-DNG var. *e:* Newton, 1 Feb., 9 June 1902; and ibid., King, 15 Jan. 1904 to Stone-Wigg.

38. CEA-DNG var. *e:* Dakers to Stone-Wigg, 24 Sept. 1907.

39. Malinowski 1967, 182.

40. CEA-DNG 1900–1926: Monckton to Stone-Wigg, 25 Apr. 1901.

41. Davidson Papers: Bishop Montgomery to Archbishop Davidson, 5 Aug. 1909.

42. *Annales* 1892, 627–628; Navarre var. *b:* 1892, 12–13; Monckton 1921, 60.

43. B. T. Butcher Papers: to wife, 27 Feb. 1920.

44. MMSA 1913: Burgess to Wheen, 25 Nov. 1913 and encl. Similar allegations were made at times against Anglicans Tomlinson and Kennedy, and LMS

missionaries Holmes and Baxter-Riley. Hubert Murray recorded in his diary (18 Feb. 1913), for instance, that there was a suspicion that Riley had "seduced two of his girls and finding them to be pregnant, murdered them before his wife's return." The other allegations, though less fanciful, were equally unsubstantiated and almost certainly false.

45. See, for example, Gunson 1978, 153–159.

46. CEA-DNG var. *e:* Dodds, Snodgrass to Stone-Wigg, 24 Dec. 1904, defending Dodd's lapse.

47. Saville 1902–1930: letter to bro., 15 Feb. 1906.

48. Ibid.

49. Holmes Diary, 18 Mar. 1899 and 23 Oct. 1900.

50. CEA-DNG var. *e:* Giblin, 17 Aug. and 21 Sept. 1904, 1 Jan. 1906; ibid.: King to Stone-Wigg, 23 Jan. 1906.

51. Ibid., Morris to Stone-Wigg, 3 Dec. 1905, and 4 Jan. 1906.

52. See C. Peter Williams 1976, 182.

53. B. T. Butcher n.d., 26, 61, 77, 89–90.

54. Ceresi 1934, 423–432; Dansette 1961, 2: chapter 7.

55. B. T. Butcher Diary, 31 Dec. 1905.

56. Fellows Diary, 31 Dec. 1891. Cf. 1 Jan. and 25 Mar. 1892.

57. See, for example, diaries of Bardsley, Holmes, Beswick, Butcher, and Eleanor Walker.

58. LMS var. *g:* Hunt to Thompson, 3 Apr. 1889.

59. B. T. Butcher Papers: to Mrs. Holtumm, 16 Feb. 1906.

60. Saville 1902–1930: letter to bro., 20 July 1902. Cf. *Annales* 1956, 125.

61. CEA-DNG var. *e:* M. Newton to Stone-Wigg, n.d.

62. LMS var. *j:* Edwin Pryce Jones Report.

63. Tomkins Papers: to bro., 11 Feb. 1901.

64. B. T. Butcher Papers: to Mrs. Holtumm, 30 July 1914.

65. *Annales* 1923, 107.

66. See Langmore (1974, 119) for Chalmers' drinking when old and depressed; see also n. 100 below for the likelihood that Maclaren was drinking in the months preceding his death; for Giblin's "drinking episode" see CEA-DNG var. *e:* Giblin, to Stone-Wigg, 1 Jan. 1906 and ibid.: Abbot, to Stone-Wigg, 7 July 1899.

67. Bardsley Diary, 30 June 1891; E. Walker Diary, 14 Dec. 1892; *MR*, Jan. 1892, 6; LMS var. *g:* Walker (12 Jan. 1893) and Clark (9 Dec. 1912) to Thompson; Holmes Diary, 14 Aug. 1893; Chignell 1913, 110; *Annales* 1889, 452; *MR*, Aug. 1895, 2.

68. LMS var. *g:* Turner to Thompson, 19 May 1909.

69. *MR*, Jan. 1892, 5; *MR*, Sept. 1895, 8; Lloyd Journal 6: 30 June 1901; Saville 1902–1930: letter to bro., 2 Dec. 1901; LMS var. *j:* Pearse, Report 1903; LMS var. *g:* Holmes to Lenwood, 1 Jan. 1915.

70. Fellows Diary, 11 Feb. 1892.

71. LMS var. *g:* Lawes to Thompson, 1 Jan. 1898.

72. E.g. *Annales* 1893, 403; *Annales* 1950, 52.

73. Bardsley Diary, 12 Aug. 1891; *MR*, July 1897, 9.

74. See S. R. M. Gill var.: Letters; CEA-DNG *Address to Conference 1899; Annales* 1893, 452.

75. Monckton 1921, 140.

76. LMS var. *g:* Dauncey (29 Jan. 1905) and Schlencker (29 Jan. 1914) to Thompson; Holmes Diary, 22 Apr. 1898; Bardsley Diary, 16 Jan. 1892.

77. Holmes Diary, 14 Mar. 1897; Navarre var. *b:* 8 Aug. 1888.

78. E.g. B. T. Butcher Papers: Diary, 28 May 1905; LMS var. *k:* Thompson to Pearse, 30 Dec. 1887.

79. *Annales* 1893, 17.

80. Ibid., 1905, 644.

81. Ibid., 1906, 400. The only non–Roman Catholic missionary known to have engaged in flagellation was Romney Gill of the Anglican mission, who required his Papuan secretary to cane him for his transgressions (Waiko 1972, app. B., 137).

82. *Annales* 1905, 643–644; *Annales* 1951, 143–144; Cadoux 1931, 6.

83. *Annales* 1890, 380.

84. Ibid., 1893, 209.

85. Ibid., 1890, 380.

86. Goyau 1938, 79.

87. Dupeyrat and de la Noë 1958, 45.

88. See for example, Turner Papers: letter of Edith Turner, 19 Apr. 1937, on the reluctance of Charles Rich to retire. Anglican missionaries Stone-Wigg and Copland King, driven away not by compulsory retirement but by ill-health, felt similar regret (Davidson Papers: Stone-Wigg to Davidson, 9 Feb. 1907; Stone-Wigg Papers: King to Stone-Wigg, 24 Sept. 1918).

89. MMSA 1913: Waterhouse to Danks, 31 Jan. 1913; George Brown MOM Letterbooks: to Bromilow, 1 Dec. 1900.

90. CEA-DNG *Anniversary Address 1899.*

91. Brother Lambert Fehrmann and Sister Paul (death certificates). Others whose mental stability was feared for were Fathers Burke and Fillodeau, Brother Luis Kuypers, Leonard Drury, Florence Thomson, Julia Benjamin, and Nurse Speers.

92. Navarre var. *a:* to Chevalier, n.d. [1895] reports Father Hartzer's dislike of "always seeing black faces and no civilisation" and Navarre (var. *b:* Apr. 1902, 152) Father Fillodeau's detestation of "the savages." Harriet Murray's nervous condition is described by Newton to Stone-Wigg (CEA-DNG var. *e:* Murray, 1 Feb. and 4 Mar. 1902).

93. Binfield (1977, 225–226 and 279–280) noted that at the commissioning of Tomkins for the mission field, less than two years before he was killed and eaten at Goaribari, cannibal jokes were enjoyed.

94. See Langmore 1974, 105–127, for an account of the deaths of Chalmers and Tomkins and reactions to them. Despite Papua's reputation for savagery, the safety record of European missionaries was surprisingly good. Three government officers were killed by Papuans in the same period. Missionaries fared worse in neighboring German New Guinea, where ten Sacred Heart missionaries were killed in one attack.

95. BNG *AR 1897–98,* xxxii.

96. E.g. Holmes Diary, 25 July 1898 and 21 Mar. 1915; LMS var. *g:* Lawes to Thompson, 5 Apr. 1886.

97. *MR,* Aug. 1895, 1; *MR,* Oct. 1895, 8; *MR,* Apr. 1899, 7; *MR,* May 1904, 6.

98. Danks Letterbooks: to Field, 26 Dec. 1898.

99. Monckton 1921, 75.

100. Chignell 1913, xi. The term 'martyr' was used loosely in the mission field. Originally applied only to those who died rather than renounce their faith, it was extended to all those who died by violent means in the course of evangelism. In the SHM it was used even more loosely to embrace all those who died during their apostolate, the victims of fever as much as the victims of "savages."

101. Synge 1908, 161. Maclaren's colleagues were also surprised at his death, having regarded him as a particularly strong man (Tomlinson Diary, 5 Jan. 1892).

102. CEA-DNG 1902–1950: King to Primate, 14 Mar. and 19 Apr. 1892; ibid., to Archbishop of Brisbane, 26 Mar. 1892.

103. Tomlinson Diary, 13 Dec. 1891.

104. LMS var. *g:* Cribb to Thompson, 25 May 1899.

105. CEA-DNG var. *e:* Ker, to Stone-Wigg, 25 May 1914. Cf. ibid., Giblin, to Stone-Wigg, 11 July 1903.

106. CEA-DNG *Anniversary Address 1903.*

107. *Annales* 1892, 632; Cf. *Annales* 1893, 450; *Annales* 1894, 692; *Annales* 1899, 427.

108. Father Louis Janet died on 15 April after three months in the mission.

109. *Annales* 1905, 514.

110. Dupeyrat 1934, 241 n.

111. Lutton 1979.

112. Beharell 1978.

113. B. T. Butcher Papers, e.g. to wife, 14 Nov. 1937.

114. Ibid., 12 Mar. 1920.

115. Musgrave var. *a:* Diary, 8 Apr. 1888; Green Letters, 17 July 1894.

116. Gunson 1978.

117. Young 1953, 4–5.

118. Strayer 1979, 6.

119. Ibid., 5.

120. Hilliard 1978, 125.

121. E.g. Hurley 1924, 63; Geil 1902, 219.

122. Some of the most notable were the Patons (Presbyterian), the Waterhouses (Methodist), the Gills and the Turners (LMS).

123. Navarre 1881–1886: Journal 1:73.

124. I Peter 2:9 (Authorized Version).

Bibliography

NOTES: The main sources for this book have been the papers of the missionaries themselves. Some are in private hands, others in individual collections, and many in mission archives. The largest and most complete collection are the papers of the London Missionary Society (LMS), now lodged at the School of Oriental and African Studies, London, and mostly available on microfilm through the Joint Copying Project. There are additional LMS collections at the Mitchell Library and in the United Church Archives (UCA), New Guinea Collection, University of Papua New Guinea (UPNG). The bulk of Methodist missionary archival material is located in the Department of Overseas Mission (MOM) Papers, Mitchell Library. It is an uneven collection with some useful manuscripts but many gaps. Other Methodist collections are the United Church Archives (UCA), UPNG, the Methodist Church Papers (MCP), Mitchell Library and the archives of the Methodist Church of Australasia, NSW at the United Church Records and Historical Society (UCR), Sydney. The Anglican Archives (AA) at UPNG provide the largest source for material on the Anglican Mission; especially valuable for this study were the Personal Files of missionaries (boxes 20–23). The Australian Board of Missions (ABM), Sydney, and the Lambeth Palace Library (LP), London, also hold relevant manuscripts. Unrestricted access to all these archives provided a wealth of material.

The archives of the Missionaries of the Sacred Heart in Rome (RA) are not open to those outside the Congregation, however most of the material relating to the Pacific has been microfilmed by the Pacific Manuscripts' Bureau (PMB) and other information was supplied to me on request by the archivist, Father Bertolini, MSC. Father John McMahon, MSC, allowed me to use material from the Congregation's archives at Bereina, Papua New Guinea (BA). The same restriction applied to archival material of the Daughters of Our Lady of the Sacred Heart, but Sister Mary Venard provided me with information from Rome and Sister Margaret Mary with material from the Yule Island Archives (YIA).

Birth, death, and marriage certificates are an essential tool for a group biography. One hundred and thirty certificates have been used, obtained from St. Catherine's House, London; the Registrar-General's Office, Papua New Guinea, and the various registrars-general's offices of the Australian states. Because of the extreme decentralization of registry offices in France, it was difficult to trace birth certificates of the French missionaries, and the requests made were not successful.

Besides the manuscript and published sources listed below, I have drawn on information provided in letters from missionary descendants, and also on personal interviews.

AAO (Australian Archives Office, Canberra)

[1880–1902]   Despatches from Secretary of State to Administrator. G3.

[1885]   Conversations with Mr Lawes re Royal Commission on recruiting. G43/1.

[1885–1886]   Correspondence for 1885 and 1886. G14.

[1885–1888]   BNG Special Commissioner, Letterbook, Home Correspondence. G4–5.

[1895–1907]   Correspondence and Papers of Administrator. G121/76–77.

[1897–1907]   Outward Letterbook, miscellaneous. G50/1.

[1900–1901]   Secret despatches from Governor of Queensland. G139/1.

[1903–1904]   Judge Robinson's Notes. G40.

[1903–1906]   Confidential despatches to Governor-General. G35/1.

[1905–1907]   Confidential Despatches. G50/1–3.

[1908–1921]   Despatches Sent. G76/1–14.

[1942]   Papua Missions: Report by missionaries re. decline in Papuan D'Entrecasteaux 1941–42. N838/1 A518.

n.d.   Folder of letters and instructions for G. Hunter. G41/1.

var. *a*   BNG Miscellaneous Papers.

var. *b*   Despatches of Lieut. Governor, Sir William MacGregor. G32.

var. *c*   Government Secretary, Letterbook. G36.

var. *d*   Private Diary of C. S. Robinson. G52/1–2.

var. *e*   Station Journals and Patrol Reports. G91.

Abel, Cecil

1978   Interview, 29 December. Alotau, PNG.

Abel, Charles W.

1900   *Kwato, New Guinea, 1890–1900.* London: C. E. Roberts.

1902   *Savage Life in New Guinea: The Papuan in Many Moods.* London: LMS.

Abel, Russell W.

1934   *Charles W. Abel of Kwato: Forty Years in Dark Papua.* New York: Fleming H. Revell Co.

Adams, A. R. D., and B. G. Magraith
    1966   *Clinical Tropical Diseases.* 4th ed. Oxford: Blackwell Scientific Publications.

Adams, Ronald W.
    1977   In the land of Strangers and Degraded Human Beings. A Culture Contact History of Tanna to 1865, with particular reference to the Rev. John G. Paton. PhD dissertation, La Trobe University, Melbourne.

Ajayi, J. F. Ade
    1965   *Christian Missions in Nigeria 1841–1891. The Making of a New Elite.* London: Longmans.

AMHS (Australasian Methodist Historical Society)
    1933–   *Journal and Proceedings.*
    1951

Anderson, R. D.
    1970   The conflict in education. In Zeldin 1970, 51–93.

    1977   *France 1870–1914.* London: Routledge & Kegan Paul.

Annales. See SMSC.

Archer, R. L.
    1921   *Secondary Education in the Nineteenth Century.* Cambridge: University Press.

Austin, Tony
    1972   F. W. Walker and Papuan Industries Limited. In *JPNGS* 6:39–62.

    1977   *Technical Training and Development in Papua, 1894–1941.* Pacific Research Monograph no. 1. Canberra: ANU.

Australia. Royal Commission of Inquiry
    1907   Report of Royal Commission of Inquiry into the present conditions, including the methods of government of the Territory of Papua and the best means for their improvement. *Votes and Proceedings of the House of Representatives with Printed Papers of both Houses.* Melbourne: Government Printer.

Australian *Annals.* See SMSC.

Australian Churchman
    1903–   Weekly. Sydney: Church of England.
    1904

Australian Temperance World
    1903   Monthly. Sydney: Independent Order of Good Templars.

AWMC (Australasian Wesleyan Methodist Church). *See also* MCA.
    1875–   *General Conference Minutes.* Sydney: Wesleyan Book Depot.
    1899

    1885   *The Laws and Regulations of the Australasian Wesleyan Methodist Church.* Melbourne: Wesleyan Book Depot.

NSW (New South Wales Conference)
    1890–   *Minutes of New South Wales and Queensland Conference.* Sydney:
    1902   Wesleyan Book Depot.

AWMMS (Australasian Wesleyan Methodist Missionary Society). *See also* MMSA.
   var. *a*   *Report of the Australasian Wesleyan Methodist Missionary Society*, 1890–1902. Sydney: Epworth Printing and Publishing House.

   var. *b*   Letters received from New Britain and Papua, 1891–1902. MOM 167/3, ML.

Ayandele, E. A.
   1966   *The Missionary Impact on Modern Nigeria, 1842–1914: A Political and Social Analysis.* London: Longmans.

Baker, Derek, ed.
   1978   *Religious Motivation: Biographical and Sociological Problems for the Church Historian.* Papers read at the 16th summer meeting and 17th winter meeting of Ecclesiastical History Society. Studies in Church History, vol. 15. Oxford: Basil Blackwell.

Banks, James A.
   1954   *Prosperity and Parenthood.* London: Routledge & Kegan Paul.

Bardsley, George
   [1892–   Notebooks (Diary). Original in possession of Mr. Howard Bardsley, 1893]   Brisbane. Ts version, PMB.

Barradale, Victor A.
   1907   *Pearls of the Pacific: Being Sketches of Missionary Life and Work in Samoa and Other Islands in the South Seas.* London: LMS.

   n.d.   *The Story of W. G. Lawes.* London: LMS.

Beattie, Betty
   1978   Interview, 17 April. Sydney.

Beharell, James
   1978   Interview, 8 November. Canberra.

Beidelman, T. O.
   1974   Social Theory and the Study of Christian Missions in Africa. *Africa* 44:235–249.

[Benjamin], Sister Julia
   1912   *Victoriana, Missionary Sister in New Guinea.* Geelong.

Berger, Peter L.
   1967   *The Sacred Canopy: Elements of a Sociological Theory of Religion.* New York: Doubleday.

Beswick, Thomas
   [1878–   Diary. NLA. 1880]

Betts, Raymond F.
   1961   *Assimilation and Association in French Colonial Policy.* New York and London: Columbia University Press.

Bevan, Theodore F.
   1890   *Toil, Travel and Discovery in British New Guinea.* London: Kegan Paul, Trench, Trübner and Co.

Biddiss, Michael D., ed.
   1979   *Images of Race.* Leicester: University Press.

Billing, M. M.
[1894– Diary. MOM 139–150.
1898]

[1895– Letterbooks. MOM 151–153.
1900]

1930   *Sister Minnie's Life and Work in Papua.* Sydney.

var.   Notebook and letters. MOM 162.

Binfield, Clyde
1977   *So Down To Prayers: Studies in English Nonconformity 1780–1920.*
        London: J. M. Dent / Totowa, NJ: Rowman and Littlefield.

Biskup, P., ed.
1974   *The New Guinea Memoirs of Jean Baptiste Octave Mouton.* Can-
        berra: ANU Press.

Black, Father Walter, MSC
1979   Interview, 20 December. Rome.

Bodger, Canon John
1979   Interview, 5 January. Alotau, PNG.

Bolt, Christine
1971   *Victorian Attitudes to Race.* London: Routledge & Kegan Paul /
        Toronto: University of Toronto Press.

Boutilier, James A., Daniel T. Hughes, and Sharon W. Tiffany, eds.
1978   *Mission, Church and Sect in Oceania.* ASAO Monograph no. 6. Ann
        Arbor: University of Michigan Press. Reprinted Lanham, MD: Uni-
        versity Press of America.

Brew, J. O., ed.
1968   *One Hundred Years of Anthropology.* Cambridge, MA: Harvard
        University Press.

Briggs, Asa
1954   *Victorian People.* London: Odhams Press.

1959   *The Age of Improvement 1783–1867.* London: Longmans.

1960   The Language of "Class" in Early Nineteenth Century England. In
        Essays in Labour History, edited by A. Briggs and J. Saville, 43–73.
        London: Macmillan.

Brisbane Courier
1885– Daily.
1908

Brisbane Daily Telegraph
1891–
1914

British New Guinea
1885– *Annual Report.* Port Moresby: Government Printer.
1906

1887   *Government Gazette.* Port Moresby: Government Printer.

Bromilow, William E.
[1891– Letters. MOM 326.
1892]

1892   Aboriginal vocabulary of Dobu. BNG *AR* 1891–1892, 106–110.

1893   Land tenure of the tribes of Nemunemu. BNG *AR* 1892–1893, 72.

1894   Notes on the tabu at Dobu. BNG *AR* 1893–1894, 78.

1910   Some manners and customs of the Dobuans. *Report* of 12th meeting of AAAS, (1909): 470–485. Brisbane.

1912   Dobuan (Papua) beliefs and folklore. *Report* of 13th meeting of AAAS (1911): 413–426. Sydney.

1914   New Guinea. In Colwell, 1914, 535–558.

1929   *Twenty Years Among Primitive Papuans.* London: Epworth Press.

Brown, George
[1890–   Journal. ML A1686/17.
1897]

[1890–   Letterbooks. ML A1686/5–7.
1909]

[1892–   Letterbooks. MOM 43–52.
1906]

[1897]   Notebooks. ML A1686/32.

1908   *George Brown, D. D., Pioneer Missionary and Explorer: an Autobiography.* London: Hodder and Stoughton.

var.   Correspondence and Papers. ML A1686/16–24.

Brown, H. A.
1956   The eastern Elema. Dip. Anthrop. thesis, University of London.

Bruce, Robert
[1894]   Voyage with J. Chalmers to the Papuan Gulf in SS *Miro*, March–April 1894. PJ, LMS.

Bulletin
1884–   Sydney. Weekly.
1914

Burns, Philp & Co.
var.   Contract (Miscellaneous) File. Burns, Philp & Co. Archives, Sydney.

Burridge, Kenelm O. L.
1973   *Encountering Aborigines.* New York: Pergamon Press.

1975   Other people's religions are absurd. In *Explorations in the Anthropology of Religion*, edited by W. E. A. van Beek and J. H. Scherer, 8–24. The Hague: Martinus Nijhoff.

1978   Missionary Occasions. In Boutilier, Hughes, and Tiffany 1978, 1–30.

Burton, John Wear
1926   *Our Task in Papua.* London: Epworth Press.

1949   *Modern Missions in the South Pacific.* London: Livingstone Press.

1955   *The First Century: The Missionary Adventure of Australasian Methodism 1855–1955.* Sydney: MOM.

Butcher, Benjamin T.
1963   *We Lived with Headhunters.* London: Hodder and Stoughton.

n.d.   *Many Faiths: one essential.* Sydney: Sven Productions.

var.   Papers (28 boxes). MS 1881, NLA.

Butcher, Marjorie
  1978   Interview, 2 September. Wentworth Falls, NSW.

Cadoux, A.
  1931   *L'Apôtre des Papous: Mgr. Henri Verjus*. Paris: Emmanuel Vitte.

Cairns, H. Alan C.
  1965   *Prelude to Imperialism: British Reactions to Central African Society 1840–1890*. London: Routledge & Kegan Paul.

Carruthers, J. E.
  1924   *Lights in the Southern Sky*. London: Epworth Press.

Cave, A.
  1898   *The Founding of Hackney College*. London.

CEA (Church of England in Australia)
  1887   *Official Year Book of the Church of England*. Sydney.

  1888   *Official Year Book. . .*

Australasian Board of Missions
  1850   *Report of Proceedings at a Meeting of the Bishops, Clergy and Laity of the Province of NSW, on Tuesday, October 29th 1850, convened for the purpose of establishing an Australasian Board of Missions*. Sydney.

ABM (Australian Board of Missions)
  1890–   *The ABM Review*. Sydney.
  1940

  1910–   *The Herald*. Sydney.
  1920

  n.d. *a*   New Guinea, Historical Notes. ABM, Sydney.

  n.d. *b*   Deceased missionaries file. ABM, Sydney.

  n.d. *c*   *The New Guinea Mission: a brief survey*. Sydney: ABM.

  n.d. *d*.   *Church Work in the Diocese of New Guinea*. Sydney: ABM.

  var.   Miscellaneous Correspondence. ABM, Sydney.

DNG (Diocese of New Guinea)
  1891–   *Address to Conference* (or *Anniversary Address*).
  1914

  1891–   *Report of the New Guinea Mission*.
  1920

  [1892–   Dogura Log, November 1892 to July 1893. Box 65, file 34, AA,
  1893]   UPNG.

  [1897–   Mission Staff Applications. Box 5, files 6–7, AA, UPNG.
  1925]

  [1898–   Dogura Log, May 1898 to September 1900. Box 65, file 4, AA,
  1900]   UPNG.

  [1899–   Diocese of New Guinea, Conferences 1899–1922. Box 2, files 48–52,
  1922]   AA, UPNG.

  [1900–   Papua, Eastern Division, Resident Magistrate 1900–1926. Box 7, file
  1926]   31, AA, UPNG.

[1902–   North East Division, Resident Magistrate. Box 7, file 37, AA, UPNG.
1909]

[1902–   Old Correspondence. Box 10, file 25, AA, UPNG.
1950]

[1904–   Roman Catholic Mission. Box 7, file 45, AA, UPNG.
1936]

[1906–   Government Secretary's Office, Correspondence. Box 7, file 33, AA,
1925]   UPNG.

[1908–   Ethnology, miscellaneous papers, 1908–1923. Box 4, file 11, AA,
1923]   UPNG.

[1910]   Album of photos by P. Money. Box 15, file 17, AA, UPNG.

[1914]   Bishop of New Guinea: Native Marriage Question and Correspon-
         dence with the Government. Box 2, file 2, AA, UPNG.

n.d. *a*   Spheres of Influence Policy. Box 1, file 1, AA, UPNG.

n.d. *b*   Death of Miss Cottingham. Box 2, file 2, AA, UPNG.

n.d. *c*   Education. Box 4, file 10, AA, UPNG.

var. *a*   Australian General Synod, Miscellaneous Papers. Box 1, file 8, AA,
           UPNG.

var. *b*   Marriage certificates, declarations etc. Box 5, file 1, AA, UPNG.

var. *c*   Station Reports. Box 5, files 28–39, AA, UPNG.

var. *d*   Annual reports, miscellaneous pamphlets, constitutions, etc. Box 8,
           AA, UPNG.

var. *e*   Personal files. Boxes 20–23, AA, UPNG.

var. *f*   *Occasional Papers.*

var. *g*   Copland King's file. Box 15, file 53, AA, UPNG.

Ceresi, Vincent
    1934   *The Life of Father Genocchi.* Translated from the Italian by Father
           Leslie Rumble. Rome: MSC.

Chadwick, Owen
    1966   *The Victorian Church.* 2 vols. London: Adam & Charles Black.

Chalmers, James
    [1877]   Rarotonga to Stacey Is. PJ, LMS.

    [1879–   Trip in the Papuan Gulf. PJ, LMS.
    1880]

    1880   New Guinea (Journey near Goldie River in 1879). RGS *Proceedings*
             n. s. 2:315–316.

    1881*a* Further explorations in New Guinea. RGS *Proceedings* 3:226–227.

    [1881*b*] Port Moresby, 1881, trip to Elema. PJ, LMS.

    1886   *Adventures in New Guinea.* London: Religious Tract Society.

    1887*a* New Guinea—past, present and future. RCI *Proceedings 1886–87*
             18.

    1887*b* On the manners and customs of some New Guinea tribes. Royal Phil-
             osophical Society of Glasgow, *Proceedings 1886–1887* 18:57–69.

1887c   *Pioneering in New Guinea*. London: Religious Tract Society.

1887d   Two New Guinea stories. In Lindt 1887, 106–117.

1887e   History and description of the pottery trade. In Lindt 1887, 118–125.

1887f   Explorations in south-east New Guinea. RGS *Proceedings* 9:71–86.

[1890a] Report of Fly River Trip. PJ, LMS.

1890b   Report of the Australasian, Papuan and Polynesian Races: New Guinea. AAAS *Report* 311–323.

[1891]   Motumotu. PJ, LMS.

1895   *Pioneer Life and Work in New Guinea*. London: Religious Tract Society.

1898   Toaripi and anthropometrical observations on some natives of the Papuan Gulf. *JRAI* 27:326–342.

[1901]   Journal, January to April. PJ, LMS.

1903a   Notes on the Bugilai, BNG. *JRAI* 33:108–110.

1903b   Notes on the natives of Kiwai island. *JRAI* 33:117–124.

[n.d.]   Autobiography: Notes for Lizzie and other papers. Papua Personal, LMS.

Chalmers, James, and W. Wyatt Gill
1885   *Work and Adventure in New Guinea 1877 to 1885*. London: Religious Tract Society.

Chalmers, James, and S. H. Ray
1898   Vocabularies of the Bugilai and Tagota dialects, BNG. *JRAI* 27:139–144.

Chaseling, Wilbur
1960   *A Boy from Geelong. The adventures of William Bromilow*. Sydney: MOM.

Chateaubriand, François René de
1802   *Génie du Christianisme ou Beautés de la Religion Chrétienne*. Paris.

Chignell, Arthur K.
1911   *An Outpost in Papua*. London: Smith, Elder & Co.

1913   *Twenty-one Years in Papua: A History of the English Church Mission in New Guinea (1891–1912)*. London: A. R. Mowbray and Co.

n.d.   Two untitled MSS. Evan Gill Collection, ML.

Chinnery, E. W. P.
1932   Applied anthropology in New Guinea. ANZAAS Congress *Proceedings* 21:163–175. Reprinted 1933, Canberra: Government Printer.

Christian World
[1890–   London.
1914]

Church Chronicle
1903   Monthly. Brisbane: Church of England.

Church Standard
1918   Weekly. Sydney: Church of England.

Church Times
1918   Weekly. Melbourne: Church of England.

Clark, G. Kitson
1965   *The Making of Victorian England.* London: Methuen.

Coghlan, T. A.
1901   *New South Wales Vital Statistics for 1901 and previous years.* Sydney: Government Printer.

Cohen, W. B.
1969   The lure of empire: Why Frenchmen enter the colonial service. *Journal of Contemporary History* 4:103–116.

Colwell, James
1904   *The Illustrated History of Methodism: Australia 1812 to 1855; New South Wales and Polynesia 1856 to 1902.* Sydney: William Brooks & Co.

Colwell, James, ed.
1914   *A Century in the Pacific.* Sydney: William H. Beale.

Cooke, C. Kinloch
1887   *Australian Defences and New Guinea.* London.

Corris, Peter
1968   Blackbirding in New Guinea waters. *JPH* 3:85–106.

Couppé, Victor
var. *a*   Correspondence. BA.

var. *b*   Correspondence. RA.

Cranswick, G. H., and I. W. A. Shevill
1949   *A New Deal for Papua.* Melbourne: F. W. Cheshire.

Crockford's Clerical Directory
1925–   Oxford University Press.
1939

Crosfield, W.
[1897]   Diary, Deputation 1897. South Seas Personal, LMS.

Cross, F. L.
1958   *The Oxford Dictionary of the Christian Church.* Oxford: University Press.

Crow, Duncan
1971   *The Victorian Woman.* London: George Allen & Unwin.

Cruse, Amy
1935   *The Victorians and their Books.* London: George Allen & Unwin Ltd.

Cuskelly, E. J.
1975   *Jules Chevalier: A Man with a Mission.* Rome: MSC.

D'Albertis, Luigi
1880   *New Guinea: What I Did and What I Saw.* 2 vols. London: Sampson Low, Marston, Searle and Rivington.

Danks, Benjamin
[1900–   Letterbooks. MOM 54–62, 230–231.
1914]

Dansette, A.
1961   *Religious History of Modern France*. 2 vols. Freiburg: Herder/Edinburgh, London: Nelson.

Dauncey, H. M.
[1891–   Letterbook and financial papers. ML 1356/15.
1893]

[1897–   Letters received. ML 1356/16.
1904]

1913   *Papuan Pictures*. London: LMS.

var.   Diary extracts and circular letter. Papua Personal, LMS.

Davidson, Randall
var.   Papers, 1907, 1910, 1912, 1925. Lambeth Palace.

Daws, C. Kingston
1962   *Methodist Ministerial Index for Australia*. Melbourne: Spectator Publishing Co.

Daws, Gavan
1973   *Holy Man: Father Damien of Molokai*. New York: Harper & Row.

1978   "All the horrors of the half known life"—some notes on the writing of biography in the Pacific. In *The Changing Pacific: Essays in Honour of H. E. Maude*, edited by Niel Gunson, 297–307. Melbourne: Oxford University Press.

Deacon, A., and M. Hill
1972   The problem of surplus women in the nineteenth century: secular and religious alternatives. In *A Sociological Year Book of Religion in Britain*, no. 5, edited by D. Martin, London: SCM Press.

De Boismenu, Alain
1905   The Catholic Church in British New Guinea. In *Proceedings of the Second Australasian Catholic Congress, Melbourne . . . 1904*. Melbourne.

1908   *Pastoral Letter*, no. 5.

1912   *Pastoral Letter*, no. 10.

1913   *Pastoral Letter*, no. 14.

1915   *Pastoral Letter*, 11 February.

Dening, Greg
1980   *Islands and Beaches: Discourse on a Silent Land, Marquesas 1774–1880*. Melbourne: University Press.

De Vaulx, Bernard
1951   *Histoire des Missions Catholiques Françaises*. Paris.

Didinger, Johannes, and Robert Streit
1951   *Bibliotecha Missionum 1525–1950. Bd 21. Missions-literateur von Australien und Ozeanien 1525–1950*. Veroffenflichungen des Internationalen Instituts fur missionswissenschaftliche Forschung. Freiburg: Verlag Herder.

Dollard, John
1949   *Criteria for the Life History with Analysis of Six Notable Documents*. New York: P. Smith.

Douglas, John M.
 1971   The Loyalty Islands and S. McFarlane 1859–1869. BA (Hons.) thesis, ANU.

Drummond, Henry
 1889   *Natural Law in the Spiritual World.* 24th ed. London: Hodder & Stoughton.

Dupeyrat, André
 1934   *Papouasie: Histoire de la Mission 1885–1935.* Paris: Dillen.

 1948   *Papuan Conquest.* Melbourne: Araluen Publishing Co.

 1951   *Le Sanglier de Kouni.* Issoudun: Archi-confrérie de Nôtre Dame du Sacré-Coeur.

 1952   *Vingt-et-un ans chez les Papous.* Paris: Arthème Fayard.

 1955   *Festive Papua.* London: Staples.

 1964   *Briseurs de la Lance chez les Papous.* Paris: Editions Albin-Michel.

Dupeyrat, A., and F. de la Noë
 1958   *Sainteté au Naturel: Alain de Boismenu, Evêque des Papous.* Paris: Arthème-Fayard.

Dyson, Martin
 1889,   *Australasian Methodist Ministerial General Index.* Melbourne: Mason, Firth & McCutcheon.
 1908

Edwards, Maldwyn
 1943   *Methodism and England: A study of Methodism in its social and political aspects during the period 1850–1932.* London: Epworth Press.

Egidi, V. M.
 1907   La tribu di Kuni and la tribu di Tivata. *Anthropos* 2:107–115, 675–681, 1009–1021.

 1909   Casa e villagio, sottotribu e tribu dei Kuni. *Anthropos* 4:387–404.

 1910   Questioni riguardanti la constituzioni fisica dei Kuni. *Anthropos* 5:748–755.

 1912   La tribu dei Kobio, British New Guinea. *Rivista di Antropologia* 16:337–354.

 1913a   La religione et le conoscenze naturali dei Kuni. *Anthropos* 8:208–218.

 1913b   Mythes et legends des Kuni, British New Guinea (part 1). *Anthropos* 8:978–1009; 9:81–97, 392–404.

 1914   Mythes et legends des Kuni, British New Guinea (parts 2, 3). *Anthropos* 9: 81–97, 392–404.

Elliott, Edmund E. R.
 1961   *Child of Calvary, Martyr of Satan: A Biography of Marie Thérèse Noblet.* Melbourne: Carmelite Fathers.

Elliott-Binns, L. E.
 1936   *Religion in the Victorian Era.* London: Lutterworth Press.

Eri, Vincent
 1970   *The Crocodile.* Milton, Qld: Jacaranda Press.

Erikson, Erik
1972   *Young Man Luther.* Paperback edition. London: Faber.

Eschlimann, P. H.
1911   L'enfant chez les Kuni. *Anthropos* 6:260–275.

Fairhall, Sister Constance
1981   Interview, 10 February. Canberra.

Farrar, F. W.
1867   Aptitude of races. In *Transactions of the Ethnological Society.* Reprinted in Biddis 1979.

Fastré, Paul
1933   *Les Origines de la Mission de la Papouasie.* Chateauroux: Imprimerie Centrale.

Fellows, Samuel
[1883–   Diaries and Papers. Australian National Gallery. Copies at MOM
1900]   and PMB.

1893   Grammar of the Pannieti dialect. *BNG AR 1892–1893* (appendix 5):79–82.

1900   Memo for HE the Governor concerning the peace-making ceremony between the Kiriwina tribes. . . . *BNG AR 1899–1900* (appendix D):20–21.

1901*a*   Atonement or peace-making ceremony of the natives of Kiriwina. *Man* 1:45–47.

1901*b*   Grammar of the Kiriwina dialect. *BNG AR 1900–1901*, 171–196.

Field, Benjamin
[c. 1868]   *Students' Handbook of Christian Theology.* Melbourne.

Field, John T.
1898   Notes on totemism, Tubetube. *BNG AR 1897–1898* (appendix CC):134.

1900   Exogamy at Tubetube: BNG and Burial Customs at Tubetube, BNG. AAS *Report* 301–307.

Figuier, Louis Guillaume
1872   *The Human Race.* London.

Findlay, G., and W. H. Holdsworth
1921   *The History of the Wesleyan Methodist Missionary Society,* vol. 3. London: Epworth Press.

Fitchett, William Henry
1914   *What Methodism Stands For.* Sydney: Methodist Book Depot.

Fletcher, C. Brunsdon
1917   *The New Pacific. British Policy and German Aims.* London: Macmillan.

1933   A footnote to the history of Christian missions. AMHS *Journal and Proceedings* 1:8–9.

1944   *The Black Knight of the Pacific.* Sydney: Australasian Publishing Co.

Forman, Charles W.
  1978   Missionaries in the Twentieth Century. In Boutilier, Hughes, and Tiffany 1978, 35–63.

Forrest, Michael D.
  1922   *Father Justin: A Story of Papua*. 2nd ed. Sydney: Sacred Heart Monastery.

Fort, George S.
  1942   *Chance or Design? A Pioneer Looks Back*. London: Robert Hale.

Fortune, R. F.
  1932   *Sorcerers of Dobu: The Social Anthropology of the Dobu Islanders of the Western Pacific*. London: George Routledge and Sons.

Frazer, Sir James George
  1949   *The Golden Bough: A Study in Magic and Religion*. Abridged ed. London: Macmillan.

Gann, L. H. and Peter Duignan, eds.
  1969   *Colonialism in Africa 1870–1960*. Vol. 1: *The History and Politics of Colonialism, 1870–1914*. Cambridge: University Press.

Garnett, W. M.
  1970   Dobu and the Missionaries 1891–1920: The problems, effects, successes and failures of the Methodist Mission on Dobu Island TPNG. BA (Hons.) thesis, ANU.

Garran, Sir Robert
  1958   *Prosper the Commonwealth*. Sydney: Angus & Robertson.

  var.   Diaries and Papers. NLA.

Garrett, John
  1982   *To Live Among the Stars: Christian Origins in Oceania*. Suva: University of the South Pacific, Institute of Pacific Studies / Geneva: World Council of Churches.

GBCO (Great Britain Colonial Office)
  [1888–   New Guinea (Papua) Sessional Papers. CO 436/1–3.
  1906]

  var.   New Guinea (Papua) Original Correspondence. CO 422/1–15.

Geertz, Clifford
  1966   Religion as a Cultural System. In *Anthropological Approaches to the Study of Religion*, edited by M. Banton, London: Tavistock.

Geil, William E.
  1902   *Ocean and Isle*. Melbourne: Wm. T. Pater and Co.

Gilbert, Alan D.
  1976   *Religion and Society in Industrial England*. London/New York: Longmans.

Gill, Eric
  1940   *Autobiography*. London: Jonathon Cape.

Gill, Evan
  var.   Correspondence. 1 vol. ML.

Gill, Stephen R. M.
  1954   *Letters from the Papuan Bush*. Liverpool: Eaton Press.

  var.   Papers: Diaries and letters. UPNG.

Gilson, Richard
 1980   *The Cook Islands 1820–1950.* Wellington: Victoria University of
         Wellington / Suva: Institute of Pacific Studies of the University of the
         South Pacific.

Glass, D. V.
 1967   *Population Policies and Movements.* London: Frank Cass & Co.

Glencross, B.
 1949   *New Guinea? Not Me!* London: Edinburgh Press.

Godwin, George
 1951   *The Great Revivalists.* London: Watts & Co.

Goodall, Norman
 1954   *A History of the London Missionary Society 1895–1945.* London:
         Oxford University Press.

 1964   *Christian Missions and Social Ferment.* London: Epworth Press.

Goyau, Pierre L. T. G.
 1938   *Le Christ chez les Papous.* Paris: Beauchesne et ses fils.

Green, John
 var.   Letters to family. PMB.

Griffin, Henry L.
 1925   *An Official in British New Guinea.* London: Cecil Palmer.

Griffiths, Deidre J. F.
 1977   The career of F. E. Williams, government anthropologist of Papua,
         1922–43. MA thesis, ANU.

Grimshaw, Beatrice
 1911   *The New New Guinea.* London: Hutchinson and Co.

 1913   *Adventures in Papua with the Catholic Mission.* Melbourne: Austra-
         lian Catholic Truth Society.

Groves, C. P.
 1969   Missionary and Humanitarian Aspects of Imperialism, 1870–1914.
         In Gann and Duignan 1969, 462–496.

Grubb, Arthur P.
 1913   *A Popular Handbook of Methodist Law and Usage.* London: Charles
         H. Kelly.

Gsell, F. X.
 1955   *The Bishop with 150 Wives.* London: Angus and Robertson.

Guis, Joseph
 1936   *La Vie des Papous.* Paris: Editions Dillen / Issoudun: Archi-confrérie
         de Nôtre-Dame du Sacré-Coeur.

Gunson, W. N. (Niel)
 1958   Evangelical Missionaries in the South Seas 1797–1860. PhD disserta-
         tion, ANU.

 1965   Missionary interest in British expansion in the South Pacific in the
         nineteenth century. *JRH* 3:296–313.

 1966   On the incidence of alcoholism and intemperance in early Pacific
         missionaries. *JPH* 1:43–62.

1969   The theology of imperialism and the missionary history of the Pacific. *JRH* 5:255–265.

1974   Victorian Christianity in the South Seas: A survey. *JRH* 8:183–197.

1978   *Messengers of Grace: Evangelical missionaries in the South Seas 1797–1860*. Melbourne: Oxford University Press.

Haddon, A. C.
1901   *Headhunters, Black, White and Brown*. London: Methuen.

1929   Obituary: The Rev. E. Baxter Riley. *Man* 29:202–203.

1935   *Reports on the Cambridge Anthropological Expedition to Torres Straits*, vol. 1. Cambridge: University Press.

var.   Papers. Cambridge University Library. PMB.

Halèvy, Elie
1961   *History of the English People in the Nineteenth Century*. Vol. 4: *Victorian Years 1845–1895*. Paperback edition. London: Ernest Benn.

Hall, A. Gratten
[c. 1921]   *Abel of Kwato*. London: LMS.

Hallden, Erik
1968   *The Cultural Policy of the Basel Missions in the Cameroons 1886–1905*. Studia ethnographica upsaliensia no. 31. Uppsala.

Harris, Marvin
1969   *The Rise of Anthropological Theory*. London: Routledge & Kegan Paul.

Harrison, Brian
1975   Christ and Culture in north-east New Guinea. MA thesis, UPNG.

Hartzer, Fernand
1888   *Cinq ans parmi les Sauvages de la Nouvelle-Bretagne et de la Nouvelle-Guinée*. Issoudun: MSC.

Hau'ofa, Epeli
1975   Mekeo: A study of a Papua New Guinea society. PhD dissertation, ANU.

Heeney, Brian
1976   *A Different Kind of Gentleman: Parish clergy as professional men in early and mid-Victorian England*. Hamden, CT: Shoe String Press.

Hely, B. A.
[1893–   Journal, 2 March 1893 to 19 April 1894. ML.
1894]

Henkelmann, A.
1928   Notice sur nos Frères Coadjuteurs Morts dans Nouvelle-Guinée. In *Annales de Notre Dame du Sacré-Coeur*.

1949   *En bourlinguant sur la Mer de Corail*. Issoudun: MSC.

Hezel, Francis X.
1983   *The First Taint of Civilization: A History of the Caroline and Marshall Islands in Pre-Colonial Days, 1521–1885*. Pacific Islands Monograph Series no. 1. Honolulu: University of Hawaii Press.

Hilliard, David
1978   *God's Gentlemen: A History of the Melanesian Mission 1849–1942.*
Brisbane: University of Queensland Press.

Hobson, John A.
1902   *Imperialism: A Study.* London: James Nisbet.

Hoffman, R.
1967   Propagation of the Faith, Congregation for. In *New Catholic Encyclopaedia* 11:840–845. New York: McGraw-Hill.

Holmes, J. H.
[1893– Diaries and Papers. LMS.
1900]

1899   Notes by Rev. J. H. Holmes on the work of the London Missionary
Society in the Gulf of Papua. *BNG AR 1898–1899* (appendix 2):98.

[1900– Papers. ML 1356/18.
1916]

1902*a* Initiation ceremonies of the natives of the Papuan Gulf. *JRAI*
32:418–425.

1902*b* Notes on the religious ideas of the Elema tribe of the Papuan Gulf.
JRAI 32:426–431.

1903   Notes on the Elema tribe of the Papuan Gulf. *JRAI* 33:125–134.

1905   Introductory notes to a study of the totemism of the Elema tribes,
Papuan Gulf. *Man* 5:2–6, 17–20.

1908   Introductory notes on the toys and games of Elema, Papuan Gulf.
JRAI 38:280–288.

1913   A preliminary study of the Namau language, Purari delta, Papua.
JRAI 43:124–142.

1924   *In Primitive New Guinea.* London: Seeley, Service.

1926   *Way Back in Papua.* London: George Allen & Unwin.

Honey, J. R. de S.
1977   *Tom Brown's Universe. The development of the Victorian Public
School.* London: Millington.

Horne, Charles S.
1904   *Story of the L.M.S.* London: LMS.

Howe, K. R.
1977   *The Loyalty Islands: A History of Culture Contact 1840–1900.* Canberra, ANU Press.

1984   *Where the Waves Fall: A New South Sea Islands History from First
Settlement to Colonial Rule.* Pacific Islands Monograph Series no. 2.
Honolulu: University of Hawaii Press/Sydney: George Allen &
Unwin.

Howe, Renata
1965   The Wesleyan Church in Victoria 1885–1901. Its ministry and membership. MA thesis, University of Melbourne.

1967   The social composition of the Wesleyan Church in Victoria during
the nineteenth century. *JRH* 4:206–217.

Hunt, Archibald E.
[1893–   Letterbook. ML.
1902]

Hunt, John
1896   *Religious thought in England in the Nineteenth Century.* London: Gibbings.

Hurley, Frank
[1921]   Diaries. NLA.

1924   *Pearls and Savages.* New York: G. P. Putnam's Sons.

Inglis, James
1880   *Our Australian Cousins.* London: Macmillan.

Inglis, K. S.
1963   *Churches and the Working Classes in Victorian England.* London: Routledge & Kegan Paul.

1974   *The Australian Colonists: An Exploration of Social History 1788–1870.* Melbourne: University Press.

Iremonger, Lucille
1970   *The Fiery Chariot: A Study of British Prime Ministers and the Search for Love.* London: Secker & Warburg.

Irvine, William
1955   *Apes, Angels and Victorians: A Joint Biography of Darwin and Huxley.* London: Weidenfeld & Nicolson.

Jenness, D. and A. Ballantyne
1928   *Language, mythology and songs of Bwaidoga, Goodenough Island, S. E. Papua.* New Plymouth, N.Z.: Thomas Avery & Sons.

Johnson, A. N.
[1907]   Diary, Deputation to Australia. LMS.

Jones, Gareth S.
1971   *Outcast London: A Study in the Relationship between Classes in Victorian Society.* Oxford: University Press.

Jones, R. Fleming
1911   The health conditions of Papua. In Pritchard 1911, 89–96.

Jones, Robert T.
1962   *Congregationalism in England 1662–1962.* London: Independent Press.

Jouet, V.
1887   *Les Missionaires du Sacré-Coeur dans les Vicariats Apostoliques de la Mélanesie et de la Micronésie.* Issoudun: MSC.

n.d.   Notes sur la Mission. RA-VAMM. PMB.

Joyce, R. B.
1971   *Sir William MacGregor.* Melbourne: Oxford University Press.

Jullien, André
n.d.   Manuscrit . . . du P. Jullien sur l'histoire antérieure des Missions [en Océanie]. RA-VANG.

Kaniku, J. W.
1975   James Chalmers at Sua'au Island. *Oral History* 3 (9):71–76.

Ker, Annie
1910   *Papuan Fairy Tales*. London: Macmillan.

Kiki, Albert Maori
1968   *Ten Thousand Years in a Lifetime: A New Guinea Autobiography*. Melbourne: F. W. Cheshire.

King, Cecil J.
1934   *Copland King and his Papuan Friends*. Sydney: The Worker Trustees.

King, Copland
1892   Vocabulary of words spoken by tribes of Wedau, Wamira and Jiwari, Bartle Bay. . . . BNG *AR* (appendix W): 92–100.

1894   Notes on tabu in Wedau and Wamira, Bartle Bay, BNG. BNG *AR, 1893–1894* (appendix 5): 76–77.

1895   Notes on native land tenure and other customs of Bartle Bay District. . . . BNG *AR 1894–1895:* 37–38.

1899   *A History of the New Guinea Mission*. Sydney: W. A. Pepperday.

1913   The Baigona Cult. *Papua AR 1912–1913* (appendix A): 154–155.

var.   Letters. CEA-DNG, box 15, file 30.

King, Joseph
1895   *Ten Decades: The Australian Centenary Story of the London Missionary Society*. London: LMS.

1909   *W. G. Lawes of Savage Island and New Guinea*. London: The Religious Tract Society.

Knowles, David
1963   *The Historian and Character, and Other Essays*. Cambridge: University Press.

Koskinen, Arne A.
1953   *Missionary Influence as a Political Factor in the Pacific*. Helsinki: Suomalaisen Kirjallisuden Seuran Kirjapainon Oy.

Kwato Mission
var.   Papers. NLA.

Landtman, Gunnar
1927   *The Kiwai Papuans of British New Guinea: A Nature-born Instance of Rousseau's Ideal Community*. London: Macmillan.

Langmore, Diane
1972   Goaribari, 1904. *JPNGS* 6 (2): 53–78.

1974   *Tamate—a King: James Chalmers in New Guinea, 1877–1901*. Melbourne: University Press.

1982a   "Where every prospect pleases." In *Melanesia Beyond Diversity*, edited by R. May and H. N. Nelson, 1:107–122. Canberra: ANU Press.

1982b   A neglected force: White women missionaries in Papua 1874–1914. *JPH* 17:138–157.

1985   "Exchanging earth for heaven": Death in the Papuan missionfields. *JRH* 13:383–392.

Laracy, Hugh
   1969   Catholic Missions in the Solomon Islands, 1845–1966. PhD disserta-
            tion, ANU.
   1976a   *Marists and Melanesians: A History of Catholic Missions in the Solo-*
            mon Islands. Canberra: ANU Press.
   1976b   Roman Catholic "Martyrs" in the South Pacific, 1841–55. *JRH*
            9:189–202.
Latourette, Kenneth S.
   1941   A *History of the Expansion of Christianity*, Vol. 4: *The Great Cen-*
            tury, A.D. 1800-A.D. 1914: Europe and the United States of
            America. New York: Harper & Brothers.
   1943   A *History* . . . Vol. 5: *The Great Century: In the Americas, Austra-*
            lasia and Africa, A.D. 1800-A.D. 1914. New York: Harper & Broth-
            ers.
Latukefu, Sione
   1974   *Church and State in Tonga: The Wesleyan Methodist Missionaries*
            and Political Development, 1822-1875. Honolulu: University Press
            of Hawaii / Canberra: ANU Press.
Lawes, Charles
   1978   Interview, 3 September. Leura, NSW.
Lawes, W. G.
   [1876] Voyage to China Strait . . . PJ, LMS.
   [1876– Voyage in the Mayri to Hood Point. PJ, LMS.
   1877]
   1879   Ethnological notes on the Motu, Koitapu and Koiari tribes of New
            Guinea. *JRAI* 8:369–377.
   1880   Notes on New Guinea and its inhabitants. RGS *Proceedings* n.s.
            2:602–616.
   1883   An excursion into the interior of New Guinea. RGS *Proceedings* n.s.
            5:355–358.
   1884   Recent explorations in south-eastern New Guinea. RGS *Proceedings*
            6:216–218.
   1886   The condition of New Guinea. BNG *AR:*24–26.
   1887   The effect of the climate of New Guinea upon exotic races. *Australa-*
            sian Medical Gazette 6:185–186.
   1890   Comparative views of New Guinea dialects. BNG *AR 1889-1890:*
            158–167.
   1891   *Speech to International Congregational Council.* London.
   1896   *Grammar and Vocabulary of the Language Spoken by the Motu*
            Tribe, New Guinea. 3rd ed. Sydney.
   var.   Diary. ML A387–389.
   var.   Letters. ML A390–391.
Lenwood, Frank
   [1897] Notebook. SSO, box 8, LMS.
   [1916] Deputation Notebook. SSO, box 8, LMS.
   1917   *Pastels from the Pacific.* London: Oxford University Press.

Les missions dans le Pacifique
  1969 *Journal de la Société des Océanistes* 25 (December). Paris. Cited as *Les missions.*

Lett, Lewis
  1949 *Sir Hubert Murray of Papua.* London / Sydney: Collins.

Lill, Maisie
  var. Papers. In possession of Rev. George Carter, New Zealand.

Lindt, J. W.
  1887 *Picturesque New Guinea.* London: Longmans Green and Co.

Lloyd, Edith
  var. Letterbooks and Journals. 6 vols. MOM.

LMS (London Missionary Society)
  1867– *Chronicle of the London Missionary Society.* London.
  1920

  1873*a* *Constitution, By-laws and General Regulations.* London.

  1873*b* *General Regulations for the Guidance of English Missionaries*

  1892 *General Regulations* . . . London.

  1897 *Centenary of the LMS: Proceedings of Founders' Week Convention.* London.

  1903 *Constitution, By-laws* . . .

  1908 *Report, Deputation to Australia, 1907.* London.

  1910 *Constitution, By-laws* . . .

  [1915] Answers to deputation questions. SSO, Boxes 10–11, LMS, SOAS, London.

  [1916*a*] Deputation to South Seas and Papua, June 1915–1916. SSO, SOAS, London.

  1916*b* *Report of the Deputation to the South Seas and Papua, June 1915–1916.* London.

  var. *a* Candidates' Answers, 1796–1899. LMS, SOAS, London.

  var. *b* Candidates' Papers, 1796–1899. LMS, SOAS, London.

  var. *c* Candidates' Papers, 1900–1940. LMS, SOAS, London.

  var. *d* Candidates' References. SOAS, London.

  var. *e* Committee Minutes, Candidates' Examinations. SOAS, London.

  var. *f* Papua Journals. SOAS, London.

  var. *g* Papua Letters. SOAS, London.

  var. *h* Papua Odds. SOAS, London.

  var. *i* Papua Personal. SOAS, London.

  var. *j* Papua Reports. SOAS, London.

  var. *k* Western (later Southern) Outgoing Letters, 1835–1914. LMS, SOAS, London.

Lockwood, David
  1958 *The Black-coated Worker. A Study in Class Consciousness.* London: George Allen & Unwin.

Lovett, Richard
  1899   *The History of the London Missionary Society, 1795–1895.* 2 vols.
          London: Henry Frowde.

  1903   *James Chalmers: His Autobiography and Letters.* London: Religious
          Tract Society.

  n.d.   *Tamate: The Life and Adventures of a Christian Hero.* London:
          Religious Tract Society.

Lutton, Nancy
  1979   Larger than life: A biography of Charles Abel of Kwato. MA thesis,
          UPNG.

Luzbetak, L. J.
  1967   Adaptation, Missionary. In *New Catholic Encyclopaedia* 1:120–122.
          New York: McGraw-Hill.

McAuley, James
  1955   Christian Missionaries. In *South Pacific* 8 (7):138–146.

  1961   My New Guinea. *Quadrant* 5 (3): 23–27.

Macdonald, Barrie
  1982   *Cinderellas of the Empire.* Canberra: ANU Press.

McFarlane, Samuel
  [1859– Journal. ML A833.
  1869]

  1873   *The Story of the Lifu Mission.* London: LMS.

  [1875– Twelve journals describing various pioneering expeditions in the *Ber-*
  1884]   *tha* and the *Ellangowan.* PJ, LMS.

  1877   Voyage of the *Ellangowan* to China Straits, New Guinea. RGS *Pro-*
          ceedings 21:350–360.

  1888   *Among the Cannibals of New Guinea.* London: LMS.

McFarlane, Samuel, and James Chalmers
  1879   *The Mission in New Guinea.* London: LMS.

MacGregor, Sir William
  [1890– Diary. 4 vols. NLA.
  1892]

MacKay, Kenneth
  1909   *Across Papua: Being an account of a voyage round, and a march*
          across, the Territory of Papua with the Royal Commission. London:
          Witherby.

Maclaren, Albert A.
  [1890] Diary, May to August 1890. AA.

  [1891] Letterbook (fragment). AA.

  [var.] Letterbooks. AA.

McLaren, Jack
  1946   *My Odyssey: South Seas Adventures.* Melbourne: Oxford University
          Press.

Maclean, Catherine M.
  1955   *Mark Rutherford: A Biography of William Hale White.* London:
          Macdonald.

McLeod, Hugh
    1973   Class, community and religion: The religious geography of the nine-teenth century. *Sociological Year Book of Religion*, 4:23–69. London: SCM Press.

    1974   *Class and Religion in the Late Victorian City*. London: Croom Helm.

McMahon, Father John, MSC
    1978   Interview, 15 July. Canberra.

Mahood, M.
    1973   *The Loaded Line: Australian Political Caricature 1788–1901*. Melbourne: University Press.

Malinowski, B.
    1967   *A Diary in the Strict Sense of the Term*. London: Routledge and Kegan Paul.

Mannoni, O.
    1956   *Prospero and Caliban: The Psychology of Colonization*. London: Methuen.

Margaret Mary, Sister, FDNSC
    1979   Interview, 16 January. Yule Island, PNG.

Martha, Sister, FDNSC
    1979   Interview, 9 February. Kensington, NSW.

Martin, D.
    1967   *A Sociology of English Religion*. New York: Basic Books.

Martin, K. L. P.
    1924   *Missionaries and Annexation in the Pacific*. London: Oxford University Press.

Mathews, Basil J.
    1917   *Dr Ralph Wardlaw Thompson*. London: Religious Tract Society.

Maugham, W. Somerset
    1956   *The works of W. Somerset Maugham: The Trembling of a Leaf*. London: W. Heinemann.

MCA (Methodist Church of Australasia). *See also* AWMC
    1904   *Minutes of General Conference*. Sydney: Methodist Book Depot.

    1905   *Laws and regulations of the Methodist Church of Australasia*.

    1907   *Minutes of General Conference*. Sydney: Methodist Book Depot.

    1910   *Minutes of General Conference*. Sydney: Methodist Book Depot.

    1913   *Minutes of General Conference*. Sydney: Methodist Book Depot.

    [NSW] New South Wales Conference
    [1885–   Minutes of Examining Committee, New South Wales. ML.
    1914]

    [1890–   New South Wales Conference Minute Books, ministerial sessions.
    1922]   UCR, Sydney.

    1902–   *Minutes of New South Wales Conference*. Sydney: Epworth Press.
    1960

    var.   Box of "characters." UCR, Sydney.

MCNZ (Methodist Church of New Zealand)
[1903– Overseas Mission Department Minutes. PMB.
1955]

Melbourne *Age*
1874– Daily.
1914

Melbourne *Argus*
1874– Daily.
1914

Methodist
1915– Published by MCA-NSW. Sydney.
1940

Meyer, Eugene
1922– Biography of André Jullien. Serialized in *Annales*.
1924

Mitchell, B. R., and Phyllis Deane
1962 *Abstract of British Historical Statistics*. Cambridge: University Press.

MMSA (Methodist Missionary Society of Australasia). *See also* AWMMS.
[1909– Letters received. MOM 114, ML.
1910]

[1911– Correspondence. MOM 115, ML.
1912]

[1913] Papua 1913. MOM 119, ML.

[1920] Missionaries 1919–1920. MOM 120, ML.

[1935*a*] Register of lay missionaries, 1916–1935. MOM 217, ML.

[1935*b*] Register of missionary sisters, 1915–1935. MOM 218, ML.

n.d. Register of missionaries. MOM 216, ML.

var. *a* *Report of the Methodist Missionary Society of Australia*. Sydney:
Epworth Printing and Publishing House.

var. *b* Papua. Photos. MOM 254–258, ML.

NGD (New Guinea District)
[1891– Journal of Synod. Box 30, UCA, UPNG, Port Moresby.
1911*a*]

[1891– Minutes of Methodist Mission, Milne Bay. Box 20, file 1, UCA,
1911*b*] UPNG.

[1891– Correspondence, Methodist Mission, Milne Bay. Box 14, file 5, UCA,
1946] UPNG.

[1903– Correspondence with Administration. Box 16, file 2, UCA, UPNG.
1911]

[1912– Record of Synod Meetings. Box 19, file 2, UCA, UPNG.
1934]

[1913– Correspondence with General Secretary. Box 16, file 5, UCA,
1914] UPNG.

n.d. White children of missionaries . . . Box 41, file 23, UCA, UPNG.

var. *a*   Miscellaneous documents. Box 17, file 33, UCA, UPNG.

var. *b*   Stipends and allowances of missionaries. Box 27, file 73, UCA, UPNG.

Mobley, Harris W.
1970   *The Ghanaian's Image of the Missionary*. Leiden: E. J. Brill.

Monckton, C. A. W.
1921   *Some Experiences of a New Guinea Resident Magistrate*. London: Bodley Head.

1934   *New Guinea Recollections*. London: Bodley Head.

Money, Percy
[1910]   Album of photos. AA box 15, file 25.

MR *(Missionary Review)*
1890–   Published by Methodist Missionary Society of Australasia (formerly
1940   AWMMS). Titled *Australasian Methodist Missionary Review* until 1914.

Murray, Charles Gideon
var.   Diary. UPNG, Port Moresby.

Murray, J. H. P. (Sir Hubert)
[1904–   Diary. ML.
1916]

1912   *Papua or British New Guinea*. London: T. Fisher Unwin.

1925   *Papua of Today*. London: P. S. King.

1930   Papuan criminals and British justice. Letter in *Man* 30:132.

n.d.   Draft history.

Musgrave, Anthony
[1889]   Memorandum on prospective establishment of a branch of the AWMMS in PNG, 27 September 1889. ML.

n.d.   Private and confidential memo. ML.

var. *a*   Papers. ML.

var. *b*   Press cuttings of New Guinea affairs. ML.

Nairne, W. P.
1913   *Greatheart of Papua (James Chalmers)*. London: Oxford University Press.

Navarre, Louis-André
[1881–   Extraits de son Journal. RA.
1886]

1896   *Manuel des Missionaires du Sacré-Coeur parmi les Sauvages*. Yule Island: MSC.

var. *a*   Correspondances. RA.

var. *b*   Notes et Journal. BA.

var. *c*   Notes sur sa Vie. BA. PMB.

Neill, Stephen
1966   *Foundations of the Christian Missions: Colonialism and Christian Missions*. London: Lutterworth Press.

Nelson, Hank
    1976   *Black, White and Gold: Gold mining in Papua New Guinea, 1878–1930*. Canberra: ANU Press.

Newton, Henry
    [1903–   Letters and photographs. UPNG.
    1947]

    1914   *In Far New Guinea*. London: Seeley Service.

    n.d.   *The Anglican Mission to New Guinea: A brief survey*. Sydney: ABM.

    [c. 1938]   *The Life Story of Rev. Frederick Robert Newton by his foster son, Bishop Henry Newton of Papua*. Sydney: Building Print.

    var.   Letters and papers. AA box 7, file 30.

Norin, G.
    1935   *Bourjade le Papou*. Paris: Dillen.

Northcott, Cecil
    1936   *Guinea Gold: The London Missionary Society at Work in the Territory of Papua*. London: Livingstone Press.

    1937   *My Friends, the Cannibals (John H. Holmes of Papua)*. London: Edinburgh House Press.

North Queensland Register
    1900   Weekly newspaper. Townsville.

Oddie, G. A.
    1974   India and Missionary Motives c.1850–1900. *JEH* 25:61–74.

Oeuvres Pontificales. *See* Society for the Propagation of the Faith . . .

Ogilvie, J. N.
    1923   *Our Empire's Debt to the Missions*. London: Hodder & Stoughton.

Oliver, Douglas L.
    1961   *The Pacific Islands*. Rev. ed. New York: Doubleday.

Oliver, Laura
    n.d.   Notes. AA box 15, file 39.

Oliver, Roland
    1952   *The Missionary Factor in East Africa*. London: Longmans, Green & Co.

Oram, N. D.
    1968   Culture change, economic development and migration among the Hula. *Oceania* 38:243–275.

    1971   The London Missionary Society pastorate and the emergence of an educated elite in Papua. *JPH* 6:115–132.

Orchard, S. C.
    n.d.   *Cheshunt College*. Cambridge.

Osborne, J. R.
    1907   *Statement concerning the Friction among Missionaries in the Papua District*. Sydney.

Pannikar, K. M.
    1959   *Asia and Western Dominance*. New ed. London: George Allen & Unwin.

Papua
  1906–   *Annual Report.* Port Moresby: Government Printer.
  1940

Paul-Marie, Sister, FDNSC
  1979   Interview, 23 December. Issoudun, France.

Pearse, Albert
  [1877– Papers. ML.
  1908]

Piggin, S.
  1978   Assessing nineteenth century missionary motivation: Some consider-
          ations of theory and method. In Baker 1978, 327–339.

PIM Pacific Islands Monthly
  1930–   Sydney.
  1960

Piolet, J. B.
  1902   *Les Missions Catholiques Françaises au XIX E Siecle. Océanie, Mad-
          agascar.* Paris.

Pitman, Emma R.
  1880   *Heroines of the Mission Field.* London: Cassell, Petter, Galpin & Co.

Pitt-Rivers, George H. L.
  1927a   *The Clash of Culture and the Contact of Races.* London: George
          Routledge and Sons.

  1927b   The effect on native races of contact with European civilisation.
          Man 27:2–10.

  1929   Papuan criminals and British justice. Letter in *Man* 29:21–22.

  1930   Papuan criminals and British justice. Letter in *Man* 30:211–212.

Porter, Andrew
  1976   Cambridge, Keswick and late nineteenth century attitudes to Africa.
          JICH 5:5–33.

  1977   Evangelical enthusiasm, missionary motivation and West Africa in
          the late nineteenth century: The career of G. W. Brooke. *JICH*
          6:23–46.

  1978   Late nineteenth century Anglican missionary expansion: A consider-
          ation of some non-Anglican sources of inspiration. In *Religious Moti-
          vation: Biographical and Social Problems for the Church Historian*,
          edited by D. Baker, 349–366. Studies in Church History, 15. Oxford:
          B. Blackwell.

Potter, Sarah
  1974   The Social Origins and Recruitment of English Protestant Mission-
          aries. PhD dissertation, London School of Economics, University of
          London.

Prendergast, P. A.
  1961   A History of the London Missionary Society in British New Guinea,
          1871–1901. PhD dissertation, University of Hawaii.

Prisk, Ethel M.
  1919   *About People in Papua.* Adelaide: G. Hassell & Son.

Pritchard, William C.
   1911   *Papua: A handbook of its history, inhabitants, physical features and resources etc.* London: Society for Promotion of Christian Knowledge.

Pryce Jones, Edwin
   var.   Letter-Diary. LMS, Papua Personal, box 7.

Pyenson, L.
   1977   "Who the guys were": Prosopography and the history of science. *History of Science* 15:158–188.

Queensland
   [1873–   *Parliamentary Papers: Correspondence relating to British New
   1884]   Guinea.* Vol 1. Brisbane: Government printer.

   [1874–   *Government Gazette.*
   1875]

   [1884–   *Parliamentary Papers: Correspondence . . .* Vol. 2.
   1889]

Quiggan, A. Hingston
   1942   *Haddon, the Headhunter.* Cambridge: University Press.

Ramsey, Arthur M.
   1960   *From Gore to Temple: The development of Anglican theology between Lux Mundi and the Second World War, 1889–1939.* London: Longmans.

Ranger, T. O., and J. Weller.
   1975   *Themes in the Christian History of Central Africa.* London: Heinemann.

Reid, R. E.
   1975   The influence of anthropology on missionary thinking at the turn of the century, with special reference to the work of J. H. Holmes in the Gulf of Papua, 1893–1917. B. Litt. Thesis, University of New England.

   1978   John Henry Holmes in Papua: Changing missionary perspectives on indigenous cultures, 1890–1914. *JPH* 13:173–187.

Reid, T. Wemyss
   1960   *A Man Like Bati.* London: Independent Press.

Rich, Clem
   n.d.   Memorial to his parents. UPNG, Port Moresby.

Richards, Noel J.
   1977   British nonconformity and the Liberal Party. *JRH* 9:387–401.

Rigg, Charles W.
   1872   *A Digest of the Laws and Regulations of the Australasian Wesleyan Connexion.* Auckland.

Riley, E. Baxter
   1923a   Dorro head-hunters. *Man* 23:33–35.

   1923b   Sago-making on the Fly River. *Man* 23:145–146.

   1925   *Among Papuan Head-hunters.* London: Seeley Service.

1932 A Vocabulary: Kiwai and English. In *A grammar of the Kiwai Language, Fly Delta, Papua*, by Sidney H. Ray, 77–173. Port Moresby: Government Printer.

Robson, William
1903 *James Chalmers: Missionary and explorer of Rarotonga and New Guinea*. London: S. W. Partridge.

Roe, Margriet
1961 A History of south-east Papua to 1930. PhD dissertation, ANU.

Rogers, Charles
1900 *Penny Post*. 21 April. Goulburn. AA.

Rogers, Edgar
1920 *A Pioneer of New Guinea: The Story of Albert Alexander Maclaren*. London: Society for the Propagation of the Gospel.

Romilly, Hugh H.
1886 *The Western Pacific and New Guinea*. London: John Murray.

1889 *From My Verandah in New Guinea*. London: David Nutt.

Ross, C. Stuart
1903 *Tamate*. Melbourne: M. L. Hutchinson.

Ross, Ronald
1923 *Memoirs, with a full account of the great malaria problem and its solution*. London: John Murray.

Rouse, Ruth
1917 A Study of Missionary Vocation. *International Review of Missions* 6:244–257.

Rowell, Geoffrey
1974 *Hell and the Victorians*. Oxford: Clarendon Press.

Rumble, Leslie
1950 *Life of Bishop Verius, MSC*. Sydney: MSC.

Rutherford, Mark
1984 *The Revolution in Tanner's Lane*. London: Hogarth Press.

Saville, W. J. V.
[1902– Letters to friends in England from Mailu. ML u.mss 328.
1930]

1912 A grammar of the Mailu language, Papua. *JRAI* 42:397–436.

1926 *In Unknown New Guinea*. London: Seeley Service.

1931 Are the Papuans naturally religious? Papua *AR 1930–1931* (appendix C): 24–25.

n.d. *A vocabulary of the Mailu language*. London: LMS.

Schlencker, H. P.
1902 Letter to Thompson, 1 May. LMS Papua Letters, SOAS, London.

n.d. Pioneer journey to Mt. Douglas. PJ, LMS.

Scott, Harry.
var. Letters from N.G. Mission, Murray Island. ML.

Seligman, C. G.
　1910　*The Melanesians of British New Guinea.* Cambridge: University
　　　　Press.

Seton, W.
　n.d.　*Chalmers of New Guinea.* London: The Sunday School Union.

[Sharp], Gerald, Bishop of New Guinea.
　1917　*Diocese of New Guinea: Its rules and methods.* Dogura: Anglican
　　　　Mission.

Sibree, James, ed.
　1923　*London Missionary Society: A Register of Missionaries, Deputations
　　　　etc. from 1796–1923.* London: LMS.

Sills, David L.
　1968　*International Encyclopaedia of the Social Sciences.* 18 vols. New
　　　　York: Macmillan and The Free Press.

Simon, Brian, and Ian Bradley
　1975　*The Victorian Public School.* [Dublin]: Gill and Macmillan.

Small, A.
　1923　*Chalmers of New Guinea.* London: Hodder & Stoughton.

SMH (Sydney Morning Herald)
　1875–　Sydney daily.
　1920

Smith, Bernard
　1960　*European Vision in the South Pacific 1768–1850.* Oxford: Clarendon
　　　　Press.

Smith, Francis Barrymore
　1979　*The People's Health, 1830–1910.* Canberra: ANU Press.

Smith, Miles S.
　1909　*Handbook of the Territory of Papua.* 2nd ed. Melbourne: J. Kemp,
　　　　Government Printer.

　1912　*Handbook . . .* 3rd ed.

SMSC (Société des Missionaires du Sacré-Coeur)
　[1880–　Les MSC en Océanie de 1880–1894. Journal. RA-VANG. PMB.
　1894]

　1885–　*Annales de Nôtre-Dame du Sacré-Coeur.* Issoudun, France. Cited as
　1950　*Annales.*

　1887–　*Annals of Our Lady of the Sacred Heart.* Randwick, NSW. Cited as
　1914　Australian *Annals.*

　[1897]　Lettre au Conseil-gen. signée des missionaires en N.G. sur le besoin
　　　　de nouveaux missionaires. RA-VANG. PMB.

　[1898]　Statistiques. RA-VANG. PMB.

　[1899]　Réglementation concernant les FDNSC en NG. RA-VANG. PMB.

　[1900]　Statistiques. RA-VANG. PMB.

　[1904]　Rapport de Mgr. Navarre sur l'état du vicariat 1902–03, 1903–04.
　　　　RA-VANG. PMB.

[1912] Rapport sur la Mission. RA-VANG. PMB.

[1918] Statistiques de 1917 et 1918. RA-VANG. PMB.

[1919] Rapport sur l'état de la Mission. RA-VANG. PMB.

n.d. *a* Documents Antérieurs. RA-VAMM. PMB.

n.d. *b* Sister Gabriel (Marie Houdmont) 1884–1974. TS. YIA.

n.d. *c* Sister Mary Madeline. TS. YIA.

n.d. *d* Sister M. Julitte. TS. YIA.

var. *a* Correspondence. BA, PNG.

var. *b* Documentation relative à la "Nouvelle-France." RA-VAMM. PMB.

var. *c* Documentation relative aux voyages des premiers MSC en Océanie. RA-VAMM. PMB.

var. *d* Mission / government relations. Two files. BA, PNG.

var. *e* Personal files of missionaries. RA, Rome.

Society for the Propagation of the Faith, and Society of St. Peter, the Apostle
1885– Oeuvres pontificales de la propagation de la foi et de Saint-Pierre-
1914 Apôtre, 1868–1964. [*Les*] *Missions Catholiques*. Lyon: Bureau de la Propagation de la Foi. Cited as Oeuvres pontificales.

Stephen, Michele J.
1974 Continuity and change in Mekeo Society 1890–1971. PhD dissertation, ANU.

Stevenson, Robert Louis
1895 *Vailima Letters*. London: Methuen.

Stone, Lawrence
1971 Prosopography. *Daedalus* 100:46–49.

Stone, Octavius
1880 *A Few Months in New Guinea*. London: Sampson Low, Marston, Searle and Rivington.

Stone-Wigg, M. J.
1912 *The Papuans: A People of the South Pacific*. Melbourne: Shipping Newspapers Ltd.

var. *a* Private papers. In possession of Mrs. S. Beattie, Sydney.

var. *b* Diary. UPNG.

var. *c* Book of newscuttings. UPNG.

Storrow, A. H.
1895 *The Cheshunt College Union*. London.

Strayer, Robert W.
1976 Mission History in Africa: New perspectives on an encounter. *African Studies Review* 19:1–15.

1978 *The Making of Mission Communities in East Africa: Anglicans and Africans in Colonial Kenya 1875–1935*. London: Heinemann Educational Books.

Strout, Cushing
1968 Ego Psychology and the Historian. *History and Theory* 7:281–297.

Stuart, Ian
1970*a* The life style of the Anglican mission. *JPNGS* 4 (2): 77–85.

1970*b*   Montague John Stone-Wigg, Anglican pioneer. Seminar paper, UPNG.

Sydney Daily Telegraph
1902

Synge, Frances M.
1908   *Albert Maclaren: Pioneer Missionary in New Guinea.* London: Society for the Propagation of the Gospel.

Teale, Ruth
1977   Matron, maid and missionary. In *Women, Faith and Fetes: Essays in the history of women and the Church in Australia,* edited by S. Willis, 117–128. Melbourne: Dove Communications in association with the Australian Council of Churches (NSW) Commission on the Status of Women.

Telford, John
1895   *Women in the Mission Field: Glimpses of Christian Women Among the Heathen.* London.

Temple, William
var.   Papers, vol. 8. Lambeth Palace.

Temu, Arnold J.
1972   *British Protestant Missions.* London: Longmans.

Thompson, E. P.
1968   *The Making of the English Working Class.* London: Victor Gollancz.

Thompson, J. P.
1892   *British New Guinea.* London.

Thompson, R. Wardlaw
1900   *My trip in the "John Williams".* London: LMS.

1908   *Education in the Mission Field.* London: LMS.

n.d.   *Industrial Missions in Theory and Practice.* London: LMS.

Times (London)
1874–
1914

Tinney, Jane
[1892–   Notebooks. 2 vols. NLA.
1902]

Tomkins, Bishop Oliver
1980   Interview, 3 January. Worcester, England.

Tomkins, Oliver Fellows
var.   Papers and Diary. In possession of Bishop Oliver Tomkins, Worcester, England.

Tomlin, J. W. S.
1951   *Awakening: A History of the New Guinea Mission.* London: New Guinea Mission.

Tomlinson, Samuel
[1891–   Diary, August 1891 to November 1892. ABM, Sydney.
1892]

[1891–   Papers: Correspondence with Canon Hughes. Thomas Collection,
1930]   ABM, Sydney.

Turner, Edith
 1920 *Among Papuan Women.* London: LMS.
 n.d. A visit to the Home of the Gods. R. L. Turner Papers, National Library of Scotland.

Turner, Robert L.
 var. Papers. National Library of Scotland. MS 9770.
 n.d. *Our Papuan Mission.* London: LMS.

Turner, William Y.
 1878 The ethnology of the Motu. *JRAI* 7:470–498.

Tylor, Edward B.
 1929 *Primitive Culture: Researches into the Development of Mythology, Philosophy, Religion, Language, Art and Custom.* 5th ed. London: John Murray.

Van Den Berghe, Pierre L.
 1967 *Race and Racism: A Comparative Perspective.* New York: John Wiley and Sons.

Vaudon, Jean
 1899 *Monseigneur Henri Verjus, M.S.C: Premier apôtre des Papous.* Paris: Victor Retaux.

Venard, Sister Mary, FDNSC
 1966 *The Designs of His Heart.* Cork: Mercier Press.

 1979*a* *The History of the Daughters of Our Lady of the Sacred Heart in Papua New Guinea.* Port Moresby: Our Lady of the Sacred Heart Provincial House.

 1979*b* Interview, 18 December. Rome.

 n.d. *History of the Australian Province of the Daughters of Our Lady of the Sacred Heart.* Sydney: FDNSC.

Verjus, Henri
 [1910] Extracts from Spiritual Journal. In *Annales.*
 var. *a* Correspondence. RA.
 var. *b* Correspondence. BA.

Waiko, John
 1972 Oro! Oro! Oro Dara: A Binandere response to imperialism. BA (Hons). thesis, UPNG.

Walker, D. P.
 1964 *The Decline of Hell.* London: Routledge and Kegan Paul.

Walker, Eleanor
 [1892– Dobu Diary, May 1892 to December 1893. ML. PMB.
 1893]

Walker, Frederick
 [1888– Journal. PJ, LMS.
 1892]
 n.d. *The Problem of the Backward Races.* London.

Walker, R. B.
 1969 Methodism in the "Paradise of Dissent" 1837–1900. *JRH* 5:331–347.

1971   The growth and typology of the Wesleyan Methodist Church in New South Wales, 1812–1901. *JRH* 6:331–347.

Warren, Max
1965   *The Missionary Movement from Britain in Modern History.* London: SCM Press.

1967   *Social History and Christian Missions.* London: SCM Press.

Watson, Foster
1968   *The Old Grammar Schools.* London: Frank Cass.

Webb, Beatrice
1926   *My Apprenticeship.* London: Longmans, Green & Co.

Webb, Sidney
1904   *London Education.* London: Longmans, Green & Co.

Weber, Max
1947   *The Theory of Social and Economic Organisation.* New York: Oxford University Press.

1965   *The Sociology of Religion.* London: Methuen.

West, F.
1968   *Hubert Murray: The Australian Proconsul.* Melbourne: Oxford University Press.

1970   *Selected Letters of Hubert Murray.* Melbourne: Oxford University Press.

Wetherell, D.
1970   History of the Anglican Mission in Papua 1891–1941. MA thesis, ANU.

1973   Monument to a Missionary: C. W. Abel and the Keveri of Papua. *JPH* 8:30–48.

1974   Christian Missions in Eastern New Guinea. PhD dissertation, ANU.

1977   *Reluctant Mission: The Anglican Church in Papua New Guinea.* Brisbane: University of Queensland Press.

White, Gilbert
1917   *Round about the Torres Strait.* London: Central Board of Missions and Society for the Promotion of Christian Knowledge.

1923   *Francis de Sales Buchanan: Missionary in New Guinea.* Sydney: ABM.

1929   *A Pioneer of Papua.* London: Society for the Promotion of Christian Knowledge.

Williams, C. Peter
1976   The recruitment and training of overseas missionaries in England between 1850 and 1900. M. Litt. thesis, University of Bristol.

Williams, Francis E.
1923   *The Vailala Madness and the Destruction of Native Ceremonies in the Gulf Division.* Port Moresby: Government Printer.

1928   *Orokaiva Magic.* London: Oxford University Press.

1930   *Orokaiva Society.* London: Oxford University Press.

1936   *Papuans of the Trans-Fly.* Oxford: Clarendon Press.

1940   *Drama of Orokolo*. Oxford: Clarendon Press.

1945   Mission influence among the Keveri of south-east Papua. *Oceania* 15:89–141.

Williamson, Robert W.
1912   *The Mafulu, Mountain People of British New Guinea*. London: Macmillan.

Wilson, George H.
1936   *History of the Universities' Mission to Central Africa*. London: Universities' Mission to Central Africa.

Wiltgen, Ralph M.
1979   *The Founding of the Roman Catholic Church in Oceania*. Canberra: ANU Press.

World Missionary Conference
1910   Report 2, *The Church in the Mission Field*. 4, *The Home Base*. London.

Young, Michael
1977   William Bromilow and the Bwaidoka Wars. *JPH* 12:153–172.

1980   A tropology of the Dobu Mission. *Canberra Anthropology* 3:86–104.

Zeldin, T.
1973   *France 1848–1945*. 2 vols. Oxford: Clarendon Press.

Zeldin, T., ed.
1970   *Conflicts in French Society: Anticlericalism, Education and Morals in the Nineteenth Century*. London: G. Allen and Unwin.

Index

Abbot, Wilfred, 28, 59, 60, 91, 105, 128, 200, 293

Abel, Beatrice, 69, 276

Abel, Charles: administrative ability of, 262; background of, 19, 23, 50, 51, 54; biography of, 283; domestic life of, 65, 66, 77; educational methods of, 154, 155, 157; family of, 260; and industrial mission, 159; marriage of, 69, 81, 164; and other missions, 232; and Papuans, 115, 118–121, 127, 131, 133, 222, 226, 237; political action of, 224–227; relations of, with LMS, 190, 191; relations of, with traders and settlers, 222, 237; settlement policy of, 156; writings of, 95, 103, 224, 225, 237, 241

Abrahama (Papuan), 138

Adams, Miss, 294

Adan, Henri, 309

Agabadi, Pilipo, 150

Agnes, Sister. *See* Maire, Marie

Aigeri, Samuel, 150

Aird Hill, 228, 241

Alcohol: attitudes of missionaries to, 93, 94; consumption of, 93, 94, 190, 257, 357n66; opposition to prohibition of, 224–225

Allera, Claudius, 95, 301

Allera, Henriette, 313

Ambrose, Frederick, 294

Andrews, John, 288

Andrews, Mrs. A. J., 279

Ange, Sister. *See* Ode, Virginie

Anglican Mission, xi, 14, 320n4; foundation of, 5, 194; organization of, 85, 86, 194, 196–200, 210; sphere of influence of, 217. *See also* Anglican missionaries

Anglican missionaries: backgrounds of, 8, 11, 14–16, 23, 24, 30–32, 131, 132, 264; and baptism, 149–150; beliefs of, 40, 43, 132, 246, 247; biographies of, 294–301; and death, 257 (*see also* Death); education of, 27, 28, 264, 324n115; and imperialism, 229; length of service of, 251, 252; lifestyle of, 85–88, 99–100, 141–142; and marriage 85, 86; on Murray, Sir Hubert, 227, 228; and other denominations, 232; and Papuans, 110, 123, 226–227; paternalism of, 127–129; salaries of, 89–91; training of, 58–60, 63; vocation of, 36, 40. *See also* Missionaries; Anglican Mission; Women missionaries

Annales de Nôtre-Dame du Sacré-Coeur, 102, 203

Anne, Clothilde (Sister Joachim), 181, 313

Annexation, 212, 214

Anthropology: influence of, on missionary thought, 99, 110–116, 120, 130, 261; missionary contributions to, 110, 112, 264

Antoine, Jean-Joseph, 309

Antoinette, Sister. *See* Belarbre, Antoinette

Arnould, Fernand, 309

Aropokina, 84

Aruadaera (Papuan), 150

Australasian Methodist Missionary Review, 179, 192, 193

Australasian Wesleyan Methodist Missionary Society (AWMMS), xi, 1, 3, 26, 191; enters Papua, 192; financial support of missionaries by, 89, 90; on marriage, 68, 70, 78; organization of, 192–193, 210; and Papuan ministry, 207, 209; and women missionaries, 168, 177. *See also* Methodist missionaries; Women missionaries

About the Author

Diane Langmore was born in Melbourne, Australia. After graduating from the University of Melbourne (BA [hons], Dip. Ed.), she lived with her husband in Port Moresby, Papua, from 1964 to 1976. While teaching history at the University of Papua New Guinea, she also obtained her MA. Her study of the flamboyant, unconventional missionary James Chalmers, *Tamate: A King—James Chalmers in New Guinea*, was published by Melbourne University Press in 1974 and led to an interest in missionaries as a social group. Returning to Australia in 1976, she received her PhD from the Australian National University and has since worked for the *Australian Dictionary of Biography* at the Research School of Social Sciences, Australian National University. Dr. Langmore has published on Papua New Guinean as well as Australian history in periodicals and edited collections. She is married with three daughters.

Production Notes

This book was designed by Roger Eggers.
Composition and paging were done on the
Quadex Composing System and typesetting
on the Compugraphic 8400 by the design and
production staff of University of Hawaii
Press.

The text typeface is Compugraphic Caledonia
and the display typeface is Compugraphic
Palatino.

Offset presswork and binding were done by
Vail-Ballou Press, Inc. Text paper is Glatfelter
Offset Vellum, basis 45.

Tokyo
JAPAN
Midway
International Dateline
CHINA
Wake
NORTHERN
MARIANA
ISLANDS
Saipan
GUAM
MARSHALL ISLANDS
Ratak Chain
Ralik Chain
Majuro
Kwajalein
Manila
PHILIPPINES
Yap
Truk
Pohnpei
Kosrae
Sunday
Saturday
BELAU
FEDERATED STATES OF MICRONESIA
Gilbert Islands
K I R I
equator
NAURU
Banaba
New Ireland
New Britain
Bougainville
SOLOMON ISLANDS
TUVALU
INDONESIA
Santa Cruz Islands
Guadalcanal
Wallis & Futuna
PAPUA
VANUATU
FIJI
Vanua Levu
Viti Levu
Lau Group
Coral Sea
Loyalty Islands
NEW CALEDONIA
AUSTRALIA
Brisbane
Norfolk
Sydney
Auckland
Tasman Sea
NEW ZEALAND
Tasmania
145°E
160°E
175°E
130°E
115°E